Europe *by* Eurail

2002

Europe by Eurail 2002

How to Tour Europe by Train

Twenty-Sixth Edition

written by

LaVerne Ferguson-Kosinski

rail schedules by

Stephanie Bell

The Globe Pequot Press

Guilford, Connecticut

The author and the publisher gratefully acknowledge the kind permission of Eurostar Passenger Service and its Web site, Deutsche Bahn and its Web site, Brittany Ferries, Hoverspeed UK Limited, Irish Ferries U.K. Limited, P &O Stena Line, SeaFrance Limited, DFDS Seaways, and Stena Line to use their resources in the compilation of the timetables in this text.

The "International Services" rail map on pp. vi–vii is reproduced courtesy of the *Thomas Cook European Timetable.*

Cover photographs by PhotoDisc
Cover design by Laura Augustine
Text design by *osprey*design

ISSN: 1081–1125
ISBN: 0–7627–1201–5

Printed in Canada
Twenty-Sixth Edition/First Printing

About the Author

In 1976, author LaVerne Ferguson-Kosinski and her former husband, Lt. Col. George Ferguson, first coauthored *Europe by Eurail*—a unique and comprehensive how-to guide for independent travelers touring Europe with a Eurailpass. After battling a long illness, George, who was globally and affectionately known as "Mr. Eurail," passed away in 1997.

LaVerne wanted to ensure that accurate British and European rail travel information would continue to be available. She is devoted to producing comprehensive, practical, yet friendly guidebooks for the independent rail traveler or armchair dreamer. Her technical writing and editorial background; academic education in English, world history, and communications; plus her experience in research and development for an international research institute have added considerable substance to her twenty-six years of traveling the rails in Europe.

LaVerne's dream of exploring the world began in third-grade geography class when she first began collecting travel brochures. She attended the Ohio State University, lived in and traveled throughout Europe, and is now studying for her realtor's license. Her husband, Joe Kosinski ("the Steel Man"), is a structural engineer and they reside in Fort Myers, Florida, with one of their six children. Europe, however, will always be her "backyard."

LaVerne thanks her entire family, especially husband, Joe, and son Matthew Palma, whose expertise and support of her career have been invaluable in enabling her to continue writing both *Britain by BritRail* and *Europe by Eurail*.

Heartfelt thanks and appreciation also go to you, the readers, whose comments, suggestions, and corrections help keep both guidebooks accurate and up-to-date. Send them directly to:

LaVerne Ferguson-Kosinski
Author of *Europe by Eurail*
PMB #160
6900-29 Daniels Parkway
Fort Myers, FL 33912
E-mail: laverne@railpass.com
Web site: www.railpass.com

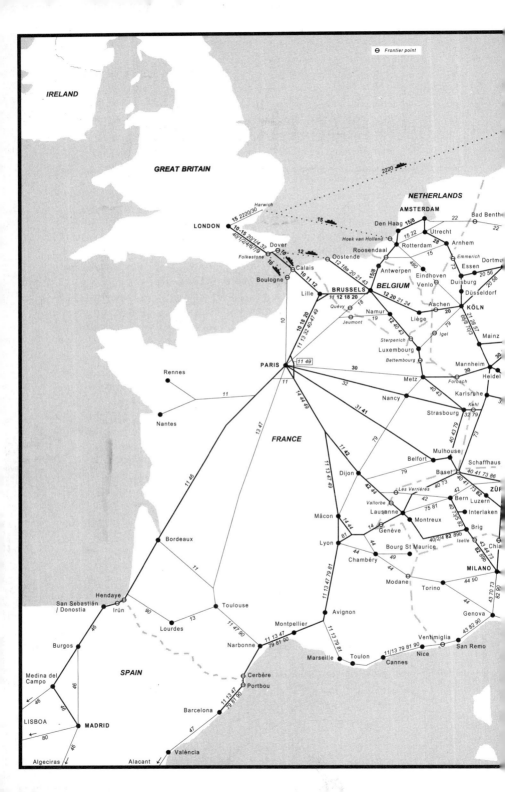

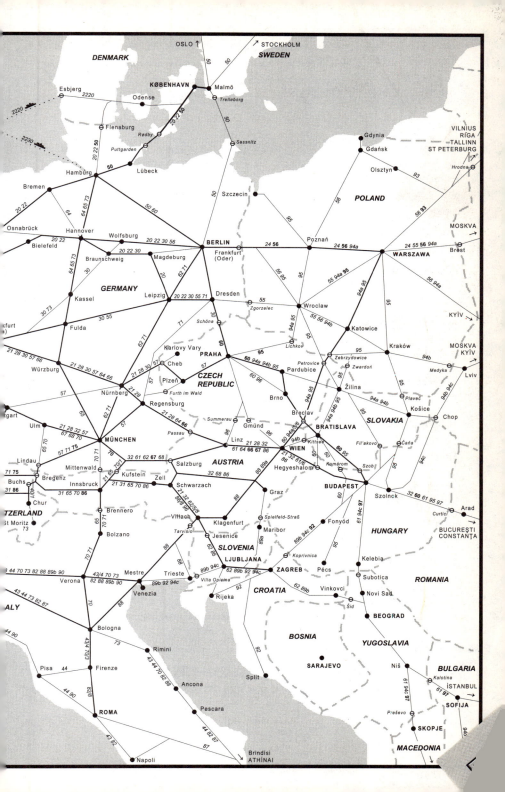

To:	Europe By Eurail Reader
Cc:	
Subject:	Request information via e-mail

Dear Traveler,

The Rail Experts will automatically reply to any email that you send to an address below with comprehensive information sheets on that subject. The information will be sent as an Adobe Acrobat attachment. Just enter "INFO please" in the SUBJECT line.

Also included in that reply will be links to the appropriate area of RAILEXPERTS.com so that you can find the information you are looking for quickly and easily online.

info@railexperts.com Pass prices, frequently asked questions (FAQ), rules and regulations, and much more. All the information you'll need to answer most of your questions regarding traveling Europe by rail.

eurostar@railexperts.com Detailed information on the Chunnel train service connecting London with the continent. Prices, FAQs, schedules and ordering information.

p2p@railexperts.com Detailed information on purchasing point-to-point tickets for train travel within Europe.

reservations@railexperts.com High speed and specialty trains, couchettes and sleepers – all the information you need to make European train reservations.

Help us Help You.... feedback@railexperts.com

We welcome and encourage your feedback. If you are happy with our service please tell others, if you aren't, please tell us. We also love hearing your tips, anecdotes, stories and any other feedback.

NO handling fees • NO busy signals • NO lines • NO hassles

GUARANTEED BEST PRICES

To order visit **www.RAILEXPERTS.com**
Or call *toll free* **1-866-RAIL-PASS** (1-866-724-5727)

Contents

About RailPass.com

Author LaVerne Ferguson-Kosinski is the founder and former Chief executive officer of RailPass.com, previously known as RailPass Express. An extraordinary small-business success story, RailPass.com was created in 1980 from a humble beginning in the Ferguson home—with a couple of desks, a toll-free telephone number, and a singular idea to provide the best customer service for the independent traveler. Incorporated in 1986 by the Fergusons, RailPass.com has blossomed into one of the largest independent, consumer-focused European railpass sales outlets in the world.

The expertly trained (pun intended) and well-traveled staff at RailPass.com provides the informational resources and travel products necessary to pursue the concepts and itineraries as outlined in the guidebooks. The team of international researchers shares LaVerne's enthusiasm for the exciting world of train travel—its comfort, speed, and continuous adventure—and is devoted to producing this comprehensive, practical-yet-friendly guidebook to touring Europe by train:

Matthew Palma, president of RailPass.com, has long provided valuable input for the guidebooks *Britain by BritRail* and *Europe by Eurail,* as well as strategic business planning to keep RailPass.com on the right track. As LaVerne's son, Matt had the privilege of growing up in the British and European rail travel business and participated in his first group tour of Europe at the age of nine.

Stephanie Bell, promotional/design editor of RailPass.com and schedule editor of *Britain by BritRail* and *Europe by Eurail,* also employs her promotional, marketing, and design skills at RailPass.com. A multifaceted graduate of fine arts with an extensive publicity and creative background, she contributes her valuable abilities in their print and Internet design areas, as well.

Mary Kish, general manager, devotes her excellent managerial and business acuity to RailPass.com. She is instrumental in streamlining operations and keeping RailPass.com moving at high speed while making customer service standards even better.

Lesley Tate, financial assistant, integrates operational systems and procedures and attends to customer service overflow.

Rich Jacko, systems engineer, maintains our award-winning Web site, www.railpass.com. The site contains information on *Britain by BritRail* and *Europe by Eurail,* an extensive British and European rail-related database, plus a secure online ordering system for railpasses and other travel products. Rich's natural ability to solve numerical problems and think analytically has enabled him to further automate RailPass.com.

Sheila Clowes is the "Lady of the Lines" on the RailPass.com voice-mail system. Originally from London, England, she is our "resident expert" on all things British. Actually, her official title is training coordinator, and we credit her with maintaining the highest-quality customer service standards in our representatives.

Ellen Byrnes heads the EuropeanVacation department. She has traveled most of Europe and is full of globe-trotting stories and expertise. Assisting her are **Mary Ellen Baker, Susan Beougher,** and **Linda Rence.** As rail reservation, tour, and information specialists, they decipher complicated point-to-point timetables for the best and most convenient trains, schedules, and itineraries. They love to share travel stories while assisting travelers. EuropeanVacation also offers tours, including luxury train tours, and group rates and discounts. Visit www.railpass.com on the Internet or call (877) RAILPASS (877–724–5727) toll free for an enjoyable and easy way to book a tour, order point-to-point tickets, or make seat and sleeper reservations.

Other RailPass.com customer service specialists and researchers for the guidebooks include **Colleen Beader, Leah Orolin,** and **Debbie Wanstrath-Norwich.**

Researchers for *Europe by Eurail* also included Major Robert Bean, Margaret Keith, Joseph Kosinski, and Adam Price. **Major Robert Bean,** a true train enthusiast, has played an ongoing, much appreciated role with both *Europe by Eurail* and *Britain by BritRail* for several years. His attention to minute details and knowledge of rail travelers' needs is superb. **Margaret Keith,** a certified Red Badge Guide for France, an artist, and a long-time European rail expert, has provided her invaluable input to *Europe by Eurail* since 1982. **Joseph Kosinski,** a.k.a. "the Steel Man," has been instrumental in Internet research, setting up databases, and accompanying his wife/author, LaVerne Ferguson-Kosinski, on her treks throughout Europe. Foremost a top structural design engineer in Florida with his own firm, J.C. Kosinski Engineering, Inc., Joe's creativity and attention to details are unsurpassed as can be seen in his design of the Pentagon renovations in Washington, D.C. **Adam Price,** the youngest of the researchers has lived and studied in Spain, and travels extensively throughout Europe by rail.

We also wish to extend thanks to Jan Cronan of the Globe Pequot Press; Raffaela Essayan, Frank Berardi, David Brever, Bill Schroeder, and the entire staff of CIT Tours; Heinz Wesner, Barbara Schmidt, Mary Stiller, and the entire staff of DER Travel Services; Jean Heger of Rail Europe Group; our many, many friends in the European tourist offices; and our travel partner professionals throughout Europe.

Train schedules, prices, and conditions of use appearing in this edition are updated at press time and are subject to change by the railways. The information is to assist with trip planning only. We cannot be held responsible for accuracy. Please check with the railways or RailPass.com toll-free at (877) RAILPASS (877–724–5727), or visit www.railpass.com for the most recent information.

Introduction

"To travel by train is to see nature and human beings, towns and churches and rivers, in fact to see life."—*Agatha Christie*

This twenty-sixth edition of *Europe by Eurail* reflects the "new" Europe and the energy and exuberance of its rail system. It's dynamic, it's futuristic, and it's on the move—accelerating with the high-tech boldness and immense speed of the world's finest transportation system.

Train travel is an enigma for most non-Europeans who either have forgotten or have never had an opportunity to learn what travel by train is like. *Europe by Eurail* takes the puzzlement out of European rail travel—like having a friend along who takes you by the hand and shows you how to use the world's finest transportation network to see and learn about European life and culture. Toward that end, this guide provides specific, pragmatic information with step-by-step directions.

Europe by Eurail is a train traveler's how-to book. *Europe by Eurail* deals primarily with the necessities of train travel in Europe and offers guidance for appreciating the educational and cultural sites and events that abound along the right-of-way of the Continent's magnificent rail system. It is not a hotel/restaurant guide, but rather tells you *how* to locate them. Certain hotels and restaurants do occasionally gain mention, however, especially if they add to the graciousness and enjoyment of a train trip or a stay in a city.

"See Europe by Train" has been a favorite slogan of Europe's railways for decades, but never has it been as full of meaning as it is today. You will never be bored traveling on a high-speed train, because rail travel is still leisurely enough to fully enjoy the constantly changing scenes of hills and hamlets, farms and forests, and cities and countrysides. Each country has its own special attractions to offer rail travelers as they speed through, ensconced in

1

comfort and free from worry. Added to the passing scenes is the opportunity for leisurely dining and drinking while chatting with fellow passengers, most of whom are the Europeans you hoped to meet.

Travel by train in Europe is a unique and pleasurable experience. All aboard—and take your imagination with you.

Why Eurail?

Many visitors to Europe fail to realize that the European rail network (which we refer to simply as "Eurail") can take you to practically every nook and cranny on the Continent, so they assume they must rent a car. At first glance, those European fly-drive packages might appear enticing, but the more you investigate them, the less appealing they become. In general, car rentals have one basic fault—the price you are quoted may not be the price you pay; it usually is higher. One important facet of a fly-drive package is the VAT (value added tax), which ranges from 6 to 33 percent in European countries. In some countries, foreign tourists are eligible for refunds on certain purchases (contact 800–KNOW VAT or visit www.globalrefund.com for more information), but there are no VAT refunds on car rentals. Reference to the VAT may be tactfully avoided in car-rental information or perhaps hidden in the fine print of the terms. After determining the low cost of a rental car with unlimited mileage privileges (which also includes the privilege of buying unlimited gasoline), don't forget to multiply the bottom line by the VAT of the country and add that figure to the cost.

Another item frequently overlooked is insurance. As a rule of thumb, add to the quoted rental cost another 20 percent for personal accident insurance, collision insurance, and taxes. After that, prepare yourself for another shock—the price of gasoline in Europe is about three times what you'd pay in the United States, plus gasoline stations are not nearly as numerous as they are stateside.

Also consider that the number of European road-traffic fatalities is more than four times that in North America, and that watching the road ahead is not really what most folks go to Europe to do, nor is deciphering the signs an easy feat. Most European automobiles are small, compact vehicles. That four-passenger economy car you're thinking of renting could never carry four passengers and their luggage—so, bring on the Mercedes at three times the price and double the gas. By now, you will realize why Europeans park their own cars and ride the trains themselves.

The more you open your eyes to rail travel, we think, you'll find there is no better way to go.One key reason for going to Europe is to mingle with Europeans. Traveling day after day in a motor coach filled with other American tourists or riding for hours in a small rental car with your spouse helping you navigate and the kids crammed in with the suitcases is not, in our opinion, the best way to mingle. Europeans use their trains. They will be sitting next to you or across from you in the diner. You will be sharing the same experiences, so conversation will come easily. It's a great way to make new friends.

Those traveling with children across the Continent will find the trains to be a fun and intriguing blessing. The kids can eat, get a drink, take a nap, or go to the restroom just as often as their little hearts desire while you enjoy the scenery en route.

Trains have always held an aura of romance and charm that cannot be experienced in any other mode of transportation. The mere mention of *The Orient Express*, for example, sparks visions of glamour, intrigue, mystery—and sumptuous dining. Although many of the original famous trains have been replaced by high-speed, high-tech international express trains, that special thrill of rail travel is still there.

The Europeans know how to run a railroad. The Eurail network connects more than 30,000 cities, villages, and hamlets with more than 90,000 daily train departures on more than 160,000 miles of track. And the system is getting faster, more efficient, and more elegant. Unlike the airlines' sardine-like accommodations, European trains are comfortable, stylish, and loaded with amenities to please the tourist and business traveler alike.

Originally, the idea of purchasing a pass for unlimited travel by train within a specified time period, for example, 1 month, on the Eurail system was a simplistic one. One type of railpass, called a **"Eurailpass,"** was offered to non-European residents as a way to encourage independent travelers to use Europe's rail network.

Although today's European railpasses encompass a wide variety of options, time periods, and countries, using a railpass is still the most economical, convenient, and flexible way to get the most out of the European rail network. A point-to-point ticket enables you to travel from one point to another but does not provide the flexibility to change your plans. Railpasses, on the other hand, provide unlimited rail travel each day within a specified time frame. They eliminate the hassle of standing in long lines to purchase tickets, and they can save you a bundle of money if you are making long or frequent journeys.

For details on the various kinds of European railpasses available to non-European residents, please consult the European RailPasses section later in this introduction, or contact RailPass.com toll-free at (877) RAILPASS (877–724–5727) or (614) 889–9100; *Internet:* **www.railpass.com.**

Remember . . . purchase your railpasses before leaving for Europe!

The Base City–Day Excursion Concept™ combined with the appropriate railpass provides greater flexibility to see more of Europe at its best—by train. Many of our cost-conscious readers modify the concept by using the less expensive suburban area of a major city or one of our day-excursion points as their "base." With any one of the various types of railpasses available today, it's easy to modify our comfortable rail travel concept to suit your budget and itinerary. Armed with a railpass and a current copy of *Europe by Eurail,* you become your own tour guide, packing and moving on only when you want to. For the experienced traveler or the novice, it's the only way to go.

How to Use *Europe by Eurail*

Base City–Day Excursion Concept

In 1976 *Europe by Eurail* first launched a new concept for easy, comfortable, hassle-free train travel by combining the economy of a Eurailpass with the Fergusons' Base City–Day Excursion method of touring Europe. Now proudly in its twenty-sixth edition, *Europe by Eurail* has proven to be a most useful tool for travelers using any type of railpass that allows access to any or all of the 17-country Eurail system.

We identify base cities throughout Europe in which you may stay in comfort and from which you may make numerous day excursions to interesting places, returning each night to the same hotel room. This concept eliminates the hassles of daily packing and unpacking and luggage lugging. This more relaxed approach to rail travel is not only an enjoyable way to visit Europe but also affords the time to see and do a delightful variety of things outside of the major cities.

You do not have to be a geographer to use *Europe by Eurail*. It is conveniently arranged alphabetically—first by country, then by base city. Rail system maps accompany each country chapter.

Europe by Eurail picks up the traveler disembarking from the train on arrival from another base city (or at the airport if it is the traveler's entry point to Europe) and leads him or her *step-by-step* through the essentials of European rail travel.

We take a pragmatic approach to European rail travel by providing explicit walking directions and explanations based from rail stations. For example, a bewildered tourist standing on a train platform in one of Brussels's *three* train stations needs practical, no-nonsense information—in a hurry:

> *The Grand'Place? How do I get there?*
>
> *Where's the tourist information office?*

Europe by Eurail leads you with specific directions: "To reach the Grand'Place from Gare Centrale (Central Station), walk downhill in the direction of the Town Hall's spire until you reach the square. The tourist office is to the right of the spire when you are facing the Town Hall."

Country sections explain what types of tourist railpasses are accepted, specify what kinds of bonuses are available, and provide specific information about rail travel within that country. These sections also list each country's tourist information office locations in North America, their telephone/fax numbers, and, where applicable, Internet site and e-mail addresses.

Some base cities have a single train station; others have multiple stations. Under **train station descriptions** are the subsections concerning

- Exchanging money and using ATMs
- Locating tourist information
- Locating and using luggage facilities
- Securing hotel accommodations

- Obtaining train information and reservations
- Obtaining railpass validation

Base city **tourist information offices** and **hotel reservation information** are listed with addresses, telephone and fax numbers, Internet and e-mail addresses (if available), hours of operation, and, of utmost importance, how to reach those offices from the rail station.

Connections from each base city to others are listed at the end of each base city section. Not all base cities can be reached from another in the same day, although most can.

A **sight-seeing, attractions,** and **special tour** information section for each base city provides a general introduction to what to see and do and how to do it.

Day excursions begin with the distance and average train time and include train schedules to/from the base city. Trains departing a base city are usually in the morning, and trains returning from the day excursions are usually in the late afternoon or early evening.

A brief history and highlights of each day excursion enable you to decide which ones are of the most interest. Then, *Europe by Eurail* again provides *step-by-step* directions on how to get from the rail station to the tourist information offices and to the day excursion sights and attractions.

Special Features

Special features in the Appendix of this edition of *Europe by Eurail* include

- **Sample 15-Day Itineraries**
- **International Calling & Dialing Codes**
- **Glossary of Rail Terminology**—In four languages.
- **Point-to-Point Fares**—Cost of a single train trip between base cities to aid in determining if a railpass is more economical than purchasing separate tickets. Nine times out of ten, a railpass will come out dollars ahead.
- **European Tourist Offices in North America**—Where to get advance destination information.
- **U.S. Passport Offices**
- **Airline and Hotel Information**
- **Reader Card**—We want to know more about our readers' travel needs, and we appreciate any comments and/or suggestions. We'll send you additional information about any special promotions and discounted rail travel in Europe—FREE! Please answer the questions on the card and mail it to **RailPass.com** 2737 Sawbury Boulevard, Columbus, OH 43235. Or, if you have Internet access, e-mail us at **laverne@railpass.com.**

INTRODUCTION

Planning a Eurail Trip

Planning Pays Off

Depending on who you are, your concept of a "plan" can vary. We have observed two general types of rail travelers—one conservative, the other adventurous. One traveler may require a detailed, hour-by-hour schedule for a day's activities; another may merely get up in the morning and see what happens that day.

The first questions to answer when planning a trip are, "When can I go and how much time can I spend there?" April through October are the most popular months for touring in Europe and for many events. When planning your trip, take bank holidays into consideration, since banks, postal services, most shops, and many attractions are closed, and some transportation services are reduced.

Whether or not you admit it, everyone has a problem budgeting vacation time. It's human nature to try to see as much as possible in as little time as possible. This "sightseer's syndrome" could be dangerous to your vacation. Avoid it by planning an itinerary that allows ample "free time." Also, vary the day excursions by going on a short one following a particularly long outing away from the base city. Try to see and do too much on your vacation and you will return home looking as if you desperately need another one.

How long should your Eurail tour be? There are many factors bearing on such a determination, the most important being the individual. How much annual vacation time do you have? How do you use it—all at one time or in two or more segments? Railpasses can accommodate just about anyone's personal needs, with Eurailpasses ranging from 15 consecutive days to 3 months of travel and flexible Europasses with options of 5, 6, 8, 10, or 15 days of travel in 2 months. In 2001 the "design-your-own" Eurail Selectpass became available for rail travel within *any* three adjoining countries in the Eurail 17-country system. When you add the wide variety of regional and individual country railpasses available, it may, at first, seem confusing. But *Europe by Eurail* and the European rail experts at **RailPass.com** can help you. Call toll-free (877) RAILPASS (877–724–5727) or check out www.railpass.com.

Even if you don't have 2 weeks or more for that grand tour of Europe, travel magazines and the travel sections of the Sunday newspapers plus the Internet are usually loaded with 1-week bargain fares to almost anywhere, mainland Europe included. By coupling our Base City–Day Excursion mode with a railpass, you can maximize the time you do have to spend in Europe.

After determining the length of time you will have for your European rail trip, the next step is to develop a clear idea of **where you want to go**, what you want to see, and what you want to do. Develop your objectives well before your departure date. We disagree with those who believe that anticipation of travel is more rewarding than its realization. But we do agree that the planning phase can also be a fun part of your trip. Properly done, this "homework" will pay substantial dividends when travel actually begins.

To get things started, write to, telephone, e-mail, or visit the Web sites of the **tourist offices** of each country you plan to visit (addresses in North America are listed in the Appendix). Be specific. Indicate **when** you will be going, **where** you wish to go, and **what** in particular you would like to see. If you have any special disabilities or interests and hobbies, be sure to mention them. By spelling out your information needs, you will obtain better responses.

Don't overlook the **Internet** and your local library as valuable information sources. Travelers who have computers and access to the Internet can do an incredible amount of research and planning in the comfort of their own homes or offices. You may want to start with some basic Web sites about each country in general and then do city-specific searches. For example, to obtain general information on Germany, start with the German National Tourist Office Web site: **www.germany-tourism.de**. Other sources of information can be found in each country chapter or see the Appendix.

Seek out friends and neighbors who have been to Europe. No doubt you'll find their experiences flavored with their own likes and dislikes, but their stories may just spark some new ideas for your plans. A great way to enhance this guidebook and your railpass is to get an inside look at European rail travel with the video *Europe by Train*. This video demonstrates tips and practical information on the services offered, and includes footage of the premier, scenic, and Eurostar trains. To order, call (800) 722–7151 or visit www.railpass.com.

You are now ready for the decisive phase of your trip planning— **constructing an itinerary**. First, draw a blank-calendar–style form or use a calendar form on your computer covering a period from at least 1 week prior to your departure to a few days following your return. (Make extra copies of the form—you'll need them. Changes are common in this project!) Now begin to block your itinerary into the calendar form, being mindful that the itinerary can be changed but the number of days in a week remains fixed. Possibly by the third time through the exercise, you'll begin to see the "light at the end of the tunnel." It's only human to try to cram too many activities into a day, but it's better to discover your planning errors *before* starting your trip rather than in the middle of it.

With your itinerary in a calendar format, you can now determine your housing requirements, seat and sleeper reservations, and other facets of your forthcoming trip. The days blocked out in advance of your departure can show your "countdown" items—stopping the newspaper, having mail held at the post office, and so on. Make several copies of your completed itinerary and leave some behind for the folks with whom you want to stay in touch. Above all, take copies of your itinerary with you—you'll be surprised how beneficial they are, and you will refer to them frequently.

One item that you can't leave home without is a **passport**. U.S. citizens are admitted to European countries with only a passport; a visa is not required. If you do not have one or if yours has expired, write immediately to one of the U.S. passport offices listed in the Appendix (*Internet:*

INTRODUCTION

http://travel.state.gov/passport_services.html). Allow a minimum of 1 month to obtain your passport. There are ways to expedite the process, but be safe by planning ahead and making this the first order of business when you've decided to make your trip abroad.

"**Know before you go**"—the slogan of the U.S. Customs Service that pertains to what you can return with—also applies to the financial aspects of vacation planning. The fluctuation of the dollar's purchasing power in Europe over the past few years has left a lot of us wondering whether or not we could afford a vacation on the other side of the Atlantic. It is sometimes difficult to determine what effect Europe's inflation will have on your dollars once you're there. Planning in advance and purchasing most of your vacation needs in advance (particularly transportation) in American dollars are probably the most effective ways to combat inflation and price fluctuations. Buy as many of your vacation needs as you can before you go and plan to limit your out-of-pocket costs paid in foreign currency to a minimum. This way, you are protected against fluctuating currency values.

Accommodations usually account for the greatest share of a traveler's budget. Low-cost airfare and transportation bargains, like railpasses, can get the traveler to and around Europe, but the real bite out of the buck comes when the visitor opens his or her wallet to pay for a night's lodging. Attractively priced accommodations packages are being offered by some tour operators; but too few suit the needs of independent travelers, as is the case for travelers on a rail vacation. With advance planning and advance payment, however, you can realize significant savings if you are willing to put forth the extra time and effort to do your "homework."

Well ahead of your intended departure date—preferably 2 months in advance, but no less than 6 weeks—write to the tourist offices listed in the Appendix and request information regarding lodging in the areas you intend to stay during your rail journey. You may arrange accommodations by mail, fax, or online at **www.railpass.com** (click on the hotel link). The best assurance that you will have a room waiting upon arrival is to make an advance deposit directly to the hotel, then take care of the balance with the hotel's cashier when checking out. And always ask the hotel to confirm the room rate when you check in; doing so will avoid delays and possible financial embarrassment when leaving.

One final bit of advice on reducing the cost of accommodations in Europe: **Use your railpass.** A railpass can provide exceptional savings in housing costs by permitting you to stay *outside* the base city's center, where hotel rooms, pensions, bed-and-breakfast housing, and the like are far less expensive than their downtown counterparts. Lodgings in the suburbs, a la RailPass, can be more economical and just as convenient as those in the base cities.

Keep in mind that tourist information offices maintain extensive current lists of all types of accommodations, from hostels, bed-and-breakfast establishments or pensions, to 5-star luxury hotels.

When inquiring as to availability, you will be asked the inevitable question, "What do you want to be near?" Naturally, when you're traveling by rail, your response will be, "Near the rail station." You are in for a surprise—most major cities have multiple primary rail stations. A better site-selection statement might be to ask for a hotel near one of the major lines of the metro, or subway.

The budget-minded traveler may write to the European tourist offices in North America listed in the Appendix and ask for information about budget accommodations in the countries to be visited while in Europe. The plenitude of modestly priced lodgings and inexpensive restaurants, even in Europe's most expensive cities, will amaze you.

Those interested in staying in hostels must join **Hostelling International.** Adult (age 18–54), $25; senior citizen (age 55 and over), $15; age 17 and under, free. You may purchase the above memberships from RailPass.com at (877) RAILPASS (877–724–5727) or for further details contact HI-AYH at (202) 783–6161 or visit www.hiayh.org.

Note: We recommend having a confirmed accommodations reservation in your European arrival city for wherever you will be spending the first night.

How to Get There

Transatlantic air traffic is so frequent and varied today that no description—short of an entire book—could do it justice. Excursion fares are available in a multitudinous variety. Charter flights are available, too, and they are still mostly money savers. But some excursion rates are less expensive than charters. It is not uncommon on a regularly scheduled airliner winging its way to Europe to find that every passenger in your row of seats paid a different fare for the same flight on the same schedule with the same service!

Travel agents keep tabs on the rapidly changing airline industry. If you've dealt with a reputable travel agency over the years, contact them for air-excursion-fare options. Or, if you have lots of leisure time, call the various airlines' toll-free telephone numbers or visit their Web sites and ask them for suggestions and fare information. We have listed the contact information for a few airlines in the Appendix. Don't be disturbed if you receive a variety of responses. Internet users can search on-line for bargain fares with consolidators, travel portals, and the actual airlines as well.

Regarding charter flights, inquire about them, but investigate thoroughly before making any final decisions. Here again, get your travel agent involved, even if it's only to obtain the tickets. Even some of the most reputable air-charter carriers still operate on a "Go–No Go" basis. This means that if enough passengers sign up for the flight, it will go as scheduled; if not enough passengers are booked, the flight will be scrubbed.

European Railpasses

A railpass provides flexibility and economy if you are making several trips, especially any over long distances. A point-to-point ticket is, of course, good for travel from one city to another. You can, though, consult the fares between major cities listed in the Appendix of this edition or visit the more extensive point-to-point fares database at **www.railpass.com**. Add up the cost of each leg of your journey and then compare it to the cost of a railpass to see what economically works best for your trip.

Today's rail traveler has a wide choice of railpasses available, from the 17-country Eurailpass to regional passes encompassing groups of countries and individual, or national, country passes.

Note: A comprehensive list of prices and types of railpasses is listed in the Appendix of this edition and on the aforementioned Web site.

How Long Is a Railpass Day?

There are many different types and price ranges of railpasses available that provide *unlimited* rail transportation for a specified number of days. A "railpass day" runs from midnight to midnight, during which time it is possible to make unlimited on-and-off-the-train journeys. Those with flexible railpasses can extend the use of their pass by taking advantage of the overnight bonus. This rule allows passengers boarding overnight *direct* trains departing after 1900 to count the trip toward the next day of train travel. This is a great way to get the most out of your pass on long treks, plus be rested for a full day of sightseeing. Flexible passes are described later in this section.

Railpass Validation

You have 6 months from the issue date of the railpass (the date of purchase stamped on your pass) in which to begin using it. Prior to boarding your first train in Europe, present your pass for validation at the rail station. Allow for a little extra time for the validation process, but once your pass is validated, that ends standing in line to buy another ticket—a real convenience.

- Do not make any entries (such as filling in your passport number) prior to validation.
- Although it is not a part of the validation process, write the starting and ending dates of your pass validation period on a piece of paper and hand it to the clerk along with your pass and passport. (Remember, Europeans write the day before the month; thus, 10/07/02 would mean July 10, 2002.)
- Be certain the clerk agrees to the dates before he or she enters the validity period on your pass.
- Double-check the validation dates before accepting the pass. If an error is made in either the dates or your passport number, have it corrected immediately.
- The clerk then enters your passport number and stamps the pass.
- Do not remove the pass from its cover.

Note: Once validated, your pass is neither refundable nor replaceable.

Pass Protection Program

Guard your railpass with the same attention you give to your cash, traveler's checks, and passport. Lost or stolen passes are not, however, refundable; RailPass.com offers a pass protection program that reimburses its clients in full for the unused portion of the railpass in case of loss or theft, and the cost is only an additional $15 per pass.

Eurail Passes

Eurail passes are valid for unlimited rail travel (in the class indicated on the pass) on the national railways and some private railway companies in the following 17 countries: Austria, Belgium, Denmark, Finland, France, Germany, Greece, Hungary, Ireland (Republic of), Italy, Luxembourg, The Netherlands, Norway, Portugal, Spain, Sweden, and Switzerland.

Note that some premier trains, such as AVE, Eurostar, and Thalys, require a supplement. Eurail passes, however, provide a substantial discount on the fare, as well as free or reduced-rate travel on selected ferries, lake steamers, and some buses. More detailed information on travel bonuses offered by each country is listed in the individual country chapters of this edition. A complete list of bonuses, a Eurail map, and timetable also come free with your railpass.

There are two basic types of Eurail passes—consecutive-day and flexible-day passes. **Consecutive-day passes** are valid for an unlimited number of rail journeys during the number of railpass days you purchase, which constitutes the pass's "validity" period. For example, if you purchased a 15-day Eurailpass and took your first train trip on January 1, your pass would be valid for use as many times as you want in any of the aforementioned countries until midnight on January 15. We call it the "tick-tock" pass.

Flexible-type Eurail passes provide exactly what the "Flexipass" name implies—flexibility. Flexipasses work especially well if you plan to stay in one place and not travel for a few days. You choose the number of travel days, either 10 or 15, and use any or all of them within a 2-month validity period. Thus, while you're not traveling, your railpass is not "ticking" away. For example, if you purchase a 10-day Eurail Flexipass, you will have ten boxes on your pass to write the dates of the days on which you use the train(s). We recommend, however, that you write in the date *on* the date that you travel, rather than in advance, just in case you want to change your travel plans at the last minute. When entering the date, remember the format: day first and then the month.

Eurailpass

Valid for unlimited **first-class** rail travel. Choose from five consecutive-day durations: 15 days, 21 days, 1 month, 2 months, or 3 months. Go as you please, stop where and when you want. This pass is an excellent value for anyone visiting several countries.

Eurail Saverpass

Unlimited **first-class** rail travel for 2, 3, 4, or 5 people traveling together at all times in any or all of the previously listed 17 European countries, with the same privileges and choice of validity periods as the Eurailpass.

Eurail Youth Pass

For those who are still **younger than age 26** on their first day of train travel, this pass provides unlimited **second-class** rail travel in any or all of the aforementioned 17 countries. It entitles you to the same privileges and choice of validity periods as the first-class Eurailpass, except it is valid for second-class travel only.

Eurail Flexipass

Unlimited **first-class** rail travel in any or all of the aforementioned 17 countries. Buy either 10 or 15 travel days and use them within 2 months.

Eurail Saver Flexipass

Unlimited **first-class** rail travel for 2, 3, 4, or 5 people traveling together at all times in any or all of the aforementioned 17 countries. Purchase either 10 or 15 travel days to be used within 2 months.

Eurail Youth Flexipass

Unlimited **second-class** rail travel for passengers younger than age 26 on their first date of travel. Purchase either 10 or 15 days of travel to be used within 2 months.

Eurail/Drive Pass

Designed for those who use the rail network for most of their travels but who occasionally want an automobile to explore the local countryside. Includes 4 days of unlimited first-class rail travel throughout the 17 Eurail countries and 2 days of car rental vouchers that can be used at any time, and not necessarily consecutively, within a 2-month period. You can purchase up to 5 additional rail days and an unlimited number of additional car days.

Eurail Selectpass

This railpass is versatile but somewhat more complicated than other passes. It provides unlimited first-class rail travel for 5, 6, 8, or 10 days within a 2-month validity period in any 3 adjoining countries in the 17-country Eurail system. The travel days may be used consecutively or nonconsecutively. The countries you choose must be adjoining by country border and must be connected by *direct* train service (i.e., not by rail service through another country) or by ship. Confused? The following list clarifies which countries qualify:

INTRODUCTION

Country	Connected by train or ship to
Austria	Germany, Hungary, Italy, Switzerland
Benelux*	France, Germany, Ireland
Denmark	Germany, Norway, Sweden
Finland	Germany, Sweden
France	Benelux*, Germany, Ireland, Italy, Spain, Switzerland
Germany	Austria, Benelux*, Denmark, Finland, France, Switzerland, Sweden
Greece	Italy
Hungary	Austria
Ireland	Benelux*, France
Italy	Austria, France, Greece, Switzerland
Norway	Denmark, Sweden
Portugal	Spain
Spain	France, Portugal
Sweden	Denmark, Finland, Germany, Norway
Switzerland	Austria, France, Germany, Italy

*For the purposes of this pass, the countries of Belgium, Luxembourg, and The Netherlands are considered one country—Benelux.

Eurail Selectpass Saver

Same benefits and conditions as the aforementioned Eurail Selectpass, but designed for two or more persons traveling together. Each person receives a 15 percent discount.

Eurail Selectpass Youth

Travelers must be under the age of 26 on the first day of travel. Valid for unlimited second class rail travel in three adjoining countries of your choice. Other benefits and conditions are the same as the first-class Eurail Selectpass.

Europass

If your rail travel will be limited to **Germany, France, Italy, Spain, and/or Switzerland,** consider this "design-your-own" flexible multicountry pass for unlimited first-class rail travel. Choose 5, 6, 8, 10, or 15 days of rail travel to be used within 2 months. As with the other Flexipasses, the travel days need not be consecutive.

You can really get creative by now adding up to 2 of the following geographical "areas" to your pass for an additional fee (see the list in the Appendix for all prices):

Benelux (includes Belgium, the Netherlands, and Luxembourg)
Austria and Hungary
Greece (includes ferry crossing from Italy to Greece)
Portugal

Youth Europasses for unlimited second-class rail travel are available to those younger than age 26 on their first day of travel.

Europass Saverpass

Unlimited first-class rail travel for 2 to 5 persons traveling together at all times to the five countries covered by the Europass plus up to two additional zones. Choose 5, 6, 8, 10, or 15 days of unlimited first-class rail travel within a 2-month period.

Europass Rail/Drive

Similar in concept to the Eurail/Drive Pass but valid only in the same countries as the regular Europass. It includes 3 days of unlimited first-class rail travel and 2 days of car rental vouchers. Unlimited additional car rental days may be purchased, up to 7 additional rail days. Zones are not available.

Europe's Passenger Trains

Europe's passenger trains range from perky little cogwheel rail cars that ascend the Alps to the sleek, high-tech, high-speed trains that whisk you to your destination at an average speed of 186 mph. In between are international **EuroCity** (EC) express trains running on the main lines, national **InterCity** (IC) and regional trains providing express services within a country's borders, and the extensive collection of rail cars that ply suburban lines.

The basis of Western Europe's high-speed rail traffic is a flawless rail bed equipped with endless-welded track, which enables the trains to glide smoothly enough to permit dining without fear that the next curve might slosh your coffee. The newer high-speed passenger trains include a whole stable full of various passenger car (carriage) types, including plush compartment interiors, comfortable seats, a children's play area, and businesslike amenities such as computer hookups and telephones.

TGVs (*train à grande vitesse,* or train of great speed) and **Thalys** trains are at the very heart of the European high-speed rail network connecting France with Belgium, The Netherlands, Germany, and Switzerland. The TGV Atlantique cruises at speeds up to 186 mph to link Paris with western and southwestern France and holds the world's speed record at 320 mph (515 km/h). France's newest high-speed line (June 2001), **TGV Mediterranee** (TGV Med), connects Paris with Avignon in 2 hours 40 minutes, Marseille in only 3 hours, Montpellier in 3 hours 15 minutes, and Nice in 5 hours 36 minutes. Travel time to 140 cities was reduced by up to one hour and frequency of service increased on the Paris-Marseille route from 11 to 17 trains per day and on the Paris-Nice route from 3 trains per day to 6.

TGV Med is a double-decker train that can accommodate up to 1,056 passengers in total comfort. TGV high-speed lines also connect Paris's Charles de Gaulle Airport and Disneyland Paris with many other major French cities.

Germany's **InterCity Express (ICE)** service provides cars with increased leg room, headphones, and even some video systems built into the seat backs. The new ICE 3 train was unveiled in Berlin at Expo 2000. This new member of the ICE family is now the fastest not only in speed, but in acceleration.

Italy has not only a "tilting tower" (the Leaning Tower of Pisa) but also "tilting" trains termed **Eurostar Italia.** You can sit back and relax with snacks and an espresso while the comfortable *ETR 500 Pendolino* trains whisk you to your destination at an operating speed of more than 150 mph. And the powerful dual-voltage **Cisalpino** trains, the world's first international tilting trains, easily climb the mountain routes between Italy and Switzerland. The high-speed **Artesia** connects Italy with France.

The British-Belgian-French–modified TGVs, known as **"Eurostar"** trains, connect Britain with Continental Europe. Connecting through London and the English Channel tunnel (Chunnel) to Paris or Brussels, the Eurostar trains make the British connection between London's Waterloo International station in the city's center and Paris's Gare du Nord or Brussels's Midi stations in less than 3 hours. Even the airlines can't get you there any faster if you consider the amount of time it takes from city center to the airport, going through security and customs, and then transportation from the arrival airport to city center.

The "Chunnel" and Eurostar Trains

On May 6, 1994, England's Queen Elizabeth II and France's President François Mitterand inaugurated a new era in European train travel—the linking of England and France via a tunnel that runs underground and beneath the English Channel. More than 17 million tons of earth were moved to build the two rail tunnels (one for northbound and one for southbound traffic) and one service tunnel. The Chunnel has proven to be one of the world's largest undertakings. The project cost more than $13 billion and took 7 years to complete.

Napoleon's engineer, Albert Mathieu, planned the first tunnel in 1802, incorporating an underground passage with ventilation chimneys above the waves. For obvious reasons the British were nervous. Later, in 1880, the first real attempt at a tunnel was undertaken by Colonel Beaumont, who bored 2,000 meters into the earth before abandoning the project. When work on another tunnel began in 1974, the Beaumont tunnel was found to be in good condition. Construction of the current tunnels began in 1987; they are 38 kilometers in length undersea and have an average depth of 40 meters under the seabed.

Operated by a British railway operating company (Eurostar) and by the French (SNCF) and Belgian (SNCB) railways, the Eurotunnel provides three different types of service between England and the Continent. Eurostar provides passenger service, and Le Shuttle provides automobile, coach, and lorry service between Folkstone and Calais. International rail freight rounds out the list.

Travel times from London to Paris are reduced from more than 9½ hours to under 3 hours; Brussels is only 2 hours and 40 minutes away, thus making a European Capitals tour nothing more than a day excursion. *Eurailpass* holders receive a discount on Eurostar tickets. Eurostar also serves Lille and Calais in Northern France, Marne-la-Valle to Euro Disney just east of Paris, and Ashford in England.

The sleek **Eurostar** trains (*Trans Manche Super Trains*) each carry nearly 800 passengers (25 in premium first class, 206 in first class, and 548 in second class) and reach speeds of 186 mph in France and 100 mph through the Chunnel and in England. The train is based primarily on the TGV but was redesigned to accommodate the three different voltage types encountered en route. The trains are accessible to disabled passengers and those with special needs. Arrangements may be made up to 48 hours prior to departure by calling Eurostar Complimentary Assistance Service in the United Kingdom at 44 (1233) 617575. Sufficient storage for luggage is provided.

Families traveling with children may opt for coaches 1 or 18 where facilities are offered for baby changing and flip-up seats allow more room for kids. Ask the train manager for a children's pack of things to do while traveling.

You are required to check in at the Eurostar terminal at least 20 minutes prior to departure. We suggest allowing a bit more time. This train is long (nearly a quarter of a mile) and the walk to your seat may be a lengthy one. After check-in and passing through the security and passport control, you will find a boarding area lounge, cafeteria, bar, and shops.

Those taking advantage of a trip from Paris or Brussels to London on a Eurostar train are in for a treat. The trains offer the comfort and amenities comparable to few other trains in the world. From departure you're in store for a smooth, quiet ride, and even when you enter the tunnel, the only noticeable change is the sudden darkness outside the windows. Those concerned with changes in air pressure needn't worry. Air flow through the tunnel is regulated to minimize changes in pressure, and few passengers, if any, notice discomfort.

Eurostar staff are multilingual and are available to provide assistance from the minute you enter the terminal to the minute you exit the platform. You'll notice them right away, dressed in navy blue uniforms with accented yellow scarves or ties. If you have any questions, don't be shy—they're there to serve you, and serve you they do.

Passengers traveling first class are treated to an onboard gourmet meal with wine ranging from breakfast to dinner, depending upon the time of day. Second-class passengers won't starve either, as a buffet car and roving refreshment-cart services are available at reasonable costs.

Given the frequency of rail service and the speed of travel, it's easy to see

London Waterloo Station—Brussels Midi/Zuid

Depart London	Eurostar Train No.	Arrive Brussels	Notes
0550	9106	0937	Not Saturdays
0614	9108	0959	Saturdays only
0653	9110	1037	Not Saturdays
0827	9116	1210	
1027	9124	1405	
1123	9128	1507	Saturdays only
1227	9132	1610	
1423	9140	1802	
1627	9148	2010	
1719	9152	2106	Fridays only
1723	9152	2110	Saturdays only
1927	9160	2310	

Brussels Midi/Zuid—London Waterloo

Depart Brussels	Eurostar Train No.	Arrive London	Notes
0701	9109	0843	Sarurdays only
0701	9109	0850	Mondays to Fridays: also runs Saturdays from 14 July to 1 September
0801	9113	0939	Fridays and Saturdays only
0857	9117	1039	
1101	9125	1243	
1301	9133	1443	
1456	9141	1639	
1701	9149	1843	
1756	9153	1939	Not Saturdays
1856	9157	2039	
2101	9165	2242	

how a "quick trip" to Paris, Brussels, or any Continental destination can be accomplished. Above are the schedules for Eurostar trains running between London and Brussels. On the following pages are the schedules of Eurostar trains running between London and Paris.

Notes

- Holders of Eurailpass, Europass, Britrail Pass, Benelux Tourrail Pass, and France Pass receive discounts on Eurostar services.
- Eurail/Europass, Benelux Tourrail, and France Pass cannot be used for rail travel in Britain.
- All Eurostar trains are nonsmoking.

To purchase one-way or round-trip Eurostar tickets or for scheduling information on trains to other cities, call toll-free (877) RAILPASS (877–724–5727), fax (614) 764–0711, or visit www.railpass.com/eurostar.

Paris Nord—London Waterloo

DEPART PARIS	EUROSTAR TRAIN No.	ARRIVE LONDON	NOTES
0637	9005	0839	Saturdays only
0637	9005	0846	Saturdays only
0716	9007	0909	
0813	9011	1013	
0843	9013	1043	Saturdays only
0910	9015	1113	
0943	9017	1143	Runs Mondays; also runs Fridays 12 July to 30 August
1019	9019	1209	
1113	9023	1313	Runs Fridays; also runs Saturdays from 13 July to 31 August
1143	9025	1343	
1219	9027	1409	
1304	9031	1509	
1416	9035	1609	Runs Fridays; also runs Saturdays from 13 July to 31 August
1443	9037	1643	
1519	9039	1709	Runs Mondays, Fridays and Saturdays only; also runs Tuesdays to Thursdays 16 July to 29 August
1543	9041	1743	Fridays only
1607	9043	1813	
1710	9047	1909	Not Saturdays
1710	9047	1913	Saturdays only
1743	9049	1943	Not Saturdays
1743	9049	1943	Saturdays only
1816	9051	2009	
1843	9053	2043	Runs Mondays 15 April to 26 August
1919	9055	2113	
2007	9058	2213	
2043	9061	2246	Fridays only
2113	9063	2316	
2131	9065	2350	Runs Fridays 12 July to 30 August

London Waterloo—Paris Nord

DEPART LONDON	EUROSTAR TRAIN NO.	ARRIVE PARIS	NOTES
0515	9078	0923	Mondays to Fridays; also runs Saturdays from 13 July to 31 August
0619	9002	1023	
0653	9004	1059	Saturdays only
0723	9006	1123	
0753	9008	1157	Mondays, Fridays, and Saturdays only
0823	9010	1223	
0853	9012	1253	
0923	9014	1323	
0953	9016	1353	Mondays, Fridays, and Saturdays only
1023	9018	1417	
1053	9020	1453	Fridays and Saturdays only
1153	9024	1559	
1223	9026	1623	Runs Fridays 12 July to 30 August
1253	9028	1647	
1323	9030	1723	Runs Fridays; also runs Mondays to Thursdays and Saturdays from 13 July to 31 August
1353	9032	1753	
1523	9038	1923	
1553	9040	1947	Runs Fridays; also runs Saturdays from 13 July to 31 August
1623	9042	2023	
1648	9044	2059	
1715	9046	2117	Not Saturdays
1748	9048	2153	Not Saturdays
1753	9048	2153	Saturdays only
1853	9052	2253	Not Saturdays
1923	9054	2323	Fridays only
1953	9056	2347	
2023	9058	0017	Runs Fridays 12 July to 30 August

London—Disneyland Paris

DEPART LONDON	EUROSTAR TRAIN NO.	ARRIVE DISNEYLAND PARIS
0927	9074	1329

DEPART DISNEYLAND PARIS	EUROSTAR TRAIN NO.	ARRIVE LONDON
1935	9057	2139

Eurostar Fares

Eurostar fares are provided in U.S. dollars, one-way, in either direction and are subject to change at the discretion of the railways. For tickets, schedules, group rates, and for other cities serviced including Ashford, Lille, Calais-Frethun, and Marne-la-Vallee, contact RailPass.com toll-free at (877) RAILPASS (877–724–5727); *Fax:* (614) 764–0711; *Internet:* www. railpass.com.

LONDON TO/FROM PARIS OR BRUSSELS

	First Class	Second Class	Notes
Adult Fare	$279	$199	1
Senior Fare	$189	S159	2
Youth Fare	$165	S79	3
Child Fare	$109	$69	4
Adult Fare w/railpass	$155	$75	5
Leisure Fare (round trip)	$438	$278	6

1. Ages 26 and over
2. Ages 60 and over
3. Ages 12–25; railpass discount not available for youths
4. Ages 4–11; railpass discount not available for children
5. Discounted ticket available with the purchase of a Eurailpass, Europass, SelectPass, France Pass or BritRail Pass
6. Saturday overnight or 3-night minimum stay required
   Seat reservations are mandatory on all Eurostar trains
   Tickets issued include reservation on the same voucher (inclusive price)
   Youthpass holders can utilize second class only
   First class includes a gourmet meal

Night Trains/Hotel Trains

Although we usually advocate going to Europe to see it, not sleep through it, today's European overnight trains provide a most comfortable and convenient means of transport over long distances. And there's an aura of romance on Europe's luxurious hotel trains.

There is a great variety of accommodations (and prices) on night trains, ranging from comfortable reclining seats in second class on certain trains, termed "sleeperettes," to luxurious hotel-style trains complete with a lobby area, concierge, and dining car. There are three main categories on hotel trains: Tourist, First, and Luxury Class. Tourist Class provides four beds in one compartment. First Class has one- or two-bed compartments. Toilet facilities are at the ends of the rail cars. Luxury Class features one- or two-bed compartments, complete with toilet and shower *inside* the compartment.

All night trains require reservations, and railpasses do not cover the cost of sleeping accommodations. You must pay a supplement, which varies according to the type of accommodations and type of train. For example, the supplemental cost per person to railpass holders for a reclining seat on the CityNightLine trains connecting Germany with Switzerland and Austria is only $11 U.S.; a six-bed couchette, $18; Economy double, $60; and Deluxe double, $109.

Traditional night trains usually do not have full restaurant service, but the steward can provide drinks and snacks, or, of course, you can bring your own. They are normally comprised of standard sleeping cars, couchette cars (with six berths per compartment in second class and four-berth compartments in first), plus seats.

EuroNight (EN) trains are usually air-conditioned and provide additional comfort and services with the same basic facilities as the traditional sleeping car trains. EN trains complement EuroCity daytime trains and offer a wash basin with soap, towels, and a power plug; a real bed with sheets, pillows, and blankets; complimentary mineral water, snacks, and a continental breakfast served in the cabin.

For luxury, comfort, and privacy, Europe's high-tech, high-comfort hotel trains are top of the line—DB-Nachtzug (German Rail), CityNightLine (based in Switzerland), Elipsos (Spanish Rail) and InterCityNight trains (Italian). A Nachtzug cabin contains its own private shower, toilet, and wash basin, and beds are aligned in the direction of travel. Popular routes include Berlin-Munich, Hamburg–Munich, Hamburg–Frankfurt–Stuttgart, and Munich–Copenhagen (via Stuttgart/Frankfurt). Railpass holders receive a discount on cabin rates.

CityNightLine trains feature high-quality, double-decked, hotel-style sleeping accommodations and single-level sleeperette cars with reclining seats and couchettes. The Deluxe category provides spacious two-bed compartments, shower, toilet, and panoramic windows. For budget travelers, the Economy category features two- and four-bed compartments and quads with washing facilities. CityNightLine routes include Zürich to Berlin (via Frankfurt), Dresden (via Leipzig), and Hamburg (via

Dortmund); Dortmund to Vienna (via Cologne–Frankfurt).

The tilting Spanish **Elipsos** trains operate within Spain and internationally into Portugal, France, Italy, and Switzerland. The Gran Clase sleeping cars include private toilet and shower facilities; Turista Class offers four-berth compartments; or, for economy, choose the sleeperette seats. Trains carrying the Gran Clase cars include the famous *Pau Casals* (Barcelona–Geneva, Bern, and Zürich), the *Antonio Machado* (Barcelona–Seville/Malaga), the *Joan Miro* (Barcelona–Paris), *Francisco de Goya* (Paris–Madrid), *Salvador Dali* (Barcelona–Milan), and the *Lusitania* (Madrid–Lisbon).

Generally speaking, the least expensive trains with sleeping accommodations are in southern and eastern Europe; northern and central Europe are the most expensive. The sleeperette, or reclining seat, is the least expensive type of accommodation, and Luxury Class on hotel trains is the most expensive.

The **OverNight Express** (Dutch) runs from Amsterdam to Milan daily, except Saturday, and from Milan to Amsterdam daily, except Sunday. Choose from three options: the traditional sleeper, a couchette (four per compartment), or the more economical reclining seat. You can have dinner on the train, sleep, and have breakfast the following morning—a great way to arrive refreshed, well rested, and ready to explore your new destination.

Seat Reservations

Most international and long-distance trains *require* seat reservations, including TGVs, Eurostars, InterCity and AVEs, EuroCity trains, Cisalpino and Artesia trains, some ICEs, and specialty sight-seeing trains such as those in Switzerland (*Glacier Express, Bernina Express, Crystal Panoramic*, and *The William Tell Express*).

A computerized reservation system linking the European rail routes is available in every major rail terminal in Europe. Check the train departure board—if there is an **"R"** next to that train, then seat reservations are mandatory, and you should not board without one. Seat reservations for TGVs and many other types of trains can be made at automatic reservation-ticket dispensers in the rail stations.

Seat reservations in Europe cost about $5.00 each, and this cost is *not* included in a railpass. Advance seat reservations may be made from North America; however, they are more expensive and nonrefundable. If you choose to make seat reservations from North America, you may make them through the same place you purchase your railpass. We do recommend making them for long distance/express trains during high season and if traveling on or near a holiday. The Point-to-Point and Reservations Department of RailPass.com can help with itinerary planning and seat reservations. *Tel:* (877) RAILPASS (877–724–5727) or (614) 793–7650 from 0900 to 1600 EST Monday through Friday.

The farther south you travel in Europe, the more important it becomes to have seat reservations, even if they are not required. *Always* have seat reservations when traveling in Italy and Greece. Seat reservations are not, however, accepted for most local trains, nor for trains traveling *within* the borders of Belgium, the Netherlands, Luxembourg, or Switzerland, with the exception of specialty trains.

To ensure that you receive the proper reservation:

- **Determine the day and date of your travel.** Remember, Europeans reverse the order of the month and day when writing dates. Day, month, and then year is the standard reading. For example, June 15, 2002, appears as 15/06/02 and *not* as 06/15/02.
- **Check the train schedules** posted in the rail stations for the train number, its departure time, and arrival time at your destination.
- **Print this information** on a piece of paper, starting with the date, the train number, and the departure time. Draw a short arrow, and then add the arrival time of the train and the name of your destination.
- **Indicate the number of seat reservations required.** Your seat reservation will identify the class of travel (first or second), smoking or nonsmoking, car number, and, in most cases, the seat number(s).

Plan to be on the train platform several minutes prior to scheduled departure. European trains stop only for a short time at intermediate stations to let passengers on and off, and stops of only 1 or 2 minutes are usual. To save a lot of scurrying around when the train arrives, **check the illustrated train composition diagrams** displayed on the platforms to determine the approximate positioning of your train's first- and second-class coaches.

Then, as your train approaches, look for *either* a large number "**1**" on or near the doors *or* a yellow stripe above the train windows to indicate first-class cars if you have a first-class railpass and/or a first-class seat reservation. Second-class cars are indicated with a large "**2**" on or near the doors.

Train Schedules

Most European rail stations have train arrival and departure times prominently posted, usually by huge digital display boards. The printed ones posted are easily recognized by their background color—**departure times are printed on yellow; arrival times on white.** Intermediate stops, train platform, and track numbers are posted as well. In case of discrepancy, the digital display boards take precedence. Although the time schedules may change, the track numbers seldom change.

Schedules are listed chronologically in **24-hour time** from 0001 (1 minute after midnight) to 1200 (noon) and to 2400 (midnight)—for instance, a departure time of 1843 would be equal to 6:43 P.M. **Note:** Arrival times for overnight/sleeper train schedules in this book show "+1" after the arrival time. This means your train arrives at the listed time on the following day.

Train information and reservation offices in the stations also provide printed mini-schedules listing rail services between two specific points. They're free. These offices have national and international schedules as well.

Train schedules presented in this edition of *Europe by Eurail* are updated to press time. They are, however, *for planning purposes only.* When purchasing a railpass, you are entitled to receive a **free timetable and map** of the major rail connections.

Train Splitting

When international trains in Europe have multiple destinations, some-times passenger coaches are "split" en route, with cars going to different cities. To make certain you end up where you want to be:

- **Check the train sideboards** displaying the departure point, stops en route, and the final destination.
- **Announce your destination** to the conductor as he or she checks your railpass.
- **Stay in your seat** when the train halts at a terminal for "splitting" the coaches. Since the splitting process occurs quickly, if you are in another part of the train you could easily end up at the wrong destination—sans suitcase and your fellow travelers.

There may also be times when two trains are scheduled to depart on the same track—one in each direction, of course. Check for your train's depar-ture position; otherwise you might be standing at the wrong end of the track as your train pulls away.

Trip Tips

Before You Go

If there have been any break-ins in your neighborhood, you should take steps to ensure that a break-in doesn't happen to you while you are gone. Alert the neighbors to keep a watchful eye for suspicious people and their activities. Many professional thieves have been known to park in a driveway in broad daylight with a moving van. The police should be advised regarding your absence. Also, check with the insurance agency that writes your homeowner's policy. Ask the same question they ask in those television commercials: "Am I covered?" You may need additional coverage during your absence. One final caution: Don't announce your forthcoming vacation plans in the newspapers. Thieves can read, too. Save the social column for your return.

What to Take?

Half the clothes and twice the money! Obviously, the practical answer to this question is, "As little as possible." We usually tend to pack everything we might conceivably use during a vacation, lug it everywhere, use it very little, and return home with longer arms. In these days of wash-and-wear fabrics (and deodorants), such an approach is not necessary. A good rule of thumb is to take **one medium-size suitcase with wheels** and a shoulder bag or two small bags. Hold to this rule and you will have a more comfort-able trip. Regardless of how comfortably warm you expect the weather to be at your destination, pack a **sweater.** Brief cold spells in Europe are not uncommon. Stow a small pocket **flashlight** in your shoulder bag together with a collapsible **umbrella** or rain hat in the "unlikely event" that you may need them.

Bring a **washcloth** if you normally use one, since they generally are not found in European hotels. Take an **electrical converter** and **adapter plugs** for your **electrical appliances**, such as electrical razors and hair dryers. Travel-size, dual-voltage hair dryers are more convenient—you only need to switch the voltage to the European 220 and add the appropriate adapter plug.

If you must take expensive jewelry with you, take a copy of its **insurance appraisal** as proof of purchase to customs officials upon your return. The same for watches produced by foreign manufacturers. You may have bought that solid-gold Rolex in a St. Louis pawnshop for a song, but the customs inspector could have you singing a different tune if you can't come up with the paperwork! Also bring **proof of purchase** on any expensive items you are traveling with, such as your laptop computer or video camera.

If you wear prescription eye glasses or contact lenses, **take a copy of the eyeglass or contact lenses prescription** with you. The same applies for **prescription medications.** Even if you use only over-the-counter drug products, we suggest taking an adequate supply of the item in its original container. Many such products are not available in Europe or are sold under a different label or packaging.

We heartily recommend luggage with wheels. Samsonite, the luggage manufacturer, has published an interesting booklet on the subject of suit-cases and travel. With the catchy title *Lightening the Travel Load—Travel Tips and Tricks,* it is crammed with helpful tips, everything from analyzing your packing and luggage needs to safeguarding your possessions on a trip. Helpful hints on carry-on luggage, how to tip, how to clear customs, and how to stay healthy are also included. For a free copy write to Samsonite Traveler Advisory Service, P.O. Box 39603, Denver, CO 80239. Include a self-addressed business envelope with postage affixed to cover up to 2 ounces of first-class mail.

Cash, Currencies, and Cards

Effective January 1, 2002, the **euro** (abbreviation is EUR; symbol €) is the legal tender for 12 of the 17 countries in *Europe by Eurail:* Austria, Belgium, Finland, France, Germany, Greece, Republic of Ireland, Italy, Luxembourg, the Netherlands, Portugal, and Spain. At press time, each country's national currency is to be withdrawn from circulation by February 28, 2002. Based on the decimal system, 100 "cents" equals 1 euro and there are eight different coins and seven different banknotes. Each country may use a different term for the sub-unit "cents." For example, France is permitted to use the term "euro-centimes" and Germany to use "euro-pfennig." Coins are issued in 1, 2, 5, 10, 20, and 50 euro cents, as well as 1-euro and 2-euro coins. Banknotes are issued in 5, 10, 20, 50, 100, 200 and 500 euro denominations.

The following conversion table was used to convert prices from each country's national currency to euro. At press time, all converted prices mentioned in each country chapter are subject to "rounding up" and/or change without notice.

Euro Conversion Rates

Country	Currency	1 euro =
Austria	ATS	13.7603
Belgium	BEF	40.3399
Finland	FIM	5.94573
France	FRF	6.55957
Germany	DEM	1.95583
Greece	GRD	340.750
Ireland	IEP	0.787564
Italy	ITL	1936.27
Luxembourg	LUF	40.3399
Netherlands	NLG	2.20371
Portugal	PTE	200.482
Spain	ESP	166.386

At press time, $1.00 U.S. = €1.10 EUR. For more information on converting from U.S. dollars to euros and to other countries' national currencies, visit the Web site **www.xe.net** or create your own "Cheat Sheet for Travelers" online at **www.oanda.com/cgi-bin/travel.** You can print out the conversion rates in a wallet-size format for each country you intend to visit. You can also purchase an electronic foreign exchange rate converter to carry with you.

Don't carry more cash than you can afford to lose; use **ATMs** (automated teller machines) or carry traveler's checks. You will, of course, need some cash on your flight to pay for tips, snacks, refreshments, and taxi fares at your arrival city. U.S. currency will usually do, but don't carry it all in one big roll—distribute it around in pockets, briefcase, money clip, and/or money belt. A money belt is an ideal way to carry larger notes. Getting some smaller denominations of the local currency is always a great idea for tipping, plus those coins and bills will make great souvenirs once the Euro is in place!

ATMs offer the best exchange rate on foreign currencies, but if you plan to use them, do your homework first. Ask your bank for a list of ATM locations in the countries where you plan to travel and whether or not your magnetic imprint needs to be modified to work in foreign ATMs. Be certain to know your PIN number, and inquire if the bank will charge you per overseas cash withdrawal. Also, remember that ATM PIN numbers in Europe are four digits; six digits will not work. The two largest international ATM networks are Visa/Plus and MasterCard/Cirrus. To find out which network your bank uses, you can look on the back of your card for the network logo. To find the ATM locations abroad for Visa/Plus, write to Visa International, 900 Metro Center Boulevard, M1-9C, Foster City, CA 94404, or access the Web site at www.visa.com; for MasterCard/Cirrus, call (800) 4–CIRRUS, or access its Web site at www.mastercard.com.

Although U.S. banks levy surcharges for the luxury of using their machines, these charges do not extend to U.S.-issued cards at machines overseas. Remember, though, that a cash withdrawal on a credit card is like a "temporary mini-loan," and there is an interest charge.

You can avoid interest charges by using a **debit card** (whereby cash withdrawals and purchases are deducted from your checking account). You probably will still pay a fee of around $2.00 per withdrawal with a debit card. If you do carry traveler's checks, cash them at the branch-bank facilities located in or near railway stations and airports. Banks and official currency-exchange services are required to pay the official exchange rates. Hotels and stores seldom give you the full exchange value and often add substantial service fees. Credit cards are handy for paying the larger expenses, such as hotels and restaurants. The charge is converted into dollars at the applicable exchange rate on the date the charge is posted.

Make a list of credit card, traveler's check, airline ticket, and railpass numbers that you plan to take. With a computer and a scanner, you can put copies of your documents on disk. When purchasing your railpass, inquire about Pass Protection, a type of travel insurance covering any unused portion of the pass in case of loss or theft while abroad. Leave a copy of your list at home and pack one in your suitcase or carry-on bag. Make **two copies of your passport.** Leave one copy at home and take the other one with you. Carry a certified copy of your birth certificate and a few extra passport photos. Taking the time to do this will save you days of delay on your trip if your passport is lost or stolen. If your passport is lost or stolen, report it to the local police and contact the nearest U.S. Embassy or Consulate.

Cameras, Film

If you plan to take an expensive foreign-made camera that you purchased in the United States, bring the sales slip. Otherwise, go to a U.S. Customs Office before leaving the country and have your equipment registered. Carry a copy of the sales slip or the registration form with your passport and keep a spare copy tucked away in the camera case or your shoulder bag.

Despite what airport officials tell you, their electronic luggage-checking devices could fog your film. The best way to avoid that is to not have film in your camera when you go through airport security, and place unboxed film in clear plastic bags. Ask that your cameras and film be inspected by hand. Above all, do not pack film in your check-through luggage. Although special lead-lined bags are available at most camera stores, luggage is subjected to a high level of radiation, and the film can still be damaged.

Color film in Europe is usually more expensive than if it were purchased at home. The solution? Prepare and take all the film you'll need with you. The same principle applies for those videotaping their adventures. We found it to be a stress reliever to have extra film and batteries on hand. Just recharge every evening, and you won't miss a shot.

We have had fun with digital cameras. Just carry a box of computer disks, which takes up as little room as 4 rolls of film, and have a go at it. Review pictures as soon as you take them and delete any that are not up to par. Plus, you can label the disk immediately with the city and site names for reference. When home, enjoy viewing them on your PC, use them as screen-savers, or take them to a local photo lab and have actual prints made from the images on your disk files.

En Route Tips

With all the luxuries of flight that aircraft offer, something about flying makes it more demanding on your system than a similar amount of time spent at home or in the office. For North Americans, it takes an entire day to reach Europe by air and an entire day to return. A transatlantic trip with a minimum of inconveniences is what we're after. Here are some suggestions that we've found helpful on our flights.

In-Flight Comfort. If you plan to catch some shut-eye en route, ask for a seat alongside a bulkhead. Bulkheads don't mind being leaned on, but passengers do. If you need more legroom, sit in an emergency exit row, but only if you are physically capable of standing and opening the exit hatch if necessary. Also, be sure your seat reclines. On some planes the seats in front of the emergency exits do not recline. Opt for seats in the forward section of the airplane; passengers in the forward section generally experience less vibration and engine noise.

Wear loose clothing. Unfasten your shoes, but don't take them off. Your feet will swell following several hours of immobility at airplane altitudes. The best remedy is to walk the length of the aisle in the airplane every hour or so. Try deep knee bends. To reduce swelling, consider wearing elastic stockings.

Flying dehydrates your body. Drink lots of water and watch what you mix with it—alcohol and soda drinks dehydrate, too. Special meals for special diets are no problem with the airlines, but requests should be made at the same time as reservations and reconfirmed 48 hours prior to departure.

Jet Lag—What to Do About It. Although the flying time aboard most commercial jet airliners ranges from 7 to 8 hours, airport to airport, it will be Day 2 before you arrive in Europe. (There are a few daytime eastbound transatlantic flights, but most depart at night during Day 1 and arrive the following morning; that is, Day 2.) During the flight you will be exposed to a cocktail hour, a dinner hour, and a break for an after-dinner drink, followed by a full-length feature movie. In the morning, as the sun rises in the east over Europe, you'll be awakened for breakfast an hour or so before landing.

Add up the time consumed by all the scheduled events while en route, and you'll quickly conclude that your night spent in the sky over the Atlantic Ocean consisted of many things—except sleep. Even if you did manage to sleep during the entire trip instead of eating, drinking, and watching movies, your body and all its functions will be arriving in Europe a few hours after midnight by North American time. You will crave adjustment to the phenomenon known as jet lag, which will be trying its best to interrupt your plans for a carefree vacation.

The following explanation of what jet lag is and some means to combat it should prove helpful to any traveler undergoing 4 or more hours of time change.

The human body has numerous rhythms; sleep is one of them. Even without sunlight, as in a cave, the body will still maintain a 24-hour awake/asleep cycle. The heart rate falls to a very low ebb in the early hours of the morning, when you are usually asleep. Body temperature, which affects the mental processes, also drops during this time. Consequently, if an air traveler is transported rapidly to a time zone 5 or 6 hours ahead of that of the departure point, even though it may be 8:00 or 9:00 A.M. at the arrival point in local time, the traveler's body functions are at a low ebb. As a result, the traveler feels subpar, and this feeling can persist for as long as 2 or 3 days unless something is done to correct it.

To cope effectively with jet lag, start varying your normal sleep-eat-work pattern a week or so before your departure. If you are normally up by 7:00 A.M. and in bed around 11:00 P.M. or so, get up earlier and go to bed later for a few days. Then reverse the procedure by sleeping in a bit in the morning and going to bed ahead of your normal time. Vary your mealtimes, possibly putting off breakfast until lunchtime. This will condition your body to accept changes in routines. In turn, when the big transatlantic change comes, it won't be as much of a shock on your system.

Remember, to lessen the effects of jet lag en route, avoid excessive drinking of alcohol and soda and eating. Set your watch to local time at your destination as you descend on your flight. By doing this, you subconsciously accelerate your adjustment to the new time zone. For example, how many times have you looked at your watch and *then* realized you were hungry? After your arrival, exercise the first day by taking a vigorous walk, followed by a long nap. Then take it easy for the rest of your arrival day. From now on begin doing everything you normally do back home according to the new local time.

Some seasoned transatlantic travelers take even stronger precautions to avoid jet lag. They follow the rule of "no coffee, tea, food, wine, beer, or liquor" on the day of the flight to Europe. They do, however, advocate lots of fruit juices, vegetable juices, and water (no carbonated drinks). This method follows the theory that your body clock will then go on hold, waiting for you to restart it with breakfast the day you arrive in Europe.

Resist the temptations of the airlines up to the point of breakfast and try to get some sleep. Some current studies have shown the hormone melatonin to be useful in combatting jet lag, but as with any other over-the-counter drug, you should first consult your physician. And then there's the "light theory"—that using a blue light source behind your elevated kneecaps will eliminate jet lag. Regardless of which remedies you choose, respect jet lag by taking some precautions and taking it easy on yourself, and you'll enjoy your vacation.

Tax-Free Purchases. Tax-free shopping in Europe ended in 1999 between European Union (EU) countries. This change should have little if any effect on U.S. and other non-EU travelers as long as travel is to or from a non-EU destination. The EU consists of Austria, Belgium, Denmark, Finland, France, Germany, Great Britain, Greece, Italy, Luxembourg, the

Netherlands, Portugal, Spain, and Sweden. Every international airport, as well as many ferry ports and train stations, currently has a "tax-free" shopping service. The routine is generally the same: You select your purchase, pay for it and add it to your carry-on luggage, find safe storage for it during the flight, and then haul it off the airplane. There are variations.

For example, at JFK in New York you select the items from a sample or catalog. The items are then delivered "for your convenience" to your departure gate for pickup. The hazards of this system are many. If the delivery person gets things mixed up and fails to make the right gate at the right time, you'll be off into the wild blue yonder sans purchases. Or if you are late passing the pickup point, sometimes an unknown "benefactor" will try to help by taking your purchases onboard the plane ahead of you—then finding this so-called benefactor can prove to be difficult.

Solution? Buy your "booty" aboard the airplane while en route. Most international airlines carry aboard a good stock of "tax-free" items that you can purchase from the cabin crew. It's always best to check at the airline counter, however, to be certain that this in-flight service will be available on your particular flight. *Tax-free,* by the way, is a misused term. Most items, with the exception of alcohol and tobacco, normally may be purchased more cheaply in the arrival city. Many airports are planning to create specialty shopping outlets to compensate for revenue losses. If you're taking any Eurostar or Channel crossing trips while abroad, the taxes in Belgium and France are lower than in Britain.

Keep in mind that everything you purchase, "tax-free" or otherwise, is subject to customs duty when returning home. Shipped items are processed separately. Consequently, know your quotas and attempt to stay within them to avoid paying duty and experiencing the ensuing delays involved. Good luck with customs. And remember, honesty is always the best policy!

Prior to Landing. Fill out all the customs and immigration forms your flight attendant may give you and keep them with your passport and airline ticket. Keep this packet handy but secure, until your credentials are required by the customs or immigrations officials at the arriving airport.

Train Travel Tips

"What affects men sharply about a foreign nation," wrote G. K. Chesterton, "is not so much finding or not finding familiar things, it is rather not finding them in the familiar place."

Going to Europe for the first time can mean a confusion of terminology that causes us to learn too late that what we sought was actually available throughout our visit. Our problem can be merely not knowing where to look and what to ask for. The following tips should help you enjoy your rail adventures:

Travel for the Disabled. Rail travel is becoming more and more a chosen method of transportation and recreation for disabled persons.

Many aids for the disabled have been incorporated into rail station design. Trains are being designed with wider doors for wheelchair access; some even have a removable seat to make room for a wheelchair. Ramp access to toilets, buffets, and other facilities is being provided. Folding wheelchairs are also available at main stations so that occupants can be transferred to a regular seat once aboard the train.

The European railways are eager to provide as comfortable a journey as possible for the disabled passenger. To do this, advise authorities of your intended travel plans before departure.

In the United States contact Mobility International USA, P.O. Box 10767, Eugene, OR 97440 (*Tel:* 541–343–1284; *Fax:* 541–343–6812); visit www.miusa.org, or e-mail info@miusa.org for information about services and referrals to international affiliates. They also produce helpful booklets for travelers upon request.

If you plan to travel in Europe with a disabled person, as soon as you establish your itinerary, contact one of the tourist offices listed in the Appendix and begin making arrangements. The same applies to the airline you'll be using for your transatlantic flight. Give details of your itinerary, the nature of the disability, and any other information that will help them to help you, such as whether a wheelchair is needed at departures and arrivals. Specifically, provide information regarding special diets, medications, and toilet and medical-attention requirements. With these details attended to, you can look forward to a pleasant journey.

Baggage Carts. Many otherwise able train visitors to Europe impose a severe disadvantage upon themselves by arriving with more luggage than anyone could possibly carry. Train porters are nearly an extinct species, and their demise was expedited by the luggage trolley—Europe's version of our baggage cart—an elusive device that, whatever your position on the train platform, haunts the extreme opposite end and requires insertion of coins to use.

Our number-one trip tip to all train travelers is to "go lightly." We repeat: At most, take **one medium-size suitcase with wheels or two small bags,** augmented by a modest shoulder bag. There will still be times when you wish you could discard your suitcase. Pack lightly and leave room for souvenirs, or you'll just need to purchase another piece of luggage.

If you have purchased a model with built-in wheels, however, it usually will follow at your heels like a well-trained dog as you apply minimum pulling power. Unlike a dog, the wheeled suitcase cannot climb stairs by itself, so be prepared to lift it on and off the train and in some stations without elevators.

Consider investing in your own baggage cart to take with you if you wish to use the luggage you have. There are many types available. You will see more and more train travelers proceeding through rail stations in Europe with wheeled equipment.

When loading your luggage onto a baggage cart or station trolley, keep the load as narrow as possible. The trolleys provided by the station should not be taken aboard the train, although we've seen it tried. Again, if you are taking your own cart with you, fold it before boarding. If you don't, you may spend an embarrassing 10 minutes or so on the station platform extracting a hapless fellow traveler from it as your train eases out of the station without you.

Porter Services. Porter service is on the wane but still available in some train stations, particularly the larger ones. The best way to locate a porter is to inquire at the LEFT LUGGAGE (baggage storage) area. Most stations also offer luggage lockers (some stations have stopped this service and, for security reasons, have even removed trash containers). If your luggage has been checked in at the station, there will be a handling charge, but the tip remains a personal transaction between you and the porter.

Most porters will take your bags to the train and place them aboard in the luggage racks over your seat. Porters are rather scarce on arrival platforms. If you must have assistance, approach the stationmaster's office or the train conductor prior to departure, with the request that a porter be asked to meet your train upon arrival at your destination.

If you are transferring between base cities or changing hotels from one city to another, you can request the hall porter at the hotel you are leaving to arrange for the arriving hotel's hall porter to meet your train upon arrival. A small tip should arrange everything.

A Few More Train-Travel Tips. A few more train travel tips to make your trip more enjoyable:

• Show your pass or rail ticket, upon request, and in the case of the pass, have your passport handy should the conductor want to see it.

• Don't place your feet on the seats of the train unless you have removed your shoes or have provided a protective covering for the seat.

• Place your luggage in the overhead racks (or the luggage vestibules) provided for that purpose—not on the seats so that other passengers won't be able to crowd you.

• Observe the smoking/nonsmoking areas and rules. There are rather stiff fines for smokers who violate the nonsmoking regulations.

• Observe seat reservations. Seating that has been reserved is marked, usually by a ticket inserted at the top of the seat. Even though it is apparent that a seat is unoccupied, if there are other passengers seated opposite, ask whether the seat is open—doing so will avoid embarrassment later if the person holding the reservation happens to return.

• Arrange dining-car reservations on long-distance trains soon after boarding. Ask the conductor. If he or she cannot make the reservations for you, a member of the dining-car crew will do so. Generally, these crew members pass through the train prior to the first serving for that purpose. Usually there are two servings, so be prepared to select the one to your liking. You can also ask about the menu at the same time. The second serving is scheduled so that the dining-car crew has time to tidy up before the train reaches its destination. Therefore, the first serving is preferred by many because it does not seem to be as rushed.

• If you plan an overnight journey on a sleeper, ask the attendant to explain how the equipment in your compartment operates. For example, newer sleeping cars have electric shades. A push of the button and they open; another push of the same button and they close. If you did not know the button's function, you just might try pushing the button while the train was standing in a station and you were not dressed for the occasion!

• Tip the attendant on a sleeper for his or her services; the appropriate time to do so is when breakfast is served.

Not by Bread Alone

Oddly enough, the reader who exists on hamburgers and milk shakes back home will find such a diet expensive to maintain in Europe. Europe abounds in good, wholesome food. Practically every major railway station has a cafeteria where the food is displayed along with the prices. "Order the spaghetti Bolognese," was the advice of one tourist official in Switzerland. "You can't go wrong," he declared, and he was right.

Many of the railway stations have cafes and dining-room facilities, and some even have gourmet restaurants. Most European restaurants offer a tourist menu at a fixed cost. Look for the MENU sign, posted outside, showing the prices and food selections.

If you are puzzled by foreign menus, take heart. Many European restaurants have menus that have been translated into your language. Although the translated versions may take some of the "adventure" out of eating in a foreign country, they may save an embarrassing moment—such as ordering the poulet, which you recognize as chicken, and ending up with a whole roasted chicken!

To help hold the food price line, determine if your hotel includes breakfast with the accommodations and, if so, what kind of breakfast and how much the room is without it.

On day excursions, pack a picnic-style lunch. Bread, cheese, pastry, cold cuts, fruits, soft drinks, and beer or wine—all are available from local shops. If you give advance notice, perhaps the hotel will prepare a basket lunch for you.

For the most part, meals served aboard the trains are, naturally, on the expensive side. In many cases, though, the food is excellent and well worth the premium you pay for enjoying it as you speed along with the scenic countryside. Many trains provide buffet and cafeteria services, and you can usually count on a food trolley being aboard for drinks and sandwiches. On some premium trains, such as the TGV, gourmet meals are served at your seat—airline style. One fact remains: The least expensive food aboard a train is that which you brought. Again, plan ahead and save.

Dos & Don'ts Safety Tips

• Picking pockets is an art that is seemingly practiced throughout the world and most commonly occurs in crowded public places. Be leery of being bumped or of someone causing a distracting incident. Don't carry anything more valuable than a handkerchief in hip pockets. Money belts, holster wallets, or pouches that can be hidden are the safest way to carry cash and other valuables.

- If you do not have a concealable money belt, holster wallet, or pouch, women should place the straps of their purses across their chests and carry the purses in front—not on the side with the straps only on the shoulder. Motorcycle thieves can grab the purse from your shoulder very easily. Men should modify the inside pocket of a coat or jacket with a zipper or Velcro. Or sew a medium-size button both above and below the pocket opening. Loop a piece of shoestring or other strong string around the buttons when carrying valuables. Don't let the thought of someone picking your pocket alarm you. Just be aware of it and take the proper precautions.
- Don't leave cash, cameras, and other valuables in the hotel room or locked up in a suitcase. Take them with you or leave them in the hotel safe. We advocate leaving expensive jewelry at home, but if you must take it with you, leave it in the hotel safe when you're not wearing it.
- Don't dangle your camera from around your neck or wrist; keep it in an inexpensive-looking camera bag.
- Don't designate one individual to carry everyone's passport or other valuables, and don't carry all of your own valuables in one place. Split up documents and money in various safe holding locations.
- Stay alert.

For further peace of mind, review the Web site www.travel.state.gov/asafetripabroad.html for insightful tips and suggestions for "A Safe Trip Abroad." It contains ideas on what to bring and leave behind, what to learn and arrange before you go, as well as helpful tips for public transport safety.

Remember, visitors are always subject to the law of the land, so pay attention to media reports and research some of the local laws and customs prior to departure. Also consider visiting the U.S. State Department's Internet site, www.state.gov, which contains up-to-date information on foreign affairs. You may also contact the U.S. Department of State Consular's Office for information on travel warnings and public announcements by calling (202) 647–5225; *fax:* (202) 647–3000; or visit www.travel.state.gov.

Several pamphlets are available as well from the Superintendent of Documents, U.S. Government Printing Office, Washington, DC 20420, *tel:* (202) 512–1800. At about $1.00 each, they include *Your Safe Trip Abroad, Tips for Americans Residing Abroad,* and *Travel Tips for Older Americans.*

Austria

Austria's central location in Europe and its six international airports of the Imperial Cities—Vienna (Wien), Graz, Innsbruck, Klagenfurt, Linz, and Salzburg—make it a convenient gateway country for European travelers. Although German is the native language of Austria, most tourism officials also speak English. With a smile on your face, try the informal German greeting "Grüss Gott," and ask slowly and distinctly, "Do you speak English?" A smile almost always elicits a cooperative attitude.

Austria is more than museums and antiques; it is also music, gorgeous scenery, and gourmet foods. Austria is a country where one can easily overindulge in temptingly tasty pastries and piles of *schlagobers* (whipped cream)—and what a way to go. We discovered why the *schlagobers* is so delicately delicious—it's the *real* thing.

As the Austrian National Tourist Office succinctly states: "Austria is more than 1,000 years old. So far, so good." For more information and pretrip planning tips, be sure to visit Austria's Web site: **www.experienceaustria.com**, or contact the Austrian Tourist Offices in North America:

> *New York:* P.O. Box 1142, New York, NY 10108–1142, *Tel:* (212) 944–6880; *Fax:* (212) 730–4568; *E-mail:* info@oewnyc.com
>
> *Toronto:* 2 Bloor Street East, Suite 3330, Toronto, Ontario M4W 1A8, Canada. *Tel:* (416) 967–3381; *Fax:* (416) 967–4101; *E-mail:* anto-tor@sympatico.ca

Banking

- **Currency:** Euro (€)
- **Exchange rate at press time:** € 1.10 = U.S. $1.00
- **Hours:** 0800–1230 and 1330–1500 Monday–Friday; closing at 1730 on Thursday; closed Saturday and Sunday. Banks in most

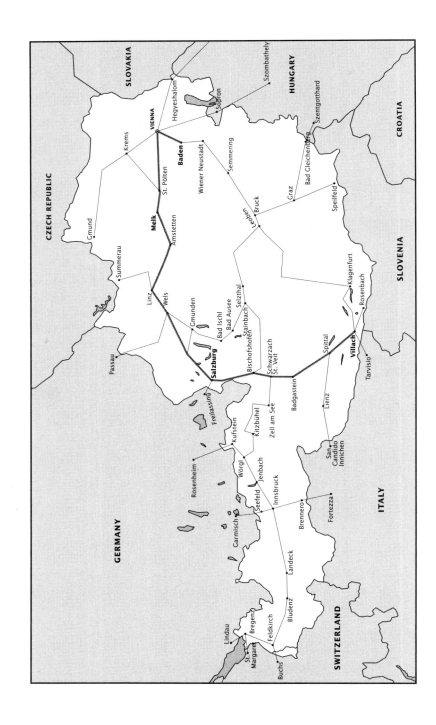

airport and rail terminals are open 7 days a week, 0800–2000; until 2200 in Vienna.

Communications

- **Country Code:** 43
  For telephone calls within Austria, dial a zero (0) preceding area code.
- **Direct dial:** AT&T Direct: 0800 200 288; Canada Direct: 0800 200 245; MCI WorldPhone: 0800 200 235; SprintExpress: 0800 200 236

It may be worth your while to buy a Telephone–Wertkarte at a post office and make your calls from a card-operated pay phone. Avoid placing lengthy long-distance phone calls from your hotel, since hotel surcharges can be astronomical.

Rail Travel in Austria

The Austrian Federal Railways, or Österreichische Bundesbahnen (ÖBB), operates the 5,800-kilometer rail system and accepts the **European East Pass**, the variety of **Eurail passes** (including Eurail Selectpass), and **Europasses** with purchase of the **Austria/Hungary** associate country and the national **Austrian Railpass**. (See Appendix for list of railpass types and prices or consult the Web site at www.railpass.com). Remember to purchase your railpasses prior to your departure for Europe. *Internet:* www.oebb.at.

The aforementioned railpasses include the following discounts within Austria:

- 50 percent discount on boats operated by BSB, SBS and ÖBB on Lake Constance
- 50 percent discount on boat day trips operated by Wurm & Köck Steamers on the Danube between Linz and Passau (Germany)
- Special discount on bicycle rentals at 130 rail stations
- 20 percent discount on boats operated by ÖBB on Lake Wolfgang May–October
- 15 percent discount on boats operated by DDSG–Blue Danube Schiffahrt between Melk, Krems, and Vienna
- 15 percent discount on the St. Wolfgang–Schafbergspitze rack railway
- 10 percent discount on the Puchberg am Schneebert-Hoch-Schneeberg rack railway

The basic **Austrian Railpass** is valid for 3 days of rail travel within a 15-day period. First Class, $158; Second Class, $107. Additional rail days available for $20, First Class; $15, Second Class. Child rates are half of the adult fare for ages 6–12; under age 6 travel free.

Seat reservations for both national and international travel may be made at any rail station. Eurail Aid offices are located in Innsbruck Hauptbahnhof, Salzburg Hauptbahnhof, and Wien Westbahnhof (Vienna West Station).

Base City:

Vienna
(Wien)

Internet: www.info.wien.at
City Dialing Code: 1

Arriving by Air

Schwechat Airport, *Tel:* 7007–22233 for information, including transport to the city center. *Internet:* www.viennaairport.com

Located 19 kilometers from the city center, Schwechat Airport is the home base for Austrian Airlines, which offers nonstop flights between the United States (New York) and Vienna and serves more than 30 other international airlines. Tourist information is available in the "arrivals hall."

Airport–City Links: Trains run every 30 minutes from the airport into Wien Mitte and Wien Nord stations. The price to Mitte is €2.90 (approximately $2.50 U.S.) During heavy morning and evening traffic, the train is the best way to go. At other times, we recommend the airport bus service, which connects with the Westbahnhof (West Station) and Südbahnhof (South Station), as well as with the city air terminal (next to the Hilton Hotel). The fare is €5.09; time en route, 20 minutes. The bus-departure point is immediately outside and to the left of the arriving-passenger exit. Purchase tickets on the bus. Buses depart every 20 minutes.

If you purchase a Vienna Card at the tourist information office in the arrivals hall of the airport ("Tourist Board") you'll pay only €4.36 on the Vienna Airport Lines bus. See "Getting Around in Vienna" for details.

Taxis are available just outside the arrivals area. Fare to city center is about €26; journey time, 20–30 minutes.

Arriving by Train

The Westbahnhof and Südbahnhof are Vienna's major railway terminals. Westbahnhof is the gateway to Germany, Switzerland, and the rest of northern and central Europe; Südbahnhof is the gateway to southern and eastern Europe. Wien Mitte and Wien Nord are commuter-type stations. For train information on the *Internet:* www.oebb.at.

Westbahnhof has two levels. Arriving by train, you will be on top of the elevated level. The taxi stand is on the left as you leave the train platform. The main station concourse is at street level.

- **Baggage storage** located on main station concourse level. After descending on the escalator from track level, turn left and go to the far end of the concourse.
- **Money exchange** (*Exchange-Wechselstube*) located to the left of the escalators on the top level. Daily hours: 0700–2200.
- **Train information**, reservations, and railpass validation may be made at *Reisebüro am Bahnhof,* located in the glass kiosk.

Südbahnhof is a three-level terminal with the train platforms located on the middle and top levels.

- **Money exchange** located in lower level immediately to the right of the main staircase. Daily hours: 0630–2200.

Tourist Information/Hotel Reservations

- City center **main tourist office:** Albertinaplatz on the corner of Maysedergasse (behind the Vienna State Opera House). *Tel:* 211 14 222 (0800–1800 Monday-Friday); *Fax:* 216 84 92; *Internet:* www.info.wien.at; *Email:* info@info.wien.at
  Hours: 0900-1900 daily
  To get there from the Westbahnhof (West Station) by public transport, take the U-Bahn (underground) Line U3 to Volkstheater and on the Ringstrasse, take Tram 2, D, or J for the two stops to the Opera House. From the Südbahnhof (South Station), only Tram D will take you to the Opera House.
- Schwechat Airport, located opposite the baggage carousels in the Arrivals Hall.
  Hours: 0830–2100.
- Verkehrsbüro Travel agency: in the Westbahnhof (West Station), located in the entrance hall on the ground floor.
  Hours: 0700–2200.
- **Hotel reservations** may be made at the tourist information offices and by: *Tel:* 1–244 14 444 (0800–1800 Monday-Friday, 1000–1800 Saturday-Sunday); *Fax:* 1–211 14 44; *Internet:* www.info.wien.at; *E-mail:* rooms@info.wien.at

Getting Around in Vienna

The most economical and convenient way to discover Vienna is with the **Vienna Card.** For only €15.26, you'll have access to Vienna's public transportation network for 72 hours, plus discounts at many museums, attractions, concerts, shops, theaters, restaurants, cafes, and Heurigen (wine taverns). All the benefits are described in the 64-page Vienna Card coupon book.

Purchase the Vienna Card at tourist information offices, your hotel, or

Vienna Transport (Wiener Linien) information offices, located in many underground stations. Or order the Vienna Card with your credit card by telephoning 43 (Austria country code) 1–798 44 00 28. For Vienna Transport information, dial 7909–105.

Vienna's efficient transportation network includes the U-Bahn underground, trams, S-Bahn (rapid-transit intracity trains), and bus service. The best bargain is the Vienna Card that covers more than just the transportation network. But there are other choices for transportation only: A single ticket is €1.38, a 24-hour network pass is €4.36, a 72-hour net work pass is €10.90 and an 8-day strip ticket is €21.80. Children under 6 travel free.

These transportation tickets can be purchased from tobacconists, at vending machines in the underground stations, or even at reception desks in many Viennese hotels. Single-trip tickets from vending machines in trams and buses cost €1.60. A punched single ticket is valid for one trip, including changing lines. Purchase a public transportation map for €1.45.

Sights/Attractions/Tours

Vienna tourist-office personnel are highly qualified professionals who can help you find a variety of ways to see Vienna, and one of the best ways to really get to know the city is on foot. Ask for the brochure *Walks in Vienna* (*Internet:* www.wienguide.at). Choose from sixty walking tours; each has a different theme spanning the spectrum from "Pure Hapsburg, The Hofburg and its Emperors" to "Chow-houses, Boozers, Brothels, and Other Houses of Ill Repute." Reservations are not required; just show up at the point mentioned in the brochure for the particular tour you choose. Cost: €10.17 per person; under age 18, €5.09 with a Vienna Card, €8.36. Duration of the walking tours is 1½–2 hours. Private guided tours may also be arranged through Vienna Guide Service (*Tel:* 440 3094; *Fax:* 440 2825; *E-mail:* office@vienna-guide-service.com). For a real moving experience, tour Vienna by bicycle. Call Bike & Guide at 212 1135.

You can see Vienna at your own pace with the "Hop-on, Hop-off" bus tours (discount with the Vienna Card). *Tel:* 712 46 830; *E-mail:* vst@via.at; *Internet:* www.viennasightseeingtours.com. For a leisurely view of Vienna, take a cruise aboard the ship MS *Vindobona* from the Danube Canal onto the Danube. The ship departs from Schwedenplatz for a cruise to Reichsbrucke. You can return to the city via the underground or the MS *Vindobona*. Departures are at 1000 and 1400. One-way, €9.45; round trip €13.08 (10 percent discount with Vienna Card; reduced rates for children). Ask the tourist office for the DDSG Blue Danube Ships' brochure detailing their cruise programs or call 588 80 0; *Fax:* 588 80 440; *Internet:* www.ddsg-blue-danube.at; *E-mail:* info@ddsg-blue.danube.at.

Vienna is many things, but primarily it is music. Visit the **Vienna State Opera House,** a preeminent point of European music. The Schoenbrunn Palace, former summer residence of the Hapsburg Empire, is truly worth seeing. Get there by taking the U4 line on the Underground. See operas and operettas performed at the **Court Theatre at Schoenbrunn**. On the palace grounds, wander through the New Maze that was patterned as closely as possible to the original design created between 1698 and 1740.

Visit the Strauss home where the "Blue Danube Waltz" was written. Thrill to the harmonious voices of the famous **Vienna Boys' Choir**, or marvel at the white Lipizzaner stallions as they dance to music in the **Spanish Riding School**. For information: *Tel:* 535 01 86.

Vista of Vienna

The pace is slower in Vienna; Vienna developed the waltz and the city's tempo has moved in leisurely three-quarter time ever since.

Vienna's coffeehouses are oases of good living at a leisurely pace. Visiting them during your stay is a must. Our favorite coffeehouse happens to be the original one in Vienna, the **Sacher Café**, a part of Hotel Sacher immediately behind the Opera House. It has a semiformal but friendly atmosphere. By all means, try the *Sachertorte* (chocolate cake) and don't miss the *Apfelstrudel* (apple cake). Expensive? Well, yes, but it's worth it.

The Viennese "invented" coffee. According to legend, in 1683 the Turks were defeated and abandoned their three-centuries quest to conquer the heart of Europe at the gates of Vienna. In their hasty departure, they left some bags of coffee beans behind. The local folks swarmed out of the city and carried the bags back behind its protective walls and began experimenting. A gentleman by the name of Kolschitzky evolved a clear brew—unlike the Turks who, to this day, serve it with the grounds—and the people of Vienna were so elated that they erected a bronze statue to his memory.

The Viennese like to eat well, and they take great pride and pleasure in giving their visitors every opportunity to do likewise. Choose from a dazzling array of eateries from stand-up snack bars and simple little pubs, known as Beisel, to ethnic specialties and gourmet restaurants. Since good food deserves good libation, try the tasty and strong Austrian beer or some of Austria's great vintages. These are bottled and aged; but young, fresh wine is rushed to the taverns, where locals and visitors alike consume it as though it might lose its freshness between sips.

Since Hungary accepts Eurailpass and Europass (if the Austria/Hungary associate zone option has been purchased), many Eurail travelers transit Vienna on through trains such as the *Wiener Walzer* without stopping. Take advantage of the frequent rail service and stop for a few hours in Vienna en route to Budapest. Baggage can be stored in the *Gepackaufbewahrung* (temporary baggage storage facility) in the Westbahnhof main concourse level.

Day Excursions from Vienna

Because of its location on the Danube River and the eastern reaches of the Alps, Vienna can offer some unusual day-excursion opportunities.

Train Connections to Other Base Cities from Vienna (Wien)

VIENNA

Depart from Vienna West station (Wien Westbahnhof), unless otherwise noted

DEPART	TRAIN NUMBER	ARRIVE	NOTES
		Amsterdam Centraal	
1925	D 224	0940+1	R, Sleeper
		Berlin Zoobahnhof	
1025*	EC 172	2031	
2120	EN 228	0817+1	R, Sleeper
		Bern (Berne)	
0716	EC 160	1813	1
0916	EC 162	1943	2
		Brussels (Bruxelles) Midi/Zuid	
1916	EN 224	0941+1	R, Sleeper
		Budapest Keleti	
0825	D 343	1133	
1007	IC 345	1303	
1433	EC 63	1713**	
1603	EC 25	1843**	
1936	347/341	2233	
		Hamburg Hauptbanhof	
1016	ICE 90	1951	
1025*	EC 172	2300	
1945	EN 490	0755+1	R, Sleeper
		Munich (München) Hauptbahnhof	
0546	EC 16	1036	
0846	EC 64	1336	
1546	EC 62	2036	
2020	EN 262	0120+1 (Ost)	
2325	268	0603+1	R, Sleeper
		Paris Gare de l'Est	
0846	EC 64	2220	
2020	EN 262	2023+1	R, Sleeper
		Rome (Roma) Termini	
1929*	EN 235	0904+1	R, Sleeper
		Zürich Hauptbahnhof	
0716	EC 160	1627	
0916	EC 162	1827	
2115	EN 466	0627+1	R, Sleeper

Daily, including holidays, unless otherwise noted
R Reservations required
+1 Arrives next day
* Departs from Vienna South station (Südbahnhof)
** Arrives Budapest Déli
1. Arrive in Zurich Hbf at 1627. Change to IC 932 departing at 1704.
2. Arrive in Zurich Hbf at 1827. Change to IC 736 departing at 1834.

Among them are cruises on the Danube to **Melk** or tours through the Vienna Woods and the **Austrian Alps** by train.

Local trains can take you to **Baden,** one of the most famous sulfur-bath spas in Austria. Express trains can whisk you from Vienna to Salzburg in time for lunch—followed by dinner—and still return you in time to slumber in your base city Vienna.

Day Excursion to

Austrian Alps Tour
via Villach and Salzburg

Depart from Vienna South Station (Südbahnhof)
Distance by Train: 541 miles (871 km)
Average Train Time: 14 hours, 40 minutes

The Austrian Alps probably provide more beauty than all of the fine-art masterpieces in the world laid end to end. The fact that you can watch the splendor of their alpine panorama unfold from the comfort of a train compartment makes this a most unusual and thrilling day excursion.

Take an adequate, large-scale map of Austria along, and try to select a day when good visibility is forecast. For the latter, your hotel should be able to provide a weather forecast, and an ideal map is the one published by Kummerly and Frey. You'll find it in newspaper kiosks or station newsstands.

This day excursion requires changing trains in Salzburg with the option of changing trains en route to Salzburg at Villach. The time between trains in Villach and Salzburg varies according to the schedule you select. Consider having lunch in Villach followed by dinner in Salzburg. Dining aboard is also possible, since all of the trains listed on the schedule haul dining cars.

The Alps in Austria are divided from north to south into three chains: the **northern limestone Alps,** the **central high Alps,** and the **limestone Alps of the south.** These chains are separated from each other by the great furrows that form the river valleys of the Inn, the Salzach, and the Enns in the north and the Drava and Mur in the south. The route we have selected for this day excursion takes you through all three alpine chains.

Even if the weather is good when you leave Vienna, the climate of the Alps varies considerably with differences in altitude. Expect some changes in the temperature and visibility while en route. It is not unusual to enter a tunnel with the landscape bathed in sunlight only to emerge at the other end into a storm.

Vienna is 580 feet above sea level. Leaving the city, the train moves along the edge of the Vienna woods. Before arriving in Bruck, you will get an occa-

VIENNA *Austrian Alps Tour*

Vienna (Wien)—Austrian Alps Tour

DEPART VIENNA SÜDBAHNHOF	TRAIN NUMBER	ARRIVE VILLACH
0658	IC 531	1137
0858	EC 31	1337
1058	IC 535	1537

DEPART VILLACH	TRAIN NUMBER	ARRIVE SALZBURG
1211	EC 112	1448
1411	IC 793	1644
1611	IC 691	1848

DEPART SALZBURG	TRAIN NUMBER	ARRIVE VIENNA WESTBAHNHOF
1532	EC 163	1850
1610	IC 649	1942
1710	IC 741	2042
1732	EC 569	2050
1805	EC 65	2120
1810	IC 743	2142
1910	IC 691	2242
1932	EC 161	2250
2005	EC 17	2320
2015	IC 747	2358
2132	EC 661	0057+1

Daily, including holidays
+1 Arrives next day
Distance: 541 miles (871 km)

sional glimpse of the **Raxalpe Peak** (6,630 feet). This steep-sided limestone massif, due to its proximity to Vienna, has become very popular with city-based mountain climbers. Here, the train follows the first mountain railway (**Semmeringbahn**) built in Europe (1848–54), which runs between Gloggnitz and Murzzuschlag.

From Murzzuschlag to Bruck, the train parallels the Murz River through the last really mountainous pass leading out of the Alps and on to the broad plains fed by the Danube. Bruck lies at the confluence of the Mur and the Murz Rivers in the pleasant setting of the **Styrian Alps.** After passing Unzmarkt, the peaks of the Zinken (7,255 feet) and the Greimberg (8,115 feet) Alps are visible. You then arrive in **Klagenfurt,** 1,472 feet above sea level. Summers here are extremely hot, for the town lies in a basin shielding it from the moderating effects of the Mediterranean.

Between Klagenfurt and Velden, the train passes along Lake Woerth before arriving in Villach. Leaving Villach and approaching the Tauern Tunnel (5 miles long), you will be able to view Mount Hochalm (11,020 feet). As you exit the tunnel, Edelweiss-Spitz (8,453 feet) stands guard on the left while Mount Gamskarspitze (9,296 feet) looms on the right.

After pausing briefly at **Badgastein**—the highest en route station, at 2,838 feet above sea level—the train gradually descends into Schwarzach and parallels the Salzach River, which flows past Bischofshofen and the city of Salzburg. Your return train to Vienna arrives at Westbahnhof (West Station).

Day Excursion to

Baden

Baths, Cures, and Casino

Depart from Vienna South Station (Südbahnhof)
Distance by Train: 17 miles (27 km)
Average Train Time: 20 minutes
City Dialing Code: 2252
Tourist Information Office: Brusattiplatz 3, (Leopoldsbad), A-2500 Baden bei Wien
Tel: 22600–600; **Fax:** 80733
Internet: www.tiscover.com/baden-bei-wien and www.baden-bei-wien.at
E-mail: touristinfo.baden@netway.at
Hours: May 1–October 31, 0900–1800 Monday–Saturday; 0900–1200 Sunday; November 1–April 30, 0900–1700 Monday–Friday; closed Saturday and Sunday.
Notes: Proceed to level 3 for trains departing on tracks 11 and 19 for Baden in direction of Graz. To get to the tourist information office from the rail station, use the station underpass to the town side of the tracks. Walk directly through the park in front of the station and bear right onto Bahnstrasse (Station Street) at the end of the park. Two blocks farther along, you will see a Fussgängerzone (pedestrian area). Turn right and walk to the town square. Pass the Rathaus (city hall) on its left side and proceed toward the end of the pedestrian area through Grüner Markt (the marketplace). The tourist office is just behind Grüner Markt.

Baden is situated on the eastern edge of the Vienna woods and surrounded by extensive vineyards and woodlands. Because it also lies on the edge of Europe's great eastern Pannonian plain, it enjoys a moderate climate, much sunshine, and favorable temperatures. In fact, Baden is in the warmest part of Austria, and it is well known as a health resort.

Baden sits on 15 ancient **thermal water springs**—with a regular temperature of 36 degrees Celsius (97 degrees Fahrenheit). These sulfurous thermal springs form the basis for treatments and cures; some 4

VIENNA
Baden

Trains depart Vienna Südbahnhof for Baden daily every 47 minutes past the hour. Plus commuter trains departing at 0822, 0922, 1022 and other frquent service. Check schedules for track Nos. 11 and 19 on top (third) level of the Südbahnhof (South Station). Most trains departing for Graz stop at Baden.

Trains depart Baden for Vienna Südbahnhof daily at 29 and 59 minutes past the hour. Plus commuter trains departing at 1513, 1613, 1713 and continuing until late evening. Check schedules in Baden railway station.

Distance: 17 miles (27 km)

million liters of it are used daily. The early Romans were always keen on baths, and they spent hours soaking in the medicinal, hot sulfur springs of the area they called "Aquae" and its thermal springs. In the nineteenth century, Baden became the center of social life for Vienna's growing sphere of influence. Today, it is a world-renowned spa full of charm, flowers, and more swimming pools than one can possibly enter in a single day excursion.

Swimming is a year-round pastime, either outdoors in the thermal and mineral pools or indoors at **Römertherme.** The thermal public swimming pool (*Thermalstrandbad*), with its Art Deco–style, 5,000-square-meter pool area and extensive sandy beach, is an adventure-bath for the whole family. In 1930 a section of the park lands of Castle Weilburg was added, making it one of the largest open-air baths in Austria.

Baden offers other forms of relaxation, ranging from quiet paths leading in and around the eastern edges of the Vienna woods to a lively game of blackjack in the **Casino Baden** opposite Kurpark. The casino opens daily at 1500. Baden is also ideal for shopping—its entire center is a pedestrian zone filled with small specialty shops. When you tire of bargain hunting, retreat to the city rose garden in **Doblhoff Park** to watch chess played on a larger-than-life chessboard.

Another interesting pastime is visiting the informal **wine taverns** scattered throughout the town. Since the Middle Ages, every citizen of Baden has had the right to sell self-produced wine, as well as meat and sausage specialties. These "taverns" are identified by a pole decorated with fir twigs, or you can seek them out by following the tavern signs displayed throughout the town. Visitors engaged in "researching" taverns might do well to come to Baden as early as possible and leave only when they have discovered the best vintage—or spend the night in Baden, depending upon how much research they conducted.

Day Excursion to
Melk
Alternative Cruise Up the Danube

Depart from Vienna West Station (Westbahnhof)
Distance by Train and Boat: 102 miles (192 km)
Total Time: 7 hours, 40 minutes
City Dialing Code: 2752
Tourist Information Office: Tourismusbüro, Babenbergerstrasse 1, A-3390 Melk
Tel: (02752) 52307 410; *Fax:* (02752) 52307 490
Internet: www.tiscover.com/melk
E-mail: melk@smaragd.at
Hours: April: 0900–1200 and 1400–1800 Monday–Friday; 1000–1400 Saturday.
   May–June 0900–1200 and 1400–1800 Monday–Friday; 1000–1400 Saturday–
   Sunday. July–August: 0900–1900 Monday–Saturday; 1000–1400 Sunday.
   September: 0900–1200 and 1400–1800 Monday–Friday; 1000–1400 Saturday–
   Sunday. October: 0900–1200 and 1300–1700 Monday–Friday; 1000–1400
   Saturday.
Ardagger ship line: Tel: (7479) 6464–0; *E-mail:* dsa@pgv.at
Brandner ship line: Tel (7433) 2590–0; *E-mail:* schiffahrt@brandner.at; *Internet:*
   www.brandner.at
DDSG ship line: Tel: (4315) 8880; *Fax:* (4315) 888–0440; *E-mail:* info@ddsg-blue-
   danube.at; *Internet:* www.ddsg-blue-danube.at
Notes: As you emerge from the bahnhof (rail station), walk toward the abbey, which
   dominates the foreground. The tourist office is in the town hall which sits at the
   base of the abbey, three blocks from the station.

The **Danube** is Europe's grand river, second in length only to the Volga and stretching almost 1,800 miles across 8 countries. As plains, hills, and mountains succeed one another along its course, the Danube can be sluggish, swift, or even wild. The Danube rises in Germany's Black Forest— the length of a football field away from the watershed of the Rhine. By the time its waters reach the German city of Ulm, the Danube becomes navigable by river craft. Between Ulm and Vienna, the Danube takes on an alpine character. The Danube is unusual among the rivers of the world in that it flows from west to east. At its delta, it empties into the Black Sea.

"The Blue Danube Waltz" is a musical expression of the attractiveness and charm of Austria along the banks of the Danube. The vast countryside— fringed by the Austrian Alps on the south—offers a vista of natural beauty. Although the waters of the river, especially in times of flood, do not always display the color of which the song sings, the beauty of the countryside through which the Danube flows makes it easy to forget that the waters are actually milky white throughout most of the spring and summer.

Vienna (Wien)—Melk—Up the Danube (Donau)

VIENNA *Melk*

There is no longer a regular Danube (Donau) steamer service between Vienna and Melk. However, on Sunday from May through Sept, there may be a sailing if sufficient passengers request reservations. Should such sailings occur, the timetable would be:

Depart Vienna Reichsbrücke dock at 0845, arrive Krems an der Donau at 1355. A regularly scheduled service sails from Krems an der Donau from May through Oct; depart Krems an der Donau at 1540 and arrive at Melk Altarm dock at 1840. Take a taxi or bus from Melk Altarm dock to the Melk Bahnhof (station) for return to Vienna by train. Direct sailings run Sun from end of April to the first week of October from 0730–1530.

Return train schedules from Melk Bahnhof to Vienna (Wien) Westbahnhof are:

DEPART MELK	TRAIN NUMBER	ARRIVE VIENNA WESTBAHNHOF	NOTES
1816	D 525	1933	
1917	R 2033/IC 547	2034	Sat, Sun, holidays
1920	IC 741	2042	1
1954	E 1627/EC 65	2117	1, Mon–Fri
2043	E 7025/EC 23	2150	1, Mon–Fri
2125	R 2043/IC 691	2242	1
2301	IC 945	0005+1	1

Daily, unless otherwise noted
1. Change trains at St. Polten
Distance: 53 miles (85 km)

We recommend taking the 0829 train to Melk, the point from which the cruise down the Danube begins. It will bring you to Melk in time for unhurried connections with the ship, but Melk itself is steeped in history and warrants your visit. The earlier train will permit you to wander about Melk's ancient streets, still guarded by the watchtowers of its town wall, and to visit Melk's **Benedictine Abbey,** the epitome of Baroque architecture in Austria. To book a guided tour of the abbey: *Tel:* 02752 555 232; *Fax:* 02752 555 249; *E-mail:* kultur.tourismus@stiftmelk.at.

Have lunch and sample the fine regional wines in one of Melk's charming *Heurigen* taverns before you walk or taxi to the DDSG pier, known locally as "Schiff Station." Check with the information desk on the pier for boarding instructions.

Carry a map of the Danube and refer to it often, for it's one fine scene after another. The market town of **Spitz,** on the Danube's left bank, is readily recognizable because it nestles at the base of the *Tausendeimer* mountain. The name of the mountain ("a thousand vessels") doesn't refer to the river traffic—it refers to the fact that the vineyards on its sides, in a good year, can produce a thousand vessels of wine.

When the ship calls at **Durnstein,** with its red roofs, you should recall that it was here that King Richard I, the Lionhearted of England, was captured and held prisoner when he returned from the Third Crusade. The next port of call will be **Krems,** which marks the eastern area of the Wachau. Since olden times, Krems has been the hub of the Wachau wine trade. Here, the Danube becomes dotted with islands as the ship draws nearer to Vienna.

Day Excursion to

Salzburg
Fortress City

Depart from Vienna Westbahnhof*
Distance by Train: 196 miles (315 km)
Average Train Time: 3 hours, 11 minutes
City Dialing Code: 662
Train Information: Hauptbahnhof, Südtiroler Platz 1, 5020
Tel: (662) 05 17 17; *Fax:* (662) 93000–3159
Internet: www.oebb.at
E-mail: wien.ticketline@pv.oebb.at
Tourist Information Offices:
Hauptbahnhof (Central Station) Information, Platform 2a; *Tel:* 88987–340
Mozartplatz Information Office, Mozartplatz 5; *Tel:* 88987–330
Salzburg-Mitte Information Office, Münchner Bundesstrasse 1; *Tel:* 88987–350
 (Easter–October)
Salzburg-Süd Information Office, Park & Ride Parkplatz, Alpensiedlung-Süd,
 Alpenstrasse; *Tel:* 889 87360 (Easter–October)
Flughafen, Ankunftshalle; *Tel:* 85 80 79 11; *Fax:* 85 34 59
Salzburg-Nord, Autobahnstation Kasern; *Tel:* 889 87 370 (June–September)
Internet: www.salzburginfo.at or www.city.salzburg.com
E-mail: tourist@salzburginfo.at
Hours: Daily 0845–1945 or 2100 (depending on time of the year)
*Salzburg is also a popular day excursion from Munich. Distance by train: 95 miles
 (153km); average train time: 1 hour, 30 minutes

If Vienna gives you the impression that it is musically inclined, wait until you see and hear Salzburg. It has been described as a music festival that never seems to end. No wonder—Salzburg is the birthplace of Mozart. His home is now a museum, and his music has become the very soul of Salzburg.

Music isn't the only thing that makes Salzburg an interesting city. It has the largest completely preserved fortress in central Europe—the **Hohensalzburg Fortress** (circa 1077). You can reach it by taking the cable car from Festungsgasse 4 (*tel*: 84 26 82), located right behind the **Neptune Fountain.** The cable car can whisk you to the top of Salzburg and the Hohensalzburg Fortress in a minute. There is a foot path leading to the top, but it takes a lot of huffing and puffing. Conducted tours include the **State rooms, Fortress Museum,** and **Rainer Museum.** The tour with an audio guide takes about 40 minutes. Opening hours: June 15–September 14, 0900–1800; September 15–March 14, 0930–1700; March 15–June 14, 0930–1730. Tour costs: adults, €3.56; children 6–15, €2.03; Family Pass (2 adults and up to 5 children), €8.72. There is a terrace restaurant on the fortress' south side where you may view the mountains as you dine (in summer).

The **Salzburg Card,** available at the tourist information offices and hotels, provides admission to all of the attractions in Salzburg, free access to public transportation, and many discounts. Choose a 24-, 48-, or 72-hour card for €16.72, €23.26, or €29.80, respectively. If you're using Salzburg as a base city, inquire about the all-inclusive **Salzburg Plus Card** to include accommodations, all meals, attractions, and cultural events. Prices start at €94.40. Find out more by visiting the Salzburg Web site or e-mailing cards@salzburginfo.at.

To conduct your own tour, begin in the old section of the city. Board bus No. 1, 5, 6, or 51 at the bus stop in front of the railway station and ride to the Staatsbrucke, the fifth stop. This places you on the perimeter of the Old Town, where most of the sightseeing is located. Orient yourself with the **Kapitelplatz** (Capital Place), and you are right in the center of everything.

The music-festival season starts in January and ends in December. In other words, it never ends. Afternoons in Salzburg may be spent in one of its comfortable coffeehouses watching theatergoers and opera buffs flocking to a performance—many in formal attire. Elegance is a way of life.

Salzburg has a charming narrow street, **Getreidegasse**, which is lined with gilt and wrought-iron trade signs, pictorial devices dating back to the time when few people could read. This is one of the best areas in town to find authentic Austrian souvenirs.

Mozart's birthplace, **Mozarts Geburtshaus,** is located at No. 9 Getreidegasse (*tel*: 84 43 13) and is probably one of the most visited houses in the city. Open daily 0900–1730 (until 1830 in July and August). Birthplace of Wolfgang Amadeus Mozart in 1756, it is now a museum. The Mozart family lived in the third-floor apartment from 1747 to 1773. Here you will see paintings and original instruments belonging to Mozart, including his childhood violin. Only about five minutes from Mozart's Birthplace is The Mozart Residence, or **Mozart-Wohnhaus** (*tel*: 87 42 27–40), across the Salzach River at No. 8 Markartplatz. Special audio and visual exhibits document the life of the Mozart family. It was here that Mozart lived and composed until 1780. His famous piano-forte, Mozart

Vienna (Wien)—Salzburg

Depart Vienna Westbahnhof	Train Number	Arrive Salzburg	Notes
0546	EC 16	0858	2
0620	IC 940	0948	3
0645	EC 662	0953	2
0716	EC 160	1027	2
0720	IC 690	1048	2
0820	IC 544	1148	3
0846	EC 64	1154	2, 4
0916	EC 162	1227	2
0920	IC 546	1248	2

Salzburg—Vienna (Wien)

Depart Salzburg	Train Number	Arrive Vienna Westbahnhof	Notes
1510	IC 941	1842	3
1532	EC 163	1850	2
1610	IC 649	1942	2
1710	IC 741	2042	3
1732	EC 569	2050	2
1805	EC 65	2120	2,4
1810	IC 743	2142	3
1910	IC 691	2242	2
1932	EC 161	2250	2
2005	EC 17	2320	2, 3
2015	IC 747	2358	3
2132	EC 661	0057+1	1,2

Daily unless otherwise noted
+1 Arrives next day
1. Train runs Mon–Fri, Sun
2. Restaurant car in this train.
3. Snacks and drinks available on this train.
4. EC 64 and EC 65 are named the *Mozart,* a popular train; seat reservations are suggested.
Distance: 196 miles (315 km)

family portrait, and instruments from that era are on exhibit in the Dancing Master's Hall.

Mozart died a pauper in Vienna at age thirty-five, and his body was dumped into an unmarked grave. His life story supports the expression applicable to too many of the world's great artists: "To be appreciated, one must die first."

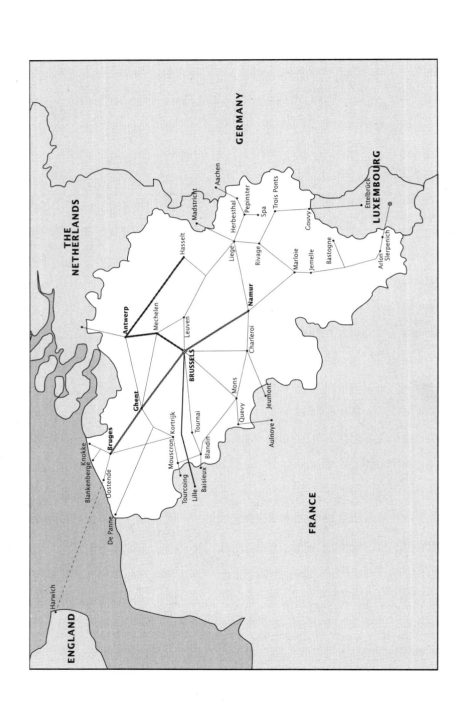

Belgium

Belgium may be small in size—about the size of Maryland in the United States—but it is large in its significance to the European Community. Belgium played an important role in creating the European Union, which now comprises fifteen members. The Treaty on the European Union was signed in Maastricht in 1992 in an effort to safeguard peace in Europe and to move toward economic and monetary union with intergovernmental cooperation. Belgium's capital city, Brussels, is the seat of the European Union, NATO, and many other world trade and finance companies.

In 1830, Belgium gained its independence. No longer a part of the Netherlands, Belgium became a federal state of communities and regions. The three communities are based on the Dutch, French, and German languages and culture—the Flemish Community, the French Community, and the German-speaking Community. The three regions (Flanders, Brussels Capital, and Wallonia) were based on economic concerns.

Belgium has a hereditary constitutional monarchy, but the king does not "govern"; he serves as protector of the country's unity and independence. King Albert II became Belgium's sixth king in 1993.

Perhaps not as well known is Belgium's significant gastronomic role in western Europe. After all, it was the Flemish Benedictine monks who invented beer, and the beers considered to be "the best" are the ones still brewed traditionally in Belgian monasteries. Restaurants of the Ardennes are well known for their wild game, and the coastal restaurants serve some of the finest North Sea fish and shellfish dishes. A not so well known culinary fact about Belgium: The ratio of restaurants to population is equal to that of France.

For more information about Belgium, use the Internet address **www. visitbelgium.com** or contact the Belgian Tourist Office in North America:

New York: 780 Third Avenue, Suite 1501, New York, NY 10017. *Tel:*

(212) 758–8130; *Fax:* (212) 355–7675; *Internet:* www.trabel.com; *E-mail:* info@trabel.com

Banking

* **Currency:** Euro (€)
* **Exchange rate at press time:** €1.10 = U.S. $1.00
* **Hours:** 0900–1530 or 1600 Monday–Friday; closed Saturday, Sunday, and holidays.

Communications

* **Country Code:** 32
  For telephone calls within Belgium, dial a zero (0) preceding area code.
* **Direct dial:** AT&T Direct: 0–800–100–10; MCI: 0–800–100–12; Sprint: 0–800–100–14

Rail Travel in Belgium

The Belgian railways were the first to be constructed on the continent of Europe, and Belgian National Railways (SNCB) is said to operate one of the densest rail networks in the world (3,396 kilometers). *Internet:* www.b-rail.be. Brussels serves as an international crossroads. InterCity (IC) trains connect the main towns and regions of Belgium; the Inter-Regional (IR) trains include stops at local stations. Rail service is frequent—usually every hour between most major cities and towns, and with SNCB's integrated schedules, you need not wait long for train connections.

TGV Thalys trains link Brussels to Paris in 1 hour and 25 minutes and to Amsterdam in the Netherlands in only 2 hours and 40 minutes; the high-speed Eurostar trains can whisk you from Brussels to London in only 3 hours.

The Belgian National Railways accepts the variety of **Eurail passes**, **Europass** (with the purchase of the Benelux [Belgium/Netherlands/Luxembourg] Associate Country), and the regional **Benelux Tourrail Pass**, which provides unlimited rail travel for any 5 days within a 1-month period in Belgium, the Netherlands, and Luxembourg. If you are two adults traveling together, purchase the special "Tourrail for Two" pass and save a total of $108 first-class or $77 for second-class passes.

Benelux Tourrail Pass

5 days in 1 month	1st Class	2nd Class
Adult	$217	$155
Youth (age 4–25)	—	$104

Benelux Tourrail for Two Pass

5 days in 1 month	1st Class	2nd Class
2 people traveling together, price per person	$163	$116.50

Base City:

Brussels

(Bruxelles)

Internet: www.tib.de
City Dialing Code: 2

Brussels (Bruxelles) has stood for more than 1,000 years as a signpost of ideals and ideas, a crossroad of people and events. Less than 150 miles from Amsterdam and 200 miles from Paris, Brussels is a bonanza for travelers desiring to see Europe by train. Few people realize how short distances actually are in Belgium, of which Brussels is the capital. Its most opposite points are only 195 miles apart.

Latin and Nordic cultures meet in Brussels, making it a city of contrasts. French is spoken by the Walloon people of French origin, and Flemish is the tongue of the nation's Germanic inhabitants. French, German, and Flemish are official languages in Belgium. Consequently, most signs are trilingual in Brussels. English is spoken in all of the train stations, hotels, and (the majority of) public places.

Brussels is old; it celebrated its millennium in 1979. Brussels is new; it's the headquarters of the European Common Market and the North Atlantic Treaty Organization (NATO). It is amazing that the people of Brussels have been able to preserve the city's quaint atmosphere while immersed in all this international activity. Brussels has played vital cultural and commercial roles in Europe for more than 1,000 years.

Arriving by Air

Brussels National Airport, B-1930, Zaventem, *Tel:* (322) 753–3913 (0700–2200), *Internet:* www.brusselsairport.be. Located 14 kilometers from city center.

Airport–City Links: Airport City Express trains depart from the airport every 20 minutes for Brussels Gare du Midi (South Station), Gare du Nord (North Station), and Gare Centrale (Central Station). Journey time—about

20 minutes. Fare one-way €3.59 first class; €2.35 second class. (Eurailpass/Europass not accepted).

Bus station located on ground floor, beneath Arrivals Hall. Take escalators/elevators through the Diamond Area of the terminal.

Taxis about €29.75, tip included. Available outside Arrivals Hall. Look for yellow and blue logo on taxi. Save 20–50 percent by phoning for a Brussels taxi instead of using the vehicles waiting at the airport. *Tel:* (322) 721–4190. Avoid using unmetered taxis!

Money Exchange: "GWT" located in Arrivals Hall

Arriving by Train

Brussels has three train stations along its main line: one in the north (Gare du Nord), one in the south (Gare du Midi), and a midcity underground station (Gare Centrale). EuroCity trains and the major express trains do not stop in the central station. Change at either the north or south station and then transfer to a local train if Gare Centrale is your destination. Those arriving in Brussels on the Eurostar train from London will arrive at Brussels Midi.

North Station (Nord Bruxelles or Gare du Nord), Rue du Progrès 85. Gateway to the Netherlands, Germany, Switzerland, Italy, and eastern France.

- **Money exchange:** In a corridor to the left when exiting from the trains into the main station area. Hours: daily, including Sunday, 0800–2000.
- **Hotel reservations:** At the information booth in the departure hall. Hours: 0900–1700 Monday–Friday.
- **Train information:** In the corridor off the left-hand side of the main station area as you exit from the trains. Hours: 0700–2100 daily, except Sunday.
- **Train reservations:** Ticket window No. 3 or No. 4 in the main station area.
- **Railpass validation** is at window No. 3 or No. 4.

A railway museum is located on the mezzanine of the North Station. Turn right when entering the main station from the train area and walk up the stairs at the end of the concourse. The museum holds an interesting collection of rail-transportation vehicles, ranging from the first Belgian steam locomotive to some of the present-day diesel and electric traction units. The museum is well worth the time of your visit. Admission is free.

Central Station (Gare Centrale), Carrefour de l'Europe 2. Links both North and South Stations via underground trackage. Many of the express trains do not stop here. You may, however, board any of the local trains as a shuttle to either of the main stations and vice versa. Therefore, it is possible to establish yourself in one of the downtown hotels or pensions quite near

Central Station yet be able to make any train connection with a minimum of inconvenience.

- **Money exchange:** Center hall of the station. As you stand looking at the train information board above the ticket windows, the office is on your right. Hours: daily, 0800–2000.
- **Hotel reservations:** Can be made at the Reservations booth in the center hall of the station. Hotel accommodations can also be obtained by visiting the tourist information center in the town hall facing the Grand'Place. (Refer to the section "Tourist Information/ Hotel Reservations.") Open daily 0900–2100.
- **Train information:** Displayed in the main station area immediately above the ticket windows. This is hourly information. Regular printed schedules are also displayed.
- **Train reservations:** Available only at North and South (Midi) Stations.
- **Railpass validation** must be completed at either North or Midi Station.

South Station (Gare du Midi), Rue de France 2. Gateway to Great Britain (via Eurostar trains through the Channel tunnel), France, and Spain. On the main floor you will find all the necessary train and tourist services. The tracks are located on the floor above, and each track has its own escalator leading to it. The underground metro station is underneath the rail station.

- **Money-exchange:** Left side of the main hall as you enter from the street. Daily hours: 0700–2300.
- **Hotel reservations:** "Information" booth in the center of the main hall. Hours: 0900–1700 Monday–Friday. If this booth is closed, use the Brussels Tourist Information Office (T.I.B.) in the Grand'Place.
- **Train reservations and railpass validation:** Local trains, at the ticket counters in the main hall. Reservations for international trains, including the Eurostar, must be made in the Relations Internationales Office on the far right-hand side of the main hall. Take a number from the ticket machine to wait for your turn. Railpasses may be validated at this office; Eurostar has its own terminal where its tickets are validated.
- **Eurostar Terminal:** Right side of the main hall as you enter from the street. Automatic ticket check-in (a simple insertion of your ticket into a machine) begins one hour prior to departure. Then enter the main terminal, which consists of a large waiting room, cafes, and duty-free stores. Keep in mind that you will carry your luggage onto the train as there is no baggage check-in. If you did not purchase your Eurostar tickets before departing for Europe, they may be purchased at the Relations Internationales Office.

Tourist Information/Hotel Reservations

*   *Tourist and Information Office of Brussels (T.I.B.):* Town Hall, Grand'Place, 1000 Brussels *Tel:* 32 2 513 89 40; *Fax:* 32 2 514 45 38; *Internet:* www.tib.be; *E-mail:* tourism.brussels@tib.be

Hours: 0900–1800 Monday–Saturday; Sunday 0900–1800 April 1– September 30 and 1000–1400 October 1–November 30; hotel reservations available.

To reach the Grand'Place from Gare Centrale (Central Station), walk downhill in the direction of the Town Hall's spire until you reach the square. The tourist office is to the right of the spire when you are facing the Town Hall.

The T.I.B. has everything you will need to make your visit to Brussels enjoyable. In addition to tourism information and hotel reservations for Brussels, this office can also provide guides to restaurants, museums, and monuments; tickets to shows; city tours; public transport information; and books and maps.

*   *Belgian Tourist Office:* Rue du Marché-aux-Herbes 63, B-1000 Brussels. Information/hotel reservations for all of Belgium. *Tel:* 504 03 90; *Fax:* 504 02 70; *Internet:* www.opt.be

Hours: June 1–September 30, daily 0900–1900; November 1–March 30, Monday–Saturday 0900–1800 and Sunday 1300–1700; April–May and October, daily 0900–1800.

Located one block north of the Grand'Place.

Getting Around in Brussels

Brussels boasts a highly efficient public transport system encompassing metro, tram, and bus (STIB, Societé des Transports Intercommunaux Bruxellois). **Transport information:** *Tel:* (322) 515–2000. A free map is available from the tourist office. The signs for the metro are blue with a white letter "M"; tram and bus stop signs are red and white. Many of the metro lines also have aboveground bus and tram connections. Note that the trams and buses stop "on request." This means you should raise your hand to signal the driver to stop.

Purchase transport tickets at metro stations, STIB offices, or newsstands: one single ticket, €1.24; card for five journeys, €5.95; card for ten journeys, €8.18; one-day card for use on all STIB transport whenever you wish during the same day, €3.22. The one-day pass is also available at tourist information offices.

Sights/Attractions/Tours

The city abounds in things to see and do, ranging from its elegant Grand'Place to historic Waterloo. If you visit Brussels during the summer, sign up at the tourist office for what we believe is the best way to browse Brussels—"Summer Routes"—attractive, unique theme packages and tours incorporating trams, coaches, boats, or bikes, as well as feet. These are not the usual whistle-stop tours; you get off the beaten track, and you can choose the theme tour that appeals to you. The T.I.B. also conducts other city tours—in 14 languages!

If you want to conduct your own tour, arm yourself with maps and information from the T.I.B. Then head for the **Grand'Place.** You can reach it from the Central Station (Gare du Centrale) by walking downhill toward the spire of the Town Hall. When you reach the square, take a minute to drink in the splendor of the ornate medieval guild houses facing the square. You will realize immediately why it is called the most beautiful square in all of Europe. If you are looking for a souvenir or a gift for someone, we can suggest pralines (hand-dipped chocolates), speculoos (brown sugar biscuits), or some fine Brussels lace. All three of these Belgian specialties are available from shops in and around the Grand'Place.

Following your map, proceed down C. Bulstraat (just to the left of the Town Hall as you face it). The name changes to Stoofstraat. At the corner of Eikstraat and Stoofstraat, you can view one of Brussels's most beloved, albeit somewhat irreverent, symbols—**Manneken Pis.** It's a fountain statue—sometimes costumed—doing just what its name implies.

Want to see Brussels and the rest of the European Community in one day? You can. Ask the tourist information office for details about **Mini-Europe** (*Tel*: 478 05 50) in Bruparck (metro stop: Heysel). You'll see Europe in miniature—more than 300 models of famous buildings and monuments of the European members constructed on a scale of 1:25, complete with animation and sound effects. Watch a TGV glide by, an Airbus take off, or Mt. Vesuvius erupt simply by pushing a button. Open April–December; admission €10.41 (children under 12, €7.93). *Internet:* www.minieurope.com.

Bits and Bites of Brussels

Brussels's cosmopolitan population knows how to enjoy itself. Eating and drinking well in Brussels is not a problem. Succumbing too easily to gastronomic temptation is the real difficulty. Bruxellois, it is said, is like French cuisine served in German portions—although some lighter touches of the nouvelle cuisine have inched their way into Brussels's menus. For the finest gourmet dining, experience the city's most famous culinary establishment, **Comme Chez Soi** at 23 Place Rouppe. For reservations call 512 29 21 (closed Sunday and Monday). It's only a 15-minute walk from the Grand'Place, at the end of Rue du Midi.

In Belgium, beer is not just beer; it's an art form, and the local cafes and bistros are as much an attraction as are the brews they dispense. In Brussels, some offer more than one hundred different labels of Belgian beer alone. Curious? Order a "gueuze," "lambic," or a "krik" (cherry beer?).

For bistro-type dining with a modest price tag, we suggest that you head for the pedestrian-only **Rue des Bouchers** (Street of the Butchers), a stone's

Train Connections to Other Base Cities from Brussels

BRUSSELS

Depart from Brussels (Bruxelles) Midi/Zuid South Station

DEPART	TRAIN NUMBER	ARRIVE	NOTES
		Amsterdam Centraal	
0637	606	0938	1

and then hourly at 37 minutes after the hour until 2037, plus Thalys* trains departing at 0828, 0928, 1128, 1428, 1728, 1828, 2028

DEPART	TRAIN NUMBER	ARRIVE	NOTES
		Barcelona Sants	
1811	Thalys 9350*	0853+1	R, 2
		Berlin Zoobahnhof	
0813	IR 2341	1416	R
1013	IR 2343	1616	R
1413	IR 2345	2016	R
2013	1949	0636+1	Sleeper
		Bern (Berne)	
0716	EC 91	1511	R
0839	D 415	1811	3
1215	EC 97	2011	R, 4
1310	Thalys 9330*	2123	R, 10
2231	D 499	0708+1	R, Sleeper
		Budapest Keleti	
1425	Thalys 9433*	0913	R, 10, Sleeper
1910	EN 225	1303+1	R, 8, Sleeper
		Hamburg Hauptbahnhof	
0652	D 411	1410	3
0825	Thalys 9409*	1444	R, 3
1025	Thalys 9417*	1710	R, 3
1225	Thalys 9425*	1847	R, 3
1425	Thalys 9433*	2110	R, 3
1625	Thalys 9441*	2244	R, 3
2338	NZ 237	0721+1	R, Sleeper
		Luxembourg	
0636	IC 2106	0933	

and hourly at 36 minutes past the hour until 2036 and other frequent service.

DEPART	TRAIN NUMBER	ARRIVE	NOTES
		Lyon Part-Dieu	
0747	Thalys 9912*	1150	R, 12
0810	Thalys 9310*	1255	R, 9
0911	Thalys 9414*	1355	R, 9
1125	TGV 9830	1505	R
1310	Thalys 9330*	1801	R, 9
1517	TGV 9834	1905	R
1619	Thalys 9968*	2009	R, 12
1710	Thalys 9346*	2201	R, 9
1810	Thalys 9350*	2255	R, 9
		Milan (Milano) Centrale	
0716	EC 91	1925	
0810	Thalys 9310*	1755	R, 9
1125	TGV 9830	2150	R, 11
1913	D 299	0705+1	R, Sleeper

DEPART	TRAIN NUMBER	ARRIVE	NOTES
		Munich (München) Hauptbahnhof	
0839	D 415	1816	3
1025	Thalys 9417*	1913	R, 3
1225	Thalys 9425*	2113	R, 3
1425	Thalys 9433*	2316	R, 3
1910	EN 225	0622+1	R, Sleeper
2025	Thalys 9457*	0722+1	R, 3, Sleeper
		Nice Ville	
0925	TGV 9826	1739	R
1040	Thalys 9420*	1923	R, 9
1125	TGV 9833	2006	R, 13
1310	Thalys 9330*	2127	R, 9
1932	1177	1053+1	R, Sleeper
		Paris Gare du Nord	
0710	Thalys 9306*	0835	R, 1
0740	Thalys 9308*	0905	R
0810	Thalys 9310*	0935	R
0840	Thalys 9312*	1005	R, 5
0911	Thalys 9414*	1035	R

and hourly at 40 minutes past the hour until 2140 plus other frequent service.

DEPART	TRAIN NUMBER	ARRIVE	NOTES
		Vienna (Wien) Westbahnhof	
0652	D 411	1950	3
0839	D 415	2150	3
1652	D 431	0850+1	6
1910	EN 225	0955+1	R, Sleeper
		Zürich Hauptbahnhof	
0716	EC 91	1500	7
1215	EC 97	2000	
1310	Thalys 9330*	2242	R, 9
2231	D 499	0700+1	R, Sleeper

Daily, unless otherwise noted
R   Reservations required
*   Thalys high-speed train, supplement required
+1 Next day
1.   Monday–Friday.
2.   Change to sleeper train 477 in Paris Austerlitz station, departing 2047.
3.   Change trains in Cologne (Köln).
4.   Change trains in Basel, Switzerland.
5.   Monday–Saturday.
6.   Change to sleeper train CNL 213 in Cologne (Köln), departing 2023.
7.   Change to EC 103 in Basel, Switzerland.
8.   Change trains in Vienna (Wien).
9.   Change trains in Paris.
10.   Change trains in Cologne (Köln) and Vienna (Wien).
11.   Change trains in Lyon.
12.   Change trains in Marne la Vallée.
13.   Change trains in Valence.

throw from the Grand'Place. For lobster with morels or shrimp served in an art-deco atmosphere, try **Aux Armes de Bruxelles** at No. 13 (*Tel:* 511 55 98). Or, if you prefer quaint, rustic decor, try **Le Marmiton** (*Tel:* 511 79 10) at No. 43. Don't miss having mussels in Brussels—**Chez Leon** on Rue des Bouchers serves mussels a myriad of ways, and we love them all. Along with the gastronomy, in the evening the area presents numerous sidewalk displays by local artisans.

If you've never eaten a **Brussels waffle**, you haven't lived a full and rewarding life. We are not referring to the "Belgian waffle" that you'll find at concession stands at every state fair, nor do we refer to the highly touted desserts served by fancy restaurants using a waffle as a base piled high with candied fruits and buried in whipped cream. These confections are good, mind you, but nothing in the world can surpass the kind of waffle that Brussels offers. There's nothing fancy about a Brussels waffle. The vendor will hand it to you wrapped in a small napkin.

Brussels waffles are a part of the environment—you can buy them from several small waffle shops located in the area around the city's opera house, and you should only buy them from a shop that actually makes the waffles right on the premises. Look for the sign GAUFRES in French or WAFELS in Flemish.

Day Excursions

It is difficult to choose from the numerous day excursions Brussels has to offer. With its central location and plentiful trains available, a day excursion to Paris, Amsterdam, Luxembourg, or Köln (Cologne) is quite feasible. Via the Channel Tunnel and its Eurostar trains, even London becomes a day excursion. We, however, present four day excursions going to various points within Belgium itself. We offer **Antwerp**, city of diamonds and Rubens; **Bruges** and its famous Markt; **Ghent** with its Flower Show; and **Namur**, gateway to the beautiful Ardennes.

Day Excursion to

Antwerp (Antwerpen)
The Diamond City

Depart from Brussels Midi/Zuid Station
Distance by Train: 35 miles (57 km)
Average Train Time: 40 minutes
City Dialing Code: 3
Tourist Information Office: Grote Markt 15, B–2000 Antwerp
Tel: 232 01 03; *Fax:* 231 19 37
Internet: www.dma.be/english

E-mail: toerisme@antwerpen.be

Hours: Monday–Saturday 0900–1800; Sunday 0900–1700

Notes: To walk there takes about 15 minutes. Antwerp's metro system can also get you there, but first stop at the metro office in the railway station for fare and routing information. In a hurry? Follow the pictograms to the taxi queue.

Train-departure information for your return trip to Brussels can be found on the many train bulletin boards located throughout the station. A train information office is on the street side of the station, between the two main exits. The train information office does not dispense tourist information, but they can assist you in finding the tourist office.

If you are convinced that diamonds are a girl's best friend or the kids are hankering to see one of Europe's finest zoos, go to Antwerp. Be certain the train you take from Brussels is marked "Antwerp Central." EuroCity and other through trains continuing to Amsterdam stop only at stations on the edge of Antwerp. The central station is right in the city center near the diamond district. If you do end up in one of Antwerp's suburban stations, board an inbound local train.

The city's name is spelled three ways: "Antwerp" is the English version; in French it is "Anvers"; and its Flemish title is "Antwerpen." Call it what you will, this fine city with nearly half a million people is a marvelous place to visit. Its contrasts will amaze you. Antwerp is Belgium's second city, the third largest port in the world, reputed to be the world's diamond center (for more than 500 years), and a Renaissance treasure house.

Because Antwerp is one of the world's major seaports, it offers an unusual harbor tour that the entire family can enjoy. During the summer, motor launches depart from the Steenplein on the river. With more than 3,000 acres of docks, seventeen dry docks, and six locks (including the largest in the world), the harbor is a spectacle you should not miss. There are a variety of waterborne tours to select from, and a short trip on the river Scheldt takes fifty minutes. The port sight-seeing tour that we recommend takes two and a half hours. A combination zoo-harbor ticket is available, too. This will take care of the kids, but we doubt that anyone will forget the diamonds.

Many guided or self-directed walking tours of the city and sites are available. Plus, ferry, tourist trams, bicycle, horse-drawn trams and carriages, and rickshaw tours are among the choices offered as well. Just inquire at the tourist office.

Antwerp boasts twenty museums, among them the **Plantin-Moretus,** featuring a sixteenth-century printing press. Most of Antwerp's museums are closed on Monday, but the zoo, which is just to the right as you exit from the railway station, is open daily until sunset. If you are interested in the **Zoo-Harbor Tour** combo ticket, check with the city tourist information office and pick a time to participate.

Brussels (Bruxelles)—Antwerp (Antwerpen)

64

BRUSSELS *Antwerp*

DEPART BRUSSELS MIDI/ZUID	TRAIN NUMBER	ARRIVE ANTWERP CENTRAL	NOTES
0735*	IC 4507	0820	
0752	IC 2007	0844	Sat, Sun
0820	IR 3306	0909	Mon–Fri
0831	IC 4508	0920	Sat, Sun
0852	IC 2008	0944	Mon–Fri
plus other frequent service			

DEPART ANTWERP CENTRAL	TRAIN NUMBER	ARRIVE BRUSSELS MIDI/ZUID	NOTES
1454	IR 2836	1552	Mon–Fri
1504	IC 4536	1553	Sat, Sun
1516	IC 2036	1608	Mon–Fri
1540	IC 4536	1626	Mon–Fri
1541	IC 636	1623	Sat, Sun
1554	IR 2837	1653	Mon–Fri
1604	IC 4537	1653	Sat, Sun
plus other frequent service until 2304			

Daily, unless otherwise noted.
* Departs 2 minutes later Sat–Sun.
All departing trains en route to Antwerp also stop at Brussels Central Station then at Brussels Nord Station; trains returning to Brussels from Antwerp stop first at Nord, then Central, and then Midi/Zuid Station.
Distance: 35 miles (57 km)

Most seasoned travelers put **Rubens's House** (open Tuesday–Sunday, 1000–1645) at the top of their list of sight-seeing "musts." Rubens bought a beautiful patrician dwelling where he lived with his family from 1615 until his death in 1640. Works of the great Flemish master also are kept in many of the museums and churches in Antwerp. Rubens is buried in **St. James Church,** where you may view the painting *Madonna with Child and Saints,* which shortly before his death, he directed be placed on the altar. Rubens and Antwerp remain inextricably linked.

Other sight-seeing musts are the **Cathedral of Our Lady** (largest Gothic church in Belgium), containing four Rubens masterpieces; the **Grote Markt** (marketplace); and the **Open Market** (known locally as the Birds Market). The **Birds Market** is open on Sunday morning, when miscellaneous wares are sold. All these city highlights will be on the map you receive at the city tourist office, and all are within reasonable walking distance.

The Flemish term, *De Rubenswandeling,* means **The Rubens Walk.** It's all laid out for you in a colorful brochure, its map detailing eleven points of interest associated with Rubens. For variety, there is a Stadswandeling/Rondwandeling—city round-trip walking tour—prepared in a similar format. Both are available at the tourist office.

According to legend, the site of Antwerp was once inhabited by a giant who extracted tribute from all who navigated the river and cut off a hand of those who refused to pay. He was slain by a Roman soldier, who cut off the giant's hand and threw it into the river. Thus, the city's name: *Ant* (hand) and *werpen* (from the verb "to throw"). In support of the legend, the city fathers erected a statue of the Roman soldier, Silvius Brabo, in front of the city hall. Those not subscribing to the legend say the name was derived from *Aenwerpen* (higher land). There's always someone who doesn't believe in the tooth fairy.

Day Excursion to

Bruges (Brugge)
Old Lace and Church Spires

Depart from Brussels Nord Station
Distance by Train: 65 miles (105 km)
Average Train Time: 1 hour, 7 minutes
City Dialing Code: 50
Tourist Information Office: Toerisme Brugge, Burg 11, B–8000 Brugge
Tel: 44 86 86; **Fax:** 44 86 00
Internet: www.brugge.be
E-mail: toerisme@brugge.be
Hours: April–September: Monday–Friday 0930–1830; Saturday–Sunday 1000–1200 and 1400–1830. October–March: Monday–Friday 0930–1700; Saturday–Sunday 0930–1300 and 1400–1730.
Notes: Arriving in Bruges, check schedules posted in the station for your return train to Brussels. The train information office is inside the station on the left side as you exit from the train platform (*Tel:* 50 38 23 82). Tourist information is available outside the station near the Video Palace, or go to the central tourist office in Burg Square.

To get to the tourist office in Burg Square, board any bus stopping in front of the railway station that is marked Centrum at the entrance side of the bus. The bus will take you to the Markt. It stops in the center of the square in front of the Provincial Palace. To return to the station, board the bus marked O Station at the library on the square close to the Markt, which can be reached by walking through Kuiperstraat off the Markt.

Declared the "cultural capital of Europe" in 2002, Bruges is where the arts reign supreme. New venues range from the Japanese-designed pavilion for the Burg to the new Concertgebouw—an arts center of distinction. According to the Bruges tourist office, "This will bring about a fruitful interchange between city, artists, residents and visitors; an interchange that scintillates long into the future." *Internet:* www.brugge2002.be.

Bruges has magnetic attractions—many of which date from the Middle Ages and the Renaissance—as well as picturesque canals, art treasures, and antiques shops. Probably the most interesting sight is the **Burg,** where history has been in the making since the ninth century. Surrounding the Burg are museums of all descriptions, spectacular church spires, peaceful canals, and fascinating alleyways. Next to the Burg is the **Markt** (Marketplace), where you will find the **Town Hall** and the **Belfry,** a remarkable building that dominates the Markt with its famous 280-foot-high octagonal tower. If you are up to it, climb up the Belfry for a panoramic view.

During the thirteenth and fourteenth centuries, Bruges stood at the crossroads of traffic between the Mediterranean and the Baltic. Rich cargoes piled high on its docks, and its warehouses held treasures of spices, cloth, and other luxuries. Bruges was bursting at the seams during this period. Hundreds of ships dropped anchor in its harbor. In its medieval magnificence, Bruges boasted a population double that of London. There was no equal to the grandeur of its court—and no one seemed alarmed that the estuary linking Bruges with the North Sea was growing narrower and shallower as the silt from the River Zwyn slowly oozed seaward.

Inexorably, the waterway began to close. Deep-draft ships could no longer navigate the estuary. The docks were abandoned, and Bruges became a victim of its own progress, a landlocked city. Today, Bruges is a museum of the Middle Ages, with gabled roof lines casting shadows on its cobblestone streets. Despite the loss of its commerce with the sea, Bruges has managed to maintain its former opulence.

Remnants of grand days past, the canals of Bruges, graced by a bevy of swans, weave in and around the city. Oddly enough, the birds' presence is attributable to a murder. In 1488, the good people of Bruges beheaded a tyrant named Langhals ("Long Neck"). Miffed by this deed, the counts of Flanders decreed that the "long necks," the symbolic swans, would be kept at public expense forever—and they are.

Although walking is the best way to see Bruges, there are other interesting ways of getting around the city, one being by canal boat—board behind the Belfry. The trip lasts thirty-five minutes. Or, if pedal power appeals to you, rent a bicycle at the station. Yet another, and no less pleasant, way of seeing the city is by horse-drawn cab. The cabs wait at Markt Square.

In addition to all the sights of historic significance in Bruges, there are

Two or more trains per hour from Brussels Midi/Zuid to Bruges at 10 and 37 minutes after the hour; journey time 50 minutes. The same trains depart first from Nord station, then Central, and finally Midi/Zuid. **67**
Returning trains (2 or more each hour) depart Bruges at 23 and 59 minutes after the hour; journey time 50 to 55 minutes. Trains arrive first at Midi/Zuid, then Central, and then Nord.
Note: The rail route from Brussels to Bruges is the main line to the port of Oostende. Consequently, most of the trains going in that direction stop at all three of the main Brussels stations. Check departure information in the station you plan to depart from in Brussels.
Distance: 65 miles (105 km)

many stores selling exquisite, handmade Flemish lace; excellent reproductions of Flemish paintings; and colorful ceramics. In general, prices are slightly lower than in Brussels, and the quality is as high.

Day Excursion to

Ghent (Gent)
Historic Beauty

Depart from Brussels Nord Station
  Most trains from Brussels to Ghent stop in all three of Brussels's metropolitan train stations. Check departure information in your station.
Distance by Train: 40 miles (64 km)
Average Train Time: 45 minutes
City Dialing Code: 9
Tourist Information Office: Inquiry desk in the Crypt of the Belfry, Sint-Baafsplein 17A, B-9000 Ghent
Tel: 266 52 32
Internet: www.gent.be
E-mail: toerisme@gent.be
Hours: November 5–March 31, 0930–1630 daily; April 1–November 3, 0930–1830 daily
Notes: To reach the tourist office, take tram No. 10, 11, 12, or 13 to the town center at Korenmarkt.

Ghent is one of the true Flemish water towns. Three rivers—the Schelde, the Lys, the Lieve—plus a canal flow through it. This accounts for its more than one hundred bridges and its Celtic name,

At least three trains per hour depart Midi/Zuid at 10, 15, and 35 minutes after the hour; journey time approximately 30 minutes. Trains depart first from Nord, then Central, and then Midi/Zuid. Returning trains (at least three each hour) depart Ghent at 15, 22, and 56 minutes after the hour; journey time approximately 30 minutes. Trains arrive first at Midi/Zuid, then Central, and then Nord. Distance: 40 miles (64 km)

"Ganda," meaning a place of confluence. In the fourteenth century, Ghent was the second largest city north of the Alps after Paris. In 1827, the cutting of the Terneuzen canal made Ghent the second largest seaport in Belgium. In more modern times, Ghent has become world famous for its flower show and the International Ghent Fair. Both are held in the Flanders Expo, a trade fair complex a few kilometers from the center of Ghent.

Ask for a free brochure, *All Information for Tourists,* at the tourist office. The brochure includes a map with different walking tours. Each is color-coded, and places of interest are indicated. During the season, guided walking tours for individuals start at the tourist office every day. Or what about enjoying a carriage trip or a boat excursion?

Saint Michael's Bridge, in the heart of the city, is a good place to begin your walking tour. The view from here is impressive, with church towers and guild houses rimming the skyline. In the distance you can see the **Castle of the Counts,** one of the most imposing feudal fortresses in Europe today. It played a prominent role in Ghent's history during feudal times. The tradespeople had united in a number of strong guilds and could offer armed resistance against their feudal lords, the counts, when said gentry came to collect the rent. The town hall and the Belfry, symbols of civic freedom, were also erected during that period. The Castle of the Counts was completely restored in 1887 and is well worth your inspection.

The **Kouter** is a favorite place for the citizens of Ghent to start their Sunday walks. Every morning there is a flower market here, which on a Sunday takes over the whole area. In the summer, bands from Ghent and the province play in the wrought-iron bandstand in the middle of the square. The vegetable and fruit markets are open Monday through Saturday at the **Groentenmarkt**. As the commercial activity diminishes, the social activities gain tempo.

In early times Ghent, like many other Flemish towns, was involved in warding off the Norse invaders coming off the beaches of the North Sea to loot and plunder. Later, Ghent was able to turn to more peaceful activities. Growing in opulence, Ghent fostered the emerging artists of Flanders and today is considered the cradle of Flemish art.

Each September and October, Ghent plays host to the **Flanders Festival of Music**. Some of the world's greatest musicians and the most celebrated Belgian orchestras and choirs perform. Many other annual events take place. International regattas are held every May at the **Watersportbaan**. From April 1–October 31 daily and during the winter season on Friday and Saturday many of the city's historic places, such as the Castle of the Counts, are illuminated at night. Check with the tourist office for a list of events and festivals.

Hungry? With more than 350 restaurants to choose from, something will suit your taste buds—Italian, Greek, French, Chinese, vegetarian—you name it, you can find it. Opposite the town hall, try the **Hotel Cour St. Georges**. Although Ghent lies inland from the North Sea, it is, in fact, a seaport and offers some exceptional seafood. If you enjoy shellfish, order the Belgian specialty, moules mariniers (steamed mussels).

Day Excursion to

Namur
Gateway to the Ardennes

Depart from Brussels Midi Station
Distance by Train: 43 miles (69 km)
Average Train Time: 50 minutes
City Dialing Code: 81
Tourist Information Office: Square de l'Europe Unie B–5000
Tel: 22 28 59 or 24 64 49; **Fax:** 24 23 60
Internet: www.ville.namur.be or www.ftpn.be
E-mail: tourisme@ville.namur.be or tourisme@ftpn.be
Hours: 0930–1800 daily
Notes: In the Namur station, leave the train-platform area via an underground ramp. Once on the ramp, walk past sortie 1 to sortie 2 and take the stairs to the street level. Bear towards the right around the "C & A" store and proceed to the park, where the tourist office will be in plain view.

I f you would like to revisit the eighteenth century, go to Namur. It is one of the most attractive towns in Belgium. The tourist office offers several excellent walking tours and theme tours. It can also provide personalized tours upon request. For the footsore and those wanting to range farther afield, book an **"All-in-One"** ticket that includes boat tours, harborside attractions, and the Citadel of Namur, complete with underground explorations.

On Saturday morning, don't miss the colorful flower market at the **Place du Palais de Justice** and the **Leopold Square** shopping center. Probably you will not find such a concentration of museums and monuments anywhere else in Europe.

The dominating landmark of Namur—**the Citadel**—looms on its skyline. It is in the center of the **Parc du Champeau**. The walk there can be delightful. The tourist bureau will provide full details. You can also reach the Citadel by bus. Board bus No. 3 in the town square, adjacent to the railway station. A tour of the Citadel is included in the "All-In-One" ticket, along with a ride in the tourist office's shuttle.

The Citadel of Namur sits at the confluence of the Meuse and the Sambre. Two thousand years of history are contained within its walls. Originally a Celtic stronghold with primitive fortifications, it was altered into a strongly defensive castle. Underground fortifications were added in the fifteenth century and again expanded century after century until modern weaponry brought a cessation of such defenses in the eighteenth century. Throughout its history, however, the Citadel, as one of the most important strongholds of Europe, faced twenty sieges!

Namur's tourist office has a wide selection of excursions for you to select from. Here are but a few: **The Gardens of Annevoie,** famous for its eighteenth-century style of flowers and fountains, are open 0900–1900; a visit can be made in minutes. A restaurant and tavern are on the grounds. **Cruises on the River Meuse** are available in a variety of schedules, including a picnic onboard or ashore.

For aquatic buffs, a kayak or boat trip down the river Lesse is available, with departures daily throughout the season at 1000 and 1400. Looking for something a bit less strenuous? Perhaps a water tour of the **Caves of Neptune** would fill the bill. It's a 45-minute tour and includes a 20-minute boat ride plus a sight and sound show. There are other ways to discover the Lesse and the valley area—try the rail/bike ride on an old railway line.

Namur is the gateway to the Ardennes, the forests and mountains of Belgium, with all the amenities of a holiday resort. Should you find yourself with time to spare (a very unlikely thing), take a stroll on the **Boulevard de la Sambre,** an attractive, tree-lined avenue. If, on the other hand, you are looking for exquisite gifts, the **Rue de l'Ange** has excellent shops. Or enjoy Brasseries (Breweries) du Bocp and des Fagnes.

We highly suggest visiting Namur during the season of festivals. This is the best way to experience the local folklore of the Stiltwalkers of Namur; the looming giants, the Royal Society of Moncrabeau; the bright-yellow uniformed Canaris regiment; or the choreographed lunacy of the dancing Chinels.

Brussels (Bruxelles)—Namur

At least 2 trains hourly depart Midi/Zuid at 6 and 36 minutes after the hour; journey time 1 hour. Trains depart first from Midi/Zuid, then from Central, and then from Nord.
Returning trains depart Namur at 23 and 53 minutes after the hour; journey time 1 hour. Trains arrive first at Nord, then Central, and then Midi/Zuid.
Distance: 43 miles (69 km)

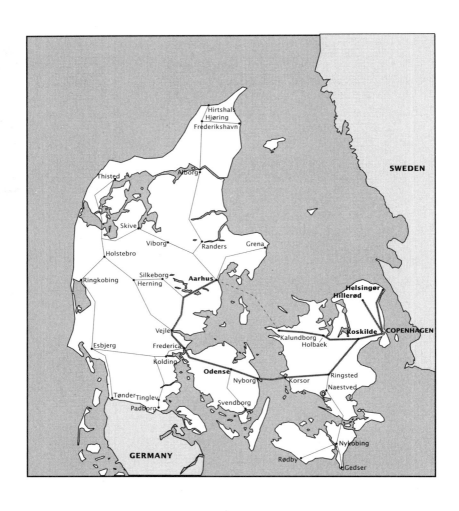

Denmark

anes are a fun-loving people, and their sparkling humor is unsurpassed. For example, Victor Borge, one of Denmark's leading expo-
nents of such jocularity, explains that his ultra-expensive, concert grand
piano is "every bit as good as a Rolls-Royce, except," quips Victor, "it has
smaller wheels." This is typical Danish humor, and this fairy-tale land of
Denmark abounds in it. No doubt you will find the Danes to be the most
happy and humorous of all Europeans. Why are they that way? One of our
Danish friends explains it in this manner: "For centuries, we Danes were the
most feared of the Vikings, destroying and plundering at will. Now, we've
got that all out of our system and have nothing left to do except to be
happy!" This happy attitude seems to exist throughout the country.

Legend has it that the ancient Vikings, fierce as they were, never missed
the chance to throw a party, and apparently their descendants are just as
enthusiastic when it comes to having a good time. In summer, there are
festivals throughout Denmark where eating, drinking, singing, and dancing
are the orders of the day. In winter, the Danes go inside for their celebrations, where eating, drinking, singing, and dancing are the orders of the day.
Oddly enough, this never seems to be monotonous to the Danes—or their
visitors. With the completion of the Øresund Fixed Link—the bridge
linking Copenhagen, Denmark, with Malmö, Sweden—it is even more
convenient to visit both countries.

For more information about Denmark, contact the newly merged Danish
and Swedish Tourist Board in North America:

New York: P.O. Box 4649, Grand Central Station, New York, NY 10163-
4649. *Tel:* (212) 885–9700; *Fax:* (212) 885–9710; *E-mail:* info@
goscandinavia. com; *Internet:* **www.goscandinavia.com** or **www.
dt.dk**

DENMARK

Banking
- **Currency:** Danish Kroner (DKK)
- **Exchange rate at press time:** DKK 8.14 = U.S. $1.00
- **Hours:** 0930–1600 Monday–Friday; Thursday until 1800

Communications
- **Country Code:** 45
  No city codes required for calls within Denmark. Danish phone numbers are usually 8 digits.
  Direct dial: AT&T Direct: 8001–0010

Shopping
- **Hours:** Monday–Thursday, 0900/1000–1730/1800; Friday, 0900/1000–1900/2000; Saturday, 0900/1000–1200/1300/1400 (until 1700 for most shops in Copenhagen)

Denmark has a hefty 25 percent VAT (value added tax). It may be avoided in two different ways: Have your purchases sent home. This way, you pay only the purchase price of the item plus shipping and insurance. Second plan, take the goods home yourself by paying the VAT; save your purchase slips and get the VAT refunded at the Copenhagen Kastrup Airport tax-free shop. In that case, plan to arrive at the airport an hour ahead of your original reporting time.

Rail Travel in Denmark
The dynamic Danish State Railways (DSB) is on the move (*Internet:* www.dsb.dk). In June 1997, the newly opened tunnel and bridge made crossing the Great Belt by train more than an hour faster than going by ferry. The "Lyntog" (high-speed diesel) trains cruise from Copenhagen to Aarhus in only 2½ hours instead of 4. In July 2000, the 16-kilometer rail and motorway tunnel/bridge complex connecting northeast Denmark and southern Sweden was completed. The Øresund Bridge connects Copenhagen and Malmö, creating the largest domestic market in northern Europe (equalling Berlin, Hamburg, and Amsterdam).

Denmark's InterCity and Lyntog trains feature seats with headphones for listening to music, 220-volt outlets for computers, and play areas for children. In first class, passengers can help themselves to tea, soft drinks, and newspapers. The DSB wants to make your trip fast but comfortable. It is advisable to have seat reservations on all IC and Lyntog trains.

The following bonuses apply if you have any of the **Eurail passes:**
- **Stena Line** ships, Frederikshavn–Göteburg (Sweden); 50 percent discount. No discount on cabins or couchettes.
- **Scandlines** ships, free ferry transport: Helsingør–Helsingborg (Sweden); (when your railpass is valid in both Denmark and Sweden)
- **Color Line** ships, 30 percent discounts on day crossings:

Frederikshavn/Skagen–Larvik (Norway); Hirtshals–Kristiansand (Norway).

- **Scandlines/DFO,** free ferry crossing Rødby Faerge to Puttgarden, Germany (railpass must be valid in both Denmark and Germany)
- **Hjørring Privatbanen** railways, Hjørring–Hirtshals v.v.—50 percent discount
- **Skagensbanen** railway, 50 percent discount Frederikshavn-Skagen.
- **Danish Railway Museum** in Odense—25 percent discount

If your European travels are all within Scandinavia, consider the **Scanrail Pass** that you can purchase in North America. It provides unlimited rail travel in Denmark, Finland, Norway, and Sweden, plus discounts on certain ferry crossings and private railways. Although you can purchase a Scanrail Pass at train stations in Scandinavia, it is considerably more expensive than if you purchase it in North America. Call toll-free (877) RAILPASS (877–724–5727) or contact RailPass.com on-line at www.railpass.com to order.

Scanrail Pass

	Adult	Child	Senior	Youth
5 days within 2 months				
1st Class	$290	$145	$258	$218
2nd Class	$214	$107	$190	$161
10 days within 2 months				
1st Class	$388	$194	$345	$291
2nd Class	$288	$155	$256	$216
21 days consecutive				
1st Class	$448	$224	$399	$336
2nd Class	$332	$166	$295	$249

Scanrail 'n Drive Pass

(Purchase only in North America; car rental not available in Finland.) Prices are per person. Valid for 5 days of unlimited rail travel and 3 days of car rental to be used within a 15-day period. Able to add unlimited number of car days.

	1st Class		2nd Class		Additional
	2 Adults	1 Adult	2 Adults	1 Adult	Car Day
Economy	$304	$354	$242	$297	$60
Compact	$324	$399	$262	$337	$78
Intermediate	$344	$419	$272	$357	$88

Base City:

Copenhagen
(København)

**Internet: www.visitcopenhagen.dk
or www.copenhagencity.dk**

Arriving by Air

Kastrup Airport: Tel: 3231–3231; Fax: 3231–3132; *Internet:* www.cph.dk
Located 8 kilometers southeast of Copenhagen. Most international flights to and from Denmark use Kastrup (Copenhagen) Airport. More than 60 airlines have regular services to Copenhagen, and there are several daily connections to/from all other major European airports.

Airport–City Links: The airport rail terminal links the airport to the Copenhagen main railway station (København H.) by train; departures every 10 minutes. The rail ticket office is located in Terminal 3 above the platforms. One-way ticket, DKK 18.

Frequent airport-coach, public-bus, and taxi service is available also. A shuttle bus operates between Kastrup Airport and City Central Railway Station 0630–2310 (weekends/holidays 0545–1110). Journey time: 20–30 minutes. Intervals: 10–15 minutes. From Central Railway Station to Kastrup Airport, 0542–2145 daily. The ride to the downtown SAS terminal (located at the main railway station) costs 40 kroner (DKK). For only DKK 16.50, public bus No. 250S will take you from the airport to the Town Hall Square, near Tivoli Gardens, and to the railway station, where your ticket entitles you to transfer to another bus within one hour from the time of purchase.

Taxi service from the airport to city center costs DKK 120–140 depending on time of day (price includes taxes/tips). You can pay by credit card.

There are banks and ATMs in Terminal 3 (the arrival hall for all international flights); one is in the corridor leading to Terminal 2. Hours: 0630–2200 daily. There is a DSB (Danish Railways) ticket office near the escalators leading to the train platforms in Terminal 3, straight ahead after exiting from Customs.

Open 0600–2300 daily, this office can validate your railpass.

Arriving by Train

There are direct train connections from Copenhagen to major cities in Europe, including Stockholm, Oslo, Hamburg, and Basel.

Copenhagen has four major railway stations, but, unlike the situation in Paris, primarily the central station, **København Hovedbanegaard,** is of concern to railpass travelers. Signs in and approaching the station are marked københavn h. The abbreviation of Hovedbanegaard (Central Station), an "H," reflects the efficiency of this huge train complex right in the heart of the city. The tracks run below street level, and the architecture of the station blends well with the locale. København H. is suggestive of a great Viking hall with two great wooden archways that span its enclosed area.

The station is served by twelve tracks joined by six exits as you ascend from train level to the station's arrival area. For your orientation, upon arrival you may exit in a northerly or an easterly direction. Tivoli Gardens flank the station's east side, and a huge square fronts the station to the north. The arrival hall serves mainly for baggage handling. The lost-and-found office and the politi (police station) are alongside tracks 11 and 12.

Most services are located in the north departure area. Here you will find the SAS coach terminal, a cafeteria, and an excellent restaurant in the northwest corner. Taxi service is available at both the north and the east exits. City bus lines also serve the station, but inquire at the train information office before using one. Train arrival-and-departure information is displayed in bulletin form at both the arrival exits and the east and west entrances. Modern, airport-style digital displays give train-departure information automatically at each departure gate and on the train platforms. Elevator service, as well as stairways, is available between the station and the train platforms. If you are using a baggage cart, be certain to use the elevators to move your baggage.

- **Baggage Storage.** Lockers are available in two sizes—the small one is DKK 25; the large one is DKK 35 for 24 hours. Baggage carts require a DKK 10 or DKK 20 coin (the carts accept either) refundable deposit.
- **Money Exchange.** Den Danske Bank is located along the northwest side. It also has ATMs. Hours of operation are 0800–2000 daily. A similar banking facility (FOREX) may be found in the row of shops on the ground level near the Bernsdorffsgade side. Hours are 0800–2100.
- **Train Information.** *Tel:* 3314–1701. A train information window, opposite McDonald's (near the bank), is open daily 0700–2100. For complicated questions, go to the train information office (RejseCenter) around the corner in the lobby leading to the Vesterbrogade exit; open 0800–1900 daily. Take a numbered ticket from the distributor near the entrance. Push "Domestic" if your question refers to local travel within Denmark; push "International" for

travel outside of Denmark, or to have your railpass validated. Train information departures (yellow) and arrivals (white) bulletins are displayed. Small monitor screens at the top of the escalators leading to each platform give arrivals/departures from that track. Other monitors showing all arrivals/departures within the next hour or so are near the two main entrances to the station and along the wall between tracks 6 and 7.

- **Train Reservations.** RejseCenter on the north side of the station, just opposite the departure gates for tracks 1/2 and 3/4. Inside the office, take a number for domestic or international assistance. Hours: 0800–1900 daily. International Reservations: *Tel:* 3314–3088; Domestic Reservations: *Tel:* 3314–8800.
- **Railpass validation** is in the same office where international tickets are purchased, 0630–2400 daily.
- **Inter-Rail Center,** in the middle section of the south side of the station between tracks 2 and 4. Enter by showing your railpass. You can pick up information on what's going on in the *Copenhagen This Week* pamphlet, and the center personnel can help with reservations for youth hostels. For a few kroner you can even take a shower.

Tourist Information/Hotel Reservations

- **København Turistinformation:** Bernstorffsgade 1, DK–1577 København V, Denmark. *Tel:* 7022 2442; *Fax:* 7022 2452; *Internet:* www.visitcopenhagen.dk. *E-mail:* touristinfo@woco.dk

Hours: May 1–September 15, 0900–2100 daily; September 16–April 30, 0900–1700 Monday–Friday, Saturday 0900–1400, closed on Sunday.

To reach the tourist office on foot, exit the central station and walk toward the corner on the right side, toward the front of the Tivoli Gardens. Turn right at this point. The office will be on your right and readily identifiable by the familiar i sign.

- **Hotel reservations** (*Tel:* 3312–2880; *Fax:* 3312–9723) can be made at the tourist office. The personnel are authorized to accept advance payments on behalf of the hotels to ensure reservations.

For convenience and comfort, we can recommend the four-star Sofitel Plaza Copenhagen at Bernstorffsgade 4, DK–1577 (*Tel:* 3314–9262; *Fax:* 3393–9362). *Internet:* www.accorhotel.dk; *E-mail:* sofitel@accorhotel.dk. Room rates range from DKK 1695 and up for a single; doubles begin at DKK 1895. The Library Bar was awarded as one of the best five bars in the world by *Forbes Magazine.*

Getting Around in Copenhagen

In Copenhagen an electrified metropolitan S-train railway network connects the city center with the suburban areas at frequent intervals. The metro, City Line, runs every 1½ minutes during rush hour.

A great convenience is the **Copenhagen Card,** which entitles you to unlimited travel by buses and trains in the entire metropolitan area as well as the whole of North Zealand, Roskilde, and Køge, plus free entrances to more than 70 museums, attractions, and sights, including Tivoli and Tivoli Museum, Believe It or Not!, Danish Toy Museum, Frederiksborg Castle, and many more. A comprehensive guide booklet accompanies the card and includes a map of the city. And that's not all—you also receive a 25–50 percent discount on four ferry crossings to Sweden and a 20 percent discount on canal tours and the city tour. What a bargain! Cards are issued for 24 hours (DKK 175), 48 hours (DKK 295), or 72 hours (DKK 395). Children age 5–11 pay 85, 145, or 195 DKK.

Copenhagen has invested heavily in putting bicycle paths alongside many of its main streets, and the city provides more than 2,000 free bicycles for visitors to use while sight-seeing. Look for one of the 110 Citybike parking areas located throughout the city center, deposit a DKK 20 coin, and start pedaling. When you return the bike, you get your money back. Check with the tourist office for more details.

Sights/Attractions/Tours

Tivoli Gardens (*Tel:* 3315–1001; *Fax:* 3375–0381; *Internet:* www. tivoligardens.com) is generally open from mid-April through mid-September. Hours: 1100–2400 Sunday–Thursday; 1100–0100 Friday–Saturday. Check the Tivoli Web site for special Christmas Market dates and opening hours. It's not the world's largest amusement park, but it is unique. It has been in business since 1843. Each year, people come from all over the world to enjoy its very special blend of old and new attractions. Tree-lined walks, resplendent with flowers and sparkling illuminations, form the backdrop to its theaters and open-air amusement areas. There are more than 20 restaurants to choose from. Four evenings each week, the park closes with a fireworks display.

During its day of entertainment for young and old alike, international artists appear at the Tivoli Concert Hall, Gilbert & Sullivan scenarios are acted out at the Pantomime Theater, and the Tivoli Boys Guard parades frequently to the delight of all. There's also an impressive assembly of quality rides to thrill you, games to play, and seven great restaurants to select from when you get hunger pangs. Tivoli cannot be described adequately in words; it must be experienced.

Amalienborg Palace is a beautiful example of Rococo architecture and has served as the permanent residence of the Danish royal family since 1794. See the changing of the Royal Guard at 1200 every day in the palace square.

Those with more prurient interests may want to visit the **Museum Erotica** at Købmagergade 24, 1150 København K, *Tel:* 3312–0311, to experience the "Love Life of Homo Sapiens." Hours: 1000–2300.

Tour the colorful **Nyhavn canal** area with its quaint restaurants or take the city harbor tour—a comfortable way to see beautiful Copenhagen.

Want more? Tour the city's world-famous breweries, Carlsberg and

Tuborg. Get details from the tourist office. Yes, they provide samples of their products. Contact Carlsberg in advance by calling 3327–1314.

The **New Museum of Modern Art Arken** (the Ark) is a favorite among those interested in contemporary art (*Internet:* www.arken.dk). The building itself is a fascinating structure.

Year-round, visit **Den Lille Havfrue ("The Little Mermaid")**, symbol of today's Copenhagen. It is an enchanting, soul-touching statue, and next to Queen Margrethe it is probably Denmark's most famous female.

Shopping? Copenhagen can accommodate you. You'll learn quickly about **Stroget** (pronounced "stroy-it"). It's not one but actually five different shopping areas, each designated pedestrian-only and lined with shops that might make you want to hide your credit cards. All the well-known Danish specialties are in profusion here. Just north of the Stroget in the Latin Quarter there are some good cafes and restaurants, so you can get anything from a hot dog to a five-course banquet. Try the world-famous Danish delicacy *smorrebrod*, which usually consists of rye bread topped with marinated herring or liver pâté and onion rings.

For the best salmon specialties, we enjoyed the **Queen's Restaurant & Pub** at Vester Voldgade 25. For reservations telephone 3312–5902. For an extraordinary evening, **St. Gertruds Kloster** at 32 Hauser Plads can provide you with an unforgettable dinner in a fourteenth-century atmosphere—in medieval monastery vaults—accompanied by the romantic light of 1,500 candles. For reservations call 3314–6630 or *Fax:* 3393–9365.

If you have a sweet tooth, please, don't go home before you have tried the Danish waffle–ice cream combination.

Day Excursions

Five delightful day excursions await whenever you can break away from the charm that is distinctly Copenhagen's. Admittedly, this is a difficult thing to do because the Danish capital has so much to offer, what with its Tivoli Gardens and pedestrian-only shopping streets; but leave it you must. The entire country is a fairyland. Go out and enjoy it.

Jutland is the Danish mainland, the tip of the European continent that reaches northward toward the Scandinavian peninsula. **Aarhus** is Jutland's cultural center and Denmark's second largest city. Fans of William Shakespeare will, no doubt, make **Helsingør** (Elsinore) their prime day-excursion choice. Castle buffs will head for **Hillerød** and its gracious Frederiksborg Castle. **Odense**, birthplace of Hans Christian Andersen, will delight day excursioners of all ages. **Roskilde** is loaded with Danish folklore and history, including a Viking-ship museum, Museum Island, and Denmark's most important medieval building—the Roskilde Cathedral—for centuries the final resting place of Denmark's royalty.

Train Connections to Other Base Cities from Copenhagen (København)

Depart from Copenhagen (København H) Station

DEPART	TRAIN NUMBER	ARRIVE	NOTES
		Amsterdam Centraal	
0752	EC 38	1749	1
1147	EC 36	2149	1
1851	NZ 40483	0856+1	R, Sleeper, 2
2100	R 1102	1349+1	R, 6, 7, Sleeper
		Berlin Zoobahnhof	
0752	EC 38	1523	R, 3
1147	EC 36	1923	R, 3
1547	EC 32	2336	R, 3
2040	R 1102	0646+1	R, 6, Sleeper
		Brussels (Bruxelles) Midi/Zuid	
1747	EC 30	0609+1	R, Sleeper, 5
		Hamburg Hauptbahnhof	
0752	EC 38	1216	R
1147	EC 36	1616	R
1547	EC 32	2016	R
1747	EC 30	2216	R
		Munich (München) Hauptbahnhof	
0752	EC 38	1900	R, 3
1147	EC 36	2259	R, 3
1547	EC 32	0704+1	R, 5, Sleeper
1851	EN 483	0918+1	R, Sleeper
		Oslo Sentral	
0820	R 1026	1645	9
1336	X 2000 490	2145	R, 10
2212	EC 37	0700+1	R, 8, Sleeper
		Paris Gare du Nord	
1747	EC 30	0908+1	R, 5
1851	NZ 40483	1205+1	R, Sleeper, 4
		Stockholm Central	
0836	X2000 530	1340	R
1236	X2000 538	1740	R
1436	X2000 542	1940	R
1836	X2000 550	2340	R
2212	EC 37	0610+1	R, 9, Sleeper
		Vienna (Wien) Westbahnhof	
1547	EC 32	0855+1	R, 5
		Zürich Hauptbahnhof	
0752	EC 38	1958	R, 3
1851	NZ 50483	1058+1	R, 11, Sleeper

Daily, unless otherwise noted.
R Reservations required.
+1 Arrives next day
1. Change trains in Hamburg and Osnabrück.
2. Change trains in Duisburg.
3. Change trains in Hamburg.

COPENHAGEN

4. Change trains in Cologne (Köln).
5. Change to sleeper train (R) in Hamburg.
6. Change to sleeper train (R) EN 111 in Malmö.
7. Change trains in Berlin.
8. Change to overnight bus in Malmö.
9. Change trains in Malmö.
10. Change trains in Göteborg.
11. Change trains in Frankfurt.

Day Excursion to

Aarhus (Århus)
World's Smallest Big City

Depart from København H. Station
Distance by Train: 139 miles (223 km)
Average Train Time: 2 hours, 36 minutes
No city code required
Tourist Information Office: Town Hall, DK–8000 Aarhus
Tel: 89 40 67 00; **Fax:** 86 12 95 90
Internet: www.visitaarhus.com
E-mail: info@visitaarhus.com
Hours: June 19–September 10: Monday–Friday 0930–1800, Saturday 0930–1700, and Sunday 0930–1300. September 11–April 30: Monday–Friday 0930–1630, Saturday 1000–1300. May 1–June 19: Monday–Friday 0930–1700, Saturday 1000–1300
Notes: To reach the tourist office, exit the station and cross the street. Turn left, proceed to the first traffic light, and cross the street to the Scandic Hotel Plaza. From this point, you will see the town hall close by on the left. Entrance is at the tower. Money-exchange service is available at the Unibank at Søndergade 44 (*Tel:* 8933–3333) 0600–1400 daily.

The Great Belt Tunnel decreased the travel time between Copenhagen and Aarhus from 4 hours to 2 hours, 36 minutes via express InterCityLyn service. And travel aboard the Danish Railways (DSB) InterCity trains is comfortable and a pleasant way to see the Danish countryside. When you arrive in Aarhus, disembark and follow the signs to the main rail station, where you mount stairs leading to the station's main concourse. Lift (elevator) service and escalators are available. After turning left, walk to the end of the corridor. The train-information office is to the left at the end of the corridor (open daily 0800–1900).

Aarhus has many other worthwhile attractions. It's Denmark's second largest city and Jutland's uncontested cultural center. So welcome to the "world's smallest big city."

People have lived in Aarhus ever since the Vikings settled at the mouth of the river, where it meets the bay. There the Norsemen constructed a harbor, built houses, and erected a church. During the 1960s, contractors excavating under a bank in Aarhus came upon the remains of a semicircular rampart that the Vikings of a thousand years ago used to protect their small community.

Today the site is a museum where you can see the reconstructed ramparts with a typical house of that time, together with tools and other belongings used by the first inhabitants of Aarhus. There is also a collection of 75 historic buildings that have been transferred there from every region of the country to re-create an entire seventeenth-century Danish market town, complete with narrow cobbled streets, shops, public squares—even a mill-race. Known as The Old Town, it is the largest museum in Jutland. Here you can wander through Danish history from the Vikings to Hans Christian Andersen.

To reach **The Old Town,** follow the city map for a 10-minute walk, or take bus No. 3. In June–August it is open 0900–1800 daily; April, May, September, and October 0900–1700; November and December, 1000–1600; January–March, 1100–1500. Admission: DKK 60 adults; DKK 15 children.

Admission to the **Viking Museum** is free, and it's only three blocks from the tourist office at Clemens Torv in the basement under Unibank. Only open during banking hours.

You may want to visit other attractions by taking the bus. You can purchase a **Tourist Ticket** (DKK 45), which is valid for an unlimited number of bus rides in the Borough of Aarhus for 24 hours. It includes a 2½ hour guided city-bus tour, which departs daily from Park Allé, the tourist office, at 1000 from June 12 to September 10. Buy it at most newsstands or at the tourist office. Remember to make a reservation in advance either by telephone or in person at the tourist office. If you plan to stay longer or make Aarhus your base city, you can buy the **Aarhus Passet** (Aarhus Pass) for one day (adults, DKK 88; children under age 16, DKK 44), two days (adults, DKK 110; children, DKK 55), or for one week (adults DKK 155; children, DKK 75), which gives you unlimited access to public transport as well as free entrance to many of the town's attractions.

South of Aarhus you'll find the **Prehistoric Museum** at Moesgård, one of Denmark's top attractions. (Hours: daily 1000–1700 in summer; closed Monday during winter.) The museum contains collections from the Stone Age, the Bronze Age, the Iron Age, and the Viking period. To get there, take bus No. 6 from the railway station.

Between Odden and Aarhus, there is a hydrofoil ferry service that takes only 90 minutes. You can return to Copenhagen via this same route, but we recommend the "great circle" tour, which includes stops at the cities of **Fredericia** and **Odense**.

Copenhagen (København)—Aarhus (Århus)

DEPART KØBENHAVN H.	TRAIN NUMBER	ARRIVE AARHUS STATION	NOTES
0700	IC 121	1008	
0756	Lyn 23	1044	Mon–Sat
0800	IC 125	1108	
0856	Lyn 27	1144	Mon–Sat
0900	IC 129	1208	
0956	Lyn 29	1244	Mon–Sat
1000	IC 133	1308	
1056	Lyn 41	1344	
1100	IC 137	1408	

DEPART AARHUS	TRAIN NUMBER	ARRIVE KØBENHAVN H.	NOTES
1402	IC 140	1718	
1430	Lyn 44	1727	
1502	IC 144	1818	
1530	Lyn 46	1827	Mon–Fri, Sun
1602	IC 148	1918	
1630	Lyn 50	1922	Mon–Fri, Sun
1702	IC 152	2018	
1730	Lyn 54	2022	Mon–Fri, Sun
1802	IC 156	2118	
1830	Lyn 56	2122	Mon–Fri, Sun
1902	IC 160	2218	
2002	IC 164	2318	

Daily, unless otherwise noted

Note: Reservations are recommended for travel on all IC and Lyntog trains in Denmark. Passengers may board the train without a reservation but are not guaranteed a seat.

Distance: 139 miles (223 km)

Day Excursion to

Helsingør
Hamlet's Hideaway

Depart from København H. Station
Distance by Train: 29 miles (47 km)
Average Train Time: 52 minutes
No city code required
Tourist Information Office: Helsingør Turistbureau, Havnepladsen 3, DK–3000 Helsingør
Tel: 49 21 13 33; **Fax:** 49 21 15 77
Internet: www.helsingorturist.dk
E-mail: info@helsingorturist.dk

Hours: June–August: Monday–Friday 0900–1800 and Saturday 1000–1500. September–May: Monday–Friday 0900–1600 and Saturday 1000–1300.
Notes: Located just across the street on the left side of the station. Look for the TURIST AGENCY sign at the end of tracks 1 and 2 for more explicit directions. Words of caution: Obey the traffic signals when crossing to the tourist office, and use the designated walkway. A local, private railroad uses the street as a siding, and it could be hazardous to your health.

Helsingør (sometimes referred to by its older name, "Elsingore" or Elsinore) is one of Denmark's oldest populated places. Documents dating back to 1231 record its development. In the vaults under **Kronborg Castle**, there is a statue of Holger Danske, a Viking chieftain who voyaged to the Holy Land as a crusader about A.D. 800, and there are many buildings of ancient vintage. For example, nearby No. 27 Strandgade is the oldest half-timbered house in town. It was built in 1577. Other structures date back to the fifteenth century.

It's the lure of Shakespeare's *Hamlet* that usually brings visitors to Helsingør. The town has many other attractions, however, not the least of which is the world's biggest and best ice cream cone. Read on, Macbeth!

Local train service between Copenhagen and the town of Helsingør runs every 20 minutes throughout the day and is interspersed with frequent express train service.

The Helsingør railway station is the terminus for the train ferries that ply between Denmark and the town of Helsingborg in Sweden. The distance across the sound is less than 3 miles. This is why Helsingør was founded there and also why it flourished from 1426 through 1857 by the collection of the "sound dues" from all merchant ships that passed.

If you are interested in maritime ferry operations, Helsingør is the place to observe it. Arrivals and departures take place almost endlessly throughout the day and into the night.

One of the tourist office's publications is *Helsingør Tourist Guide*. It describes, in great detail, Kronborg Castle, the churches of Saint Olai and Saint Mary, and the Carmelite monastery. These highlights of Helsingør are all nearby.

The **Kronborg Castle** (*Tel:* 4921–3078; *Internet:* www.kronborg castle.com) the city's most famous landmark, was built by Christian IV between 1574 and 1582. With this formidable fortress came the rapid development of the town under its protective shelter. For several centuries Helsingør was the second largest city in Denmark. The castle is open May–September, 1030–1700. During April and October, hours are 1100–1600 (closed Monday); November–March, 1100–1500 (closed Monday).

Hamlet's residency in the castle was imaginary, but the play was performed there from 1916 until 1954, when performances were curtailed

From Copenhagen to Helsingør:
Trains depart daily every 20 minutes at 1, and 21, and 41 minutes past the hour from 0701 to 0041. Journey time is approximately 52 min. Check with the train-information office in the København H. station.

From Helsingør to Copenhagen:
Trains depart daily every 20 minutes at 5, 25, and 45 minutes past the hour, 0425–2345 (service begins at 0539 on Sunday). Check with the train-information office in the Helsingør train station.

Ferries between Helsingør, Denmark, and Helsingborg, Sweden:
Copenhagen–Helsingør trains connect with ferries to Sweden on Scandlines. Eurail pass is accepted for passage. Several ferries depart every 20 minutes per hour beginning at 0700 until 2200 with less frequent service outside of these hours. Service in either direction takes about 20 minutes. If desired, you may combine a day excursion to Helsingør, Denmark, with a round-trip ferry crossing to Helsingborg, Sweden. Return trips are similar, beginning at 0510 and returning until 2340.
Distance: 29 miles (47 km)

for financial reasons. It was again performed in 1979, but there are no definite plans for the future. In the castle the King's Chamber, the Queen's Chamber, and the Great Hall must be seen to appreciate the once great splendor of this fortress. Cannons still stand along the seawall.

While admiring the Great Hall, you'll probably note that there are no fireplaces or other heating devices. Apparently, they were overlooked by the royal architect. This created no problem for the royal occupants, however, when they wanted to lay on a royal midwinter bash; they merely marched several thousand men of the royal guard into the area, and the troops' body heat sent the mercury soaring—along with a few other atmospheric additives, no doubt.

While in Helsingør, make certain that a part of your tour includes a stop at the **Raadhus** (town hall). In its council chamber, you can see a stained-glass window that depicts the history of the town. Outside of the town hall you will see a narrow street (Brostraede) leading to the sea. Follow it. The ice cream shop is there.

Day Excursion to

Hillerød

Picture-Book Scenery

Depart from København H. Station
Distance by Train: 19 miles (30 km)
Average Train Time: 40 minutes
No city code required
Tourist Information Office: Hillerød Turistbureau, Slangerupgade 2, DK–3400 Hillerød
Tel: 48 24 26 26; **Fax:** 48 24 26 65
Internet: www.hillerodturist.dk
E-mail: turistbureau@hillkomm.dk
Hours: June–August: Monday–Friday 1000–1900 and Saturday 1000–1700; September–May: Monday–Friday 1000–1700 and Saturday 1000–1300.
Notes: To get there, follow the signs to the castle, starting just outside the station building (about a 20-minute walk). The tourist office is across the street from the main entrance to the castle. If you like, you can obtain a brochure in the railway station that contains a city map to help guide your way. Or take bus No. 701 or 702 in the direction of either Ullerød or Sophienborg and ask the driver to let you off at the tourist information office. You can buy tickets on the bus for DKK 12.

COPENHAGEN *Hillerød*

Hillerød can become the crowning touch to your visit to Denmark. The town has an atmosphere distinctly its own with beautiful woodlands surrounding it. A picture-book lake rests in the town's center, faced on one side by the old town and its market square and on another by the majestic **Frederiksborg Castle**. There are few places in the world where nature and culture blend so perfectly.

No doubt the Frederiksborg Castle will be the first stopping point on your tour of Hillerød. A tour boat plies along the "most beautiful nautical mile in Denmark" between the castle and the marketplace from May through September, a delightful way of seeing both the city and the castle. (DKK 20 for adults, DKK 5 for children.)

The castle actually spans three islands. The first of its structures, erected by Frederik II in 1560, occupied the largest island. The balance of this imposing castle complex was built by Christian IV between 1600 and 1620. Between 1570 and 1840, Danish monarchs were anointed in the castle chapel, and it was used for the wedding of Danish Prince Joachim and Alexandra Manley from Hong Kong in 1995.

In 1859, a disastrous fire destroyed the interior of the main building, and irreplaceable treasures were lost forever. The chapel and all of its valuable contents, however, remained relatively undamaged. Among those items was the celebrated chapel organ built by Esaias Compenius in 1610. The

Trains depart København H. at 0554 and then every 10 minutes Mon–Fri and every 20 minutes Sat and Sun.
Trains depart Hillerød at 1506, then every 10 minutes Mon–Fri and every 20 minutes Sat and Sun.

Daily, including holidays
Journey time: 39 minutes
Distance: 19 miles (30 km)

88

COPENHAGEN *Hillerød*

chapel organist plays every Thursday between 1330 and 1400. The castle has been restored, at first by royal contributions and public donations, and, more recently, by philanthropic support from J. C. Jacobsen, former owner of the Carlsberg Brewery and the Carlsberg Foundation. The museum is open daily 1000–1700 April–October; 1100–1500 November–March; (admission: DKK 50, adults; children, DKK 10). There is an interesting museum of local and regional history, known as the **North Sealand Folk Museum,** by a small pond in a corner of the castle's gardens, and the castle itself now houses the Museum of Natural History.

The castle gardens, water canals, and fountains are among the most exquisite. In 1996, the reconstruction of the Baroque Garden was finished and inaugurated by Danish Queen Margrethe II; it resembles the original park from 1720. In another section of the castle garden, known as the *Indelukket,* you can inspect a charming little country house built in 1562 for the king to conduct informal entertainment. Several guided tours are offered of the sites, castles, museums, forest, and parklands of Hillerød. Contact the tourist center for arrangements.

The shop-'til-you-drop group will enjoy Hillerød's shopping center, the **"SlotsArkaderne"** (Castle Arcades), with more than 47 specialty shops. It, too, is conveniently located on Slotsgade. When you are coming from the railway station, the glass-covered SlotsArkaderne shopping mall is on the left-hand side of Slotsgade.

The **Money Historical Museum,** at No. 38 Slotsgade, is on your way to the castle. It should attract coin collectors of all ages as it comprises a very fine collection of Danish and foreign coins as well as other means of payment used in ancient times. Illustrations tell the story of political, historical, and cultural aspects of money and coinage.

At Slotsgade 52 E, visit the **Hagenglas**—a glass-blower's studio and shop. You can watch artist/designer Rikke Hagen create her modern glass designs and one-of-a kind pieces. *Tel:* 45 48 24 62 60. *Hours:* Monday–Friday 0930-1730; Saturday 1000-1300.

Just outside Hillerød, you may want to visit the exhibit *Mode i Mini* of costumed dolls. You can reach it on bus No. 736. The display features seventy dolls with handmade costumes that present the history of dress as well as the history of humankind. You'll see everything from Queen Victoria to the kind of bustle that your great-grandmother might have worn.

Day Excursion to
Odense
Home of Hans Christian Andersen

Depart from København H. Station
Distance by Train: 103 miles (165 km)
Average Travel Time: 1 hour, 17 minutes
No city code required
Tourist Information Office: Odense Turist Bureau, Rådhuset (Town Hall), DK–5000 Odense C
Tel: 66 12 75 20; *Fax:* 66 12 75 86
Internet: www.odenseturist.dk
Hours: June 15–August 31: Monday–Saturday 0900–1900 and Sunday 1000–1700. September 1–June 14: Monday–Friday 0930–1630 and Saturday 1000–1300.
Notes: When you arrive in the Odense railway station, look for the train-information booth on the second floor. There you can obtain train information and a map of Odense showing how to get to the Turist Bureau at the Rådhuset (Town Hall). Information booth hours: Monday–Saturday, 0600–2100; Sunday, 0700–2200.

Hans Christian Andersen, Denmark's famous teller of fairy tales, was born in a tiny yellow house in Odense on April 2, 1805. One hundred years later, the city bought the house and turned it into a museum—probably the best investment that the city ever made. Tourists of all ages still flock to this magic point to see what his early life was like and to wonder what developed an imagination that could captivate the entire world.

Many of Andersen's stories were set in or near Odense. Most of the locations can be seen today. The small, half-timbered house where he was born, now the nucleus of the **Hans Christian Andersen Museum**, is set in a cluster of other small houses from the same period. A visit there is like stepping back into the nineteenth century.

The Hans Christian Andersen house (near the tourist office, about a 10-minute walk from the rail station) is open daily (except Monday) June 16–August 31 0900–1900; September 1–June 15, 1000–1600. The area surrounding Hans Christian Andersen's home, with its little colored houses and cobblestone streets, is very attractive.

If you are visiting the museum area at mealtime, we suggest that you eat

At least two trains depart København H. hourly on the hour and half-hour; journey time on IC trains is 1 hour 29 to 32 minutes (a few minutes faster Sat–Sun). Lyntog trains (departing at 0656, 0756, and 0856) take only 1 hour 16 minutes. At least two trains depart Odense hourly at 15 and 47 minutes after the hour; journey time for IC trains is 1 hour 30 minutes. Lyntog trains (departing at 1506, 1606, 1706, 1806, and 1906) take 1 hour 16 minutes.
Note: Seat reservations are recommended on all IC and Lyntog trains in Denmark. Passengers may board the train without a reservation but are not guaranteed a seat.
Distance: 103 miles (165 km)

in a charming little restaurant nearby at Overgade 23, **Den Gamle Kro,** (*"The Old Inn"*). *Tel:* 66 12 14 33. It's but one of a score of excellent restaurants in Odense. The tourist office has a handy pocket guide describing many of these eating establishments. You'll find an interesting selection—including such names as **Jensen's Boefhus** and **Den Lille Café Olivia.**

The house of Hans Christian Andersen is not the only attraction in Odense. With more than 185,000 inhabitants, the city is Denmark's third largest. Industrial and vigorous in its lifestyle, Odense has smart shops, spacious parks, and sparkling residential areas. Situated in the center of Denmark's second largest island, the Isle of Funen, the city is the focal point for those wishing to explore the island's rolling countryside.

The German emperor Otto III officially mentioned Odense for the first time in a letter dated March 18, 988. Although there were people living there at the time and a church had been previously erected, the present-day residents applied the emperor's date as a benchmark and declared 1988 as the "1,000th Anniversary of Odense."

A Hans Christian Andersen fairy tale is presented from mid-July through the first week in August at the **Open Air Theater** in Funen Village. The village is one of the largest open-air museums in Denmark, characterized by a coherent layout of landscape and a real village of seventeenth-century houses assembled from the Island of Funen and the surrounding islands. Here you will find farms with animals, a rectory, a school—even a brickyard and a forge. The theater seats 2,000 people.

Odense has a museum for every interest—from art to transportation. **The Brandts Klaedefabrik Art Gallery, Danish Museum of Printing, Danish Press Museum,** and **Museum of Photographic Art** are all located in Brandts Passage. The **Danish Railway Museum** is next to the railway station at Dannebrogsgade 24 (*Tel:* 6613–6630). Experience 150 years of train and ferry history. It is open daily from 1000 to 1600.

The **Odense Adventure Pass** will provide free public transport within the Odense area and either free or reduced-price admission to Odense's museums, sights, and the zoo. A 24-hour pass costs DKK 85 for adults and

40 for children, and the 48-hour pass costs DKK 125 for adults and 60 for children. The Adventure Pass can be purchased at the Odense Tourist Bureau. To reach the zoo, board one of Odense Aafart's covered cruise boats for a relaxing journey.

Day Excursion to

Roskilde
The Viking Ship Museum and the Cathedral

Depart from København H. Station
Distance by Train: 19 miles (31 km)
Average Train Time: 25 minutes
No city code required
Tourist Information Office: Roskilde-Egnens Turistbureau, Gullandsstraede 15, Postboks 637, DK–4000 Roskilde
Tel: 46 35 27 00; **Fax:** 46 35 14 74
Internet: www.visitroskilde.com
E-mail: info@destination-roskilde.dk
Hours: July–August: Monday–Friday 0900–1800 and Saturday 1000–1400; September–December: Monday–Thursday 0900–1700, Friday 0900–1600, Saturday 1000–1300; January–March: Monday–Thursday 0900–1700, Friday 0900–1600, Saturday 1000–1300; April–June: Monday–Friday 0900–1700, Saturday 1000–1300..
Notes: Ten-minute walk from the railway station, or take a taxi for about DKK 50. If walking, exit the station and proceed downhill to the main street. Turn left at this point to the city square. The tourist office is only about 300 yards off the pedestrian street in Gullandsstraede.

Since Roskilde is so close to Copenhagen, you might think that it would be so much like Denmark's capital city that a day excursion there would be pointless. On the contrary, Roskilde is as different from Copenhagen as night is from day. Known as the "Town of Viking Ships and Royal Tombs," Roskilde warrants a visit. In fact, it is difficult to see all that you might want to see in Roskilde in just one day.

We recommend at least three things to do during your day excursion: (1) visit the cathedral, (2) take a guided tour, and (3) visit the Viking Ship Museum. If you decide to stay over, Roskilde offers one of the most beautiful campsites with waterfront and fjord views, plus 11 chalets available to rent. The area also has modern hotels and beautiful manor house accommodations. Consider contacting the tourist office prior to departure for the *Destination Roskilde* guide.

Trains run about every 15 minutes from Copenhagen to Roskilde all day beginning at 0500 through 0030; a couple of trains also run during the middle of the night. Distance: 19 miles (31 km)

Roskilde's twin-spired, redbrick **Domkirke** (cathedral) dominates the city's skyline. Its construction was begun in 1170 on the same site where King Harald Bluetooth erected a church in A.D. 960. Today it's considered Denmark's most important medieval building and is now inscribed on the World Heritage List. It is an international attraction primarily because it has been the burial place of Danish royalty for centuries. Thirty-nine kings and queens of Denmark are buried there, representing the longest reign of family monarchy in the world.

The cathedral is one of Denmark's first brick buildings, and it is said that it has as many tales to tell as it has bricks in its walls. Originally, a limestone edifice was erected on the foundation of Harald Bluetooth's church, only to be torn down and slowly replaced by the present brick structure, which was completed in 1280.

Some less significant but nevertheless interesting features of the cathedral are its granite measuring column and a 500-year-old clock. The column was used to measure the height of royal visitors. The tallest, Peter the Great of Russia, checked in at 6 feet 10 inches! The clock features Saint George and the dragon. For nearly 500 years, Saint George has mounted his trusty horse each hour and attacked the dragon, which screams in pain before going off to dragon heaven to be refurbished for the next hour's performance. The cathedral is open (except when services are being conducted) April–September: Monday–Friday 0900–1645, Saturday 0900–1200, and Sunday 1230–1645. October–March: Tuesday–Friday 1000–1545, Saturday 1130–1545, and Sunday 1230–1545. Admission is DKK 15 for adults; DKK 10 for children. Guided tours offered by Roskilde-Egnens Turistbureau (*Tel:* 46 35 27 00).

If you visit Roskilde on a Wednesday or a Saturday morning, you will find the city's **market** in full operation. The market is unique in that it isn't limited to the sale of meats, poultry, fish, and produce—the usual bill of fare that you find throughout Europe. The market activities include a flea market that could rival the best American garage sale ever held. All of this activity takes place in the town square, the Staendertorvet, fronting the Town Hall.

The **Viking Ship Museum** is an interesting addition to Roskilde's many attractions (open daily May–September, 0900–1700; October–April, 1000–1600). In summer admission is DKK 54 for adults, DKK 30 for children; in winter DKK 45 for adults, DKK 28 for children. Family tickets are DKK 138 in summer and DKK 98 in winter. Proceed downhill from the cathedral. Expansions since 1997 to the museum island include the Boat Yard, Visitor's and Archaeological Workshops, plus sailing trips from June to August are offered in Viking-ship replicas for all Viking wanna-bes.

Viking ships, circa A.D. 1000 to 1050, have been restored piece by piece in this most modern of maritime museums, on the banks of the Roskilde fjord. For centuries legend had it that a barrier at the fjord's narrowest point actually had a Viking vessel beneath it. The legend was only partially correct in that a cofferdam operation in 1962 revealed that not one but five vessels had been sunk there to protect Roskilde's harbor from enemy fleets.

Just 6 miles west of Roskilde is the **Prehistoric Village–Historical–Archaeological–Experimental Centre** at Lejre, representing one of the most profound studies of prehistoric housing. Ask the tourist office about bus connections from the small station in Lejre to the center.

And if you visit during late June, be sure to check out the **Roskilde Festival,** the greatest rock-and-jazz fest in northern Europe. Visit www.roskilde-festival.dk to keep up with the latest news and ticket information. The 2002 festival dates are June 27–30. *Internet:* www.roskilde-festival.dk.

All ages will enjoy "one of the most beautiful houses in Scandinavia," **Ledreborg Palace,** an impressive example from the Rococo period. Tours of the palace are DKK 50 for adults and DKK 25 for children. *Tel:* 46 48 00 38 or *Fax:* 46 48 04 80 or visit www.ledreborgslot.dk for more details. Admire exquisite landscape, architecture, paintings, and furnishings from more than 250 years ago; see the home's servant quarters, and even visit the dungeon. Don't forget your children (in the dungeon area, that is), as they will not want to miss the treasure hunt in and around the park or trying to find their way through one of Europe's most amazing mazes. Summers provide concerts on the green.

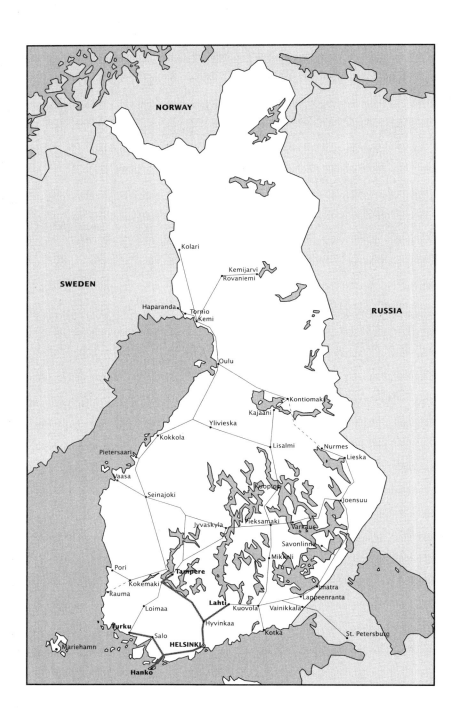

Finland

Finland is well known for its unique natural beauty, including 188,000 lakes, 179,000 islands, and Europe's biggest archipelago. Known as the "Land of the Midnight Sun" in summer, it is an artistic array of color in autumn, dazzling white in winter, and awash in green beauty in spring. Finland definitely is a country for all seasons.

Finnish and Swedish are the two languages spoken most frequently. English is a second language for many Finns, particularly for those involved in tourism and transportation, which is common in most European countries.

Since they share a common border, Finland has long been associated with Russia in one way or another. During the Napoleonic Wars, Russia invaded Finland, and it became a Russian grand duchy in 1809. Finnish nationalism grew, however, and the Finns proclaimed their independence in 1917. The Finns were again defeated by Soviet troops in the beginning of World War II. In the late 1980s, the Soviet's political demise fostered development of closer relations with Western Europe, and in 1995, Finland joined the European Union.

Finland is still considered a gateway between East and West. If you've always wanted to visit Russia now's your chance. There are daily rail connections from Helsinki to Vyborg, St. Petersburg, and Moscow.

For tourist information, contact the Finnish Tourist Board Offices in North America:

New York: P.O. Box 4649, Grand Central Station, New York, NY 10163-4649. *Tel:* (212) 885–9700; *Fax:* (212) 885–9710; *E-mail:* info@ goscanavia.com; Internet: **www.goscandinavia.com** or **www.mek.fi**

Ontario: P.O. Box 246, Station Q, Ontario, CAN M4T 2MI. *Tel:* 800–FININFO; *Fax:* (416) 964–1524

Banking
- **Currency:** Euro-€
- **Exchange rate at press time:** €1.10 = U.S. $1.00
- **Hours:** 0900–1600 Monday. Hours may vary regionally. Foreign currency and traveler's checks can also be exchanged in the following currency exchange offices: Katajanokka Harbor, Helsinki, open daily 0900–1899 and during the arrival and departure of ships, and the Helsinki-Vantaa Airport, open daily 0630–2300.

Communications
- **Country Code:** 358
- For telephone calls within Finland, dial a zero (0) preceding area code.
- Direct dial: AT&T Direct: 98100–100–10

Rail Travel in Finland
The Finnish Railways (VR Ltd.; *Internet:* www.vr.fi) operate Finland's mass transportation system. High-speed Pendolino S 220 trains and InterCity and express trains provide long-distance services, and local and commuter trains provide connections for shorter routes. The variety of **Eurail passes** is accepted on the national rail network of Finland, and the group/student rate applies on the crossing by Finnjet from Helsinki to Rostock (Germany) and is available when reservations are made 7 days before departure in Budget or Tourist IS class. Free transport is also offered on buses operating as train substitutes during certain hours. The national rail pass, **Finnrail Pass**, and the regional **Scanrailpass** are also accepted.

Finnrail Pass

Valid for any 3, 5 or 10 days of rail travel within one month.

	ADULT		CHILD	
	1ˢᵗ Class	2ᴺᴰ Class	1ˢᵗ Class	2ᴺᴰ Class
3 days	$162	$108	$81	$54
5 days	$216	$144	$108	$72
10 days	$291	$194	$145.50	$97

Scanrail Pass
Unlimited train travel in Denmark, Finland, Norway, and Sweden for a specified number of days. Also includes 20–50 percent discounts on certain ferries and bus connections. The passes range from 5 days of travel within a 2-month period ($290 Adult First Class) up to 21 consecutive days of travel ($448 Adult First Class); special Senior (age 60 and over), Youth (age 12–25), and Child (age 4–11) rates.

See Appendix for a more detailed list of railpass types and prices.

Base City:

Helsinki

Internet: www.hel.fi
City Dialing Code: 9

Arriving by Air

Vantaa Airport: *Tel:* 9 82771 or 9 61511; *Internet:* www.ilmailulaitos.com
Location: 20 kilometers north of Helsinki, 25 kilometers northeast of Espoo.

Airport–City Links: By bus: Finnair buses to Helsinki city center depart from Platform 1A outside the international terminal every 20 minutes 0545–0110; journey takes 35 minutes. Fare: €5.04. Local bus service: Operated by Sirolan Liikenne Oy, take bus No. 615 or 617 from Platform 1B between the airport and the station square two to four times an hour; trip takes 40 minutes.

By taxi: Airport to the Central Railway Station takes 25–40 minutes. Fare about €25.22. Airport Taxi is a service requiring a minimum of three passengers to share the ride. Fare: €10.09 per person.

Passengers should check in at the airport a minimum of 45 minutes before departure time for overseas flights. Contact Finnair several hours before flight time to check weather conditions at the airport. Duty-free shops at the airport are loaded with gifts of Finnish origins.

Arriving by Train

Helsinki is served by a single train terminal, the **Central Helsinki Railway Station,** which is considered one of the most famous works of Finnish-American architect Elier Saarinen. The terminal lies right in the heart of Helsinki and is close to everything. The train platforms have a total of nineteen covered tracks.

- **Baggage storage** is available on the far right of the main hall entering from the trains. Baggage lockers are available in various sizes at a standard charge. There is also a Left Luggage office on the left-hand side arriving from the trains. Pictograms will lead you to it.
- **Money exchange** is located in the main hall. There are two Forex

money exchange desks open daily 0700–2100. Banks are open 0915–1615 Monday through Friday.

- **Hotel reservations** may be made at the booking center on the right-hand side as you exit the trains. Pictograms will lead you. *Tel:* (0)9 2288 1400; *Fax:* (0) 9 2288 1499; *Internet:* www.helsinkiexpert.fi; *E-mail:* hotel@helsinkiexpert.fi.
  Hours: September 1–May 31: Monday–Friday 0900–1700; June 1–August 30: Monday–Saturday 0900–1900 and Sunday 1000–1800.
- **Train information** is on the right-hand side of the station's main hall. *Tel:* 0307 20 900; *Internet:* www.vr.fi; *E-mail:* info@vr.fi.
- **Seat reservations** can be made at ticket counters 1 to 10 in the ticket office.
  Hours: 0800–2130 Monday–Friday; 0930–2130 Saturday–Sunday.
- **Railpass validation** can be made at counters 14 to 17 at the VR International Tickets section.

There are many cafeterias and restaurants in the station. All information is in three languages—Finnish, Swedish, and English. Helsinki's Central Station connects with an underground shopping area—a great place to pick up a loaf of crusty bread, tasty cheese, and a beer when returning late from a day excursion.

Arriving by Ship

The Silja Line ferries from Stockholm arrive at Helsinki's Eteläsatama dock. Silja Finnjet and Viking Line ferries dock at Katajanokka Pier. Each ferry company maintains spacious passenger facilities complete with food services, lounges, currency exchanges, and connections to public transportation. Shipping activities in the harbor present many photographic opportunities. If you are continuing your Eurail journey back aboard the Silja Line, a money-exchange service is offered aboard by the ship's purser. The rates are governed by the Swedish banks but have basically the same exchange rates as the onshore facilities in Helsinki.

- **Silja Line,** Mannerheimintie 2, Helsinki, FIN 00100. *Tel:* 9 180 41; *Fax:* 9 1804 279; *Internet:* www.silja.fi
- **Viking Line,** P.O. Box 35, Mariehamm, FIN 22101. *Tel:* 18 26001; *Fax:* 18 15811; *Internet:* www.vikingline.fi

Tourist Information/Hotel Reservations

- *Helsinki City Tourist Information Office:* Pohjoisesplanadi 19, 00100 Helsinki; *Tel:* 9 16 93 757; *Fax:* 9 16 93 839; *Internet:* www.hel.fi; *E-mail:* tourist.info@hel.fi
  Hours: Summer, 0900–1900 Monday– Friday and 0900–1500 Saturday and Sunday; October–April, 0900– 1700 Monday–Friday, and 0900–1500 Saturday; closed Sunday.

Located in the market square area of the harbor. To reach this office, board tram No. 3T immediately in front of the train station. The fare for adults is €1.34; for children, €0.84. In about 10 minutes, the tram will pass the Silja Line Terminal for Stockholm ferries. Disembark at the next stop, which is the market square on the harbor. Look for the green i sign.

Getting Around in Helsinki

The Helsinki Card is a veritable key to the city. This card not only grants you free travel on buses, trams, trains, and the Metro in the metropolitan area but also provides free entry to about fifty museums and other places of interest in and around Helsinki and includes a free guided sight-seeing tour by bus. Showing the card in department stores brings you a free gift; it will spoil you in many of the city's restaurants, theaters, the opera, and concerts. A ninety-six-page brochure describing the scores of opportunities the Helsinki Card provides may be obtained from the Helsinki City Tourist Office or in the Hotel Booking Centre at the railway station, as well as at some travel agencies, hotels, and department stores. The cards are issued for periods of 1 day for €24, 2 days for €31, and 3 days for €36. Kids ages 7 to 16 pay €10, 11, and 13, respectively. It's a value you can't refuse.

Sights/Attractions/Tours

During the summer, Helsinki operates an unusual form of sightseeing—a tram (streetcar) named "3T." It circles the city and takes in most of its important sightseeing points. Board the tram and pay your fare to the driver. Pick up a pamphlet containing a map and descriptions of the sights you'll see on your tour from the city tourist information office. The round trip takes about 60 minutes. Fare: €1.34 (€1 when purchased in advance); kids age 7–16, €0.84.

Another way to become acquainted with the city is to take a guided bus tour. City tours depart from the Station Square June–August at 1100 and 1300 daily. The fare is €15.13 (70 percent discount for Helsinki Card Holders), the duration is 1½ hours. The same tours are conducted on a more limited schedule throughout the year. Check with the Helsinki tourist information office for details.

For a more intimate way to get to know Helsinki, ask the tourist office for the brochure See Helsinki on Foot. Tour No. 5—Market Square–Kaivopuisto–Eira—interested us. Just follow the route on the map in the brochure. The sights are numbered and explained. If you begin at Market Square, one of the first sights will be the **Havis Amanda** (a beautiful mermaid) fountain by the sculptor Ville Vallgren, created in 1908. Next you'll see the first public monument in Helsinki—the **Czarina's Stone,** designed by C. L. Engel to commemorate the Czarina Alexandra's visit. About midway through your tour, you may want to stop at the **Ursula Seaside Café** (No. 33 on the map).

Other tours originate at the Silja Line or Viking Line terminals in the harbor area. These tours run 2 hours, and some schedules include lunch. Again, the tourist information office has the details.

Highlights of Helsinki

Helsinki is a city born of the sea, and it is from the sea that it draws its soul and nature. It is the beautiful daughter of the Baltic—a sparkling jewel with the blue sea as its setting. Helsinki is a modern city. Here the visitor does not come face to face with the past as he or she does in many other long-standing European capitals. Great fires destroyed the original Helsinki many times, but it was always rebuilt. The only original remains of the trade-and-seafaring town that Swedish king Gustav Vasa founded in 1550 at the mouth of the Vantaa River are the foundations of a church.

Helsinki did not become Finland's capital until 1812. It is very cosmopolitan, the heart of cultural and artistic experiences for the Finns. The city's colorful market square on the harbor is characterized by the glittering sea and an abundance of flowers and fruit, white seagulls, and busy salespeople. Helsinki has an ambience that is all its own, supported by a friendly population and the physical comforts to enable you to fully enjoy its many features.

Helsinki's market square, besides presenting flowers, fish, vegetables, fruits, and souvenirs, can also provide visitors with coffee and delicious sugared buns at the square's tent cafe. Market hours: 0700–1400 Monday–Saturday. From mid-May through August, the evening market hours are 1530–2000 Monday–Friday. Most shops in Helsinki are open 0900–1800 (or 2000) weekdays and 0900–1400 Saturday.

Surrounded as the city is by the sea, there is a lot of island hopping you can do while visiting Helsinki. A ride on a ferryboat will take you to **Korkeasaari Island,** Helsinki's zoo; by ferry you can also reach **Suomenlinna,** a fortress island started by the Swedes, captured by the Russians, and shelled by the British before being given to Finland, which used it as part of its sea defenses until 1973. Should you tire of all this activity, you can plan to relax in one of Helsinki's excellent saunas.

Day Excursions

When you have finally broken the fine Finnish spell Helsinki casts over its visitors, you will want to venture forth into the Finnish countryside. We have selected four such adventures for your pleasure. They are **Hanko, Lahti, Tampere,** and **Turku.** Hanko, Finland's southernmost city, is a very popular summer resort with miles of wide beaches, good fishing, sailing, and all types of amusements. Lahti is about 65 miles north of Helsinki and provides an opportunity to ride trains between Helsinki and St. Petersburg. Also north of Helsinki lies Tampere, Finland's third-largest city. Both industrial and recreational, Tampere has much to offer visitors year-round. Turku, Finland's gateway to the west, was its former capital and an important cultural center before Helsinki was founded. Wherever you go, the friendly Finns will make you feel right at home. Enjoy Finland as the Finns do.

Ferry Connections Helsinki—Stockholm

See Appendix, Ferry Crossings section, for detailed information.

Silja Line ferries depart Helsinki Olympiaterminaali (Olympia Terminal), Eteläsatama port, at 1700 daily and arrive Stockholm Värtahamnen port at 0930 next day.

Viking Line ferries depart Helsinki Katajanokka dock at 1730 daily. Arrive Stockholm Stadsgården dock 0930 next day*.

Train & Ferry Connections Helsinki—Stockholm via Turku

DEPART HELSINKI	TRAIN NUMBER	ARRIVE TURKU HARBOR
0550	121	0823
1804	143	2032

Arrives Turku Satama (harbor train station)

Silja Line ferry MS *Silja Festival* departs Turku Harbor daily at 0910, arrives Stockholm Värtahamnen port 1915; and MS *Silja Europa* departs at 2115 for arrival at 0700 next day*. During September 3, 2001–mid-May 2002, the *Silja Europa* departs Turku daily at 1830 for arrival Kapellskar 0630 the next day*.

Viking Line ferries depart Turku Linnansatama dock daily at 0845, arrive Stockholm Stadsgården dock at 1855; and depart at 2100 for arrival at 0630 next day*. Bus connections between Stadsgården port and Cityterminalen (bus terminal) near Stockholm Central Station in connection with arrival/departure of ships.

*Confirm sailing dates and make advance reservations by telephone, fax, or Internet.

Day Excursion to

Hanko (Hangö)
Southernmost City

Depart from Helsinki Station
Distance by Train: 85 miles (137 km)
Average Train Time: 1 hour, 54 minutes
City Dialing Code: 19
Tourist Information Office: 5 Raatihuoneentori, P.O. Box 14, 10901 Hanko
Tel: 2203 411; *Fax:* 2203 261
Internet: www.hanko.fi
E-mail: tourist.office@hanko.fi
Hours: April–September: 0900–1700 Monday–Friday; October–March: 0800–1600

Monday–Friday; in June and July, also Saturday 1000–1400.

Notes: To get to the Hanko tourist office, depart the station and proceed along the overpass crossing the railroad, which will be on your left as you arrive. Walk over the bridge and continue past the market square on your right. Turn left on Bulevardi Street. The tourist office is in the town hall, on the corner of Bulevardi and Vuorikatu Streets.

Hanko (Hangö) is Finland's southernmost town. It is best known as a summer resort, but as the climate in this part of Finland often is very mild, you can visit Hanko in any season. In September, for example, the seawater is still warm enough for swimming. If you do not want to swim, you can lie on the beach, take a walk in the surrounding area, go for a bicycle tour, hire a horse, or just relax. Hanko in autumn is an unusually peaceful place. No matter when you go there, you will find clean water, lots of fresh air, and lots of things to do.

The peninsula where Hanko lies, known long ago among seafarers, was used for centuries as a harbor where sailing vessels could seek refuge from storms or winter ice packs. With time on their hands, many navigators, merchants, and soldiers kept themselves busy by carving their names or family coats of arms in the rocks along the shoreline of the harbor. More than 600 of these carvings have been found. Due to these inscriptions, the area gained the title "Guest Book of the Archipelago." You can inspect this handiwork during the sight-seeing cruises available in the harbor area.

Hanko did not begin as a town until the 1870s. With the introduction of iron ships, winter navigation became possible, and Hanko's peninsula was found to be well suited as a year-round harbor. Both a railway and a harbor were constructed, and Hanko was well on its way to becoming an important part of the Finnish economy.

By the end of the nineteenth century, Hanko was a fashionable summer resort, especially among the Russians coming from the St. Petersburg area. The Russian influence is visible in the architecture of many wooden villas in Hanko, most of which are in the **Spa Park.** The peninsula on which Hanko lies was ceded to the Soviet Union in 1940 but was regained in 1941.

Hanko is inseparably linked to the sea. The sunny south of Finland has about ninety islands just within its town limits! The town has four small boat harbors, including the largest harbor for visiting boats in all of Finland, two commercial harbors, and four industrial harbors. None of this activity is detrimental to tourism; in fact, it attracts it. More than 200,000 tourists visit Hanko annually. They come not only for the long sandy beaches and aquatic sports but for the various events that take place every year.

The day excursion to Hanko requires a change of trains at **Karjaa,** which you reach in a little more than an hour from Helsinki. In Karjaa, you will transfer to a local train that makes an interesting trip through southern Finland's woods and quaint little rail stations before reaching Hanko. The

Helsinki—Hanko (Hangö)

Depart Helsinki	Train Number	Arrive Hanko	Notes
0550	121/352	0825	
0904	IC 125/354	1055	R
1204	IC 131/356	1355	

Depart Hanko	Train Number	Arrive Helsinki	Notes
1410	357/138	1558	R
1615	359/IC 142	1802	R
1810	361/IC 146	2002	R

Daily, including holidays
R Reservations required, supplement required
Change trains in Karjaa
Distance: 85 miles (137 km)

Hanko station is the last stop on the line, so there's no chance of missing it.

Between 1880 and 1930, thousands of emigrants set off from Hanko for the United States, Canada, and Australia. In 1967, a statue commemorating this period was erected near the beach, a short distance from the tourist office. Depicting wild birds in free flight, this **"emigration monument"** is well worth the visit. Also worthwhile is the **Fortress Museum** (*Tel:* 2203 223) in the Eastern Harbor and the **Municipal Art Gallery** (*Tel:* 2203 317), which features exhibitions from local, Finnish, and foreign artists.

To experience Hanko's spa history, visit the famous **Summer Restaurant Casino,** one of the largest summer restaurants in Finland. To get there, head down Bulevardi toward the sea. Turn left onto Appelgrenintie. As you enter the Spa Park, you will see the beaches on your right. The villas in the park once housed Russian nobles and their families as guests.

Hanko has several other interesting restaurants, some of which are open year-round in the Eastern Harbor area. You can find seafood, Italian-style entrees, or homemade Finnish fare.

Other tours of Hanko and its surroundings can be arranged through the City Tourist Office. Brochures, maps, and special information leaflets are available, and guides can be hired. Sea cruises operate every day from mid-June to the end of August. You can visit the highest lighthouse in the Nordic countries by a tour to **Bengtskär** (6–7 hours; *Tel:* 02 466 7227 or 050 353 6933) or take a shorter trip to **Pike's Gut** (Hauensuoli), the "Guest Book of the Archipelago." This is a narrow strait between two islands, Tullisari and Kobben. The sea tours start at the Eastern Harbor. Tickets are sold onboard. Fishing trips may also be arranged, but before angling off, check with the tourist office and obtain a general fishing permit from the town's post office. Hanko is packed with exciting as well as relaxing things to do.

Day Excursion to

Lahti

Ski, Skate, Sail, or Cycle

Depart from Helsinki Station
Distance by Train: 81 miles (130 km)
Average Train Time: 1 hour, 30 minutes
City Dialing Code: 3
Tourist Information Office: Aleksanterinkatu 13, PL/Box 175, SF–15111 Lahti
Tel: (3) 877 677; *Fax:* (3) 877 6700
Internet: www.lahtitravel.fi
E-mail: info@lahtitravel.fi
Hours: June–August: Monday–Friday 0800–1700 and Saturday 1000–1500. September–May: Monday–Friday 0900–1700; Saturday 1000–1400.
Notes: When you arrive in Lahti from Helsinki, exit on the left side of the train. Use the underground exit and walk toward track No. 4 to the station. Exit the terminal and proceed along Rautatienkatu Street to Aleksanterinkatu Street, where you turn left. Walk straight on. Tourist office is located on the left-hand side of the street. Tourist information is available in the rail station, as well as in the Sports Centre and the Passenger Harbour, throughout the summer.

Lahti is the seventh largest city in Finland, with nearly 100,000 inhabitants. It is particularly noted for its timber and wooden furniture, brewers' products, and clothing and is equally famous as a winter sports center. Sporting events have always played a prominent role in Lahti's lifestyle. The **Salpausselkä Ski Games,** as well as the **Finlandia** and other skiing events, have made Lahti world famous.

Perhaps the most spectacular sight in Lahti is its 116-meter ski jump, located in the **Lahti Sports Centre.** The jump is about a 15-minute walk from the tourist information office and merits everyone's inspection. An observation platform on top of the jump can be reached by elevator and is accessible to visitors daily during summer months and on weekends during low season. In addition to the 116-meter ski jump, there are smaller ski jumps and practice areas nearby. The ski-jump area actually is a year-round attraction for tourists. In addition to the observation platform, there is an open-air, heated swimming pool at the foot of the ski-jump complex.

The Sports Centre is not the sole attraction in Lahti. In the 1920s and 1930s the city had the most powerful broadcasting station in Finland. The station now stands as a Radio and TV Museum. The museum contains more than a thousand items of great interest in the field of radio technology.

In Lahti, general fitness is a feature of everyday life. There are illuminated trails for walking, jogging, and skiing—about 40 kilometers of them—as well as nonilluminated trails. Summer weekly events include

Helsinki—Lahti

DEPART HELSINKI	TRAIN NUMBER	ARRIVE LAHTI	NOTES
0734	R 71	0904	
0914	NR	1052	
1026	R 3	1154	
1106	R 73	1232	
1224	R 21	1352	Mon–Fri, Sun

DEPART LAHTI	TRAIN NUMBER	ARRIVE HELSINKI	NOTES
1500	8	1630	
1634	24	1806	except Sat
1733	IC 10	1858	
1830	78	1956	
2100	14	2224	

Daily, unless otherwise noted
Distance: 81 miles (130 km)

outdoor theater, concerts, a lively marketplace, and hiking.

The city is unique in that it is one of the few metropolitan areas where you can live in a one-family house in the center of the city on the shore of a lake. (We suggest that the city planners of America go to Lahti to pick up a few pointers.) Much of Lahti's housing is spread over a wide area, along the city's green hillsides and lakeshores. Many visitors are surprised to find Lahti so sophisticated and versatile. The infrastructure of quality department stores, good hotels, and good restaurants coupled with civic convention centers capable of handling large numbers of people are the elements of Lahti's success. Lahti is modern yet traditional.

The old Vesijarvi Harbor has turned into a second living room for Lahti citizens and visitors with its musical and cultural events. There you can find the new **Sibelius Hall Congress and Concert Centre,** the largest wooden building constucted in Finland. This is where the world-famous Lahti Symphony Orchestra may be heard.

Shopping for excellent Finnish glassware can be a full-time occupation. Numerous Lahti department stores, as well as specialty shops, feature fine Finnish glassware and other high-quality items. The city is well known for its ready-to-wear garments for both men and women. The Finnish furniture industry is centered here, and Lahti bread and beer are known all over Finland for their quality.

In summer, Lahti's cultural life includes performances in the **Kariranta open-air theater** and the open-air concerts at the **Mukkula Tourist Centre.** Lahti provides an interesting as well as relaxing day-excursion site; it's a year-round attraction you shouldn't miss.

Sights to see while in town include the **Historical Museum**, the **Museum of Military Medicine, the Ski Museum,** and the **Museum of Art.** The Lahti Tourist Office conducts a 2-hour city tour every Wednesday starting at 1800 from June 1 through August 2.

Lahti has been described as Finland's most American city. Founded in 1905, Lahti is, historically speaking, a young city, but it has grown more rapidly than towns of similar age or older. One reason for its vigorous development is its geographic position in the center of southern Finland, at the junction of major traffic routes. Another, we might add, is its friendly, courteous people.

Day Excursion to

Tampere
City of Theaters

Depart from Helsinki Station
Distance by Train: 116 miles (187 km)
Average Train Time: 1 hour, 55 minutes
City Dialing Code: 3
Tourist Information Office: Verkatehtaankatu 2, Box 487, FI-33101 Tampere
Tel: 3146 6800; **Fax:** 3146 6463
Internet: www.tampere.fi
E-mail: touristbureau@tampere.fi
Hours: June–August: Monday–Friday 0830–2000 and Saturday–Sunday 1000–1700. September–May: Monday–Friday 0830–1700.
Notes: To get there, walk from the rail station down Hämeenkatu Street, which lies directly in front of the station. After four blocks, just before the river, turn left to Hatanpaan Valtatie. The city tourist information office, housed in a redbrick building beside a small park, will then be in front of you.

Known as "the cradle of Finnish industry," Tampere is the youngest of the "triangle towns" of Finland, the others being Helsinki and Turku. The reference to a triangle comes from the fact that all three cities are approximately 93 miles (150 kilometers) apart from each other. The town of Tampere was granted its charter in 1779 by Gustavus III, who was king of both Sweden and Finland at that time. From a modest start, Tampere developed into an industrial and resort center early in the nineteenth century. Today, with its 195,000 inhabitants, it is the third largest city in Finland.

Tampere is a city of lakes and parks. Its two major lakes are connected by rapids flowing over three waterfalls. Tampere is considered to be a "small" city. The city center is located on a narrow isthmus that is divided by the rapids. The "smallness" actually means that all shops, stores, restaurants, hotels, and other sights are within easy reach of each other, which makes Tampere an easy city to explore on foot.

Many tours are offered through the tourist office, such as the **Rapids Walk,** through the heart of the city, and the **Pispala Walk,** to the top of the ridge for a spectacular view, then to the bohemian historical district. Learn about Finland's Grand Duchy past during the **In the Footsteps of the Tsar** tour, or take the **Art Tour,** the **Guided Shopping Tour,** or the **Tour of Churches.** Visit the Web site of the tourist board for more listings. Many lake cruises are offered as well.

Among the noteworthy places to see and visit in Tampere is the **Sarkanniemi Adventure Park,** which contains an amusement park and a children's zoo, both of which are open daily in summer. An aquarium, a dolphinarium, a planetarium, an observation tower, and the **Sara Hilden Modern Art Museum** are also located in the complex. These attractions are open daily throughout the year.

In the Sarkanniemi aquarium, you will find some 2,000 fish of more than 200 species from all over the world. See Eevertti, the newest addition to the dolphinarium. In the completely renovated multimedia planetarium, a veritable sea of 6,000 twinkling bodies will open up before you. Here you will see both past and future movements in space projected on the planetarium's dome ceiling in a 30-minute space adventure. The new Orion space adventure has opened also.

The Sarkanniemi amusement park area also contains roller coaster rides, big and small bumper cars, and many other attractions. The ultimate experience is the Rapids Ride, a 490-meter-long track excavated out of the rock. For more thrills and chills, try the new Tornado roller coaster. The little ones in the family will love getting to know all of the fluffy animals in the children's zoo.

Art lovers will enjoy the Sara Hilden Modern Art Museum, with its outstanding collection of contemporary art. The paddle-wheel boat *Finlandia Queen* starts its 1½-hour cruises from the quay nearby from June through August, running several days a week. Need we say more—except that the Sarkanniemi is the place to be?

Another place of interest in Tampere is the revolving auditorium of the **Pyynikki Summer Theater.** It is world renowned and was the first of its kind when it opened in 1959. Nearby Pispala Ridge, with its old timbered houses and Pyynikki Park, are also worth visiting.

The **Museum Centre Vapriikki** is located in a former engineering plant by the Tammerkoski Rapids. Site of the 1999 preliminary European Union (EU) summit meeting, the collections of five formerly separate museums form the basic exhibition in addition to several international exhibitions.

Tallipiha (Stable Yards) is a family attraction located right in the heart of idyllic old Tampere. Formerly stables for the Nottbeck family horses,

Helsinki—Tampere

DEPART HELSINKI	TRAIN NUMBER	ARRIVE TAMPERE	NOTES
0658	IC 49	0858	1
0758	IC 91	0957	1
0858	R 163	1105	

and later service at hourly intervals.

DEPART TAMPERE	TRAIN NUMBER	ARRIVE HELSINKI	NOTES
1500	R 52	1702	
1520	NR	1742	
1555	R 172	1802	
1702	IC 94	1902	1
1729	NR	1942	
1755	R 54	2002	
1825	R 174	2030	
1956	R 176	2155	
2102	IC 58	2258	1
2118	IC 96	2325	1

Daily, unless otherwise noted
R Reservations required
1. A supplemental fare is charged on all IC trains. If the supplemental fare is paid in advance of boarding the train, a seat reservation is included at no extra charge; the supplemental fare may be paid aboard the train, but such payments do not guarantee seat availability.
Distance: 116 miles (187 km)

horsemen, and carriages, the area has been restored and houses a cafe, artisans' shops, and a chocolate shop. Horse-drawn carriage rides, among other activities, are offered. Open 1000–1800 daily in summer; shorter hours Monday–Saturday during the remainder of the year.

In Tampere, you can find a good cross section of Finnish architectural history. It ranges from charming wooden houses and Art Nouveau houses in the center of the city to the most modern designed office buildings and redbrick factory buildings at the city's rapids. Tampere's oldest building is the **Messukyla stone church,** which dates back to the fifteenth century. The city's cathedral, with its architecture and frescoes, is an outstanding example of Finland's Art Nouveau period. A newer place of worship is the **Kaleva Church,** a strikingly modern construction completed in 1966. Another fine example of modern Finnish architecture is the city's main library, the **City Library Metso.** The **Moomin-Valley Museum,** in the same building, is also worth a visit. The Moomin collection includes more than 1,000 fairy-tale sketches and illustrations by the author-artist Tove Jansson and can be enjoyed by all ages. If you are interested in architectural design, Tampere can come up with a good serving of it.

In the center of Tampere, there is the **Verkaranta Arts and Crafts Center,** with Finnish articles of high quality on exhibition. Close by, you can browse about in Tampere's colorful old market hall and the outside markets that surround it. If you happen to be in town during the summer (June–August), there's a concert at 1900 at the Old Library Park in the city center on Tuesday and Thursday. Folk dance groups perform at 1900 on Wednesday.

Day Excursion to

Turku
Finland's First Capital

Depart from Helsinki Station
Distance by Train: 124 miles (200 km)
Average Train Time: 2 hours
City Dialing Code: 2
Tourist Information Office: Turku Touring, Aurakatu 4, Turku–20100
Tel: 262–7444; *Fax:* 262–7679
Internet: www.turku.fi or www.turkutouring.fi
E-mail: tourist.info@turku.fi
Hours: April 1–September 30: 0830–1800 Monday–Friday and 0900–1600 Saturday and Sunday. Remainder of the year, Saturday and Sunday hours are 1000–1500.
Notes: Turku's tourist information office can be reached by proceeding from the rail station down Humalistonkatu (Humlegardsgatan). Turn left at Eerikinkatu and proceed for two blocks, then turn right onto Aurakatu. The tourist information office will be at your right near the city hall. If arriving at the harbor from Stockholm, check with the Silja Line desk for city information and directions to the city.

Turku is a city of contrasts, where past and present meet and blend. Finland's oldest established town, Turku celebrated its 770th anniversary in 1999. Turku was never founded; it seems it was always there. It developed naturally at the crossing of the northern trade routes at the mouth of the Aura River. The present population of approximately 170,000 is hardworking, industrious, and friendly.

With a railpass, you can choose from two forms of traveling to Turku. You can go by train on a day excursion from Helsinki, or you can take the Silja ferry from Stockholm. Whether you go by train or ferry, Turku deserves an extended examination because it has many interesting sights to offer.

Turku has three rail stations. Arriving from Helsinki, your train will make a brief stop at the Kupittaa suburban station before arriving in the city's main station. Do not detrain at Kupittaa. If you arrive in Turku on a day excursion from Helsinki and your train is scheduled to terminate at the ferry port (the third stop), rather than getting off at the main station (second stop), stay aboard the train and ride to the end of the line. There you can, time permitting, visit the nearby Great Castle of Turku. Farther along the river Aura, by the Martinsilta Bridge, is the sailing ship *Suomen Joutsen* (the "Swan of Finland"), the best-known tourist attraction in Turku. If you prefer a taxi, the fare is approximately €6; the walk from the port to the station should take about 20 to 30 minutes, and there's a lot to see en route. Bus service is also available. Bus No. 1 plies between the town's marketplace and the port. The bus fare is €1.70.

Tours depart the Aurakatu tourist office Monday through Saturday from mid-June through August. Check with either of the city's tourist information offices for full details regarding sightseeing opportunities in and around Turku.

The **Great Castle of Turku,** which is only a brief walk from the Silja Line, was begun in the 1280s. It is the largest castle in Finland and once served as a prison, but now it provides a magnificent banquet hall for state and civic functions. Also of interest to visitors is the historical museum that is housed in the Great Castle. Its collection provides insight regarding 400 years of Finnish history. Hours of operation are 1000–1800 daily from April 16 to September 15; 1000–1500 from September 16 to April 15.

An interesting museum combination is the **Aboa Vetus Museum** and the **Ars Nova Museum.** *Internet:* www.aboavetusarsnova.fi. The Aboa Vetus tells of how life in Turku developed since the fourteenth century, while Ars Nova focuses on twentieth-century art. Multimedia programs help guide you through the museums. The museums are open daily 1100–1900 May 2–September 3; Thursday–Sunday 1100–1900 the rest of the year.

The **Turku Cathedral,** another thirteenth-century structure, is open throughout the year. The cathedral is open to visitors 0900–2000 in summer and 0900–1900 daily in winter. Turku Cathedral, the major medieval ecclesiastical building in Finland, is regarded as the national shrine. You will see many interesting Neoclassical buildings surrounding the cathedral. Turku boasts two major universities—one Finnish and one Swedish—with a combined student body exceeding 20,000.

During the early hours of the day, the bustling marketplace is full of life. There you will see brisk bargaining amid a brilliant display of flowers, fruit, vegetables, and fresh fish. Fire destroyed a major part of Turku in 1827, but Cloister Hill, a neighborhood of carpenters and stonemasons, escaped damage. Today the area houses the unique **Luostarinmäki Handicrafts Museum,** with some thirty workshops that reflect the eighteenth and nineteenth centuries. It's open daily 1000–1800 April 16–September 15 and 1000–1500 Tuesday–Sunday, September 16–April 15.

The word turku means "marketplace." The city, born out of the needs of commerce, is still one of the largest commercial centers in Finland. The

Helsinki—Turku

Depart Helsinki	Train Number	Arrive Turku	Notes
0550	121	0807	continues to Turku Harbor, arriving 0819
0734	S 123	0926	R, Mon–Sat
0904	IC 125	1107	R
1106	S 129	1254	R
1204	IC 131	1407	R
1304	133	1508	Mon–Fri
1404	IC 135	1607	R
1504	IC 137	1707	R
1602	IC 139	1822	
1702	S 141	1852	1
1804	143	2007	Continues to Turku Harbor, arriving 2030
2006	S 147	2154	R, 1
2130	IC 149	2333	R

Depart Turku	Train Number	Arrive Helsinki	Notes
0545	IC 122	0754	Mon–Fri
0630	S 124	0830	R
0738	S 126	0930	R, Mon–Fri
0854	128	1102	departs from Turku harbor at 0844
1058	132	1302	R
1151	IC 134	1402	R
1408	S 138	1558	R
1458	IC 140	1702	
1558	IC 142	1802	R
1708	S 144	1858	R, 1
1751	IC 146	2002	R
1858	148	2102	
2008	S 150	2158	R, 1
2122	152	2334	departs from Turku Harbor at 2110

Daily, unless otherwise noted
R train with supplement
1. Daily except Saturday
IC Intercity train. Conveys Business Plus, Business, and 2nd class
S Pendolino S 220 train (high-speed train). Conveys Business Plus, Business, and 2nd class

Hansa Shopping Center, the country's largest, is adjacent to the city's marketplace and features more than one hundred shops and boutiques— plus a supermarket. Also there are hotels, theaters for movies and live performances, more than one hundred restaurants, and four banks.

If you, too, are a rail travel enthusiast, be certain to stop at **The Blue Train Café** in the market hall. Its decor originates from a wooden long-distance Finnish railway car built in 1952 and is typical of the Finnish passenger rail cars of the 1950s.

France

"How can you be expected to govern a country that has 246 kinds of cheese?"   —*Charles de Gaulle, 1962*

Now, France has more than 340 different kinds of cheese and more than 450 types of wines. France is western Europe's largest and probably its most diverse country. Each of France's 22 regions has its own culture and scenery, its own style of architecture and art, its own gastronomy and lifestyle, and, in many cases, its own dialect. This delightful diversity makes travel in France so intriguing.

The primary language is, of course, French, but most tourism officials and rail personnel speak at least un peu (a bit) of English. The best way to obtain the most help and cooperation in France is to first of all smile and then ask *in French, "Excusez moi, parlez-vous Anglaise?"* Even if your pronunciation makes the French language unrecognizable, the idea that you at least attempted to ask in French makes a big impression.

For more information on France, contact the French Government Tourist Offices. *Tel:* (900) 990–0040 in the United States (charge is 50 cents per minute) or (410) 286–8310; *Internet:* **www.francetourism.com** or **www.france.com.**

New York: 444 Madison Avenue, Sixteenth Floor, New York, NY, 10022–6903. *Tel:* (212) 838–7800; *Fax:* (212) 838–7855

Chicago: 676 North Michigan Avenue, Suite 336, Chicago, IL 60611. *Tel:* (312) 751–7800; *Fax:* (312) 337–6339

Los Angeles: 9454 Wilshire Boulevard, Suite 715, Beverly Hills, CA 90212–2967. *Tel:* (310) 217–6665; *Fax:* (310) 276–2835

Montreal: 1981 McGill College Avenue, Suite 490, Montreal, Quebec PQH3A 2W9, Canada. *Fax:* (514) 845–4868

Banking

- **Currency:** Euro (€)
- **Exchange rate at press time:** €1.10 = U.S. $1.00
- **Hours:** 0900–1400/1600 Monday–Friday (Some are open Saturday and closed Monday)

Communications

- **Country Code:** 33
  For telephone calls within France, dial the two-digit prefix applicable for the area as listed below, and then the 8-digit phone number:
  01– for Paris numbers
  02– for the northwest of France
  03– for the northeast of France
  04– for the southeast of France
  05– for the southwest of France
  All calls within France must use the full 10 digits. When placing calls to France from another country, use the country code 33 and drop the initial zero. (As an example, to call the Lyon Tourist Information Office from the United States, you would dial 011 + 33 + 4 + 72 + 77 + 69 + 69.)
- **Direct dial:** AT&T Direct: 0800 99 00 11

Rail Travel in France

Seemingly, France has more varieties of trains than it has cheeses. The French lead the world in rail technology, and their TGV *(train à grande vitesse)* trains hold the world's friction rail speed record at 320 mph.

French National Railroads (Société Nationale des Chemins de Fer Français, or SNCF) operates some 21,100 miles of rail lines, supplemented by SNCF buses in mountainous areas. For train information and reservations for all of France, call 08 36 35 35 39. *Internet:* www.sncf.com.

French National Railroads accepts the variety of **Eurail passes, Europass,** and their own **France Pass.** Bonuses in France include:

- Paris, France–London, England, via Eurostar thru the Chunnel— Special discounted fares for railpass holders.
- SeaFrance—50 percent discount on Calais-Dover (England) ferry crossing
- Irish Ferries: Cherbourg and Roscoff—Rosslare, Republic of Ireland: 50 percent discount on standard foot passenger fares (advance booking recommended). Sailings April–September.
- 50 percent discount on Chemins de Fer de la Corse between Ajaccio, Calvi, and Bastia.
- 25 percent discount on Chemins de Fer de la Provence between

Digne and Nice.

- 30 percent discount on ferry crossings from Marseilles/Nice/Toulon to Ajaccio/Bastia/Propriano (Corsica) operated by SNCM and Ferry France.
- 20 percent discount on Chemins de Fer du Montenvers—Mer de Glace.

The **France Pass** provides any 3 days of unlimited rail travel in France within a 1-month period. Purchase additional travel days (up to a maximum of 6 extra days) for $30 per day. The 1st Class France Pass is $210; 2nd Class, $180. Senior (age 60 and over) $199 1st Class and $159 2nd Class. Children age 4–11 travel at half the adult fare, and children under age 4 travel free. The France Saverpass for two or more people traveling together is $171 for 1st Class; $146 for 2nd Class. The France Pass also provides discounts on the Paris metro and bus pass and discounted fares on the Thalys train supplements.

Base City:

Lyon

Internet: www.lyon-france.com

Lyon bustles with industry, trade fairs, and business. Its origins, however, go back to Roman times. Founded in A.D. 43, its old town stands on a hillside of volcanic soil containing some of the richest archaeological sites in France and still contains an unspoiled area of fourteenth- and fifteenth-century houses.

Lyon also claims to be the gastronomic capital of the world, and it has some impressive credentials to back its claim. The gastronomic tradition comes from its geographic position in the center of such great culinary areas as Bourgogne, Savoy, Beaujolais, and many others. With tongue in cheek, Lyon citizens say that the whole world cannot come from Lyon—there has to be at least a little from elsewhere. With our tongue in cheek, we note that Lyon also has several American-style fast-food establishments. Touché!

Although proud of its history and devoted to preserving its antiquity, Lyon forges ahead with a continuous modernizing, building-and-expansion program that rivals even that of Paris. Part-Dieu, a complete and separate metropolis on the left bank of the Rhône, rises like a modern phoenix above the rest of Lyon, most of which was built during the eighteenth century. Lyon's contrasts are great. By virtue of these contrasts, Lyon is becoming one of the great cities of France and of Europe.

Arriving by Air

Lyon Saint Exupéry International Airport (*Internet:* lyon.aeroport.fr), 15 miles (25 kilometers) to the east of Lyon. International air service between Lyon and New York is provided by Air France and Delta Airlines. Frequent air service to Paris, Frankfurt, Brussels, and Amsterdam provides additional connections for passengers with North American destinations.

Airport–City Links: Airport bus (Satobus) service to Lyon's Perrache and Part-Dieu stations. Every 20 minutes 0600–2300 daily. From Lyon's Perrache and Part-Dieu stations to the airport, every 20 minutes 0500–2100 daily. Journey time: about 45 minutes; fare, €7.55.

Limousine service is also available direct to most of the city's hotels. Journey time: about 45 minutes.

Taxis: €30.50 (daytime) and about €46.00 (nighttime).

Arriving by Train

Most of the TGV Duplex (double-decker) trains from Paris to Lyon terminate at Part-Dieu, but a few continue on to terminate at Perrache.

The facilities provided by **Gare de Perrache** have been expanded by the ultramodern annex appended to the front of the present station building. This annex houses a bus terminal, the terminal for the city's metro system, and a bevy of offices, shops, snack bars, and restaurants. The terminal for the airport bus and local taxi services is also located in the annex.

Access to the annex is gained by escalators immediately in front of the station's main doors. Pedestrian traffic, moving from the station through the annex and into the city, uses another escalator system to exit into Lyon's **Place Carnot.** The square, with its statues, fountains, and waterfalls, is one of the city's showplaces.

Gare de Perrache, together with its annex, is a large and sprawling complex. Access to train platforms is through two underground passage-ways—Sortie Nord and Sortie Sud (north and south exits)—and escalators that descend from the ticket office and the waiting-room areas. Use of either passageway will take you to platform No. 1 and, in turn, to exits leading to the street side of the station. Fortunately, there's an abundance of pictographs throughout the station.

If you have baggage, be prepared to carry it. Baggage carts for passenger use are not available, probably due to the platform stairways. The escalators serve only the tracks reserved for express-train service.

Train-departure signs are displayed in the underground passageways at the bottom of the platform stairways. The north passageway, however, will not list a southbound departure, nor the south a northbound one, unless it is a train running through Lyon Perrache and not originating there. All train departures are displayed over the ticket windows in the main station hall.

- **Money exchange** services are available at the Thomas Cook Bureau de Change in the Perrache station. Hours: 0800–2000 daily. From the train information area, follow the pictographs and proceed by either escalator or elevator to the station's TGV departure lounge on the second level.

To reach the **bank**, Société Générale, use the escalator on the side of the station annex facing Place Carnot, the city square immediately in front of the station. When you reach ground level, walk down the steps alongside the waterfall to the fountain at the bottom. At this point, turn to the right between the fountain and the waterfall, and then proceed across the square. The bank is at No. 12 Place Carnot. When you approach the first street, you will see the bank across the intersection to your left. This is the only bank in the vicinity of Place Carnot.

- **Train information** office is within the main building of the Perrache station. Use the main entrance, turn right once you have entered the hall, and proceed through an archway to the train information office. *Hours:* 0900–1900 Monday–Saturday; 0900–1830 Sunday/holidays.

The French National Railroads produces *Le Fiches Horaires* (mini-timetables), which are free. A selection is normally kept immediately outside the train information office door and inside the office on the left-hand wall. These timetables may eliminate standing in line to make inquiries.

- **Train reservations** may be made in the train information office at any one of the operating windows. We did not find the train information staff too adept at English. Consequently, we recommend submitting your reservation requests in writing.
- **Railpass validation** is handled at any window in the train information office. Write the starting and ending dates on a piece of paper and obtain concurrence from the attendant before the entry is made on your railpass.

Lyon's ultramodern Metro (subway) system serves both Gare de Perrache and Gare Part-Dieu rail stations.

Tourist Information/Hotel Reservations

- *Lyon Tourist Information (central office):* Lyon Convention and Visitors Bureau, Place Bellecour, BP 2254, 69214 Lyon cedex 02 (two Metro stops from Gare de Perrache); *Tel:* 04 72 77 69 69; *Fax:* 04 78 42 04 32; *Reservations Desk:* 04 72 77 72 50; *Internet:* www.lyon-france.com

Hours: April 15–October 15; 0900–1900 Monday–Saturday, 1000–1800 Sunday. October16–April 14: 1000–1800 Monday–Saturday, 1000–1730 Sunday.

Hotel reservations for within the city of Lyon may be made at the tourist information office Reservations Desk.

Getting Around in Lyon

Lyon has an ultramodern Metro (subway) system. One of its main terminals is in Gare de Perrache; there's another in the rail terminal at Part-Dieu. Trains run every 3 to 10 minutes from 0500 to 2400 daily. A single-ride ticket costs €1.30; a book of 10 tickets, €10.44; 1-day tourist ticket, €3.74.

The best way to discover Lyon is with the tourist office's **"Lyon City Card."** Valid for 1, 2, or 3 days (at €13.72, 24.39, and 30.49; reduced rates for those under age 18), this card covers city transport on buses and the metro as well as entrance to museums, guided tours, and river cruises. You can even save 10 percent on shopping (excluding some promotional items) at Galeries Lafayette Part-Dieu.

LYON

Sights/Attractions/Tours

Lyon Vision operates a 1½-hour sight-seeing bus tour of Lyon April 1–October 31. The buses are equipped with headsets providing explanations of the tour sights in five languages, including English. Fare for adults, €15.25; 1 child rides free for each paying adult. Buses depart daily at 1040, 1345, 1545, and 1745 from Place Bellecour No. 25. Ask for a folder at the tourist office.

Or, join the Lyon Tourist Office's guided tour, "A Stroll Through Old Lyon," which is conducted on foot over a 2-hour period. Departures are daily throughout the tourist season at a charge of €7.62. An evening tour is also available. The tourist office also offers World Heritage Guides of five walking tours of Lyon for €5.34. Check with the tourist office for the daily schedule.

Le Vieux Lyon (Old Lyon) is a charming area to visit. For your convenience use the *funiculaires* (funicular) to gain the summit. Take bus No. 44 from the station annex and ask the driver to let you off at the St. Jean bus stop. The funicular station is located at rue St. Jean and avenue Max, immediately to the left of **place St. Jean**.

Old Lyon is said to be the most extensive Renaissance area in France. It covers about 1 mile along the right bank of the Saone River at the foot of **Fourviére Hill**. In 1998, the historic area of Lyon, the Fourviére Hill, Croix-Rousse Hill, Renaissance Quarter, and the Peninsula were recognized as UNESCO World Heritage architectural sites. While visiting the Fourviére Hill area, check out Lyon's answer to Paris's Eiffel Tower, located behind the basilica. The Lyonese claim their tower is 5 feet higher than the Parisians', and it is—above sea level, that is.

Day Excursions

Contrasts continue in the selection of day excursions from Lyon, the third largest city in France. A scant 25 miles short of Geneva, the town of **Annecy** and its crystal-clear lake wait to charm you. Annecy's old quarter, lying back from the lake, has one of Europe's finest marketplaces.

Dijon vies with Lyon for gastronomic honors. During your visit to Dijon, you will want to shop for its world-renowned product, mustard. But that's

Train Connections to Other Base Cities from Lyon Part-Dieu

DEPART	TRAIN NUMBER	ARRIVE	NOTES
		Amsterdam Centraal	
0630	TGV 6642	1407	R, 1
0756	TGV 9856	1539	R, 2
0900	TGV 6610	1707	R, 1
1200	TGV 6616	2007	R, 1
1300	TGV 6618	2107	R, 1
1640	TGV 9868	2339	R, 2
2000	TGV 6632	0710+1	R, 1, Sleeper
		Barcelona Sants	
1515	TGV 9833	2148	R, 3
2115	RE 96528	0901+1	R, 4, Sleeper
		Bern (Berne)	
0605	D 4696	1013	R, 4
0629	4449	1113	R, 4
0738	RE 96500	1213	4
0934	RE 96504	1313	4
1050	RE 96508	1513	4
1240	RE 96512	1713	4
1446	TGV 6864	1813	4
1533	TGV 6866	1913	R, 4
1720	RE 96516	2113	4
1836	RE 96520	2213	4
		Brussels (Bruxelles) Midi/Zuid	
0756	TGV 9856	1217	R
1546	TGV 9866	1959	R
1640	TGV 9868	2026	R
		Madrid	
1700	TGV 6626	0858+1	R, 1
		Milan (Milano) Centrale	
0707	EC 142	1245	R
1608	EC 138	2150	R
2150	RE 91442	0845+1	R, 5, Sleeper
		Nice Ville	
0906	TGV 5103	1324	R
1141	TGV 5149	1602	R
1531	TGV 6819	2006	R
1801	TGV 6829	2225	R
		Paris Gare de Lyon	
0630	TGV 6642	0824	R
0700	TGV 6604	0855	R
0800	TGV 6608	1001	R
0900	TGV 6610	1055	R

and then hourly service until 2100, plus 1730.

		Rome (Roma) Termini	
0707	EC 142	1830	R, 6
1836	RE 96520	0935+1	R, 5, Sleeper

Depart	Train Number	Arrive Zürich Hauptbahnhof	Notes
0605	D 4696	1126	R, 4
0629	4449	1226	R, 4
0738	RE 96500	1253	4
0934	RE 96504	1426	4
1050	RE 96508	1553	4
1240	RE 96512	1753	4
1446	TGV 6864	1953	R, 4
1533	TGV 6866	2026	R, 4
1720	RE 96516	2226	4
1836	RE 96520	2334	4

Daily, unless otherwise noted
R Reservations required
+1 Arrives next day
1. Change trains in Paris.
2. Change trains in Brussels.
3. Change trains in Perpignan.
4. Change trains in Geneva.
5. Change trains in Dijon.
6. Change trains in Milan.

not all it has to offer. The history of Burgundy breathes in Dijon, its capital, and you will want to catch its scent.

Grenoble is situated in the midst of a breathtaking panorama of mountains. A ride on its téléphérique will provide an even more remarkable view of the city and the countryside surrounding it.

Vienne, 20 miles to the south, is almost a suburb of Lyon, but it is very different. It has some of the best preserved Roman buildings and amphitheaters in all of Europe and one of the world's finest restaurants, La Pyramide.

Day Excursion to

Annecy
Alpine Lake

Depart from Lyon Part-Dieu Station
Distance by Train: 99 miles (160 km)
Average Train Time: 2 hours, 25 minutes
Tourist Information Office: Bonlieu Center, 1 rue Jean Jaurés, 74000 Annecy
Tel: 04 50 45 00 33; *Fax:* 04 50 51 87 20
Internet: www.lac-annecy.com
E-mail: ancylac@cybercable.tm.fr
Hours: April–November, 0900–1830 daily, 0900–1200 and 1500–1800 on Sunday.

If this office is closed, go to the bureau of information in the city hall, which is open until 1900 daily, except Sunday and holidays.

Notes: Reach the information office via bus No. 1 from in front of the station to place de la Liberation, where you'll find the office in the Bonlieu Center. On foot, use the underground pedestrian passageway to the left of the station as you exit. Continue to walk a block ahead to rue Vaugelas. Here, you turn left and walk four blocks to where rue Vaugelas ends at place de la Liberation (a large open area).

Annecy (pronounced "Ahn-see") still remains largely undiscovered by North Americans, although it has long been a retreat of the French themselves. A crystal-clear lake, a spectacular view of the Alps, foothills that touch the town, an old quarter where quaint canals cross arcaded lanes, an engaging market selling everything from apples to zinnias—these are Annecy.

Annecy is a health spa as well as a popular holiday center. It has innumerable hotels, casinos, and, best of all, the lake. The basin in which the lake lies is so protected against pollution that the latter is almost transparent in its purity. The Thiou River, flowing out of the lake and through the old quarter of Annecy, runs through canals and meanders around islands en route to the Rhône and the Mediterranean.

Tour-boat operators offer a wide variety of tours around the "sea" of Annecy. Rapid tours, lasting a little more than an hour, have frequent departures. The more vigorous traveler can opt to cycle around it. Either mode will provide a spectacular view of alpine meadows, rivers, waterfalls, and the bountiful natural riches surrounding the lake.

Visit the town hall, **Hôtel de Ville,** just a short walk along **quai Chappuis.** But exercise caution when crossing the street—the locals stage a "Grand Prix" on occasion.

The tourist information office has several brochures describing the city and its lake, including an illustrated booklet, *Through the Old Town.* The office also contains bulletin boards with numerous announcements of cultural events in Annecy.

From the bridge crossing the Thiou River, you will catch your first glimpse of the **Palais de l'Isle** sitting astride the river. As its name suggests, this curious palace was an island stronghold, and it remains one of the most arresting monuments of Annecy. Its oldest sections date from the twelfth century. At one time it housed Annecy's municipal offices, the high judges' private apartments, and also served as a dungeon.

Beyond the Palais de l'Isle lies the enchanting marketplace of Annecy's **Old Quarter.** A network of narrow streets filled with every type of shop imaginable is augmented on market days by hundreds of stands erected in the streets, where only pedestrians are allowed to pass.

Along with the chic boutiques and appliance shops, the marketplace vends every imaginable food product, pastry, flower, and condiment.

Lyon—Annecy

DEPART LYON PART-DIEU	TRAIN NUMBER	ARRIVE ANNECY
0646	—	0915
0806	—	1024
1246		1455

DEPART ANNECY	TRAIN NUMBER	ARRIVE LYON PART-DIEU
1549	—	1811
1708	—	1923
1918	—	2112

Daily, including holidays
Distance: 99 miles (160 km)

Lavender, picked in the Alps, and locally manufactured culinary wares are also available.

The picturesque medieval appeal of Annecy stems from both the French and Italian civilizations as a result of having changed sides several times during its 2,000-year existence. The area became a part of the French empire in 1792, although it reverted to the Italian Kingdom of Sardinia in 1815. It was not until 1860 that all of Savoy, where Annecy is situated, was again reunited with France as a reward to the French for helping Italy in its war with Austria.

Annecy slipped quietly into the twentieth century with the introduction of TGV train service directly from Paris. The distance from the Gare de Lyon station in Paris to Annecy is covered in about 3½ hours—a trip that formerly consumed at least 8 hours. Currently, there are four trains daily that depart in the morning, making the possibility of a day excursion to Annecy from Paris a reality.

Departing Paris Gare de Lyon station on a TGV at 0644, you would arrive in Annecy at 1029; boarding TGV 6984 departing Annecy at 1902, you would be back in Paris by 2231. It's a full day, but a fun-packed one, too.

Day Excursion to

Dijon
Cutting the Mustard

Depart from Lyon Gare de Perrache or Part-Dieu
Distance by Train: 122 miles (197 km)
Average Train Time: 1 hour, 30 minutes

Tourist Information Office: Place Darcy
Tel: 03 80 44 11 44; **Internet:** www.ot-dijon.fr
E-mail: infotourisme@ot-dijon.fr
Hours: May 1–November 15, 0900–2100 daily; 0900–1300 and 1400–1900 daily the remainder of the year
Notes: Exit through the main doors of the station and bear to the right onto avenue Maréchal Foch. Average walking time: 5 minutes. Use the Hotel Climat de France as a landmark. Proceed along avenue Foch for one block. As you approach place Darcy, you will find the tourist information office on the left-hand side of the street.

LYON
Dijon

Say "Dijon" to any American who likes to eat well, and the response will be "mustard." Mention Dijon to any Frenchman, and his eyes will roll and his hands will fly as he describes the gastronomic wonders of the Burgundian city's pastry shops, restaurants, cassis (black-currant liquor), and mustard—but not necessarily in that order. Dijon, the ancient capital city of Burgundy, has something for everyone. It sets a fine table, lives its history, and preserves its art.

Dijon is the gateway to France's most famous wine region, the Côte d'Or. Important historically in 1015 when Robert I, Duke of Burgundy, made it the capital of his duchy, today it produces more than 40 million bottles each year. The city's most brilliant era, however, was from the fourteenth through the eighteenth centuries, when it gained most of its art and beautiful monuments.

Dijon cannot be visited in a hurry. Actually, an entire day can easily be spent visiting its **Palace of the Dukes of Burgundy** and the **Museum of Fine Arts,** which is housed in the palace. The museum, founded in 1783, is the most important in France after the Louvre in Paris. Don't miss the huge banquet room of the palace. It is identified as the Guards Room, and the tombs of the dukes are located here. The tombs provide some descriptive background as to how the populace rated the four "Valois" Dukes of Burgundy: Philip the Bold, Jean the Fearless, Philip the Good, and Charles the Rash.

Modern art has made an entry in the palace in the form of a department housing an exhibition of Impressionist works from the Granville collection. There's also a gallery devoted completely to the works of local artists from the Burgundy area.

The city is particularly proud of its artists, among them François Pompon (1855–1933). Sculptor Pompon began his career as a Burgundy marble cutter. He attended Dijon's school of fine arts before further studies and apprenticeships in Paris. He sculpted 300-plus works, almost all depicting animals. His fresh, clear style has astonishing simplicity.

Engrossing as Dijon's works of art can be, don't forget to break for lunch—another Dijon work of art that can't be hurried. Whatever entree

DEPART LYON PART-DIEU	TRAIN NUMBER	ARRIVE DIJON	NOTES
0649	4306	0833	
0851	TGV 6852	1026	1
0929	5070	1125	
1155	TGV 5171	1335	
1350	TGV 5198	1531	1

DEPART DIJON	TRAIN NUMBER	ARRIVE LYON PART-DIEU	NOTES
1515	4232	1656	
1600	TGV 5117	1734	1
1623	TGV 6829	1755	1
1644	—	1849	
1821	—	2017	
1935	5073	2139	
2047	4206	2229	

Daily
R Reservations required
1. Snack car
Distance: 122 miles (197 km)

125

LYON
Dijon

you select, we are certain that you will want to enhance it with a dab or so of Dijon mustard. A word of caution—make that dab a small one, and determine first if it suits your palate. Dijon's favorite condiment has some varieties that exceed the fire power of any Mexican pepper.

Dijon's railway station is unique in that its main hall is circular. Train information is available in the area marked INFORMATION VOYAGEURS on the right as you enter the main hall of the station. Hours: 0830–1900 Monday–Friday; 0830–1830 Saturday. A map showing the location of the city's tourist information office in relation to the rail station is displayed prominently in the station's foyer.

The tourist office displays a room-availability list immediately outside the office entrance. This depicts the number of vacancies existing in the various hotels of Dijon and its surrounding areas. Within the tourist office, you will find hotel-reservations facilities and money-exchange services. There is a nominal fee for each call within Dijon to secure hotel reservations.

The **Saint Benigne Cathedral** probably holds the record for being destroyed and rebuilt more times than any other place of worship in France—four times since its origins back in the sixth century! The present church was built between 1281 and 1325.

Also constructed in the thirteenth century, the **Church of Notre Dame** in Dijon fared better over the centuries. Both edifices are typical Burgundian Gothic.

One of the newer attractions in Dijon includes the **University of**

Bourgogne. The Centre International d'Etudes Françaises attracts students from all over the world to study the French language and culture.

Day Excursion to

Grenoble

And the Bastille Cableway

Depart from Lyon Part-Dieu Station
Distance by Train: 80 miles (129 km)
Average Train Time: 1 hour, 30 minutes
Tourist Information Office: 14, rue de la République
Tel: 04 76 42 41 41; *Fax:* 04 76 00 18 98
E-mail: office-de-tourisme-de-grenoble@wanadoo.fr
Hours: 0900–1900 daily year-round
Notes: Located some distance from the railway station in a labyrinth of winding streets. Reach it by either of the tramways in the direction of Grand Place, Universités, or Auguste Delaune. Your stop is Hubert Dubedout/Maison du Tourisme. MAISON DU TOURISME signs are displayed at many intersections.

Grenoble will remind many North Americans of Denver, Colorado. Lodged on a wide plain, butted against the swift waters of the Isere River, and backdropped by the French Alps, it is a breathtaking scene of man and nature in concert.

Known as "the capital of the French Alps," Grenoble lies at the feet of three majestic mountain ranges at the crossroads of a number of large valleys. Its Isere River was first bridged by Roman legion engineers in 43 B.C.; Napoleon employed the concealment of the area to move his armies into the Italian campaign. Modern mountaineering was born on its towering peaks.

Grenoble unfolds the past as well as the present in its monuments and art. The **Musée de Grenoble** houses one of the finest collections of old and modern masters in France. The classics of Rubens and Watteau, along with those of Utrillo and Picasso, adorn its galleries. The **Cathedral of Grenoble** dates to the twelfth century. In the center of Grenoble, in the oldest part of the town, you will find the **Musée de l'Ancien Evêché.** Begin by exploring an area below the surface of the outside square to see the remains of the town wall and Grenoble's first baptistery, then continue on to the old bishop's palace. The early **Renaissance Palace of Justice** was built in the sixteenth century.

The **University of Grenoble** was founded in 1339—making it one of the oldest in Europe—and is considered by many academics to be one of the

Lyon—Grenoble

DEPART LYON PART-DIEU	TRAIN NUMBER	ARRIVE GRENOBLE	NOTES
0719	—	0848	
0826	—	0956	
0834*	—	1026	Mon–Fri
0920	—	1050	
1024	—	1154	
1215*	—	1418	

DEPART GRENOBLE	TRAIN NUMBER	ARRIVE LYON PART-DIEU
1315	4376	1445
1418	—	1548
1556	4338	1731
1621	—	1754
1710	—	1843
1815	—	1945
1925	—	2151**
2004	—	2133
2114	—	2244
2200	—	2339

Daily, unless otherwise noted
* Departs Lyon Perrache
** Arrives Lyon Perrache
Distance: 80 miles (129 km)

best in France. Grenoble's student population exceeds 50,000, more than 8,000 of whom are foreigners from 150 different countries. With university students near snow-covered slopes, it was inevitable that winter sports should develop. The 1968 Winter Olympics were hosted by Grenoble, and many other sports gatherings, including the Davis Cup finals, have taken place in the city's magnificent Sports' Hall.

To ride the **Téléphérique de la Bastille,** wend your way to the banks of the Isere River and then to the Jardin de Ville (city garden). From practically any point on the riverfront, you can see the "bubbles" of the cableway flying up and down the hillside in groups of three. A photographic hint: Ride the rear "bubble" up and the front one down for better views of Grenoble and its environs.

The terminal at the top of **Guy Pape Park** provides a spectacular view of the city and its surrounding countryside. Dominating the heights is the **Bastille,** a nineteenth-century fortress housing a military museum and a restaurant featuring traditional, regional cuisine. On a suitable day, you may opt to descend on foot through Guy Pape Park to the **Jardin des Dauphins** (Dauphins' garden) on the banks of the Isere. Contact the tourist office for bicycle rental information, then search for and explore the gardens, the fountains, or the famous "grey gold" (concrete) buildings of Grenoble.

TGV service makes a Grenoble day excursion from Paris practical. Departing Paris Gare de Lyon at 0640 on TGV 6901 places you in Grenoble at 0935. There are six TGVs departing from Paris Gare de Lyon Monday–Friday, four TGVs on Saturday, and five on Sunday. The last daily TGV returning to Paris departs Grenoble at 1916 and arrives at Gare de Lyon in Paris at 2211. On Sunday, the latest TGV departs Grenoble at 2040 for arrival at 2339 in Paris.

Day Excursion to

Vienne
Of Roman Origin

Depart from Lyon Gare de Perrache or Part-Dieu
Distance by Train: 20 miles (32 km)
Average Train Time: 24 minutes
Tourist Information Office: No. 3 Cours Brillier, 38200 Vienne
Tel: 04 74 53 80 30; *Fax:* 04 74 53 80 31
Internet: www.vienne-tourisme.fr
Hours: Mid-June–mid-September, 0900–1200 and 1330–1830 Monday–Saturday; 1000–1200 and 1330–1730 Sunday
Notes: About a 10-minute walk from the railway station. Depart from the statue in front of the rail station down Cours Brillier to the tourist pavilion on the left-hand side of the street.

Turn a corner in Vienne, and you turn a page of history. Roman in origin, this charming city lies on the Rhône River to the south of Lyon but so close (20 miles) that it could be mistaken easily for a Lyon suburb. Such is not the case. Vienne is distinctly different.

Among the remains of this once great city of the Roman Empire, and dating from the first century B.C. to the end of the third century A.D., stand a temple, an amphitheater, and a pyramid that was once the center of a Roman circus. Roman Vienne spread to both sides of the Rhône River, where ruins of a warehouse and baths have been uncovered.

A statue to the fallen during 1914 and 1940 stands in the square fronting the railway station. Take a moment to pause and reflect here. Note, too, that many of the names have family extensions in North America.

Attendants at the tourist office will assist by marking a suggested walking tour on your map. The majority of the city's sights, concentrated in the old north quarter, allow visitors to move quickly from one attraction to another.

Collections of bronze, ceramics, and jewels are on display at the **Museum of Fine Arts.** Perhaps the most impressive Roman ruin of Vienne

Lyon—Vienne

DEPART LYON PERRACHE	TRAIN NUMBER	ARRIVE VIENNE	NOTES
0755	—	0854	Mon–Sat
0835	—	0853	
0925*	—	0945	
1115*	—	1135	
1145	—	1203	Mon–Fri

DEPART VIENNE	TRAIN NUMBER	ARRIVE LYON PERRACHE	NOTES
1329	—	1349	Mon–Sat
1404	—	1423	Mon–Fri
1648	—	1707	
1819	—	1839**	
1839	—	1900 (1905 Su)	
1930	—	1956**	
2023	—	2043**	
2035	—	2054	Mon–Fri
2210 (2208 Su)	—	2229 (2234 Su)	

Daily, unless otherwise noted
* Departs Lyon Part-Dieu
** Arrives Lyon Part-Dieu
Distance: 20 miles (32 km)

is the **Temple of Augustus and Livia,** which is perfectly preserved. One almost expects toga-clad senators to step through its portals and into a local pastry shop. The temple is surrounded by more modern structures in the center of the city. No doubt the proximity of other buildings has helped shield and preserve the temple through the ages.

The great **amphitheater of Vienne** was cleverly built into the slope of the hillside on which the town now stands. In its original state, it could hold 13,000 spectators. It was covered entirely by soil in the first century A.D., but excavations between 1922 and 1938, when activities were curtailed by World War II, have brought to life some very beautiful remnants of statuary, coins, and jewels from the era.

The amphitheater, modernized with stage lighting, is now the scene of many fine theatrical presentations in Vienne for thousands of spectators throughout the summer season, including the Vienne Jazz Festival. Similar lighting of the Temple of Augustus and Livia makes an evening visit to the city a memorable one.

The **pyramid** was erected in the center of a Roman circus to guide the racing chariots, but it was never completed. For centuries it was believed to be the tomb of Pontius Pilate, who, according to a twelfth-century legend, had died in Vienne while living there in exile. Little else remains of the circus site, but it stirs your imagination.

The city's famous restaurant, **La Pyramide** (named for its location on boulevard Fernand-Point at the former Roman circus), has been endorsed by many gourmets as the world's finest. Reservations are recommended at La Pyramide, which is closed every Wednesday and Thursday at noon in season and annually from November through mid-December. Call ahead at 04 74 53 01 96 or fax them at 04 74 85 69 73. It's expensive, but you only live once!

When departing from the main part of town, you can reach Vienne's pyramid and the restaurant La Pyramide by taking the main road running to the south, cours de Verdun (RN 7), to boulevard Fernand-Point, on your right. When proceeding from the tourist information office at cours Brillier, head south on quai Riondet and turn left onto boulevard Fernand-Point.

Vienne also has its share of medieval buildings. Most of them are still being lived in and look very much as they probably did back in the fifteenth and sixteenth centuries.

Although its industrial history is not as well known, for more than 200 years Vienne was an important center for textiles, especially carded wool and a cloth called "Renaissance." The **Musée de la Draperie,** housed in the Saint Germain building, is worth a visit. Hours: April 1–September 30, 1430–1830; closed Monday and May 1. Still a center of a lively wool trade, the town manufactures chemicals and flourishes from other industries, too. The people of Vienne are justly proud of their industrial endeavors, set in the midst of a richly wooded countryside.

Base City:

Nice

Internet: www.nicetourism.com

Nice, "the gateway to southern Europe," has changed more in 50 years than it did over the past two centuries. According to Nice's Convention and Visitors' Bureau, Nice's "history advances, but its past remains."

In the days before World War I, the Riviera was a haven for rich Russian dukes and English lords seeking escape from the rigors of a more northerly winter. When such aristocracy, particularly the Russian version, began to fade from the scene, summer became the popular season, bringing with it hordes of Americans and others seeking the sun and all sorts of fun, including the nocturnal varieties.

The Riviera began to change. Towns and fishing villages that earlier visitors knew have grown together into an almost continuous resort town stretching from Saint-Raphael to the Italian border. Nice, the largest community in the area, lies about halfway between these two points and is our base city for numerous day excursions in either direction. However, because of the relatively short distances between points and excellent rail service, one could select any one of the day excursions (Cannes, Monte Carlo, or Saint-Raphaël) as a base city.

Arriving by Air

Nice Côte d'Azur Airport, 4 miles (9 km) west of the city. *Internet:* www.nice.aeroport.fr.

The airport has a convenient Rendezvous (meeting place) just beyond the arrival gates and a Bureau des Change (**money exchange**) and **information** desk farther into the international terminal, Terminal 1. Terminal 2 is for flights within France. If you are not certain of your transportation mode to your final destination, inquire at the airport's information desk or at one of the airline counters inside.

Airport–City Links: An **airport bus** and **limousine** service are available between the airport and the Nice Ville railway station. Bus fare: €3.35; departs every 20 minutes. It makes three stops between the airport and the station. Journey time is about 30 minutes. Connections can be made in the front-left section of the airport building as you exit.

Taxis are available at the exit from the airport terminals. Fare between airport and rail station: €21.34–27.44. Journey time: about 15 minutes. Taxi and intercity bus service between the airport in Nice and the resorts of Cannes and Monte Carlo are also available.

Several resort hotels offer free or reduced-rate transportation to their locations along the Riviera. Inquire at the airport information desk.

Arriving by Train

Nice Ville Station—Gare SNCF Centrale, avenue Thiers. *Tel:* 08 36 35 35 39 (in English) and then press number 2.

Nice is a major rail terminus for the Mediterranean region, with 30 daily connections from France's largest cities and 27 from other countries.

The exterior of the central station in Nice is deceptive. There is a lot more activity and more facilities than those you see. Although it is smaller than most major train terminals in Europe, it seems to function equally well, with the exception of long ticket lines. Here again, a railpass will prove to be an invaluable convenience.

Manual lockers are available (*Tel:* 04 92 14 82 68).

If your luggage is lost or stolen, if you missed your train, or if you need help with a disabled or elderly passenger, don't panic. The railway station provides a helpful service—the **SOS Voyageurs SNCF** (Travelers' SOS Service). *Tel:* 04 93 16 02 61 Monday–Friday, 0900–1200 and 1500–1800, for assistance. (Closed Saturday and Sunday.)

- **Money-exchange office** is outside the main station and on the right as you exit from the trains (Tel: 04 93 82 13 00). Hours: June–September, 0700–2130 daily; remainder of the year, 0800–2000 daily.

- **Train-information, reservations,** and **railpass validation** office is inside the main station on the extreme left side when exiting from the trains. The office is marked reservation information—renseignements. Hours: 0830–1830 Monday–Saturday; 0830–1115 and 1400–1730 Sunday/holidays.

Remember, when having your pass validated, write out the starting and ending dates on a piece of paper and get the railroad clerk to agree to the correctness of the dates before the validation information is entered onto your railpass.

Tourist Information/Hotel Reservations

- The *Office du Tourisme (Tourist Bureau)* has three offices in the city of Nice, plus one at the international terminal at the airport (*Tel:* 04 93 21 44 11; *E-mail:* info@nicetourism.com). The one in the railway station can probably best serve all of your needs. It is located outside the station and beyond the train administration office on the left.

Hours: June–September 0800–2000 daily; October–May 0800–1900 Monday–Saturday. If you need to call ahead to the tourist office in the rail station, the number is 04 93 87 07 07 (*Fax:* 04 93 16 85 16); or call or fax the tourist office on the Promenade des Anglais (*Tel:* 04 92 14 48 00; *Fax:* 04 92 14 48 03; *E-mail:* info@nicetourism.com).

- **Hotel reservations** may be booked at any of the tourist offices or via the *Web site:* www.nicetourism.com. Room vacancies in Nice and throughout the Riviera are extremely hard to come by during June, July, and August, as well as during the winter holiday period. If possible, reserve your accommodations well in advance by writing ahead.

Hotel rates in Nice and the rest of the Riviera vary according to the season of the year, so be specific when requesting reservations. The most expensive time of the year is between late March and the end of October. If you are looking for bargain rates, late October through January is when the rates are lowest.

Getting Around in Nice

The best way to get around in Nice is on foot, by bicycle/scooter, or by bus.

- Agence Sunbus, 10 avenue Felix Faure (*Tel:* 04 93 13 53 13 [0715–1900 Monday–Friday; 0715–1800 Saturday])
- Eden Tour Minibus, 21 Bd. Raimbaldi (*Tel:* 04 93 92 55 85; *Fax:* 04 93 92 56 20)
- Glaude Transport Service (GTS) (*Tel:* 04 92 29 50 19; *Fax:* 04 92 29 50 10)

Train Connections to Other Base Cities from Nice

DEPART	TRAIN NUMBER	ARRIVE	NOTES
		Amsterdam Centraal	
0936	TGV 6174	2107	R, 1
1031	TGV 9864	2139	R, 2
1141	TGV 6176	2307	R, 1
1556	TGV 6180	0710+1	R, 1, Sleeper
1846	TGV 5770	1338+1	R, 1, 2, Sleeper
		Barcelona Sants	
1031	TGV 9864	2148	6
		Berlin Zoobahnhof	
1345	TGV 6178	0821+1	1
		Brussels (Bruxelles) Midi/Zuid	
0715	TGV 6172	1550	R, 1
0936	TGV 6174	1750	R, 1
1031	TGV 9864	1836	R
1842	1170	0946+1	Sleeper
		Luxembourg	
2018	4330	0850+1	R, Sleeper
		Lyon Part-Dieu	
0605	RE 17426	1226	
0924	TGV 5198	1344	R
1017	TGV 6864	1440	R
1535	TGV 5184	1950	R
1634	TGV 6876	2058	R
1753	RE 17434	2357	
		Madrid Chamartin	
1010	4758	0700+1	R, 7, Sleeper
		Milan (Milano) Centrale	
0707	1143	1345	R
1002	IC 343	1450	R
1830	347	2310	R
		Munich (München) Hauptbahnhof	
1002	IC 343	2230	R, 3
		Paris Gare de Lyon	
0715	TGV 6172	1251	R
0936	TGV 6174	1511	R
1141	TGV 6176	1721	R
1345	TGV 6178	1921	R
1556	TGV 6180	2141	R
1643	TGV 6182	2221	R
1733	TGV 6184	2311	R
2049	5770	0745+1	R, 5, Sleeper
2100	5772	0815+1	R, 5, Sleeper
		Rome (Roma) Ostiense	
0821	4679	1644	4
1002	IC 343	1930	3
2035	369	0657+1	R, Sleeper

Daily, unless otherwise noted
R Reservations required
+1 Arrives next day
1. In Paris, transfer to Nord station.
2. Change trains in Brussels.
3. Change trains in Milan.
4. Change trains in Ventimiglia.
5. Arrive Paris Austerlitz.
6. Change trains in Marseilles–St-Charles and Montpellier.
7. Change trains in Montpellier and to sleeper in Barcelona Sants.

- Bikes: Arnaud, 5 rue François Ier (*Tel:* 04 93 87 88 55; *Fax:* 04 93 88 34 40 [bikes, mopeds, scooters)
- Nice Location Rent, 12 rue de Belgique (*Tel:* 04 93 82 42 71; *Fax:* 04 93 87 76 36) for bikes, mopeds, scooters, roller blades.

Sights/Attractions/Tours

Nice boasts more than 200 hotels and 1,000 restaurants. Most of these facilities are located in the modern section of Nice, west of the Paillon River, which divides the town in two.

The Riviera is noted for its spectacular scenery. Every proper ingredient of sea, shore, cliffs, and mountains is present. Grapes and flowers are the predominant crops of its highly cultivated farmlands. It is one of the great flower-growing areas of Europe and probably the most famous center in the world for perfume production.

The Riviera is also a center for modern art. The works of many twentieth-century artists can be found in its numerous museums and exhibition halls. Picasso spent the last years of his life in a villa overlooking the Mediterranean.

In selecting Nice as the base city for the day excursions in the Riviera area, we considered the variety of features and attractions that the city has to offer, and they are many.

In the maze of Old Nice's narrow streets, you will discover, in variations of light, shade, and fragrances, the **fish market**, the **Palais Lascaris**, the public squares of the city—each one different in function but all with an air of grace—and, in a sudden burst of sunlight, the beaches.

To the east, the old town and port offer many attractions to those who have a feeling for the past. At 300 feet above the **Old Town**, in a public park where once a fortress stood, the views are unforgettable. Streets and houses in the Old Town date from the sixteenth century.

The **Marché aux Fleurs** (Flower Market), one of the most beautiful and truly native sights in the Old Town of Nice, is held daily except Monday in the **Cours Saleya**, a block south of the **Prefecture Palace** near the opera. At Cours Saleya, you'll discover what makes Nice so fragrant and colorful. You will also discover what makes the cuisine of the area so appetizing: A fruit-

and-vegetable market flourishes right in the midst of the floral beauty. Mondays are a bit different in the Cours Saleya, since that's when the market is reserved for antiques dealers. But here again is another opportunity to delve into the priceless things that make Nice so nice.

There are ten casinos within 40 miles of Nice and three international ski resorts only 2 hours away. The world-famous **Nice Carnival** takes place every February. Other festive events, however, are to be found in Nice throughout the year. The King Carnival takes place just before Lent and rivals New Orleans's Mardi Gras.

Turn from the sea in Nice, and your eyes confront **Mont Alban** and its fortress overhanging the harbor. If you choose to go to the alpine area behind the city, there's a charming private narrow-gauge railroad, **Chemin de Fer de Provence** (Railroad of Provence), that will transport you through rocky gorges and sheer cliffs and Lingostiere, on the invasion route used by Napoleon, to an exceptional panorama of the Alps and the Mediterranean Sea.

For another train ride, this one within the city, board the **Nice "little train"** at its station on the Promenade des Anglais for a scenic ride through the shady, narrow streets of the Old Town to **Castle Hill** for a vista of the Baie des Anges (Bay of Angels) and the Port of Nice.

Day Excursions

With Nice as their pivot point, four wonderful day excursions have been selected. **Cannes** was picked for its beaches and bikinis (or something even less); **Marseilles**, melting pot of the Mediterranean, because of its flair for bouillabaisse and its Bogart background; **Monte Carlo (Monaco)** for its coastline and casino; and **Saint-Raphaël**, the resort on the Riviera with something for everyone, and at popular prices.

Day Excursion to

Cannes
Top of the Riviera

Depart from Nice Ville Station
Distance by Train: 19 miles (31 km)
Average Train Time: 25 minutes
Tourist Information Office: Cannes Syndicat d'Initative in the rail station, Office de Tourisme, place de la Gare, 06400 Cannes
Tel: 04 93 99 19 77; *Fax:* 04 93 39 40 19
Internet: www.cannes-on-line.com
E-mail: semoftou@palais-festivals-cannes.fr
Hours: 0900–1830 Monday–Saturday
Notes: Reach it by turning left in the main station hall, then take the stairs located

immediately outside. Elevator service is also available. Look for the sign that reads Service du Tourisme de la Ville de Cannes, Syndicat d'Initiative Accueil de France, Syndicat des Hoteliers.

- **Cannes Tourisme Information Office,** Palais des Festivals, boulevard de la Croisette, across from the Majestic Hotel
Hours: 0900–1830 Monday–Saturday; during July–August, 0900–2000 daily
- *Croisette Change* (money exchange), 3 boulevard de la Croisette, 06400 Cannes. *Hours:* 0900–1800 Monday–Friday

Cannes has been described as a magnet that attracts the famous, the rich, and the dreamers. It also has a reputation of being impossibly expensive. No doubt this is true of **La Croisette**—the waterfront boulevard of Cannes lined with sandy beaches, extravagant restaurants, and elegant hotels. But this reputation does not apply to all of Cannes.

Cannes is a large resort with nearly 5,000 hotel rooms within its city limits and that many again in its suburbs. A hundred yards or so back from the waterfront, hotels charge a fraction of the rates extracted from the famous, the rich—and the dreamers—who insist on living at the water's edge.

The Cannes railway station is modern and efficient. All services are grouped conveniently in or near its main hall. As you exit from the track area, you can reach the **train information and reservations office** via the escalator to your right. Summer hours: Monday–Saturday 0900–1230 and 1400–1830; winter hours: 0900–1900 Monday–Friday. Coin-operated baggage lockers are available on the main level at either end of the station.

Walking through Cannes is enjoyable and easy. Certainly no one would want to miss a stroll along the Promenade de la Croisette, one of the most beautiful and highly celebrated seaside walks on the Riviera. It borders the Bay of Cannes for about 2 miles until you reach its extreme eastern end at the Palm Beach Casino—with its gaming rooms and gala evenings—on place Franklin D. Roosevelt.

Along the way, you will see some of the world's finest yachts berthed close by magnificent rose gardens in the Port Pierre-Canto and the famous **Palais des Festivals et des Congrés,** home of the International Film Festival. Walk along the old port to the old part of town called **"Le Suquet,"** which overlooks the harbor and offers a marvelous view of the bay.

Except for the brief period in the late fall when the Mistral winds make things a bit uncomfortable, the climate of Cannes is wonderfully mild and temperate. Because of a few canes and reeds growing in the bay, the Romans named the spot "Castrum de Canois," and for centuries Cannes remained a small village inhabited only by fishermen.

History relates that in 1834, the Lord Chancellor of England, Lord Brougham, "whilst" en route to Nice, was prevented from reaching there due

There are at least 3 trains per hour in each direction throughout the day from 0500 to 2300; journey time, 25–30 minutes. Distance: 19 miles (31 km)

to a cholera quarantine and paused briefly in Cannes. Taken by the place, his lordship decided on the spur of the moment to build a house in Cannes and did so, straight away—the transaction in real estate taking a matter of only eight days. For the next 34 years, until the time of his death, Lord Brougham left the winter fogs of London for the sunshine of Cannes.

His lordship's example was quickly followed by other English aristocracy, and Cannes' population began to swell accordingly. Alluding to the eight days required to get Cannes under way, locals point out that God took only seven days to create the universe—so Cannes, necessarily, is a cut above all else.

The center of Cannes is ideal for strolling and shopping. Locals claim that you get more than what you pay for because the area has a theatrical atmosphere about it, and the show is free. Not so on the Croisette, the waterfront. Here the most elegant of shops extol the virtues of high fashion at equally high prices. Window shopping, however, is free to all.

Excursion-boat services from the main port take you to the islands of **Sainte-Marguerite** and **Saint-Honorat**. Sainte-Marguerite's prison incarcerated the Man in the Iron Mask, and the island named after Saint Honorat has the remains of the monastery the saint started in the fourth century. Boats run daily throughout the year.

Another very delightful boat ride provides an unequaled panorama of the Mediterranean and the Alps each afternoon from June through September. This excursion departs at 1430, cruises the Bay of Cannes and the **Esterel Coast,** and returns at 1730. If you don't happen to be one of the millionaires with a yacht tied up in Port Pierre-Canto, now's your chance to enjoy the same exhilarating view that they enjoy—at a more reasonable price.

Day Excursion to

Marseilles
City of Intrigue

Depart from Nice Ville Station
Distance by Train: 140 miles (225 km)
Average Train Time: 2 hours, 15 minutes
Tourist Information Office: Maison du Tourisme Marseilles, 4 La Canebiere, 13001 Marseille

NICE
Marseilles

137

Tel: 04 91 13 89 00; *Fax:* 04 91 13 89 20
Internet: www.marseille-tourisme.com
E-mail: info@marseille-tourisme.com
Hours: July–August: Monday–Saturday 0900–1930; Sunday 1000–1800.
September–June: Monday–Saturday 0900–1900; Sunday 1000–1700.
Notes: Located adjacent to the municipal docks. Via Metro, take Line 1 in the direction
"La Timone" to stop "Vieux Port–Hôtel de Ville." You may taxi there just by
showing the driver the address. To reach it on foot—about a 15-minute walk—
leave the railway station by descending the steps to street level. Directly in front is
the boulevard d'Athens (a promenade from the original settlers, no doubt). Follow
this street to the third traffic signal, including the one at the foot of the train-station
steps. Turn to the right onto boulevard La Canebiere, and just beyond the second
traffic light now in front of you, look for the tourist office in the last building on the
left-hand side of the street just before the small boat harbor.

Also, there is a small tourist office in the train station on the track level that
is open 1000–1800.

Marseilles, the great port of France, is second only to Paris in population and is one of the oldest surviving towns in the world.
Although French in character, Marseilles is distinctly Mediterranean, with
an international flair. There is much to compare in the character of
Marseilles to the contents of its epicurean delicacy, bouillabaisse, and the
three ingredients so essential in its making.

Greeks, fleeing out of Asia Minor from the Persians, founded Massalia
(Marseilles) in 600 B.C. Their enterprising nature disturbed the Ligurians,
who came from Italy, as well as the Iberians coming from Spain, and a lot of
head smashing took place until the Greeks appealed to Rome for help.
Romans came by the legions and promptly named the area a Roman
province. Hannibal and his elephants created some disturbance, but nothing
like that of 360,000 Teutonic warriors in 102 B.C. who were seemingly bent
on destroying the civilized world and all that was in it.

Rome, again to the rescue, dispatched Caius Marius to the province; he,
in turn, disposed of 100,000 Teutons near Aix-en-Provence, just north of
Marseilles, thus saving the day for the province and impacting the future of
modern-day France. Even today, the most popular name for men in this
region is Marius.

The French national anthem, *The Marseillaise,* was composed in
Strasbourg by a young French military officer, Rouget de Lisle. The battle
song was published and reached Marseilles just at the time when the city
was giving a send-off banquet to 500 volunteers bound for Paris and the
revolution. Someone sang the new song, and immediately the banquet room
picked it up in chorus.

The song was an immediate success, and the volunteers sang it in unison
at every stopping place en route to Paris. By the time they reached Paris they
had become somewhat of an accomplished choir, which electrified the

Nice—Marseilles

Depart Nice Ville	Train Number	Arrive Marseille St-Charles	Notes
0656	—	0906	
0721	17476	0949	Mon–Fri
0839	—	1114	
0900	17484	1126	
0924	TGV 5198	1157	R
1010	4758	1241	
1017	TGV 6864	1252	R
1031	TGV 9864	1305	R

Depart Marseille St-Charles	Train Number	Arrive Nice Ville	Notes
1507	TGV 9826	1739	R
1609	—	1843	Mon–Fri
1646	4656	1909	
1728	TGV 6818	2006	R
1950	TGV 6829	2225	R
2029	4662	2256	
2055	5634	2328	Fri
2132	17495	2354	except Sat
2208	TGV 6183	0035+1	R

Daily, unless otherwise noted
R Reservations required
+1 Arrives next day
Distance: 140 miles (225 km)

Parisians as they marched through the streets of Paris singing the stirring words at the tops of their voices.

All the foregoing was given to set the mood for your arrival in Marseilles. Although the city is not famous as a tourist center, it is a very enjoyable place to visit. Its unusual character and mixture of peoples cannot be found anywhere else in the world.

Not far from the tourist office, you will find the **Vieux-Port** and its fish market, which defies description. This is one of the few places in the world where you can obtain those three essential ingredients for bouillabaisse: red gurnet, conger eel, and a Mediterranean fish known locally as *rascasse*. Nearby restaurants serve it to perfection.

Here in the Vieux-Port, from a pier known as the quai des Belges (Belgian Wharf), you can take a ferry for the 15-minute crossing to the island of **Chateau d'If,** made famous in *The Count of Monte Cristo* by Alexandre Dumas. The castle is an interesting place to visit, and your guide will dramatically conclude your tour by showing you the opening through which the count was said to have made his escape. The visit to the island takes about 1½–2 hours, including the tour of the dungeons where the Man in the Iron Mask and many other political prisoners were imprisoned.

Monte Carlo (Monaco)
Roulette and Relaxation

Depart from Nice Ville Station
Distance by Train: 9 miles (14 km)
Average Train Time: 20 minutes
Tourist Information Offices: Monte Carlo Tourist Information, 2a Boulevard des Moulins
Tel: 377 92 16 61 16
Internet: www.monaco-tourism.com
Hours: Monday–Saturday 0900–1900; Sunday 1000–1200
Notes: The bus terminal is a short distance downhill from the railway station. Board bus No. 4 and ask the driver to let you off at the Office National du Tourisme (the National Tourist Office). From June 15 to September 30, there's a small tourist information kiosk in the station lobby open daily 0800–2000.

The Principality of Monaco lies 4,092 miles east of Philadelphia—two cities inexorably linked by the memories of their princess, Grace Patricia Kelly, who died as the result of a tragic accident in 1982.

Monaco consists of 0.7 square miles (453 acres) of rocky coastline along the Riviera. It has been ruled by members of the Grimaldi family for the past ten centuries. Its famous gambling casino is located in Monte Carlo, one of four sections that make up the principality. The other three are Monaco-Ville itself (the capital and site of the palace), La Condamine (a commercial and residential area), and Fontvieille (a residential and light-industries section).

Monaco operates a highly efficient bus system consisting of five major lines: No. 1 (Red), No. 2 (Blue), No. 4 (Gold), No. 5 (Brown), and No. 6 (Green), which serves the Fontvieille-Larvotto (beach) area. These are augmented by Line No. 3, serving the beach area during the summer.

French francs are the legal tender in Monaco, so there is no need to change your currency. Traveler's checks can be cashed at "Credit Lyonnais," a bank opposite the train station, 0845–1155 and 1330–1600 Monday through Friday. The American Express office is just to the west of the casino at 2 avenue de Monte Carlo.

If cracking casinos is your cup of tea, Monte Carlo's public gambling rooms open at 1000 daily. You must be twenty-one to enter. Youngsters are not barred, however, at the National Museum and Collection of Dolls and Automats of Yesteryear, located at 17 avenue Princesse Grace. Hours: daily April–September, 1000–1830; daily October–March, 1000–1215 and 1430–1830. Admission, €4.57, adults; children age 6–14 and students, €3.05.

Pomp and ceremony still prevail in Monte Carlo. The changing of the guard takes place daily in front of the **Place du Palais** exactly at 1155. The

There are at least 2 trains per hour—often 3 or 4—from 0525 to 2300+ throughout the day in both directions; journey time is about 20 minutes. Distance: 9 miles (14 km)

charge for visiting the Prince's **Palace State Apartments** is €4.57; children 8–14, €2.29. Tours are conducted daily June–September, 0930–1830, and during October, 1000–1700. One of Europe's greatest aquariums, the **Musée Oceanographique**, lies near the palace on the seaside. Hours: April–September 0900–1900; October–March 1000–1800. Admission: adults, €10.67; children, €5.34.

While at the Place du Palais, you should visit the **Museum of Napoleonic Souvenirs and Collections of the Palace Historic Archives.** Hours: 0930–1830 daily June–September; reduced hours during the balance of the year. Admission: adults, €3.05; children 8–14, €1.52.

Other attractions include the **Wax Museum of the Princes of Monaco,** the **Museum of Old Monaco,** and the **Museum of Prehistoric Anthropology,** the last featuring the Exotic Gardens and the **Observatory Cave.** The tourist office publishes a brochure listing all places of interest, opening times, and admission fees. Also available is a map showing the city's "semi-pedestrianized" zone, 12 public lifts, and the bus system.

The grandeur of the Monaco yacht harbor may be viewed from many vantage points. The view from the casino's restaurant **Le Prive** is impressive—expensive, too. Probably the best site (at popular prices) is a canopy-covered table at the **Portofino Restaurant,** which clings to the cliff just above the quai President Kennedy.

Day Excursion to
Saint-Raphaël
"In" Place on the Riviera

Depart from Nice Ville Station
Distance by Train: 37 miles (59 km)
Average Train Time: 50 minutes
Tourist Information Office: Office de Tourisme, Rue Waldeck-Rousseau, B.P. 210, 83 702 Saint-Raphaël
Tel: 04 94 19 52 52; *Fax:* 04 94 83 85 40
Internet: www.saint-raphael.com
E-mail: touroff@clubinternet.fr
Hours: September–June: 0900–1230 and 1400–1830 Monday–Saturday. July and August: 0900–2000 daily.

Located across the street and to the left of the main entrance to the railway station. It is identified by a white i sign together with TOURISME in brown letters.

If you arrive late, there is also a tourist information stand available on the Veillat Beach, one block from the main tourist information office. It is open 0200–2200.

Saint-Raphaël is the Riviera resort that has something for everyone— and at popular prices. Its primary asset is its delightful weather, which is mild in the winter and moderate throughout the entire summer.

Before leaving the railway station, check the departure schedules for trains returning to Nice. There is a train information office in the station on your right as you exit the train platform. Hours: Monday–Saturday 0800–1930. *Tel:* 36 35 35 35.

With such a richly diverse area, Saint-Raphaël is a year-round destination. Sports enthusiasts are attracted by water sports, sailing, diving, and four beautiful golf courses—two 18-hole courses and two 9-hole courses located in three different areas. Situated between the Mediterranean Sea and Limestone Provence, the Esterel mountain—a volcanic range encompassing 79,000 acres—offers many nature activities such as hiking, horseback riding, and mountain biking.

The fishing-boat dock in Saint-Raphaël is not far from the railroad station. The tourist office can point the way. Here you will find some unusually fine local restaurants where, in the summer, you can dine at tables set under trees close to the boats. It is a relaxing atmosphere.

Saint-Raphaël has an interesting history. Its modern origins stem from the era of the Roman Empire, when it was a fashionable suburb of the Roman port of Frejus. Napoleon passed through Saint-Raphaël in both victory and defeat. In 1799, the emperor and his generals disembarked there upon returning from Egypt; a pyramid standing in the town still commemorates the event. In 1814, he sailed again from Saint-Raphaël, this time for Elba and exile. On April 28, as Napoleon, overcome with emotion, was saying good-bye to the soil of France, the English frigate he was to sail in fired a salute of twenty-one guns.

The site where the present town of Saint-Raphaël now stands has played an exciting part in the history of the Mediterranean. Because of its natural harbor, which is deep enough to accommodate even the deepest-draught warships, the Romans developed it first as a holiday center. The town's casino is built over the original foundations of the Roman baths and a fish-holding tank. Villas of the rich Romans who had come to Saint-Raphaël to "take the sea air" were destroyed by Saracen pirates. By the time the pirates were driven from the area in the tenth century, the land lay deserted.

Much of Saint-Raphaël's modern development has been due in great part to the establishment of the cut-flower industry started there in 1880 by

Nice—Saint-Raphaël

DEPART NICE VILLE	TRAIN NUMBER	ARRIVE SAINT-RAPHAËL	NOTES
0715	TGV 6172	0806	R
0721	RE 17476	0813	
0753	RE 81130	0903	
0900	RE 17484	0948	

and continuing with 3 to 4 trains each hour until 2231

DEPART SAINT-RAPHAËL	TRAIN NUMBER	ARRIVE NICE VILLE	
1606	RE 81197	1716	
1633	TGV 6175	1726	R
1646	TGV 9827	1739	R
1714	RE 81217	1837	
1821	4657	1909	
1832	TGV 6177	1923	R
1839	RE 81229	1956	
1917	TGV 6819	2006	R
2037	TGV 6179	2127	R

then five more trains until 2343

Daily, unless otherwise noted
R Reservations required
Distance: 37 miles (59 km)

Alphonse Karr. Although its biggest revenues today are developed by the tourist industry, Saint-Raphaël is still a large and prosperous center for cut flowers.

An excellent excursion-boat service operates from Saint-Raphaël. The tourist information office will have to provide you with schedules and fares, as they are too varied to mention here. There are short cruises on the Mediterranean as well as full-day excursions to many ports of call on the Riviera.

Saint-Tropez, summer home of Brigitte Bardot and one of the better "topless" beaches of France, can be reached from Saint-Raphaël by bus (*Tel:* 04 94 83 87 63) or boat (*Tel:* 04 94 95 17 46). Journey time: 1 hour, 25 minutes in each direction, but connections can be made that allow almost 7 hours of visiting and sight-seeing in this quaint resort town. For details on bus service between Saint-Raphaël and Saint-Tropez, consult the rail information office in Nice or Saint-Raphaël, or ask for assistance from the tourist office in Saint-Raphaël. There is no rail service between Saint-Raphaël and Saint-Tropez.

PARIS

E very traveler has two cities," wrote Edna St. Vincent Millay, "his own and Paris." Besides being one of the most beautiful and captivating cities in Europe, Paris is the center of one of the most interesting regions of France. Local people call the area around Paris the **Ile de France** (Island of France), for it is here that the nation began in the forested lands stretching out in all directions around Paris. The city is not only the political capital of France; it's the country's industrial and commercial center as well. To understand and appreciate it, follow the suggestion of British poet and novelist Lawrence Durrell and watch it "quite quietly over a glass of wine in a Paris bistro."

Arriving by Air

Charles de Gaulle Airport, 17 miles (23 km) north of the city center (*Tel:* 01 48 62 22 80). Two major terminals; Terminal 2 is split into five. Majority of flights from North America arrive at Terminals 2A, 2B, 2C, 2D, or 2F. Signs are posted in both French and English, and information is available in other languages. Terminal T9 handles seasonal charter flights.

- **Money exchange:** TRAVELEX just outside customs area in Terminal 2C. Hours: 0615–2300. ATM at Sortie (Exit) 6.
- **SNCF (French Rail) office hours:** 0730–2015. You can board a train to Lyon, Avignon, or Nice without having to transfer to Paris.

Airport–City Links

- **RER** (Regional Express Railway) Line B trains run every 7–15 minutes 0545–2300 to stations Gare du Nord, Chatelet-les-Halles, St. Michel, Luxembourg, Port Royal, and Denfert-Rochereau; journey time 35 minutes; fare €5.34. Plenty of luggage space. RER station is to the right of the customs area, Terminal 2C.
- **Roissybus** departs every 15 minutes 0545–2300 between Roissy Terminal 2 and Opera; journey time about 40–60 minutes; fare €6.10.
- **Air France Bus** departs every 15–20 minutes 0540–2300 to rail station Gare Montparnasse, and Métro stops Porte Maillot (Air France City Terminal), Palais de Congres, and place Charles de Gaulle Étoile; journey time 40–60 minutes; fare €7.32.

- **Taxis** take about 45 minutes; average fare, €38.11; higher night rates.

Orly Airport, 10 miles (14 km) south of Paris (*Tel:* 01 49 75 15 15). Terminal West for Air France, Iberia, and TAP flights; Terminal South for most airlines.

Airport–City Links
- **RER (Regional Express Railway)** Line C trains run every 15 minutes 0545–2315 to stations Gare d'Austerlitz, St. Michel, Invalides, and Porte Maillot.
- **Air France Bus** departs every 15–20 minutes 0540–2300 to Gare d'Austerlitz, Gare Montparnasse, or St. Michel; journey time about 25 minutes; fare €6.10.
- **Orlybus** departs every 15 minutes 0600–2300 to and from the Métro/RER stop Denfert-Rochereau; journey time about 40 minutes; fare €4.95.

Arriving by Train

Paris has six major railway stations, but arriving there by train from one of the other base cities listed in this edition of *Europe by Eurail* will place you either in Gare du Nord (North), Gare de l'Est (East), Gare de Lyon, Gare d'Austerlitz, or Gare Montparnasse. Details of these stations follow.

Transfers between rail stations in Paris may be made by bus, Métro, or taxi. If you have baggage, a taxi is your best bet. There are, however, interstation buses that provide baggage storage. Rule out the Métro unless you are without baggage. Suggestion: Consult the conductor on your train at least 30 minutes prior to arrival. If you are transferring between stations to continue your journey, the railroad is obliged to assist you. For train information in France, call 08 36 35 35 39.

The Railway Stations

Gare du Nord (North Station), 18 rue de Dunkerque, 75010 Paris

The terminal for Eurostar and Thalys trains. Gateway to the channel ports of Calais and Boulogne plus Belgium, Germany, The Netherlands, and London via Eurostar.
- **Money-exchange office:** In the station concourse area across from platform 3. Hours: 0615–2230 daily, except holidays. ATM, Point Argent, across from platforms 3 and 4.
- **Train information:** Displayed in digital format throughout the station. A rail information office is located across from platform 1. Hours: 0600–2300 daily, including holidays.
- **Seat reservations,** including TGV and sleeping cars, may be made in the train information office. A layout of the station can be seen on a chart across from platform 5.
- **Eurostar** has its own terminal, reservations, and waiting room upstairs from the main part of the station. The well-marked signs will direct you to it.

Gare de l'Est (East Station), place du 11 Novembre 1918, 75010 Paris
Gateway to eastern France, Germany, Luxembourg, Austria, and
Switzerland. Located a short distance from Gare du Nord and can be
reached on foot or by the Métro.

- **Money exchange:** In the main reception hall area opposite platforms
  25 and 26. Hours: 0645–2200 daily.
- **Train information:** Displayed in digital format throughout the
  station. A rail information office is located on the left-hand side of
  the station coming from the trains, between platforms 6 and 7.
  Hours: 0845–2000 every day, although on Sunday for information
  only (no reservations).
- **Seat reservations:** May be made in the train information office.

Gare de Lyon (Lyon Station), 20 boulevard Diderot, 75012 Paris
Gateway to the Riviera, southern France, Italy, and western Switzerland.
Located on the right bank of the Seine, some distance south of the north and
east terminals.

- **Money exchange:** On the left side of Sortie (Exit) 1 as you enter the
  station and proceed toward platform A. Hours: 0630–2300 daily.
- **Train information:** In digital format throughout the station. The
  office for train information, marked INFORMATION AND RESERVATIONS, is
  in the center of the station, to the left of the *Billets Grandes Lignes*
  area. Hours: 0800–2200 Monday–Saturday; 0800–1900 Sunday/
  holidays. **Train reservations** at the same office.
- **Tourist information/hotel reservations:** In the Paris Convention
  and Visitors Bureau, located in the main ticket hall. Hours:
  0800–2000 Monday–Saturday.
- **Restaurant le Train Bleu** is located on the mezzanine of Gare de
  Lyon. Without doubt, it is the most elegant restaurant of any train
  station in the world. Opened in 1901, it was originally called the *Buffet
  de la Gare de Lyon.* Quickly, however, it became the fashionable place
  for well-heeled passengers to partake of a late supper prior to boarding
  Le Train Bleu, the stylish sleeper that traveled between Paris and the
  French Riviera, and so it was renamed. The food is good, and the
  decor is France at the turn of the twentieth century at its opulent best:
  crystal chandeliers, shimmering brass, and mahogany.

Gare d'Austerlitz (Austerlitz Station), 55 quai D'Austerlitz, 75013 Paris
Gateway to central and southwest France as well as Spain and Portugal.
Located on the left bank of the Seine, a short distance from Gare de Lyon,
which may be reached on foot or by the Métro.

- **Money exchange:** Within the main hall of the station, close to the
  ticket windows. Hours: 0630–2300 daily.
- **Train information:** Displayed in digital format. A rail information
  office is located in the foyer of the station just before entering the
  main hall. Hours: 0730–1945 Monday–Saturday.
- **Seat reservations:** May be made in the train information office.

Other major railway stations in Paris include **Gare Saint-Lazare** (north and west of France) and **Gare Montparnasse** (west of France). There are four Métro stations (Routes 4, 6, 12, and 14) in or adjacent to the Montparnasse railway station. Consequently, it is easy to reach from other parts of the rail network. Route 4 connects directly with Gare du Nord (North Station) and Gare de l'Est (East Station). Trains departing Paris for Chartres from Montparnasse also stop in Versailles, but this station is some distance from the Palace of Versailles and should not be used for that day excursion.

In these railway stations, the **reservation offices** are open 0800–2000 daily. Train information and reservations for all France: *Tel:* 08 36 35 35 39.

In addition to the six major railway stations of Paris, there are five smaller or suburban-type stations of importance to *Europe by Eurail* readers.

- **Gare des Invalides,** another station that begins underground with its trackage until well past the Eiffel Tower, is exclusive for trains running to the Palace of Versailles.
- **Gare Bercy** and **Gare Charolais** are two auxiliary stations serving the Gare de Lyon complex on the right bank of the Seine.
- On the Rive Gauche (Left Bank) side, **Gare Tolbiac** serves the Austerlitz station network, and **Gare Vaugirard** performs the same function for the extensive train trackage terminating in the Montparnasse station compound.

A system of buses connects the major Paris stations, Gare St. Lazare, Gare du Nord, Gare de l'Est, Gare de Lyon, Gare Montparnasse, and Gare d'Austerlitz. Operated privately, the system charges a fare slightly higher than that of the Métro, but it is much more convenient for passengers with luggage than the Métro or regular city buses.

Tourist Information/Hotel Reservations

- Office de Tourisme et des Congrès de Paris, 127 avenue des Champs Elysées, 75008 Paris; *Tel:* 08 36 68 31 12 (€0.33/min.); *Fax:* 01 49 52 53 00; *Internet:* www.paris-touristoffice.com; *E-mail:* info@paris-touristoffice.com

Hours: 0900–2000 daily

Branch office at Eiffel Tower open May–September 1100–1800 daily

Notes: Free maps of Paris are available at most hotels, or you can purchase one at tourist offices. You may also consult the Galeries Lafayette travel agency, 40 boulevard Haussman. Hours: Monday–Saturday 0930–1900 (until 2100 on Thursday). Tel: 01 42 85 21 20.

Getting Around in Paris

The mainstay of transportation within Paris is its subway system, the Métro. It has sixteen lines, several with rubber-tired coaches that sort of sneak up on you in the station. The system covers all of the city and much of its suburbs. You can reach all the railway stations in Paris via the Métro. *Internet:* www.rapt.fr.

Obtain a map of the Métro system from one of the tourist offices and ask for a brief explanation of its operation or call toll-free (877) RAILPASS (877-724-5727) for a free city map of Paris, including Métro, Bus, and RER Lines. Many of the Métro stations have an illuminated map in their entrances, where, by pushing the button of your desired destination, the entire route will light up showing what line to take, in what direction, and, when necessary, where to make transfers.

The French refer to transfers as *correspondances*. Although the lines are numbered, the reference you should remember is the direction, which refers to the last station on the end of the line in the direction in which you are traveling. For example, Line No. 1 has two directions: Grande Arche de la Défense in the west, Château de Vincennes in the east. If you were visiting the Louvre and wanted to see the Place de la Concorde next, look for the direction Grande Arche de la Défense because your destination lies to the west.

At transfer points, watch for the orange CORRESPONDANCE sign, then disembark and look for the direction sign for the line you want to transfer to. Proceed to that platform and there determine from the line map how many stops to your destination.

Purchase a **Paris Visite** (tourist pass) valid for 1, 2, 3, or 5 consecutive days, which provides for travel on public transportation in Paris and surrounding areas using the Métro, bus, tram, Montmartre funicular, or RER and SNCF (French National Railways) lines within Ile-de-France as far as Euro-Disneyland, Versailles, Fontainebleau and the airports. The Paris Visite also includes discounts at many museums and monuments; a €22.87 reduction on the purchase of two dinners/shows at Paradis Latin, and many other valuable perks. Prices vary according to the number of zones selected.

If you are staying in Paris for the prescribed number of days and plan to make more than three one-way trips on the Métro or bus systems per day, the pass will definitely save you money, and the convenience is invaluable. These passes may be purchased in all of the main Métro and train stations in Paris, at the international airports, Paris tourist offices, and wherever you see the RATP logo.

Acquaint yourself with the **Paris RER** (Regional Express Railway), the high-speed, limited-stop rail service that runs *under*—that's right, *under*—the regular Paris Métro. If you need to get somewhere in a hurry, the RER's the way to go. For example, we have ridden from Gare de Lyon to the Arc de Triomphe (the Étoile) in less than ten minutes. Call 08 36 68 41 41 for information.

The RER consists of four lines. RER color-coded lines appear on maps as follows: Line A = Red, Line B = Blue, Line C = Yellow, and Line D = Green. *Line A* goes west to east from St. Germain-en Laye, La Défense, the Étoile, Auber, Châtelet, Gare de Lyon, and the Marne Valley. *Line B* goes north to south from Roissy-Charles de Gaulle Airport to Gare du Nord, Châtelet, Pont St. Michel, Luxembourg, and the Chevreuse Valley. *Line C* runs from Versailles and follows the Seine through Paris to Orly airport. *Line D* runs

Paris Visite Pass Prices in Euros

	1–3 Zones	1–5 Zones	1–8 zones
1 Day	8.38	16.77	23.63
2 Days	13.72	26.68	34.30
3 Days	18.29	37.35	42.69
5 days	26.68	45.73	53.36

from Orry-la-Ville Coye through central Paris then splits at the Villeneuve-St-Georges to Meluri or around to Malesherbes.

Note: Eurail passes are not accepted on RER lines within the Paris region.

- **Train information:** *Tel:* 01 36 35 35 39. Request an English-speaking operator. Available 0800–2000 daily.
- **Bus information:** *Tel:* 01 43 46 14 14.
- **Taxi:** *Tel:* 01 47 39 47 39, 01 45 85 85 85, 01 49 36 10 10, or 01 41 27 27 27. To reserve a taxi for the airport, call before 2100 the night before.

Sights/Attractions/Tours and Paris Potpourri

Musts during your stay in Paris include:

- A visit to the **Louvre** to view the *Mona Lisa* and *Venus de Milo*.
- A cable-car ride up to **Montmartre** for a view of the "City of Light" or by elevator up the **Eiffel Tower** to the highest point in Paris.
- Walk the **Champs Elysées** to the **Arc de Triomphe** and look deep into its "flame of remembrance" for the faces of France and its allies who fought and died in the two world wars.
- Lunch at a sidewalk cafe.
- Ride the **Seine** on a *bateau* (boat).
- Get a gargoyle's point of view from high atop **Nôtre Dame**.
- Dine at **Maxim's** (if your waistline and wallet can afford it).
- Take in a dazzling dinner/show at the great Parisian cabaret **Paradis Latin**.

Paris has triumphed once again in the arts—this time in a museum that served the city as a train station for nearly 40 years. **Gare du Quai d'Orsay** was inaugurated on Bastille Day 1900 and included a 400-room hotel. By 1939, the Gare d'Orsay was obsolete, its platforms too short to accommodate the longer, electrified trains of the day. In 1971, the city of Paris reluctantly scheduled the structure for demolition, creating an uproar from its citizens. Under pressure, the government reversed itself and saved both the station and the hotel, which became the **Musée** (museum) **d'Orsay.**

Located at 1 rue de la Légion d'Honneur (at entry to Quai d'Orsay RER station and near Solférino Métro stop), Musée d'Orsay boasts a glorious collection of nineteenth-century French painting and sculpture. Hours:

Train Connections to Other Base Cities from Paris

Depart from Paris Gare du Nord station, unless otherwise noted

DEPART	TRAIN NUMBER	ARRIVAL	NOTES
		Amsterdam Centraal	
0655	Thalys 9309*	1107	R
0955	Thalys 9321*	1407	R
1655	Thalys 9349*	2107	R
		Barcelona Sants	
1324	TGV 6211	2148	R, 1, 2
2032	Hotel 477	0824+1	R, 3, Sleeper
2156	3731	1149+1	R, 4, Sleeper
		Berlin Zoobahnhof	
0855	Thalys 9417*	1735	R, 5
1055	Thalys 9425*	1935	R, 5
1255	Thalys 9433*	2142	R, 5
2046	—	0821+1	R, Sleeper
		Bern (Berne)	
0744	TGV 9281	1229	R, 1
0840	TGV 6565	1413	R, 1, 6, Mon–Fri
1030	TGV 6569	1613	R, 1, 6
1304	TGV 9269	1813	R, 1, 5
1340	TGV 6573	1913	R, 6, Exc. Sat
1440	TGV 6577	2013	R, 1, 6
1644	TGV 9285	2123	R, 1
1740	TGV 6581	2313	R, 1, 6
1804	TGV 9297	2244	R, 1
1818	TGV 427	2300	R, 1, 7
		Brussels (Bruxelles) Midi/Zuid	
0655	Thalys 9409*	0820	R
0731	Thalys 9311*	0859	R, Mon–Fri
0755	Thalys 9313*	0920	R

plus hourly Thalys* train service at 55 min past each hour (but not 1355) until 2155. Arrive in Brussels at 20 min past each hour (but not 1520) until 2320.

DEPART	TRAIN NUMBER	ARRIVAL	NOTES
		Budapest Keleti	
1347	EC 67	0913+1	R, 8, 10, Sleeper
1749	EN 263	1303+1	R, 8, 9, Sleeper
2227	D 261	1713+1	R, 9, 10, Sleeper
		Copenhagen (København) H.	
1655	Thalys 9449*	0959+1	R, 11, Sleeper
2046	NZ 237	1159+1	R, 12, Sleeper
		Hamburg Hauptbahnhof	
0655	Thalys 9409*	1510	R, 5
0855	Thalys 9417*	1710	R, 5
1055	Thalys 9425*	1910	R, 5
1255	Thalys 9433*	2110	R, 5
		Lisbon (Lisboa) Santa Apolónia	
1555	TGV 8543	1045+1	R, 13, Sleeper
		Luxembourg	
0655	EC 203	1035	8, Exc. Sun
0854	EC 57	1234	8

DEPART	TRAIN NUMBER	ARRIVAL	NOTES
1054	EC 357	1435	8, Exc. Sun
1719	EC 53	2052	8
1821	EC 207	2206	8
1950	355	2345	8

Lyon Part-Dieu

0730	TGV 6643	0931	R, 1
0800	TGV 6605	0955	R, 1,
0830	TGV 6645	1025	R, 1, Exc Sun
0900	TGV 6607	1055	R, 1, Exc. Sun
1000	TGV 6609	1155	R, 1

then hourly until 2200.

Madrid Chamartin

0725	TGV 8505	2050	R, 14
1943	Hotel 409	0858+1	R, 3, Sleeper
2250	TGV 8597	0858+1	R, 14, Sleeper

Milan (Milano) Centrale

0804	TGV 9251	1455	R, 1
1104	TGV 9255	1755	R, 1
1430	TGV 6943	2150	R, 1, 15
2220	EN 217	0845+1	R, 16, Sleeper

Munich (München) Hauptbahnhof

0749	EC 65	1615	8
1347	EC 67	2217	8
2227	D 261	0851+1	R, 8, Sleeper

Nice Ville

0754	TGV 6171	1338	R, 1
0934	TGV 6173	1512	R, 1
1150	TGV 6175	1726	R, 1
1350	TGV 6177	1923	R, 1
1554	TGV 6179	2127	R
1653	TGV 6181	2232	R, 1
2117	5771	0759+1	R, 3, Sleeper
2230	TGV 6185	0644+1	R, 1, Sleeper, Fri only

Rome (Roma) Termini

0804	TGV 9251	2111	R, 1, 8
1104	TGV 9255	0103+1	R, 1, 10
1909	EN 213	0957+1	R, 17, Sleeper
2220	EN 217	1330+1	R, 1, 17, Sleeper

Vienna (Wien) Westbahnhof

0749	EC 65	2120	8
1749	EN 263	0842+1	R, 8, Sleeper

Zürich Hauptbahnhof

0744	TGV 9281	1346	R, 1, Exc. Sun
0801	1841	1558	R, 8, 18, Sun only
1316	1745	1825	R, 8, 19
1444	1747	2120	R, 8, 18
1644	TGV 9285	2242	R, 1
2243	469	0620+1	R, 8, Sleeper

Daily, unless otherwise noted
R Reservations required
* Thalys high-speed train, supplement required
+1 Arrives next day
1. Departs Paris Gare de Lyon station.
2. Change trains in Montpellier.
3. Departs Paris Austerlitz station.
4. Sleeper train to Portbou. Depart Portbou 0950 on Talgo (R) 377.
5. Change trains in Cologne (Köln).
6. Change trains in Geneva.
7. Change trains in Lausanne.
8. Departs Paris Gare de l'Est (East) station.
9. Change trains in Vienna (Wien).
10. Change trains in Munich (München).
11. Change to sleeper train in Cologne (Köln).
12. Change trains in Hamburg.
13. Departs Paris Montparnasse station. Change to sleeper train in Irún.
14. Departs Paris Montparnasse station. Change trains in Irún.
15. Change trains in Chambéry.
16. Departs Paris Gare de Bercy.
17. Change trains in Milan (Milano).
18. Change trains in Basel.
19. Change trains in Mulhouse.

Mid-June–September 0900–1800 Tuesday–Saturday; 1000–2145 Thursday; closed Monday. Opens 1000 during winter. Admission: €6.10. It is usually most crowded on Thursday night and the weekend. Reduced price, €4.57, on Sunday. *Internet:* www.musee-orsay.fr.

An interesting mix of Egyptian and European art can be found at the **Musée du Louvre.** Its glass-pyramid entrance, designed by I. M. Pei, has sparked much controversy, similar to that brought about by Gustave Eiffel and his tower. Referred to by the writer Guy de Maupassant as the "disgraceful skeleton," the Eiffel Tower became the city's most recognizable landmark. The Louvre is open 0900–1800 daily except Tuesday and certain public holidays. Evening hours are extended to 2145 on Monday and Wednesday. (*Tel:* 01 40 20 53 17; *Internet:* www.louvre.fr). Admission: €7.01. Reduced price (€4.57) after 1500 and all day Sunday.

To avoid queueing up and having to buy a separate ticket for each museum and monument, consider purchasing the **Carte Musées et Monuments,** which covers entry to about 65 museums and monuments in Paris and Ile de France.

1-day pass	*€12.19*
3-day pass	*€24.39*
5-day pass	*€36.58*

Purchase the pass at any of the museums, at more than 100 Métro stations, or at tourist offices.

No stay in Paris is complete without a visit to one of its great cabarets. Our favorite is **Paradis Latin** at 28 rue du Cardinal Lemoine (*Tel:* 01 43 25 28 28; *Fax:* 01 43 29 63 63; *Internet:* www.paradislatin.fr). This beautiful and elegant theater–dining hall played an interesting role in Parisian history. Its foundation dates back to the twelfth century, and its walls date back to 1803 when Bonaparte decided to construct his "Theatre Latin." It burned down during the siege of Paris in 1870, and Gustave Eiffel (the Eiffel Tower architect) was appointed to design and rebuild it. It reopened with great success in 1889. Then, in the early twentieth century, it was transformed into industrial workshops.

The theater was accidentally rediscovered in 1972 and meticulously restored to its former glory by 1977. According to Harold Israel, "At the Paradis, we decided that not only should the show be enchanting, but also the cuisine should be of excellent quality as well," and it is. Dinner's at 2000 and the dazzling show starts at 2130. Enjoy!

The Champs-Elysées is the most famous thoroughfare in Paris, but you should also see Paris from its most beautiful avenue, the River Seine. Aboard a *bateau* (boat), sights such as the Louvre, Nôtre Dame, and the Eiffel Tower take on a different perspective—particularly at night, when the floodlights of the *bateaux* illuminate the passing scenes. **Bateaux Parisiens**, Port de la Bourdonnais (at the foot of the Eiffel Tower). *Tel:* 01 44 11 33 55 for schedules, rates, and reservations. *Bon voyage!*

Day Excursions

Three of the six Paris day excursions have been selected to introduce the traveler to Ile de France: **Chartres, Fontainebleau,** and **Versailles.** These places are every bit as important to what Paris is today as the Louvre, the Place de la Concorde, or the Eiffel Tower. The three remaining day excursions venture farther afield in express trains to visit **Caen and the Normandy Beaches, Rennes,** and **Rouen.**

Day Excursion to

Caen
and the Normandy Beaches

Depart from Paris St. Lazare Station
Distance by Train: 148 miles (239 km)
Average Train Time: 2 hours, 20 minutes
Tourist Information Office: Office de Tourisme, Place Saint-Pierre, F-14000 Caen
Tel: 02 31 27 14 14; *Fax:* 02 31 27 14 18
Internet: www.ville-caen.fr or visit the Normandy Tourism Board's Web site at: www.normandy-tourism.org
E-mail: tourisminfo@ville-caen.fr
Hours: July–August: Monday–Saturday 0930–1900; Sunday 1000–1300 and 1400–1700. September–June: Monday–Saturday 0930–1300 and 1400–1800; Sunday and bank holidays 1000–1300.

More than five decades have passed since one of the greatest battles in history took place in Normandy. At dawn on June 6, 1944, American, British, and Canadian forces, together with elements of the Free French, assailed the Normandy beaches along a broad spectrum of the coastline at five preselected landing points, Utah, Omaha, Gold, Juno, and Sword. Preceded by the drop of three airborne divisions during the predawn hours, between 0630 and 0730, 120,000 soldiers and about 20,000 vehicles were landed from the sea. The assault upon Adolf Hitler's "Fortress Europe" had begun.

By the night of August 21, 76 days later, the **Battle of Normandy** was over. The German Seventh Army had been encircled and forced to surrender. It had cost the Germans 640,000 soldiers—killed, wounded, or taken prisoner. Allied losses were tallied at 367,000 dead or wounded. American losses were set at 127,000 casualties—31,000 of that number died in battle.

The town of Caen was the pivot of the battle and paid heavily for its part in the conflict. By the second day of the invasion, the whole of the town center had been flattened by Allied bombing. The German garrison fought fiercely. It wasn't until July 9 that the British and Canadian troops were able to take the town. The Germans, however, retreated to the right bank of the Orne River, where they continued to direct mortar fire into the ruined town. Caen was not completely liberated until August 9. The Battle of Caen lasted more than two months. Seventy-five percent of the town was destroyed.

For years following the war, Caen was one vast building site in which life gradually began to return to normal. Reconstructed and restored, the town decrees that now is the time for all men of goodwill to be reconciled. To that purpose, the **Caen Memorial** was established on the site of one of the bloodiest battles in history to take you on a compelling journey from the dark years of world wars to a vision of peace.

The memorial is unlike any other museum devoted to the theme of warfare. It employs audiovisual presentations to explain the sequence of events that led up to the outbreak of hostilities in 1939, the suffering of the people involved, the preparation for the invasion, and the strategies behind it. Peace can never be taken for granted; consequently, the memorial ends its presentation with a powerful and moving film emphasizing the need for vigilance if we are to have peace in our world in our own time and in our children's.

Allow one day for the Caen Memorial and sight-seeing in Caen—a typical day excursion. If you want to tour the landing beaches and the memorial, consider purchasing a rail/drive package (see rail/drive package types and prices in the Appendix). Ask the tourist office for the brochure, *The D-Day Landings and the Battle of Normandy*. The **Hertz** office in Caen is directly across from the rail station (closed Sunday). Reserve your first car

Paris—Caen

DEPART PARIS ST. LAZARE	TRAIN NUMBER	ARRIVE CAEN	NOTES
0712	3303	0857	Mon–Fri
0810	3333	1019	Sat
0840	3337	1045	Mon–Fri
0908	3305	1058	Sat–Sun
1010	3339	1218	Sat–Sun
1036	3307	1227	Mon–Fri
1043	3307	1230	Mon–Fri
1200	3343	1406	Sat
1225 (1305 Sa)	3309	1409 (1449 Sa)	Mon–Sat

DEPART CAEN	TRAIN NUMBER	ARRIVE PARIS ST. LAZARE	NOTES
1424	3354	1633	Mon–Fri
1508	3308	1712	Sat
1516	3310	1702	Mon–Fri
1520	3312	1706	Sun
1630	3336	1836	Daily
1641	3356	1853	Daily

and other frequent service until 2132 on Sun, 1955 on Mon–Sat
Distance: 148 miles (239 km)

rental on your rail/drive package at least 7 days prior to your departure for Europe by calling Hertz at (800) 654–3001.

Another option is to take the train from Paris Saint-Lazare station to Caen and purchase the Discovery Stay package which includes a visit of Caen Memorial, a 4-hour guided tour of the D-Day Landing Beaches, a book on the D-Day Landing (in English) and one night in a one-, two-, or three-star hotel, including breakfast. Prices start at €71.65 per person, based on double occupancy. Make your reservations in advance with a credit card: *Tel:* 2 31 06 06 44 (0900–1800 Monday–Friday); *Internet:* www.memorial-caen.fr.

This day excursion is a pilgrimage that every American should make. Arriving in Caen, you can proceed directly to the memorial on city bus No.17 going in the direction of the memorial. It departs from the bus station outside the rail station on the right.

The memorial is open daily, 0900–1900 (until 2000 during July and August). A half-day tour time is recommended. Check at the information desk for the starting times of the English-language programs. A cafeteria is located on the second floor for refreshments.

Returning from the memorial to the station, take bus No. 17 in the direction of **Grace de Dieu**. The bus makes a stop in the center of the town at Tour Leroy near the tourist office (Office du Tourisme). Walk along **boulevard des Allies** and proceed one block to where it intersects rue

Saint-Jean. From this point, the tourist office sign may be seen across the street to the right. The tourist office can advise on accommodations in Caen and the Normandy towns close to the beaches. For each full-priced ticket purchased at one of the museums, you get reduced rates at all the other ones in the D-Day Landings and the Battle of Normandy region.

Tours of the invasion beaches start in Caen and proceed west through the Anglo-Canadian sectors of Sword, Juno, and Gold before arriving in the American sectors of Omaha and Utah. With a Hertz rental car, proceed west from Caen on Route 13 past Bayeux, LaCambe, and Carentan until reaching Ste.-Mere-Eglise, the first town in France to be liberated on D-Day, June 6, 1944. Visit the Airborne Museum with its CG4-A glider and a C-47 airplane and gaze in wonder at the Eighty-second Airborne paratrooper's predicament when his parachute caught on the church steeple opposite the museum.

Proceed from there to the **Utah Beach Landing Museum** at Ste.-Marie-Du-Mont. An audiovisual presentation explains how Utah beach was used to land about one million soldiers on its shores. Your next stop should be **Pointe-Du-Hoc,** which was captured by the Second Ranger Battalion in a spectacular assault on June 6, 1944, scaling 100-foot cliffs to destroy a German battery of coastal guns. The Rangers made it, but they paid a high price for their valor—77 dead, with an overall casualty rate of about 60 percent.

Leaving Pointe-Du-Hoc, head east to **Colleville-St.-Laurent,** where on a summit overlooking Omaha beach, you enter the American cemetery. Pay your respects to the 10,000 Americans resting there. To paraphrase Sir Winston Churchill, "This part of a foreign field shall forever be American."

En route back to Caen, stop in Bayeux at the **Memorial Museum** that you passed earlier while en route to Ste.-Mere-Eglise—time permitting. Otherwise, plan to return there the following day and visit the Anglo-Canadian sectors as well. Take advantage of your rail/drive package.

Day Excursion to

Chartres
Cathedral Country

Depart from Paris Saint Lazare Station
Distance by Train: 55 miles (88 km)
Average Train Time: 1 hour
Tourist Information Office: Chartres Office de Tourisme (tourist information), place
de la Cathedrale, B.P. 289, 28005 Chartres
Tel: 02 37 18 26 26; *Fax:* 02 37 21 51 91
E-mail: chartres.tourism@wanadoo.fr
Hours: April–September: Monday–Saturday 0900–1900 and Sunday 0930–1730.

October–March: Monday–Saturday 1000–1800, Sunday 1000–1300 and 1430–1630

Notes: Exit the station, cross the street in the direction of the cathedral, and continue straight ahead until you come to a large square. Bear left at the square and follow the cathedral signs that you will begin to see from that point onward. The tourist information office is in a building at the far end of Cathedral Square. Its sign reads, OFFICE DE TOURISME.

Mention Chartres and anyone who has been there recalls the Cathedral of Nôtre Dame but not much more. But Chartres has many other attractions. To mention a few, we start with the town itself. Beguiling, gabled houses line the streets. Make it a point to stroll through the **old quarter** of town along streets with the appealing names of rue du Soleil d'Or (Street of the Golden Sun) or rue des Ecuyers (Street of the Horsemen). The tourist office has a special walking-tour program for the Old Town that includes the rental of a headset and a prerecorded audio guide in English. The length of the walking tour is 1½ hours.

Food is another one of Chartres's attractions, so plan to dine there during your visit. There are many excellent restaurants—the one in the ancient **Inn of the Grand Monarque** at 22 place des Épars, for example.

On arrival in the Chartres station, check the train departures for Paris on the posters displayed in the main hall near the ticket windows. The cathedral is illuminated at night, so if you would like to see this, check for a later train departure.

The **Cathedral of Nôtre Dame** in Chartres is in plain view from the railway station and will draw you like a magnet. It is said to be the most beautiful Gothic cathedral in Europe. To get there, just follow the aforementioned directions from the station to the tourist office, which is located in the same area. The cathedral's stained-glass windows, the superb lines of its pillars and vaulting, and its interior are overwhelmingly beautiful. Fire destroyed the original eleventh-century building. The present cathedral was rebuilt between 1194 and 1220.

It is interesting to note that the cathedral has two nonmatching spires. The plain one of simple architecture was built first; the elaborate spire in late Gothic followed later. On Sunday afternoons at 1645 during July and August, you can enjoy the organ recitals at the cathedral. Admission to these performances is free.

The district surrounding the cathedral is noted for its medieval houses. Time permitting, you should walk down to the river for a look at the old houses and bridges close to the restored Romanesque **Church of Saint André.**

The Cathedral of Chartres may be the most famous attraction in the city. There is a lot more to this ancient town, however. In addition to the Church of Saint André, there are others that warrant your inspection. The

DEPART PARIS MONTPARNASSE	TRAIN NUMBER	ARRIVE CHARTRES	NOTES
0700	—	0758	
0720	—	0830	except Sun
0815	—	0927	
0856	—	0955	
0915 (0910 Sa, Su)	—	1024	Sat, Sun
0930*	—	1032	
1025	—	1132	Mon–Fri
1115	—	1226	
1215	—	1326	except Sun
1230	—	1334	except Sun

DEPART CHARTRES	TRAIN NUMBER	ARRIVE PARIS MONTPARNASSE	NOTES
1526	—	1631	
1539	—	1635	
1550	—	1701	Mon–Fri
1648	—	1757	
1712	—	1800	Mon–Fri
1720	—	1831	Mon–Fri
1750	—	1901	
1822 (1824 Sa, Su)	—	1924 (1921 Sa, Su)	

and other frequent service until 2106
Daily, unless otherwise noted
* Mon–Fri Paris Montparnasse 3 Vaugirard
Distance: 55 miles (88 km)

Church of Saint Pierre is a Gothic masterpiece. Its stained-glass windows dating back to the fourteenth century, when added to those of the cathedral, make Chartres the metropolis of stained glass.

The **Episcopal Palace,** now the Museum of Fine Arts, has a lovely seventeenth-century facade in addition to its interesting contents. The exhibit includes a unique collection of harpsichords, painted wood carvings and art from Oceania, and many French, Flemish, and Italian paintings.

Chartres is bountiful in its art and has many museums and galleries to enjoy, such as the **International Stained Glass Center, La Maison de l'Archeologie,** and the **Maison Picassiette,** as well as the **Natural History Museum,** the regional **School Museum,** and the **Agriculture Museum** (COMPA).

To see all of the city's attractions, hop aboard *Le petit Chart' train* (The little train of Chartres). From April through October, the "train" departs daily on the hour from in front of the cathedral on a 35-minute tour of "Old Chartres." The first departure is at 1000; the last departure, at 1800. Adults, €4.88; children, €2.74. All aboard!

Fontainebleau
Palace of Kings

Depart from Gare de Lyon
Distance by Train: 37 miles (60 km)
Average Train Time: 45 minutes
Tourist Information Office: Office de Tourisme, 4 rue Royale
Tel: 01 60 74 99 99; **Fax:** 01 60 74 99 98
Hours: 0800–dusk daily, except Tuesday. Royal Apartments tours conducted 0930–1700 in June; 0930–1800 July–August; 0930–1230/1400–1700 November–May.
Notes: To reach the palace from the railway station in Fontainebleau, take the No. 1 bus marked Château from the station to the palace. The ride takes 10 minutes. No admission charge to palace grounds.

The Palace of Fontainebleau is most famous today as the residence of Napoleon Bonaparte, but the site attracted the presence of the kings of France and other royalty as far back in history as the twelfth century. For many, Fontainebleau signifies the spirit of France more so than does Versailles.

In 1169, Louis VII had the chapel of his manor at Fontainebleau consecrated by Thomas à Becket, the famous English archbishop of Canterbury. The palace that stands today probably owes more to the imagination of Francis I of France than any other of its monarchs. In 1528, he had the remains of prior centuries torn down and rebuilt; he then filled the new structure with sumptuous jewels, weapons, statues, and pictures—among them the *Mona Lisa* (which graced the bathroom)—as a suitable reclining palace for his mistress, the Duchess d'Etampes. In 1539, with the place set in order, he received his great rival, Emperor Charles V, in the new digs.

The fortunes of Fontainebleau slumped under the reign of Louis XIV. He was giving more attention to his new project at Versailles and his dalliances with Madame de Maintenon; but his successors, Louis XV and Louis XVI, were faithful to the palace as an autumn residence. Slowly, Versailles became the "in place" with French courtiers, and only the old retainers showed up to probe the forest surrounding the château for wild game. Fortunately, Fontainebleau survived the French Revolution much better than did Versailles and other royal residences closer to Paris. (Suburban living had its advantages even then.)

Fontainebleau has probably bedded more queens, court favorites, and royal mistresses than other palaces in France. (Versailles had its headliners, like Pompadour and Du Barry, but Fontainebleau was more discreet.) Under the new management of Francis I, the Duchess d'Etampes was granted a

Paris—Fontainebleau

In addition to the trains listed below there is frequent commuter train service to and from Fontainebleau.

DEPART PARIS LYON	TRAIN NUMBER	ARRIVE FONTAINEBLEAU -AVON
0717	5903	0753
0827	TER 91005	0904
1134	—	1212

DEPART FONTAINEBLEAU-AVON	TRAIN NUMBER	ARRIVE PARIS LYON
1504 (1519 Sa)	TER 91024	1545 (1558 Sa)
1719	5856	1802
1939	TER 91032	2030
2032	5920	2104

Daily, unless otherwise noted
Distance: 37 miles (60 km)

PARIS
Fontainebleau

chamber that later became known as the "King's Staircase" when Louis XV needed freer access to her apartments. Madame de Maintenon moved to Fontainebleau under the auspices of Louis XIV in 1686 and into a room that bears her name even today.

Since the beginning of the seventeenth century, every queen of France has slept in the queen's bed chamber within the palace. Marie Antoinette ordered the bed that now graces the chamber, but because of unfortunate developments, she never had the opportunity to lay her head upon its pillows.

When Napoleon Bonaparte became Emperor of France in 1804, he had Fontainebleau refurbished and refurnished to receive Pope Pius VII, who had come to crown him. From 1812 to 1814, the pope was also in residence in Fontainebleau—only this time he was not an invited guest but Napoleon's prisoner.

Not all of Napoleon's residence at Fontainebleau was surrounded with the fringe benefits befitting an emperor of his stature; he had some bad days, too. He signed his abdication in a room known now as the "Abdication Chamber" (formerly a bathroom) on April 6, 1814. Nineteen days later, he bade farewell to his officers and bodyguard in the Court of the White Horse from the horseshoe-shaped grand staircase that is now the main entrance to the palace.

Fontainebleau, unlike Versailles, possesses the secret of intimacy, no doubt due to the fact that each successive generation of kings or emperors added a wing of his own to the structure. The palace is full of nooks and crannies. There are back staircases and tapestries that pull aside to reveal secret hallways. Living in Fontainebleau, its occupants were surrounded by romance and intrigue. In a sense, it probably was the earliest version of the present "no-tell motel," but it had far more class!

The Germans used Fontainebleau as a military headquarters during World War II. Following the war, it served as a seat of the North Atlantic Treaty Organization (NATO) until 1965, when it became a public museum.

If you take the tour, and you should, your tour guide will lead you first through the Red Room, scene of Napoleon's abdication, then, in turn, through the Council Room, the Throne Room, and the Queen's Bedroom. From there, you pass through the Royal Apartments, then down the King's Staircase to the Oval Court, where the tour ends. It's intriguing.

The gardens and parks surrounding the palace are lovely throughout the year. You are invited to bring your own picnic lunch and spread it out on the royal grass as long as you don't litter the imperial landscape.

Day Excursion to
Rennes
Capital of Brittany

Depart from Paris Montparnasse Station
Distance by Train: 232 miles (374 km)
Average Train Time: 2 hours, 4 minutes
Tourist Information Office: Chapelle Saint-Yves, 11 rue Saint-Yves, CS 26410, F-35064 Rennes
Tel: 02 99 67 11 11; *Fax:* 02 99 67 11 10
Hours: April–September: 0900–1900 Monday–Saturday, 1100–1800 Sunday; October–March: 0900–1800 Monday–Saturday, 1100–1800 Sunday.
Notes: From the rail station, take avenue Janvier to the River Vilaine, where a left turn puts the office in view two blocks farther on.

There's an expression that has been making the rounds of the travel trade for some time now, "Half the fun is in the going." Rennes fully qualifies as such a day excursion, since you can go there on the TGV *Atlantique,* the pride of the French rail fleet and holder of the friction-rail speed record.

Once outside of Paris and onto its special right-of-way, the TGV (*train à grande vitesse,* or train of great speed) cruises at 186 mph, and you will be experiencing some of the finest rail travel in the world. Be certain to have seat reservations. It's not a "seat belt" ride—it's smooth and totally enjoyable. Outbound in the morning, you can enjoy breakfast as the French countryside flashes by; inbound returning to Paris, you are in for a "Happy Hour"

Paris—Rennes

DEPART PARIS MONTPARNASSE	TRAIN NUMBER	ARRIVE RENNES	NOTES
0635	TGV 8601	0852	Mon–Fri, 1
0705	TGV 8703	0908 (0926-A)	Mon–Sat, 1
0735	TGV 8607	0949	Mon–Fri
0805	TGV 8609	1020	
0905	TGV 8713	1108	
1005	TGV 8715	1208	
1105	TGV 8717	1325 (1321 A)	Mon–Fri, 1

DEPART RENNES	TRAIN NUMBER	ARRIVE PARIS MONTPARNASSE	NOTES
1605	TGV 8746	1825	
1705	TGV 8752	1910	
1735	TGV 8656	2000	except Sat, 2
1805	TGV 8760	2010 (2025 Sa)	
1835	TGV 8762	2040	3, B
1905	TGV 8770	2110	
1935	TGV 8774	2140	Sun
2005	TGV 8780	2215	

Reservations required on all TGVs
Daily, unless otherwise noted
A runs mid-July through end of August.
B Sat runs end of June through August, TGV 8658.
1. runs from end of August through mid-July.
2. Daily, mid-July through August.
3. Daily, end of June through August.
Distance: 232 miles (374 km)

you'll never forget!

Rennes is unique in that it doesn't remind you so much of France as it does the area around Cornwall in Britain. As the cultural capital of the French province of Brittany, it has some strong ties to its Celtic origins in its architecture and gastronomy. Rennes stands at the confluence of the Ille and the Vilaine Rivers. This junction of waterways came to the attention of Julius Caesar, and in 56 B.C., his legions conquered its original Celtic settlers, the Riedones. After this flurry of activity, however, things settled down for the balance of the Middle Ages.

At the beginning of the eighteenth century, Rennes still looked as it had for several hundred years—with narrow alleys and houses constructed of lath and plaster and no running water for sanitation or firefighting. History records that in the evening of December 22, 1720, a drunken carpenter set fire to a pile of shavings, which, in turn, set fire to his house and then spread rapidly throughout much of the town, destroying more than a thousand other buildings before it burned itself out.

The part of the wooden town destroyed by that fire was rebuilt with granite arches and stone along well-ordered lines. Gabriel, architect to the French king Louis XV, then designed a new Town Hall. Thus, Rennes developed its "New Town" that stands yet today and awaits your inspection following your arrival in its ultramodern train station designed specifically for the high-speed TGV *Atlantique*. Rennes's aesthetic value embraces its vibrant past, present, and future by offering visitors a wealth of architectural variety. It rightfully claims to be one of the prettiest cities in Brittany.

With a population of 200,000, Rennes describes itself as youthful, well-established, and dynamic. Well equipped with prestigious theater and museum facilities and augmented with a city orchestra and the **National Centre for Dramatic Art,** the city plays a major role in the cultural activities of the region.

In the first week of July, during the *Tombées de la Nuit* (Summer Festival), Old Rennes is illuminated with spotlights while ballets, songs, plays, or visual arts presentations are performed. Daytime attractions include the contemporary architecture of the Law Courts, *Le Triangle,* and the cultural center. Saturday mornings are always special with the open-air market.

Guided tours depart from the main tourist information office at Pont de Nemous daily at 1030 (also at 2100 on Tuesday and Thursday only) and at 1500 July 1–August 31. City tours in English are offered Wednesday at 1500 during summer months.

Evenings in Rennes are pleasant. The city is home to numerous eating places offering a wide range of local or exotic cuisine—each establishment exhibiting a character all its own. Located close to the Atlantic Ocean as well as the English Channel, Rennes offers a selection of seafood second to none. For fine seafood served in an authentic fifteenth-century house, dine at **l'Auberge St. Sauveur,** at 6 rue St. Sauveur (*Tel:* 02 99 79 32 56). As this is a university city, the bars in rue Saint-Michel and rue Saint-Malo attract the younger set, and there are plenty of concerts, plays, or films to keep the elders fully occupied, too.

TGV *Atlantique* service to Rennes opens up another day excursion opportunity, **Mont-Saint-Michel,** one of the great wonders of France. Operated by Les Courriers Breton, a special luxury bus runs between the rail station in Rennes to Mont-Saint-Michel, taking only 1 hour and 10 minutes. The bus runs daily during summer and Friday through Sunday only during the balance of the year. For details check with the House of Brittany in Paris, the Tourist Information Office in Rennes, or Les Courriers Breton in Saint Malo (*Tel:* 02 99 56 79 09).

Rouen
Joan of Arc Memorial

Depart Paris St. Lazare Station
Distance by Train: 87 miles (140 km)
Average Train Time: 1 hour, 15 minutes
Tourist Information Office: Office de Tourisme et des Congres, 25 place de
la Cathédrale
Tel: 02 32 08 32 40; *Fax:* 02 32 08 32 44
Internet: www.mairie-rouen.fr
E-mail: otrouen@mcom.fr
Hours: May–September: Monday–Saturday 0900–1900, Sunday 0930–1230 and
1400–1800. Remainder of the year: Monday–Saturday 0900–1800, Sunday
1000–1300.
Notes: The office is 5 minutes away from the station by taxi; 10 minutes on the
underground, which stops at the Théâtre des Arts, just two blocks away from the
office. Walking—and it's downhill all the way—takes about 20 minutes. Follow
rue Jeanne d'Arc from in front of the station, turning left at rue du Gros Horloge
(Big Clock). After walking under the clock, bear right at the cathedral plaza for a
few yards to the tourist office.

Rouen was established by the Romans, who selected the site as the
first point from the sea where a bridge could be built across the
Seine. Rouen became the capital of Normandy at the beginning of the
Christian era, and, despite many thrashings in many wars, it still contains a
number of lovely churches, towers, and other reminders of its colorful past,
such as half-timbered houses and town clocks.

Rouen is steeped in history and is considered one of the capitals of
stained glass. We told you Rouen was colorful! During the Hundred Years'
War, the city was held by the English from 1419 to 1449. **Joan of Arc** was
burned at the stake in Rouen by the English in 1431. Her memory is
commemorated during the last week of May every year during the Joan of
Arc Festival. Highlights include music and street entertainment, a medieval
market, parade, and fireworks.

Your train from Paris will arrive in Gare Rive Droite, the rail station in
Rouen on the right bank of the Seine. Several hotels, restaurants, and bars
are clustered about the station's plaza. The city abounds with eating and
drinking establishments—even McDonald's—so finding refreshments in
Rouen during your visit will be no problem.

The tourist office has prepared an English-language pamphlet describing
a tour itinerary that takes about 2 hours. It starts at the tourist office and
takes the visitor to the principal points of interest within the boundaries of

Depart Paris St. Lazare	Train Number	Arrive Rouen Rive-Droite	Notes
0732	3133	0838	except Sun
0806	13101	0934	
0807	13141	0915	Mon–Fri, 1
0816	13103	0943	Mon–Fri
0839	13103	1010	Sat
0915	3135	1021	
1051 (1044 Su)	3193	1157	
1204	13105	1336	except Sun
1240	3139	1345	except Sun

Depart Rouen Rive-Droite	Train Number	Arrive Paris St. Lazare	Notes
1418	13114	1544	except Sun
1424	3144	1532	Sun
1458	3146	1604	except Sun
1604	13148	1714	Sun
1611	13150	1721	Fri
1642	—	1825	Sun
1659	3192	1809	Mon–Fri
1719	3194	1843	Sat, Sun
1724	13116	1848	Mon–Fri
1737	3148	1846	Sun
1801	3104	1907	

and other frequent service until 2045

Daily, unless otherwise noted
1. Runs September through June
Distance: 87 miles (140 km)

165

PARIS *Rouen*

the historical town center. The railway station appears on the map, so you need not worry about finding your way back to the station.

First stop on the tour is the city's **cathedral**, which stands as one of the most beautiful examples of French Gothic architecture. Construction began in the twelfth century. It was leveled by a devastating fire in 1200 and it was not until the fifteenth century that it began to take on its present appearance. The cast-iron spire atop the cathedral's central tower is a nineteenth-century addition. Heavily damaged during World War II, the cathedral's restoration work still continues.

In order to rebuild the cathedral, Rouen had to revive the medieval skills of its original creators. The cathedral's structure was said to have gained its name from the fact that it was built with money paid by the faithful members of the parish for the privilege of consuming butter during Lent.

Following the tour itinerary suggested by the tourist office, the midway point of the tour will be the **Palace of Justice**. Three short blocks beyond, you will enter Rouen's **old market area**, with its narrow streets and half-timbered houses. There are more than 800 structures in Rouen that illustrate the typical architecture of the city from the Middle Ages to the end of the eighteenth century. The houses were termed *half-timbered* because their external and internal walls were constructed of timber frames, and the spaces between the structural members were filled with brick plaster or wattle—woven reeds covered and plastered with clay. You'll note that the upper stories of many half-timbered houses in Rouen project out over the ground level. This arrangement allows the lower part of the house to be protected against inclement weather.

Born a peasant in 1412, Joan of Arc believed she heard celestial voices. In 1429, during the Hundred Years' War when the English were about to capture Orleans, Joan convinced Charles VII (then Dauphin of France) of her divine mission and led the resistance against the English at Compiegne in 1430. Subsequently, she underwent fourteen months of interrogation by her captors and was then burned at the stake in the Old Market Square at Rouen on May 30, 1431. The Maid of Orleans, national heroine and patron saint of France, decisively turned the Hundred Years' War in France's favor.

The place in the old market where Joan of Arc met her fate is marked by a huge cross of concrete and metal. Towering over it is a modern church, completed in 1979, its roof representing the flames of the stake. It blends masterfully into the scene against a background of black-and-white timbered houses. The impact of history can be felt here.

Last stop is that huge clock you may have passed en route to the tourist office. It was positioned at ground level until 1527, when the people of Rouen asked that it be raised so they could see it better. The city council obliged by housing it in the elegant Renaissance structure you see today. The clock is unique in that it has only one hand. The globe at the top, which is no longer functioning, used to indicate the phases of the moon. Although the clock was converted to electricity in 1928, the original mechanism is still in place.

Day Excursion to

Versailles
Celebrated Site of France

Depart Paris for Versailles from any station on RER Line C
Distance by Train: 11 miles (18 km)
Average Train Time: 30 minutes
Tourist Information Office: Office de Tourisme, 2 bis, avenue de Paris
Tel: 01 39 24 88 88; **Fax:** 01 39 24 88 89
Internet: Tourist Office: www.versailles-tourism.com. Château: www.chateau versailles.com. Ville: www.mairie-versailles.fr
E-mail: tourism@ot-versailles.fr
Hours: April–September, 0900–1900 daily; October–March, 0900–1800 daily
Notes: To get to the tourist office, turn right as you exit the Rive Gauche station.

In the left margin:

PARIS *Rouen*

166

Walk about 100 yards to the next intersection, then turn left. You will find the tourist office and the palace about 20 yards farther on the left.

Paris's RER Line C runs between Orly Airport and Versailles. Suggested stations are Austerlitz, Orsay, Pont St. Michel, or Invalides, the railway station close to the Hotel des Invalides, which was founded by Louis XIV to serve as a military hospital and home for veterans. Gare Invalides can be reached via Métro line 8 or 13. Get off at the "Invalides" Métro stop.

Trains for Versailles also run from Montparnasse station, but the station in Versailles to which this line connects is a considerable distance from the palace. Trains running from Gare Invalides, however, take you to within easy walking distance. Trains on RER Line C from Gare d'Austerlitz in Paris terminate in Versailles. Therefore, stay on the train until it reaches the end of the line. The main function of this station appears to be assisting visitors coming to Versailles to see **the palace**. Bilingual signs and voice announcements will assist you.

Hours: May–September, 0900–1800 daily except closed on Monday; October–April, 1000–1200 and 1400–1700 Tuesday–Friday, 0900–1700 Saturday–Sunday.

Admission:

Passport (day pass): Chateau, Trianons, Groves	€13.72
Chateau, Grand Apartments	€7.47
Grand Trianon & Petite Trianon	€5.03
Guided Tour of the Groves (1100–1600)	€3.05

Note: All prices subject to change. Reduced fares after 1530. Separate tickets required for the King's Bedchambers and Private Apartments, Royal Chapel, Opera (guided tours only), and the Museum of French History. Audioguides available for rent.

You may purchase "e-Tickets" online at www.chateauversailles.com, which enable you to use the express line. Just pick up your tickets at the e-Ticket booth on the day of your visit (present a photo ID).

The only way to understand the powerful influence that France exerted during the centuries of monarch rule is to visit Versailles. Here, only at Versailles, can you come to appreciate the spiritual, artistic, and political renown of France and its lineage of kings.

In 1623, Louis XIII (1601–1643) ordered a hunting lodge built on a hill named Versailles in place of a windmill that had occupied the site until then. The lodge was erected in 1624. Liking the spot so well, he then ordered the lodge replaced by a grand mansion, which was completed in 1634.

His son, Louis XIV (1638–1715), the Sun King, liked the spot, too, hated the crowds in Paris with equal vigor, and envied his finance minister's fine home at Vaux le Vicomte to the extent that he came up with an order that put his dad's to shame—"Build a palace at Versailles to surpass all

Paris—Versailles

Frequent service to/from Versailles: RER Line C trains depart Gare d'Austerlitz every 15–30 minutes and terminate in Versailles Rive Gauche (Chateau) Station; journey time about 40 minutes Rive Gauche Station is significantly closer to the Palace of Versailles than the alternative RER Line C service to Versailles Chantiers or the SNCF station, Versailles Rive Droite.
Distance: 11 miles (18 km)

palaces!" Orders being orders, before long 36,000 laborers aided by 6,000 horses were at work building palace walls, digging lakes with canals to connect them, and transplanting a forest when the king and his gardener decided that God had planted it in the wrong place to begin with. Work continued on **the Palace of Versailles** over a period of 50 years.

The Sun King made certain that nothing from the outside world would be imported for Versailles if it could be created or found in France. The result was an extraordinary showcase of French culture.

Urged on, first by Madame de Pompadour and then by Madame du Barry, Louis XV (1710–1774) also ordered additions to the palace, including the Petit Trianon, which Louis XVI (1754–1793) gave to his wife, Marie Antoinette, when he came to the throne.

Despite the splendor of this edifice, Marie and her courtiers were drawn to the fantasies of a hamlet erected for her by her loving husband. There, among other rural objects, stood a dairy barn complete with cows, among which Marie and her companions would cavort—much to the consternation of the bovines, who had never observed such carefree antics before among the peasants of the land.

Versailles is an extraordinary complex of marvels where the kings of France stood in insulation against the distant horrors of the Revolution. Its restoration to the original is a marvel in itself—a testament to the heirs of its tradition.

Let your imagination run by visualizing throngs of court favorites, courtiers, teams of prancing horses pulling royal carriages over the cobblestones of the courtyard, chambermaids scurrying about, valets rushing with the linens of the gentry, and butchers carving the roasts for the banquets under the surveillance of the king's hounds—all of this seventeenth-century tumult, cacophony, and frenzy taking place on a scale many times greater than that of any Cecil B. DeMille production.

It is impossible to see Versailles completely in one visit—three perhaps, but nothing less than that. Consequently, set priorities (and this may sound silly) by going there the first time and just wandering around. Go back the second time and take the tour. Return the third time to see the things you missed or wanted to see again from the times before.

Germany

Germany's reunification, symbolized by the fall of the Berlin Wall in late 1989, had a great impact on the overall German economy and way of life; it also opened new doors to tourism. Unifying public transportation systems of the East and West did, of course, play a major role in the total reunification process.

Germany is a land based on a rich, complex history on track to a vibrant future. In recent years, Germany has seen an influx of refugees and foreigners that has fostered a political culture more tolerant of the customs and traditions of others.

Located in the heart of Europe, Germany makes a convenient starting point for travel, especially by rail, to nearly anywhere in Europe. Major airports for North Americans are Berlin, Dusseldorf, Frankfurt, Hamburg, and Munich, each of which is connected by rapid transit (S-Bahn) to the city's center.

The Germans are famous for brewing some of the tastiest beer in the world, and they love celebrating dozens of national, regional, and local holidays, holy or otherwise, with great passion, beer and wine tents, pageants, beer and wine, parades, beer and wine, festivals, beer and wine, markets, and lots of beer and wine.

The most well-known festivals include the German Mardi Gras, also known as Fasching, Fastnacht, or Fastnet, which includes masked balls; Munich's Octoberfest, which attracts people from all over the world; and the Hamburg Dom, Nuremberg's Christ Child's Market at Christmas and the Onion Market in Weimar.

Don't let the guttural German language frighten you; many Germans, particularly tourism and train personnel, are multilingual. It's the majority of Americans who are "unilingual."

For more information on delightful Germany, contact the German

Tourist Offices in North America: *Internet:* **www.germany-tourism.de**

New York: 122 East Forty-second Street, Fifty-second Floor, Chanin Bldg., New York, NY 10168–0072; *Tel:* (212) 661–7200; *Fax:* (212) 661–7174; *E-mail:* gntony@aol.com.

Toronto: 175 Bloor Street East, North Tower, Suite 604, Toronto, Ontario M4W 3R8, Canada. *Tel:* (416) 968–1570; *Fax:* (416) 968–1986; *E-mail:* germanto@idirect.com

Banking

- **Currency:** Euro (€)
- **Exchange rate at press time:** €1.10 = U.S. $1.00
- **Hours:** 0830–1300 and 1430–1600 Monday–Friday. Currency exchange offices are found at mainline railway stations, airports, and border crosspoints. They are generally open 0600–2200.

Be aware that many establishments in Germany do not accept credit cards. Major hotels, restaurants, and department stores do; but have cash handy for the smaller establishments that do not.

Communications

- **Country Dialing Code:** 49
- **Direct Dial:** AT&T Direct: 0130–0010; MCI 0130–0012; Sprint 0130–0013

Rail Travel in Germany

Deutsche Bahn AG (*Internet:* www.bahn.de), or GermanRail, operates more than 25,000 miles of the unified rail networks of the former East and West Germany. Massive investments in infrastructure and train stock, including use of tilting trains, have benefitted schedules and shortened journey times.

Germany's top-of-the-line, high-speed, long-distance **ICE** (InterCity Express) trains are big, bold, and beautiful, with an emphasis on passenger comfort and a wide range of services. There are 216 ICE trains of five different types, with the ICE 3 being the fastest at 300 kilometers per hour to reduce the travel time between Cologne (Köln) and Frankfurt from 2 hours 14 minutes to under 1 hour. ICEs, reaching speeds of up to 175 mph, depart hourly every day for major centers within Germany and into the Swiss cities of **Basel, Bern, Interlaken,** and **Zurich,** as well as **Vienna, Austria.** The network connects all major cities.

Each train has a restaurant car, termed **BordRestaurant,** with two sections—a traditional-style dining car and a self-service bistro. They're big on other amenities, too, such as headphones; private lockers in which to stow purses, cameras, or other valuables while you visit the BordRestaurant car; and some have video systems.

Changing trains in Germany is a snap. In many cities, platforms are designed in such a way that the train you need to transfer to may be

German Railpass

Railpass

| 4 days in 1 month | First Class | $260 |
| | Second Class | $180 |

Children age 7–11 travel at half the adult fare; under age 6 travel free.

German Rail Twin Pass
Price is total for 2 people traveling together

| 4 days in 1 month | First Class | $390 |
| | Second Class | $270 |

German Rail Youthpass
For travelers age 12–25, Second Class Rail Travel

| 5 days in 1 month | | $142 |

Additional Rail Days on German Passes

up to a total of 10 days	First Class	$34
	Second Class	$22
	Youth Second Class	$18
Twin Pass additional days	First Class	$48
	Second Class	$33

standing immediately across the platform from the train in which you arrive. Since most GermanRail trains are often configured the same—first-class cars in the front, second-class cars in the rear—you merely cross the platform to find the same type of accommodation on the connecting train.

Train platforms are divided into sections A to E. If you are traveling on a long-distance train, consult the train configuration display to easily determine where you will be sitting.

Just when we thought porters went the way of the dinosaur, **porter service** is available in Dresden, Frankfurt am Main, Hamburg, Leipzig, Munich, Stuttgart, and Berlin Zoo stations. The porters wear blue uniforms and red caps. (€2.56 for first 2 items of luggage; €1.28 for each additional item.) Luggage requires a deposit of €0.51 or €1.02.

ICE2s have even more legroom, electronic destination indicators on the *outside* of the train cars, digital display seat reservation units above the seats, electronic 220V sockets for laptop computers, and increased facilities for the disabled, and one car has a family compartment. The new ICE3 (NeiTec, or tilting) trains are even more high-tech and able to "tilt" to round curves at higher speeds.

Germany's **EuroCity (EC), InterCity (IC), D,** and **InterRegio (IR)** trains round out the mainline service. Regional services are provided by trains designated RE, RB, and SE. The **S-Bahn** ("Schnell," or "fast") rapid-transit system provides service to and from the suburban areas of Berlin, Cologne (Köln), Frankfurt, Hamburg, Hannover, Leipzig, Munich, Nuremberg, and Stuttgart.

Eurailpass, Eurail Selectpass, Europass, and **German Railpass** are accepted on the above-mentioned trains. Bonuses include:

- Scandlines/DFO–Free transport on the Puttgarden–Rødby Faerge (Denmark) and Sassnitz–Trelleborg (Sweden) ferry crossings (railpass must be valid in both Germany and Denmark).
- KD German Rhine Line boats between Cologne (Köln) and Mainz, and Koblenz and Cochem (extra charge for hydrofoil transport).
- EUROPABUS, 75 percent discount on the following routes (reservations in advance recommended highly): EB 189 Burgenstrasse (Castle Road): Mannheim–Heidelberg–Heilbronn–Rothenburg ob der Tauber–Ansbach–Nuremberg, *May to September.* EB 190/190A Romantische Strasse (Romantic Road): Frankfurt am Main–Rothenburg ob der Tauber–Augsburg–Munich–Füssen, *April to October.*
- Ferry Crossings, 50 percent discount with TT-Line crossing Travemünde–Trelleborg (Sweden); TR-Line crossing Rostock–Trelleborg (Sweden); Finnjet crossing Rostock–Helsinki (Finland) in Budget or Tourist IS classes (must book 7 days in advance).
- Group/student rate for Finnjet crossing Rostock–Helsinki (Finland).
- Wurm & Köck boat day trips between Passau and Linz (Austria), 50 percent discount.
- Mountain railroad Garmisch Partenkirchen–Grainau–Zugspitzplatt and on some cable cars in the summit area, 25 percent discount; plus reduced fare on the Freiburg–Schauinsland rack railway.
- 50 percent discount on boats operated by BSB, SBS, ÖBB, and URH on the Rhine River between Constance and Schaffhausen on Lake Constance, calling at Bregenz, Constance, Friedrichshafen, Kreuzlingen, Lindau, Romanshorn, Rorschach, Radolfzel, Ueberlingen, and the Isles of Reichenau and Mainau.

Base City:

Berlin

Internet: www.berlin.de or www.berlin-tourism.de
E-mail: information@btm.de
City Dialing Code: 30

Although eons apart, the modern city of Berlin and the ancient city of Jericho shared a common occurrence—their walls "came a tumblin' down." The Bible (Joshua 6) is a bit vague concerning the actual date of the occurrence in Jericho, but we do know the Berlin Wall "fell" on November 9, 1989, 28 years after it was built. Berlin became a whole city; Germany became one country; Berlin is the capital of the new Germany; communism is on the wane worldwide; and this city again has the largest Jewish community in Germany.

For Berlin, World War II ended on the afternoon of May 2, 1945. Of the 245,000 buildings in Berlin before the war, 50,000 had been destroyed or rendered beyond repair. There was no electricity, no gas, no water. Before the war, Berlin had 4.3 million inhabitants; in May 1945, the remaining 2.8 million began the task of clearing away the debris.

In July of that year, Berlin became a four-power city with a joint Allied administration composed of Britain, France, Russia, and the United States. This division into zones turned the former German capital into an island of occupation surrounded completely by a sea of Soviets. East and West were in complete agreement about abolishing Nazism, but they had no common or precise answer as to what would replace it. Moreover, it quickly became evident that the Soviet intention was to gain complete control of the city.

On June 24, 1948, the Soviets sealed off the West's section of the city and, on the basis of "technical disorders," shut off their supply of electricity. They were left with a meager 36-day food supply. A disaster appeared imminent, but two days later the largest airlift in history began. From July 1948 to May 1949, the Western Allies transported, in some 213,000 flights, more than 1.7 million tons of food and other supplies to the beleaguered city. While operating the airlift, seventy members of the Allied Air Forces lost their lives. On May 12, 1949, the siege was lifted. Berliners began demonstrating their political choice by moving en masse to the Western sectors.

By August 1961, faced with mass evacuation of their sector, the Soviets began erecting the Berlin Wall. In 1989, after 28 years of division, the wall that Winston Churchill called the "Iron Curtain" was breached in one night. Before it "fell," more than one hundred people lost their lives while attempting to cross it. The eastern part of Berlin, including its historic center, is once again easily accessible to visitors. The infamous Checkpoint Charlie was dismantled. Its guardhouse is now a museum piece. Except for a small section that will stand as a mute reminder, every vestige of the Berlin Wall has been removed.

With the demise of the Wall, Berlin nearly doubled in size. The reunited metropolis rediscovered the traditional rhythm that made it famous throughout the world and added some new ones. This city now offers incredible nightlife and never sleeps a wink. Hmm, did you pack your dancing shoes? Travelers from around the world are passing the word, "Berlin is worth the trip."

Once again, Berlin is without boundaries. As it's been explained to us, "Berlin is more than the sum of two halves," and we agree.

Arriving by Air

Tegel (TXL), Tempelhof (THF), and Schönefeld (SXL). All three airports are connected with the city center by buses and trains. *Internet:* www.berlin-airport.de

Tegel Airport, 5 miles northwest, is your most likely arrival airport. Exiting from Customs, you'll see an information office between two rows of ticket counters. Go there for transportation information. From that position, look over your right shoulder and you will see the money exchange office across the hall. ATMs are available near gates 4 and 10. Tel: 41 01 2306 from 0500–2300.

- **Airport–City Links:** Bus line X9, 109, or 128, as well as the Airport Transport, takes you from Tegel Airport to Berlin Zoo rail station in about 20 minutes. If you have baggage, the Airport-Transport system is recommended.

Schönefeld Airport is served by many European airlines; you should check with the airline taking you into Berlin as to its landing airport. Express train service to Berlin Zoo station (RE4, RE5) every half hour 0430–2300.

Tempelhof Airport is in the southwest section of the city. Surrounded by a sea of buildings, it is used for regional flights.

- **Airport–City Links:** Airport-Transport or S-Bahn lines S-9 or S-45. Both connect with the Berlin Zoo rail station. The No. 171 bus connects the terminal with Rudow U-Bahn (underground) station, Line U-7.

Arriving by Train

There are two major railway stations in Berlin: Zoologischer Garten (Zoo), and Ostbahnhof (formerly Hauptbahnhof or Hbf.). If you disembark at the Zoo Station, Berlin's main tourist information office is located nearby. There's ample time to get off the train, since it will stand in the station at least five minutes before proceeding on to Ostbahnhof. The S-Bahn trains and the city's U-Bahn (subway) connect the two stations. Train information for all of Berlin: (030) 19419 (0600–2300 daily).

Berlin Zoo Station

Centrally located in the western sector of Berlin. The majority of the city's hotels, pensions, hostels, restaurants, shopping centers, and entertainment is also in this area.

- **Baggage storage:** Berlin Zoo is not a baggage cart station, since ramps to the train level are nonexistent and elevators normally are not available for public use. Porters are available by prearrangement, but the best insurance for a no-hassle visit to Germany's capital is to observe the golden rule of rail travelers: Take one medium-size suitcase or two small ones—nothing else.
- **Money exchange:** Available at the DVB Bank Zoo. Use the Kaiser-Wilhelm Gedachtniskirche exit. Bank hours 0730–2200 Monday through Saturday and 0800–1900 Sunday. An ATM is available outside the bank.
- **Train information, reservations, and railpass validation:** As you descend from the trains into the main hall of the Berlin Zoo Station, there's a train information office in the *Reisezentrum* (Travel Center) to the far left. Open daily 0600–2300. A rail schedule machine allows you to look up train schedules and receive a printout. Facing the Reisezentrum, you'll find lockers on the left-hand side. Train departure and arrival information is posted on boards above the stairway.
- **A EurAide office** is located between the Reisezentrum and the station post office. During summer it is open daily; closed on Sunday and holidays during the remainder of the year. This office (like the one in Munich) is designed specifically to assist English-speaking travelers.

Berlin Ostbahnhof (formerly Hauptbahnhof)

Deutsche Bahn AG (DB), or GermanRail, service counter is located in the center of the main hall. The personnel can give schedule information 24 hours a day, 7 days a week, but don't count on their speaking English.

- For detailed information and to make reservations, go to the **Reisezentrum** (Travel Center), located along the back wall of the station, opposite the street exit. Hours: 0600–2300 daily. Lockers are to the right of the Reisezentrum as you face it.

- **Money exchange:** Facilities can be found by ascending either flight of stairs and walking toward the back hall. Hours: Monday–Friday, 0700–2200; Saturday, 0700–1800; Sunday, 0800–1600. There's also an ATM behind the DB service center.

Tourist Information/Hotel Reservations

For written information in advance, write to *Berlin Tourismus,* Marketing GmbH, am Karlsbad 11, D–10785 Berlin. *Tel:* (information/reservation hot line from U.S.) 011–49 1805 754040; *Internet:* www.berlin-tourism.de; *E-mail:* information@berlin-tourism.de

Hours: Monday–Friday 0800–1900; Saturday–Sunday 0900–1800

The city's main tourist information office is within easy walking distance. To reach it, leave the Berlin Zoo Station via the **Kaiser-Wilhelm-Gedächtniskirche** (Kaiser Wilhelm Memorial Church) exit and walk toward the ruins of the church. Its jagged steeple is a stark reminder of war's destructive power. You will see the **Europa Center** and its globe fountain, which Berliners affectionately refer to as "the wet dumpling." Stay on the left side of the Europa Center. The tourist information office is on the street side of the center, just before the Palace Hotel. *Address:* Budapester-Strasse 45, 10787 Berlin. *Tel:* (030) 250025. *Hours:* Monday–Saturday 0830–2030; Sunday 1000–1830.

Another tourist information office is located at Brandenburg Gate and offers the same services as the one in the Europa Center. *Address:* South Wing, Pariser Platz, 10117 Berlin. *Hours:* 0930–1800 daily. Both tourist offices can make hotel reservations (charge, €2.56).

For those interested in economical hostel-type accommodations, try **David's Home for Backpackers,** a privately owned hostel—no curfews, and you get your own key and a modest buffet breakfast. It's located about 7 minutes' walking time from the Berlin Zoo rail station (3 minutes by Metro, or U-Bahn). Cost is €17.90 the first night; additional nights are only €15.34. Advance reservations are necessary. Telephone from outside Germany: (4930) 395-7788; within Berlin, just dial 395-7788; *E-mail:* David. Berlin@hotmail.com or Fabian.Berlin@mailcity.com.

Getting Around in Berlin

One of the first things visitors should do on arrival in Berlin is acquaint themselves with the city's phenomenal fast-train system—the S-Bahn ("S" is for schnell—fast) and the U-Bahn (underground train or subway). During rush hours, trains run every 3–5 minutes and approximately every 5–10 minutes at other times. The S- and U-Bahn systems are augmented by trams and buses. You can purchase an excellent city map for €0.51, and the map of the S-Bahn and U-Bahn system is free of charge.

Standard tickets (*Einzelfahrschein*) for all forms of Berlin transportation cost €2.05.

The **Berlin Welcome Card** provides 3 days of free travel on all buses and trains operating within the A, B, and C fare zones of the Berlin and Potsdam public transport network (BVG) for only €16.36. Purchase the card at all BVG ticket offices, tourist information offices, and at many Berlin hotels. The card also includes vouchers for discounts of up to 50 percent at numerous museums, sightseeing tours, theaters, and other attractions.

Sights/Attractions/Tours

Top Tour is an innovative tourist bus system that makes 20 stops within the city, ranging from the Zoological Gardens in the west to Alexanderplatz in the east. You are free to hop off the red double-decker bus whenever you fancy and hop back on another one as you please. You get a free street map and information describing the stops. Another sightseeing bus line from the Zoo to Michelangelostrasse-Prenzlauer Berg was introduced in 2000. A 40-minute ride is €2.05. Contact BVG Call Center at 301 9449 or visit www.bvg.de. If you happen to be in Berlin in July, ask about special rave tickets and trains for the Love Parade, the largest annual techno rave demonstration. Call the tourist office.

Berlin is such a fascinating, pulsating metropolis full of attractions, nonstop activities and events that we can list but a few here. Don't miss a walk on Berlin's shopping and entertainment streets—**Kurfürstendamm** and **Friedrichstrasse**. Stop at No. 207–208 Kurfürstendamm for a journey through "A Story of Berlin," a multimedia presentation documenting the city's 800 years of history.

The **Friedrichstadtpalast** is Europe's largest light entertainment theater that features gala performances, artistic displays, dancers and solo singers, and a live orchestra. The **Berlin Zoo** is one of the finest in Europe, and there's no better place to relax than in the attractive **English Gardens**, dedicated by Sir Anthony Eden. Berliners call it the "Garden of Eden."

The dome of the **Reichstag** has become one of the main attractions. At 23.5 meters high and 40 meters wide, it proudly stands in solitary splendor over the renovated Reichstag, which inaugurated the German Bundestag in April 1999. Climb to the top for an enjoyable view of the city.

Berlin claims they have more museums than they have rainy days. You can obtain a 3-day **Museum Pass** for €8.18 from the tourist information points in the Europa Center and at Brandenburg Gate. It provides entry to more than 50 museums and collections over 3 consecutive days. There are more than 170 museums housing collections of art, original artifacts, and other intriguing creations. Following Germany's reunification, the state museums were restored and new ones built, including the **Vitra Design Museum** and the **Jewish Museum**. The **Gemäldegalerie** reunited an internationally renowned collection of more than 1,300 paintings from the 13th to the 18th centuries that had been separated since the end of World War II. Part of the collection went to the United States and part to Russia. The **Old National Gallery** reopened, as well. The **Berlin Teddy Museum** has a collection of some 3,000 teddy bears on display. It's located at No. 147

Train Connections to Other Base Cities from Berlin

Many trains make stops at several Berlin train stations on arrival and departure from the city. The primary station used other than Berlin Zoobahnhof is the rebuilt Berlin Ostbahnhof that was named Berlin Hauptbahnhof by the German Democratic Republic government. After its reopening in 1998, the name reverted to the one used before 1945. Other stations used are Berlin Wannsee, Berlin Spandau, Berlin Lichtenberg, and Berlin Schönefeld. Consult the detailed timetables of www.railpass.com.

Depart Berlin Zoo Station (Zoobahnhof) unless otherwise noted.

BERLIN

DEPART	TRAIN NUMBER	ARRIVE	NOTES
		Amsterdam Centraal	
0734	IR 2344	1435	
1134	IR 2342	1835	
1534	IR 2340	2235	
2256	NZ 1948	0935+1	R, Sleeper
		Brussels (Bruxelles) Midi/Zuid	
0622	ICE 825	1407	1
0721	ICE 944	1435	1
0821	ICE 827	1622	1
then hourly until 1322, followed by 1522			
2104	NZ 242	0609+1	R, Sleeper
		Budapest Keleti	
0741	EC 171	1958	2
1955	EN 229	1133+1	R, Sleeper
		Copenhagen (København) H.	
0634	IC 632	1359	3, R
1034	IC 872	1759	3, R
1434	EC 176	2159	3, R
2254	EN 110	0859+1	R, 2,4, Sleeper
		Hamburg Hauptbahnhof	
0634	IC 632	0857	
0751	ICE 1634	0959	
0834	IC 874	1057	
0951	ICE 1616	1159	
and continuing service (ICE, EC, and IC trains) at about 1 hr intervals until 2034.			
		Luxembourg	
0922	ICE 942	1721	5
2104	NZ 242	0939+1	R, 6, Sleeper
		Munich (München) Hauptbahnhof	
0626	ICE 1513	1309	2
0810	ICE 1515	1507	2
0841	ICE 593	1622	
1027	ICE 1517	1711	2
1041	ICE 595	1826	
1227	ICE 1519	1909	2
1427	ICE 1611	2109	2
1441	ICE 599	2226	
1627	ICE 1613	2309	2
2221	NZ 1901	0646+1	R, Sleeper
2256	NZ 51948	0918+1	R, Sleeper

Depart	Train Number	Arrive	Notes
		Paris Gare du Nord	
0722	ICE 944	1605	1
0922	ICE 942	1805	1
1122	ICE 940	2005	1
1322	ICE 848	2205	1
2140	NZ 242	0908+1	R, Sleeper
		Stockhom Central	
2254	EN 110	1240+1	R, 2, 4, Sleeper
		Vienna (Wien) Südbahnhof	
0941	EC 173	1933	
1955	EN 229	0821+1	R, 7, Sleeper
		Zürich Hauptbahnhof	
0841	ICE 593	1658	5
0939	ICE 795	1847	9
1139	ICE 797	1958	8
1339	ICE 799	2202	R, Sleeper
2121	CNL 479	0916+1	R, Sleeper

Daily, unless otherwise noted
R Reservations required
+1 Arrive next day
1. Change trains in Cologne (Köln).
2. Departs Berlin Ostbahnhof.
3. Change trains in Hamburg.
4. Change trains in Malmö.
5. Change trains in Bonn.
6. Change trains in Brussels.
7. Change trains in Vienna Hütteldorf station.
8. Change trains in Mannheim.
9. Change trains in Stuttgart.

Kurfürstendamm. Hours: Wednesday–Friday, 1500–1800; donations welcome. *Tel:* 893 39 65.

At some point during your visit, stand at the **Brandenburg Gate**—on either side—and feel democracy in action. Or, take Europe's fastest lift up 90 meters to the platform on the **Daimler Chrysler Building** for a spectacular panoramic view of this great city. Admission: €3.07; it operates daily 1100–2000.

Day Excursions from Berlin

Three day excursions have been selected. All of them—**Dresden, Leipzig,** and **Potsdam**—are typical German cities in their own right. Since the end of World War II, and until the "Fall of the Wall," they had been a part of the then German Democratic Republic, more often referred to as "East Germany." Consequently, tourist and transportation facilities are still being improved.

Dresden is an important city in the historic German state of Saxony, and probably best known for its product Dresden china. **Leipzig** is also a part of Saxony and owes much of its prestige to its cultural accomplishments. Potsdam owes its appeal to Frederick the Great, who took the concept of *sans souci* (without care or worry) and transformed it into the reality of the delightful Sans Souci Palace. It was also the scene of the Potsdam Conference in 1945, where Harry (Truman) met "Old Joe" (Stalin) and got to like him—at least for a little while.

Day Excursion to

Dresden
China, Carillons, and Culture

Depart from Berlin Zoobahnhof or Ostbahnhof
Distance by Train: 117 miles (189 km)
Average Train Time: 2 hours, 30 minutes
City Dialing Code: 351
Tourist Information Office: Dresden Tourist Board, Ostra-Allee 11, 0106 Dresden
Tel: 49–1920; **Fax:** 49 192 116
Internet: www.dresden-tourist.de
E-mail: info@dresden-tourist.de
Hours: April–October: Monday–Friday 0900–2000; Saturday 0900–1600; and Sunday 0900–1400
Notes: In the winter, the center is open on weekdays, but for fewer hours. A 5-minute walk on Prager Strasse, across the street from the rail station, will take you there.

Dresden's name is derived from *Drezdzane*, the old Slavic word for "forest people," who were the early settlers in the area. Dresden is situated in the wide, gentle valley of the Elbe River, about 19 miles (30 kilometers) from the northwest border of the Czech Republic. Although the city's fame comes mainly from its past cultural achievements, Dresden is also economically important and is best known for its Dresden china.

From its beginnings as a small Slavonic fishing village, Dresden developed a delightfully harmonious relationship with the river and the forest. As it grew, its scenic beauty was enhanced in the seventeenth and nineteenth centuries by builders who erected fine examples of Baroque and Rococo architecture. This, in turn, attracted a great number of artists and writers as Dresden grew into a modern, confident city of a half million citizens. With its architectural landmarks and its art treasures of Dutch, Flemish, and Italian collections, Dresden gained the well-deserved title "Florence of the Elbe."

On February 13, 1945, more than a half million bombs rained down on Dresden from Anglo-American aircraft. Thirty-five thousand citizens died, and more than 15 square miles of the inner city were reduced to rubble. The air raid devastated nearly all of the city's cultural monuments. Dresden was declared dead.

But Dresden is rising like a Phoenix. Dust from the air raid scarcely settled before restoration began on the **Semper Opera House.** Forty years to the day, on February 13, 1985, Dresden's population celebrated the reopening of this world-famous theater, and many other cultural and historic edifices have been rebuilt.

Dresden's *Altmarkt* (old market) is the historic center of the city, which was rebuilt between 1953 and 1956. The city's botanical gardens, completely destroyed in 1945, were rebuilt in 1950. Only nine zoo animals survived the air attack, but in 1961 the zoo reopened with a stock of more than 2,000 animals representing nearly 500 species.

With typical Dresden determination, on February 13, 1992, the city announced that the **Frauenkirche** (Church of Our Lady)—decried by the communists to stand in ruin forever—would be rebuilt.

The church's dome dominates the scene. The Frauenkirche is the largest German Baroque and Protestant church and also the world's largest centrally planned Protestant church. It is undergoing archaeological reconstruction, that is, incorporating the remaining fragments in the reconstruction. Another feature is **Raphael's** *Sistine Madonna.*

The church's reconstruction site is near the **Albertinum Museum** at Brühlsche Terrace. The Albertinum houses the New Masters Picture Gallery, the "Green Vault," treasure chamber, and numismatic and sculpture collections. Hours: 1000–1800 daily, except Thursday.

Beginning with a group of only 55 dedicated members, the Society to Promote the Rebuilding of the Frauenkirche now numbers more than 5,000 members in Germany, with active supporters from more than twenty other countries. Out of the ruin long seen solely as an admonition against war, the Frauenkirche is rising again as beautiful as ever—a symbol of the healing of war's wounds, with a resounding message of a strong desire for peace.

Obtain the *Tourist City Guide* from the tourist office. It contains a city map, places of interest, sight-seeing tours, and just about everything you might ever want to know about Dresden. The **Old Town** is on the left bank of the Elbe, and the **New Town** is across the river on its right bank. If you are an average sightseer, as we are, you can reach the Old Town area on foot from the city center in no more than 15 minutes.

Ask about the **Dresden Card** (€13.80; valid for 48 hours), which provides for free transportation on all tram and bus lines plus ferries on the Elbe, free entrance to many museums, and discounts on city tours. In typical German fashion, the city's *Rathaus* (town hall) has a *Ratskeller* (restaurant) in its cellar, where you may enjoy a cold draft and a sample of Saxon food before setting out to see Dresden.

Berlin—Dresden

DEPART BERLIN ZOOBAHNHOF	TRAIN NUMBER	ARRIVE DRESDEN HAUPTBAHNHOF	NOTES
0526	IC 879	0741	Mon–Fri
0722	EC 171	0952	1
0926	EC 173	1152	1
1126	IC 871	1341	
1326	EC 175	1541	

DEPART DRESDEN HAUPTBAHNHOF	TRAIN NUMBER	ARRIVE BERLIN ZOOBAHNHOF	NOTES
1416	IC 870	1631	
1616	EC 174	1831	
1816	EC 172	2031	
2016	EC 170	2231	1

Daily, unless otherwise noted
All trains also stop at Berlin Ostbahnhof
1. Also stops at Dresden Neustadt.
Distance: 117 miles (189 km)

One of the many magnificent edifices vying for your attention during your Dresden visit is the **Zwinger**. It is known as the most important Late Baroque building in Germany. The name "Zwinger" is a term used in the construction of fortresses and defines the space between the outer and inner ramparts. Heavily damaged in 1945, the Zwinger reconstruction was said to have begun "instantaneously" despite communist objections. It was restored to its present condition by 1963.

If you cross the Elbe, be sure to use Dresden's famous **Loschwitzer–Blasewitzer Bridge**. Opened in 1893, it was the only bridge to remain intact by 1945. The complex WWII German political and military organization known as the SS had the bridge set for destruction, but two Dresdeners, each unaware of the other's action, cut the wire to the explosives. The grateful populace of Dresden now refers to the bridge as the "Blue Miracle."

Make it a point to visit the **Old Masters Picture Gallery** in the Zwinger Semperbau and examine the famous views of the court painter Bernardo Bellotto. They show the city at the peak of its splendor.

Day Excursion to

Leipzig
Bach and Mendelssohn Memories

Depart from Berlin Zoobahnhof
Distance by Train: 113 miles (182 km)
Average Train Time: 2 hours
City Dialing Code: 341
Tourist Information Office: Richard-Wagner-Strasse 1, D–04109 Leipzig
Tel: 7104 260/265; *Fax:* 7104 271/276
Internet: www.leipzig.de
E-mail: lipsia@aol.com
Hours: 0900–1900 Monday–Friday; 0900–1600 Saturday; 0900–1400 Sunday; 1000–1600 holidays
Notes: Located directly opposite the rail station—5-minute walk

Like many cities and towns in Europe, Leipzig has an old and a new section. Leipzig's old town is located between three rivers: the Parthe, the Elster, and the Pleisse. No doubt the site selection had much to do with safety, and the proximity to three navigable rivers also indicates an early interest in trade. Leipzig has been known for its great trade fairs that date back to the Middle Ages and still attract businesspeople from all over the world.

The city's name is derived from *Lipsk,* the original Slav settlement named for the lime trees *(lipa)* growing there. Leipzig was built as a walled city in the eleventh century; the walls surrounding the old town were replaced in the eighteenth century by a ring of parks and promenades. Subsequently, Leipzig expanded in all directions by gradually incorporating the suburbs that were growing up around it—a tactic followed by many American cities.

Reconstructed from 1996 to 1998, Leipzig's main rail terminal (Hauptbahnhof) has 23 platforms (plus 4 outside platforms) and is the largest rail terminal in Europe. The three-level station houses restaurants, shops, cafes, meeting rooms, travel agencies, money exchange, and other tourist facilities. More than 800 trains move through the terminus daily, carrying an estimated 75,000 passengers. There's no need to worry about its size, since the Hauptbahnhof comes well equipped with pictographs.

The **Leipzig Card** provides transport on trams and buses and on the city railway to the **New Trade-Fair Centre.** There are also reductions on city tours, museums, concerts, Bach Festival tickets, and in selected restaurants. There are three types: 1-Day €5.26 (1 person); 3-Day €10.74 (1 person); 3-Day Group €17.38 (2 adults + up to three children under 15). Purchase at the tourist office, rail station, and many hotels or order online.

The main attraction on the old town's market square is the **old town**

Berlin—Leipzig

DEPART BERLIN ZOOBAHNHOF	TRAIN NUMBER	ARRIVE LEIPZIG HAUPTBAHNHOF
0610	ICE 1513	0801
0810	ICE 1515	1001
1010	ICE 1517	1201
1210	ICE 1519	1401

DEPART LEIPZIG HAUPTBAHNHOF	TRAIN NUMBER	ARRIVE BERLIN ZOOBAHNHOF
1554	ICE 1518	1746
1754	ICE 1516	1946
1954	ICE 1514	2147
2148	ICE 1512	2346

Daily
Distance: 113 miles (182 km)

hall. It was built in the record time of nine months in 1556 by Hieronymus Lotter. The building is one of the oldest Renaissance town halls still standing on German soil. Although severely damaged by fire during the Allied air raid on December 4, 1943, the building's facade remains almost unchanged from the sixteenth century. The city was governed from here until 1905, when a new town hall was erected in a more spacious area. Since 1909 the building has been the **Museum of History of the City of Leipzig.** Its attractions include the Old Council Chambers and special exhibits.

The **new town hall,** built between 1899 and 1905 on the foundations of earlier buildings, will also attract your attention with its 115-meter tower. It houses both the mayor and the city council.

Within the rim of the old town, the spires of the **Church of Saint Nicholas** (Nikolaikirche) and the **Church of Saint Thomas** (Thomaskirche) stand as sentinels over the scene. The first mention of Saint Nicholas was made in 1017; Saint Thomas was erected between 1212 and 1222 as the collegiate church of the Augustinian Choir. Its Late Gothic hall was added at the end of the fifteenth century.

The stained-glass windows of Saint Thomas, dating from the end of the nineteenth century, depict four historical personalities closely associated with Leipzig: Johann Sebastian Bach, Felix Mendelssohn Bartholdy, Martin Luther, and King Gustav Adolf II of Sweden. Saint Thomas became world famous from its association with Johann Sebastian Bach. The composer served as cantor of the church from 1723 to 1750. Since 1950, the remains of the great composer have lain in the church. For more information about the 4-day Leipzig Bach Festival (May 8–12, 2002), contact Bach-Archiv Leipzig, Thomaskirchof 16, PF 10139, 04013 Leipzig; *Tel:* 964–4182 or *E-mail:* jsbach@rzaix530.rz.uni-leipzig.de. Contact the tourist office for a highlights list of other 2002 events in Leipzig.

The **Church of Saint Nicholas,** although containing some of the oldest building remains in Leipzig, recently played an important part in the reunification of Germany. From 1982, the prayers for peace held every Monday under the sheltering roof of the church "transmitted" loud and clear signals to the Leipzig demonstrators—impulses that, during the days of October and November 1989, brought about the "gentle revolution" that led to the downfall of the communist dictatorship.

Music lovers also will not want to miss the **Mendelssohn House,** where the innovative composer Felix Mendelssohn Bartholdy lived and died. The Mendelssohn House has been restored to its original grandeur.

Outside Leipzig's old town you can visit the **Leipzig Zoo,** which was founded in 1878. The city information center will tell you it's "only a 15-minute walk," but perhaps a taxi would be better. Although the entire zoo remodeling project will not be finished until 2010, the world's largest primate area (30,000 square meters) opened in 2001. It includes a jungle landscape, tropical hall, and a research camp for chimpanzees, gorillas, and orangutans. The zoo is noted for its lions and tigers, including the breeding of some 2,500 purebred Berber lions. An unusual feature of the zoo is its "shop-window," whereby spectators are separated from the animals only by a moat—a *deep* moat.

From the rubble left at the end of World War II the city constructed a stadium seating 100,000 spectators. The stadium was the first major building project in Leipzig following the war. Three million cubic meters of rubble were used for the 23-meter-high terraces. At press time, the stadium is being modernized to hold 45,000 covered seats. The project is to be completed in 2002 in time for the German Gymnastics Festival.

Day Excursion to

Potsdam
Where Harry Met Joe

Depart from Berlin Zoobahnhof or Wannsee Station, or use S-Bahn
Distance by Train: 22 miles (36 km)
Average Train Time: 26 minutes
City Dialing Code: 331
Tourist Information Office: 5, Friedrich-Ebert-Strasse D–14412 Potsdam
Tel: (0331) 27–5580; *Fax:* (0331) 275–5829
Internet: www.potsdam.de
Hours: April–October: Monday–Friday 0900–1900, Saturday–Sunday 1000–1600. November–March: Monday–Friday 1000–1800 and Saturday–Sunday 1000–1400.
Notes: Located in the old market, a 5- to 10-minute walk from the railway station.

Turn right out of the station and walk across the Lange Brucke (Long Bridge) and up the Friedrich-Ebert-Strasse to the center, which is located on the right side of the street. Ask for the illustrated pamphlet *Info—Stadtplan Potsdam*.

Originally a small settlement of Slavs, Potsdam first appeared in German chronicles under the name *Poztupimi* (Under the Oak Trees) in a Deed of Gift dated July 3, 993. There are virtually no oak trees left in present-day Potsdam, but from days gone by you will find a large number of handsome oak mansions and palaces surrounded by beautiful parks.

After a period of almost total insignificance during the Middle Ages, Potsdam eventually entered the sphere of German history in the seventeenth century when Frederick William, the Elector of Brandenburg, decided to make Potsdam his place of residence.

In the eighteenth century, during the reigns of King Frederick William I and his son Frederick II, known as Frederick the Great, Potsdam grew to be a prestigious royal seat and garrison town. Frederick William I established a military orphanage where the boys "learned to work" in nearby factories and also drilled in "square bashing," which came in handy whenever the impoverished peasants could no longer stand their plight and chose to demonstrate in the town square.

Unlike many towns emerging from the Middle Ages, Potsdam was not surrounded by a wall until the eighteenth century. Oddly enough, the wall served not so much as a military protection as it did a device to prevent soldiers from deserting and dishonest folks from smuggling. Whether the wall contributed to the growth of the town is not known, but Potsdam did flourish under the Fredericks. The *Alten Markt* (old market), the *Hollandisches Viertel* (Dutch quarters), the Brandenburger Strasse, and the **Sans Souci Park and Palace** date to the era of their reign.

Frederick II was growing a bit "long in the tooth" and decided he wanted to live "without cares" *(sans souci)*. So, beginning in 1744 and during the following three decades, "Old Fritz" supervised the building of the palace and several other buildings, including his own tomb as a last resting place beside the palace.

The Rococo Sans Souci Palace was built from sketches by the king himself, together with designs by his architect, Knobelsdorff. With further additions made during the nineteenth century, Sans Souci stands today on a 717-acre complex as one of the largest and most significant parks in Europe.

But "Old Fritz" would not rest. After the Seven Years' War, in which he lost all the battles but won the war, he celebrated his "victory" by building another palace—the **Neues Palais** (New Palace).

The Potsdam Information Center conducts a bus tour from April to October that includes a tour of the **Sans Souci Palace** and its gardens. The tour (3 hours) leaves the center at 1100. Cost: €19.94. Open year round and closed Monday.

Berlin S-Bahn trains run frequently between many Berlin stations and Potsdam—4 or 5 trains each hour all day. In addition, Potsdam is a stop for many Deutsche Bahn mainline trains between Berlin and cities to the west—typically 3 or 4 trains each hour in both directions run from Berlin Ostbahnhof and from Berlin Zoobahnhof (some also stop at Berlin Wannsee Station). Journey time from/to Berlin Ostbahnhof is about 35 minutes, from/to Berlin Zoobahnhof about 20 minutes, and from/to Berlin Wannsee about 8 minutes.

Distance: 22 miles (36 km)

If you like palaces, you've come to the right place. **Charlottenhof Palace,** a part of the Sans Souci complex, comes complete with Roman baths. The baths, by the way, were not intended for the purpose of hygiene but formed a part of a museum-like dream world reflecting the romantic yearnings of Crown Prince Frederick William (Fat William).

The **Marble Palace** and the **New Garden**—called "new" in contrast with the "old" gardens at Sans Souci—were ordered built by "Fat William" when he was crowned in 1786. Hours: April–October, Tuesday–Sunday 1000–1700; November–March, 1000–1600 weekends only. Guided tours are €3.07; self-guided visits are €2.56. *Tel:* (0331) 969–4200 for more information.

Potsdam's **old town** is a great place to browse. Right in the center of it you feel as though you've been transferred to Holland. To attract Dutch craftsmen to Potsdam, more than one hundred middle-class Dutch Baroque-style houses were built between 1734 and 1742. The project failed in that it did not attract Dutchmen in the number expected, but the houses were inhabited, in turn, by Potsdam's craftsmen, artists, and military. Sometimes things just don't work out the way you want them to. Perhaps that is Potsdam's penchant—read on.

The son of Kaiser Wilhelm, Crown Prince William, built a second palace at the New Garden from 1913 to 1915. He named it **Cecilienhof** after his Crown Princess. Unlike his father, who never returned from his Dutch exile, the ex–Crown Prince did move back into Cecilienhof Palace in 1923 and stayed there until 1945, bringing a number of interesting guests.

From July 17 until August 2, 1945, Cecilienhof played host to the Potsdam Conference, the third and final meeting of Churchill, Stalin, and Truman. One of the conference aims was the unity of Germany, though what followed was actually its division. Harry Truman returned from the conference stating that he "liked old Joe." But just like the time when Harry met Sally, things didn't quite work out the way they wanted them to.

Base City:

Hamburg

Internet: www.hamburg-tourism.de
E-mail: info@hamburg-tourism.de
City Dialing Code: 040

189

HAMBURG

The Free and Hanseatic City of Hamburg is an impressive title—for an equally impressive city. Its 1.7 million residents are proud of their city and are eager to show it. Hamburg is the largest in a league of "Hansa" cities in Germany that medieval merchants organized to secure greater safety and privileges in trading. For a long time nobility was barred from entering this affluent city, which sits poised between the Elbe River and Alster Lake.

Hamburg is full of surprises. It has more bridges than the combined total of Amsterdam and Venice. The city's harbor is one of the leading ports in Europe and ranks as one of the top ten largest ports in the world—notwithstanding the fact that it is 68 miles inland from the North Sea!

Chartered in 1189, Hamburg occupies a 288-square-mile area, 20 percent of which is covered by water. To the delight of residents and visitors alike, about 10 percent of the city's total area has been landscaped into public parks. Many of these areas date back to the eighteenth century, when landscaping was fostered by the city's wealthy residents as one of the arts.

Hamburgians have their port to thank for the development of their city to its present stature—an expansive metropolis of international business and culture. During the first weekend of May, the Hamburgians begin a three-day celebration to commemorate the year 1189, when Emperor Frederick Barbarossa granted Hamburg its "free port" status. The term free port means that transit cargo is exempt from custom duties. Not all of the harbor area, however, is classified as a free port.

Arriving by Air

Fuhlsbüttel International Airport, 8 miles north of the city center. Although the airport has four terminals, all international arrivals and departures utilize Terminal 4. Icelandair, SAS, and Lufthansa operate transatlantic services between Hamburg and North America. Airport information: *Tel:* (040) 5075–0; *Internet:* www.ham.airport.de.

Airport–City Links: Express bus service between the airport and a nearby U-Bahn station where frequent train service into Hamburg is available. If you are burdened with baggage, use the Airport Express No. 52 bus;

departures every 15–20 minutes, 0539–2044, for Hamburg's Hauptbahnhof (main rail station). Journey time: 25–30 minutes. Fare, €4.35; round trip, €6.39. From city center to airport, service 0500–2020. Taxi stands in front of Terminals 1 and 4 (Tel: 66 66 66, 21 12 11, 22 11 22), follow the pictographs. Average taxi fare to the city center, €15.34.

- **Money exchange and ATMs:** Deutsche Bank in the arrivals hall of Terminal 4, hours 0630–2200 daily.

Arriving by Train

The Hamburg **Hauptbahnhof** (main rail station) appears as though it was constructed to handle the dirigible *Hindenburg*. Its immensity is impressive. There are 14 Gleise (tracks). Gleise 1–4 serve the S-Bahn, the suburban rail service; Gleise 5–14 are for regular train service. Most InterCity Express (ICE) trains glide in and out of the Hauptbahnhof on Gleise 13 and 14.

For a full-service restaurant, visit the InterCity Restaurant, accessible by elevator, on the station's second floor front. The Gourmet Station on the main floor features national and international dishes. It's informal. Opposite the Gourmet Station are various boutiques in the "Wandelhalle."

- **Baggage storage** carts are scarce. The baggage room is the best source for a cart or a porter.
- **Money exchange** hours, 0730–2200 daily.
- **Post office** hours, Monday–Friday, 0700–2100; Saturday–Sunday, 0800–2000.
- **International telephones** are on the second floor of the post office.
- **Train information** is in the *Reisezentrum* (Travel Center). Hours: 0530–2300 daily.
- **Railpasses** can be validated at window 20 or any window marked AUSLAND. Information windows are 21 to 24. If the attendant does not speak English, you will be referred to one who does.
- **Tourist office** in the main rail station open daily, 0700–2300 (*Tel:* 300 51 201 or 202).

Tourist Information/Hotel Reservations

- The *Hamburg Tourist Board* has an information office in the main rail station; exit Kirchenallee. For advance planning contact. Hamburg Tourist Board, P.O. Box 10 22 49, D-20015 Hamburg, Germany; *Tel:* from outside Germany, 49–40–300–51300; *Fax:* 49–40–300–51333; *E-mail:* info@hamburg-tourism.de
- Hot line for **hotel reservations** (0800–2000): 40 3005–1300; or use the Internet hotel booking service: www.hamburg-tourism.de

In addition to general information, the board's information service can provide accommodation bookings; bookings for port tours and Alster cruises; arrangements for guides; and tips on sight-seeing, dining, and shopping.

HAMBURG

Getting Around in Hamburg

Purchase a **Hamburg-CARD** at tourist information offices, from U-Bahn (metro) station vending machines, and at most hotels. The CARD is a real bargain. It entitles you to travel free on the city's bus and train systems, subways, and port ferries at any time within the card's period of validity. It also provides free admission to 11 museums and includes reductions up to 30 percent for such activities as the Alster tour, the Port tour, and the entrance fee to Hamburg's famous Hagenbucks Zoo.

The Hamburg-CARD is available as a daily card (€6.54 for 1 adult and up to 3 children age 12 or under, or €12.53 for up to 5 persons) or a 3-day card (€13.50 for 1 adult and 3 children or €21.99 for up to 5 persons). The tourist information office will provide you with a brochure, *City Map and Tips from A to Z*, which explains the card's features. Those under age 30 should consider the **Hamburg Youth Pass**—1 day for €6.39 and €2.81 for each additional day up to seven days.

Sights/Attractions/Tours— Hamburg Highlights

A tour of the harbor by launch is available year-round. (The launches are heated in winter.) In summer, the tour operates every half hour from 0900–1800; for winter tours contact the tourist information office. The launches sail from St. Pauli pier. From the Hauptbahnhof, take either the U-Bahn line U3, or S-Bahn lines S1 or S3 to the Landungsbrücken station. Tickets: €7.67 adults; €3.83 children. Hamburg-CARD holders pay €5.62 and €3.32, respectively. The tour takes about one hour. Ask for a launch with an English-speaking captain.

From April through October, leisure cruise boats depart from the quay at Jungfernstieg—Hamburg's elegant shopping street—to **cruise on Lake Alster**. Actually, the Alster is not really a lake. It is a tributary of the Elbe River that has been widened into a lake just before it flows into the Elbe River. This 460-acre lake, an area larger than the entire principality of Monaco, was created when the Alster was dammed in the early thirteenth century.

There is a wide selection of tours available on the Alster boats, including a one-hour trip along its shoreline, a tour of the city's canal system, a bridge tour where you'll see a sampling of the city's 2,400 bridges, and a twilight tour. A guided tour of the **Inner and Outer Alster** operates every half hour, 1000–1800; tour duration, about 50 minutes. Adults: €8.18; children, €4.09; Hamburg-CARD holders receive a discount. Even in winter, the Alster boats cruise the lake for the popular "punch" cruises. To inquire, visit the **Alster-Touristik office** on the quay where the boats depart (*Tel:* 3574240). Brochures are also available in all of the Hamburg tourist offices.

Take a ride on the **Hamburger Hummelbahn**. Hamburg-CARD holders get a substantial discount. *Hummel* is German for "bumble bee," and this amazing form of transportation literally "buzzes" all over town. The train does

Train Connections to Other Base Cities from Hamburg

Depart from Hamburg Hauptbahnhof, unless otherwise noted.

DEPART	TRAIN NUMBER	ARRIVE	NOTES
		Amsterdam Centraal	
0647	IC 703	1149	1
0847	IC 705	1349	1
1115	MET 1036	1656	2
1247	IC 601	1749	1
1515	MET 1032	2054	2
1647	IC 603	2149	1
		Berlin Zoobahnhof	
0654	EC 173	0923	
0800	ICE 1517	1007	
0900	IC 871	1123	
and continuing hourly service until 2108.			
		Bern (Berne)	
0824	ICE 73	1611	
1935	CNL 471	0811+1	R, 3, Sleeper
		Brussels (Bruxelles) Midi/Zuid	
0647	IC 703	1407	4
0747	EC 109	1435	4
0847	IC 705	1622	4
then hourly departures until 1347 (plus 1115) followed by 1547, and			
2236	NZ 236	0609+1	R, Sleeper
		Budapest Keleti	
0803	ICE 91	2233	5
2038	EN 491	1303+1	R, 5, Sleeper
		Copenhagen (København) H.	
0728	EC 31	1159	
0928	EC 33	1359	
1328	EC 35	1759	
1728	EC 37	2159	
		Milan (Milano) Centrale	
0620	ICE 775	1835	3
0824	ICE 73	2035	3
0924	ICE 575	2245	6
1935	CNL 471	1235+1	R, 3, Sleeper
2203	NZ 1989	1450+1	R, 7, Sleeper
2241	NZ 1907	1645+1	R, 6, Sleeper
		Munich (München) Hauptbahnhof	
0603	ICE 783	1212	
0708	ICE 583	1258	
0905	ICE 585	1458	
1003	ICE 787	1612	
and continuing ICE service at hourly intervals until 1906, then			
2203	NZ 1989	0704+1	R, Sleeper

DEPART	TRAIN NUMBER	ARRIVE	NOTES
		Paris Gare du Nord	
0747	EC 109	1605	R, 4
0947	IC 505	1805	R, 4
1147	IC 801	2005	R, 4
1347	IC 507	2205	R, 4
2286	NZ 236	0908+1	R, Sleeper
		Rome (Roma) Termini	
1403	ICE 881	0817+1	R, 7, Sleeper
1424	ICE 79	0935+1	R, 3, Sleeper
1935	CNL 471	1830+1	R, 8, Sleeper
		Stockhom Central	
0728	EC 31	1740	R, 10
0928	EC 33	1940	R, 10
1728	EC 37	0610+1	R, 9, Sleeper
		Vienna (Wien) Südbahnhof	
0803	ICE 91	1747	
2038	EN 491	0855+1	R, Sleeper
		Zürich Hauptbahnhof	
0620	ICE 775	1358	3
0824	ICE 73	1558	3
1024	ICE 71	1758	3
1224	ICE 77	1958	
1424	ICE 79	2202	
1935	CNL 471	0816+1	R, Sleeper

Daily, unless otherwise noted
R Reservations required
* Thalys high-speed train, supplement required
+1 Next day
1. Change trains in Osnabrück.
2. Change trains in Düsseldorf.
3. Change trains in Basel.
4. Change trains in Cologne (Köln).
5. Change trains in Vienna (Wien) Westbahnhof.
6. Change trains in Stuttgart.
7. Change trains in Munich (München).
8. Change trains in Zürich then Milan.
9. Change trains in Mälmo.
10. Change trains in Copenhagen.

not run on tracks. Its open platforms are ideal for photographing. It's a fun trip.

Prefer a frightening one? Visit 2,000 years of terror and pain at the **Hamburg Dungeon** (€9.20 adults; children under 12 must be accompanied by an adult, and it's recommended to not bring them at all). Perhaps a gruesome souvenir would suffice instead. Open daily 1000–1900. *Tel:* 040 3600 5500; *Internet:* www.thedungeons.com.

If you are in Hamburg on a Sunday, reserve a good part of the day for a visit to the **Fischmarkt** (fish market). Dating from about 1703, it is the oldest licensed market in Hamburg. Fish? Well, fish have become incidental to the market's activities; freshly caught fish, however, are still sold any day of the week from fishing boats at the city's pier.

On Sunday mornings, the pubs scattered around the fish market area draw crowds of early risers and late-night revelers alike. Take in the Sunday-morning auction activities held in the **Fischauktionshalle** (fish auction hall). The auction hall opens promptly at 0500 (0700 in winter) and lasts only until 1000, so hurry. Following the auction, treat yourself to a jazz breakfast right in the Fischauktionshalle.

Shopping is an international pastime, and Hamburg is a wonderful place to pursue such interests. No city on the Continent has so many covered shopping arcades. As a jumping-off place, start at the **Jungfernstieg**, where the white ferries depart for water tours of the Alster Lake. Here, you will find covered arcades where shoppers may stroll regardless of the weather. For big department-store shopping, head for **Monckebergstrasse**, directly east from the **Rathaus**, Hamburg's city hall. Or, get off to a flying start right after arriving by train in Hamburg at the Wandelhalle, the covered mall above the train platforms in the Hauptbahnhof.

A unique memory will be a visit to the **Speicherstadt**, built in the late nineteenth century. This historic warehouse complex was built during the growth of the free port and served as storehouses along the crisscrossing canals of the day. Hamburg abounds in museums. Two museum ships are the *Rickmer Rickmers*, a reminder of bygone days when sailing ships ruled the waves, and the *Cap San Diego,* the "White Swan of the South Atlantic." Both offer discounts to Hamburg-CARD holders and are open daily starting at 1000.

At night, **St. Pauli,** the entertainment district, offers numerous pubs, restaurants, and discos along the (in)famous **Reeperbahn, Hans-Albers-Platz,** and **Grosse Freiheit.** Yes, this is the area the beer (St. Pauli Girl) is named after.

Special events for the year include the 2002 Port Birthday May 9–12; and the wonderful Hanseatic Christmas Market at the end of November. Call the tourist office for details and information on other events.

Day Excursions

Hamburg is situated in the center of a vast railway network. Consequently, the availability of day-excursion opportunities is virtually limitless.

Bremen, another great Hanseatic city of Germany, is quite a contrast to Hamburg, although jointly the two provide the largest operation of seaports within Germany today.

To the south of Hamburg, in the midst of the Weser Hills, stands the fascinating town of **Hameln,** where the tale of the legendary Pied Piper is reenacted every Sunday.

Ride the pride of the German fleet—the German ICE (InterCity

Express)—to **Hannover** for a rewarding day of sight-seeing amid the city's beautiful parks and gardens.

Lübeck is Germany's largest Hanseatic port on the Baltic and one of the oldest and most beautiful towns in Germany today. Go early and enjoy!

Day Excursion to

Bremen
And the Town Musicians

Depart from Hamburg Hauptbahnhof
Distance by Train: 76 miles (120 km)
Average Train Time: 55 minutes
City Dialing Code: 421
Tourist Information Office: Findorffstrasse 105, D-28215 Bremen
Tel: 01805–101030; *Fax:* (0421) 30 800–36
Internet: www.bremen-tourism.de
E-mail: btz@bremen-tourism.de
Hours: 0930–1830 Monday–Friday (until 2000 on Thursday and Friday); 0930–1600 Saturday–Sunday
Notes: A tourist information office is at the railway station.

Bremen is Germany's oldest maritime city. Bremen got its start as a port city in the tenth century when Emperor Otto I approved the construction of its docks. It lies on the Weser River, 44 miles upstream from the mouth. Bremen is the second largest port in Germany. With so much to see and do in Bremen, rail travelers visiting Bremen for the first time may want to confine their sight-seeing to the area in and around the city's market square, then follow up with a second visit to the city's extensive harbor facilities. Certainly the charm of the market and its immediate surroundings will beckon the traveler to return again.

Finding your way from the Bremen railway station to the **market square** is an easy task. Attendants there can give you a considerable amount of information regarding Bremen. Particularly informative is a free brochure entitled *Bremen, Everything at a Glance.* The brochure contains background information on all aspects of Bremen.

The most direct route to the market square is down **Bahnhofstrasse,** which begins in front of the station. Proceed to where it intersects with Sogestrasse and crosses a former moat. A landmark at this point is a large windmill, seen in the distance on the right when crossing the bridge. Proceeding two blocks straight ahead on Sogestrasse brings you to the threshold of the old city center. A short walk through a shopping area and

IC trains depart Hamburg Hauptbahnhof hourly at 47 minutes past the hour from 0847; journey time to Bremen Hbf is 58 minutes.
Trains depart Bremen Hbf hourly at 14 and 24 minutes after the hour until 2114, and then at 2218, 2233, and 2318; journey time is 54 minutes.
Distance: 76 miles (120 km)

HAMBURG *Bremen*

you are in the market square, where the **cathedral**, the **Rathaus** (city hall), and the **Liebfrauenkirche** are all clustered.

Bremen's oldest resident, the statue of *Roland*, which was erected in 1404, is the center attraction in the market square. Roland is a symbol of justice and freedom. Legend has it that Bremen will not pass away as long as the stone giant is still standing in the marketplace. Legend also has it that the city fathers have a replacement ready—just in case.

No one is quite certain as to Roland's origins. City history first mentions the existence of the knightly statue in the marketplace in 1366, but it was made of wood and went up in flames. So did its wooden replacement. The stone statue has fared better.

The seventeenth-century facade of the Rathaus makes it one of the most photographed public buildings in the world. Rising above the town hall are the twin towers of the eleventh-century **Saint Peter's Cathedral**, site of an ancient sand dune where the earliest Bremeners sought refuge from the surging tides of the Weser River.

Seek out the cellar of the town hall. It is said that the people of Bremen are most at their ease in a cellar—and this cellar is one of the best. It's a Ratskeller with more than 650 varieties of German wines to sample. Chances are if you find it, it may be a while before you see the light of day again.

The bronze statue of Bremen's *Four Musicians* (the donkey, dog, cat, and rooster) is stashed away in a cranny between the Rathaus (town hall) and the Liebfrauenkirche, the Church of Our Blessed Lady. Be certain you find and photograph it, or your kids will never forgive you. The *Four Musicians* is one of several statues erected in Bremen honoring the Brothers Grimm fairy tales. If you delve into the true origins of the odd assortment of these domestic animals, apparently they are symbolic of a peasants' revolt against aristocracy rather than the Grimms' version of frightening off robbers—but don't tell the kids. A free open-air stage performance at Liebfrauenkirchhof Square takes place on Sunday at noon and 1330 (May–September).

The **Böttcherstrasse**, a narrow street leading off the market square, was redeveloped as a center for arts and crafts, with shops, workshops, art collections, and fine restaurants—even a casino. At the end of the street you will come to the Martini Church on the banks of the Weser—the area known as "the **Schlachte Embankment**." Here, the recently redesigned riverside promenade is inviting for leisurely strolls and a myriad of restaurants and cafes offer national and/or international cuisine. Boat tours of the

Bremen harbor, the Island of Heligoland (tax-free shopping), and other destinations depart from the piers immediately in front of the church.

Another area that you can reach on foot by walking upstream along the banks of the Weser is the **Schnoor.** The oldest surviving residential area within the city of Bremen, it boasts quaint little houses, inns, and workshops dating back to the sixteenth, seventeenth, and eighteenth centuries.

City sight-seeing tours depart daily from the bus station in front of the main railway station at 1030. Tickets (€14.57 adults; children up to age 12, €9.20) must be obtained beforehand at the tourist information office. Trips around the harbor depart the Martini Church jetty daily at frequent intervals from March through October. The trip lasts 1¼ hours.

Anywhere in Bremen, the marketplace, the Böttcherstrasse, and the Schnoor included, you may come upon a chimney sweep garbed in traditional swallow-tailed coat and high, black hat. Reach out and touch him, for it is said that doing so brings good luck. Everyone does, and it's quite an exciting time when one passes through a crowd. Legends old and new abound in Bremen. Enjoy your visit.

Day Excursion to

Hameln
Where the Pied Piper Played

Depart from Hamburg Hauptbahnhof
Distance by Train: 148 miles (233 km)
Average Train Time: 2 hours, 25 minutes
City Dialing Code: 5151
Tourist Information Office: Hameln Marketing and Tourismus GmbH, Deisterallee 1,
   D-31785 Hameln
Tel: 95 78 23; *Fax:* 95 78 40
Internet: www.hameln.de
E-mail: touristinfo@hameln.de
Hours: May–September: Monday–Friday 0900–1900, Saturday–Sunday 0930–
   1600. October–April: Monday–Friday 0900–1800
Notes: A short walk from the Hameln railway station. Walk through the square in
   front of the station, turning right onto Bahnhofstrasse. At the first traffic light,
   turn left onto Deisterallee. When you note a modern glass building on the right
   of the main street (Deisterallee), you are in front of the tourist information office.

Hameln's Old Town will hold you spellbound with its cobblestone walks, ancient facades, and cozy eating places. If a time machine is ever invented, its first journey might well be to Hameln to confirm—or

Hamburg—Hameln

HAMBURG-HANNOVER-HAMELN
trains depart at 24 and 28 minutes past the hour. Journey time 2 hours 15 minutes.
HAMELN–HANNOVER–HAMBURG
trains depart at 20 and 50 minutes past the hour until 2120. Journey time averages
2½ hours.

Change trains in Hannover. S-Bahn trains for Hannover–Hameln
Distance: 148 miles (233 km)

HAMBURG *Hameln*

dispel—the *Legend of the Pied Piper.*

Fact or fable, the town's archives reflect that on June 26, 1284, an itinerant *Rattenfänger* (rat catcher) attired in a multicolored costume trilled his flute, and 130 children followed him out of town to an unknown fate. Only three children survived—one boy had returned for his coat and was left behind, a little blind lad lost his way, and a mute youngster returned but was unable to tell the story.

This most famous kidnapping supposedly happened in retribution for the town's elders' not paying the Pied Piper for his previous performance, when he trilled the town's burgeoning rat population to the Weser River, where they drowned. Moral of the story: You have to "pay the Piper."

The story of **Hameln's Pied Piper** is the most well known of all German folklore. It appeared in the *Brothers Grimm German Legends* and has been translated into at least thirty languages. There are probably as many theories as to what actually happened as there are children who disappeared—maybe more. The most probable explanation relates to the colonization of an area in the Czech Republic to which many citizens of Hameln migrated after being recruited by wealthy nobles during the same time in history. Peasants were referred to frequently as the children of towns, so it is quite possible that the tales became tangled. The present citizens, however, appear to be happy that it worked out the way the Brothers Grimm recorded it.

Every Sunday from mid-May through mid-September, a live reenactment of the event is staged in the town square. The colorful Piper, plus 50 or so of the town's children (attired in charming "rat" costumes) and another 20 adults representing the town mayor and citizens of Hameln, begin their performance promptly at noon.

You will have about 20 minutes to change trains in Hannover. You will realize you are approaching Hameln when you see the silhouette of the famous Piper on the railroad control tower. If you plan to arrive in Hameln for the performance at noon on Sunday, go directly to the town square.

Adjacent to the main tourist office at Deisterallee on the right is a beautiful park, the **Burgergarten.** The park is readily identified by its pleasant green gate with the silhouette of the Pied Piper. The tourist information office conducts 1-hour guided walking tours (in German) every day from

April through October at 1500 (cost €3.07 per person). Ask the tourist office for prices of English-speaking tours. You can even arrange for a tour with the Piper himself, including an autograph!

If you're making your own walking tour, turn right when leaving the tourist information office and take the pedestrian underground route. Follow the signs reading ALTSTADT (Old City). When you leave the underground passageway, you will be on Osterstrasse. The **Gaststatte Rattenfängerhaus** (Pied Piper House), which is a charming restaurant, will be to your immediate left. Either pause for refreshments here or proceed on Osterstrasse to the town hall, situated at the end of the street by the marketplace. En route, you will find several other attractive restaurants and cafes.

The Pied Piper isn't Hameln's only attraction—sight-seeing in the Altstadt alone could fill your entire day. During the summer, it is possible to take a steamboat trip on the Weser River or stroll through the extensive woods surrounding Hameln. Visit **Museum Hameln** on Osterstrasse. Hours: 1000–1630 Tuesday–Sunday. It contains an extensive collection of civic art and culture dating back to the origins of Hameln, including the Pied Piper legend.

You can observe the 2,000-year-old craft of glass-blowing and engraving in the historical **Pulverturm** (glassworks). The old and the new have been blended successfully in Hameln.

Day Excursion to

Hannover
Follow the Red Thread

Depart from Hamburg Hauptbahnhof
Distance by Train: 111 miles (178 km)
Average Train Time: 1 hour, 30 minutes
City Dialing Code: 0511
Tourist Information Office: Hannover Tourist Service, Ernst-August-Platz 2, D-30159 Hannover, *Tel:* 168–49700; for packages, *Tel:* 168–49701/2; *Fax:* 168–49707. Hotel Bookings: *Tel:* 168–49816/17/18; *Fax:* 168–49709
Internet: www.hannover-tourismus-service.de
E-mail: tourismus-service@hannover-stadt.de
Hours: 0900–1900 Monday–Friday; 0930–1500 Saturday
Notes: Exit the station and turn to the right. The tourist office is on the right in the Hauptpost (main post office) building. Watch for the "Red Thread," a painted red line that runs directly to the information office.

H annover is known throughout the world as a commercial center dating back almost 900 years. Ideally located in the center of Europe, it is well served by rail and air. As a world leader in hosting international events, Hannover hosted the first world's exposition ever to be held in Germany—EXPO 2000: Humankind–Nature–Technology—and unveiled Germany's new ICE3 trains.

The history of Hannover is interesting in that it produced the lineage of Britain's present royal family. George I of England was born in Hannover, as was his son and successor, George II. Thoroughly German in tastes and habits, both monarchs made frequent trips back to Hannover, where they also ruled under the title of "Elector." George III, who presided over the loss of Britain's American colonies, was the grandson of George II and the first English King George to be born on British soil.

Hannover's rail station, constructed initially between 1876 and 1879, has had numerous improvements, although it has retained its original nineteenth-century facade. Fourteen tracks serve passenger traffic from an elevated platform. A concourse at ground level connects all the tracks with the main station area. Running under the main station area and extending under the station's plaza and into the city is a shopping mall.

The **"Red Thread"** (the painted red line on the ground) is actually an unusual walking tour of the city. Follow the red line that runs through the city's sight-seeing points, but do it with a Red Thread booklet that you can pick up at the tourist office for a nominal charge. The booklet fits easily in your hand—or it's small enough to slip into your pocket if you want to avoid looking like a tourist. It contains a map outlining the 2-hour walking tour and describes 36 points of interest you will pass while following the Red Thread. Take a camera with a wide-angle lens. Each point of interest has been numbered and the number placed so that if you stand on the number while photographing the scene, you'll have the best shot possible.

Highlights of the Red Thread walking tour include the **Gallerie Luise,** a pedestrian shopping area; the city's **1852 Opera House;** the old city wall; and the new city hall. Hannover's oldest half-timbered building, dating from 1566, is also seen on the tour, which ends "under the stallion's tail"—unless you have succumbed on the tour route to the charm of the local fräuleins or bierstube.

Bus tours are conducted daily. The tour, which is described in English, takes 2½ hours; ticket, €12.78 for adults and €7.67 for children up to age 14 and college students.

Purchase a one-day **HannoverCard** at the tourist information office for €6.65 (single) and receive a 40 percent reduction on the tour. Other benefits include free travel on all GVH buses and trams in fare zones 1 and 2 and a myriad of other sight-seeing reduced fares, including a cruise on Hannover's downtown lake, Maschsee.

Frequent service of at least two trains per hour in both directions from about 0700 to near midnight daily.

DEPART HAMBURG	TRAIN NUMBER	ARRIVE HANNOVER
0708	ICE 583	0826
0724	ICE 573	0839
0729	ICE 1081	0900
0803	ICE 91	0923
0824	ICE 73	0939
0908	ICE 585	1026
0924	ICE 575	1039
1003	ICE 787	1123
1024	ICE 71	1139
1108	ICE 587	1226
1124	ICE 577	1239

DEPART HANNOVER	TRAIN NUMBER	ARRIVE HAMBURG
1618	ICE 72	1733
1634	ICE 788	1750
1718	ICE 576	1846
1732	ICE 586	1851
1818	ICE 70	1932
1834	ICE 90	1951
1901	IC 1080	2030
1918	ICE 574	2032
1932	ICE 584	2050
2018	ICE 974	2136
2020	ICE 774	2136
2034	ICE 786	2152
2118	ICE 572	2236
2132	ICE 582	2250
2243	ICE 782	2359
2344	ICE 589	0105

Distance: 111 miles (178 km)

Hannover's Zoo is less than five minutes from the central station by U-Bahn Line 6 or by bus No. 128 from the central station. With the Gorilla Mountain, Jungle Palace, Zoo Farm and the Zambezi Savannah landscape, the Hannover Zoo has become one of the most attractive in Germany.

The **Great Herrenhausen Garden and Garden Theater** is one of Europe's greatest tourist attractions. In its 300-year-old landscaping, you will find the only example in Germany of early Baroque gardens that have survived in their original form. Herrenhausen Avenue, facing the gardens, is lined with 1,219 lime trees set in four rows; they link Hannover's inner city with the gardens of the former summer residence of the Royal House of Hannover in Herrenhausen. Many sections of the garden have remained unaltered through the centuries. A new highlight of the gardens is the unique **Regenwaldhaus (Rainforest House)**.

The garden is open 0800–1630 in winter and until 2000 in summer. Throughout the summer, the ornamental fountains of the garden operate from 1100–1200 and 1500–1800 daily. Either U-Bahn No. 4 or No. 5 will take you to the Herrenhausen Garden, or you will be able to see a portion of the gardens during a stop on the city bus tour.

Hannover has several museums spanning 6,000 years of history including the **Sprengel Museum** (Modern Art), **Kestner Museum** (Egyptology, Greece, Middle Ages), **Hannover Museum of History** (local social history), and the **Busch Museum** in the **Georgengarten**, a natural park developed in the eighteenth century. In sharp contrast to the baroque world of the Herrenhausen Garden, the Georgengarten is a mature example of English landscape gardening.

Many of Hannover's residents believe that a day in their city should have 48 hours. The refurbished city center alone—an ambler's paradise (reserved entirely for pedestrians) with shops, cascading fountains, and cafes—can captivate you. With the frequent train service between Hamburg and Hannover, you can easily extend your stay into evening.

Day Excursion to

Lübeck
Renaissance and Rotspon

Depart from Hamburg Hauptbahnhof
Distance by Train: 39 miles (62 km)
Average Train Time: 38 minutes
City Dialing Code: 451
Tourist Information Office: Breite Str. 62, D-23552 Lübeck
Tel: 01805-882233; **Fax:** 0451 1225419
Internet: www.luebeck-tourismus.de
E-mail: tb-breite@luebeck-tourismus.de
Hours: 0800–1600 Monday–Friday
Tourist information: In the train station opposite track No. 1.

    Hours: 0930–1900 Monday–Friday; 1000–1600 Saturday; 1000–1500 Sunday.

    Note: To get to the tourist office at Breite Strasse (pedestrian area) from the rail station, pass by the Holstentor and continue through Holstenstrasse. Cross the marketplace area on the left-hand side and continue through the Townhall Arcades to the Breite Strasse. Turn left again. In about 300 meters you will see the Tourist Information on the left side.

Hamburg—Lübeck

Depart Hamburg	Train Number	Arrive Lübeck	Notes
0705	RE 35200	0750	
0728	EC 31	0805	R
0805	RE 35222	0850	
0835	IR 2506	0910	
0905	RE 35202	0950	
0928	EC 33	1005	R
1005	RE 35224	1050	
1105	RE 35204	1150	

pattern continues until 1905 followed by hourly service until 2320

Depart Lübeck	Train Number	Arrive Hamburg	Notes
earlier trains with about the same frequency as these:			
1805	RE 35211	1849	
1905	RE 35233	1949	
1939	EC 32	2016	R
2005	RE 35213	2049	
2105	RE 35235	2149	
2139	EC 30	2216	R
2205	RE 35215	2249	
2305	RE 35143	2349	

R Reservations required
Distance: 39 miles (62 km)

HAMBURG Lübeck

The Hanseatic City of Lübeck extends its hospitality in a phrase, "Welcome, to yesterday, today, and tomorrow." The city's origins go back to the year 1000, when "Liübice" was established as a royal seat, artisan settlement, and trading center on the banks of the Trave River near the Baltic Sea. Today, parts of the old town of Lübeck have become a UNESCO World Heritage Site, and tomorrow is well in the hands of its energetic citizens, who number more than 210,000.

Destroyed by fire in 1157, the city at present dates from 1159, when it was rebuilt. In 1358, it was chosen as the administrative headquarters for the Hanseatic League. Between 1806 and 1813, Napoleon I held Lübeck as a part of his empire. Until the turn of the twentieth century, when it began to build its own industries, Lübeck was known only as a Baltic port. Its industrial strengths and strategic maritime location, however, brought destruction to Lübeck during World War II, when most of Lübeck's industrial complex and some one-fifth of its Old Town were destroyed by Allied aerial bombardment. In 1949, the reconstruction of Lübeck, including the historic Old Town, began. As Germany's largest Baltic port, this proud city has once again become a center of economic, cultural, and commercial interests.

Lübeck is noted for two culinary specialties that you should sample during your visit—marzipan and rotspon. **Marzipan**, as a sweet specialty, is produced in a countless variety of forms. Try a piece of marzipan cake and visit the Marzipan Museum at Cafe Niederegger. The origins of marzipan are hidden in history. Lübeck's version is that during the famine of 1407, bakers produced a bread made from the stocks of almonds, since wheat flour was unavailable. Others believe that marzipan originated in Venice, and the recipe came to Lübeck through trade links.

In the early days, when salt was used to preserve fish, ships sailing from Lübeck began carrying salt mined in the Lübeck area to fishing ports along the French coast of Biscay. Rather than return empty, the ships brought back casks of French wine to mature in Lübeck prior to bottling. A combination of sea climate and storage in Lübeck's wine cellars brought about an amazing improvement in the quality of the wine. This was first discovered in 1806 during Napoleon's occupation, when French officers found that the Bordeaux wine from Lübeck's wine cellars tasted considerably better than at home. Try a glass of *Lübeck er rotspon* and judge for yourself.

Lübeck's architecture ranges from Gothic to Neoclassical, and you can find typical examples of these as well as Renaissance, Baroque, and Rococo in almost every part of the town's old section. You can see all five styles mix in harmonic unity within one block, starting with the College of Music at the head of Grosse Petersgrube.

With Lübeck's illustrated brochure in hand, you can become your own tour guide, or you might want to opt for one of the town's regular guided walks that start from the tourist office in the marketplace. The guided walks take about 2 hours to complete. The tourist office in the train station can give you directions for finding the marketplace.

After you leave the train station, your point of reference will be the **Holstentor,** an imposing structure perched prominently at the head of the harbor just before the bridge leading over the Trave River into Old Town. Built between 1464 and 1478, more as a prestige symbol for the town than to protect its harbor, the unique design of its twin towers has become the symbol of Lübeck. The museum of city history housed in the Holstentor is very interesting and features a model of Lübeck in 1650.

After crossing the river, follow **Holsten Strasse**, which leads directly to Lübeck's **Rathaus** (town hall), in the marketplace. It is one of the oldest town halls built in Germany between the thirteenth and sixteenth centuries and is certainly one of the most beautiful. The **Ratskeller Restaurant** in the basement of the Rathaus is a delightful place to pause for lunch or to sample a glass of rotspon. We can also recommend the **Schiffergesellschaft Restaurant** at No. 2 Breite Strasse, site of a meetinghouse built in 1535 for shipmasters and brimming with treasures from the world of shipping. Bring money—lots of it—the ambience and food are worth it. (Closed on Monday.)

For an aerial view of Lübeck, cross Holsten Strasse from the marketplace to **Petrikirche** (St. Peter's Church). Here you can ride the elevator to a viewing platform 162 feet (50 meters) above the city.

Base City:

Munich
(München)

Internet: www.muenchen-tourist.de
E-mail: tourismus@ems.muenchen.de
City Dialing Code: 089

Munich (München), the capital and heart of Bavaria, is situated in the center of a vast plain washed by the Isar River. Founded in 1158, it was given the status of a town in 1214. The immaculate and astonishing beauty of its countryside is visible in any direction. Rimmed by the Alps to the south and dark green pine forests in all other quadrants, Munich becomes the gateway to day excursions galore. With a population of more than a million, Munich is Germany's third largest city, but it still retains its unmatched roisterous elegance.

Munich's mood is always festive, but twice a year the tempo soars even higher as the city observes Fasching and Oktoberfest. Fasching celebrations are held during January and February. The festivities could be compared to Mardi Gras, only Müncheners get a head start on everyone by cranking up just after New Year's Eve and never letting up until the sun sets on Ash Wednesday!

During this period of Fasching revelry, thousands of masked balls and parties are staged. Many are in fancy dress, and sometimes masks are worn because individuals don't wish to reveal their identities to their partners—who are seldom the ones they came in with. It's often a complete surprise when the inevitable unmasking takes place.

The coming of Lent doesn't dampen Munich's spirits one drop, for it marks the beginning of the strong beer season. Munich's monks, limited to one meal a day throughout Lent (but with no limit on their drinking), started this ancient custom that still prevails today. They asked the brewmasters if, during Lent, they could increase the regular alcoholic content of their product; the brewmasters agreed—and everyone apparently has lived happily ever after. There are six major breweries in Munich.

Oktoberfest, instituted by a Bavarian king in 1810 on the occasion of the marriage between Princess Therese von Sachsen-Hildburghausen and Prince Ludwig (later King Ludwig I), actually takes place during the latter part of September and ends the first weekend in October. About 660,000 gallons of beer are produced by the city's breweries and dispensed directly from huge, chilled barrels in enormous tents serving as beer halls. Bands play throughout the day and long into the night while drinkers wash down sausages, roast chicken, and oxen with five to six million liter-size drafts of the world's finest brews.

Colorful road signs on just about every highway entering Bavaria declare it to be *Freistaat Bayern,* the Free State of Bavaria. Insurrection? Not really. It is the manifestation of the free and roisterous spirit of its citizens, who love their homeland and feel that there is no place quite like it anywhere else in the world.

Arriving by Air

Munich International Airport is located 28 kilometers northeast of the city center. *Tel:* 9752–1313 (for flight information). *Internet:* www.munich-airport.com

The airport features a system of passenger modules connected by walkways, referred to as PTS (Passenger Transport System), that run the entire length of the terminal on level 03. The PTS also connects with the central area, where there is a 24-hour information area staffed by multilingual personnel.

Railpasses may be validated at the GermanRail counter (MVV, Munich Integrated Transport System) in the central area of level 03.

Airport–City Links: Munich's rapid transit rail system, S-Bahn No. 8 line, or No. 1 line, which stops at the Marienplatz (city center) and the Hauptbahnhof (main rail station). Journey time, 40 minutes to the Hauptbahnhof. From the central area, descend to level 02. Trains depart every 20 minutes 0355–2455. Fare: €7.77 for a one-way ticket, which you can purchase from machines at the airport (near the escalators leading to the S-Bahn). Eurail passes, Europasses, and GermanRail passes are valid on the S-Bahn, but if this is the only rail trip you'll be making that day, we suggest you purchase the one-way ticket and validate your railpass when you're ready to journey out from Munich.

Lufthansa Airport Bus departs from the stop at Terminal Area A every 20 minutes for Munich Hauptbahnhof 0617–2137 daily; from the airport main concourse 0620–2140; from Terminal Area D 0625–2145. From Munich Hauptbahnhof to airport, buses depart every 20 minutes, 0510–1950. Tickets: €9.20; round-trip, €14.32. Travel time, about 45 minutes. Tel: 32 30 40; Fax: 32 32 594.

Taxi stands in front of areas A, B, C, D, and E. Due to traffic congestion, the time it takes to travel between the airport and the city by road can exceed 1 hour and can cost €51–61. Check at the taxi information desk in the central area of the airport. For advance taxi arrangements and information, Tel: 21610 or 19410 in Munich or Fax: 7470260.

Arriving by Train

Munich has several suburban stations, but most international trains stop only at the Hauptbahnhof.

Munich's Railway Station—The Hauptbahnhof is actually a city within a city. It even has its own hotel. In addition to the regular rail-station services, all you need do is descend one level on any one of the station's many escalators to discover a veritable city of shops, ranging from bakeries, *bier* (beer) *stubes*, and fruit stands to supermarkets, as well as the subway entrances to many of Munich's department stores. This shopping colossus extends from the Hauptbahnhof all the way to Karlsplatz-Stachus—more than ¼ mile. Most shops in the immediate Hauptbahnhof area are open late during the week as well as on weekends and holidays.

- **Money exchange** (Geldwechsel-Exchange-Cambio): Located in the far left corner (as you exit) of the main station hall next to the main entrance. Hours: 0600–2300 daily. This facility is operated by the Deutsche Verkehrs-Kredit-Bank (DVB) and offers a service not usually found in other exchanges. It will accept foreign coins (except coins from eastern Europe). Most exchanges will only accept notes.

An ATM is located on the left-hand side as you face the bank. A walk-up currency exchange office operated by DVB may be found by turning right when exiting the trains, by track 11 at the street exit. Hours: 0730–1900 daily. There is also an ATM just before the Bayerstrasse exit.

The EurAide office is located in Room 3 next to track 11 in the Hauptbahnhof. It is open primarily during the summer months: 0730–1200 and 1300–1630 daily in May; 0730–1200 and 1300–1800 daily from June 1 to the end of September.

- **Tourist Information/Hotel Reservations** may be made in the tourist information office. To reach it, exit through the Bahnhof Platz exit and turn right. It is the second office on the right, next to the ABR Reisebüro. It is within the station complex but can only be reached from the outside. A nominal charge is made for reservations. The attendants are very helpful in finding local reservations. *Hours:* 0900–2000 Monday–Saturday; 1000–1600 Sunday. *"InfoPool–Young People's Guide"* lists youth accommodations and activities.

The four-star **InterCity–Hotel München** is located conveniently in the train station. As you are exiting from the train-platform area, turn to the right just past the first main concourse shops and walk to the street entrance. The hotel will be on the left just before the doors leading to the street. It's convenient, but get reservations early—it's also popular. *Tel:* 54 55 60; *Fax:* 54 55 66 10; *E-mail:* reservierung@inter-city-hotel.de.

- **Train reservations** for EuroCity, InterCity, ICE, and express-train services can be made in the **Reisezentrum** (Travel Center), located in the center of the station in front of tracks 21 and 22. Hours: 0900–1800 Monday–Friday; 0900–1200 Saturday. It can be very crowded, particularly on weekends and during the summer tourist season. You must make train reservations at least one day in advance. They can also be made at counters that have signs reading RESERVIERUNGEN.

- **Railpass validation and train information** also can be obtained in the Reisezentrum. Use window 19, 20, or 47 for railpass validation. For train schedules only (international or domestic), use window 2 or 3 or the service counter in the middle of the station across from tracks 18 and 19. The sign reads DB SERVICE.

Prior to entering the train information office, prepare a list or an itinerary of the rail trips you intend to make. Too many people enter the office without a thought of where they want to go or when they want to arrive. This office can tell you what train to take and the time that it leaves the Munich Hauptbahnhof. They are not a travel agency, however, and you should not ask for suggestions of things to do.

- **Food services** are available in several parts of the station. The most famous is the stand-up wiener-and-beer stube immediately to the right of the entrance into the main station concourse. Behind it, there are three full-service restaurants with posted prices and menus.
- **Luggage lockers** are available in four areas of the station. Look for signs reading SCHLIESSFÄCHER. There is also a luggage-checking office on the main floor under the Burger King.
- Another **tourist information office** is located in the New Town Hall in Marienplatz (same building as the glockenspiel). Hours are Monday–Saturday 1000–2000; Sunday 1000–1600. This office also will make hotel reservations.

Getting Around in Munich

Munich's fine S-Bahn (rapid train) system is operated by Deutsche Bahn (DB). The variety of Eurail and Europasses and GermanRail Pass are accepted for travel throughout the entire S-Bahn system. The aforementioned railpasses are not accepted on the U-Bahn (underground or subway system) or on the trams (*Strassenbahnen*).

The S-Bahn has eight main operating lines, S-1 through S-8. All of these lines converge on the Marienplatz and Hauptbahnhof. You can obtain maps and fare information at the tourist information office.

A U-Bahn (subway) station is located directly under the plaza in front of the railway station. The Munich Hauptbahnhof is the center of train, tram, bus, suburban train, and subway services for the entire city.

A great value is the MVV-Single (valid for one person) or Partner (valid for two adults) Tageskarte (Day Tickets). The Day Ticket provides unlimited travel on the S-Bahn (rapid transit line), U-Bahn (subway), streetcars, and buses on the date of validation until 0600 the following day. A Single Day Ticket for Munich's entire transport network costs €9.20; Partner Day Ticket, €14.32 (5 adults). Remember to have your ticket "stamped/validated" by using any one of the machines near and in any station.

All of Munich's public transportation operate on the honor system. You must have a ticket for any conveyance you board, but you may not be asked to show it—then, again, you may. If you are apprehended without a valid ticket, you will be fined €30.68 on the spot.

The **München Welcome Card** is a great combination of city transport and sight-seeing savings. Travel is free on all public transport within Munich's boundaries with the card, and up to 50 percent discounted entrance is offered for museums, cinemas, gardens, castles, horse-drawn carriage rides, and walking and sight-seeing tours. A Single Day Ticket costs €6.14; Single 3-Day Ticket costs €15.34; Partner 3-Day Ticket costs €22.50. The card is available at the Main Rail Station (Hauptbahnhof), Bahnhofplatz 2, the Town Hall, and at many hotels.

Sights/Attractions/Tours

Munich's heart pulsates at the Marienplatz, the city's central square. From the tower of the new town hall in the center of the Marienplatz, a glockenspiel chimes every morning at 1100 and 1200 (again in summer at 1700) and is followed by a performance of mechanical figures, including knights on horseback and a crowing rooster. You will have to see it to believe it.

Dallmayr's Delicatessen is nearby—one of the finest delicatessens in the world. Facing the glockenspiel, walk around the right side of the town hall to the smaller square in the rear. Dallmayr's store will then be in plain view immediately across the street to your right, at 14 Dienerstrasse. (*Tel:* 213–5100) Hours: Monday–Wednesday 0930–1900; Thursday–Friday 0930–2000; Saturday 0900–1600; closed Sunday. Extravagant beyond description, it demands to be seen. If for no other reason, go to Munich to savor the sights and scents of Dallmayr's! There are a restaurant specializing in seafood and a unique gift shop on the second floor. This is not your usual "deli"; you'll find rich German chocolates, caviar, lobster, fine wines—order a gourmet lunch "to go."

Munich has a great variety of things to see and do. There are approximately 100 historic buildings, 2 castles, 200 churches, 46 art collections and museums, and 58 performing theaters—all within the city limits and most of them within reasonable walking distance from the Marienplatz. Ask the tourist information office for the folder containing a city map showing the exact location of each of the points of interest, including the **1972 Olympic Park**, identified by color-coded squares. For admirers of the brewmaster's art, the map also pinpoints 12 of Munich's most famous beer gardens.

The **Hofbräuhaus** (the state-owned beer hall) is a short walk from the Marienplatz via Dallmayr's delicatessen. (It would be un-American not to stop!) The Hofbräuhaus dates back to 1591. It is no longer operated as a brewery, but beer is drayed in to be consumed daily from 1-liter (1¾-pint) mugs while bands play lively tunes, often accompanied by the singing of the drinkers. There's a full-service restaurant on the second floor, where decorum is a bit more in evidence. **Planet Hollywood** is directly across the street from the Hofbräuhaus.

If you tire of city dining, take a southbound S-1 train on the S-Bahn

Train Connections to Other Base Cities from Munich

Depart from Munich Hauptbahnhof

DEPART	TRAIN NUMBER	ARRIVE	NOTES
		Amsterdam Centraal	
0858	ICE 680	1749	1
1029	ICE 826	2054	2
1237	ICE 794	2054	3
1258	ICE 586	2149	1
1336	ICE 592	2154	3
1446	EC 12	2354	2
2249	D 222	0941+1	R, Sleeper
		Berlin Zoobahnhof	
0639	ICE 1612	1346	
0851	ICE 1610	1546	
0933	ICE 596	1719	
then hourly departures at varying times until 1641, followed by			
1928	NZ 40482	0636+1	R, Sleeper
2306	NZ 1900	0705+1	R, Sleeper
		Bern (Berne)	
0814	ICE 92	1343	4
1213	EC 94	1743	4
1354	EC 196	1943	4
1811	EC 98	0017+1	4
		Brussels (Bruxelles) Midi/Zuid	
0846	IC 710	1807	3
1029	ICE 826	2007	3
1046	EC 18	2007	3
1142	IC 112	2035	3
1342	IC 522	2307	3
2249	D 222	0941+1	R, Sleeper
		Budapest Keleti	
0925	EC 63	1713	5
2345	EN 269	0913+1	R, Sleeper
		Copenhagen (København) H.	
0658	ICE 682	1759	6
1058	ICE 588	2159	6
1928	EN 482	0959+1	R, Sleeper
		Hamburg Hauptbahnhof	
0658	ICE 682	1250	
0747	ICE 882	1350	
0858	ICE 680	1452	
0947	ICE 880	1553	
hourly departure pattern continues until 1747, then			
2258	NZ 1988	0752+1	R, Sleeper
		Luxembourg	
0846	IC 710	1633	7
2054	D 260	0624+1	R, 8, Sleeper
		Milan (Milano) Centrale	
0730	EC 81	1450	
1330	EC 89	2050	
2340	D 289	0821+1	R, Sleeper

MUNICH

DEPART	TRAIN NUMBER	ARRIVE	NOTES
		Nice Ville	
0730	EC 81	1958	9
		Paris Gare de l'Est	
0742	EC 66	1622	
1348	EC 64	2220	
2054	D 260	0659+1	R, Sleeper
		Rome (Roma) Termini	
0930	EC 85	2002	
2030	EN 287	0817+1	R, Sleeper
		Vienna (Wien) Westbahnhof	
0925	EC 63	1420	
1625	EC 65	2120	
1825	EC 17	2320	
2345	EN 269	0605+1	R, Sleeper
		Zürich Hauptbahnhof	
0814	ICE 92	1227	
1213	EC 94	1627	
1354	EC 196	1827	
1811	EC 98	2223	

Daily, unless otherwise noted
R Reservations required
+1 Arrives next day
1. Change trains in Hannover.
2. Change trains in Cologne (Köln).
3. Change trains in Mannheim.
4. Change trains in Zürich.
5. Arrive Budapest-Deli station.
6. Change trains in Hamburg.
7. Change trains in Koblenz and Trier.
8. Change trains in Metz-Ville.
9. Change trains in Milan.

from the main transfer station under the Marienplatz and get off in the **Village of Aying**—about a 40-minute ride. Walk four blocks toward the church steeple to the Aying Hotel, where you'll find the best Bavarian food, beer, and atmosphere.

Those visiting Munich for the first time probably will want to take a guided tour by bus. A 4-hour leisurely paced bicycle tour is also available for about €18. For information call Mike's Bike Tours. *Tel:* 651–4275; *Internet:* www.mikesbiketours.com.

Day Excursions

South to the Alps and **Garmisch**. Into the Alps to **Berchtesgaden**. Through the Alps to Austria and its beautiful cities of **Innsbruck** and **Salzburg**. North to **Nuremberg, Ulm**, or **Rothenburg** and the **Romantic Road**. For a special adventure ascend the peak of Germany's highest mountain, the **Zugspitze**. Take your choice—and go at your leisure.

Day Excursion to

Berchtesgaden
Alps, Lakes, and Salt Mines

MUNICH
Berchtesgaden

Depart from Munich Hauptbahnhof
Distance by Train: 112 miles (180 km)
Average Train Time: 2 hours, 40 minutes
City Dialing Code: 4
Tourist Information Office: (Kurdirektion), Berchtesgadener Land, Köenigsseer Strasse 2, D-83471; opposite the railway station
Tel: (0) 8652–9670; **Fax:** (0) 8652–967400
Internet: www.berchtesgadener-land.com
E-mail: info@berchtesgaden.de
Hours: June 15–October 15: Monday–Friday 0800–1800; Saturday 0900–1700; Sunday 0900–1500. October 16–June 14: Monday–Friday 0800–1700; Saturday 0800–1200, and closed Sunday.
Notes: To reach the tourist information office, cross the street in front of the station at the traffic light and incline to the left, following the KÖNIGSSEE sign. The office is located in a large cream-colored building on the right-hand side.

Don't let the train time to Berchtesgaden deter you from making this day excursion. The train follows a route that passes through some of the most beautiful countryside in the world, and the tours waiting for your arrival in Berchtesgaden are simply out of this world.

After Adolf Hitler seized power in 1934, he ordered the expansion of the facilities in **Obersalzberg,** an appendage to Berchtesgaden, with the intent of making it the equivalent of a summer White House. His dream was destroyed, however, when the greater part of Obersalzberg was demolished by an air attack on April 25, 1945.

If possible, take the early train out of Munich to have ample time to select a tour and have a relaxing lunch in one of Berchtesgaden's charming inns. Current schedules are always posted in the main hall of the station.

Berchtesgaden Mini-Bus Tours (located in the tourist office) specializes in English-speaking historical tours of Berchtesgaden's sights, including the Obersalzberg and **Eagle's Nest.**

The village of Berchtesgaden has many attractions. Among them is the Folk Museum housed in the **Adelsheim Castle** (Schloss Adelsheim), where you will find displays of wood carvings and the famous Berchtesgaden wood-shaving boxes.

For one of the most spectacular scenic views in the world, take the Jennerbahn two-person cable cars to the top of Mount Jenner above **Lake Königssee** (literally translated "Royal Lake"). Start from the valley station at Lake Königssee. Your breathtaking, 20-minute ascent to 1,834 meters (6,017

Munich (München)—Berchtesgaden

DEPART MÜNCHEN HBF	TRAIN NUMBER	ARRIVE BERCHTESGADEN	NOTES
0633	RE 31001	0924	1
0741	IR 2091	1021	1
0833	RE 31003	1112	1
0937	IC 717	1220	1

DEPART BERCHTESGADEN	TRAIN NUMBER	ARRIVE MÜNCHEN HBF	
1347	RB31918	1620	1
1547	RB31922	1820	1
1747	RB31926	2020	1
1839	RB31928	2127	1
1947	RB31930	2220	1
2039	RB31932	2327	1

1. Change trains in Freilassing
Distance: 112 miles (180 km)

feet) unveils vistas of mountain summits stretching as far as the eye can see. This wondrous landscape once caused Bavarian writer Ludwig Ganghofer to cry out: "Lord, if you love anyone, then set them down in this land!"

In addition to sight-seeing in Berchtesgaden and its immediate surroundings, there are many interesting guided tours that can be taken outside of the village. The most popular ones for North Americans are visits to Obersalzberg, the Salt Mines, the Königssee, the Sound of Music/Salzburg Tour, and the Eagle's Nest. All tours are available year-round with the exception of the Eagle's Nest, which is open from mid-May to mid-October.

The **Obersalzberg tour** features a visit to the former location of the Berghof, Adolf Hitler's official home and the site of many pre–World War II conferences. Included on the tour is a trip through its air-raid shelters and bunkers, which provided protection to the conferees in the event that the Allied air forces wanted to disrupt the proceedings.

The **Salt Mines** are located a few miles outside the town of Berchtesgaden. If you have chronic respiratory problems, you may sigh a breath of relief in the specially treated air of the new curative salt mine tunnel. The guided tour is a thrilling experience. In miner's protective clothing, you ride a mine train, slide down chutes, and cross over subterranean lakes. What an adventure!

The **Königssee** is considered the pearl of Berchtesgaden and provides some of the most romantic scenery in Upper Bavaria. In order to preserve the quietness of the lake and the clearness of its waters, electric boats have been the only crafts permitted to navigate there since 1909. A tour aboard an electric boat runs daily whenever the lake is ice-free. Midpoint in the cruise, the captain shuts down the motor and, in the silence of the lake, lets go with a blast on a trumpet that resounds and resounds for as many as seven times off the alpine palisades surrounding the lake.

The **Eagle's Nest** tour begins in May and is conducted daily until winter snows block its access. A bus conveys you to a height of 5,600 feet, where an elevator lifts you the final 400 feet to a never-to-be-forgotten experience. Despite the publicity gained by the Eagle's Nest's connection with Adolf Hitler, he visited there only about five times. The road running to the elevator that takes you to the summit is beyond doubt a uniquely daring feat of road building. It's a white-knuckle ride all the way. The tour itself is far less strenuous than that of the Salt Mines, but the weather is all important.

Despite its ancient facade, Berchtesgaden is actually very modern in its tourist and recreational facilities. Should its charm overcome you—as it does many—consider an overnight stay. The Berchtesgadener Land tourist information office, opposite the rail station, can assist you in finding accommodations.

For lunchtime try the **Gasthof Neuhaus**, opposite the fountain in the town square. Its selection of *Schmankerl* (Bavarian specialties) is a treat, and its ice cream specialties will make you forget all about Baskin-Robbins.

Day Excursion to

Garmisch-Partenkirchen
Bavaria at Its Best

Depart from Munich Hauptbahnhof
Distance by Train: 63 miles (101 km)
Average Train Time: 1 hour, 30 minutes
City Dialing Code: 8821
Tourist Information Office: Kurverwaltung, Postfach 1562, 82455 Garmisch–
   Partenkirchen
Tel: 180–700; *Fax:* 180–755
Internet: www.garmisch-partenkirchen.de
Zugspitze Internet: www.zugspitze.de
Zugspitze E-mail: zugspitzbahn@zugspitze.de
Hours: 0800–1800 Monday–Saturday and 1000–1200 Sunday
Notes: Reach the information office by turning left outside the station and walking
   downhill about 300 yards to Bahnhof Strasse. Turn left and walk about 150
   yards to Richard Strauss Platz and the Kongresshaus (Congress Hall).

Bavaria's eccentric King Ludwig II spent lavishly, admired Wagner, and went mad—though not necessarily in that order. Two of his famous castles, Neuschwanstein and Linderhof, can be visited on tours from Garmisch-Partenkirchen, as well as the village of **Oberammergau** (home of the Passion Play) and the Zugspitze, Germany's highest mountain.

Tourism started in the area with the building of a railroad between Munich and Garmisch-Partenkirchen in 1889. Prior to that time, the area waned or prospered according to who was in town. The Romans occupied the area as far back as the first century B.C. At the beginning of the eighteenth century, the area was suppressed by the Spanish and then by the Austrians and the French. It wasn't until 1802 that the area was finally made a part of Bavaria. Because of its interest in winter sports, in 1966 the twin-city of Garmisch-Partenkirchen became the sister city of Aspen, Colorado, ski capital of the United States.

DER, a German tour agency, offers a wide selection of tours in the Garmisch-Partenkirchen area, including tours of King Ludwig's **Neuschwanstein Castle** and his **Linderhof Castle.** The DER agency is immediately adjacent to the Garmisch-Partenkirchen rail station.

Proceed to track No. 1 by turning to the left at the bottom of the stairs leading from the arriving train platform. DER is visible from the rail station lobby. Most tours are conducted daily.

Garmisch-Partenkirchen (actually two villages that united in 1935) hosted the 1936 Winter Olympics and the World Alpine-Ski Championship in 1978. Just visiting the Olympic facilities can consume an entire day. A downtown shopping spree can do the same, but with more injury to pocketbooks. In wintertime, the Winter Olympics ski jump provides spills and chills, and the Olympic Ice Stadium is open year-round.

The alpine ski runs extend 68 miles in length, and there are 93 miles of tracks for the growing sport of cross-country skiing. Two of the most popular alpine cable-car runs in summer are the **Eibsee-Zugspitze** system (9,678 feet) and the **Wank Bahn,** which takes you to the promontory of the Wank Alp (5,874 feet). There are others as well. One that is particularly convenient starts at the Olympic Ski Stadium on the fringe of Garmisch-Partenkirchen and scales the Eckbauer Alp to a height of 4,127 feet. From any of these points on a clear day, the view is extraordinary.

Near the Ski Stadium, you can hike through the Partnachklamm gorge, which has a trail cut into the rock. The trail follows the course of the Partnach Stream for more spectacular views. Want more? There's also the Hollentalklamm. Begin your hike at Hammersbach, about 3 kilometers west of Garmisch, a stop on the Zugspitzbahn. Hike a couple of kilometers up the mountain to the beginning of the gorge. The trail continues to the top of the Zugspitze. The tourist office can fill you in on all the details.

The **Zugspitze** is the highest mountain in Germany—9,718 feet, to be

Munich (München)—Garmisch-Partenkirchen

DEPART MUNICH HBF	TRAIN NUMBER	ARRIVE GARMISCH
0700	RB 5405	0823
0800	RB 5407	0921
0900	RB 5409	1023
1000	RB 5411	1121
1100	RB 5413	1223
1200	RB 5415	1321

Zugspitze trains depart Garmish at 39 minutes past the hour from 0839 to 1439.

DEPART GARMISCH	TRAIN NUMBER	ARRIVE MUNICH HBF
1532	RB 5424	1653
1631	RB 5426	1754
1733	RB 5428	1854
1831	RB 5430	1955
1931	RB 5432	2052
2029	RB 5434	2153
2131	RB 5436	2252
2229	RB 5438	2352

Zugspitze trains returning to Garmisch depart Zugspitzplatt station hourly 1000–1600.
All trains are daily, including holidays
Distance: 63 miles (101 km)

exact. A cog railway was completed in 1931 to the Zugspitzplatt, along with a cable car that scaled the last 2,000 feet to the top. Another cable car running from Eibsee, a station stop on the cog railway at the 3,500-foot level, was placed in operation during 1963. This system lifts passengers directly to the peak in a spectacular 10-minute ride.

These two systems make a circuitous routing possible—up one way and down another. The round-trip fare from Garmisch is €41.41 (discount for GermanRail and Eurail railpass holders). The ticket entitles you to ride on any part of the total system. When you arrive in the Garmisch-Partenkirchen station, walk about 100 yards to your right to the cog-railway station. The cog railway stops in Eibsee about 30 minutes after departing Garmisch. Transfer at this point to the Eibsee cable car.

The cable-car trip from Eibsee to the top of the Zugspitze takes about 10 breathtaking minutes. If you are in a hurry to return to Garmisch, you could retrace your trip by returning to Eibsee on the cable car, but we recommend that you proceed to the **Sonn Alpin Glacier Restaurant** via the "Gletscherbahn" cable car. At the Sonn Alpin, you join up with the cog railway, which terminates there in a huge vaulted hall blasted out of solid rock. Trains depart on the hour, and the trip back to Garmisch takes 1 hour and 10 minutes.

Day Excursion to

Innsbruck, Austria
Jewel of the Alps

Depart from Munich Hauptbahnhof or Ostbahnhof
Distance by Train: 107 miles (172 km)
Average Train Time: 1 hour, 53 minutes
Austria Country Dialing Code: 43
City Dialing Code: 512
Tourist Information Office: Innsbruck Tourismus, Burggraben 3, A–6021 Innsbruck
Tel: 598500; *Fax:* 598507
Internet: www.innsbruck-tourism.at and www.ski-innsbruck.at
E-mail: info@innsbruck.tvb.co.at
Hours: Monday–Friday 0800–1600, Saturday 0800–1200
Hotel Information: Innsbruck Hauptbahnhof
Tel: (0512) 583766; *Fax:* (0512) 583767
Notes: A tourist office is located in the train station on the east side. One is also on the outside of the station. To get to the other offices, leave the main station hall by the exit on the left-hand side and proceed past the "Checked Baggage" area. To get to the office in town, follow Salurner Strasse to the Triumphal Arch; make a right and follow Maria-Theresien Strasse directly to the tourist office at the Burggraben crossroad entrance to the old town.

Located less than 2 hours away by train, Innsbruck is a convenient excursion to make from Munich. Translated, *Innsbruck* means "bridge over the Inn River." Situated at the junction of the Inn Valley and the Sill Gap, on the road and railroad route running into Italy through the Brenner Pass, the city is the cultural and tourist capital of the Austrian Tyrol and brings together nature, culture, sport, and tradition.

Innsbruck is surrounded theatrically by its mountains. There is a mountain view from nearly every street corner and every window in town. Looking northward from its main street, **Maria-Theresien Strasse,** you will confront the towering Alps, which seem to encroach upon the city. The scene is breathtaking.

This day excursion offers an opportunity to explore the **Tyrolean Alps** in a cable car—plus a visit to one of the most picturesque "old towns" in Austria. To top it off, a circuitous return on the **Mittenwald railroad** is possible; it takes you on a fantastically scenic rail route straight through the heart of the Austrian and Bavarian Alps en route back to Munich via Garmisch-Partenkirchen. Guided tours are offered twice daily from the main train station in the summer (1200 and 1400) and once daily at 1200 in winter. Railpass holders get a 15 percent discount on the Seegrube-Hafelekar cable car. The Patscherkofel does not offer it, and the Mutterer

Alm is being rebuilt. The cost of a cable-car ride is equivalent to the Innsbruck Card, which includes a cable-car ride plus more.

You are in for an eye-filling day. Even the regular rail line running out of Munich is loaded with alpine scenery. Take a seat on the right side of your coach outbound from Munich for the best views.

The **Innsbruck Card** includes admission fees for many sights, museums, and other attractions (even a free welcome drink at the casino) and unlimited use of the public transportation network within the city. The card is a great bargain and is valid for a period of 24 hours at €16.70, 48 hours, €21.80, 72 hours, €26.80.

Also purchase the large guide map if you plan a walking tour of the city, then head west for a few blocks to Innsbruck's **Arc de Triumph.** From this point, turn north and wend your way slowly through the Altstadt (Old Town), which lines both sides of the street all the way to the **Goldenes Dachl** (Golden Roof) at the end of Herzog-Friedrich Strasse. Try your luck in the Casino, a tasty aperitif in the Piano Bar, or a culinary feast in the Guggeryllis Restaurant. It may come as a disappointment, but the so-called Golden Roof is made of heavy, gilded copper.

Bus tours of the city are available throughout the year. A city tour by bus departs the Central Bus Station daily at 1200 and 1400 June–September. Biking tours are a great way to see Innsbruck, too. Or, take the 60-minute guided "City Walk" through the historic center of Innsbruck at 1100 and 1400. Cost: €8.

We suggest you eat lunch in the **Goldener Adler** (Golden Eagle), the oldest inn in the city, founded in 1390! It is around the corner on the left and can best be described as a delicious experience. If you go there for dinner, enjoy Tyrolean music in the cellar restaurant. It will complete a perfect evening, although an expensive one. Another option is the **Ottoburg,** which is just past the Goldener Adler and serves good traditional meals. Here is an insider's tip on where many locals eat lunch: try the **Fischerhäusl,** a cute little house with a garden located between the cathedral and congress center.

Every year on August 15, the Austrian Philharmonic Youth Orchestra performs in Innsbruck to celebrate the King of the Waltz—Johann Strauss— with the "hottest Strauss event in Austria," according to the 120 participating young musicians. For tickets: *Tel:* 0512 56 15 61; *Internet:* www.Innsbruck-ticket-service.at; *E-mail:* ibk.ticket@netway.at.

In the winter Innsbruck is an alpine sports paradise, with 7 skiing regions, including the magnificent Stubai Glacier, 62 lifts, 55 marked ski runs, 130 kilometers of well-maintained ski trails, and 9.5 kilometers of high-altitude cross-country trails. Telephone, fax, or e-mail the Innsbruck Tourist Office for holiday and ski package information.

DEPART MUNICH HBF	TRAIN NUMBER	ARRIVE INNSBRUCK
0730	EC 81	0922
0800	RB 5407	1057
0930	EC 85	1122
1000	RB 5411	1250
1130	EC 87	1322

DEPART INNSBRUCK	TRAIN NUMBER	ARRIVE MUNICH HBF
1437	EC 88	1630
1637	EC 84	1830
1837	EC 86	2030
1901	RB 5434	2153
2037	EC 80	2230

Daily, including holidays
Distance: 107 miles (172 km)

Day Excursion to

Nuremberg (Nürnberg)
Beer, Gingerbread, and Toys

Depart from Munich Hauptbahnhof or Pasing
Distance by Train: 125 miles (201 km)
Average Train Time: 1 hour, 40 minutes
City Dialing Code: 911
Tourist Information Office: Nürnberg Congress und Tourismus Zentrale, Frauentorgraben 3, D–90443 Nürnberg.
Tel: 2336–123; **Fax:** 2336–166
Internet: www.nuernberg.de
E-mail: tourismus@nuernberg.de
Hours: 0900–1900 Monday–Saturday.
Notes: A tourist information pavilion is in front of the main railway station.

Although Nuremberg (Nürnberg) is more than 950 years old, it is a lively, modern city. A mecca for lovers of markets, music, and museums, Nuremberg must have originated the "Day Excursion"!

On December 7, 1835, the first German train chugged its way from Nuremberg to Furth, a neighboring city, with honored guests *and* two barrels of beer. But on this day excursion ICE trains average 76 mph between Munich and Nuremberg—considerably faster than in 1835—and Nuremberg's brew is every bit the match for Munich's, for Nuremberg is a part of Bavaria, too. Get ready for an enjoyable day out.

When you arrive in Nuremberg, you will find the tourist office in front of the railway station, which at press time is undergoing extensive renovation. Another tourist information office is on the main market square at Hauptmarkt 18.

Conducted tours of the city from May to October and in the Christmas season depart daily at 1300. Individual tours may be arranged at any time; one of the Tourist Board's experienced city guides will serve as escort. *Tel:* 233–6123. Or put your own tour together with the **Nuremberg Cultour Ticket,** available at the tourist office. This 2-day ticket offers entrance to many museums and sites. If you decide to stay over, hotel guests get free public transport in Nuremberg, Fürth, and Stein with the card as well. Ask about the Welcome Pack at the tourist office if you do book a hotel. You'll be in for a nice surprise.

Train schedules, posted in several prominent locations in the station, will confirm the departure time and track location of your return train to Munich, no matter how long you decide to stay.

One of the main gates of the old walled city of Nuremberg, the **Kingsgate,** is directly across from the railway station. Picking up Königstrasse (King Street) at this point, you can follow it to the heart of the old walled area known as the Hauptmarkt (Central Market). Plan to be there at noon; a mechanical clock will entertain you at the stroke of twelve with its seven electors paying homage to the emperor. Then look for a nearby pub . . . shouldn't be too hard, as they seem to be everywhere.

What goes better with beer than an authentic "Three in One"? Famous for their sausages, these Nuremberg minnies may only be as big as your little finger, but they are spicy—and famous across Germany. Now, about that beer. . . .

Connoisseurs of the brewer's art won't want to miss a visit to Nuremberg's **Museum Brewery** and **Medieval Cellars.** The museum is really the Altstadthof brewery, who's motto, "Beer like our Forefathers," is observed today by the use of only the finest materials and brewing methods, which date from the nineteenth century. The cellars, going down 85 feet through solid rock, form a labyrinth of tunnels dug in the fourteenth century for the storage of beer. A guided tour is available.

Nuremberg offers not only beer, but gingerbread and toys as well. The aroma of Nuremberg's special gingerbread, *Lebkuchen,* fills the Hauptmarkt every Christmas. At other times, including the pre-Christmas period (which starts in mid-August), the same aroma may be savored—and tasted—in the many pastry shops throughout the city. The traditional recipes of the original gingerbread are kept secret by the bakeries that produce it. Companies

Munich (München)—Nuremberg (Nürnberg)

DEPART MUNICH HBF	TRAIN NUMBER	ARRIVE NUREMBERG HBF
0747	ICE 882	0930
0851	ICE 1610	1028
0947	ICE 860	1130
1029	ICE 826	1224
1051	ICE 1518	1229
1147	ICE 868	1330

DEPART NUREMBERG HBF	TRAIN NUMBER	ARRIVE MUNICH HBF
1430	ICE 867+787	1612
1530	ICE 1517	1711
1630	ICE 869	1812
1730	ICE 1519	1909

plus hourly service at 30 minutes past the hour until 2130.

Daily, unless otherwise noted
Distance: 125 miles (201 km)

such as Lebkuchen Schmidt invite visitors to sample their products. Arrangements may be made by either of the tourist offices. Trying to save purchases can be tempting. To avoid teasing your tastebuds and have gifts for those left behind, we suggest having the bakery shop ship some home for you.

Toy shops are in profusion, and the **Toy Museum** on Karl Street, two blocks from the Hauptmarkt via Augustinerstrasse, has a splendid display of dolls, puppets, and tin soldiers. The museum also houses an interesting model-railway layout, featuring—of all things—the train station in Omaha, Nebraska.

Nuremberg's most famous citizen was Albrecht Dürer, a man who towered above his time. The stately home in which he lived, from 1509 until his death in 1529, is located two blocks north of the Toy Museum, past the Wine Market, on Albrecht Dürer Strasse. The house holds a collection of the famed artist's works. The area surrounding it is probably the most interesting section within the walled city. Unfortunately, Dürer's most famous work, *The Four Apostles,* now rests in Munich, but a number of his paintings are exhibited along with a multilingual film presentation on his life and works. The New Museum features exhibits showing free form, applied arts, and modern design.

If you have any doubt about that first day excursion by train originating in Nuremberg, check in at the **Verkehrsmuseum (Transportation Museum)**, three blocks to the right of the train station as you face it. The museum is open 0900–1700 Tuesday–Sunday. There you will find the *Adler* (Eagle), the first German locomotive, complete with the two beer barrels mounted on its tender.

If you are a model-railroad fan, you will be pleased to note that, in addition to the Toy Museum, two of Germany's largest manufacturers of HO- and N-gauge equipment, **Arnold and Fleischmann,** are located in Nuremberg. **E. P. Lehmann,** the manufacturer of G-scale equipment for the increasingly popular outdoor garden railways, is located at Sagnerstrasse 1–5 (*Tel:* 83 40 21). It has operating layouts, and visitors are welcome. The operating hours are seasonal, so check with one of the tourist information offices if you would like to visit.

Day Excursion to

The Romantic Road
Delightfully Medieval

Depart from Munich Hauptbahnhof
Distance: 172 miles (276 km) by bus and 173 miles (278 km) by train
Total Journey Time: 12 hours, 36 minutes
City Dialing Code for Rothenburg ob der Tauber: 9861
Tourist Information Office: Rothenburg o.d. T. Tourist Office, Marktplatz 2, D-91541
Tel: 4 04 92; *Fax:* 8 68 07
Internet: www.rothenburg.de
E-mail: info@rothenburg.de
The Romantic Road, Deutsche Touring GmbH, Am Romerhof 17, 60486
  Frankfurt/Main
Tel: 49-89593889; *Fax:* 49–895503965

Too long and too far? Not in the least. **The Romantic Road,** packed with superb scenery and delightful medieval villages, is worth every minute. The Deutsche Bahn (German Railroad) bus that takes you from Munich to **Würzburg** makes two stops en route: one in **Dinkelsbühl** for lunch and one in **Rothenburg** for sight-seeing. After these pleasant interludes, plus a return trip to Munich on one of Germany's lightning-fast InterCity Express trains, you will wonder where the day has gone.

The Romantic Road bus carries an English-speaking guide. This trip has become so popular that seat reservations are necessary. Reservations can be made at the EurAide, Inc. office in the Munich railway station opposite track No. 11 in the main hall, three doors down from the line of four telephone booths. The office is open 0800–1600 Monday–Friday (*Tel:* 089 59 38 89). Seat reservations are €5.11, and the Eurailpass, Europass, and GermanRail Pass provide a 60 percent discount.

Munich (München)—The Romantic Road

Romantic Road excursion by bus from München to Dinkelsbühl to Rothenburg ob der Tauber to Würzburg; return to München by train.
Schedule shown is valid from April 1 to October 31, 2002, but subject to change without notice.

Europa Bus Trip 190:

Depart München Hbf Starnberger Bahnhof	0900
Arrive Dinkelsbühl (Schweinemarkt)	1245
Depart Dinkelsbühl (Schweinemarkt)	1400
Arrive Rothenburg ob der Tauber (Bahnhof)	1450
Depart Rothenburg ob der Tauber (Bahnhof)	1615
Arrive Würzburg (Busbahnhof)	1830

DEPART WÜRZBURG HBF	TRAIN NUMBER	ARRIVE MUNICH HBF
1928	ICE 863+883	2212
2033	ICE 683	2259
2036	ICE 921	2337
2128	ICE 865+885	0012+1 (next day)
2229	ICE 923	0126+1 (next day)

Distance: 172 miles (276 km) by bus, plus 173 miles (278 km) by train

For detailed information and registration, contact:
EurAide, Inc.
München Hauptbahnhof
Bahnhofplatz 2
D-80335 München Germany
Tel: (089) 59 38 89
Fax: (089) 550 3965
E-mail: euraide@compuserve.com

Deutsche Touring Gmbh
Am Römerhof 17
60486 Frankfurt (Main) Germany
Tel: 49 (0) 8959 38 89
Fax: 49 (0) 89 550 3965

Note: Eurail passes, Europasses, and GermanRail passes are valid for a 60 percent discount on this excursion. Credit cards accepted.

MUNICH *The Romantic Road*

The Romantic Road bus has no special markings. Ask for its departure position (which is usually No. 20/21) when you make reservations. Your reservation ensures you a seat on the bus, but not a specified seat. Be at the bus station at about 0830, therefore, to ensure getting a window seat.

Rothenburg is one of the most frequently visited places in Germany.

Every year thousands of visitors from all parts of the world come to this ancient walled city. You will see why Rothenburg is picturesque and photogenic. Be sure to take a camera. Probably more photographs have been taken of its **Kobolzeller Tor** and **Siebers Tower** than of any other scene in Germany.

The town is a museum piece of medieval character. Most of its 12,500 citizens living within or just outside the city's walls work to serve the tourist in some manner. This town has survived, even in the twenty-first century, as the "Jewel of the Middle Ages."

Enjoy your visit in Rothenburg, but keep your eye on the town clock, for the Romantic Road bus continues on its journey to Würzburg and its final destination, **Frankfurt,** promptly at 1615. If for some reason you do miss the 1615 bus departure, the German railroad also operates another bus line between Rothenburg and Steinach, where you can connect with train service back to Munich.

Arriving in Würzburg at 1830, you have the opportunity of returning to Munich at 1928 aboard ICE 863 or 883; or, you might want to have dinner and linger. A later departure would allow you to stay in Würzburg for several hours. The last train departs Würzburg at 2229. There are several restaurants immediately across from the park fronting the east side of the Würzburg rail station where you could enjoy dinner.

Rothenburg is loaded with living legends. One concerns the salvation of the town from certain destruction by its wine-drinking mayor. In 1631, during the Thirty Years' War, the town was captured by imperial troops under the command of General Tilly. While the general toyed with the idea of destroying the town and executing its councilors, he was handed a tankard holding more than three quarts of heavy Franconian wine to aid his meditation.

The general promised mercy to Rothenburg if one of its councilors could drain the "bumper" in one mighty draft. Mayor Nusch did and thus saved the town. Although he slept for three days and nights following the mighty quaff, apparently he suffered no other ill effects, for he lived another 37 years and died at the age of 80—with a smile on his face. The historic deed is reenacted daily by a glockenspiel installed in the gable of the Councilors' Tavern at 1100, 1200, 1300, 1400, 1500, 2000, 2100, and 2200. Be there!

Day Excursion to

Ulm
World's Tallest Cathedral

Depart from Munich Hauptbahnhof
Distance by Train: 92 miles (148 km)
Average Train Time: 1 hour, 13 minutes
City Dialing Code: 731
Tourist Information Office: Tourist-Information Ulm/Neu-Ulm, Stadthaus,
    Münsterplatz, D-89073 Ulm.
Tel: (0731) 161–2830; *Fax:* (0731) 161–1641
Internet: www.tourismus.ulm.de
E-mail: info@tourismus.ulm.de
Hours: 0900–1800 Monday–Friday, 0900–1300 Saturday, and 1100–1400 Sunday
    (May–October)
Notes: A display of tourist information is in the railway station to your left upon en-
tering the station from the train platforms.

S ilhouetted against a blue sky, the Gothic spire of the **Ulm Cathedral** is a scene you are not likely to forget. Poised on the banks of the swift-moving Danube, Ulm is a picturesque representation of a typical Swabian city. Birthplace of Albert Einstein, Ulm has withstood the onslaughts of many conflicts, including Napoleonic campaigns, with great dignity. Considered a miracle, its cathedral escaped damage throughout World War II, although serious damage was inflicted on the town by Allied bombing. All of Ulm's original facades have now been repaired or replaced.

With a skyward thrust of 528 feet, the spire of the cathedral is the tallest in the world. Although the foundation stone was laid in 1377, the two towers and the spire were not completed until 1890. When the central nave was completed in 1471, it could hold 20,000 people—twice as many as the town's population at that time. Truly, this was an ambitious undertaking right from the start.

The clear vertical lines and the lightness of the cathedral's architecture are beautiful. The interior is open 0900–1700 daily with extended summer hours, except when services are being conducted. There is no entrance fee, but there is a small admission charge to ascend the spire.

Speaking of the spire, a breathtaking panorama of Ulm, the Danube, and the surrounding area rewards those who climb its 768 steps. A word of caution: the climb is rigorous and should not be attempted unless you have good physical stamina. Back on the Münster square in front of the cathedral, you will notice the remarkable contrast of the old Gothic style and the contemporary architecture of the **Stadthaus** (Town House), built by Richard

Munich (München)—Ulm

DEPART MUNICH HBF	TRAIIN NUMBER	ARRIVE ULM HBF
0733	ICE 598	0849
0742	EC 66	0903
0833	ICE 798	0949
0846	IC 710	1003
0933	ICE 596	1049
1036	ICE 796	1149
1046	EC 18	1203
1137	ICE 594	1249
1142	IC 118	1303

DEPART ULM HBF	TRAIN NUMBER	ARRIVE MUNICH HBF
1408	ICE 793	1522
1455	EC 65	1615
1508	ICE 593	1622
1608	ICE 795	1722
1655	IC 517	1816
1708	ICE 595	1824
1808	ICE 797	1924
1855	IC 611	2016

and continuing frequent service until 2315

Daily
Distance: 117 miles (189 km)

Meier in 1993. This modern building offers a variety of activities, including exhibitions, concerts, conferences, and tourist information, plus magnificent views of the cathedral.

You will get a brief view of the Danube and the cathedral when crossing the railroad bridge entering Ulm. Watch on the right-hand side of the train immediately after passing the Neu-Ulm (New Ulm) station. The railroad bridge has a pedestrian crossing, so you may want to return to that vantage point again for a more prolonged observation. The bridge can be reached after leaving the station by walking to the right and following the railroad. Continue straight ahead, not turning with the trolleys, on the promenade to the river's edge and the approach to the bridge. Cross onto the bridge to stand on the federal state borderline separating Bavaria and Baden-Württenberg right over the middle of the Danube.

Another route to the Danube is through the **Fischerviertel** (Fishermen's Quarter), which lies to the south of the cathedral. En route, you will pass the picturesque **Schiefes Haus** (Crooked House), which has settled over a canal. If you walk downstream on the Danube's left bank, the river promenade will bring you to the **Metzgerturm** (Butcher's Tower), another Ulm landmark. Walk on the ancient city wall and see the old traditional Ulm river boat—the *Ulmer Schachtel*—on the other bank of the Danube.

Walking to the city center from the Metzgerturm, you'll reach the **Rathaus** (Town Hall) from 1370, famous for its opulent frescoes and ornamental carved figures. On the east gable is a beautiful astronomer's clock (1520).

Visit the **Ulm Museum,** where you will find displays of art and culture ranging from the Middle Ages to modern times. Notable features are the collections of modern graphics and important examples of Late Gothic art, as well as prehistoric finds such as the 30,000- to 40,000-year-old figure "Lion Man." There are also exhibits concerning some of Ulm's famous citizens, such as the physicist Albert Einstein, and Albrecht Berblinger, the "tailor of Ulm," who in 1811 made man's first serious attempt to fly. A model of his hang glider is on exhibit in the covered courtyard of the Rathaus. The funny Einstein Fountain, in front of the former Imperial city's arsenal ("Zeughaus") at the east of the old city center, merits a short visit.

Although the cathedral dominates the scene, a stroll through Ulm will reveal its other aspects—exclusive shops, boutiques, and department stores. For refreshment in between sight-seeing, you will find traditional old taverns, pleasant restaurants, comfortable inns, and good hotels where you may enjoy Swabian specialty dishes accompanied by drafts of good Ulm beer.

Unique in the field of museums is Ulm's **German Bread Museum** (Salzstadelgasse 10, D-89073 Ulm; *Tel:* 69955; *Fax:* 6021161), situated in the beautifully restored salt warehouse from 1592. It presents an impressive display of the major ingredient of our daily diet for the last 8,000 years. The museum is open 1000–1700 daily. It's only a 10-minute walk from the rail station. Not only does the museum effectively tell the story of breadmaking, it makes you aware of how serious hunger can be.

Very remarkable and to be noticed everywhere in Ulm and Neu-Ulm are the buildings and installations of the former Federal Fortification Ulm ("Bundesfestung"). Important landmarks of Europe's largest remaining nineteenth-century fortifications are the **Citadel Wilhelmsburg** on the "Michelsberg"—from where you have a splendid view of the city—Blaubeuren Gate or the "Glacis" bastion, now Neu-Ulm's municipal park.

Ulm University offers a Path of Art. More than 60 large works by artists of repute such as Niki de Saint-Phalle or Max Bill are presented along a 1½-kilometer tour around the university and Science Park Ulm. To get there, take bus line 3 or 5 from the central station to James-Franck-Ring.

Wiblingen Monastery (founded in honor of St. Martin in 1093), with its Baroque basilica and splendid Rococo library, is only 5 kilometers away (bus line 3 from Hauptbahnhof to Pranger). The famous library is open 1000–1200 and 1400–1700 except Monday (April–October). Church visit is free, but there is an admission charge for the library.

With so much to see and do, the **Ulm Card** may be just the ticket for your visit. It costs €4.60 per person or €9.71 per family. Prices include transport on buses and trams, benefits, and reduced prices for sites, guided tours, and a map of Ulm and Neu-Ulm. The Ulm Card is available at the tourist office, along with the monthly schedule of events.

Greece

I nasmuch as Greece is most famous for its archaeological finds and significance in antiquity, many visitors are astounded to learn this scenic, sun-drenched country also includes about 1,400 islands and more than 7,500 caves, many of which contain subterranean rivers, lakes, and waterfalls. Complementing this varied geographic wonder are the mountain ranges such as the Pindus and, of course, the waters of the Mediterranean, the Aegean, and the Saronic Gulf linking Attica (Athens area and its port Piraeus) to the Peloponnese.

CHAT Tours, a leading tour operator in Greece, offers many delightful sight-seeing tours and cruises to the Greek islands. The tour campus is located at 4, Stadiou Street, Athens, Greece (*Tel:* 323 0827, 322 2886, or 322 3137; *Fax:* 323 5270 or 323 1200).

For tourist information contact the Greek National Tourism Organization in North America:

New York: Olympic Tower, 645 Fifth Avenue, 5th Floor, New York, NY 10022. *Tel:* (212) 421–5777; *Fax:* (212) 826–6940; *Internet:* **www.gogreece.com** or **www.gnto.gr**; *E-mail:* gnto@orama.com

Chicago: 168 North Michigan Avenue, Suite 600, Chicago, IL 60601. *Tel:* (312) 782–1084; *Fax:* 782–1091

Los Angeles: 611 West Sixth Street, Suite 2198, Los Angeles, CA 90017. *Tel:* (213) 626–6696; *Fax:* 489–9744

Toronto: 1300 Bay Street, Upper Level, Toronto, Ontario M5R 3K8. *Tel:* (416) 968–2220; *Fax:* (416) 968–6533; *Internet:* **www.gogreece. com** or **www.aei.ca/~gntom**; *E-mail:* grnto.tor@sympatico.ca

Montreal: Office National du Tourism Greece, 1233 Rue De La Montagne, Suite 101, Montreal, Quebec H3G 1Z2. *Tel:* (514) 871–1535; *Fax:* 871–1498

GREECE

Banking

- **Currency:** Euro (€)
- **Exchange rate at press time:** €1.10 = U.S. $1.00
- **Hours:** 0800–1400 Monday–Thursday; 0800–1300 Friday

Communications

- **Country Code:** 30
- **Direct dial:** AT&T: 00–800–1311; MCI: 00–800–1211; Sprint: 00–800–1411. Phone cards may be purchased at most kiosks and Greek Telecommunications offices. Public red phones and gray phones at kiosks are metered for long-distance calls. Pay the kiosk owner for number of units charged.

Rail Travel in Greece

The rail system of Greece is limited and presents a challenge to rail travelers. The trains can be too few and too slow. With a little perseverance, however, traveling by train in Greece can be charming, especially on overnight trains in first-class sleepers.

The line from Athens to Thessaloniki in the north has been modernized, and several other major modernization programs are underway by the Hellenic Railways Organization (OSE). Narrow-gauge lines serve the Peloponnese, the southernmost part of Greece. Both networks serve Athens.

The OSE (*Internet:* www.ose.gr) accepts a variety of multicountry railpasses, including **Eurailpass, Europass** (with purchase of the Greece add-on), the **Eurail Selectpass,** the **Balkan Flexipass,** and the national railpass—the **Greek Flexipass**—for travel solely within Greece. (See the Appendix for prices and types of multicountry rail passes.)

Eurail bonuses include:

- Free ferry crossings (railpass must be valid in Greece) from Patras, Igoumenitsa, and Corfu to Brindisi (Italy) on Hellenic Mediterranean Lines (HML) and Blue Star Ferries. A $20 U.S. surcharge applicable in July/August. Port taxes are extra.
- Free ferry crossings (railpass must be valid in Greece) from Patras and Igoumenitsa to Ancona and Bari (Italy) on Superfast Ferries. A $20 U.S. surcharge applicable in July/August. Port taxes are extra.
- 25 percent discount on a 1-day cruise—Athens to Aegina-Poros-Hydra through ETOS Travel; plus reduced hotel rates. *Tel:* 30 1 522 6138 for reservations.

Greek Flexipass

Provides unlimited first-class rail travel for any 3 or any 5 days within a 1-month period.

	Adult	Child	Youth
3 days/1 month	$86	$58	$62
5 days/1 month	$120	$85	$89

Child: age 2–11; under age 2 travels free.
Youth: age 12–25

Greece to Italy via Ferry—Crossing the Mediterranean

Attika Superfast Ferries operate daily, departing in the evening for arrival on the following day. The shortest journey time to Italy is Patras—Brindisi in only about 14 hours; to Bari, about 15 hours; and to Ancona, 19 hours. To reach the Patras Superfast ferry terminal from the rail station, turn left as you exit the station and walk along the street side of the quay about 300 yards.

Advance reservations are highly recommended, especially during June through September. Prices vary according to accommodations (from Pullman seats to deluxe cabins). For complete details, sailing dates, and fares, contact the individual ferry companies or their sales agent.

Superfast Ferries Headquarters:
146, Vas. Pavlou Str. 16673 Voula, Athens
Tel: (01) 89119900; *Fax:* (01) 8919999
Internet: www.superfast.com

Superfast Ferries Sales Agent in U.S:
Kompas Holidays International
2826 E. Commercial Blvd.
Fort Lauderdale, FL 33308
Tel: 954–771–9200; *Fax:* 954–771–9841
E-mail: info.usa@superfast.com

Other ferry companies offering Eurail and Europass (with Greece option) discounts are:
Hellenic Mediterranean Lines
HSAP Building
PO Box 80057
GR-185 10 Pireaus, Greece
Tel: 30 1 4225341; *Fax:* 30 1 4225317
Internet: www.hml.it

Adriatica (Tirrenia Lines)
Zattere 1411
30123 Venezia, Italy
Tel: 39 41 781611; *Fax:* 39 41 781894
Internet: www.adriatica.com

Athens

(Athinai)

City Dialing Code: 1

Arriving by Air

Athens International Airport—Eleftherios Venizelos. Athens' newly opened (2001) international airport (*Internet:* www.athensairport-2001.gr) is located 27 kilometers northeast of Athens. The new airport meets the goal of enhancing tourism to Athens in preparation for the Olympics in 2004.

Airport–City Links: Airport Express Bus Line E95 connects the airport with Syntagma Square (Athens city center). Buses run every 25 minutes 0630–2120; less frequent service throughout the night. Fare €2.93. Plans are to develop a suburban rail link to connect the airport with downtown Athens in 2003.

Money exchange, ATMs, and **tourist information** are available in the Arrivals area, Level 0, of the main terminal.

If you are departing Athens by air, the airport's tax-free shopping area offers a wide selection of Greek apparel, liquors, and delicacies. Unlike many tax-free shopping facilities, the one in Athens's airport has some reasonable values, but you can't bargain with the salespeople—leave that for shopping in the city.

Arriving by Train

Arrivals from eastern European countries and points in northern Greece terminate in Athens's Larissa Station, a standard-gauge facility. If you are traveling via Attika's Superfast Ferries or Hellenic Mediterranean Lines ferries to the port of Patras, the Peloponnese Station (narrow gauge) will be your arrival point. The two stations lie parallel to each other, with a connecting, overhead footbridge. Each has a train-information booth with a limited amount of city information available.

Both stations have taxi stands and bus service, but we recommend that new arrivals use the taxi. The taxi fare from the station area to the tourist office on Syntagma (Constitution) Square is inexpensive, about €3 plus baggage charges, and well worth it.

Larissa Station serves the standard-gauge rail lines to the north.

- **Money exchange:** At the north end of the train platform. The sign reads BANK. Hours: 0800–1830 Monday–Friday; 0900–1400 Saturday; 0900–1300 Sunday.
- **Train information:** In a booth to your immediate left when entering the station from the train platform area. Open daily, 0600–2330. *Tel:* 823–7741.
- **Baggage storage:** In room marked Left Baggage Office located to the left as you enter the station from the track side (open 0630–2300).
- **Train reservations:** Are best obtained at the Greek Railways office at No. 1–3 Karolou Street or No. 6 Sina Street. Get taxi instructions from the tourist office on 2 Amerikis Street.
- **Railpass validation:** Also available at the Greek Railways main office. Railpasses can also be validated at ticket windows in the stations, but only on your departure day.

Athens's **Peloponnese Station** serves the narrow-gauge lines to the south.

- **Money exchange:** Not available. Use the footbridge to cross to the Larissa Station Bank, or use the exchange services in the tourist information office on Syntagma Square.
- **Train information:** In a booth to your immediate left when entering the station. Open 0730–1900 daily throughout the summer. The hours are split, 0730–1230 and 1630–1900, the rest of the year. *Tel:* 513–1601.
- **Train reservations:** Are best obtained at the **Hellenic Railways** office at No. 1–3 Karolou Street or No. 6 Sina Street. Get taxi or bus instructions from the tourist office on Syntagma Square.
- **Railpass validation:** Available at ticket windows in the stations, or go to the aforementioned Hellenic Railways office.

Tourist Information/Hotel Reservations

- *Hellenic Tourism Organization:* No. 2 Amerikis Street, Box 1017, Syntagma, Athens 10110; *Tel:* 322 3111; *Fax:* 322 2841

Money exchange hours: 0800–1830 daily

Tourist information hours: 0900–1900 Sunday–Friday; 1000–1600 Saturday

Notes: Located in the vicinity of Syntagma Square. When you are facing the Parliament Building from the bottom of the square in the cafe area, the tourist information office is just across the street on the left. The tourist office also offers money exchange services.

Hotel and pension reservations: Hellenic Chamber of Hotels, located in the National Bank at 2 Karagiorgi Servias Street, Syntagma Square. *Tel:* 322 2545 and 331 0022. For reservations by mail, the address is Festival Office, Stadiou Street, Athens. *Tel:* 322 1459.

Getting Around in Athens

Getting around in Athens is easy with its extensive bus and trolley-bus system. Obtain a public transport map showing routes and Metro stations at any of the tourist information offices. The Metro is slowly being modernized and expanded in preparation for the 2004 Olympics in Athens. Formerly called the "Athens-Piraeus Electric Railway," there were three lines open at press time. Additional services and expansions will continue to take place. Progress was slowed somewhat by archaeological finds. Even now, though, you can marvel at the extensive use of marble in the Syntagma station.

Sights/Attractions/Tours

Most of the tours offered are bus tours that include some walking. Consequently, you should inquire as to the tour's duration and terrain before signing up, and don't forget to wear comfortable walking shoes. To avoid the daytime heat, select an evening tour, when available. Most of the tourist attractions are illuminated.

The city tourist office is an excellent source for information concerning other areas of the country. Be certain to inform the attendant you speak with that you hold a Eurailpass. Otherwise you might find yourself signing up for a bus tour when a rail trip would suffice for the transportation to the site you want to see.

Although there is more to Athens than the **Acropolis,** it should be the first place to visit during your stay in the city. If you use the ISAP electric railway, detrain at Thission for the Acropolis. All else in and around Athens becomes secondary to this symbol of classic perfection that has stood majestically above Athens for about 2,500 years. Don't rush your visit, or you will regret it. Plan to spend an entire day, and if you go there during the summer months, go prepared with some sunscreen, sun hats, bottled water, and comfortable walking shoes.

The **Parthenon** is the focal point of the Acropolis, but there is much more to see. Study the **Propylaea**, the impressive entrance to the sanctuary, along with the **Temple of Athena-Niki** and the elegant row of maidens along the facade of the Erechtheion. You can peer down on the Theater of Dionysius from the rim of the Acropolis, but go there later to feel its "presence."

During the tourist season, a light-and-sound show of the Acropolis is presented in several languages. Don't miss it. The program in English starts at 2100. The tourist office can provide you with more details. You view the show from an opposite hillside, and it can cool down considerably. You may want to take a light sweater or pullover.

The Romans made their presence known in Athens, too. A group of ruins dating back to the days of Julius Caesar clusters about the **Roman Forum** at the beginning of Aeolou Street. There are so many other sights to be seen that we recommend a guided tour as the only means of possibly scratching the surface of this wonderful city where Western civilization began.

With Athens's extensive history, expect to find a full retinue of museums. You won't be disappointed. Be aware that you may be required to check any bags, including purses, and that most museums charge a fee for videotaping within the museum. If your stay in the city is limited, visit the **Benaki Museum,** located on the corner of Vassilissis Sofias Avenue and Koumbari Street (*Tel:* 361–16178). In its 28 chambers, you will see exhibits ranging from the Bronze Age to the beginning of the twentieth century. As you pass through the centuries of statuary development, note the style by which the sculptors slowly developed the technique of depicting fingers and toes.

The modern city of Athens also holds much interest for visitors. You must visit the **Tomb of the Unknown Warrior,** with its colorful guards. Go to a cafe on **Syntagma Square** for coffee and pastry. Climb the time-worn steps leading through the **Plaka Quarter,** which hugs the base of the Acropolis. Take the Metro to Faliro Station and sample the fruits of the sea at one of Mikrolimano's charming seafood restaurants.

Despite being one of the easternmost cities in Europe, Athens has a distinct Western appearance. Modern Athens surrounds the splendor of its ancient Acropolis, which has a nobility that survives time and change. That first glimpse of the Parthenon from the window of the plane or train that brought you to Athens remains a once-in-a-lifetime experience.

Addendum to Athens

Select one of Athens's "tavernas" and enjoy its food, music, and dancing. To experience a popular form of Greek entertainment, visit a Bouzouki nightclub. Bouzouki music is similar to American blues in that the music reflects the pain and pathos often present in love and friendships. Before you participate in the traditional plate breaking, check with the management as to the cost per dozen. You could end up spending a lot of euros.

Tourists are targets for ploys and pranks throughout the world. Athens is no exception. A waiter may suggest that you consume bottled water with your meal. After all, you may have been warned not to drink the regular water. Bottled water is a good idea, but insist that the waiter open the bottle at your table. Otherwise, you might receive an opened bottle of water that was just recently filled from the water tap in the kitchen. Or order a bottle of carbonated water. That's hard to bootleg!

Day Excursions

Riding a narrow-gauge train through areas steeped in the history of Western civilization is sufficiently stimulating to make the traveler overlook the lack of air-conditioning, posh dining cars, and other amenities. Our day excursion to **Argos,** the oldest continuously inhabited town in Greece, is one such adventure. **Corinth,** both modern and ancient, is rich in Greek history, from Alexander the Great down through Roman rule. **Patras,** port city and scene of the most spectacular carnival in Greece, is still another

Train/Ferry Connections to Other Base Cities from Athens (Athinai)

Depart Athens Peloponnese Station by train to Patras (see rail schedule in "Day Excursion to Patras" section). Depart Patras by ferry to Brindisi, Italy (see previous section "Greece to Italy via Ferry—Crossing the Mediterranean"), and then depart Brindisi by train to the selected base city:

Brindisi—Rome (Roma) Termini Trains

DEPART BRINDISI	TRAIN NUMBER	ARRIVE ROME TERMINI
0647	ES 9352	1244
1054	ES 9354	1650
1647	ES 9358	2256
2246	ICN 782	0629+1

Brindisi—Milan (Milano) Centrale Trains

DEPART BRINDISI	TRAIN NUMBER	ARRIVE MILAN CENTRALE
0748	ES 9416	1655
1348	ES 9420	2255
1949	ICN 762	0715+1

Reservations required
+1 Arrives next day

Note: Although rail travel is possible on the Athens (Athenai Larissa station), Thessaloniki-to-Budapest route, Eurail passes do not cover travel through Yugoslavia and other eastern European countries (except Hungary). Also, travelers are warned of the hazards of traveling in politically unstable areas. The potential traveler choosing this route is urged to consult a European rail ticket agent for detailed schedule information and for information about procedures and visa requirements in eastern European countries.

place to see on the Peloponnese. **Piraeus,** main port of Athens, provides culinary delights from the surrounding sea.

An InterCity train between Athens and **Larissa** provides an opportunity to spend several hours in Larissa during a day excursion out of Athens. Depart Athens at 0800, arrive in Larissa at 1200, and depart at 1811 to arrive back in Athens by 2217. Or, depart Larissa at 1953 for arrival in Athens at 0009. Although the IC 60 does not haul a restaurant car, there are beverages and some food available. Also, you will find an abundance of cafes and patisseries on the town square. Larissa, the "citadel," is the capital of Thessaly, and for a time it was the home of Hippocrates, the Father of Medicine.

Argos (Arghos)
Oldest Greek Town

Depart from Athens Peloponnese Station
Distance by Train: 89 miles (144 km)
Average Train Time: 2 hours, 30 minutes
City Dialing Code: 751

Argos does not have a tourist information office. Neither does it have a tourist police office such as one finds in many of the smaller towns throughout Greece. But these absences present no great hardship, for most of its sights are within the city limits. The area must be the birthplace of all Greeks who have ever worked in the United States as waiters. We met two of them by just standing on a corner and looking perplexed.

The railway station is about a kilometer from the town square in Argos. To reach the town square on foot, walk straight out of the station to the main road, where a road sign points to the right in the direction of town. Taxis are available for a nominal fare.

For sight-seeing, orient yourself with the church in the town square. From its front door, you can reach the **Argos museum** by crossing the street, turning left, and proceeding to the first cross street, where you then turn right. The museum is half a block farther on the left-hand side of the street and is open daily, except Tuesday. Admission is charged. This museum has an excellent collection of archaeological exhibits.

The **ancient theater and Roman ruins** lie on the outskirts of town, in the direction of the hillsides. They are a 5-minute taxi ride or a 15-minute walk from the museum. On foot, turn left at the next street beyond the museum and walk until you reach the next main intersection. Turn right, and walk straight ahead to the site. If there is the slightest tinge of archaeology in your blood, you'll love this spot.

The theater has ninety tiers, which were cut into the hillside on rather a steep angle, making it possible for a perfect, uninterrupted view of the stage area from any seat in the house. Oddly enough, the 20,000 seating capacity of this amphitheater is more than adequate for the present 19,000 population of Argos.

History comes out to meet you on this day excursion. Argos lies in the plain of Argolis on the Peloponnese peninsula, land of myth and magic. Your mind can run rampant as you journey there. The *Iliad*, the *Odyssey*, and the beautiful Helen hover over all travelers who enter.

Modern history appears first as the train crosses the Isthmus of Corinth. Below the railroad bridge lies the canal connecting the Aegean and Ionian Seas. Alexander the Great, Caesar, and Nero all failed in their attempts to

Athens (Athinai)—Argos (Arghos)

DEPART ATHENS PELOPONNESE	TRAIN NUMBER	ARRIVE ARGOS
0700	IC 08	0924
0724	1430	1017
1035	422	1326
1507	424	1802

DEPART ARGOS	TRAIN NUMBER	ARRIVE ATHENS PELOPONNESE
1511	423	1800
1852	1433	2142
2024	IC 09	2248

Distance: 89 miles (144 km)

construct the waterway through 4 miles of solid rock. A French engineering firm finally succeeded in 1893. Watch for it about 1 hour and 20 minutes after leaving Athens. The best view is from the right side of the train. The railroad bridge is only 108 feet long; if you intend taking pictures, have everything poised and ready to go, for it passes quickly.

Medieval history is next in line as you approach Argos, where the hillsides northwest of the city reveal at their highest point a Venetian fortress, which dominates the **White Chapel of the Prophet Elias** and **Our Lady of the Rocks Convent** lying below.

Ancient history unfolds in Argos itself, with the 20,000-seat theater, and 5 miles east of the town with the **Argive Heraeon** and the scattered remains of Greece's oldest recognizable temple (800 B.C.). **Tiryns**, legendary birthplace of Hercules, is also in the area. These last two sights are not on the rail line and are best visited by taxi from Argos.

Argos is the oldest continuously inhabited town in Greece. Many archaeologists suspect that it may be the oldest in all of Europe. Legends, many of them the basic stuff from which most of Greek mythology sprang, have their origins in Argos and the area surrounding it. In the legendary time of Danaus, storytellers relate how his fifty daughters slew their husbands on their wedding night and then tried to make amends with the devil by trying to fill a bottomless cask with water carried in sieves from the Lake of Lerna.

The legend does, however, have a happy ending. One of Danaus's daughters, realizing that it could ruin her honeymoon, let her spouse escape the murderous nuptial-night activities. For this she was rewarded by becoming the ancestral matriarch of a long line of mythological heroes.

The modern town of Argos was built up over ancient ruins from previous centuries of conflict. The last ethnic group to participate in that form of urban renewal was the Turks, who ravaged the town in 1397. As a result, Argos has scant visible remains of its ancient origins except the theater and the Roman baths.

Day Excursion to

Corinth (Korinthos)

And the Isthmian Canal

Depart from Athens Peloponnese Station
Distance by Train: 57 miles (91 km)
Average Train Time: 1 hour, 32 minutes
City Dialing Code: 741

ATHENS *Corinth*

This day excursion runs from modern Greece back through the millennia to the Bronze Age. You have the opportunity to see modern Corinth (Korinthos), a typical "new" Greek city, and its port on the Peloponnese. You may delve as well into the hillside of ancient Corinth, where Saint Paul established a church, Nero fiddled around with a canal, and Julius Caesar implemented an earlier version of the Marshall Plan.

En route to Corinth, the railroad skirts the Aegean Sea and crosses the Isthmian Canal. Watch for the canal when the train is about 1 hour and 20 minutes out of Athens. The center of the canal runs 285 feet deep through solid rock. The railroad bridge passes 200 feet above the level of the water for a spectacular view.

Greek and Roman rulers (the infamous Nero included) periodically attempted to breach the isthmus with a canal, but until a French company using modern methods succeeded in 1882–1893, all had failed. The ancients hauled their small ships across the isthmus on rollers. Vestiges of the portage road are still visible just after the train crosses the bridge. Watch on the right side of the train for the best view. Have your camera poised and ready—the train traverses the area quickly.

The present "new" city of Corinth, moved to its site in 1858 after an earthquake destroyed "old" Corinth, was leveled by an equally devastating earthquake in 1928. The site has had its share of earth tremors; ancient scribes record devastation in A.D. 522 and 551. Called an "undistinguished town," new Corinth is interesting in that it represents a community rebuilt on anti-seismic principles of low buildings that, paradoxically, give it an air of impermanence.

In fear of pirates, old Corinth was built well back from the sea. This strategic position served the city well. It prospered and became one of the three great city-states of Greece, along with Athens and Sparta. Things went reasonably well until Corinth led the Achaean League against the Romans in 146 B.C. The Romans won the ball game and, a la Carthage (as was the custom in those days), laid waste to Corinth. After the city withstood a hundred years of total desolation, Julius Caesar decided to rebuild Corinth, and it blossomed into one of the great trading cities of the Roman Empire.

Athens (Athinai)—Corinth (Korinthos)

Depart Athens Peloponnese	Train Number	Arrive Corinth
0724	1430	0919
0849	IC 20	1022
0937	302	1135
1035	422	1226
1207	IC 10	1339

Depart Corinth	Train Number	Arrive Athens Peloponnese
1417	IC 23	1549
1611	423	1800
1659	303	1900
1829	IC 11	2001
1954	1433	2142
2033	IC 25	2204
2117	IC 09	2248

Distance: 57 miles (91 km)

During his eighteen-month sojourn in Corinth, Saint Paul became alarmed about the sinful ways of the Corinthians and frequently "read the riot act" to the city fathers. Because of his violent condemnation of moral laxity, he was charged with inciting a riot. Instead of dispensing punishment, the city fathers issued Saint Paul a reprimand—and the suggestion that he leave town as soon as possible, which he did.

Historians estimate that at one time the ancient city of Corinth had a population of more than 460,000; today, its citizens number about 21,000. Although termed a *citadel,* the old city was attacked repeatedly and conquered through the ages. During their sweep through Greece, the Turks took over the city in 1458 and again in 1715. In 1458, the Turkish conquest ended when they retreated hastily in ships. The siege of the city in 1715 was described in prose by Lord Byron. There is little Turkish architecture visible in the Corinthian area, due mainly to the short time they were on the premises.

There is excellent bus service between the city and the **archaeological site.** Departures are daily on the hour from 0615 to 2100. The bus terminal is on the south side of the city park. The sign over the terminal reads ΑΡΧΑΙΑ. A taxi will take you there from the railway station for a nominal fare.

To reach the bus station on foot, turn left after leaving the station and then right onto Damaskinou Street and right again onto Ermou Street, just before the Hotel Belle Vue. Turn left at this point and, three blocks later, you'll arrive at the bus terminal on the far left-hand corner of the city park.

For further information check with the **"Tourist Police."** Walk through the park past another bus terminal to a pharmacy on the right-hand side. Turn right and find the police station half a block farther on the left-hand side.

Excavations have been in progress on the site of old Corinth for many years. Literature describing the excavations and the contents of the museum is available as you enter the site. Between 1925 and 1929, extensive excavations were made. Among the findings, an inscription was found that recorded the story of Androcles and the lion. According to Roman history, Androcles removed a thorn from a lion's paw. Later, when he was sentenced to death and thrown to the lions, the lion remembered Androcles's kindness and let him off without a scratch.

In ancient Corinth, you must pay for admission to the grounds and an additional fee to enter the museum. Hours: Monday–Friday 0730–2100 (or sunset); Sunday 1000–1300 and 1500–1900. Plan to spend a minimum of 4 hours at the site. There is a lot of walking. Several canteens serve refreshments outside the main entrance.

Day Excursion to

Patras
Port City

Depart from Athens Peloponnese Station
Distance by Train: 138 miles (222 km)
Average Train Time: 3 hours, 49 minutes
City Dialing Code: 61
Tourist Information Office: Peloponnese and Western Greece Tourism Bureau, 110 Iroon Politehniou, Glyfada, P.C. 262 23 Patras
Tel: 65358–61; *Fax:* 423866
Hours: Daily, 0900–1400
Notes: Ask at the rail station or the ferry terminal for directions. Otherwise, turn right at the quay and walk well beyond the ferry terminal and look for the signs leading to the office. There also is an information office at the entrance of the port of Patras (at Glyfada).

The railway station in Patras lies on the quay, but it's about 500 yards from the pier where ferries depart for Brindisi. You'll spot the pier to the right as the train slows for its stop in the Patras station. A **tourist information** booth is located at the entrance to the ferry terminal. For complete information regarding Patras and its surroundings, visit the Peloponnese and Western Greece Tourism Bureau at the aforementioned address.

Patras is the fourth largest city in Greece. It is also the country's western

Athens (Athinai)—Patras

DEPART ATHENS PELOPONNESE	TRAIN NUMBER	ARRIVE PATRAS
0629	300	1044
0849	IC 20	1215
0937	302	1418
1207	IC 10	1533

DEPART PATRAS	TRAIN NUMBER	ARRIVE ATHENS PELOPONNESE
1354	303	1859
1635	IC 11	2001
1838	IC 25	2204
1959	305	0016+1

+1 arrives next day
Distance: 138 miles (222 km)

gateway. Located at the entrance to the **Gulf of Corinth,** Patras has been a Greek seaport since the beginning of recorded history. Ships large and small are constantly arriving in, and departing from, its harbor. The ferry services of Adriatica (Tirrenia Line) and Hellenic Mediterranean Lines ply between Patras and Brindisi, Italy. Attica Enterprises (Superfast Ferries) ply between Patras and Bari. If you are traveling with a railpass, no doubt you will either enter or leave Greece through the Port of Patras.

Patras is the port where the majority of Greek emigrants sailed for the United States. It is interesting to note that in 1922, refugees fleeing Asia Minor arrived at the pier in Patras penniless. Many of them paid for their passage to America by selling their Oriental carpets, which they had carried from their homelands. Since the early 1960s, Patras has developed into a major Adriatic ferry port.

Spreading below its Venetian castle, Patras is where **Saint Andrew** taught Christianity and was crucified. The saint's head rests in a shrine following its return from Saint Peter's, Rome, in 1964. It was here in Patras in 1809 that Lord Byron first set foot on Greek soil.

The quay is an interesting part of Patras. The long mole, with its benches for resting, extends into the harbor and is a favorite place from which to watch the activity in the harbor. From it you can photograph the arrival of the ferryboats running between the ports of Patras and Brindisi. Patras is not just a busy harbor, however. Its eucalyptus-soaked shorelines, topaz waters, and vast sandy beach at Kilini have made it well known for its spas since antiquity.

Patras has two noteworthy celebrations: the stately procession of Saint Andrew on November 30 and a spectacular carnival during the last ten days before Lent. The city also conducts a classic-theater season during the summer. We suggest a walking tour of Patras starting at the **Trion Symmahon Square,** across from the station and on the right. The long arcaded avenue leading off the park in the direction of the city's heights is studded with stores, restaurants, and specialty shops.

Continue walking on this avenue (Ayiou Nikolaou) to the foot of a broad flight of steps, which will bring you to the site of the ancient **Patras Acropolis.** Enjoy a wonderful view of the city, its harbor, and the surrounding hills and mountains from here. Return to the base of the steps and proceed to the left on Yeoryiou Street, which will lead you to the **Odeum,** a characteristic Roman theater. It was discovered in 1889, but enterprising building contractors subsequently removed much of its marble, requiring the theater to be restored extensively in 1960.

Visitors seeking **Saint Andrews Church** should begin their quest at the Trion Symmahon Square and walk southwest along Andreou Avenue to the church, which stands by the sea at the avenue's end. A park dedicated to Andrew, the patron saint of Scotland, is across from the church.

To reach the city's museum, turn left at the Trion Fountain in Trion Symmahon Square and walk for two blocks, then turn right and walk for two more. The museum has an extensive collection of classic Greek and Roman statues plus a collection of prehistoric pottery. There is an admission charge.

The area surrounding Patras is steeped in history. Use Patras as a "base city" when visiting **Olympia,** original site of the Olympic Games. In Olympia, you can visit the site of the Olympic flame, which is carried by runners to any point in the world where the games are to be held. Also of interest is the arch commemorating Nero's "victory" in a chariot race staged in A.D. 67. The emperor's chariot was pulled by ten horses, while all other competitors had to make do with four—needless to say, Nero won.

Another interesting side trip can be made to the **Achaia Clauss Winery,** 5 miles outside Patras, to view the wine-making process and sample a bit of the product. If interested in either excursion, obtain information at one of the tourist offices.

Culinary delights abound in Patras. A sea-bass dish, *tsipoures,* is a specialty of the area. This and other Greek dishes are available in the tavernas scattered throughout the upper part of town. An American-style restaurant lies just before the Hellenic Lines office on the quay. Customers may stow their suitcases and backpacks there free of charge while waiting for the ferry.

Day Excursion to

Piraeus
Seafood by the Seaside

Depart from Athens Peloponnese Station
Distance by Train: 5 miles (8 km)
Average Train Time: 20 minutes
City Dialing Code: 1
Tourist Information Office: Diikitirio Building, East Central Greece Islands, Marina
  Zeas, 18504
Tel: 4522586; *Fax:* 4522591

Y ou won't need your railpass for this day excursion. You'll be traveling
on Athens's privately owned electric line—ISAP. The line is the
"subway" for the city. A major portion of the rails running to Piraeus,
however, are above ground.

Begin your journey from **Omonia Square** in the city. It connects with
Syntagma (Constitution) Square via Stadhiou Street, which starts right
outside the entrance to the tourist information office. The entrances to the
underground terminal are clearly marked. Be certain to purchase and validate your tickets before boarding. The station uses a center platform for all
trains, so check the directional signs for Piraeus before boarding.

Travel at off-peak hours to avoid the crowds. Service is frequent
throughout the day. Train etiquette in Greece dictates that men relinquish
their seats to the ladies and that the young do the same for elders. When in
Greece, do as the Greeks do.

Leave the electric train at the end of the line in Piraeus. The terminal lies
right at the harbor. To stroll along the quay, exit the station straight ahead,
turning left at the side along the sea. Commercial ships and ferries to
hundreds of island points occupy the piers along the waterfront of the main
harbor. The railway station serving the Athens-Peloponnese Line is to the
right of the subway terminal. Trains for Patras, Corinth, and Argos originate
from there, but passengers are not accepted for the short ride between
Piraeus and Athens.

Throughout the centuries, Piraeus has had successes and failures. In 86
B.C., the Roman general Sulla destroyed the city and its docks, and for
centuries Piraeus was considered an unimportant village. Reconstruction
began only in 1834, when Athens became the capital of Greece. Resettled by
islanders, Piraeus grew rapidly throughout the nineteenth century and
played a large part in the revival of Athens.

Between 1854 and 1859, Piraeus was occupied by an Anglo-French fleet
to prevent Greek nationalists' forays against Turkey, an Allied power in the
Crimean War. In World War II, the port was put out of action in April 1941

ATHENS *Piraeus*

Athens (Athinai)—Piraeus

DEPART ATHENS PELOPONNESE	TRAIN NUMBER	ARRIVE PIRAEUS
0918	1431	0945
1032	IC 21	1056
1309*	IC 53	1338
1355	1421	1418
1446	301	1520

DEPART PIRAEUS	TRAIN NUMBER	ARRIVE ATHENS PELOPONNESE
1342	IC 22	1406
1439	424	1507
1454	304	1526
1536	1432	1603
1751	IC 24	1820
2145	306	2219
2236	426	2310

Other frequent local trains run between Athinai Omonia station and Piraeus on the Athinai Electric Railway; journey time is approximately 20 minutes.

Larissa Station
Distance: 5 miles (8 km)

by a German air attack. The ammunition ship *Clan Fraser,* carrying 200 tons of TNT, together with two other ships loaded with ammunition, exploded and destroyed the port.

In addition to its main harbor, Piraeus has two small-craft harbors, **Zea** and **Mikrolimano.** Zea shelters pleasure craft, and Mikrolimano features fishing craft and seafood restaurants, the latter rimming its waterfront like pickets of a fence. Bus No. 20 will take you to either of the smaller ports. Board it from the bus terminal on the left side of the train station. Bus No. 20 stands in the far line, facing away from the sea.

After skirting the main harbor, the bus passes through a built-up area before it again sides with the sea at Zea. If Mikrolimano is your destination, ride four stops beyond Zea and dismount. **The Castella Hotel** is on the left side at the bus stop. From there, walk down to the harbor. If you're going for lunch, try to arrive before 1230, when the area is invaded by a horde of tour buses packed with hungry tourists. At night the tables in the restaurants overlooking the sea groan under their loads of fresh fish, luscious lobsters, and opulent oysters. Top off your evening by climbing the hill behind Mikrolimano for a magnificent view of the Mediterranean's Saronic Gulf.

Piraeus, main port of Greece, basks in the warm embrace of the Saronic Gulf, just a few miles and minutes outside the heart of Athens. Piraeus today is one of the principal ports of the Mediterranean and serves both commercial shipping and pleasure craft. Most tourists go to Piraeus not to view its remains of antiquity but, rather, to enjoy the picturesque atmosphere of its port and to indulge in some of the wonderful seafood served in its restaurants.

Many restaurants employ solicitors to influence your selection of eating places. You can ignore them. We have found that the better places lie to the right of the harbor. **Kanaris 2** is one of the more expensive restaurants, but it is well worth it. While on the subject of price, a word of caution: check menu prices carefully before ordering. Many menu prices are given for 1 kilo (2.2 pounds) of fish—a price that the government requires the restaurants to list. Certainly, your platter won't hold that much, but some places will try to charge you on that basis. *Caveat emptor*—let the buyer beware.

During the summer, Piraeus is considerably cooler than Athens. Should the temperatures soar during your stay in the Greek capital, take a quick trip on the Athens subway to the seaside at Piraeus. In the evening, the tavernas and nightclubs there provide a resort-type lifestyle. The city's nightspots feature popular singers.

Lacking museums, Piraeus's archaeological discoveries are displayed in the Athens National Museum. Of particular interest is a collection of statuary stored and forgotten by General Sulla in 86 B.C. Perhaps the general lost his claim check.

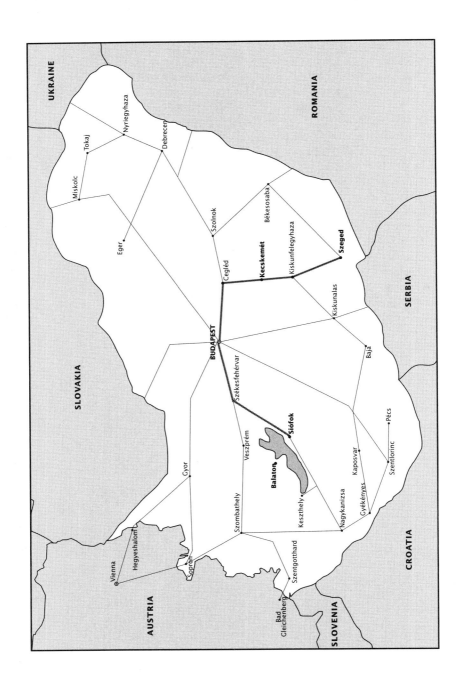

Hungary

Hungary lies in the Carpathian Basin of Central Europe where the jewel of the Danube still shines with facets of multiple architectural styles. Hungary was the seventeenth member country to join the Eurail Community and the first Eastern European nation to do so. Of the country's 10.1 million inhabitants, 1.8 million live in its capital city of Budapest.

Present-day Hungarians descended from the Magyars, a nomadic, horse-riding people who conquered the land in the ninth century. The Magyars spoke a language unlike any other language of Europe, except Finnish, and even today other Europeans have difficulty understanding it. English and/or German, however, are spoken by many Hungarians in the tourism industry, particularly in hotels and restaurants.

Hungarian cuisine is hardy and flavorful. When dining on one of the many specialties made perhaps from cabbage, peppers, pork, and paprika, be sure to add a little *Bull's Blood* (wine) from Eger. For a marvelous treat do not pass up the fine pastries and baked goods of the region.

During World War II, the Hungarian government sided with the Axis powers. In April 1945 the country fell to Russian troops. Encouraged by the Polish defiance of the Soviet Union, Hungarians staged an uprising in 1956 that was quickly suppressed by Soviet troops and tanks. Hungary was under the "Iron Curtain" until 1989. The last Soviet troops left the country in June 1991. The Hungarian People's Republic became the Republic of Hungary with a newly elected democratic government—a coalition of six parties.

Hungary has six UNESCO World Heritage sites including the scientifically significant Baradla-Domica cave system of Aggtelek and Hortobágy's National Park, one of Europe's largest protected grasslands.

For more information on Hungary, visit **www.hungarytourism.hu**, E-mail tourinform@hungarytourism.hu, or contact the Hungarian National Tourist Office in North America:

New York: Hungarian National Tourist Office, 150 East 58th Street, 33rd Floor, New York, NY 10155-3398. *Tel:* (212) 355–0240; *Fax:* (212) 207–4103; *Internet:* www.gotohungary.com; *E-mail:* info@gotohungary.com

Banking
- **Currency:** Hungarian Forint (HUF)
- **Exchange rate at press time:** HUF 281 = U.S. $1.00

Communications
- **Country Code:** 36
- **Direct dial:** first dial 00 and wait for second dial tone, then dial AT&T: 800–01111; MCI: 800–01411; Sprint: 800–01877.

Rail Travel in Hungary

The Hungarian State Railways (Magyar Allamvasutak, or MAV) includes more than 4,844 miles (7,750 kilometers) of rail lines with 1,423 miles (2,277 kilometers) electrified. Fifty-four international trains per day arrive in Budapest, including Euronight (EN) service from Zürich and Bucharest. All international trains have dining and sleeping facilities; however, many of the Hungarian intercity and express trains still do not afford all of the same amenities that can be found on the trains of Western Europe.

The Hungarian State Railways (MAV) accepts the variety of **Eurail** passes, **Europass** (with purchase of the Austria/Hungary Danube Zone), the **European East Pass**, and its own national pass—the **Hungarian Flexipass.**

Hungarian Flexipass

5 days travel within 15-day period	$67.00 (U.S.)
10 days travel within 1-month period	$84.00 (U.S.)

Children age 5–14, half adult fare; children under age 5 travel free.

European East Pass
Valid for travel in Austria, Czech Republic, Hungary, Poland and Slovak Republic
First Class

5 days travel in 1 month	$210 (U.S.)
Additional days	$24 (U.S.)

Up to 5 additional days may be added. Children age 4–11 half adult fare; under age 4 travel free.

For more detailed information on types and prices of other railpasses, please see the European RailPasses listed in the Appendix.

HUNGARY

Base City:
Budapest

City Dialing Code: 1

Budapest's tree-lined boulevards and spacious public squares bordered by magnificent buildings make it one of the most beautiful capitals of Europe. Hungary welcomes more than 24 million visitors annually, the majority of whom pass through Budapest, pausing to enjoy its special charm and atmosphere.

The city is a combination of two ancient towns, Buda on the west bank of the Danube and the community of Pest on the east bank. Buda stands on a terraced plateau and contains relics of a Turkish occupation; Pest rises from a plain and is the site of the Houses of Parliament, the Palace of Justice, the Museum of Fine Arts, and the National Museum. Buda and Pest are linked by six bridges over the Danube, including the beautiful Stone Chain Bridge.

Budapest's origins date back to about 10 B.C. when the Romans established the colony of Aquincum on what is now Buda. The Vandals took it over from the Romans in A.D. 376, and, in turn, management changed hands frequently during invasions by the Tartars and the Turks until armies under Austrian leadership liberated what was left of the towns in 1686. Some Roman ruins withstood the assaults and may be seen even today.

You'll find many reasons to enjoy Budapest, known as the "Pearl of the Danube." Beyond the panorama (a UNESCO World Heritage Site), the healing waters of the springs, and the hospitality of the people, there is much to see and do and just take in. You'll be back.

Arriving by Air

Budapest's international airport, **Ferihegy,** consists of two terminals. Ferihegy 2A is about 20 kilometers southeast of the city center and Ferihegy 2B is 24 kilometers. Terminal 2A handles flights for Malév Airlines and terminal 2B is for international flights.

Terminal 2A	Telephone
Flight information (arrival, departure)	357–7155
Luggage location service	357–7690

Terminal 2B
Flight information

Departures	357–7000
Arrivals	357–8000
Luggage location service	357–8108
Customs information	357–8306

Airport-City Links: Bus Service departs from either Terminal 2A or 2B. The bus stop at the airport is located immediately to the right of the main exit.

Airport Minibus (fixed-route taxis); (*Tel:* 357–8555), operates between the two terminals and any address in Budapest. Fare: HUF 1,500.

Budapest Transport Enterprise (BKV) services, bus No. 93 between Terminal 2 and terminus M3 metro line Köbánya-Kispest.

The airport **taxi** stand is farther to the right, about 200 feet beyond the bus stop. Taxi service is available twenty-four hours a day. All taxis in Hungary must have yellow license plates and meters that print out receipts.To reserve a taxi: City Taxi, *Tel:* 211–1111; Fotaxi, *Tel:* 222–2222; Palotaxi, *Tel:* 272–0616; Radiotaxi, *Tel:* 377–6766; or Tele 5 Taxi, *Tel:* 355–5555.

Tourist information: Terminal 2A at the airport. You will find it on your right as you approach the main exit. Hours: daily 0800–2300.

Customs control uses the red-green corridor system just like the Western European countries. If you have nothing to declare, you should use the green corridor.

Arriving by Train
The Hungarian State Railways (MAV)
Tel: 461–5400 Domestic train information
461–5500 International train information.

Both numbers give information on trains departing and arriving at Keleti, Deli, and Nyugati stations. You can also visit www.mav.hu (in Hungarian).

Keleti (East) **Station** is the terminus for most international express trains, with exception of the *Adriatica, Agram, Lehar EuroCity, Maestral,* and *Graz* trains, which terminate in Budapest Deli (South) Station. Although it has undergone extensive improvements and restoration since its original construction in 1884, the old charm is still evident. Statues of George Stephenson, the inventor of the locomotive, and James Watt, creator of the steam engine, grace its entrance. The modern touch is found in the digital departure boards displayed at the platform entrances.

BUDAPEST

Stairs at the front of the station take you to the city's Metro, a modern three-line subway system, but arrivals burdened with luggage should opt for the taxi queue immediately outside the station on the right. A word of caution: Be sure that the taxi you hail has a meter—and uses it. The best taxi service is City Taxi and most drivers speak English. Call them at 211–1111 and tell the English-speaking operator the telephone number you called from and a taxi will arrive in just a few minutes. Any "no-name" taxi is almost certainly a rip-off.

Keleti Station has all of the usual tourist services. For rail reservations, proceed to the sign FOREIGN RAILWAY TICKETS—SEAT RESERVATIONS on your right when exiting from the trains. Note that window 2 is for currency exchange, window 3 for hotels, and window 6 is where you request tickets and seat reservations. Pay for all services in cash (U.S. dollars; forints not accepted).

Deli (South), a modern concrete edifice on the Buda side of the Danube, features a huge supermarket on the ground level. Trains arrive overhead on uncovered platforms that lead to a covered concourse, with an enclosed waiting room and ticket office just beyond. The designation of Deli as Budapest's "south" station is a bit confusing in that it actually lies to the west of the city. A visit to the supermarket is a must. The products and produce selections offered may be fewer than those offered by even your local 7-Eleven store, but it's a great place to pick up the local flavor and mix with the citizens.

The Metro Line 2 (or Red) terminates at the Deli Station, with direct connections to the other two rail stations, Keleti and Nyugati. To access, follow the "M" pictographs leading from the train level; same for taxis.

Nyugati (West) stands at the head of Teréz Boulevard just before Nyugati Square. Nyugati Station has a TOURINFORM office as well as the usual amenities found at Keleti and Deli.

Train schedules and information are available by contacting RailPass.com toll free at (877) RAILPASS (877–724–5727) or by visiting www.railpass.com.

Tourist Information/Hotel Reservations

- *Tourism information office:* TOURINFORM, Main Hall, Nyugati (West) Rail Station; *Tel/Fax:* 302–8580; *Internet:* www.tourinform.hu

The National Tourism Information Service has 754 travel offices in Hungary and offers information about tourism office hours and services for visitors, including money exchange, hotel reservations, travel reservations (including rail and air), tour bookings, and general tourist information. The main tourist office in Budapest is located at 1052 Süto u.2 (Deák tér). *Tel:* 317–9800; *Fax:* 317–9656; *E-mail:* hungary@tourinform.hu. Hours: 0900–1900 Monday–Friday and 0900–1600 Saturday and Sunday.

If you are interested in organized tours, TOURINFORM offers quite a selection of sight-seeing and tour activities. The "City Tour" is a three-hour sightseeing adventure by bus to Budapest's famous spots, including Castle

Train Connections to Other Base Cities from Budapest

Depart from Budapest Keleti station unless otherwise noted.

DEPART	TRAIN NUMBER	ARRIVE	NOTES
		Amsterdam Centraal	
1530	IC 344	0941+1	R, 1, Sleeper
		Berlin Ostbahnhof	
1005	EC 170	2216	R
1250	EC 62	0705+1	R, Sleeper, 6
1745	EN 342	0817+1	R, Sleeper
2050	374	1216+1	R, Sleeper, 8
		Bern (Berne)	
1745	EN 342	0745+1	R, Sleeper, 2
		Brussels Midi/Zuid	
1530	IC 344	0941+1	R, 1, Sleeper
		Copenhagen (København) H.	
0920	EC 24	0959	`0
1530	IC 344	1359+1	R, 3, 4
2010	EN 268	1759	R, 4, 6
		Hamburg Hauptbahnhof	
0605	EC 76	2106	R, 8
0920	EC 24	2152	11
1250	EC 62	0752+1	R, Sleeper, 6
1530	IC 344	0755+1	R, Sleeper, 1
1745	342	1057+1	R, Sleeper, 3
		Luxembourg	
1700	262/296	0859+1	R, 5, Sleeper
		Lyon Part-Dieu	
2010	EN 268	1650+1	R, Sleeper, 6, 12
		Munich (München) Hauptbahnhof	
1250	EC 62	2036	R
2010	EN 268	0603+1	R, Sleeper
		Paris (Est)	
1250	EC 62	0659+1	R, 6
1530	IC 344	1023+1	R, Sleeper, 1
2010	EN 268	1622+1	R, Sleeper, 6
		Rome (Roma) Termini	
1530	IC 344	0904+1	R, Sleeper, 7
		Vienna (Wien) Westbahnhof	
0920	EC 24	1200	R,
1250	EC 62	1530	R,
1530	IC 344	1830	R
1745	342	2046	R
1855	EC40	2126	R, 13
		Zürich Hauptbahnhof	
0600	346	1827	R, 1
1745	342	0627+1	R, Sleeper

Daily, unless otherwise noted

R Reservations mandatory
+1 Arrives next day
1. Change trains in Vienna (Wien).
2. Change trains in Zürich.
3. Change trains in Berlin (Zoobahnhof Station).
4. Change trains in Hamburg.
5. Change trains in Strasbourg.
6. Change trains in Munich (München).
7. Change from Wien Westbahnhof to Wien Südbahnhof Station.
8. Change trains in Prague (Praha).
9. Change trains in Breclav.
10. Change trains in Nurenburg (Nürnberg).
11. Change trains in Würzburg.
12. Change trains in Heidelberg.
13. Arrive Wien Südbahnhof Station.

Hill for a panoramic view. Narrow-gauge train runs through gorgeous hillsides may be arranged through the offices, or you may also want to take a two-hour sightseeing cruise on the Danube.

For "the whole city in your pocket" do not pass up the Budapest Card (available for 2 days HUF 2800 or 3 days for HUF 3400). The card offers free transportation around the city and discounts on shopping, restaurants, sightseeing, and cultural and folklore programs. Pick up the card at the tourist information offices, hotels, and underground ticket offices.

For a night on the town, you have the option of a Goulash Party with wine and a show, or you can pull out all the stops with the "Budapest by Night" tour, which offers dinner, a floor show, dancing, and wine tasting accompanied by folk music. If visiting in August, plan ahead for the Buda-Fest by calling the tourist office for a list of highlights for this summer cultural event. If you can work it in, the full-day Danube Bend bus tour on the right bank of the Danube to the towns of **Esztergom, Visegrad,** and **Szentendre** is well worth the expense for the experience. The area is not accessible by train, and the vistas along the river are captivating.

Day Excursions

Four day excursions from two of Hungary's nine tourism regions have been selected for your Hungarian explorations. (Call the Hungarian Tourist Board or visit their website for further information on the other regions.) Two excursions are to Balaton and Siófok, resort towns bordering what the locals call the Balaton, the long, great lake lying south of Budapest. Two other excursions, Kecskemét and Szeged, take you south through the Great Plain region.

Although **Lake Balaton** is shallow (12.4 meters at the deepest point), it actually has waves created by the wind over the northern hills and offers watersports such as boating, yachting, sailing, fishing, and hunting, as well as horseback riding, and giant slides for kids of all ages. You may explore a number of beautiful towns and villages, including **Siófok** (considered the best bathing resort on the Lake), with the Balaton Daily Ticket. The Balaton ticket is available for HUF 1500 and is valid for unlimited rail travel around the lake. You can get the card from the Hungarian Tourist Board or at rail stations in Hungary.

Considered "the capital of Lake Balaton," Siófok is 72 miles away from Budapest, and is easily reached by train. Siófok's railway station and harbor were built in 1863, nearly 800 years after the city was founded. Today green parks and flowering gardens transform the city into a paradise on and off shore. Notice the landscape of Millenium Park as soon as you step off the train in front of the station. Historic and modern structures provide an interesting mix while a variety of outdoor sculptures stand on public display in open-air exhibitions. The city has many organized programs and tours; check with the tourist office for offerings.

From the waters of Lake Balaton we go to the relaxing lifestyle of the Kiskunság region. **Kecskemét** is our next stop. The largest city of the Southern Great Plains (the area lying between the Danube and Tisza rivers), Kecskemét has an impressive town square with a majolica-tile decorated Town Hall. The architecture is particularly stunning, with the Cifrapalota or Ornamental Palace, Katona Jozsef Theatre, and a 19th-century Moorish-style synagogue which today is the House of Science and Technology. Every August since 1934, the Hirös Festival has been held here. It highlights the traditional crafts, agriculture, and culture of the area.

Szeged, also in the Southern Great Plains, is often called the City of Sunshine, averaging 2000 hours of sunshine a year—a bit warmer than the rest of the country. The city was devastated by a flood in 1879, but the Szeged Synagogue, the Votive Church, the Greek Orthodox Serbian Church and other examples of architectural magnificence help this city shine in wonder. For a special treat visit during the open-air festival July-August, but plan ahead as this festival is popular around the world.

The Southern Great Plains is abundant in traditional folk art such as motif painting, weaving, slipper crafting, egg painting, and the very popular and intricately decorated embroidery work and pottery. Contact the tourist boards for programming or shops to visit. You may even be lucky enough to experience a Hungarian folk dance show.

We also encourage you to try the cuisine as testimony to the rich history and flavors of the different regions. Of course there is the *gulyás* (goulash) stew made with red paprika and multitudes of noodle dishes, but try the famous *halászlé* spicy fish soup and pike-perch of the Balaton; the wheat and vegetable dishes of the Great Plains made with cream, and desserts such as cottage cheese pie or cabbage strudel. Don't forget to try a glass of the king of wines, the wine of kings, *Tokaj* and a delicious apricot.

Prefer a different indulgence? The thermal bath is taken seriously in Hungary. Over 1000 natural thermal springs throughout the country allow for a variety of spas to be incorporated into your stay. Whether enjoying the original Roman-built spas (three still exist today: Császár, Király, and Rudas), a modern hotel spa, or many of the resort spas in the countryside near Lake Balaton, a little pampering never harmed any traveler's soul. Besides, thermal bathing is part of the Hungarian culture and actually is quite affordable.

For more information on some of the day excursions contact:

Lake Balaton, there are several TourInform locations surrounding the lake or www.balaton.net

Siófok, 8600 Víztorony, Pf.:75. *Tel:* 84–315–355 *Fax:* 84–310–117; *E-mail:* siofok@tourinform.hu

Kecskemét, 6000 Deák F. tér 3. *Tel:* 76–412–750 *Fax:* 76–412–750; *Internet:* www.kecskemet.com

Szeged, 6720 Victor Hugo u. 1. *Tel./Fax:* 62–425–711, 62–420–509

Budapest—Balatonszentgyörgy

Depart Budapest	Train Number	Arrive Balaton	Depart Balaton	Train Number	Arrive Budapest
0650 Dél	IC 200	0913	1551	8503	1933 Dél
0725 Dél	852	1012	1625	8403	1952 Klt
0825 Dél	8502	1201	1746	851	2043 Dél
0925 Klt	5209	1253	1830	IC 201	2103 Dél
			1847	8501	2218 Dél

Daily
Distance: 112 miles (180) km
Note: Budapest Keleti station is designated as Klt and Budapest Déli station is designated as Dél.

Budapest—Siófok

Depart Budapest	Train Number	Arrive Siófok	Depart Siófok	Train Number	Arrive Budapest	Note
0650 Dél	IC 200	0822	1523	IC 1875	1703 Dél	R
0725 Dél	852	0906	1730	8503	1933 Dél	
0825 Dél	8502	1022	1746	8403	1952 Klt	
0925 Klt	5209	1125	1856	851	2043 Dél	
0950 Dél	IC 1872	1122	1923	IC 201	2103 Dél	R
1015 Klt	5609	1213	2024	8501	2218 Dél	

R Reservations required
Daily
Distance: 72 miles (115 km)

BUDAPEST

Budapest—Kecskemét

Depart Budapest Nyugati	Train Number	Arrive Kecskemét	Notes
0705	IC 700	0832	R
0805	752	0954	
1005	712	1147	
1105	IC 702	1232	Fri, R
1205	714	1351	

Depart Kecskemét	Train Number	Arrive Budapest Nyugati	Notes
1436	713	1616	
1533	IC 703	1657	R
1634	753	1812	
1837	711	2014	
1933	IC 701	2057	R
2034	1711	2212	Sat, Sun
2113	14701	2317*	Mon–Fri

* Arrives Budapest Keleti
R Reservations required
Daily unless otherwise noted.
Distance: 66 miles (106 km)

Budapest—Szeged

Depart Budapest Nyugati	Train Number	Arrive Szeged	Notes
0605	710	0858	
0705	IC 700	0937	R
0805	752	1108	
1005	IC 712	1258	
1105	IC 702	1337	Fri, R

Depart Szeged	Train Number	Arrive Budapest Nyugati	Notes
1425	IC 703	1657	R
1520	753	1812	
1720	711	2014	
1825	IC 701	2057	R
1920	1711	2212	Sat, Sun
1930	14701	2317*	Mon–Fri

* Arrives Budapest Keleti
R Reservations required
Daily unless otherwise noted
Distance: 119 miles (191km)

BUDAPEST

Ireland

Known as "the Emerald Isle," Ireland is no doubt the greenest country of Europe. According to legend, a true Irishman can recognize at least forty shades of green. The breeze that blows across the seas to Ireland drops its moisture from the time it touches the Irish shoreline on the Atlantic Ocean until it's well out into the Irish Sea. A raincoat or an umbrella—or both—is essential equipment for your visit, and a sweater, even in summer. But the sun also shines a bountiful bit of the time, and most of the time showers disappear as quickly as they come.

Today's tourists to Ireland are discovering a new Ireland. Tourism to Ireland is growing rapidly, and Dublin was one of the most rapidly changing capitals in the 1990s. To accommodate these increases, Ireland has expanded all forms of its public transportation. Even Ireland's five international airports—Dublin, Shannon, Cork, Knock, and Belfast (in Northern Ireland)—have undergone major expansions, reflecting the increase of air traffic from all parts of the world.

With all of the enhancements in Ireland, some things remain unchanged—Irish friendliness. Its citizens still seem to have the time to be genuinely interested in you and are wondrously literate when discussing almost any subject. Even if scurrying for a bus, the Irish will stop to chat when they spy a friend—after all, there's always another bus. In Gaelic, *céad mile fáilte* means "one hundred thousand welcomes!" You'll hear it frequently.

For more information about Ireland, contact the Irish Tourist Board offices in North America:

New York: 345 Park Avenue, New York, NY 10154; *Tel:* (212) 418–0800; *Fax:* (212) 371–9052; *Internet:* **www.ireland.travel.ie**; *E-mail:* info@ irishtouristboard.com

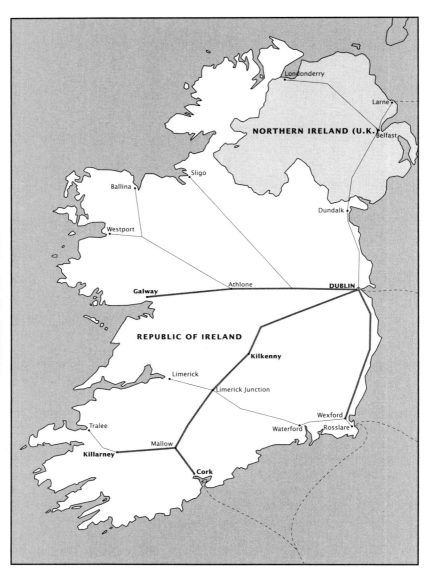

IRELAND

Northern Ireland Tourist Board:
New York: 551 Fifth Avenue, Suite 701, New York NY 10176; *Tel:* (800)
326–0036 or (212) 922–0101; *Fax:* (212) 922–0099
Toronto: 3 Bloor Street West, Suite 1501, Toronto, Ontario M4W 3E2.
Tel: (800) 576-8174 or (416) 925-6368; *Fax:* (416) 925–6033;
Internet: **www.northernireland.tourism.com**

Republic of Ireland
- Currency: Euro (€)
- Exchange rate at press time: €1.10 = U.S. $1.00

Communications
- Country Code: 353
- Direct dial: AT&T: 1–800–550–000; MCI: 1–800–551–001; Sprint: 1–800–552–001

Rail/Bus Travel in Ireland
Irish Rail (Iarnród Éireann)
Internet: www.irishrail.ie
Tel: 01 836 6222

Irish Bus (Bus Eireann)
Internet: www.buseireann.ie
Tel: 01 836 6111

Dublin Bus
Internet: www.dublinbus.ie
Tel: 01 873 4222

Northern Ireland Railways
Internet: www.nirailways.co.uk
Tel: 028 9089 9411

Ulsterbus (Northern Ireland)
Internet: www.ulsterbus.co.uk
Tel: 028 9033 3000

Because the country is only about the size of the state of Pennsylvania in the United States, travelers can easily discover Ireland by using the rail and bus systems. **Irish Rail** (Iarnród Éireann)—a subsidiary of Coras Iompair Éireann (CIE), Ireland's transport company—has been upgrading its railroads and rail facilities as an essential part of Ireland's development plan, with the goal of reliable, convenient, and fast passenger travel throughout the country. Visit their Web site at **www.irishrail.ie**. Much of the equipment compares favorably with the EuroCity trains operated on the Continent.

If wishing to travel strictly within Ireland, then in North America contact **CIE Tours International,** P.O. Box 501, Cedar Knolls, NJ 07927–0501 (*Tel:* 800–243–8687; *Fax:* 800–338–3964). Otherwise, use your Eurailpass or Eurail Selectpass for rail travel on the Emerald Isle.

Ireland's high-speed trains are modeled after the futuristic TGV-style Eurostar trains and aptly dubbed "the trains of the future." The *Enterprise* is one of the high-tech trains that connects Dublin with Belfast in Northern

Ireland. The air-conditioned carriages include digital displays and satellite route maps.

First class is referred to as "super-standard," and second class is known as "standard." First-class railpass holders are entitled to travel in super-standard coaches without payment of supplements. First-class coaches are equipped with reclining seats and headphones, with a choice of listening to radio, cassette tape, or CD unit. A facsimile service is provided, as are "Silver Service" meals served at the seats.

Standard-class coaches include a "family room" at one end of the car for those with children. Light meals are available from the mobile food service cart and the buffet (pronounced "buffey" in Ireland) area of the coach.

Some trains operate with standard-class (second-class) coaches only. Standard-class seats are not reservable for individuals, only groups (no seat reservations on bank holidays or weekends). You are required to show your ticket (or railpass) when entering the train platforms in Irish rail stations, so have it handy.

Food and beverages are served by Irish Rail's own catering service. The service varies according to the type of train. Full-service restaurant cars are hauled on main-line routes, but most catering consists of buffet cars or snack-bar service. Food carts are used on some routes. When traveling on a train hauling a restaurant car, super-standard passengers are provided with in-seat catering. In buffet cars, you can obtain hot food, but trains equipped with snack-bar service offer only sandwiches and other prepared food. You may take your own food and beverages aboard. Take some candy treats with you—it's a good way to get acquainted with other passengers.

Service to the cities in the Republic slated for faster, more efficient service include Galway, Sligo, Westport, and Tralee.

Eurailpasses and **Eurail Selectpasses** are accepted for rail travel in the Republic of Ireland, but not in Northern Ireland. Eurail bonuses include:

- 50 percent discount on Irish Ferries crossing Rosslare to Cherbourg and Roscoff (France) April–September. Advance booking recommended.
- Reduced fare on Bus Eireann's 3-day Rover ticket valid on Bus Eireann Expressway and Provincial Services and on Bus Eireann services in the cities of Cork, Limerick, Galway, and Waterford. The ticket is valid for any 3 days' travel within an 8-day period.

The **BritRail Plus Ireland Pass** is accepted in both the Republic of Ireland and Northern Ireland, as well as in England, Scotland, and Wales, and covers a round-trip connection on your choice of three **Stena Line** ferry routes: between Dun Laoghaire and Holyhead, Rosslare and Fishguard, or Belfast and Stranraer.

For more detailed information on travel in Britain, please read our other rail guidebook, *Britain by BritRail—How to Tour Britain by Train,* published by The Globe Pequot Press.

A variety of railpasses and rail/bus combination tickets are available to help in exploring the Emerald Isle.

The **Irish Explorer Pass** covers the Republic of Ireland; **Irish Rover Pass** and **Emerald Card** cover both the Republic of Ireland and Northern Ireland.

Irish Explorer Pass–Rail
Valid for any 5 days within a 15-day period. Unlimited standard-class rail travel in Republic of Ireland and local rail services in Dublin area:
Adults: $106; Children under 12: $53

Irish Explorer–Rail & Bus
Valid for any 8 days within a 15-day period. Unlimited standard-class rail travel in Republic of Ireland, local rail services in Dublin area, and city bus services in Cork, Galway, Limerick and Waterford:

Adults:	$158
Children under 12:	$79

Irish Rover–Rail Only
Valid for any 5 days within a 15-day period. Unlimited standard-class rail travel on Irish Rail (in the Republic of Ireland) and Northern Ireland Rail, local rail services in Dublin area, and suburban rail services in Northern Ireland.
Adults: $132
Children under 12: $66

Emerald Card–Rail & Bus
Valid for any 8 days within a 15-day period or any 15 days within a 30-day period. Unlimited travel on Irish Rail, Northern Ireland Rail, Irish Bus, Ulsterbus, local rail services in Dublin area, and city bus service in Belfast, Cork, Dublin, Galway, Limerick and Waterford.

	Adults	Children
8 days in 15-day period	$182	$91
15 days in 30-day period	$316	$158

2002 prices unavailable at press time. Tel: 800-CIE-TOUR or visit www.cietours.com for price updates.

See the Appendix for a detailed list of individual country passes and the Ferry Crossings section for detailed information on sailing connections from Ireland to France and Britain.

Base City:

Dublin

Internet: www.dublintourist.com or
www.visit.ie/dublin
City Dialing Code: 1

About one-third of the Republic of Ireland's population lives in or near Dublin. The city is as intoxicating as its national brew, Guinness, which is also lovingly referred to as Dublin's "water supply."

O'Connell Street is Dublin's somewhat tarnished "Main Street," the pulsating heart of the old city and Ireland's broadest boulevard. A grand statue of the Irish patriot Daniel O'Connell, *The Liberator,* stands at the foot of O'Connell Street, where O'Connell Bridge crosses the River Liffey. A new sculpture of James Joyce's river spirit, *Anna Livia,* is one of the many statues of national heroes posed along the way to the Garden of Remembrance at Parnell Square.

Art galleries, museums, shopping areas such as the Powerscourt Townhouse Center and Grafton Street, famous cathedrals, and elegant cafes are within walking distance of O'Connell Street. The best-preserved examples of eighteenth-century houses are also found nearby. **St. Stephen's Green,** at the top of Grafton Street, is ringed with magnificently restored, stately Georgian residences with solid-colored enameled doors and sparkling brass fixtures.

Arriving by Air

Ireland has two main gateways for air travelers: **Shannon International Airport,** on the west side of the Republic, and **Dublin International Airport,** 12 kilometers northeast of the city's center. (*Internet:* www.aerrianta.ie) Aer Lingus, American Trans Air, Continental, and Delta service both Shannon and Dublin. Other air carriers stop only in Shannon, which has a world-famous, duty-free shopping area featuring items produced in Ireland.

Airport–City Links: Shannon connects with the rail station in Limerick by airport bus service. Journey time: 45 minutes; fare, €5.08.

Dublin International Airport's Tourist Information and Reservations Centre is on the arrivals concourse next to the main arrivals door. Hours: 0800–2200 daily.

Airport–City Links: Air Coach operates an express bus service between Dublin Airport and St. Stephen's Green, Fitzwilliam Square, Merrion Square, Ballsbridge, and Donnybrook. Journey time: 25 minutes; fare, €5.08. Taxi fare to city center, about €19.05.

Arriving by Train

Connolly Station and DART: 35 Lower Abbey Street (*Tel:* 01 836–6222)

Connolly Station is the terminal in Dublin for trains arriving from Northern Ireland and for boat trains connecting with the Irish ferries that sail from the port of Rosslare, south of Dublin, to the French ports of Cherbourg and Le Havre.

Coming from London by train requires a transfer to either a Stena Line or Irish Ferries ferry at Holyhead. The Stena Line ferries serve the port of Dun Laoghaire, a suburb of Dublin, where passengers can transfer to the center of the city by the local rapid transit train service, DART.

The northwestern coastal city of Sligo is also reached by train service departing from Connolly Station, as are the towns of Wicklow and Wexford, located south of Dublin in the direction of Rosslare.

Heuston Station: west of city center on the River Liffey (*Tel:* 01–677–1871)

Heuston Station serves as the departure point for *Europe by Eurail* day excursions to Cork, Galway, Kilkenny, and Killarney.

City buses depart from the head of track No. 5 in Heuston Station and take passengers near the O'Connell Bridge. There is also a taxi stand on the opposite side of the station immediately beyond track No. 1 and outside the ticket-office entrance.

Heuston Station has eight main tracks. Ticket offices are located on the side of the station serving track Nos. 1 and 2. Train information and railpass validation are available at any of the ticket windows.

Advance seat reservations may be obtained from the Iarnrod Eireann (Irish Rail) ticket office at Connolly and Heuston Stations as well as at the Irish Rail Travel Centre at 35 Lower Abbey Street. Reservations can be made up to 1700 on the preceding day. If you don't have seat reservations, we suggest arriving in the station about a half hour before your train's scheduled departure time just in case the travel is heavy on the day you have selected for your excursion.

Shopping for Waterford crystal? Depart Heuston Station via Kilkenny to the town where it's made—and take money, lots of it!

Tourist Information/Hotel Reservations

Tourist Information Office: Dublin Tourism Centre, Suffolk Street, Dublin 2; *Tel:* 01 605–7700; *Fax:* 01 605–7725; Reservations *Tel:* 011–800–6686–6866; *Fax:* 011–353–6697–92116; *Internet:* www.visitdublin.com; *E-mail:* information@dublintourism.ie.

Dublin is well equipped to offer a wide range of accommodations to visitors. Two exceptions, however, come during the Dublin Horse Show in early August and St. Patrick's Day in March. The principal sporting and social event of the year in Ireland, the horse show attracts thousands of visitors from all parts of the world. Don't plan to be in Dublin during the horse show unless you have confirmed reservations. The city is filled to overflowing at that time. If you are planning a visit to Dublin on St. Patrick's Day or during the summer months, it would be wise to check well in advance with the Irish Tourist Board in New York for accommodation arrangements.

Travelers looking for homelike accommodations can purchase the Irish Tourist Offices' *Self Catering* **Services Guide,** which describes apartments or houses for short-term rent (for a few days, a weekend, or a week). For reservations, contact the Dublin Tourism Centre.

Bed-and-breakfast establishments are also a viable alternative to large, expensive hotels. Again, the Irish Tourist Offices maintain current descriptions. Mary and Brian Bennett's extraordinary guest house, **Number 31,** at Leeson Close, Dublin 2 (*Tel:* 01 676–5011), is the former home of Sam Stephenson, one of Dublin's renowned architects.

For those who wish to experience the ambience of one of Dublin's newest landmark hotels, we suggest the Brooks Hotel, 59–62 Drury Street, Dublin 2 (*Tel:* 01 670–4000; *Fax:* 01 670–4455; *E-mail:* reservations@brookshotel.ie). Room rates range from standard to superior executive suites, and the location places you in the heart of the city, with Grafton Street, Temple Bar, and Trinity College only a short walk away.

Getting Around In and Outside Dublin

- **DART,** 35 Lower Abbey Street; *Tel:* 01 836–6222
- **Bus Eireann,** Store Street; *Tel:* 01 836–6111

DART, or Dublin Area Rapid Transit, is the electric commuter service running around Dublin Bay and provides the fastest way of getting around Dublin as well as convenient access to the many resorts and other attractions outside of Dublin.

Much of the route is coastal and gives many different views of the bay. It's excellent for short excursions to places such as the charming fishing village of Howth at its northern end or Dun Laoghaire, the busy harbor for the Stena Line ferry service to England via Holyhead. DART accepts Eurailpass, as well as the various Irish Rail and/or Bus combination passes.

Dublin's DART has expanded to include stations at Clontarf Road, Kilcock, and Drumcondra, and work has begun on an extension to Greystones. Improvements have been made to the public address system, electronic information displays, signs, and lighting. In addition, easier accessibility for the disabled has been provided.

Service to the cities in the Republic slated for faster, more efficient service include Galway, Sligo, Westport, and Tralee.

Sights/Attractions/Tours—Discovering Dublin

Dublin, with a population of more than one million people in its greater metropolitan area, offers the excitement of a vital city yet the ambience of an old-world town.

Sight-seeing on foot is easy. During your visit to the Dublin tourist information office, purchase the walking tour guide booklets that are of interest to you: *Heritage Trails,* or the *Rock 'n Stroll Trail* (significant sites in Dublin's music history), which is popular among the younger set. The success of bands like U2 and the Cranberries and singers like Sinead O'Connor, who began her career by singing traditional Irish songs, has made Dublin a rock music capital.

Each of these brochures describes specially selected, sign-posted walking tours through the center of Dublin and includes many points of interest. The tours are so designed that you can pick up the trails anywhere within the downtown area. The routes cover much of what is of interest historically and culturally to visitors and take about 3 hours.

If you plan to visit the **Dublin Writers Museum,** the **Joyce Tower, Shaw's Birthplace,** the **Viking Adventure, Malahide Castle, Newbridge House,** and the **Fry Model Railway Museum,** purchase the **Dublin Super Saver Card** at the tourist office and save 25 percent off the total admission charges (€24.12 adults; €17.78 seniors and students; €11.43 children; and €62.22 families).

One of Dublin's sights to see is **O'Connell Street.** A block away on the river's south bank stands **Parliament House** (now the Bank of Ireland), which faces the entrance to Trinity College, founded in 1592. The **Book of Kells,** considered its greatest treasure, is housed in the Collonades. Tourist trails lead from that point to **St. Stephen's Green,** at the top of Grafton Street, where its 22 acres are surrounded delightfully by splendid Georgian houses.

Most shops in these areas are open Monday–Saturday from 0900 to 1730 or 1800, with extended hours on Thursday. Plus many shops are now open on Sunday from 1200 to 1800.

For an insight into Irish life, visit **a Dublin pub.** In general, the Irish treat their pubs as a second home. The French seem to spend a relatively short time in a cafe before heading off for lunch, dinner, or whatever. The English go to a pub for a chat with friends and the barmaid and perhaps a game of darts before heading homeward. But the Irish, when they have the time (and they generally seem to), are in the pub for the entire evening.

The main pub activities are drinking and talking, although many serve appetizing meals and snacks and provide entertainment in the form of traditional music and song. You are free to sit and watch or join in. To take the latter option, merely turn to your neighbor and mention the weather. With that, the ball's in play. What is revealed then is fascinating. You'll find that everyone has positive but sensible opinions about a myriad of subjects. Make certain that what you say about a topic is relevant, for unlike most bar conversationalists, the Irish listen when you speak. Listening is an art that can be developed to a fine degree in a Dublin pub. Unless you are a Scot, try not to match the Dubliners' drinking ability or verbal athletics.

Suburban Dublin Day Excursions

Travelers can stay in Dublin, their "base city," and easily make day excursions to visit other areas outside of Dublin. Or, they can use the "flip side" of the base city–day excursion concept by taking advantage of less expensive accommodations outside the city and making day excursions into Dublin.

One Dublin suburban-area day excursion is to **Dun Laoghaire**, a charming, lovely port on the Irish Sea that can be reached in only 15 minutes by DART from Dublin's Connolly Station. The ferry terminal and DART station are much more convenient for travelers than the former underground facility. The Stena Line's HSS (High-speed Seacat Service) catamaran provides inexpensive passage to and from Great Britain in less than 2 hours. A variety of hotels, bed-and-breakfast establishments, hostels, and the new "self-catering" apartments and houses are available in Dun Laoghaire for those who prefer to stay just outside of Dublin.

For a high-standard hostel on a low-cost budget, consider **The Old Schoolhouse**, Eblana Avenue, Dun Laoghaire (*Tel:* 01 280–8777; *Fax:* 01 284–2266). It's a former Christian Brothers school that was renovated to create a modern, comfortable hostel that includes a laundry, a television room, and use of fully equipped kitchen facilities.

Other Dublin suburban areas within easy reach via DART, Suburban Rail, and the Arrow lines include:

Bray, 30 minutes from Dublin, is where writer James Joyce and artist Neil Jordan once lived and where rock star Bono of U2 makes his home. Connecting buses can take you to the quaint little village of **Enniskerry,** with its delightful cafes, coffee shops, and comfortable bed-and-breakfast facilities.

Howth, only 25 minutes from Connolly Station via DART, is a charming fishing village on the northern side of Dublin Bay.

Naas, southwest of Dublin, can be reached by the Arrow train line departing from Heuston Station. Naas is famous as a center for horse breeding, and race horse owners from all over the world attend the October yearling sales held nearby.

Kildare, also famous with the equestrian set as a center for horse breeding and home of the Irish National Stud, is only 48 kilometers away and is the last stop on the Arrow line trains departing from Dublin's Heuston Station. For luxurious resort-type accommodations (at resort-type prices, of course), the Kildare Hotel and Country Club is top notch. The transformation of the former fifth-century Straffan mansion into a luxury hotel took

Train Connections to and from Port of Rosslare for Ferry Connections to Cherbourg

Dublin—Rosslare Europort

DEPART DUBLIN CONNOLLY	ARRIVE ROSSLARE EUROPORT	NOTES	DEPART ROSSLARE EUROPORT	ARRIVE DUBLIN CONNOLLY	NOTES
0814	1142	exc. Sun	0720	1023	exc. Sun
1000	1307	Sun	0845	1144	Sun
1325	1635		1445	1800	
1830	2141		1820	2125	

Daily, unless otherwise noted
For more information telephone (01) 836622
Standard class only on all trains
Distance: 95 miles (168 km)

more than 2 years to complete. The clubhouse and 18-hole golf course were designed by Arnold Palmer.

Waterford, a twelfth-century Norman fortress positioned on the banks of the Suir, has been a significant port since the sixteenth century. The Dominican Blackfriars and ruins of the French Church are reminders of medieval times, as is the twelfth-century Reginald's Tower, where the city's museum is located. In 1170 Strongbow was married to Princess Aoife, daughter of the King of Leinster, in Christ Church Cathedral, where today an audiovisual presentation using the excellent acoustics of the nave re-creates a 1,000-year-old history of the area. Hook Tower, one of the oldest lighthouses in Europe, stands proudly at Hook Head at the beginning of the estuary in Waterford Bay. Waterford is home to Waterford Crystal, the largest crystal factory in the world (*Internet:* www.waterford.com). From April through October the **Waterford Crystal Visitor Centre** is open seven days a week from 0830 to 1800. Tours and audiovisual presentations are available April through October, and the gallery features some of the most unique and valuable crystal pieces ever created.

Waterford Castle (*Tel:* 05–187–8203; in the United States, *Tel:* 800–221–1074), located on an island, began as a monastic settlement in the sixth century. It ultimately became one of the estates of the Fitzgeralds, who were the kings of Ireland during the fifteenth and sixteenth centuries. Purchased by Eddie Kearns in 1987, it was developed into a luxurious hotel and country club. The castle's guest rooms are comfortable and bright, with beautiful views of the estate. Conference facilities are available, and special arrangements are made for business entertaining. The main dining room seats 65 guests and often hosts a resident pianist. Hunting and polo are available, as is deep-sea and freshwater fishing. Croquet is played on the castle lawns. An excellent country club, championship golf course, and luxurious leisure center also grace the island.

More Day Excursions

Other day excursions made conveniently with Irish Rail/Bus are **Cork, Galway, Killarney,** and **Kilkenny.** Cork provides a double treat when you tread its fascinating quays and kiss the renowned stone at nearby Blarney Castle. Galway, the western capital of Ireland, has all the charm of an ancient city, plus the vitality of expanding industries and popular holiday-resort attractions. The combination of Kilkenny Town and Kilkenny Castle offers a delightful variety of attractions, from cats and choir lofts to castle tours and witches' tales.

Day Excursion to

Cork
And the Blarney Stone

DUBLIN

Depart from Dublin Heuston Station
Distance by Train: 165 miles (266 km)
Average Train Time: 2 hours, 20 minutes
City Dialing Code: 21
Tourist Information Office: Tourist House, Grand Parade
Tel: (021) 4273251; **Fax:** (021) 4273504
Internet: www.cork-kerry.travel.ie
E-mail: info@corkkerrytourism.ie
Hours: July–August, Monday–Saturday 0900–1900; remainder of the year, Monday–Friday 0915–1730; Saturday 0930–1600; Closed for lunch 1300–1415.
Notes: To get to the tourist office on foot, exit the railway station to Railway Street and turn left to Penrose's Quay. Make a right onto Penrose's Quay to St. Patrick's Bridge. Turn left onto St. Patrick's Street until you come to Grand Parade on your left. Follow it past Oliver Plunkett Street, and you will see the tourist office on your left. To get to the bus station from the tourist office, go back to Oliver Plunkett Street, where you turn right. Turn left on Anglesea Street until you come to the bus station.

Cork, Ireland's second largest city (about 200,000 residents) and commercial and passenger port, is easily accessible from both Dublin and Shannon (via train from Limerick). From Dublin a special executive car called "City Gold" is available, with special amenities for doing business, including fax and phone.

Cork City (*Corcach* in Irish, which means "marshy place") was built

Dublin—Cork

DEPART DUBLIN HEUSTON	ARRIVE CORK	NOTES	DEPART CORK	ARRIVE DUBLIN HEUSTON	NOTES
0710	1001	exc. Sun	1425	1726	exc. Sun
0820	1119	Sat	1630	1935	Sun
0950	1310	Sun	1730	2016	exc. Sun
1050	1339	exc. Sun	1735	2008	Sun
1205	1515	Sun	1830	2125	Sun
1320	1622	exc. Sun	1905	2157	Sun
			1915	2221	

Distance: 165 miles (266 km)

upon the marshes and wetlands of the River Lee. **Saint Finbarr's Cathedral** is located where Cork's first settlement and monastery was founded by the missionary in the seventh century. The **Guinness International Jazz Festival,** held in October, attracts world-famous musicians, including famous American stars.

The moist, temperate climate of Cork makes for splendid gardens and wonderful parks. And shopping the maze of streets between Patrick Street and South Mall provides a plethora of fashions and fashionable cafes and eateries offering finely prepared foods at various prices.

The village of **Blarney** is a short, 25-minute bus ride north of the city, where the "touristy" thing to do is visit **Blarney Castle** and kiss the legendary **Blarney Stone,** which promises the gift of eloquence to anyone believing enough to be lowered backward from the battlements on the roof of the castle to achieve it. You will, of course, be adding to the lip prints of thousands of other tourists who have attempted the same thing.

Board the bus marked BLARNEY in the city's bus terminal at Parnell Place. It's only a 10-minute walk down Glanmire Road to the river and the bus station. On Sunday buses depart Cork on the hour 0900–2300 and return at 35 minutes past the hour. During the week, buses run about every 15 minutes. Check schedules with the Cork tourist office or call Bus Eireann (353) 21 4508188.

There are many legends regarding the origins of the Blarney Stone. According to one, it was brought to Ireland from the Holy Land during one of the crusades. Another theory has the Blarney Stone originating from half of the Stone of Scone, with Robert the Bruce giving the mystical rock to Cormac MacCarthy, Lord of Blarney, in 1314. Legend has it that the gift of eloquence would be bestowed upon anyone who kissed it. It was not until Cormac MacCarthy saved an elderly woman from drowning that he learned of this magical secret.

Galway
Roundstone

Depart from Dublin Heuston Station
Distance by Train: 129 miles (208 km)
Average Train Time: 2 hours, 40 minutes
City Dialing Code: 91
Tourist Information Center: Fair Green, Foster Street, across from City Hall
Tel: 091 563081; *Fax:* 091 565201
Internet: www.galway.net
E-mail: info@irelandwest.ie
Hours: Open daily May–June, September–October: 0900–1745. July–August: 0900–1945. Open November–April: Monday–Friday 0900–1745; Saturday 0900–1245.
Notes: Emerging from the railway station, you'll see Eyre Square with the Kennedy Park in its center. Turn left onto the main street. The traditional green i signs will lead you to the tourist office. Fronting the square is the Great Southern Hotel. (Turn right and right again at Victoria Place to find the new office.)

L ike some other Irish cities, Galway was established initially by foreigners. Since medieval times, it has been a significant port dominated by an oligarchy of fourteen Norman and Welsh merchant families. As a thriving trade with Spain developed, the **Spanish Arch** was erected in 1594; it was created to protect the Spanish ships as they unloaded their cargo. It still remains below the Claddagh Bridge and has an adjacent museum. The avenue leading from the arch, known as the "Long Walk," is where Spanish merchants supposedly strolled into Galway City. The area is still resplendent with Spanish architecture.

Galway has become Ireland's fastest-growing city. A university town since the fourteenth century, Galway still has a huge student population and is still a cultural center for writers and scholars. In October, March, and July, Galway (as in Dublin and Cork) hosts an **international film festival** to showcase new cinema.

Guided tours via double-decker buses depart Eyre Square every 30 minutes in the summer. **Eyre Square,** given to the city by Edward Eyre in 1710, is the heart of Galway City activity and the site where the John F. Kennedy Memorial Park is located. Fronting the square is the **Great Southern Hotel,** a hostelry combining the charm of both old and new and an ideal place to halt for a libation or a luncheon. The shopping center west of the square is also where the last section of the old wall has been preserved, along with the Penrice and Shoemaker Towers.

At 19 Eyre Square, the Bank of Ireland displays the priceless **Silver**

Dublin—Galway

DEPART DUBLIN HEUSTON	ARRIVE GALWAY	NOTES	DEPART GALWAY	ARRIVE DUBLIN HEUSTON	NOTES
0720	1013	exc. Sun	1510	1808	exc. Sun
0905	1202	Sun	1620	1925	Sun
1055	1351	exc. Sun	1805	2056	Sun
			1808	2135	exc. Sun

Distance: 129 miles (208 km)

Sword and Great Mace, the finest examples of Irish silver work remaining in the Republic.

Galway is a ferry port for the Aran Islands, which lie 30 miles offshore, as are Doolin and Rossaveal. Air service is available via Connemara airport. The islands are a tribute to traditional Irish life and culture, and, as in Galway and Connemara, Gaelic is still proudly spoken among the natives.

The **Galway Bay Conference and Leisure Centre** (*Tel:* 091 520520) is a prime example of Galway City's growth. The new deluxe facility is located on Galway's promenade, just minutes from Eyre Square and the City Center. It includes a fitness center with swimming pool, sauna, and steam room. Restaurant, bar, and lounge each have panoramic views of Galway Bay. With its proximity to **Leisureland,** the hotel is one of the most extensive conference and leisure centers in the country.

Or, if you decide to base yourself in Galway for a night or two, try Jury's Galway Inn, a mere ½ mile from Ceannt Station. The inn overlooks Galway Bay and is located in the heart of the city near the historic Spanish Arch. *Tel:* 3539–1566444; *Fax:* (353) 9156–8415.

Supposedly, the word *lynching* entered the English language through an act of Galway's chief magistrate, James Lynch-FitzStephen, elected to his post in 1493. According to a popular but dubious legend, his son, Walter, murdered a Spanish visitor and then confessed to the crime. He was condemned by his own father, but no one could be found to carry out the execution. So Judge Lynch, no doubt a firm believer in "spare the rod and spoil the child," hanged his own son and afterward retired into seclusion. **Lynch's Castle** stands today on Shop Street, and the Lynch Memorial attesting to this stern and unbending justice lies nearby, close to the **Church of St. Nicholas,** erected in 1320. Legend has it that Columbus worshiped in the church before setting out on his voyage of discovery to America.

An unusual feature of Galway is its downtown salmon weir, where shoals of salmon swim in the clear river en route to spawning grounds. This unique sight may be viewed from the **Salmon Weir Bridge,** which crosses the Corrib River by the city's cathedral.

Roundstone is a picturesque fishing village on the southern shores of Connemara. Already well known for superb seafood and quaint bed-and-breakfast-style hotels, Roundstone is also "the home of the bodhran"—a one-sided framed drum made from goatskin—Ireland's oldest product, made famous more recently when played by Christy Moore in *Riverdance*. A bus leaves daily during the summer from Foster Street in Galway City for Roundstone and Clifden.

If you have never seen *Riverdance* or heard the haunting tones of the bodhrans, you've missed one of the most exciting music and dance shows in the last 1,000 years. Visit master bodhran maker **Malachy Kearns's** (known locally as Malachy Bodhran) quaint craft and music shop. Malachy and artist-wife Anne are the only full-time bodhran makers in the world, and they've been making them for many years.

You can purchase the handmade bodhrans with Celtic designs, family crests, or names. The shop is open daily 0900–1900 (closed Sunday in winter). Malachy Kearns mixes the goatskins with secret ingredients and soaks them for 7–10 days before stretching them over a beech-wood frame. Mr. Kearns attributes the bodhran's haunting tones to the goatskins; we think his secret ingredients have something to do with achieving such extraordinary sound. It is truly fascinating!

Roundstone Music, Roundstone, Connemara, Co. Galway
Tel: 095 35808; *Fax:* 095 35980
Internet: www.bodhran.com
E-mail: bodhran@iol.ie

Day Excursion to

Kilkenny
Ghosts and Gifts Galore

Depart from Dublin Heuston Station
Distance by Train: 81 miles (130 km)
Average Train Time: 1 hour, 49 minutes
City Dialing Code: 56
Tourist Information Office: Shee Alms House, Rose Inn Street, Kilkenny
Tel: 056 51500; **Fax:** 056 63955
Hours: May–July: Monday–Saturday 0900–1800 and Sunday 1100–1700
Notes: To reach it, turn left onto John Street after leaving the station and walk to the bridge crossing the river. Cross the bridge, and John Street then becomes Rose Inn Street. Continue walking up Rose Inn Street, and you will find the office in the Shee Alms House on the right.

Kilkenny may be Ireland's smallest city, but it is one of the most popular destinations from Dublin. **Kilkenny Castle** (by guided tour

Dublin—Kilkenny

DEPART DUBLIN HEUSTON	ARRIVE KILKENNY	NOTES
0730	0925	exc. Sun
0930	1122	Sun
1130	1316	exc. Sun

DEPART KILKENNY	ARRIVE DUBLIN HEUSTON	NOTES
1519	1710	Sun
1541	1737	exc. Sun
1911	2117	exc. Sun
1920	2118	Sun

Distance: 81 miles (130 km)

only), a twelfth-century grand stone fortress on the River Nore, dominates the scene and sets the theme. It was the chief residence of the Butler family from 1391 until 1935—almost 550 years. Recently restored to the majesty of the 1820s, it is now home to the National Furniture collection and the modern Butler Gallery. The castle is impressive and reminiscent of the great bastions along the Rhine River.

Other sites include the thirteenth-century **St. Canice's Cathedral,** reputed to be one of the most beautiful in Ireland; **Rothe House,** home of the Kilkenny Archeological Society; and **Shee Alms House,** a restored sixteenth-century building that houses the tourist information office.

Though small, Kilkenny is cosmopolitan, with a pub and club life that draws visitors from major cities. In fact, the **Paris Texas Bar & Restaurant** has to close its doors by 2100 because of the crowds. **Langtons,** a four-time winner of the National Pub of the Year award, is a traditional pub and restaurant in grand surroundings, with a disco club that stays open to the wee hours of the morning. (A hotel facility is adjacent to the disco; *Tel:* 056–65133).

Another interesting landmark is **Kytler's Inn,** which has the distinction of being the oldest residence in the city and, by tradition, the house of the witch Dame Alice Kytler, born there in 1280. Dame Alice seems to have been a very nice lady except that she acquired and disposed of husbands— four in all—in rapid succession. This aroused the curiosity of the local folks, and in 1324 she was charged by Bishop de Ledrede with witchcraft, heresy, and criminal assaults upon her husbands. Brought to trial and condemned to burn at the stake as a witch, Dame Alice eluded her accusers and escaped across the Irish Sea to Scotland. Her maid, Petronilla, was not as fortunate; the bishop had her burned at the stake as a suitable substitute. Locals claim that Petronilla's ghost still haunts the cellar of what is now the Kytler Inn on St. Kieran Street—possibly asking for back wages?

Day Excursion to

Killarney
Lakes and Jaunting Cars

Depart from Dublin Heuston Station
Distance by Train: 185 miles (298 km)
Average Train Time: 3 hours, 30 minutes
City Dialing Code: 64
Tourist Information Office: Beach Road, Killarney
Tel: 064 31633; *Fax:* 064 34506; E-mail: killarney@cork-kerrytourism.ie
Hours: July–August: Monday–Saturday 0900–2000, Sunday 1000–1300/1415–1800. June and September: Monday–Saturday 0900–1900. October–May: Monday–Saturday 0915–1930 (closed for lunch 1300–1415).
Notes: To reach the tourist information office, turn left on Railway Road just after passing the Great Southern Hotel on your left as you leave the railway station. Railway Road crosses Muckross Road a short distance from the station. At the Cinema, cross to the other side of the road. The Killarney Plaza Hotel and the jaunting cars are on the right-hand side. Continue along Beech Road. Take a right turn into New Street Car Park. The tourist office is a short distance on the left-hand side.

DUBLIN
Killarney

Killarney is rivaled now by Dublin as the number-one tourist attraction in the Republic of Ireland. Horse-drawn carriages known as jaunting cars take tourists to feature sights including: **Muckross Abbey,** the ruins of a fifteenth-century Franciscan monastery; **Ross Castle,** on the banks of Lough Leane (which now offers memorable guided tours of the inner castle); and **Muckross House,** a nineteenth-century manor with a museum depicting local folk life and housing various crafts shops with blacksmiths, weavers, and potters. Muckross Traditional Farms is also a very fine attraction.

Jaunting-car rates are usually based on four passengers. If your party is fewer than four, the tourist office may be just the place to find other passengers willing to share the cost. The central jaunting-car stand in Killarney is a stone's throw from the tourist office, so you won't have to return to the railway station.

Killarney's **St. Mary's Cathedral** is an impressive Neo-Gothic structure worthy of a visit. The **Great Southern Hotel,** opposite the railway station, is a fashionable hostelry of great beauty, and its amicable Punchbowl Bar is a good place to pause for a libation and friendly conversation.

There are many eating places to choose from. We found the food at the **Flesk Restaurant** on Main Street to be tasty and satisfying. One of the favorite spots of the locals, too, the Flesk is known for its daily fresh fish specials, such as wild salmon, and its live Dingle Bay lobsters. Four-course menus range from €12.70 to €17.78.

Dublin—Killarney

DEPART DUBLIN HEUSTON	ARRIVE KILLARNEY	NOTES
0830	1211 (1156 Sun)	
0950	1423	1
1205	1600	1, Sun
1320	1700	1, exc. Sun

DEPART KILLARNEY	ARRIVE DUBLIN HEUSTON	NOTES
1430 (1428 Sun)	1825 (1755 Sun)	
1630	2005	Sun
1808	2133	Sun
1829	2221	1, exc. Sun

Daily, unless otherwise noted
1. Change at Mallow
Distance: 185 miles (298 km)

A classic Killarney countryside excursion is by bus to **Kate Kearney's Cottage**, a coaching inn, where you are fortified with Irish coffee. Then, setting out by pony through the **Gap of Dunloe,** you are refreshed again at **Lord Brandon's Cottage** before returning by boat to Lough Leane and to Killarney by jaunting car. You can obtain information on prices from the tourist office. A comprehensive guide to Killarney is the *Killarney Area Guide,* which can be purchased at the Killarney tourist office.

Italy

W hy do we find Italy so inviting? Just ask any Italian—it can be summed up in three little words: *La dolce vita,* the sweet life. Italy is pasta, Pavarotti, and the Pope; it's fashion, Ferrari, and films; it's *vino* (wine), Venus, and villas—it's all of our favorite things that culminate in *La dolce vita.*

Most visitors are aware of Italy's predominantly Catholic heritage, but not many are aware that Italy also has a rich Jewish heritage dating as early as 140 B.C. Most Italian Jews are descendants of the group Sephardim, who were expelled from Spain and Portugal in the fifteenth and sixteenth centuries. Many outstanding synagogues and other Jewish sites are most evident in Florence, Rome, and Venice.

For more information about Italy, contact the Italian Government Tourist Boards (ENIT) in North America (*Internet:* **www.italiantourism.com** or **www.enit.it;** *E-mail:* enitny@italiantourism.com):

Chicago: 500 North Michigan Avenue, Suite 2240, Chicago, IL 60611; *Tel:* (312) 644–9448; *Fax:* (312) 644–3019

New York: 630 Fifth Avenue, Suite 1565, New York, NY 10111; *Tel:* (212) 245–4822; *Fax:* (212) 586–9249

Los Angeles: 12400 Wilshire Boulevard, Suite 550, Los Angeles, CA 90025; *Tel:* (310) 820–0098; *Fax:* (310) 820–6357

Toronto: 175 Bloor Street East, Suite 907, South Tower, Toronto, Ontario M4W 3R8, *Tel:* (416) 925–4882; *Fax:* (416) 925–4799

Banking

- **Currency:** Euro (€)
- **Exchange rate at press time:** €1.10 = U.S. $1.00

Communications

- **Country Code:** 39

For telephone calls within Italy, dial a zero (0) preceding area code.

- **Direct dial:** AT&T: 172–1011; MCI: 172–1022; Sprint: 172–1877 in Bologna, Brindisi, Catania, Cozena, Florence, Formia, Genoa, Latina, Milan, Naples, Olbia, Padua, Palermo, Perugia, Pescara, Pisa, Pordenone, Trieste, Turin, and Venice. Buy telephone cards at any tobacco or newsstand.

Rail Travel in Italy

The **Italian State Railways** (*Ente Ferrovie Italiane dello Stato,* or *FS*) provides excellent and frequent train services linking all of Italy, including Sicily and Sardinia via train ferries, with Austria, France, and Switzerland (*Internet:* www.fs-on-line.com). All main lines and many minor lines are electrified. Italy's principal express train service, the **Eurostar *Italia*** (not to be confused with the cross-Channel Eurostar trains and formerly referred to as the ETR Pendolino and ETR 500 trains), are among the best in Europe.

Keep in mind that Italian trains are not just for tourists; the Italians are heavily dependent upon their rail system, and second-class rail cars are often crowded. We recommend traveling in first class when in Italy.

The Italian State Railways accepts the variety of **Eurail passes** (including the new Eurail Selectpass) **Italy RailCard, Italy Flexi RailCard,** and the **Italian Kilometric Ticket.** Eurail bonuses include:
- Free transport on FS-operated ferry crossings Civitavecchia to Golfo Aranci (Sardinia) and Villa S. Giovanni to Messina (Sicily).
- 30 percent discount on Attica Enterprises's Superfast Ferries from Bari and Ancona to Patras (Greece) and between Bari and Igoumenitsa (Greece), plus a 25 percent discount on cabin fares. *Tel:* 39 07 120 2033 for reservations.

The Italy RailCard provides for unlimited rail travel for the specified number of days consecutively, or for more flexibility, choose the Flexi RailCard for traveling the specified number of days within a 1-month period.

Italy RailCard and Flexi RailCard are valid for unlimited travel on the entire Italian State Railways network, including InterCity, EuroCity, and Rapido trains, with no surcharge. **Supplement required for Eurostar *Italia* trains.** Children under 12 years of age pay half adult fare; under 4 years of age, free.

The Italian Kilometric Pass (first class U.S. $364; second class U.S. $256) provides up to 3,000 kilometers (1,875 miles) of rail travel within a 2-month period, with a maximum of 20 single train trips. The pass may be used by as many as 5 persons, but each trip is calculated by multiplying the distance by the number of persons traveling. It also requires a supplement for traveling on all high-speed trains (and Italy has a lot of them), such as InterCity, EuroCity, Rapido, and Eurostar *Italia*. A "single trip" means boarding a single train by a single person. This pass is inconvenient in that it deviates from the general concept of a railpass because travelers must show the pass at ticket windows before each train trip.

Italy RailCard

Validity	1st Class	2nd Class
8 days	$299	$199
15 days	$373	$249
21 days	$433	$289
30 days	$522	$348

Italy Flexi RailCard

Validity	1st Class	2nd Class
4 days within 1 month	$239	$159
8 days within 1 month	$334	$223
12 days within 1 month	$429	$286

Base City:
Milan
(Milano)

City Dialing Code: 02

Milan is fashionable and futuristic—as evidenced by the growing number of high-rise structures and the accelerating pace of its population. At the same time, Milan is ancient and respectful of its glorious past. For instance, the **Duomo** (cathedral) is the second largest church in Italy, a beautiful example of Gothic stonework begun in 1386. *The Last Supper,* Leonardo da Vinci's famous painting, may be seen in the refectory of the **Santa Maria delle Grazie** convent. It was painted between 1495 and 1498. Like a typical Milanese, Leonardo was concerned with the future, and his drawings of machines in flight, together with some of his futuristic inventions, are exhibited in the **Leonardo da Vinci National Museum of Science and Technology.**

To promote its future, Milan created one of the most extensive fairgrounds in Europe; each year, thousands of businesses display or investigate products there. Milan does not live up to the stereotype of the Italian town. Lunches tend to be shorter, conversations seem more direct and to the point, and the Milanese appear to be in a bit of a hurry.

Transportation in Milan is abundant and unusually dependable. Several decades ago, the five o'clock train never left Milano Centrale on time; today, the five o'clock train leaves at five o'clock. Milan has an excellent underground transportation system (Metropolitan). A ticket costs €0.77 and is valid for 75 minutes on buses and trams, or for one underground (metro) trip. There is also a day ticket available for €2.58 and a 2-day ticket for €4.65. Hotel services rival the finest in Europe; shops are sophisticated and efficient. In a word, Milan "works."

There is one crucial thing about Milan. It is virtually impossible to get a hotel room in the city during those periods when the major fairs and fall and spring fashion shows are in progress—September, October, and early March. Forget about August. That's when the Milanese go on vacation and the majority of the hotels are closed. The larger chains, however, are open year-round.

Arriving by Air

Milan has two airports serving international travelers (*Internet:* www.sea-aeroportimilano.it). Milan's main international airport, **Malpensa**, is 28 miles northwest of the city, and 50 to 60 minutes is required to reach the downtown air terminal. Closer in, Milan's **Linate Airport** is located slightly more than 6 miles to the east of Milan. Check with your airline regarding which airport will be used for your flight. *Tel:* 02 748 5220.

Airport–City Links: Malpensa Airport Bus service connects Malpensa Airport with Linate Airport (travel time of 110 minutes) and Malpensa Airport with the Central Station (travel time of 60 minutes; fare, €6.70). Malpensa Express Train Service to the city departs every 30 minutes; journey time is 39 minutes. Fare: €7.75.

A deluxe bus service (Air Pullman, *Tel:* 02 58583185) runs every 20 minutes between Linate Airport and the Central Station from 0600 to 2300; fare, €4.13. Purchase tickets on board the bus.

Bus, limousine, and taxi services are available at both air terminals. The taxi services are quite expensive, averaging about €67 from Malpensa but only about €13 from Linate.

Arriving by Train

Milan has seven railway stations, but luckily, readers need be concerned with only one, the Milan Central Station **(Milano Centrale)**. Milan's Central Station is enormous.

- **Money exchange** offices can be reached by going through the archway leading off *binari* (tracks) Nos. 10–15. Once through the archway and into the main hall of the station, you will see several exchange offices, two of which have hours daily from 0700 to 2300. Avoid the so-called money changers who frequent this area. Like the gypsies in the Paris Métro, their main purpose is to relieve you of your money. The gypsies do it by picking your pocket; the "money changers" are much more gentle in their approach—they just short-change you. You will find the best rates inside the official exchange office at the counter.

- **Tourist information** is located on the first floor near the "Gran Bar" in the main hall. Maps and tour information are available. This office is not equipped to assist in locating hotel accommodations, but you can get directions to the central tourist office at Piazza del Duomo. Summertime hours: Monday–Friday 0830–2000; Saturday 0900–1300 and 1400–1700: Sunday and holidays 0900–1300 and 1400–1700 (*Tel:* 02 72524360/370). A hallway on the left side of the tourist office will lead you to a public telephone.
- **Train information** office is marked with a black **i** sign, located at the extreme right end of the station as you come from the trains. Illuminated flags indicate what language is spoken at the windows. The British flag means English is spoken. Hours: 0700–2100.
- **Train reservations** for Eurostar *Italia,* EuroCity, InterCity, and Rapido express-train services are made in an office separate from the one dispensing train information. To reach it, go through the main station hall and descend to the station foyer on the lower (street) level. Turn left and look for a huge door marked BIGLIETTERIA EST (ticket office east). Go through the door, and take a number from the ticket machine to wait your turn. You will see counter Nos. 49–53, labeled PRENOTAZIONI (Reservations). Hours: 0800–2200 Monday through Friday and 0800–1300 on Saturday and Sunday.
- **Railpass validation** requires that you descend to the street level via the escalator in the middle of the station, make a right turn, and look for a sign, BIGLIETTERIA OVEST. Then proceed to window 20 or 22, marked INTERNATIONAL TICKETS.
- **Food services** range from trackside vendors to a full-service restaurant. The restaurant, with a large and efficient self-service cafeteria next to it, is located on the far left side of the main hall as you exit from the trains. A snack bar is also there. Downstairs near the BIGLIETTERIA OVEST sign you will find an excellent cafeteria that serves traditional Italian hot entrees and sandwiches. Just behind the cafeteria is a supermarket.

In this snack bar, as in the various smaller ones scattered throughout the main hall and track area, you need to purchase tickets for the particular food or beverage you desire from a cashier, then give the tickets to a counter attendant. The system works, but now you know how confused the Italian immigrant felt when ordering an American hamburger, especially if asked "would you like that with mustard, catsup, lettuce, tomato, pickles—and was that to go?"

If this is your first rail trip into Italy, this will probably be your first acquaintance with the trackside vendors. Similar to the pushcarts that grace many of the streets in New York City, they offer a convenient variety of refreshments—and the price is right.

- **Baggage-checking** facilities may be reached by taking the exit at the end of tracks 6 and 7. Across the main hall and to the right, you'll see a sign in red letters, DEPOSITO BAGAGLI. Rates vary according to what you store. The facility is open all the time. To store one bag costs €2.58 per 12 hours.

The main baggage room, located on the street level of the station, can be reached either from the plaza facing the Michelangelo Hotel or from the bottom of the main escalator, between the street level and the train concourse. Hours: 0700–2230 daily. Through experience, we have learned that you should check items to be forwarded at least one day in advance, and then only to other major points in Italy. We would not advise forwarding anything to France or Switzerland.

There is a checkroom in the restaurant-and-cafeteria entrance that is convenient and safe to use for temporarily storing suitcases and apparel while you are eating or searching for a place to stay. If you check your baggage here, it is most important that you find out when the attendant plans to leave. Otherwise, you could return to collect your duds only to learn they have been moved to a safe area until the operation starts again in the morning. The hours of operation are posted as 0700–2400, but it appears to be an individual enterprise rather than one under the supervision of management.

- **Station miscellany.** Milan's railway station has many other services. There is a large and rather comfortable first-class lounge leading off the street side of the main hall. Its entrance is just to the left of the tourist information office. Inside the lounge you will find a computer that can give you train information.

Milano Centrale is a multilevel station, but elevator service from the train level to the street level is available. The entrance on the train level is inside the first-class lounge. If you have a first-class railpass, you have full access to the passenger lounge and elevator service.

- **Taxi service** is available at both side entrances and the front, and **bus service** is in the Piazza Duca d'Aosta in front of the station. Pictographs of the station's facilities are located conveniently at the end of many tracks.

Double-check your departing train number and platform location. For example, when departing Milan for Munich aboard EuroCity 93 *Leonardo Da Vinci,* you will note that signs in the station indicate the train's destination as MONACO. In Italian, this means "Monk," and Munich (in German) is the "City of Monks." So, you are on the right train, and you are not bound for Monaco, which, in French, means "Monte Carlo." InterCity 341 *Ligure* is the proper train to board if you are in fact going to Monaco and Monte Carlo via Genoa.

Emerging from the train platforms, if you detect the aroma of an American-style hamburger, it's coming from Wendy's. To get there, turn right in the station hall and take the escalator at the far end to the street level. Skirt the tram terminal to the left then look for the Wendy's sign.

Tourist Information/Hotel Reservations

- *Tourist Information Office:* A.P.T., Via Marconi I, just off Piazza del Duomo; *Tel:* 02–725 24301 or 725 24302 or 725 24303; *Fax:* 02–7252 4350

Hours: Summertime, 0830–2000 Monday–Friday; 0900–1300/1400–1900 Saturday; 0900–1300/1400–1700 Sunday.

Notes: To reach the central tourist information office, take bus No. 60 in front of the station to Piazza del Duomo, site of Milan's cathedral. You can also take line 3 of the metro to the Duomo stop. Attendants in the railway station information office will direct you.

The friendly Milanese devised the "Milano for You" *Welcome Card* kit to make your stay in Milan more convenient and enjoyable. The kit includes access to art tours, cultural theme dinners, Giuseppe Verdi Symphonic Orchestra tickets, a 24-hour public transportation ticket, city map, and an opera music compact disc. It's available at the tourist information office.

There are times when Milan reaches the visitor saturation point and NO VACANCY signs go up all over town. Should you arrive in Milan without hotel reservations, you have two alternatives to consider.

If there is no housing in Milan, you can leave town. A EuroCity train can have you in Como in 30 minutes, where hotel rooms probably will be more plentiful. In fact, you may be taken with the idea of residing in this lovely lake location throughout your stay in the area. There is express-train service back to Milan every morning.

Another alternative is a fast but systematic search of the concentrated hotel area adjacent to the railway station. There is a covey of luxury and first-class hotels to the left of it. Dominating the scene is the 17-story Michelangelo, with the Bristol, the Anderson, the Andreola, and the Splendido close by.

For lower cost but comfortable lodgings, walk two blocks on Via Roberto Lepetit, beginning at the Michelangelo, to Piazza San Camillo. Within this distance, you pass the Florida, the Colombia, and the Boston hotels. No luck? Turn right at the Plaza onto Via Napo Torriani. Between this point and Piazza Duca d'Aosta three short blocks ahead (where you can again see the station), you pass on your right the hotels Berna, Atlantic, and San Carlo; on your left, the Canova, Garda, Flora, Bernina, and Augustus.

If you have not found a room by this time, head back to Milano Centrale and one of the EuroCities. By this time, you'll be sure to fall in love with Lake Como.

The main tourist office charges a nominal fee for making accommodations reservations, but they are not authorized to accept deposits to guarantee that your reservation will be honored on your arrival at the hotel or pension. If you have made a room reservation through the tourist office, proceed immediately to your hotel to confirm your reservation in person. Many Italian hoteliers operate on a "first-come, first-housed" basis, and even though you have a reservation, someone else may end up with your room.

Train Connections to Other Base Cities from Milan (Milano)

Dep rt from Milan (Milano) Centrale

DEP..R T	TRAIN NUMBER	ARRIVE	NOTES
		Amsterdam Centraal	
0810	IC 386	2154	1
2005	D 208	1037+1	R, Sleeper
		Barcelona Sants	
2000	EN 372	0901+1	R, Hotel Train, 2
1525	IC 344	0723+1	R, 1, Sleeper
		Berlin Zoobahnhof	
2125	D 200	1119+1	R, 3, Sleeper
		Bern (Berne)	
0810	EC 90	1156	
0910	IC 322	1337	4
1110	IC 324	1537	4
followed by departures at 1110, 1310, 1410, 1510, 1710, and 2010.			
		Brussels (Bruxelles) Midi/Zuid	
0810	EC 90	1945	R
2135	D 298	0929+1	R, Sleeper
		Copenhagen (København) H.	
1325	IC 252	0959+1	R, 1, 5, Sleeper
1710	CIS 46*	1359+1	R, 1, 7, Sleeper
		Hamburg Hauptbahnhof	
0715	CIS 156*	1932	R, 6
0925	EC 8	2136	1
1510	EC 79	0752+1	R, 8, Sleeper
1710	CIS 46*	0833+1	R, 1, Sleeper
2125	D 200	1032+1	R, 5, Sleeper
		Luxembourg	
0810	EC 90	1650	
2135	D 298	0624+1	R, Sleeper
		Lyon Part-Dieu	
0630	EC 136	1159	R
1315	EC 140	1856	R
1510	IC 328	2233	9
2330	EN 222	0805+1	R, 10, Sleeper
		Munich (München) Hauptbahnhof	
0910	EC 93	1630	
1510	EC 79	2230	
2222	IR 2117	0633+1	R, 11, Sleeper
		Nice Ville	
0710	IC 341	1151	R
1510	IC 345	1958	R
1815	E 1145	2354	R
		Paris Gare de Lyon	
0915	TGV 9252	1611	R
1600	TGV 9258	2251	R
2330	EN 222	0838+1	R, 12, Sleeper
		Roma (Roma) Termini	
0530	ES 9425	1030	R
0800	ES 9429	1230	R

Depart	Train Number	Arrive	Notes
1000	ES 9433	1430	R
		Roma (Roma) Termini	
1200	ES 9437	1630	R
1400	ES 9415	1830	R
1600	ES 9445	2030	R
1800	ES 9449	2230	R
1900	ES 9451	2330	R
2320	E 1913	0558+1	R, Sleeper
		Vienna (Wien) Westbahnhof	
2015	2113	0841+1	
		Zürich Hauptbahnhof	
0715	CIS 156*	1053	R
0825	IC 386	1253	R
1110	CIS 154*	1453	R
1225	IC 380	1653	R
1425	IC 382	1853	R
1625	IC 354	2053	R
1745	CIS 152*	2127	R
1915	CIS 150*	2253	R
1925	IC 356	2333	R

Daily unless otherwise noted
R   Reservations required
*   Cisalpino (CIS) trains require a supplement.
+1 Arrives next day
1.   Change trains in Basel.
2.   *Salvador Dali,* Trenhotel (hotel train), special fares required.
3.   Change trains in Mannheim.
4.   Change trains in Brig.
5.   Change trains in Frankfurt.
6.   Change trains in Zürich.
7.   Change trains in Hamburg.
8.   Change trains in Munich (München).
9.   Change trains in Geneva.
10. Depart Milano P Garibaldi Station and change trains in Dijon-Ville.
11. Depart Milano Lambrate Station.
12. Arrive at Bercy.

Day Excursions

A total of four day excursions have been selected from Milan. The first two take you south of Milan into the Italian peninsula to Italy's gastronomic capital, **Bologna,** and the birthplace of Christopher Columbus, **Genoa.** Another day excursion will take you to where Switzerland meets Italy, **Lugano,** the Swiss city with an Italian flair. The remaining day excursion will take you east to "the Queen of the Adriatic," **Venice,** and the romance of its gondoliers and grand canals. You'll enjoy each of them.

Day Excursion to

Bologna
Italy's Gastronomic Capital

Depart Milan Centrale Station
Distance by Train: 136 miles (219 km)
Average Train Time: 1 hour, 42 minutes
City Dialing Code: 51
Tourist Information Office: Piazza Medaglie d'Oro
Tel: 24–6541; *Fax:* 25–1947
Hours: Monday–Saturday 0900–1230 and 1430–1900
Notes: Piazza Medaglie d'Oro lies directly in front of the station. To reach the tourist office in the station you must first exit the main entrance of the station. Incline to the right and enter the station hallway at that exit.
Tourist Information Office: No. 6, west side of Piazza Maggiore
Tel: 23–9660; *Fax:* 23–1454
Hours: Monday–Saturday 0900–1900; Sunday and midweek holidays 0900–1400
Notes: To reach it, turn left when exiting the rail station and walk two blocks to Via Dell'Independenza, one of Bologna's main avenues. Turn right onto the avenue, and a delightful 15-minute walk will bring you to Neptune's Fountain. Then continue your walk in the same direction a short distance into Piazza Maggiore.

Bologna specializes in two areas—thinking and eating. When you think about it, you'll probably conclude, as we did, that it is not too bad a lifestyle to follow.

Bologna stands out historically and architecturally. Tourists can walk under the porticoes of the city while visiting the many monuments. If lined up, the porticoes would cover 40 kilometers!

Bologna's university, the oldest in Europe, was founded in 1088. By the thirteenth century, its student body numbered 10,000. One of its more recent students, Guglielmo Marconi (1874–1937), studied wireless telegraphy there. The university was noted for employing women professors. One professor, Novella d'Andrea, was said to be so beautiful in face and body that she had to give her lectures from behind a screen to avoid distracting her students.

Bologna is the capital of **Emilia-Romagna**, a northwest-to-southeast slice of the Italian peninsula just below its juncture with the European Continent. It is here that the "cultura villanoviana," better known as the Iron Age, began more than 4,000 years ago. After the fall of the Roman Empire, the city did not flourish again until after the eleventh century. Marvelous Etruscan and Roman examples of history can be seen at the **Civic Archaeology Museum**.

Milan (Milano)—Bologna

DEPART MILAN CENTRALE	TRAIN NUMBER	ARRIVE BOLOGNA CENTRALE	NOTES
0720	IC 589	0928	
0800	ES 9429	0944	R
0900	ES 9431	1044	
1000	ES 9433	1144	R
1100	ES 9435	1244	R
1110	CIS 153*	1300	R

plus other non-ES trains departing at 0840, 0920, and 1120

DEPART BOLOGNA CENTRALE	TRAIN NUMBER	ARRIVE MILAN CENTRALE	NOTES
1414	ES 9436	1600	R
1514	ES 9438	1700	R
1614	ES 9440	1800	R
1714	ES 9418	1900	R
1814	ES 9444	2000	R
1914	ES 9422	2100	R
2014	ES 9448	2200	R
2107	ES 9420	2255	R
2114	ES 9450	2325	R
2214	ES 9452	0005+1	R

plus other non-ES trains departing at 1522, 1632, 1832 and 2032

Daily, unless otherwise noted
R Reservations required
+1 Next day
* Supplement required on Cisalpino
Distance: 136 miles (219 km)

An economically strong region, with the nation's highest employment rate, Emilia-Romagna holds the uncontested title of the "richest gastronomic region in Italy." Endless strings of sausages and thousands of cheese varieties adorn the windows of its delicatessen shops. Restaurants line the city's arcaded streets, filled with people devouring delicacies to the accompaniment of fine wines. Many of them are in the luxury class, but you can also dine very well in the less expensive restaurants. Many maintain an "open kitchen," which you're welcome to inspect and where you may chat with the cooks.

The famous prosciutto of Parma is absolutely unlike any American prosciutto—and, like most Italian meat products, it cannot be sold in the United States.

Bologna is an ideal base for exploring the Emilia-Romagna area. Among the towns to visit are **Faenza,** for its ceramics; **Ferrara,** for its fortress; **Ravenna,** for its early Christian art; **Rimini,** for its Adriatic beach; and, of course, **Parma,** for its ham and Parmesan cheese. All are about one hour or less by rail from Bologna. All of these cities may be visited out of Milan, too. Consult the schedules in Milan's Central Station.

Bologna also has much to offer architecturally. An ensemble of rare Italian beauty is concentrated in its two enjoining squares, the **Piazza Maggiore** and the **Piazza del Nettuno**. Combined with the **Piazza di Porta Ravegnana,** the heart of Bologna even today reflects its Renaissance greatness.

Neptune's Fountain (Fontana del Nettuno) is the focal point of its piazza. Completed in 1566, it aptly depicts Bologna's vigorous nature. Saint Petronius Basilica, facing the Piazza Maggiore, was begun in 1390, but remains unfinished even today.

The Piazza Ravegnana contains not just one leaning tower, but two. The taller, built by the Asinelli family between 1109 and 1119, stands 330 feet with a tilt exceeding 7½ feet. The other, the Garisenda Tower, is only 165 feet high, but it leans out 10 feet over its foundation. If you're in good physical condition and feel like climbing 498 steps, there's a fine view from the top of the Asinelli Tower.

And if you would like to experience more of the "culta Bononia" (the Latin name for Bologna), call the tourist office for the *Not Just for the Weekend* brochure. Rates and special offers on more than 50 hotels and inns, city and "pilgrim" tours, plus events year-round are listed.

Day Excursion to

Genoa (Genova)
Great Port of Italy

Depart Milan Centrale Station
Distance by Train: 93 miles (150 km)
Average Train Time: 1 hour, 25 minutes
City Dialing Code: 010
Tourist Information Office: On the right-hand side of the Piazza Principe station foyer after the second escalator coming from the trains
Tel: (010) 2462633
Hours: 0800–2000 Monday–Saturday; 0900–1200 Sunday
Tourist Information Office: Porto Antico-Palazzina Santa Maria (old harbor-aquarium area)
Tel: (010) 248711; *Fax:* (010) 2467658
Internet: www.apt.genova.it
E-mail: aptgenova@apt.genova.it
Hours: 0900–1830 daily

Richard Wagner wrote, "I have never seen anything like this Genoa! It is something indescribably beautiful, grandiose, characteristic." According to its tourist office, Genoa is "a town that you have to know how to love . . . there can be no half measures." Genoa is a merchant town, a vertical city, a major Mediterranean port. It is a city of contrasts, mixing the ancient with the new.

To experience a taste of this interesting city, ride the InterCity 341 *Ligure* out of Milan to Genoa at 0710 in the morning. Enjoy a leisurely walk along Genoa's avenues. Lunch in full view of the city's great harbor—largest in all of Italy. Board an InterCity late in the afternoon and be back in Milan for dinner that same day. Or, fall in love with Genoa by lunchtime and return to Milan just before midnight. The relatively short time en route between these cities makes a "set your own pace" schedule ideal.

Be mindful that Genoa has two major railway stations, **Piazza Principe** and **Brignole.** If you come from Milan, Piazza Principe is the first stop after the train emerges from a tunnel. Digital schedule boards in both stations advise what time the next connecting train departs for the other station. To be certain, board your returning train to Milan from Piazza Principe because many through-trains do not call at Brignole. You can, however, ride any shuttle train from Brignole north to the next stop, which is Piazza Principe.

A boat tour of the city's harbor is an excellent way for visitors to acquaint themselves with Genoa. Tours by boat leave from the aquarium, in the old port area, daily at 1515. Organized boat trips from the Maritime Building may be arranged ahead of time. The tour runs every hour starting at 0930 and ending at 1730/1800 (or later, depending on the number of people asking for the trip), when a minimum of 10 persons is present. To reach the departure quay, proceed by bus or on foot to Piazza Caricamento, following the yellow signs to the aquarium. Cross the road and enter the old port area. You'll see the aquarium on your right. The tour boats are berthed just beside the aquarium building.

Most visitors link Genoa with Christopher Columbus (1451–1505). This association begins as you leave the Piazza Principe Station fronted by **Piazza Acquaverde,** where a statue stands in honor of Columbus. A part of the city bus tour takes you to the Church of San Stefano, where Columbus was baptized, and into the Piazza della Vittoria—a vast expanse of lawns where the three ships of his fleet, the *Niña, Pinta,* and *Santa Maria,* are depicted in grass and flowers.

Plan a walking tour of Genoa. Depart Genova Piazza Principe Station and follow Via Balbi to Via Cairoli, which connects with "the street of Kings"—Via Garibaldi. At the end of Via Garibaldi, turn right (south) and proceed to the city's center, Piazza de Ferrari. From this point, you can continue along Via XX Settembre to the park in front of the Brignole Station

Milan (Milano)—Genoa (Genova)

Milan (Milano)–Genoa (Genova)
Departures hourly alternating at 10 or 15 minutes past the hour begininning at
0710. Journey time 93 minutes to 1 hour and 50 minutes.

Genova (Genoa)–Milan (Milano)
Departures at 18 and 58 minutes past the hour every other hour, then 1857
followed by 6 trains until 2158. Journey time: 1 hour 47 minutes.

or return on foot to the Piazza Principe Station by turning south and
walking along the harbor. Both tourist information offices have maps to
assist you in the walking tour. Be certain to include Genoa's great aquarium.
The **Aquarium**, built in 1992 for the Columbus celebrations, is one of the
biggest in Europe and should not be missed.

The city of Genoa lies beside a fine natural harbor at the foot of a pass in
the Italian Apennines. It rivals Marseilles as the leading European port on
the Mediterranean. Genoa's harbor facilities, which were damaged heavily
during World War II, have been expanded and modernized. Shipbuilding is
the leading industry of Genoa.

Ever since its birth, Genoa's calling has been the sea. Genoese ships
transported Crusaders to the Middle East and returned laden with booty.
Genoese merchants, profiting from the newly created demand in Europe for
goods from the Middle East, expanded their operations throughout the
Christian world. Genoese forts and trading posts soon spread throughout
the Mediterranean and Aegean Seas, creating a rivalry between Genoese and
Venetians. Ask the tourist office for hours and information on the new sea
and navigation museum called **Padiglione del mare e della Navigazione** in
the Porto Antico Area.

Genoa is proud of its **Lanterna,** the lighthouse that has become the
international symbol of the city. Built on the site of an ancient tower in the
first half of the sixteenth century, it has guided mariners to its safe harbor for
more than four centuries.

In the time of Christopher Columbus, another son of Genoa, Andrea
Doria (1468–1560), did much to promote the development of the city's
maritime power. Serving as captain-general of Genoa's navy until defeated
by Spanish forces in 1522, he served the French briefly before restoring the
republic of Genoa as an ally of Holy Roman Emperor Charles V. Andrea
Doria's palace can be seen during the city tour.

Those traveling with children will not want to skip the **La Citta dei
Bambini.** This children's town is fascinating to young ones and to the
curious of any age who want to learn how scientific things work.

Day Excursion to

Lake Lugano
The Swiss Riviera

Depart Milan Centrale Station
Distance by Train: 48 miles (77 km)
Average Train Time: 1 hour, 15 minutes
Switzerland Dialing Code: 41
City Dialing Code: 91
Tourist Information Office: Palazzo Civico, Riva Albertolli, P.O. Box 2533, CH-6901
    Lugano, Switzerland
Tel: 913–32 32; *Fax:* 922–76 53
Internet: www.lugano-tourism.ch
E-mail: info@lugano-tourism.ch
Hours: April–June and September–October: Monday–Friday 0900-1830; Saturday
    0900–1200; Sunday 1000–1400. July–August: Monday–Friday 0900-1830;
    Saturday 0900–1230 and 1330–1700; Sunday 1000–1500. November–March:
    Monday–Friday 0900–1200 and 1400–1700.
Notes: To reach the official tourist office of Lake Lugano, ride the *funicolare* (cable
    railway) to Piazza Cioccaro and proceed on foot downhill to the center of
    Lugano, Piazza Riforma. As you continue downhill toward the lake, stop at the
    town hall where the tourist office is located.

    Holders of Eurail or Europasses need not purchase separate rail tickets to
make excursions from Milan into Switzerland, since both Italy and Switzerland
are included on these passes.

MILAN *Lake Lugano*

L ake Lugano, known as the Swiss Riviera, is sheltered from the north
    by the Lepontine Alps. It is favored with a climate that is exception-
ally mild and is purportedly the sunniest of all central European resorts.
Considered a year-round resort, the city of Lugano sponsors a multitude of
events to attract visitors of all ages.

Although Lugano is a very short distance from Milan, you will be
crossing the Swiss border on this day excursion. Don't forget your passport.
There is a currency-exchange desk in the railway station (open daily,
0515–2230), and the town abounds in banks and *cambio* (exchange) offices
that offer official rates.

There is a **hotel-reservations-and-information office** to your immediate right as you leave the station. Train information may be obtained in the
office bearing the i sign to the left of the main exit.

When the lake beckons, there is a choice of 8 round trips by boat, each
offering an opportunity for a special vista. If the mountains attract you,
ascent is possible by cableways and funiculars in many different directions.
Two funiculars, one at each end of Lugano, carry you swiftly up 3,000 feet
to breathtaking views of either **Monte Bre** or **Monte San Salvatore.**

Milan (Milano)—Lake Lugano

DEPART MILAN CENTRALE	TRAIN NUMBER	ARRIVE LUGANO	NOTES
0715	CIS 156	0810	R
0825	IC 386	0954	
0925	EC 8	1054	
1110	CIS 154	1210	R
and hourly at 25 minutes past the hour until 1625, then 1745, 1825, and 1915			

DEPART LUGANO	TRAIN NUMBER	ARRIVE MILANO CENTRALE	NOTES
1506	IC 253	1635	
1548	CIS 155	1645	R
1706	EC 5	1835	
and hourly until 2006, and then			
2148	CIS 157	2245	R

Daily, unless otherwise noted
R Reservations required
Distance: 48 miles (77 km)

The list of things to do and see doesn't stop there. Take a motor coach to either **Sonvico** or **Tesserete,** typical Swiss mountain villages. Even a journey to the world-renowned resort of **St. Moritz** is possible. In fact, anything's possible—just ask at the Lugano tourist information office.

For a relaxing day on the lake, select the cruise to the **Swiss Miniature Village,** a unique exhibition of towns, hamlets, castles, mountains, and railways—all on a scale of 1:25. The model railway is centrally controlled and has a length of 186 miles! Realize that this is an all-day outing, but it has wooed millions of other visitors—why not you? The village is open from mid-March through October, 0900–1800. *Tel:* 91640 1060 or *E-mail:* info@swissminatur.ch.

The tourist information office will gladly mark out a walking tour of the city and its interesting areas, or opt for a free guided walking tour every Monday morning from April until October.

For lunch in Lugano, you can make it a stand-up affair by selecting from a vendor's cart at lakeside or perhaps aboard a lake steamer. For an enjoyable sit-down meal, we recommend these quality restaurants: **Al Portone, Cantinone, Casino Kursaal, Commercianti, La Tinera, Parco Saroli, Olimpia, Orologio, Restaurant Scala,** and **Trani.** All of these are in the center of Lugano. In Paradiso, we can recommend **Osteria Calprino.**

Shopping in Lugano is a pleasant experience. The place to do this is concentrated in the market area stretching from the bottom of the *funicolare* to the city square fronting the lake. Mouthwatering food vies for your attention along with a wide selection of Swiss products and crafts. We have yet to see a visitor enter the market area around lunchtime and not emerge a few minutes later with a sandwich in hand rivaling anything that Dagwood could concoct.

Shopping in this market area is, for the most part, in the shelter of overhead arcades. If you have been looking for specialty items of the Ticino area of Switzerland, you will find them here. Although firmly Swiss, the market in Lugano does have that piquant touch of Italy.

If you are longing for a Swiss-made watch, stop by **Bucherer's** in Lugano at Via Nassa 56. It's open Monday–Friday from 0900 to 1830 and Saturday until 1800 and carries its own styles as well as the other top Swiss names.

For a special treat be certain to visit our "secret hangout," **Gandria**, a small cliffside village that clings precariously to the mountains descending from the east into Lake Lugano. Gandria has no streets, but there is a bus stop on the mountainside above. The best, and more romantic, access is by lake steamer. If you want to share in our secret, inquire at any steamer pier regarding schedules to Gandria. You will want to take the Lugano-Porlezza line and plan to have an early dinner at one of Gandria's superb restaurants.

Day Excursion to

Venice (Venezia)
Grand Canals and Gondolas

Depart Milan Centrale Station
Distance by Train: 166 miles (267 km)
Average Train Time: 2 hours, 45 minutes
City Dialing Code: 41
Tourist Information Office: In Santa Lucia rail station.
Tel: 5298711
Internet: www.turismovenezia.it
E-mail: apt-06@mail.regione.veneto.it
Notes: Proceed to the head of the train platform. Enter the main hall of the station. The train information office is on the immediate left. No tourist information is available at this office. Beyond that, you'll see a sign directing you to a self-service buffet. Digital train information is prominently displayed above the buffet sign. Telephones, ticket windows, newspaper stands, and specialty shops are on the right-hand side of the station hall. Just prior to exiting the station, you'll see tourist information.

Upon arrival in Venice (Venezia), the American humorist Robert Benchley telegraphed his publisher, "Streets are flooded, please advise." Things have changed little since. Venice is situated on 120 islands surrounded by 177 canals in a lagoon between the Po and Piave Rivers at the northern extremity of the Adriatic Sea. The islands on which the city is built are connected by 400 or so bridges. Not only by its site but also by its architecture and history, Venice is known as "the Queen of the Adriatic."

Venice was founded in A.D. 452 when the inhabitants of several northern Italian cities sought refuge there from the Teutonic tribes invading Italy during the fifth century. The Venetians improved their fortifications and erected bulwarks of masonry to protect their growing city from the sea and from their enemies.

During the Crusades, Venice developed trade with the Orient and quickly became the center for commerce with the East. Venice became the leading wartime power of the Christian world by the end of the fifteenth century. In 1797, Napoleon Bonaparte conquered Venice and turned its government over to Austria. Through subsequent political maneuvers, Venice became part of the newly established kingdom of Italy in 1866.

Be sure to obtain full details regarding the canal transportation system. Water taxis are expensive, with fares starting at €13.94, plus €0.26 for each additional 15 seconds. The public boats (*vaporetto, motoscafo,* or *motonave*) operated by ACTV are a far more affordable means of reaching the main parts of Venice. The most romantic way to traverse the canals is, of course, via Venice's famous gondolas. Fares run about €62 for 45 minutes. For only €0.36, you could use one of the seven *traghetti* (ferries) to get from one side of The Grand Canal to the other. Also, ask for a map of Venice. You'll need it. Venetian addresses are somewhat peculiar in that they consist of a number and the name of a small area that could include several streets, thus making a particular restaurant or shop difficult to find. The canal navigation services (*Linee di Navigazione Lagunare*) are described in full detail on the reverse side of the map. If in Venice on a day excursion, purchase a one-way rather than a round-trip water-bus ticket from the rail station to **San Marco** on Line 1 and return to the station on foot.

Ticket in hand, board Line 1–Accelerata at Station 2, on the left side of the rail station. The dock and vessels are marked PIAZZALE ROMA–FERROVIA–LIDO, and the boat should be moving to your left as you come from the station. Boats proceeding to the right terminate at Station 1, Piazzale Roma, where you're required to disembark and purchase another ticket to get back on course!

Line 1 moves along the Grand Canal until emerging into open water from the canal at **Piazza San Marco** (St. Mark's), the center and most frequented part of Venice. The **Grand Canal** is Venice's principal traffic artery. It is lined with churches, museums, palaces—even a fish market—so keep your guidebook open so you can recognize these landmarks as you glide by.

Go ashore at St. Mark's and revel in the staggering sights before you. St. Mark's Bell Tower dominates the scene, but it won't be long before you'll find yourself standing in front of the cathedral. If time permits, take the elevator to the top of the bell tower for a spectacular view of vibrant Venice.

With so much to see, be mindful of the time or you will miss the train back to Milan. You can't hail a taxi at the last minute, since there are none,

Milan (Milano)—Venice (Venezia)

DEPART MILAN CENTRALE	TRAIN NUMBER	ARRIVE VENICE SANTA LUCIA
0705	IC 607	0957
0805	IC 609	1057
0905	IC 611	1157

and hourly until 2105 (the 1005 and 1805 trains run Sun only) and IR trains departing hourly at 15 minutes after the hour; journey time, 3 hour 22 minutes.

DEPART VENICE SANTA LUCIA	TRAIN NUMBER	ARRIVE MILAN CENTRALE	NOTES
1500	IC 622	1755	
1600	IC 628	1855	
1700	CIS 38*	1955	R
1800	IC 630	2055	
1900	IC 634	2155	
2000	IC 640	2255	
2100	IC 1508	2355	Sun only

and other frequent service on IR trains.

Daily, unless otherwise noted
R Reservations required
* Cisalpino (CIS) trains require a supplement
Distance: 166 miles (267 km)

so allow at least 45 minutes for the return trip from St. Mark's to Santa Lucia Station by water bus. Or start ambling through Venice by following the signs, ALLA FERROVIA (to the rail station). They are posted everywhere and easy to follow. Allow 2 hours to reach the station on foot, although a reasonable pace should get you there about 30 minutes sooner.

En route, you will cross the **Rialto Bridge**—the best place to view the Grand Canal and a good place to shop, too. There are 24 shops right on the bridge and a variety of vendors selling their wares along both sides of the canal. Farther on, you will cross the **Ponte Degli Scalzi** (Station Bridge) and arrive at the rail station where you started.

We're sure you will return to Venice, but heed the plight of tourists burdened with too many bags on the water buses—come back with minimum luggage or stow it in the lockers at the Santa Lucia or Mestre Station.

Base City:

Rome

(Roma)

Internet: www.romaturismo.com
City Dialing Code: 06

Italians refer lovingly to Rome as the "Eternal City." In the days of the Caesars, all roads led to Rome. Today, the same may be said of Italian State Railways.

No one knows exactly when people first started living along the Tiber River where Rome developed. Archaeologists continue to find evidence of still earlier civilizations than that of the Romans buried under those remains they have already identified. Etruscans ruled the area long before the Romans. Remains of that earlier Mediterranean civilization continue to be discovered in and around Rome.

Rome has already had two periods of greatness in the civilized world, each of which had a significant impact. Two thousand years ago, Rome ruled a good part of Europe and the Middle East. Rome contributed roads, architecture, art, law, literature, and political experience to the entire area.

Conquered by barbarians during the fifth century A.D., the city managed to remain the home of the popes, and through them and their armies, political power was regained. During the Renaissance, Rome again became a great center of art and learning. Since 1870, when Italian troops captured the city from Pope Pius IX, Rome has been the capital of Italy.

Readers considering "open jaw" (arrive in one European city, depart from another) air transportation to and from Europe should give serious consideration to Rome as either their entry or exit point. For example, in the spring, enter Europe through Rome and wend your way northward as the weather improves. Leave from Amsterdam. In autumn, reverse the procedure. Follow those lingering fall days southward from Amsterdam to Rome. By planning a rail vacation itinerary in this manner, you can assure yourself of having more moderate weather.

As a matter of fact, the average daily temperatures of Amsterdam and Rome vary by 10 to 12 degrees Fahrenheit—Rome's, of course, being the higher. So, when in Rome, do as the Romans do—move north as the mercury soars in the summer, south again when it begins to sink.

Arriving by Air

Rome has two airports, but because Ciampino Airport is small and deals mainly with charter flights, we focus on the main airport, Leonardo da Vinci, also called Fiumicino. **Fiumicino Airport** is 22 miles southwest of Rome.

Airport–City Links: Direct train service from Fiumicino Airport to Rome's Stazione Termini (Central Station) in Rome runs 0650–2150. Journey time: 30 minutes; fare, €8.78. It leaves and arrives at track No. 22 in Roma Termini Station.

There is also another train service from Fiumicino Airport to Tiburtina Station (total travel time, 46 minutes), with stops at local stations **Trastevere** and **Ostiense**. Trains run every 20 minutes 0628–2328; fare, €4.65. If you arrive at night, there is night bus service between Fiumicino Airport and Tiburtina Station. Buses run 0115–0500; fare, €4.65.

A taxi from Fiumicino Airport to the center runs about €46.48, but we caution against using taxis unless your airline representative arranges it and determines the fare beforehand. Authorized taxis are yellow-and-white cars with meters.

Arriving by Train

When you arrive at the railway station in Rome, beware of the many willing "helpers" eager to carry your luggage and find you a cab. If you need a taxi, carry your own bag and get in the regular taxi line.

Roma Termini. Rome has several suburban stations, but the InterCity and express trains stop only in the main station—Roma Termini, which has undergone extensive renovation. It is like a city within a city. In its main concourse, the section separating the train platforms from the main hall, you will find a bar and restaurant. On the lower level of the station you will find services you normally associate only with the most modern airports—barbershops, hairdressers, showers, lounges, bookstore, drugstore, fast food, and clothing shops.

- **Money-exchange** facilities are located throughout the railway station. In the main concourse, there is an office just to the left of *binari* (track) 12, between gateways 2 and 3. Hours: daily 0830–1930, and 0830–1400 and 1400–1930 on holidays. In the main hall, another currency exchange, including an ATM, is operated by the Bank of Rome. Turn left when entering the hall from the concourse and walk past all the ticket windows to the bank. Hours: Monday–Friday 0825–1335 and 1440–1600; holidays 0825–1155; Saturday 0830–1130.
- **Hotel reservations.** Hotel reservations in Rome and other Italian cities can be made Monday through Sunday 0700–2200 directly

across from track No. 20. You are required to leave a deposit and arrive at the hotel within one hour. We found that the line was always very long. If this is the case, telephone Rome's free hotel reservation service; *Tel:* (06) 699–1000.

- **Train information** may be obtained from three free-standing computer touch-screens from which you can gather schedule information for your destinations. The computers are located across from the tracks in the center and sides of the station, across from track Nos. 1, 9, and 22. *Tel:* 848 888 088; *Internet:* www.fs-on-line.com.
- **Train reservations** can be made at ticket windows 30 through 45. There are 45 ticket windows with their services indicated in Italian. Windows 7–29, labeled BIGLIETTI ORDINARI E RIDOTTI, sell tickets. At windows 30–38, labeled PRENOTAZIONI POSTI-WL-CUCCETTE-PENDOLINO, you can make reservations, including couchette and sleeper reservations. Finally, at windows 42–45, labeled PRENOTAZIONI, PENDOLINO, PARTENZA IN GIORNATA, you can make reservations for trains leaving that day. The cost of the reservation varies depending on destination. To ensure that you receive the proper reservation, determine the day and date of your travel, the number and departure time of your train, and its arrival time at your destination. This information can be taken from any of the train schedules posted throughout the station.

Print this information on a plain piece of paper, starting with the date, the train number, and the departure time. Draw a short arrow, then add the arrival time of the train and, finally, the name of the destination. Indicate the number of reservations required, then present the information to the attendant together with the railpass you will use for the trip. Submission of this information may draw a small grin from the attendant making the reservations, but it will save time and lessen the possibilities of errors in completing your train reservations.

- **Railpass validation** may be made at a window labeled in English located in the center of the train station near the main entrance facing the bus station. It is rather hidden away, and there are not any signs directing you. Just follow the signs for taxi and bus service, and right before you exit the station behind several tobacco shops you will see several windows, including the Eurail window and other windows that can provide you with information.

If you plan an early-morning departure on the first day you use your railpass, either allow an extra hour at the station that morning or inquire at one of the validating windows midevening the night before about the possibility of predating the validation.

Tourist Information/Hotel Reservations

- Azienda di Promozione Turistica di Roma, Via Parigi, 5–00185 Roma; *Tel:* 36 00 43 99; *Fax:* (06) 481 9316
  Hours: 0830–1900 Monday–Saturday; closed Sunday/holidays.

Notes: To visit this office, exit the main entrance of Roma Termini, skirt the left side of the city square in front of the station, and proceed past Museo Nazionale Romano (the National Roman Museum) to Via Parigi. Turn right at that point, then look for the office on the left-hand side of the street.

- **"Enjoy Rome,"** a very helpful tourist office especially designed for English speakers, very close to the station at 39 Via Varese. *Tel:* (06) 4451843.

  To get there, cross Via Marsala adjacent to the station on the right as you exit the train terminal. After two more blocks, turn right onto Via Varese. Number 39 is at the end of this one-way street.

- **National Tourist Office, ENIT,** at 2 Via Marghera, one block east of the railway station. *Tel:* (06) 49711.

- For tours in Rome and vicinity, the Sestante office in the main hall of the railway station will be happy to oblige.

Rome abounds with tourist facilities. Every resident seems to know the exact location of everything and seems eager to direct you. But Rome has more than three million citizens, each with a different opinion regarding the best way to get there—even if it's only around the corner.

Consequently, depend on the official tourist office staff, hotel staff, or city policemen, not the man on the street, for reasonably correct information. Above all, watch out for the "cab-and-coin" man. He'd be more than glad to take you where you want to go, but probably at three times the regular rate. The legitimate taxicab service in Rome is moderate in price and equipped with meters. Ask your hotel personnel to hail one for you or telephone. Telephone numbers to call in Rome for radio-dispatched cabs are 3570, 4994, and 6645.

American Express has a convenient location in Rome near the Spanish Steps at 38 Piazza de Spagna (*Tel:* 67641). American Express can assist in making train or hotel reservations in Rome or any other of the base cities. They also conduct excellent tours, in English, of Rome and its surroundings.

Sights/Attractions/Tours

Rome is a great walking city. First, get a map from your hotel or the tourist office, then find your way to the **Spanish Steps** and walk down Via Condotti—with detours down some of the side streets—to the Tiber. Sightseeing musts during an initial visit include the **Pantheon,** the **Coliseum,** and, close by, the **Forum.** Set aside at least a few hours for a visit to the **Sistine Chapel** and **St. Peter's.**

Roaming around Rome is like moving through history. Columns that looked down on the mighty Caesars, walls that saw Saint Peter and Saint Paul passing, statues sculpted by Michelangelo—these are Rome, where present-day life flourishes in the midst of monuments from past civilizations. Throw a coin in the **Trevi Fountain** as a down payment on your

Train Connections to Other Base Cities from Rome

Depart from Rome Termini station unless otherwise noted.

DEPART	TRAIN NUMBER	ARRIVE	NOTES
		Amsterdam Centraal	
1530	ES 9444	1037+1	R, 1
1935	EN 314	1701+1	R, 2, Sleeper
		Bern (Berne)	
0830	ES 9430	1756	R, 1
1935	EN 314	0840+1	R, Sleeper
		Brussels (Bruxelles) Midi/Zuid	
1630	ES 9422	0929+1	R, 1, Sleeper
1935	EN 212	1220+1	R, 6, Sleeper
		Budapest Keleti	
1655	ES 9472	1203+1	R, 7, Sleeper
1907	EN 234	1303+1	R, 4, Sleeper
2110	EN 286	1713+1	R, 3, Sleeper
		Copenhagen (København) H.	
0754	EC 84	0959+1	R, 3, Sleeper
		Luxembourg	
1630	ES 9422	0624+1	R, 1, Sleeper
		Lyon Part-Dieu	
0730	ES 9428	1856	R, 1
1935	EN 212	0731+1	R, 8
		Milan (Milano) Centrale	
0730	ES 9428	1200	R
0930	ES 9432	1400	R
1130	ES 9436	1600	R
1330	ES 9440	1800	R
1530	ES 9444	2000	R
then 1730, 1830, 1930 followed by			
2225	E 824	0625+1	R, Sleeper
		Munich (München) Hauptbahnhof	
0754	EC 84	1830	R
2110	EN 286	0831+1	R, Sleeper
		Nice Ville	
1207	ES 9308	1958	R, 5
1307	IC 544	2218	R, 9
1418	IC 550	2354	R, 5, 10
2315	368	0950+1	R, Sleeper
		Paris Gare de Lyon	
0930	ES 9432	2251	R, 1
1935	EN 212	0958+1	R, 10, Sleeper
		Vienna (Wien) Südbahnhof	
0855	ES 9464	2101	R, 7
1907	EN 234	0848+1	R, Sleeper

DEPART	TRAIN NUMBER	ARRIVE	NOTES
		Zürich Hauptbahnhof	
0730	ES 9428	1653	R, 1
0930	ES 9432	1853	R, 1
1130	ES 9436	2053	R, 1
1145	IC 582	2127	R, 1
1330	ES 9440	2253	R, 13
1935	EN 314	0853+1	R, Sleeper

Daily, unless otherwise noted
R Reservations mandatory
ES (Eurostar Italia) high-speed trains require supplement
+1 Arrives next day
1. Change trains in Milan (Milano).
2. Change trains in Basel and Duisburg.
3. Change trains in Munich (München).
4. Change from Vienna (Wien) Südbahnhof station to Wien Westbahnhof.
5. Change trains in Genoa (Genova) Piazza Principe.
6. Change trains in Paris.
7. Change trains in Venice.
8. Change trains in Chambery.
9. Change trains in Ventimiglia.
10. Arrive Paris Bercy Station.
11. Change trains in Bologna.

return trip, because you will certainly want to return.

When walking in Rome, keep pocketbooks, camera bags, and so on away from the curb side of the street and on a short leash. Motor-scooter thieves find them easy targets.

So vast is the city that it is essential to take some of the organized tours in order to see all of it. We recommend the tours conducted by the CIT (Compagnia Italiano Turismo). It is the general passenger agent for the Italian State Railways, and its tours can be booked through most hotels and pensions.

To dine differently, try **Da Meo Patacca** at 30 Piazza Mercanti (*Tel:* 06–58331086)—excellent food and entertainment. For that once-in-a-lifetime splurge, dine in the rooftop restaurant of the **Hassler Hotel**, Rome's finest hostelry; it overlooks the Spanish Steps. The view of the city from there on a summer's evening is unmatched. *Tel:* 06–699340 for reservations. Ignore the cost. You only live once!

Day Excursions

Four interesting day excursions from Rome await your visit: **Anzio,** scene of an Allied beachhead during World War II; **Florence,** one of the most prominent art centers of the world; **Naples,** with its world-renowned **Isle of Capri;** and **Pisa,** where the tower really tilts.

Day Excursion to

Anzio
Historic Beachhead

Depart Rome Termini Station
Distance by Train: 35 miles (57 km)
Average Train Time: 1 hour
City Dialing Code: 06
Tourist Information Office: Regione Lazio Azienda Autonoma, Soggiorno e Turismo, Piazzo 19
Tel: 9845147; *Fax:* 9848135
Hours: June–September, 0900–1300 and 1600–1900 daily. Off-season hours 0900–1300 and 1530–1800 Monday–Saturday. If the office is closed, directions will be posted on how to reach another office in the area.
Notes: To get to the tourist office on Pia Square: When leaving the Anzio railway station, walk downhill along the palm-lined avenue to Cesare Battisti Square. Then continuing on Via dei Fabbri, you will be in the main square of Anzio, Pia Square, where you will find the city's tourist information office to the left, just near the church.

Nothing more beautiful, nothing more agreeable, nothing more peaceful," wrote Cicero about Anzio. The Roman emperor Nero was born in Anzio. The villa where he spent his childhood and studied music still stands. Anzio's sandy beach attracted many important leaders over the centuries, which made it a VIP sanctuary, so to speak. Roman emperors such as Tiberius, Hadrian, Antoninus, and Commodus found escape from Rome and their affairs of state in Anzio.

American and British forces stormed ashore at Anzio and nearby Nettuno on January 22, 1944, to establish a beachhead, which they held until the taking of Rome on June 4, 1944. The devastated town that endured both the crossfire of the Germans and the bombardment of the Allied fleet offshore during that time has been restored completely, but row upon row of white crosses mark the graves in nearby military cemeteries, where lie 7,862 American and more than 6,000 British troops killed between Sicily and Rome. Those missing in action, 3,194 of them, sleep in unknown graves. A visit to these cemeteries is sobering.

If you, like the Roman emperors, want to escape the rigors of Rome or, on the other hand, wish to pay tribute to fallen comrades, Anzio extends a warm and pleasant welcome to all.

Because of the city's proximity to Rome and frequent train connections, rail travelers might consider accommodations in the area during their visit. Anzio, together with the neighboring sea resorts stretching southward to it from **Lido dei Pini,** can offer a wide selection of housing amenities and accommodations. If interested, telephone Anzio's tourist information office

Rome (Roma)—Anzio

Depart Rome Termini
Monday–Saturday: 0650, 0755, 0825, 1025, 1125, and hourly until 2125; Sunday:
0645, 0825, 0925, 1155, 1345, 1525, 1725, 1850, 2025, and 2125.

Depart Anzio
Monday–Saturday: 1354, 1507, 1559, 1652, 1752, 1852, 1952, and 2158; Sunday:
1353, 1533, 1715, 1857, 2008, and 2158.

2nd class only
Journey time: 60–65 minutes
Distance: 35 miles (57 km)

at (06) 9845147 (*Fax:* 9848135) for details and rates. For a longer stay, villas and apartments are available for rent at moderate rates.

Commuter trains depart the Roma Termini frequently for Anzio. For complete information regarding train service, check the *Partenze* (departure) information board in the main hall of Roma Termini.

Anzio is listed in the **Roma–Nettuno** section. It is one stop before Nettuno and the end of the line. Nettuno is where the American beachhead was established in World War II. Tell the train conductor about your destination, and he or she will be glad to alert you to the correct stop.

Upon arrival in Anzio, you will find directions for reaching Nettuno and the American Military Cemetery posted inside the train station; before proceeding, check with the Anzio tourist office and obtain the details on the bus service running between Anzio and Nettuno.

Places to visit in Anzio are, of course, the beach area and the harbor, where the Allied forces landed. The beach is now lined with cabanas, and the sand is excellent and the surf usually moderate. Be certain to visit the beachhead museum on **Via di Villa Adele** near the rail station.

The harbor holds many interesting places to investigate. Watercraft of all types are moored there, and the waterfront is lined with seafood restaurants to which fishermen sell their catch right from the dock. Deciding where to have lunch can be difficult—they all look inviting. On the street side of the harbor you will find a number of smart shops with eye-catching selections of nautical clothing.

Aside from the beach and the port area, places of particular interest are **Nero's Grottoes,** those ancient warehouses of the port located at the northern end of the Riviera Mallozzi. Beyond Anzio's western harbor wall lie the remains and mosaics of Nero's villa, which runs from the beach up to the level of Via Fanciulla d'Anzio. It's an impressive sight.

At the foot of the **Innocenziano wharf** in Anzio you can examine the remains of an eighteenth-century fort, and from the wharf itself, there is a view of the gulf with the Astura Tower and Circeo visible in the distance. The monument commemorating the Allied landings in 1944 is situated nearby on the western shore.

Nettuno, a seaside town of Saracen origins, is less than 3 miles distant. The American Military Cemetery is located there. The two British cemeteries are in Anzio. En route to Nettuno, you'll pass the Villa Colonna on the right and the **Villa Borghese,** with its magnificent gardens, on the left.

Anzio's involvement with the sea is reflected in its festivals. One such festival, the "Festa del Mare" (Feast of the Sea), is held in June in honor of Saint Antony of Padua, patron saint of the town.

Day Excursion to

Florence (Firenze)
City of Beauty

Depart Rome Termini Station
Distance by Train: 197 miles (317 km)
Average Train Time: 2 hours
City Dialing Code: 055
Tourist Information Office: Via Cavour, 1 rosso, 50129 Firenze
Tel: (055) 290832 or (055) 290833; **Fax:** (055) 2760383
Internet: www.firenze.turismo.toscana.it
E-mail: infoturismo@provincia.firenze.it
Hours: March–October: Monday–Saturday 0815–1915, Sunday 0815–1345.
   November–February: Monday–Saturday 0815–1915.
Notes: Take a taxi there or board bus Nos. 1, 6, or 17. Tourist information also available in Piazza Stazione (the rail station plaza), near the church Santa Maria Novella.

Florence (Firenze) as a day excursion is suggested for the traveler on a time-compressed itinerary. It is impossible to see all the beauty of Florence in one day. A week—or even a lifetime—could easily be devoted to such a pursuit. About 60 percent of the world's most significant artworks are in Italy, and about half of them are in Florence. No other city in the world pays better homage to human genius and creativity and, in turn, beauty appreciation than does Florence.

Aside from its buildings, art galleries, museums, and parks, Florence has had an interesting and rather hectic development as a municipality and seat of government. It was ruled by the Medici family until 1737, when the family died out and its leadership was assumed by Grand Duke Ferdinand III (1769–1824). Driven out by the French in 1799, the duke made several abortive attempts to resume power. He wasn't successful, however, until 1814.

Ferdinand's successor, Leopold II (1797–1870), held on until he was

Rome (Roma)—Florence (Firenze)

DEPART ROME TERMINI	TRAIN NUMBER	ARRIVE FLORENCE SMN	NOTES
0730	ES 9428	0905	R, Mon–Fri
0830	ES 9430	1005	R
0930	ES 9432	1105	R
1030	ES 9434	1205	R
1055	ES 9466	1230	R
1130	ES 9436	1305	R

DEPART FLORENCE SMN	TRAIN NUMBER	ARRIVE ROME TERMINI	NOTES
1455	ES 9437	1630	R
1530	ES 9443	1705	R
1555	ES 9439	1730	R
1655	ES 9441	1830	R
1730	ES 9469	1905	R
1755	ES 9423	1930	R
1800	EC 85	2002	

plus other and later frequent service until 2255

Daily, unless otherwise noted
R Reservations required
Distance: 197 miles (317 km)

expelled in 1849. Florence was the capital of Italy under King Victor Emmanuel from 1865 to 1871, when the seat of government became Rome.

Although a part of Italian history since 200 B.C., it wasn't until the turn of the eleventh century that Florence began to develop power and influence. Coincident with this growth came the development of the city's powerful guilds.

Florence was established on those banks of the Arno River spanned by the bridge of the Roman road Via Flaminia and where the Ponte Vecchio (old bridge) still stands today. With the single exception of Ponte Vecchio, all of the city's bridges were destroyed in 1944 during World War II. In 1966, a major flood damaged numerous art treasures in Florence, but many have been restored in succeeding years by the use of sophisticated techniques.

Hotel reservations can also be arranged at the ITA tourist office in the railway station. The one at Via Cavour cannot make hotel reservations but gives the booking centers of Florence, which are Coopal, *Tel:* (055) 219525; Top Quark, *Tel:* (055) 462–0080; and Promothotels, *Tel:* (055) 570481. Maps are available at the tourist offices, the CIT office (the Gray Line office) outside the station, or purchase the illustrated book *Florence, Pisa and Siena* at the newsstand inside the main hall of the station. An excellent map of Florence is contained in this informative book.

A **train-reservations office** (hours 0700–2000 daily) and **money exchange** (open 0820–1920 Monday–Saturday) are located inside the main station hall.

You can see most of the city's highlights by walking and, when needed, by taxi. Start by walking or taking a taxi to **Il Duomo** (the cathedral square) in the center of Florence. Here you can examine the three huge bronze doors of the **Battistero** (baptistery), enjoy the view from the top of the cathedral's dome, and enter the **Museo dell'Opera del Duomo** (cathedral museum), where you will find the priceless Altar of Saint John the Baptist displayed.

The **Galleria dell'Accademia** (Academy Gallery) is next. Summer hours: Closed Monday; open 0830–2100 Tuesday–Friday; 0830–2400 Saturday; 0830–2000 Sunday. Winter hours: Closed Monday; open 0830–1850 Tuesday–Sunday. Walk three blocks on Via Ricasoli, off Piazza Duomo's north side, to Piazza St. Marco. Michelangelo's original *David* is displayed here.

Taxi from here to **Piazza della Signoria,** which lies on the opposite side of the cathedral near the Arno River. (A brisk walk and some expert map reading will get you there in about 20 minutes.) This is the former center of Florence. The concentration of art treasures here is immense. The building with the tower is **Palazzo della Signoria** (Palace of the Lords), also known as **Palazzo Vecchio** (the Old Palace). Among its wealth of treasures is the little chapel of Eleonora of Toledo, with its magnificent frescoes by Bronzino (1503–1572). Summer hours: Tuesday, Wednesday, and Saturday 0900–1900; Monday and Friday 0900–2300; Thursday 0900–1400. Winter hours: 0900–1900 daily; closes at 1400 Thursday. Admission: €5.58.

On the south side of the square, you will see the **Loggia dei Lanzi,** which picked up a few other names, such as "Loggia dei Priori" and "Loggia della Signoria," since it was built in 1376. Statuary such as *Hercules and the Centaur* (1599) and *Rape of the Sabine Women* (1583), both by Giambologna, surround Cellini's *Perseus* (1545).

The **Galleria degli Uffizi** (Office Gallery) is, in fact, a converted office containing the priceless works of art acquired by the Medici family. Located on the right flank of Palazzo della Signoria, it has 45 exhibit rooms. Its vast collection includes the ancient sculpture *Medici Venus* from 300 B.C., Botticelli's *Primavera* and *Birth of Venus,* Leonardo da Vinci's *Adoration of the Magi,* and Michelangelo's *Holy Family,* plus an entire roomful of Rembrandts. Summer hours: Closed Monday; open 0830–2100 Tuesday–Friday; 0830–2400 Saturday; 0830–2000 Sunday. Winter hours: Closed Monday; open 0830–1850 Tuesday–Sunday.

This concludes your "quick" tour of the world-famous "City of Art, Florence," and it's time to taxi back to the rail station for the train back to Rome—unless, of course, you have succumbed to Florence's charms. It's a difficult decision to make. If you are still ambulatory, the walk back to the station will take about 20 minutes.

Day Excursion to

Naples (Napoli)
City by the Bay

Depart Rome Termini Station
Distance by Train: 134 miles (216 km)
Average Train Time: 2 hours
City Dialing Code: 081
Tourist Information Office: Main Hall of Napoli Centrale Rail Station (English-speaking staff)
Tel: 268779 or 206666; **Fax:** 401961
Hours: 0815–2000 Monday–Saturday; 0900–1400 Sunday

Naples (Napoli) is a world apart. There is no other place in Italy quite like it. In fact, there's no place that we have visited in the rest of the world quite like Naples. When you go there, you don't really see Naples—you feel it, hear it, and taste it. After you've been to Naples, you come away either loving it or hating it. You alone must be the judge.

Naples itself is a coalescing of gaiety and sadness. Its inhabitants, the Neapolitans, are expressive, noisy, and vivacious. They are imaginative, superstitious, and (about a third of them) unemployed, either by choice or by circumstance—it's difficult to determine which. But as a consequence, crime is rampant, so watch your wallets, pocketbooks, cameras, and other valuables.

But don't go to Naples in fear for your life; just be cautious. The Neapolitans don't want to harm you; they are only interested in your valuables. They want you to enjoy yourself and come back again—with more valuables. Deal only with official agencies. If you plan to take a city tour or sign up for a trip to **Vesuvius** and **Pompeii**, do it in an office, not on the street. Ignore the uniformed people who approach you on the street or in the rail station wearing badges proclaiming they are "official guides." There are several small shops on the square facing the station where you can buy one of those badges yourself.

Now for the fun part. Spaghetti was invented in Naples, as well as Neapolitan-style ice cream. Pizza first saw the light of day in Naples. If you can, enjoy a pizza in one of the pizzerias located in the old quarter of Naples. If you do, you'll probably not patronize your local pizza parlor for at least thirty days following your return home. The Neapolitan version of a Cajun fish-fry, *frittura di pesci,* is also well worth sampling. So much for tasting Naples.

You can't avoid hearing Naples. The musical style of Bel Canto is exclusively that of the Neapolitans. *Santa Lucia, Funiculi-Funicula,* and *O Sole Mio!* are but part of the repertory you will hear being played by hurdy-gurdies, all of it mixed in with the constant background noise of the crowded streets.

Rome (Roma)—Naples (Napoli)

Depart Rome Termini	Train Number	Arrive Naples Centrale	Notes
0810	IC 725	1000	
0816	D 2387	1050	1
0832	E 287	1054	
0845	ES 9421	1030	R
0916	D 2389	1154	
1016	D 2391	1254	Mon–Sat
1045	ES 9425 (ES 9485 Su)	1230	R
1145	IC 587	1347	

Depart Naples Centrale	Train Number	Arrive Rome Termini	Notes
1600	IC 726	1750	
1606	D 2402	1844	
1658	ES 9368	1850	R, 3
1730	ES 9452	1915	R
1829	ES 34530	2030	R, 3
1853	E 286	2055	
1930	ES 9456	2115	exc. Sat
2000	IC 732	2150	
2006	D 2410	2244	
2030	ES 9362	2215	
2058	ES 9380	2250	
2123	D 2412	2350	R, 2

Daily, unless otherwise noted
R Reservations required
1. Arrives Napoli Campi Flegrei.
2. Departs Napoli Campi Flegrei.
3. Departs Napoli Piazza Garibaldi.
Distance: 134 miles (216 km)

Dray animals such as mules wear bells so that their presence can be acknowledged in the crowd.

If you haven't developed a feel for Naples after exposure to some or all of the above, you can take an early train back to Rome.

You will find the **Napoli Centrale** station in the city center and flanked by the two narrow-gauge railway stations serving the **Circumvesuviana Line** from Naples to **Pompeii** and **Sorrento.**

Money-exchange, train information, and food services are all housed within the Napoli Centrale terminal. A train-information-and-reservations office is located to the side of the main hall (open daily, 0700–2115).

Naples, a city with a population of more than one million, is just large enough so that unguided sight-seeing can become difficult. Several reputable tour operators provide excellent service, such as the **Tourcar Travel Agency,** *Tel:* (081) 552 0429. The American Express Office located at Piazza

Municipio 5/6 also provides tours under its travel agency. *Tel:* (081) 5518564; *Fax:* (081) 722242.

Local trains leave the Napoli Circumvesuviana railway station for Pompeii and Sorrento. To reach this station, walk in the direction of the *Garibaldi* statue in the center of Piazza Garibaldi. Just before reaching the statue, turn left on Corso Garibaldi and proceed to the station, which is close by. The train time from Naples to Pompeii averages about 25 minutes. To Sorrento, the average time is 60 minutes. Pompeii is 15 miles from Naples; Sorrento is 28. Check at the rail station for complete schedules. Eurail and Europasses are not accepted on this line.

Day Excursion to

Pisa
New Slant on an Old Scene

Depart Rome Termini Station
Distance by Train: 208 miles (335 km)
Average Train Time: 3 hours
City Dialing Code: 050
Tourist Information Office: In the station plaza
Tel: 42291
Tourist Information Office: Piazza del Duomo
Tel: 560464
Internet: www.pisaonline.it
E-mail: manager@pisaonline.it
Regional Information: Touristic Consortium of the Pisan Area, PO Box 215, 56125 Pisa
Booking Center: Tel: (050) 830253; Fax: (050) 830243
Internet: www.traveleurope.it/pisa.htm or www.turismo.toscana.it
E-mail: pisa.turismo@traveleurope.it or www.info@pisa.turismo.toscana.it
Notes: Take bus No. 1 from rail station plaza to Piazza del Duomo. The tourist information office is on the other side of the Leaning Tower.

M any consider Pisa to be the most beautiful city in Italy. Its location in the very heart of Tuscany may even entice you to make Pisa a base city for day excursions to its charming nearby villages. In only about an hour or so, you can venture by train or bus to other main art cities such as Lucca, Florence, Siena, Volterra, San Gimignano, and Arezzo.

Pisa is rich in artistic resources and possesses one of the loveliest architectural groupings in Europe. Known either as **Piazza dei Miracoli** (Square of the Miracles) or **Piazza del Duomo** (Cathedral Square), it contains, in addition to the famous **Leaning Tower** and the cathedral, the **Baptistery** and the Campo Santo (burial ground), each in its own stead a masterpiece of sculpture and architecture.

If you have never been to Pisa and actually stood and looked at the Leaning Tower, you are in for a surprise. Forget any photograph, painting, or motion picture you may have seen of the tower prior to your personal encounter. It is not an optical illusion—it *really* leans.

Ride bus No. 1 from Pisa's station plaza to Piazza dei Miracoli. Dismount from the bus on the southern end of the square—the direction in which the tower is leaning. You will have no doubt whatsoever that (1) the tower leans; (2) it's leaning in your direction; and (3) you had better get out of its way before it topples on you. No other work of art provokes the instinct of self-preservation like this one. You can spend hours gazing at it, but there is never a moment when you are not consciously aware of the trajectory it will take if it topples.

Bonanno Pisano began construction of the tower in 1173, but the project was not completed until 1350. The primary reason for the delay in its completion was that the tower began to tilt when it reached its fourth level. With an annual increase of about 1.2 millimeters per year, the tower was closed to public access in 1990. At press time, it is scheduled to reopen in November 2001. Only 30 people at a time, however, will be allowed inside to make the climb to the top.

By using sonar soundings of the ground, the foundation of an ancient village was discovered under the north side of the Leaning Tower. This explains why the north side has remained relatively stable, while the south side has sunk almost three-quarters of a meter. Various plans have been proposed to stabilize the tower. One plan is to use sonic waves to break up the ancient foundation under the north side so that it will sink at the same rate as the south. Another proposal requires a ring of steel to be inserted into the base of the landmark. Perhaps the Italian Public Works Ministry should expedite its plans. Studies reveal that the tower is nearly 17 feet off plumb.

For the best restaurants in Pisa, in the countryside, or by the sea, call the Touristic Consortium at (050) 830253 or inquire at the tourist offices.

When at last you can turn your attention away from the tower, you will realize that Piazza dei Miracoli holds some other fantastic sights that warrant your inspection. Among them is the cathedral, on which construction was initiated in 1063. The first work of art to catch your eye is the splendid bronze doors of its entrance. Inside the cathedral and opposite the pulpit, Lorenzi (according to legend) hung a bronze lamp on a chain so long that Galileo figured that it must be the first pendulum and proceeded to work out the theory of isochronism—one of the better "isms" existing today.

The astronomer and physicist Galileo (1564–1642) lived in Pisa and used the buildings of the **Piazza del Duomo** to conduct studies concerning the laws of gravity, the acceleration of falling bodies, and the movement of the pendulum. He used the Leaning Tower to work out his theories on

Rome (Roma)—Pisa

DEPART ROME TERMINI	TRAIN NUMBER	ARRIVE PISA CENTRALE	NOTES
0707	ES 9306	1005	R
0807	IC 536	1130	
1007	IC 538	1330	
1012	D 2338	1420	
1207	ES 9308	1505	R

DEPART PISA CENTRALE	TRAIN NUMBER	ARRIVE ROME TERMINI	NOTES
1344	D 2341	1748	
1434	IC 549	1757	
1540	D 2343	1948	
1634	IC 551	1957	
1734	IC 553	2057	
1831	ES 9309	2127	R
1931	ES 9311	2227	R
1944	D 2347	2351	1

R Reservation required
Daily, unless otherwise noted
1. Roma Tiburtina
Distance: 208 miles (335 km)

gravity and acceleration and the cathedral for the accurate measurement of time. Galileo was said to have quarreled with his scholars over his theory of the rotation of the universe. During the Inquisition, when compelled to renounce his theory that the world turned, not the universe—because the Pope thought otherwise—in despair he whispered, "Nevertheless, it does turn."

Last of the edifices within the confines of the Piazza dei Miracoli is the building known as the **Camposanto** (Monumental Cemetery). It began when 53 shiploads of earth were transported from Calvary in the Holy Lands to the site and then surrounded by the building, which, after completion in 1283 by Giovanni Pisano, was frescoed by local Tuscan artists. The structure suffered damage during World War II bombings, but repairs have all but removed those scars.

During its days of prominence, Pisa was in close touch with the Orient. As a result, you'll note an Eastern flavor in its architecture. In the ninth century, the city was a naval power of considerable proportion. Pisa and its ally, Genoa, drove the Saracens out of Sardinia and Corsica in the eleventh century. Pisa's powers, however, then went on the wane. No longer allied with Genoa, the city was taken by Florence in 1406, proving that, as is so often the case, your allies are not there when you really need them.

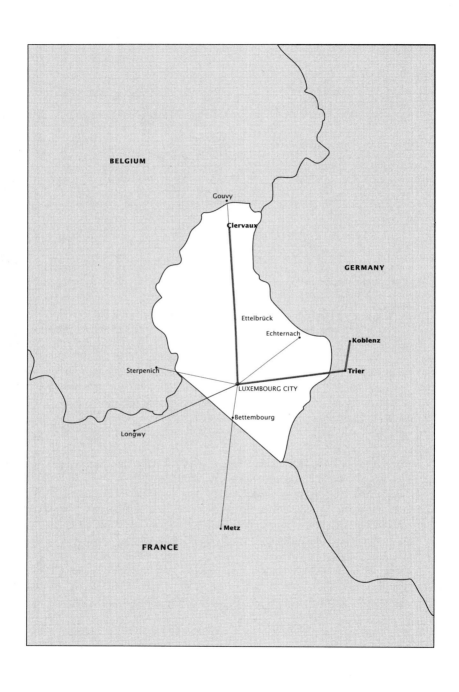

BELGIUM

Gouvy

Clervaux

GERMANY

Ettelbrück

Echternach

Koblenz

Sterpenich

Trier

LUXEMBOURG CITY

Bettembourg

Longwy

Metz

FRANCE

Luxembourg

The Grand Duchy of Luxembourg is one of Europe's small countries—51 miles (82 kilometers) long and 32 miles (57 kilometers) wide, encompassing 999 square miles (2,586 square kilometers)—a little smaller than the state of Rhode Island. It is a constitutional monarchy with a population of about 400,000. Germany borders it to the east, France to the south, and Belgium adjoins it on the north and west. Luxembourg vies with Switzerland in the field of international banking. A substantial number of corporations doing business in the European community maintain accounts there.

The Grand Duchy once dominated an area nearly 300 times its present size. In more recent times, as well as in the past, Luxembourg's fate and fortunes have been linked with those of Belgium. The forces of French king Louis XIV conquered the city of Luxembourg in the middle seventeenth century. Subsequent fortifications built by the French and succeeding conquerors earned the city the title "Gibraltar of the North."

Luxembourg was overrun by the Germans during World War I, but its independence was restored by the Treaty of Versailles. It was occupied again by German forces during World War II. During the Battle of the Bulge in December 1944, the tides of war surged around Luxembourg. Liberated earlier by U.S. forces, the city was recaptured by the Germans, who executed many members of the Belgian and Luxembourgese underground before Luxembourg was again taken by the Allied forces.

For more information on Luxembourg, contact the Luxembourg National Tourist office in North America:

New York: 17 Beekman Pl'ace, New York, NY 10022; *Tel:* (212) 935–8888; *Fax:* (212) 935–5896; *Internet:* **www.visitluxembourg.com**; *E-mail:* luxnto@aol.com

Banking
- **Currency:** Euro (€)
- **Exchange rate at press time:** €1.10 = U.S. $1.00

Communications
- **Country Code:** 352

City codes are not used when dialing within Luxembourg
- **Direct dial:** AT&T: 0800–0111; MCI: 0800–0112; Sprint: 0800–0115

Rail Travel in Luxembourg

The information service of **CFL, the Luxembourg national railways** (also gives country bus information), can be contacted by *Tel:* (352) 4990–4990 or (352) 4990–5571 (every day, 0600–2000 GMT) and by *Fax:* (352) 4990–4470.

From the capital, Luxembourg City, you are no more than 1 hour away from anywhere within the Grand Duchy of Luxembourg. The **Oeko-Pass** is available at rail stations throughout the country and at Findel airport. It covers unlimited travel on all forms of public transport (city buses, trains, and country coaches) for 1 day (which is considered to last until 0800 the following morning) throughout the Grand Duchy. It is not valid on sight-seeing buses, however. You can purchase a single ticket for €3.97 or a block of 5 tickets for €13.39.

The CFL also accepts the multicountry passes of **Eurailpass** and **Europass,** with purchase of the Benelux—Belgium, the Netherlands, Luxembourg—add-on. (See the Appendix for a detailed list of multiple-country and regional railpasses and prices.) If your travels are confined only to the Benelux countries, consider the **Benelux Tourrail Pass** for unlimited rail travel throughout Belgium, the Netherlands, and Luxembourg:

Benelux Tourrail Pass

	1st Class	2nd Class
5 days within 1 month	$217	$155
Youth: 5 days within 1 month	—	$104

Benelux Tourrail for Two Pass

2 people traveling together	1st Class	2nd Class
5 days within 1 month	$326	$233

Base City:

Luxembourg City

Internet: luxembourg-city.lu/touristinfo/
E-mail: touristinfo@luxembourg-city.lu

Arriving by Air

Luxembourg International Airport (*Internet:* www.luxair.lu) is about 4 miles (6 kilometers) from the city center. Luxembourg, because of its central European location and convenient rail connections, attracts an increasing number of visitors from North America.

Airport–City Links: Bus service from the airport terminates at the Luxembourg rail station. Municipal buses (bus No. 9) depart every half hour Monday–Friday, every 20 minutes on Saturday, and hourly on Sunday from a platform about 50 feet outside the air terminal. Journey time, 25 minutes; you can check stops, timetables, fares and extra transport like the City Night Bus or the City Shopping Bus at the *Web site:* www.luxembourg-city.lu. At present there is no underground or train service link, but there are very interesting plans proposed to link the airport to the railway station via a direct connection.

Luxair Coach to the rail station: €3.72; children under 12 years, 50 percent. No charge for luggage.

Taxis: €16–18 (supplements for nights, Sunday, and extra luggage). Journey time to city center: 15–20 minutes. All taxis are equipped with meters. No tips are expected.

Tourist information at the airport: *Tel:* 42 82 82 21. *Hours:* Open Monday and Wednesday 0930–1330 (except on holidays).

Arriving by Train

The city of Luxembourg is served by a single railway station located conveniently in the city center. Connections can be made directly to Belgium, France, Germany, Italy, the Netherlands, and Switzerland from the station. The downtown air terminal and the city bus terminal are clustered conveniently about the railway station, which, like the airport, has been modernized to handle an increasing number of passengers.

Luxembourg Central Station is actually located in what historians call the "new city." From 1855 to 1866, when the first rails were laid, the gorge of the Alzette River remained too wide to be bridged. Consequently, the rail station was established on the far side of the gorge opposite the city as it existed then, and the new section of the city began to develop around it.

The station has three platforms (*quais*) serving five tracks. Track 1 is served by platform 1, which is directly connected to the station with level access to the platform. Trains arriving on the other tracks, however, require passengers to utilize an underground tunnel, to reach the main station hall.

A system of elevators serves the outer train platforms. To access them, take the hallway off to the right of the main hall until you arrive at the entrance to the elevator service tunnel, just beyond the last ticket window and before reaching the baggage room.

The entrances to the elevators serving the train platforms are marked clearly, although it seems a bit confusing when you first use them. You descend from the train platform to a tunnel. There, you walk a short distance to another elevator, which you ascend to the station level; you then take another short tunnel into the main hallway.

- **Train information** is to your immediate left when exiting from the train platform area. Hours: 0530–2030 daily. *Tel:* 4990–4990.
- **Train seat reservations** for EuroCity, InterCity, and regular express trains can be made in the train information office. Sleeper reservations and **railpass validation** may also be made here.

Tourist Information/Hotel Reservations

- *Office National du Tourisme,* Luxembourg Central Station, Place de la Gare. *Tel:* 4282–8220; *Fax:* 4282–8230.

   Hours: June 1–September 30, 0900–1900 Monday–Saturday; 0900–1230 and 1400–1800 Sunday; remainder of the year, open daily 0915–1230 and 1345–1800. Closed November 1, Christmas, and New Year's Day.

The office is in the Central Station, on your right as you exit from the train platform area. In addition to making hotel reservations, information on youth hostels, camping grounds, and holiday flats and chalets available to tourists can be provided.

- *Luxembourg City Tourist Office (LCTO),* Place d'Armes, (P.O. Box 181, L-2011; *Tel:* 22 28 09; *Fax:* 40 70 70; *Internet:* www.luxembourg-city. lu/touristinfo; *E-mail:* touristinfo@luxembourg-city.lu.

   Hours: April 1–September 31: 0900–1900 Monday–Saturday; 1000–1800 Sunday. October 1–March 31: 0900–1800 Monday–Saturday; 1000–1800 Sunday.

The LCTO provides extensive services such as guided city tours, tourist and cultural information, hotel and restaurant details, and offers telephone cards, maps, books, and souvenirs. Students attired in "Ask Me" T-shirts also walk about the streets of the city center to provide tourist information.

- **Hotel reservations** can also be made by the tourist information offices. There are numerous hotels on the side streets near the station in addition to some charming smaller hotels within reasonable taxi or city-bus distances. The four-star **Best Western International** (*E-mail:* info@hotelinter.lu) and the **President Hotel** (*E-mail:* president@pt.lu) are across the street from the rail station. For those who prefer an American-style hotel with all the amenities, the **Sheraton Aerogolf** is located near the Findel Airport.

Our choice is a small, quaint hotel with European-style charm and service—**Hôtel Italia** (20 rooms). Located at 15–17 rue d'Anvers, Hôtel Italia is near the rail station and features an excellent Italian restaurant. *Tel:* 48 66 26–1 or *Fax:* 48 08 07; *E-mail:* italia@euro.lu. Rates range €65–73 for a single and €73–82 for a double, and major credit cards are accepted.

Getting Around in Luxembourg City

The city center is condensed, and most sights are accessible on foot, despite the cliffs and ramparts that characterize this fortress city. For longer distances use Luxembourg's efficient network of buses (single fare, €1). Taxis are metered.

The most practical way of getting around Luxembourg on your own is to purchase a **LuxembourgCard.** You get free admission to 32 tourist attractions, free use of public transportation, and a 32-page guidebook to go along with it. The Luxembourg Card is valid from Easter through October:

Luxembourg Card Prices in Euros

	Adult	Senior	Family (2–5 persons)
1 day	8.68	7.81	17.35
2 days	14.87	13.39	29.75
3 days	21.07	18.96	42.14

There is also the **Muséeskaart**—a 1-day pass offering unlimited access to Luxembourg City's major museums and monuments, including the Casino–Luxembourg–Forum of Contemporary Art, the National Museum of History and Art, and more: Adults: €6.99; Children/Seniors: €5.01.

Sights/Attractions/Tours

A basic city sight-seeing tour by bus departs from platform No. 5 at the downtown bus terminal next to the rail station. The tour takes 2 hours, 15 minutes and departs at 1415 daily from the end of March to mid-November

Train Connections to Other Base Cities from Luxembourg

LUXEMBOURG CITY

DEPART LUXEMBOURG	TRAIN NUMBER	ARRIVE	NOTES
		Amsterdam Centraal	
0721	IC 2130	1339	1
0921	IC 2132	1539	1
1021	IC 2133	1639	1
then hourly until 1521 followed by 1721 and 2021; plus other departures.			
		Berlin Zoobahnhof	
1032	IR 2431	1835	3
1432	IR 2433	2247	3
2115	IR 122	0821+1	R, 6, 8, Sleeper
		Bern (Berne)	
1002	EC 91	1511	
1502	EC 97	2011	4
		Brussels (Bruxelles) Midi/Zuid	
Service is hourly from 0621 to 2121. Journey time is 3 hours, 03 minutes.			
		Hamburg Hauptbahnhof	
1032	IR 2431	1810	3
1432	IR 2433	2210	3
2115	IR 122	0721+1	R, 8, Sleeper
		Lyon Part-Dieu	
0541	359	1135	7
0802	353	1501	10
1002	EC 91	1656	R, 7
1127	IC 2134	1905	R, 1
1556	RE 37663	2229	R, 7
		Milan (Milano) Centrale	
1002	EC 91	1925	R
2212	D 299	0705+1	R, Sleeper
		Munich (München) Hauptbahnhof	
1032	IR 2431	1816	5
1502	1835	2217	6
		Nice Ville	
0802	353	1923	R, 9
1308	EC 91	0035+1	
1946	4239	0820+1	R, Sleeper
		Paris Gare de l'Est	
0541	359	0934	R
0802	353	1138	R
1308	1835	1709	R
1634	205	2025	R
1716	1839	2106	R
		Rome (Roma) Termini	
2212	D 299	1230+1	R, 10, Sleeper
		Vienna (Wien) Westbahnhof	
1032	IR 2431	2150	5
1856	RE 37685	0842+1	R, 2, Sleeper
		Zürich Hauptbahnhof	
1002	EC 91	1458	4
1502	EC 97	2000	R

Daily, unless otherwise noted
R Reservations required
+1 Arrive next day
1. Change trains in Brussels.
2. Change trains in Nancy-Ville.
3. Change trains in Cologne (Köln).
4. Change trains in Basel.
5. Change trains in Koblenz.
6. Change trains in Strasbourg.
7. Change trains in Metz.
8. Change trains in Liege-Guillemins.
9. Change trains in Paris.
10. Change trains in Milan.

(on Saturdays only remainder of the year). It includes the Old Town, the rail station district, the fortress ruins, the casemates (underground outside fortifications), European Center, and Luxembourg's version of Wall Street—the banking district. The tour fee for adults, €11.15 children ages 6–12, €6.20.

The **Bock and Pétrusse Casemates** are two unique networks of underground fortifications, one of the most interesting being the archaeological crypt in the Bock Casemates. This room presents an audiovisual show relating the history of the casemates (open March 1–October 31, 1000–1700). Admission: €1.74 adults; €1.00 children. The Pétrusse Casemates are open from Easter, Whitsunday, and during school holidays. Guided tours are daily 1100–1600.

From April to October you can rent the tape tour "City Walk" and a Walkman for €4.71 (between the hours of 1000 and 1700 daily).

The **"City Promenade"** is a guided tour departing at 1400 daily (April–October) on foot and encompasses Place d'Armes, City Palace, the outside casemates, Place de la Constitution, the Government District, the Holy Ghost Plateau, the Corniche, the Monument of the Millennium, the Old Town, William Square, and the exterior of the Grand Ducal Palace.

The **"Vauban Circular Walk"** is an interesting historical and cultural tour that can be done either on your own or as a guided tour by making reservations through the Luxembourg City Tourist Office. This tour takes you through a part of the fortifications of the seventeenth, eighteenth, and nineteen centuries. Other interesting tours are the "Wenzel Circular Walk" or "1000 Years in 100 Minutes," and kids and families may enjoy the "City Detective Discovery Tour."

There are other tours by bus that take you through the Ardennes, or opt to see much of the area on your own during day excursions to Clervaux, Metz, and Trier.

"The soldier, above all other people," said Douglas MacArthur, "prays for peace, for he must suffer and bear the deepest wounds and scars of war." Such is the drama of 5,100 grave sites in **The American Military Cemetery** near the village of Hamm, 3 miles outside the city of Luxembourg. Among the crosses standing row upon row, you will see one marked GEORGE S. PATTON, JR., GENERAL, THIRD ARMY, CALIFORNIA, DECEMBER 21, 1945. Solemn in its simplicity, beautiful in the manner in which it attests to the American spirit, this cemetery must be seen. It is a moving, memorable moment. You can taxi there for about the same price as the airport-to-rail-station fare. Telephone for a return taxi.

Luxembourg's low value added tax (VAT) makes it a bargain base city in comparison to some other European cities. Even residents of Luxembourg's neighboring countries purchase tobacco, alcohol, and fuel in the Grand Duchy because the taxes are lower.

Although hotel rates and restaurant prices are lower than those of most other European cities, the quality is not. Some Luxembourgers actually believe "the way to a man's heart is through his stomach," and they've made believers out of us. Try the smoked pork with broad beans or the delicate Ardennes ham cut paper-thin. For a real taste treat, try trout from the Moselle accompanied by a fine Luxembourg wine—all at popular prices.

Luxembourg abounds in international cuisine. One of our favorites is the **L'Hotel-Restaurant Italia** at 15–17 rue d'Anvers (*Tel:* 48 66 26/27), which offers excellent Italian specialties. Phone ahead for reservations—it's popular with the local folks, too.

Day Excursions

Four day excursions have been selected for the Grand Duchy and its surrounding countries. Each is distinctly different in its points of interest. The day excursion to **Clervaux** takes you through the rugged north country of the Grand Duchy, where the World War II Ardennes campaign was contested bitterly in 1944. The day excursion to charming **Koblenz,** one of the oldest cities in Germany, is saturated with scenic views along the Moselle and Rhine Rivers. **Metz** measures up to a most interesting day excursion into France. The German city of **Trier,** founded by Augustus Caesar, provides an exciting opportunity to explore many Roman ruins and to titillate your taste buds with the most delectable Moselle wines.

Day Excursion to

Clervaux
Grand Duchy's Medieval Charm

Depart from Luxembourg City Central Station
Distance by Train: 38 miles (61 km)
Average Train Time: 54 minutes
Tourist Information Office: Clervaux Castle, B.P. 53, L-9701 Grand Duchy of Luxembourg
Tel: 92 00 72; *Fax:* 92 93 12

Internet: www.luxembourg.co.uk/clervaux.html or www.clervaux-city.lu

Hours: April–June: Monday–Saturday 1400–1700; July–August: daily 0945–1145 and 1400–1800; September–October: Monday–Saturday 1300–1700.

Notes: Start at the station by walking along the main street in the direction from which the train came. When you reach the town square, turn right and follow the paths and steps leading up to Clervaux Castle. The Clervaux tourist information office is located at the entrance to the castle in a towerlike structure on the right-hand side.

Clervaux is a medieval town nestled in the valley of the Clerf River, deep in the Ardennes of northern Luxembourg, through which runs the scenic rail route from Luxembourg through Liege in Belgium to Amsterdam in the Netherlands.

The scenic beauty of the train ride begins the moment you leave the Luxembourg station and the train crosses a viaduct high above the Alzette River. Take a seat on the left side of the carriage to best enjoy a spectacular view of the city of Luxembourg from the viaduct. Have your camera ready, and start shooting a moment after the train clears a short tunnel just beyond the rail station. The morning departure is best for photographing the ramparts of Luxembourg because the sun will be shining directly upon them at a rather low level at that time. You will pass the same scene on later departures; however, the sun will be at a higher angle, and the shadows will be less dramatic.

Clervaux is the fourth express-train stop en route after stops at **Mersch, Ettelbruck,** and **Kautenbach.** Beyond Ettelbruck, you enter the hilly and heavily wooded Ardennes, where the Battle of the Bulge was fought during World War II in December 1944. Some of the buildings along the right-of-way still bear the scars of this engagement. Don't be alarmed if you should spot a German or an American tank at a road intersection en route. The locals have intentionally placed it there.

The Clervaux railway station is a 15-minute walk from the town's main square. It's a delightful stroll along the river and easy to do with the aid of several maps posted along the way with "you are here" arrows to assist you.

Clervaux is packed with points of interest. Three of the most prominent ones are the **DeLannoi Castle,** the **Benedictine Abbey of St. Maurice and St. Maur,** and the **parish church.** All three tower over the town and its surrounding countryside.

The DeLannoi family are some of Franklin Delano Roosevelt's maternal descendants. The DeLannoi Castle has so much to offer that we recommend you concentrate on it first and see the rest of Clervaux's sites in the time remaining at the end of your visit. It houses the Battle of the Bulge museum, an exhibition of ancient Luxembourg castle models, and the world-famous **"Family of Man"** photo exhibition of Edward Steichen, an American citizen born in Luxembourg.

Luxembourg–Clervaux
Departures hourly at 15 minutes past the hour, plus 1145, and others throughout the day.

Clervaux–Luxembourg
Departures at 54 minutes past the hour until 2254, plus 1632 and 2207.

Journey time: 51 minutes
Distance: 38 miles (61 km)

No one is quite certain about the castle's origins. There are several hypotheses: Some historians believe that it was built on top of an ancient Roman citadel, while others speak of Celtic origins. In any event, it has been established that the oldest part of the castle dates back to the twelfth century.

There's an immediate impact upon entering the castle's outer courtyard. One of General Patton's tanks is parked there, along with its chief antagonist, a German Army 88-millimeter cannon. History buffs of all ages will enjoy climbing aboard the tank to inspect its armor and speculate as to the role it played during the liberation of Clervaux and the Battle of the Bulge. Bear in mind that by December 1944, the castle you see now was reduced to a burned-out hulk. The authentic restoration that has been accomplished by the townspeople of Clervaux and the Duchy of Luxembourg is laudatory.

The "Family of Man" exhibit and the castle model exhibit are immediately inside the first gate leading off the courtyard (open 1000–1800 daily except Monday; closed January–February). The "Bulge" museum is located farther along toward the center of the castle off an inner courtyard.

Steichen considered the Clervaux castle an ideal location for his exhibition. The collection was given to the Grand Duchy of Luxembourg by the U.S. government in 1975, three years after Steichen's death.

Day Excursion to

Koblenz
Heart of the Rhineland

Depart from Luxembourg City Central Station
Distance by Train: 101 miles (163 km)
Average Train Time: 1 hour, 14 minutes
Germany Dialing Code: 49
City Dialing Code: 261

Tourist Information Office: Koblenz-Touristik, Bahnhofplatz, Postfach 201551, D-56068 Koblenz

Tel: 261–31304; *Fax:* 261–1004388

Internet: www.koblenz.de

E-mail: touristik@koblenz.de

Hours: May–September: Monday–Friday 0900–2000; Saturday, Sunday, and holidays 1000–2000. Easter–end of April and October: Monday–Friday 0900–1800; Saturday, Sunday, and holidays 1000–1800. November–beginning of April: Monday–Friday 0900–1800.

Notes: To reach the tourist office, turn right as you exit the rail station and you will find the tourist office on the ground floor of the new rail station building.

The Koblenz railway station is just far enough away from the meeting of the Moselle and Rhine Rivers and the city's major tourist attractions to cause a "walk or ride" decision. If you decide to ride into the city center, the tourist office can help you hail a cab or provide you with the city's bus schedule and fare information. If you are planning to stay in Koblenz, tourist-office staff can make hotel reservations at no charge. Be sure to pick up a map and the brochure *Koblenz . . . Tour of The Town's Heritage* before setting out.

Just as there is a subtle difference between Rhine and Moselle wines, so is there a difference between the scenic beauty of the two great rivers from which the wines take their names. At the rivers' confluence you will be able to enjoy both. Koblenz claims that it offers more than 2,000 years of history to its visitors—and all within the span of a few hours. The historical background of this city, in the very center of Germany's Rhineland, makes this no idle boast as its claim to Germany's most beautiful corner.

The area around Koblenz was settled originally by the Celts. Julius Caesar, dividing and conquering as he went, arrived with his legions and established domain along the Rhine's western banks. Roman tranquillity thrived until the fifth century, when Rome's power weakened and the Franks took over.

Napoleon's MEMORABLE CAMPAIGN AGAINST THE RUSSIANS was inscribed on **St. Castor's fountain** in the city during 1812. In 1814, the tables were turned when the Russians captured the town and added a postscript, SEEN AND APPROVED, beneath the original inscription. At the **Deutsches Eck**, a monument erected at the confluence of the Rhine and the Moselle in 1897, the statue of the German emperor Wilhelm I was toppled into the Rhine by the U.S. Army Corps of Engineers in 1945. The base of the monument was made as a memorial to German unity in 1953 by President Theodor Heuss. Since September 1993, Wilhelm I is back—in mini-model form on top of the monument.

If you choose to see Koblenz under your own foot power, guided by the city map, a 10-minute walk down the **Markenbildchenweg** brings you to

Luxembourg City—Koblenz

DEPART LUXEMBOURG CITY	TRAIN NUMBER	ARRIVE KOBLENZ	NOTES
0722	RE 22007	0943	1
0822	IR 2535	1039	1
0922	RE 22009	1143	1
1032	IR 2431	1239	Direct

DEPART KOBLENZ	TRAIN NUMBER	ARRIVE LUXEMBOURG CITY	NOTES
1613	RE 22010	1833	1
1716	IR 2534	1933	1
1813	RE 22012	2033	1
1916	TR 2532	2133	1

You may want to spend several hours in Germany's oldest town and board a later train to Luxembourg City.

Daily
1. Change in Trier
Distance: 101 miles (163 km)

the Rhine, and a left turn at that point sends you in the direction of the Deutsches Eck, where the Rhine meets the Moselle. The riverside gardens along the Rhine join up with those on the Moselle to provide a delightful 5-mile promenade along their banks.

If you plan to whiz around the city on wheels, bus No. 1, marked RHINE (DEUTSCHES ECK) will deposit you on the promenade at a point opposite the **Rheinkran,** an antique building that once housed the harbor crane. The bus route takes you through the narrow streets of the old city along the Moselle and past the Deutsches Eck before reaching its final stop on the Rhine. Returning to the train station, the bus follows a more direct (and less interesting) route through the town's shopping areas. If your "walk or ride" decision is still up for grabs, we suggest you compromise by taking the bus outbound and returning on foot. From the river to the station, the bus is bannered HAUPTBAHNHOF. The bus ride takes about 15 minutes. Allow a little more time if you're walking.

Make the **Koblenz Weindorf** (Wine Village) a must-stop during your visit. It consists of four taverns clustered around a village square that, in turn, is enclosed within a real vineyard along the Rhine. The taverns are actual copies of half-timbered houses found in the notable German wine areas. Six hundred or more guests can be accommodated in the taverns and more than 1,000 outside when the weather is good—as it usually is.

The wine village was built on the occasion of the 1925 German Wine Exhibition. Since then, it has achieved fame for its products and romantic atmosphere. The village offers an excellent menu and wine list daily from 1100 to 2400. From November through March, an advance booking is required.

Day Excursion to

Metz
Moselle Stronghold

Depart from Luxembourg Station
Distance by Train: 39 miles (63 km)
Average Train Time: 53 minutes
France Dialing Code: 33
City Dialing Code: 87
Tourist Information Office: Office de Tourisme, place d'Armes, BP 80367, 57007 Metz, France
Tel: 33 387 55 53 76; *Fax:* 33 387 36 59 43
Internet: www.mairie-metz.fr:8080 *E-mail:* tourisme@ot.mairie-metz.fr
Hours: Mid-July–September: Monday–Saturday 0900–2100 and Sunday 1100–1700; remainder of the year: Monday–Saturday 0900–1900 and Sunday 1100–1700.
Notes: To get there, turn right leaving the arrival gate and walk the length of the station hall to the departure gate (served by the northern underground passageway). The station's north end houses the train information office and faces General de Gaulle Square. Money can be changed in the post office, the huge red building in front of the station. Board either minibus line A or B at the bus terminal directly in front of the rail station. Get off at the Hotel de Ville (town hall) stop in front of the cathedral. The tourist office will be on the right in place d'Armes.

Throughout its 3,000-year history, Metz has been a great Roman city, a religious center of the Carolingian Empire, an independent republic, a part of Germany, and a bastion of France. Throughout the ages, various cultures have left their marks in the form of various architectural styles throughout the city.

Poised at the confluence of the Moselle and Seille Rivers, Metz claims one of the oldest churches in France, the fourth-century **St. Pierre-aux-Nonnains**. The center of attraction, however, is its Gothic cathedral of **Saint Etienne** (thirteenth–sixteenth centuries). The cathedral has been described as the "apotheosis of light" due to the luminescent quality of its stained-glass windows—two of the largest surface stained-glass windows in the world. Its 300-foot-high nave is among the highest in France.

Metz further claims the largest railway station in eastern France. Due to its size, visitors arriving by rail may find the facilities somewhat confusing. When arriving from Luxembourg in the north, take the southern stairway rather than the northern one when transiting from the arrival platform to the main station hall via the underground passageway.

Obtain a map of Metz and a copy of *Transports Par Minibus,* which describes the two minibus lines from the tourist office. The two lines cover

Luxembourg City—Metz

DEPART LUXEMBOURG CITY	TRAIN NUMBER	ARRIVE METZ	NOTES
0802	353	0843	
1002	EC 91	1056	
1110	64641	1158	Mon–Fri
1308	EC 54	1355	

DEPART METZ	TRAIN NUMBER	ARRIVE LUXEMBOURG CITY	NOTES
1349	356	1435	Mon–Sat
1607	EC 90	1650	
1702	RE 64564	1755	Mon–Fri
1902	RE 64578	1950	Mon–Fri
1912	EC 96	1959	
2005	EC 53	2052	
2115	EC 207	2206	
2300	355	2345	

Daily, unless otherwise noted
Distance: 39 miles (63 km)

the city's major sights and shopping areas and terminate at the main railway station. The minibus stops throughout the city are marked with devices very similar in appearance to barber poles, to which are attached maps showing the course of the bus making that particular stop. Each pole is marked with the name of the stop, and inside the bus is a circular chart showing all of the stops that the bus makes. By noting first the name on the pole stop and then relating it to the map inside the bus, you can easily identify your position. Both minibus lines operate 0730–1930 daily except Sunday and holidays. A bus leaves the main railway station approximately every 6 minutes. Tickets are available in the bus.

Metz has many other interesting sights, such as the fourteenth-century **St. Louis market square** with its Italian influence. Its majestic buildings are constructed of yellow limestone, which seems to give them an aspect of light. The city's eighteenth-century theater, **Place de la Comédie,** is another typical example of this "brightness."

In August Metz goes "plum crazy." The golden mirabelle plum is celebrated in various deliciously edible forms—perhaps on a tasty tart or in a luscious, languid liqueur. Other gastronomic specialties include frog-legs pie, freshwater fish, and traditional stews, as well as not-so-traditional stews—snail stew.

Want to try a different type of city tour? Take a tour via Metz's **"Petit (little) Tourist Train"** (Tel: 03 87 55 53 76). It has departures at 1030, 1130, 1300, 1400, 1500, 1600, 1700, and 1800.

The Metz tourist office proposes an audio-guided walking tour that covers the highlights of the city with an English narration. If you are sight-seeing on your own in Metz, you should include the city's museum, with its Gallo-Roman collections and impressive display of seventeenth-century paintings by Dutch masters and artists of the French School. Top off your visit with a stroll along the city's Esplanade, on the banks of the Moselle River.

Day Excursion to

Trier
Germany's Oldest Town

Depart from Luxembourg Station
Distance by Train: 32 miles (51 km)
Average Train Time: 41 minutes
Germany Dialing Code: 49
City Dialing Code: 651
Tourist Information Office: Trier Stadt und Land e.V., An der Porta Nigra, D-54290
Tel: 978–080; *Fax:* 44759.
Internet: www.trier.de
E-mail: info@tit.de
Hours: April–October, 0900–1830 Monday–Saturday; 0900–1530 Sunday. Shorter hours in the winter months.
Notes: Money exchange is available in the tourist office, which is about a 10-minute walk from the rail station, or there is a taxi stand at the right-hand front of the station. On foot, proceed down Bahnhofstrasse, which runs from the station into Theodor-Heuss-Allee leading to the Porta Nigra. Located immediately in back of the Porta Nigra monument. Walking tip: Avoid the din of traffic by using the park pathways on the left of the main thoroughfare.

Welcome to Germany's oldest city! "Before Rome, there was Trier." Although this is legend, it is also a historical fact. Evidence of human settlements as early as the third century B.C. has been discovered in and around the city of Trier. Further legend attributes the founding of Trier in 2000 B.C. to the Assyrians. But history more soberly attributes its roots to Emperor Augustus, who founded (or refounded) Trier in 16 B.C., thereby beginning Trier's role in Roman history.

In A.D. 293, Trier became the capital of Rome's province of Belgica Prima and the seat of the emperor's court. History records that no less than six Roman emperors held court here. The city's population swelled to about 80,000 citizens, and its cultural growth kept pace with its expanding population. Many magnificent edifices and archaeological finds attest to this growth today.

Luxembourg City—Trier

DEPART LUXEMBOURG CITY	ARRIVE TRIER	DEPART TRIER	ARRIVE LUXEMBOURG CITY
0722	0809	1443	1533
0822	0912	1547	1633
0922	1009	1640	1721
1032	1114	1747	1833
1122	1208	1843	1933
1222	1312	1947	2033
1322	1409	2043	2133
		2147	2230
		2245	2330

Daily, including holidays
Distance: 32 miles (51 km)

Trier came to be known as the second Rome. By the end of the third century A.D., it had become a capital of the western part of the Roman Empire. Its many monuments from that time attest to its greatness. The fourth-century Roman cathedral has among its treasures the "Holy Robe," said to have belonged to Christ. In ancient Roman records, Trier was among the first places north of the Alps to bear the name of "city."

Trier's pedestrian zone begins at the town's northern edge with its prize possession—the Roman gateway building, the **Porta Nigra** (Black Gate), built in A.D. 200. Known as the "northern gate of the Roman Empire," it takes its name from the dark patina that formed over its sandstone facade. It was transformed into a church during the eleventh century, but Napoleon restored the building to its original appearance in 1804. Other Roman ruins still remaining are the **Barbara Baths** (A.D. 150), the **Imperial Baths** (A.D. 300), the **Forum Baths** (A.D. 100), the core of the **Cathedral** (A.D. 330/380), the **Amphitheater** (A.D. 100), and a bridge crossing the Moselle River.

Trier fell to the Franks in the fifth century, but the city's life did not end. During the thousand years that followed, churches, monasteries, convents, and mansions were built literally on top of, and around, its ancient structures. A cross, erected in A.D. 958 to signify Trier's right to conduct a market, marks the **Hauptmarkt** (Main Market) of today's city. On the other side of the coin, in 1818 a man was born in Trier whose ideas were in opposition to the free market concept; his name was Karl Marx.

Walks between the area of the Porta Nigra and beyond the Main Market will find you amongst stores galore. Ranging from the quaint antiques shop to the eclectic gift emporium to the modern department store. Fine wines may be found in several locations (tastings offered, of course, prior to purchase); as well as rare Roman coins at the shop Haubrich. In 1993, Trier claimed the largest antique coin discovery with a find of more than 2,500 Roman gold pieces.

Trier is an appealing city. It probably can attribute much of this appeal to the fact that it has been an imperial residence since the days of the Caesars. Strolling through Trier, you will see examples of Renaissance, Baroque, and Rococo architecture standing side by side. More recently, during the nineteenth century, several impressive citizens' houses of outstanding architectural beauty were built along with many museums, including the Archaeological Museum, Bishop's Museum, Cathedral Treasury, the Karl Marx Museum, and the newest favorite, the Toy Museum.

Sprechen Sie Deutsch? German speaking, walking, and bus tours are offered daily. City tours in English run Saturday and Sunday in April and daily from May to October at 1330. Tours last 2 hours and include entrance to Roman monuments. Arrangements may be made for private guides during the rest of the year as well. Walking tours: adults €5.11; children €1.53. Bus tours: adults €8.69; children €4.35. For more tour information, including summer boat trips down the Moselle, visit the tourist office *Web site:* www.trier.de.

Not all of Trier's attributes are readily visible, for beneath the city in the storage cellars of its wineries there are vats and casks capable of holding more than three million gallons of the Moselle, Saar, and Ruwer wines produced annually in the area surrounding the city. If you would like to enjoy a gourmet meal with a glass of the grape, settle into the **Dorint Hotel** or the **Pfeffermühle restaurants,** or taste the Mosel-Saar-Ruwer region wines and sparking wines at the new Mediterranean-style eatery, **Haus des Weines.** Wine tasting is also offered at the area's five wineries and at the vintners in Olewig.

Trier is abundant in festivals throughout the year. Celebrations include the Olewig Wine Festival, Trier Sparkling Wine Gala, Wine & Gourmet Festival in spring, and the Wine Forum, plus the Trier Summer Festival, Music Festival, and Christmas Market. Schedules are available from the tourist information office.

A small street to the side of the great cathedral in Trier is named Sieh um Dich (Look Around You)—an expression that depicts the city's greatness, for you can see 2,000 years of history in just about as many steps. In fact, one of the tours conducted by the city bears the title "Trier—2,000 steps—2,000 years." Perhaps this tour should be taken before tasting the local nectar or maybe you would prefer to ride the bus. Trier 24-hour bus tickets may be purchased for 1 or 2 adults and up to 4 children under the age of 15.

The tourist office also offers the **Trier Card** (adult, €9.71; family, €17.90) valid for 3 consecutive days. The card provides free transport on city buses, free admission to museums (except during special exhibitions), fee reductions for Trier's Roman monuments, city walking tours (in English), and city bus tours (in German).

Den Helder

Enkhuizen

Hoorn
Alkmaar

Haarlem
AMSTERDAM

Den Haag

Hoek van Holland

Rotterdam
Utrecht

Amersfoort

Vissingen

Antwerp

Eindhaven

BELGIUM

Liége

Madstricht

Aachen

FRANCE

LUXEMBOURG

GERMANY

Leeuwarden

Groningen

Leer

Zwolle

Hengelo

Rheine

Arnhem

Duisburg

The
Netherlands

Traditionally, when we think of the Netherlands, windmills, wooden shoes, wondrous flowers, and wheels come to mind. While these things probably will always be a part of Dutch traditions and landscape, there is another not-as-well-known facet to the Netherlands and its people—its important and enviable economic position in Europe and as one of the founding members of the European Union.

Dutch innovation and know-how are responsible for making the computer software Windows accessible for blind users through the use of a cordless mouse that utilizes sound instead of visual images. And, the Netherlands is the only country with an Internet 2 Abilene link with the United States.

The Dutch seem to have an idea or an answer for just about everything. One Dutch company had an answer to automobile congestion and pollution problems by developing a new concept in public transport—People Movers—a combination of ski-lift design and the already existing airport-style people movers.

Another Dutch firm, Spectrum Buoca, has targeted another type of pollution—the acrid urine odor that plagues public facilities (particularly during hot weather). Biological Urine Odour Control Agent (Buoca) is a mixture of natural enzymes and bacteria that "eats" the smelly problem.

It doesn't take too long to discover that the Netherlanders are not only multitalented; they're also multilingual. The Dutch laughingly refer to their own language as "more of a throat condition than anything else" and readily join you in your native tongue. English is the primary second language spoken in the Netherlands, but French, Spanish, German, and many others are heard daily.

Although the Dutch are seemingly inventing the future, they are not forgetting their traditions. There are still about 1,000 working **windmills** that are functioning the same way they did more than a hundred years ago. A group of 19 windmills may be found at **Kinderdijk** in the province of South Holland, some of which you may tour inside. It's amazing—mills that were built in 1740 are still running.

Wooden shoes may not be worn very often anymore, but thanks to tourists, their production has continued. Now, almost any Dutch souvenir shop sells them, and a few farmers in some rural areas still don their wooden clogs when they work in the fields or stalls.

Wondrous flowers are, of course, still in generous supply in Holland. Spanning about 70 acres, the **Keukenhof in Lisse** is the most famous and biggest bulb show in the world (*Tel:* 252 46 55 55; *Fax:* 252 46 55 65; *Internet:* www.keukenhof.nl; *E-mail:* info@keukenhof.nl.) From March to May, it is open 0800–1930 daily. More than 800,000 visitors can gaze upon some six million bulbs. Admission: €9.08 adults; €4.54 children; €7.94 age 65 and over.

For a wondrously colorful event, visit **Floriade 2002.** The Floriade only occurs every 10 years. In 2002, it is being held from April 6 to October 20 at **Haarlemmermeer,** a city just south of Amsterdam developed by land reclamation about 150 years ago. It is located near Amsterdam Schiphol Airport and close to Haarlem as well. Exhibitors from all over Europe, the U.S., Japan and India will landscape the 65-hectare area with more than 300 colorful pavilions, including a "flower valley" with more than 1 million bulbs. Contact the Amsterdam Tourist Information Office for advance information and tickets. Just show your Floriade ticket for free bus connections to the Floriade from Schiphol Airport.

Wheels, wheels, wheels! The bicycle is a common mode of transport in its own right—there are more than twice as many bikes as cars! No less than 15,000 kilometers of marked routes, special paths, and bike lanes abound. More than 300 rail stations allow transport of bikes for a supplement. Many travelers hire a bike at the station. Contact the tourist office for bike rental agency information.

For more information on the Netherlands, contact the Netherlands Board of Tourism in North America:

New York: 355 Lexington Avenue, New York NY 10017–6603. *Tel:* (888) GO HOLLAND (888–464–6552) or (212) 370–7360; *Fax:* (212) 370–9507; *Internet:* **www.holland.com**; *E-mail:* info@holland.com.

Banking

- **Currency:** Euro (€)
- **Exchange rate at press time:** €1.10 = U.S. $1.00

Communications

- **Country Code:** 31
  For telephone calls within the Netherlands, dial a zero (0) preceding area code.

THE NETHERLANDS

Rail Travel in the Netherlands

The Netherlands Railways (Nederlandse Spoorwegen, or NSB; *Internet:* www.ns.nl) has many of its own day excursions. Because the Netherlands is a very compact country, it is possible to take any one of the day excursions from any railway station within the country and return to your point of departure the same day.

Frequent trains run to every part of the Netherlands, and most of the stations are linked with bus services and train taxis. The Dutch **Rail Idee** program offers the day excursionist the convenience of a one-stop shop before hitting the rails. Travelers may purchase day passes directly from the rail station that include not only their transportation (train, bus, taxi, even bicycle rental), but also their admission to a variety of sight-seeing attractions in the Netherlands. Rail Idee ticket packages range in price according to destination and offer a choice of more than 200 attractions to visit. On average, one can save around 20 percent compared to separately buying transportation and admission tickets. The day pass also offers bonus discounts at various shops and restaurants.

To find out more about these day excursions, ask at the train information office in the Amsterdam Central Station. Or contact the Netherlands Board of Tourism.

Many Dutch cities, such as **The Hague** (Den Haag), **Rotterdam**, and **Utrecht**, are less than an hour away from Amsterdam. In just 2 hours, you could be in Antwerp, Belgium, shopping for diamonds. Add another 30 minutes, and you could hop on the fast Thalys train and have lunch in Brussels and then shop for lace. Continue your spree—the quaint town of **Delft**, where the world-renowned Delft blue pottery is made, is only 50 minutes' train time from Amsterdam.

The Netherlands Railways accepts **Eurail passes, Europass plus Benelux option**, the **Benelux Tourrail Pass**, and the **Holland Railpass.** A bonus for Eurailpass and Europass plus Benelux option holders is a 30 percent discount on Stena Line high-speed ships (HSS) crossing from Hoek van Holland to Harwich, England.

Benelux Tourrail Pass

	1st Class	2nd Class
5 days within 1 month	$217	$155
Youth: 5 days within 1 month	—	$104

Benelux Tourrail for Two Pass		
2 people traveling together	*1st Class*	*2nd Class*
5 days within 1 month	$326	$233

335

THE NETHERLANDS

Holland Railpass

3 days/1 month	Adult	Child	Senior	Youth
1st class	$98	$50	$78	—
2nd class	$65	$33	$52	$52
5 days/1 month				
1st class	$147	$74	$119	—
2nd class	$98	$49	$79	$79

Valid for travel throughout Holland; travel on bus lines not included. Senior fares valid for ages 60+. Youth fares for ages 12–25, second-class travel only; child fares, ages 4–11.

Holland Rail Twinpass

3 days/1 month	Adult	Child	Senior	Youth
1st class	$147	$75	$117	—
2nd class	$98	$50	$78	$78
5 days/1 month				
1st class	$221	$111	$180	—
2nd class	$147	$74	$120	$119

Prices are total for two persons traveling together. Valid for travel thoughout Holland; travel on bus lines not included. Senior fares valid for ages 60+. Youth fares for ages 12–25, second class only; child fares, ages 4–11.

Base City:

Amsterdam

**Internet: www.visitamsterdam.nl or
www.amsterdamtourist.nl
City Dialing Code: 20**

One of the most unusual cities in Europe and built entirely on piles, Amsterdam is a "fun city"—fun to see, fun to be in. It is a pleasant, human city where handsome houses stand on quiet canals, shoppers walk uninterrupted on streets without vehicles, and street organs play in the parks (even on rainy afternoons). It is the kind of city that, when you are lost, sends a smiling old gentleman on his bicycle or a bevy of flaxen-haired schoolgirls to your rescue. Amsterdam is a patient city whose people listen as you attempt to read Dutch expressions from a phrase book—then respond in perfect English. Amsterdam is a city to fall in love with.

Though picturesque, by European standards Amsterdam is not an ancient city. In the thirteenth century it was a small fishing village tucked behind a protecting dam on the Zuider Zee. It wasn't until the seventeenth century that it emerged as northern Europe's most prosperous port. Dutch influence declined at the end of the seventeenth century, but Amsterdam survived in style, having been built on 90 islands linked by more than 1,200 bridges arching 165 canals. Although their interiors have been altered many times, the fronts of seventeenth-century houses along the canals remain unaltered.

As the Netherlands Board of Tourism states: "Amsterdam is to the Netherlands what New York is to the United States. It is the cuckoo in the Dutch nest, the strange bird with the big mouth, New York with a more easygoing nature. But that shouldn't be surprising. After all, New York was founded by Amsterdammers. Now you are invited to discover our Amsterdam."

Arriving by Air

Schiphol Airport, P.O. Box 7501, 1118 ZG Schiphol Airport, the Netherlands; Hello Port Schiphol Information *Tel:* (31) 0900–0141 or 0900–72447465; *Internet:* www.schiphol.nl

Amsterdam's Schiphol Airport, which ranks fourth largest in Europe after airports in London, Paris, and Frankfurt, is one of the most modern and efficient air terminals in the world. Schiphol handles more than 25.4 million passengers per year and has some of the best tax-free shopping in Europe. It was built to be convenient. At last count, the airport provides flights to more than 220 destinations in 85 countries by more than 80 international airlines. After you have cleared customs, proceed to Schiphol Plaza to the **Holland Tourist Information** (HTI) center (open daily 0700–2200). There you can obtain all the information you may need for getting into downtown Amsterdam.

Airport–city links: Rail service between the airport and Amsterdam's Central Station takes about 20 minutes and costs €5.22 for a round trip. Trains run approximately every 15 minutes from 0600 to midnight. If your destination is in the southern part of the city, you can board a train for the Zuid (South) Station as well. In fact, direct train service from Schiphol Airport to many other points in the Netherlands, such as The Hague, Rotterdam, and Delft, is available. Within Holland, *Tel:* 0900–9292, for bus, tram, subway, and rail connections, or for international train information, *Tel:* 0–0900–9296.

KLM Airport Hotel Shuttle operates a bus service between Schiphol Airport and the major hotels of Amsterdam. The bus stops at the Luchthaven Schiphol, Hilton Amsterdam, Barbizon Centre, Hotel Pulitzer, Krasnapolsky, Holiday Inn, Renaissance, and Barbizon Palace hotels. The one-way fare is €7.94, and tickets may be purchased on the bus. If your hotel is not listed here, ask at the HTI desk for the listed hotel nearest to yours and get off there—first checking that your hotel is only a short distance away.

Otherwise, a **taxi** may better serve your needs. A taxi takes about 30–45 minutes and costs about €25–36. Again, the HTI desk will be helpful. Taxis can be found just outside the Arrivals Hall.

Money-exchange machine is available in the South Lounge. It changes different currencies into euros. The West Lounge has an ATM (bank cards only). The tourist office will also exchange money.

Duty-free shopping: Amsterdam's Schiphol Airport Shopping Centre is actually three centers. The Plaza totals more than 50 shops with more than 120,000 different items. The shops are open from first to last flight departure. Duty-free shopping is available only to passengers departing Schiphol to destinations outside the European Union.

Schiphol Plaza shopping is available to everyone, but normal VAT is payable. Hours: 0700–2200 daily.

Arriving by Train

The **Amsterdam Centraal Station** is the focal point of all rail, tram (trolley), bus, and Metro (subway) traffic within the city. All train service for the listed day excursions depart from, and arrive in, this station. Trams, buses, and the Metro (entrance) are available immediately in front of the station, the hub of Amsterdam's city-transportation network; practically everything in Amsterdam begins and ends here.

Although Amsterdam's Centraal Station abounds in digital train-information displays, the station still provides the standard train-departure posters with their yellow background giving train-departure information by separate directions. Rail service throughout the Netherlands is so dense—departures approximately every half hour—that these sectional timetables to Rotterdam, Utrecht, and other cities are most helpful.

Amsterdam's Centraal Station is virtually a city within a city, with many restaurants and shops operating over extended hours—a good place to stock up for a trip. It's also an originating point for long-distance express trains, including the Thalys train connections to Brussels and Eurostar to London, as well as the EuroCity network. This means lots of tourists—and tourists attract pickpockets. Watch when boarding the trains, particularly for people who are apparently traveling without luggage and are following you closely with only an empty shopping bag in hand. Chances are that they are "shopping" for your wallet and they plan to leave the train before it departs.

- **Money-exchange** office "GWK" is on the street side of the station foyer. It is open daily, 24 hours per day. Money exchange is also possible at local banks (open from 1000 to 1600).
- **Tourist information** for all of the Netherlands, including Amsterdam, is available from the VVV Amsterdam Tourist Offices located inside Centraal Station at platform 2 (Spoor 2), open daily 0800–2000 except Sunday 0800–1700; or in front of the rail station, open 0900–1700 daily; offices also located at tram stops Leidesplein, 0900–1900 daily and Stadionplein, 0930–1730 (closed Sunday).

- **Train information** may be obtained in the office of the Netherlands Railways (information for trains within the Netherlands [*Tel:* 0900–9292), located on the far right of the main station hall as you exit from the trains. This office has the familiar **i** sign. Open daily 0630–2230. Take a number as you enter.
- **Seat reservations** as well as **railpass validation** may be made in this office. Complete information regarding the Netherlands Railways day-excursion program is also available. Remember, when having your pass validated, write out the starting and ending dates on a piece of paper and have the railroad representative agree to the correctness of the dates before the information is entered on your pass.

Tourist Information/Hotel Reservations

- *VVV Amsterdam Tourist Office:* P.O. Box 3901, 1001 AS, Amsterdam; *Tel:* 20 5512525 or 0900 400 40 40. From abroad; *Tel:* 011–31 20 5512525. *Fax:* 20 625 28 69; *Internet:* www.visitamsterdam.nl; *E-mail:* info@amsterdamtourist.nl

Hours: 0900–1700 daily (July–August: Monday–Saturday 0800–2000; Sunday 0900–1700)

Notes: Located immediately in front and slightly to the left as you exit Amsterdam's Centraal Station, in the Noord-Zuidhollands (NZH) Koffiehuis.

This office can provide complete city and national information for all of the Netherlands. Hotel, hostel, camping, and apartment bookings can be made here. Maps of Amsterdam are available for €1.93. You can also call 0900–400 40 40, Monday–Friday, 0900–1700, for information. Other VVV offices are located at Leidesplein, Stadionplein, and in the Centraal Station at platform (Spoor) 2. A Holland Tourist Information center is located at Schiphol Airport Plaza.

- **Hotel reservations** can be made at the Holland Tourist Information (HTI) office at Schiphol Airport, at the VVV Amsterdam Tourist Office (aforementioned) in the Noord-Zuid Hollands Koffiehuis (NZH coffeehouse), in the VVV office in the Central Station at platform 2, or at the Leidesplein and Stadionplein VVV offices. Hotel reservations may also be made before departure through Amsterdam Reservation Centre. *Tel:* 011–31–777000888 (dialing from the U.S., Monday–Friday 0900–1700 Europe time); *E-mail:* reservations @amsterdamtourist.nl.

For convenience, comfort, and cuisine all in one place, we recommend the **Victoria Hotel**, one of the Park Plaza Hotels Benelux.

- *Convenience*—centrally located in Amsterdam and across the street from Amsterdam Centraal Station. The hotel will even send someone to help with your luggage.
- *Comfort*—the stately Victoria Hotel, built in 1890, offers all of the

AMSTERDAM

Train Connections to Other Base Cities from Amsterdam Centraal

DEPART AMSTERDAM	TRAIN NUMBER	ARRIVE	NOTES
		Berlin Zoobahnhof	
0813	IR 2341	1416	
1013	IR 2343	1616	
1413	IR 2345	2016	
2013	NZ 40371	0636+1	R, Sleeper
		Bern (Berne)	
0955	EC 105	1911	R
1923	IC 642	0708	R, 4, Sleeper
2006	D 203	0811+1	R, 1, Sleeper
		Brussels (Bruxelles) Midi/Zuid	
0656	Thalys 9316*	0932	R
0723	IC 630	1014	
0823	IC 631	1114	
0856	Thalys 9324*	1132	R
0923	IC 632	1214	
0956	Thalys 9328*	1232	R
1023	IC 633	1314	
(and hourly until 2023, then 2232)			
		Copenhagen (København) H.	
2006	D 203	0959+1	R, 3, Sleeper
		Hamburg	
0813	IR 2341	1310	5
1013	IR 2343	1510	5
1413	IR 2345	1910	5
1813	IR 2347	2313	except Sat
2023	IC 643	0721+1	R, 4, Sleeper
		Luxembourg	
0623	IC 629	1153	4
0723	IC 630	1339	4
0823	IC 631	1439	4
0925	632	1452	4
(and hourly until 2023, then 2223)			
		Lyon Part-Dieu	
0656	Thalys 9316*	1501	R, 6
0823	IC 631	1505	R, 4
0856	THA 9324*	1655	R, 6
0956	THA 9328	1801	R, 6
1123	IC 634	1905	R, 4
1256	THA 9340*	2057	R, 6
2223	D 288	1055+1	R, 6, Sleeper
		Milan (Milano) Greco	
1755	D 209	0729+1	R
		Munich (München) Hauptbahnhof	
0755	EC 3	1622	2
0955	EC 105	1826	2
1925	D 223	0622+1	R, Sleeper
plus other departures			

Depart	Train Number	Arrive	Notes
		Nice Ville	
0623	IC 629	1739	4
0956	Thalys* 9328	2127	R
2223	D 288	1357	R, 6, Sleeper
		Paris Gare du Nord	
0656	Thalys 9316*	1105	R
0856	Thalys 9324*	1305	R
0956	THA 9328*	1405	R
1256	Thalys 9340*	1705	R
1656	Thalys 9356*	2105	R
1856	Thalys 9364*	2305	R
2223	D 288	0656+1	R, Sleeper
		Vienna (Wien) Westbahnhof	
1925	D 223	0955+1	R, Sleeper
		Zürich Hauptbahnhof	
0755	EC 3	1658	R
1923	IC 642	0700+1	R, 4, Sleeper
2006	D 203	0800+1	R, 1, Sleeper

Daily, unless otherwise noted
R Reservations required
+1 Arrive next day
* Thalys high-speed train, supplement required
1. Change trains in Basel SBB.
2. Change trains in Mannheim.
3. Change trains in Duisburg.
4. Change trains in Brussels Nord Station.
5. Change trains in Osnabrück.
6. Change trains in Paris.

modern "creature comforts," such as deluxe rooms, indoor heated swimming pool, beauty salon, and fitness room—even a free first-class train ticket to and from Schiphol Airport.

- *Cuisine*—fine French and international dinners in the Seasons Garden Restaurant.

Park Plaza Hotels Benelux are located either opposite from, next to, or very close to the central rail stations in Amsterdam, Utrecht, and Eindhoven in the Netherlands, as well as in Antwerp, Belgium. In addition, they **offer *Europe by Eurail* readers a 20 percent discount off their normal rack rates**. Just mention *Europe by Eurail* when you make your reservation and present the coupon in this book upon check-in to receive your 20 percent discount. For reservations, *Tel:* (31) 2062–71 166; *Fax:* (31) 2062–52997.

Getting Around in Amsterdam

GVB: located on square opposite Centraal Station

AMSTERDAM

Tel: 0900 9292 or 460 60 60

Hours: Monday–Friday 0700–2100; Saturday–Sunday 0800–2100

Amsterdam's public transportation system encompasses 17 tram lines, more than 30 bus lines, and 4 underground systems/light rail lines, plus ferries, and canal boats. The transport office, GVB (Gemeentevervoerbedrijf), is located in front of Amsterdam's Centraal Station in Noord-Zuid Hollands Koffiehuis. Check with this office for up-to-date information, for public transportation maps, and to purchase transport tickets.

There are a variety of one-day or multiple-day transportation passes that have to be stamped only with the first use; strip tickets (strippenkaart) are also available, but they require stamping with each use unless you travel round-trip within 1 hour. The tourist transportation tickets are accepted on all trams, express trams, buses, and subways. Single day €4.99, two days €7.94, and €2.67 per additional day up to a 9-day maximum. For transportation information, *Tel:* 0900 92 92. For **boat services** contact the tourist information office for details on the Canal Bus, Water Taxi, Artis Express Rederij Lovers, and the Museum Boat. Bicycle and water bike rentals are also available.

Circle Tram 20 provides flexible access to sights and attractions, museums, hotels, and restaurants—30 different stops—in Amsterdam. Hop on and off when and where you please. Circle Tram 20 operates 0900–1900 daily and departs every 10 minutes in two directions. Purchase 1-, 2-, 3-, or 4-day tickets at the VVV Information offices, at the GVB transport offices, from the conductor at the back of the tram, or from tobacco shops and large hotels. The tickets are valid on all public transport everywhere in Amsterdam. With Circle Tram 20, a helpful conductor is onboard.

The **Amsterdam Culture and Leisure Pass** costs €29 and offers substantial discounts or free entry for various museums, including the Rijksmuseum, the Van Gogh, the Stedelijk Museum of Modern Art, and The Netherlands Maritime Museum. The pass also includes discounts on other attractions, excursions and guided tours, a 3-day public transportation ticket for the price of a 1-day ticket, a 25 percent discount on Holland International's romantic Candlelight and Wine Cruises—even a free canal boat cruise and discounts on the Museum Boat and the Canal Bus.

The Amsterdam Culture and Leisure Pass is available in 1 of 6 languages at any of the VVV Amsterdam Tourist offices, the Holland Tourist Information center at Schiphol Airport Plaza, or inquire at your hotel.

Sights/Attractions/Tours

If you'd like to see Amsterdam on foot, the VVV's color-coded signboards and map will guide you along six walking routes. More than thirty attractions are incorporated into the walking routes.

A boat trip on Amsterdam's canals and other waterways is, undoubtedly, the most relaxing way to see the city. Canal-boat terminals line the city's pier-studded canals, many of which may be found immediately outside the station. The closest of these is the **Holland International** pier (*Tel:* 622–7788). It is just across the bridge on the right. A canal tour costs €7.94 for adults and €4.54 for children age 4–12 and senior citizens over age 65. Other tour-boat terminals are scattered throughout Amsterdam.

There are several canal cruise companies to choose from—all are excellent. During summer evenings, when the buildings along the canals are illuminated and the canal bridges are outlined by tiny lights, Holland International offers a Candlelight and Wine Cruise (€24.96)—the perfect way to end your day. (Receive a 25 percent discount if you've purchased the Amsterdam Culture and Leisure Pass.)

Amsterdam's old "inner city" is famous for its compactness. Most museums, markets, monuments, shopping streets, and other attractions are all within walking distance—or a short tram ride—from your hotel. Several of the city-center shops are open on Sunday—somewhat unusual when compared to the shopping hours for the rest of Europe. Amsterdam boasts the largest historical inner city in Europe, with more than 6,800 National Trust buildings.

The city has more than 60 museums, including the famous **Rijksmuseum** (open daily 1000–1700), where you can view Rembrandt's renowned *Night Watch,* along with an extensive collection of his other dazzling works. The South Wing is devoted to a wide-ranging overview of eighteenth- and nineteenth-century Dutch Impressionist art. All the paintings now have explanations in English, and you can rent a CD-ROM player that describes in English, German, or French the 200 most significant paintings in the collection. For more details visit *Internet:* www.rijksmuseum.nl or *E-mail:* info@rijksmuseum.nl.

The **Van Gogh Museum** underwent a $15.5 million renovation and construction of a new wing in 1999. A must-see. For a preview check out *Internet:* www.vangoghmuseum.nl, or *E-mail:* info@vangoghmuseum.nl for more information.

One of the newest of Amsterdam's museums is appropriately named **"newMetropolis" Museum or "NEMO."** It is an interesting attraction designed by Italian architect Renzo Piano, due to its location on top of one of the major tunnels leading into and out of Amsterdam. Plus its roof offers a spectacular view of the city. The building appears to rise from the water of the Oosterdok as a bow of a ship. A twenty-first-century public center for science and technology, this new museum fits with our earlier statement, "The Dutch are inventing the future," by using up-to-date, hands-on techniques.

"Diamonds are a girl's best friend," and Amsterdam is a good place to see how a glassy little piece of stone can become the most beautiful, desirable gemstone in the world. With nine diamond factories to tempt you, we suggest taking a tour of the **Amsterdam Diamond Center,** located at Rokin 1–5 (Tel: 624–5787; *Fax:* 625–1220). Hours: 1000–1800 Monday–Saturday, 1000–2030 Thursday, and 1000–1800 Sunday. Although free samples are not available, a diamond sure makes a great souvenir!

Dining in Amsterdam is an exercise in international cuisine. The expression "You can eat there in any language" is no exaggeration. First decide what type of food you want—Hungarian, German, Italian, Greek, Scandinavian, Japanese, or Indonesian—then select from among the many restaurants offering such dishes. Our favorite for Indonesian food is **Restaurant Indonesia,** at 18 Korte Leidsedwarsstraat (*Tel:* 20–6232035). Take tram 1, 2, or 5 from the Centraal Station to the Leidseplein area, about a 12-minute ride. Its specialty is an eighteen-dish rijsttafel (ricetable). Go there hungry—we guarantee you won't go home that way.

For more traditional Dutch bill-of-fare, try another favorite—**Haesje Claes** at Spuistraat 275 (*Tel:* 20–624–9998; *Fax:* 20–627–4817; *Internet:* www.haesjeclaes.nl). Named after Lady Haesje Claes, this restaurant's slogan is "From canapes to caviar." Born in 1520 into a prosperous merchant family, Lady Haesje Claes was the founder and patron of the Public Orphanage, now the Amsterdam Historical Museum. Have a typical Dutch lunch or dinner in one of the eight chambers, each with its own special atmosphere. The eel and salmon with lobster is excellent.

Visitors from the United States who are hankerin' for a good U.S. steak should not miss the **Three Sisters Restaurant.** The beef is USDA Prime. There's quite a story about how the restaurant got its name. Ask the waiter for the menu with the complete version of the story of the three sisters and their New York connections.

Day Excursions

The *Europe by Eurail* day excursions described in this chapter are to **Alkmaar,** home of the world-famous cheese market; **Enkhuizen,** for its open-air Zuider Zee Museum, which depicts what Dutch life was like before the Zuider Zee was sealed off from the North Sea; **Haarlem,** for the Frans Hals Museum and more aspects of life in the Netherlands; and **Hoorn,** for browsing in a medieval market. These day excursions present a cross section of the Netherlands, from its rural to its sophisticated side.

Day Excursion to

Alkmaar
World-Famous Cheese Market

Depart from Amsterdam Centraal Station
Distance by Train: 24 miles (39 km)
Average Train Time: 30 minutes
City Dialing Code: 72
Tourist Information Office: Regio VVV Alkmaar, Waagplein 2-3, 1811 JP Alkmaar
Tel: (72) 511–4284; **Fax:** (72) 511–7513
Hours: 1000–1730 Monday, 0900–1730 Tuesday–Wednesday, 0900–2100 Thursday, 0900–1800 Friday, and 0930–1700 Saturday.
Notes: An easy route to the town square is to follow the street, Geesterweg, running perpendicular to the front of the station and the VVV signs leading you across a bridge toward a large church (Church of St. Laurens). Pass the church on its left side and pick up Lange Straat, still walking in the same direction. Pass the town hall, which will be on your right; four blocks farther, at a canal, turn left to the Weigh House, where the cheese market is held. The VVV office is located in the front of the Weigh House.

There is a cheese market in Alkmaar every Friday 1000–1230 the first Friday in April to the last Friday in September. But Alkmaar is such a picturesque town that it deserves a visit any day of the week at any time of the year. Trains run between Amsterdam and Alkmaar about every 15 minutes.

Alkmaar is famous not only for its cheese; it is steeped in Dutch history as well. It was at Alkmaar in 1573 that the Spanish were first compelled to retreat their occupying forces; hence, the Dutch expression "victory begins at Alkmaar." A festival is held annually on October 8 to commemorate the breaking of the Spanish siege.

Ask at the tourist office about seeing Alkmaar by canal, a popular way to see the town. Boats depart from Mient (near Waaggebouw). Adult fare, €4.00; children under age 12, €2.50. During the cheese market on Friday, boats sail every 20 minutes from 0930. During May, June, July, and August, they depart daily on the hour from 1100. In April, September, and October, they sail Monday–Saturday, every hour on the hour, from 1100, depending

Daily departures from Amsterdam Centraal Station every 22, and 52 minutes after the hour from 0652 throughout the day; journey time 35 minutes.
Daily departures from Alkmaar Station at 7 and 37 minutes after the hour throughout the day; journey time, 35 minutes.
Distance: 24 miles (39 km)

on the weather. The canal trip takes about 45 minutes (*Tel:* 511–7750).

The **cheese auction** is *the* thing to see in Alkmaar. The square explodes into a frenzy of color and activity as cheese porters trot across the square wearing red, blue, green, or yellow hats according to the group they represent. This auction has continued for more than 400 years and attracts thousands of tourists. It is not, however, merely a tourist attraction. It is a genuine auction, at which cheese merchants sample the product, bargain for the best price, and conclude the sale "on hand clap." From there the porters move the cheese to the Weigh House, where the weigh master checks the weight and calls it out in a loud voice; then the porters take the cheese from there to the buyers' warehouses.

Alkmaar's cheese makers founded their guild in 1622, only 2 years after the Pilgrims landed on Plymouth Rock. Unique in the curatorial world, Alkmaar's **Cheese Museum** attracts visitors from far and wide (open April–October, Monday–Saturday 1000–1600; opens at 0900 on Friday). Entrance fee, €2.50, but a **Dutch Museumpass** will get you in for free.

Another unique museum is dedicated to the history of beer production. Featuring the fine skills of brewmasters and covering 5,000 years of beer-making history, the **National Beer Museum De Boom** deals with all aspects down through the ages that have determined the various characteristics of beer, including the current Dutch favorite, pale lager. It is interesting to note that despite the complicated brewing equipment used today, the art of brewing has remained a natural process relatively unchanged from earlier times.

Both the Cheese Museum and the Beer Museum (April–September, open 1000–1600 Tuesday–Friday, 1300–1600 Saturday and 1330–1600 Sunday; November–March, 1300–1600 Tuesday–Saturday and 1330–1600 Sunday) are but a few steps from the city square, where the cheese auction takes place.

Alkmaar is a charming town. It is crisscrossed by canals that, in turn, are spanned by humped stone bridges. The shining red roofs of its old houses are guarded by the towering vaults of the aged **St. Laurens Church**, constructed in 1520. Four blocks south of St. Laurens stands **Molen van Piet,** a windmill built in 1769.

There are an amazing number of things to do and see, among them a visit to the Municipal Museum, the Dutch Stove Museum, and the Hans Brinker Museum; on a Friday, take a look at the stately wooden gabled

AMSTERDAM *Alkmaar*

house complete with an embedded cannonball as a memoir of a war now past. Sample the famous Edam cheese at either lunch or dinner. Time moves slower in Alkmaar.

Day Excursion to

Enkhuizen
Zuider Zee Museum

Depart from Amsterdam Centraal Station
Distance by Train: 42 miles (62 km)
Average Train Time: 64 minutes
City Dialing Code: 228
Tourist Information Office: VVV-Enkhuizen e.o., Tussen Twee Havens 1, 1601 EM Enkhuizen
Tel: 31 228 31 31 64; **Fax:** 31 228 31 55 31
E-mail: vvvenkhuizeneo@hetnet.nl
Hours: April–mid-October, daily 0900–1700; mid-October–March, Monday–Friday 0900–1700, Saturday 0900–1400
Notes: After disembarking from the train, bear left approaching the railway station. As you round the station, you will see the VVV tourist office. The route is well marked; just follow the signs.

This day excursion from Amsterdam was made possible by the opening of the **Zuider Zee Open Air Museum** in Enkhuizen, east of Hoorn. Purchase museum tickets at museum's ticket office. Admission: adults, €9.08; children age 4–12, €6.81 and adults age 65 and over, €7.94; children under 4 are admitted free. A visit to the Zuider Zee Museum begins with a 15-minute boat ride. After stopping at the VVV tourist office, walk along the right side of the boat yard in front of the rail station to its far end and board the launch at the pier. The boats leave every 15 minutes.

The museum was opened formally by Queen Beatrix on May 6, 1983, after 18 years of construction. It consists of 135 houses and workshops to depict the Zuider Zee culture before it was closed off from the North Sea in 1932 by the Afsluitdijk barrier dam. You will see a foundry, a steam laundry, a sail loft, and a smokehouse, to name but just a few items. There are a fishing village on the quay and a town center complete with a church and a general store, where postcards, wooden shoes, and other souvenirs are for sale.

Snacks and various Dutch food specialties are also available, as are tours led by English-speaking guides. Check at the museum office for information. You will pass it just after the foundry. The open-air museum is open mid-April to October, 1000–1700 daily. The indoor portion, known as the

Daily departures from Amsterdam Centraal station at 19 and 49 minutes after the hour from 0619 until late in the day; journey time about 64 minutes.

Daily departures from Enkhuizen station at 7 and 37 minutes after the hour from 0507 until 2107, then hourly until 2307; journey time 67 minutes.

Distance: 42 miles (62 km)

Binnen Museum, is open throughout the year (except December 25 and January 1). Reduced entrance fees when the outdoor museum is closed.

Enkhuizen has succeeded in preserving its seventeenth-century character. The old center of the city contains a picturesque fisherman's quarter and a corresponding essential (a farmer's corner) from those days. Within the old seawall, which was constructed to protect the city from storms on the Zuider Zee, you will find a shopping center, sidewalk cafes, and restaurants.

The last two Thursdays of July and the first two of August are the celebrations of Zuiderzeedag. Each Thursday brings a different theme, with old Dutch dancing groups, games for children, many types of music, a special market, contests, and much more.

Ever wonder how artisans build those beautifully detailed ship models inside glass bottles? A visit to the **Bottle Ship Museum** will reveal the secrets of this ancient sailors' handicraft. The world's largest collection of ships-in-a-bottle is housed in an early seventeenth-century building—the "Spuihuisje"—within easy walking distance of the Zuider Zee Museum. More than 500 models are contained in bottles ranging in size from small perfume bottles to a 30-liter wine flagon. Tickets may be purchased at the VVV office (adults, €2.72; children 4 to 12, €2.04).

For the small-fry, Enkhuizen offers **Sprookjeswonderland** (Fairyland). Situated in a park setting, it contains a children's zoo with a deer park, a farm, and a "hugging" barn. (Open daily, mid-April to mid-October, Monday–Saturday 1000–1730 and Sunday 1000–1730.)

The town of Enkhuizen is a living museum in itself. The Zuiderkerk church, with its spiraling tower and copper-clad roof, dominates the skyline of the city, assisted by the wooden bell tower of Enkhuizen's other church, the "Wester." Together with the ramparts and fortress walls, Enkhuizen ensures its future by preserving its rich past.

Day Excursion to

Haarlem
And the Frans Hals Museum

Depart from Amsterdam Centraal Station
Distance by Train: 12 miles (19 km)
Average Train Time: 15 minutes
City Dialing Code: 23
Tourist Information Office: Stationsplein 1, 2011 LR Haarlem
Tel: 0900 6161600; *Fax:* 23 534 0537
Hours: Monday–Friday 0930–1730, Saturday 1000–1400, closed Sunday
Notes: The **VVV tourist information office** is situated on the south right-hand
corner of the railway station as you exit. (The train bringing you to Haarlem is
headed in a westerly direction as it enters the station.) The office is marked with
an ample sign reading VVV HAARLEM and cannot be missed.

Haarlem is close to Amsterdam, and this trip has the shortest travel time of any day excursion described in this edition of *Europe by Eurail*. It is also one of the most interesting.

Haarlem remained relatively undamaged by both world wars. What you find there in the **Grote Markt** (Great Market), the old center of the town, has authentic origins dating from the thirteenth century. Haarlem was put to the sword in July 1573, when it fell to its Spanish besiegers and its citizens were butchered. Its devastation, however, was not on the scale that modern weapons could perpetrate.

With the release in 1976 of the motion picture **The Hiding Place,** the attention of the world was drawn to a quaint little watchmaker's shop established in 1837 at 19 Barteljorisstraat in the heart of Haarlem. It was here in the shop and home of a Christian, Opa ten Boom, and his family that Jewish refugees fleeing the wrath of Nazi Germany were hidden for a time during World War II. A hiding place was built in a bedroom where the refugees could go in case the Germans made a surprise inspection. The ten Boom family operated the refuge for more than 18 months, until they were betrayed on February 28, 1944.

At the time of the betrayal, six persons were concealed in the hiding place. They escaped while the Gestapo was still in the house. The ten Boom family, however, was imprisoned in a concentration camp for their acts of mercy. The ten Boom house is now a museum. It is open for visits 1000–1600 Tuesday through Saturday from April 1 through October 31. It is open 1100–1500 the rest of the year. Entrance is free, but a donation is always graciously appreciated. Check with the VVV for directions and details.

The old center of Haarlem is not so large as to require transportation to

AMSTERDAM *Haarlem*

Amsterdam—Haarlem

Daily departures from Amsterdam Centraal station at 4, 11, 34, and 41 minutes after the hour throughout the day; journey time, 16 minutes.
Daily departures from Haarlem station at 7, 10, 37 and 40 minutes after the hour, throughout the day; journey time: 15 minutes.
Distance: 12 miles (19 km)

its points of interest, but the city bus system is available to assist if necessary. You will want to visit the Great Market and see the town hall and the **Church of Saint Bavo,** then proceed to the world-famous **Frans Hals Museum** and from there to the **Teylers Museum** before returning to the railway station.

The Great Market is actually the central square of Haarlem, in which the nobles of Holland staged their tournaments during the Middle Ages. Today, it is traditionally the social gathering place of the townspeople. A part of the town hall was once a hunting club. The Church of Saint Bavo houses a pipe organ that was once played by the eleven-year-old Mozart.

On foot, head south from the station, crossing the Nieuwe Gracht (New Canal), and proceed to the city's central square, using the tower of the great church as your point of destination. As you enter the square, the church stands on your left, the town hall on your right. This square has been described as the most beautiful in the Netherlands. A pause here in one of the many restaurants, outdoor cafes, or ice cream shops is recommended.

Time permitting, before leaving the Great Market, you may wish to visit the **Meat Hall** and the **Fish Hall.** No longer functioning by their descriptive names, both structures are now employed in the exhibition of modern visual art. The seventeenth-century architect Lieven de Key designed the Meat Hall, which is said to be one of the finest examples of Renaissance architecture in the Netherlands.

From the western end of the church, follow the street running south from the square to the **Frans Hals Museum,** just before the canal. This street has several names—Warmoesstraat, Schagchelstraat, and Groot Heiligland—appearing in that order as you move to the museum through one of the most heady seventeenth-century atmospheres to be found anywhere in Europe.

The Frans Hals Museum is a moving experience. It's open Monday through Saturday, 1100–1700, and Sunday, 1200–1700. Perhaps nowhere else can you find such a perfect combination of setting and display. The building is a gorgeous sight—its inner courtyard is a magnificent example of seventeenth-century architecture. The versatility of the museum's collections is also unusual. In one section, the peak achievements of Haarlem's seventeenth-century painters may be viewed; in another wing of the museum, visitors may view an exhibition of modern Dutch art.

A left turn at the canal below the museum takes you to the **Turf Markt** on the Spaarne River, where another left turn takes you winding along the river to Holland's oldest museum, the **Teylers Museum,** just beyond Damstraat (Dam Street). Here you will be treated to a rich collection of drawings and paintings by Michelangelo, Raphael, Titian, and Rembrandt. The Coin and Medal Room displays Dutch coins and medals from the sixteenth to the twentieth centuries. The museum also includes a collection of fossils and minerals.

Day Excursion to

Hoorn
Old Dutch Market

Depart from Amsterdam Centraal Station
Distance by Train: 26 miles (42 km)
Average Train Time: 39 minutes
City Dialing Code: 229
Tourist Information Office: Veemarkt 4, 1621 JC Hoorn
Tel: 0900–403 1055; **Fax:** (0229) 215023
Hours: In summer, 1300–1800 Monday; 0930–1800 Tuesday–Friday (until 2100 Thursday); 0930–1700 Saturday; 1300–1700 Sunday
Notes: Cross the main street in front of the railway station, bear right to the first street, then turn left to the next intersection. Here, you turn left, then take the second street on your right. Green signposts scattered along this route indicate the location.

Ever since its harbor slowly silted in the eighteenth century, the city of Hoorn has taken to relaxing—except on Wednesday from July to August, when it awakens with colorful markets and fun events.

In stalls grouped around the statue of Admiral Jan Pieterszoon Coen (founder of the East India Company) in the square the town calls **Rode Steen,** Hoorn's seventeenth-century crafts of clog making, net mending, basket weaving, and many others come to life while groups of folk dancers perform with musical ensembles. If you are not particularly fond of mingling with the crowd, this colorful spectacle may be viewed from the comfort of the **Old Dutch Tavern** on Rode Steen Square.

Although the Zuiderzee has been landlocked since the strait to the North Sea was sealed off in May 1932, Hoorn has managed to maintain its status of a port by establishing four harbor areas with more than 1,100 moorings for commercial and recreational watercraft. The pursuit of water sports, including sailboarding and waterskiing, may be observed—or participated

Daily departures from Amsterdam Centraal Station at 19 and 49 minutes after the hour throughout the day beginning at 0619; journey time to Hoorn is 39 minutes.

Daily departures from Hoorn station at 4 and 34 minutes after the hour throughout the day, then 2037, 2107, 2207 and 2307; journey time: 40 minutes.

Distance: 26 miles (42 km)

in—throughout the season in Hoorn.

Steam-engine buffs will find interest in Hoorn, too. You can travel on a genuine **steam train** from Hoorn to Medemblik and back in old-fashioned coaches. The Netherlands Railways operates a day excursion, "Historical Triangle," during spring, summer, and fall. Starting either in Hoorn or Enkhuizen, a steam train plies between Hoorn and Medemblik and a boat between Medemblik and Enkhuizen. The VVV office in Amsterdam or the train information office in Amsterdam's Centraal Station can provide details for this triangle trip. Information for finding Rode Steen Square, as well as the departure point and tickets for the steam train to Medemblik, is also available in the Hoorn railway station.

On Wednesday, you'll find the market area merely by following the crowd. At other times, follow the directions to the VVV tourist office (aforementioned).

Day excursions by train to Hoorn are popular trips out of Amsterdam in the summer. Local trains bear special markings (on Wednesday) from July through August, when the market is staged. Take these trains for a festive mood; but regular train service between Amsterdam and Hoorn runs about every half hour throughout the day, so you have the option of going and returning whenever you feel like it.

The steam train operates every day but Monday from April through the end of October; so Hoorn stages this market plus many other attractions on days other than Wednesday. In fact, the steam train continues to operate through September and October from Tuesday through Sunday. (For more complete details check the Netherlands Railways day-excursion brochure.)

Wednesdays during the summer are, of course, the times of high activity in Hoorn, but you may go there anytime throughout the year and spend an enjoyable day in this ancient town on the **Ysselmeer,** a freshwater lake that was once part of the Zuiderzee. It is one of Holland's loveliest cities. As an important fourteenth-century fishing harbor, it grew in stature until the seventeenth-century East Indies trade made it rich. The warehouses and mansions of the East India merchants that still line its streets make exploring the town on foot a sheer delight. You can obtain a street map with a recommended walking tour from either the VVV office or the ticket office in the railway station.

At Rode Steen Square you may inspect the seventeenth-century **Weigh House** and the **Westfries Museum,** which houses a collection of antiques, paintings, and objects associated with the city and its surroundings. The museum is crammed with beautiful paintings of Hoorn's citizen soldiers and other memories of Hoorn's "golden age" during the seventeenth century.

Stop at the fifteenth-century calligrapher's workshop. Here is where Hoorn's wealthy merchants had their contracts and correspondence penned prior to the invention of the printing press later in the century.

Take time to smell the flowers. It took Hoorn many centuries to become what it is today. Relax and enjoy it.

Norway

"See, darling, how the departing day
On a scarlet pillow is laid away;
How the sun has set
In clouds of gold and violet."
    From the poem "Beautiful Clouds" (1839), by Henrik Wergeland

Norway—Land of the Midnight Sun (there seems to be more than one including Finland and the state of Alaska). In the upper reaches of Norway during the summer, the sun never fully sets, generating extraordinary hues of scarlet, gold, and violet in the northern skies. The Norwegian Tourist Board succinctly describes a visit to Norway as "A nature so incredibly beautiful one can't help but feel spiritual. Overall, a vacation in Norway feels like a spa treatment. Norway will capture your heart and renew your spirit."

More than 30 percent of Norway's 155,000 square miles are covered by forests, rivers, and lakes, creating majestic landscapes and mystic fjords. Norwegian beauty and charm are not confined to its landscapes—they are reflected in its people.

Norwegian is the official language, but most Norwegians speak English, and some also speak French or German. Norwegians are friendly, fun, and eager to make visitors feel welcome.

Norway is a constitutional monarchy with a Parliament, known as "Stortinget," and has been a member of NATO (North Atlantic Treaty Organization) since 1949. Oil and gas are the cornerstone of its economy, and its people have one of the world's highest per capita incomes.

From art, beauty, and culture to hiking, skiing, and whale watching, Norway has something for everyone.

For more information on Norway, contact the Norwegian Tourist Board in North America:

New York: Scandinavian Tourist Board, P.O. Box 4649, Grand Central Station, New York, NY 10163–4649. *Tel:* (212) 885–9700; *Fax:* (212) 885–9710; *Internet:* **www.goscandinavia.com** or **www. norway.org**; *E-mail:* info@goscandinavia.com or usa@nortra.no

Banking

- **Currency:** Norwegian Kroner (NOK)
- **Exchange rate at press time:** NOK 8.81 = U.S. $1.00
- **Hours:** 0815–1500 (1530 in winter) Monday–Friday, closing at 1800 on Thursday. Some banks are open longer than regular hours in larger cities. Most shorten hours during summer.

Communications

- **Country Code:** 47
  City codes are not used when dialing within Norway
- **Direct dial:** AT&T: 800–19–011; MCI: 800–19–912; Sprint: 800–19–877

Rail Travel in Norway

The **Norwegian State Railways** (NSB) successfully combines a comprehensive system (4,044 kilometers) of express and local rail service with bus and boat services.

The NSB **"Norway in a Nutshell"** package tours incorporate various transportation modes to create a great way to see Norway. These packages include hotel, breakfast, and a Norway Railpass. *Tel:* (888) 868–7404, *Fax:* (614) 764–0711 for a free *Norway in a Nutshell* brochure.

Norway's trains traverse difficult geography; consequently, train speeds are limited to a maximum speed of 160 km/h. The rail connection between Gardermoen Airport and Oslo on the *Gardermoen Express,* however, is built for 200 km/h and takes only 19 minutes. Norwegian trains are known for cleanliness and comfort.

On the night trains, sleeper cars contain 1, 2, or 3 beds per compartment, and couchettes and/or reclining seats are available on some trains.

NSB accepts the 17-country variety of **Eurail passes,** including the new **Eurail Selectpass,** the **ScanRail Pass** (for rail travel in Denmark, Finland, Norway, and Sweden), and the **Norway Railpass.** Eurail bonuses include: a 30 percent discount on the Color Line steamship fare between Norway and Denmark. Crossings: Kristiansand–Hirthals, Moss–Hirthals, Moss–Frederikshavn, Larvik–Frederikshavn, Larvik–Skagen

- Scandinavian Seaways—50 percent discount between Oslo and Copenhagen
- Ferry reduction of 50 percent on Flaggruten ANS: Bergen–Haugesund–Stavanger and on Stena Line between Oslo and

Frederikshavn (No discount on cabin/couchette supplements.)

Seat reservations are compulsory (NOK 20) on InterCity (ICE) trains and most other express trains. Supplement is charged for use of the ICE's "Bureau car," and for the "Saloon car," which includes a meal.

In June 2000, Norway's new "Signatur-trains" began operating on the Bergen Line.

Norway Railpass

	Adult		Senior	
	First Class	Second Class	First Class	Second Class
3 days within 1 month	$190	$146	$151	$117
4 days within 1 month	$236	$182	$188	$146
5 days within 1 month	$264	$202	$210	$162

Children age 4–14 travel at half the adult fare. Children under age 4 travel free; maximum of 2 children travel free per adult. Senior age 60+.

Travel on the Flam Railway Line no longer included with the Norway Pass, ScanRail Pass, or Eurail passes, but pass holders receive a discount of 30 percent.

"Signatur" Expresstrains run on the Southern Line, Dovreline and Bergen Line. Supplement required, includes meals and refreshments.

Base City:

Oslo

Internet: www.oslopro.no or www.oslo.com

Oslo, known as "the Viking Capital," is unique. If you love to bask in the sun, go to Oslo sometime between May and October, when more sunbeams fall on Oslo than on any other capital city in Europe north of the Alps. About half a million of Norway's 4 million people live in Oslo, and soaking up the sun is the thing to do in town during the summer. Sauna baths, of course, become the rage for the balance of the year.

Oslo is also Norway's business, cultural, and fun capital. Frequently referred to as the "Nightclub of the North," Oslo is Scandinavia's center for entertainment and night life. Artists and performers entertain into the wee hours of the morning.

Arriving by Air

Touted as "Europe's safest and most efficient airport," Oslo's international airport at Gardermoen is a beautiful example of contemporary Norwegian architecture. Located some 47 kilometers north of Oslo, the airport has the capacity to handle 16–17 million passengers per year. There are daily direct flights to more than 30 European cities and hourly flights to Copenhagen and Stockholm. *Internet:* www.osl.no

Airport–City Links: High-speed rail connections into Oslo on the Airport Express Train (*Flytoget*) take only 19 minutes. The rail station is located in the air terminal. Follow the pictographs. Long-distance train service provides connections to all parts of Norway and Scandinavia.

The taxi stand at Oslo Airport is on your right as you exit from the arrivals hall. Ask for "Airport Taxi" at the Taxi Information desk in the arrivals hall and expect to pay NOK 475–575 for 1–4 persons. (To book in advance: *Tel:* 47 23 23 23 23.) All taxis are equipped with meters and accept all major credit cards. Oslo Taxi service (information in Norwegian): *Tel:* 47 22 38 80 90; *Fax:* 47 22 38 85 80.

NOR-WAY Bussekspress (*Internet:* www.nor-way.no) or SAS Flybussen (*Internet:* www.osl.no/trafikanten) provide airport-to-city coach service. Fare: NOK 80, Adults; NOK 40, Seniors.

Arriving by Train

Oslo has several suburban rail stations, but all international trains stop only at the **Oslo Sentralstasjon** (Oslo Central Station). You will see the station name frequently abbreviated as "Oslo S," or shortened to "Oslo Sentral."

Within the station, rail travelers can take advantage of a mini-market area amid a variety of kiosks selling everything from apples to zircons. The nostalgic market area stands on what was once known as the East Station. The East Station was devoted to steel rails, nail-spiked wooden platforms, and tiles bearing the patina of wear from countless passengers' feet as they hurried to and from the steam-hauled trains.

Oslo Sentral Station is a model of efficiency. Access from the train platforms to the station's main hall is by ramps. A shopping mall, Byporten ("City Gate"), is connected to Oslo Sentral and has more than 65 shops, 10 restaurants, and a hotel.

- **Baggage carts** are available for a NOK 10 coin. The coin is refunded if you return your cart to a rack when you are finished. Although the carts may be used on the ramps, they cannot be used on the station's escalators. You can, however, use the large passenger elevators located at either end of the main hall when moving from one level to another. The elevators are marked *heis*, which comes close to the word *hoist* in English.

Follow the pictographs, and you will find every service you might need.

- **Baggage storage lockers** are located on a balcony to the right of the station's main exit. Access to the locker area is open 0700–2300 daily.
- **Money exchange** facilities are located on the mezzanine level of the station, directly across from the ticket windows. Follow the currency exchange pictographs. Hours: June–September, Monday–Friday 0700–1800; Saturday 0900–1500. When the money exchange is closed, you can change money in the post office or at the tourist information office in Oslo opposite the City Hall.
- **Ticket offices** are on the left-hand side of the station. Domestic tickets are available 0600–2300 Monday–Saturday; 0630–2330 Sunday. The international ticket office is located next to the domestic ticket windows (open daily 0630–2300).
- **Tourist information office** is open 0800–2300 daily and is located next to the money exchange office. It provides tourist information covering Oslo, hotel reservations, guest house and private accommodations, sales of the Oslo Card, and sight-seeing tours. To request information/accommodations in advance, write to Tourist Information, Oslo Sentralstasjon, Jernbanetorget 1, N-0154, Oslo.
- **Train information** is located in Oslo Sentral's main concourse area on the left-hand side just prior to the moving walkways. Hours: Monday–Saturday 0700–2300; Sunday 0700–2330. If possible, get the information you need from the regular arrival and departure digital bulletin boards installed throughout the station. Departures carry the heading AVGAENDE TOG, and arrivals are labeled ANKOMMENDE TOG.
- **Train reservations** and railpass validation are handled at window No. 4 in the ticket office of the main lobby. The ticket windows are marked BILLETTER, and any of the other windows can assist you if No. 4 is closed. This office can also make sleeping-car reservations.

Tourist Information/Hotel Reservations

Tourist Information Office: Brynjulf Bulls plass 1, N0250 Oslo; *Tel:* 47 23 11 78 80; *Fax:* 47 22 83 81 50; *Guide Service: Tel:* 47 22 42 70 20

Hours: October–March, 0900–1600 Monday–Friday; April–May, 0900–1700 Monday–Saturday; June–August, 0900–1900 Monday–Sunday; September, 0900–1700 Monday–Saturday

Notes: The Tourist Information Centre is located opposite Oslo's City Hall in the old railway station building "Vestbanen."

The attitude of the personnel at the Information Centre is, "If we can't tell you what you need to know, we can tell you who does and where to go to get it."

The Information Centre provides details on Oslo and its surrounding

Train Connections to Other Base Cities from Oslo

Depart from Oslo Sentral Station

DEPART	TRAIN NUMBER	ARRIVE	NOTES
		Copenhagen (København) H.	
2300	BUS 393/R 1023	0759	R, 1
		Hamburg	
2300	BUS 393/EC 38	1216+1	R, 1
		Helsinki	
0730	IC 55	0930+1	R, 2
		Stockholm Central	
0730	IN 55	1325	R
1522	IN 59	2130	R, exc Sun

Daily, unless otherwise noted
R Reservations required
+1 Arrive next day
At press time, overnight bus service replacing train service Copenhagen–Mälmo.
1. Change or board trains in Malmö.
2. Change trains in Stockholm to ship overnight, then change trains in Turku.

OSLO

regions plus selected destinations throughout Norway; houses a nice cafe, interesting gallery, gift shop, and newspaper kiosk; and it neighbors a restaurant serving "Norway's best food in a contemporary setting at an attractive price."

- **Hotel reservations** can be made in the tourist information office across from City Hall or in the one next door to the money-exchange office in Oslo Sentral Station. This service is operated by Oslo Promotion. It will make reservations for you in hotels, pensions, and private homes (NOK 20 fee per booking). Oslo Promotion has an exceptional track record. Few, if any, are ever turned away though the entire town is "fully booked." Oslo is one of the few European cities where you can arrive without an advance reservation and still be reasonably certain of lodgings that night.

Ask for the *Oslo Package* brochure. This package combines your hotel (choose from 42 selected hotels), accommodations, including breakfast, and the Oslo Card. Prices start from NOK 450 per person, per night, double occupancy.

Tourist information and hotel bookings for Oslo are also available from the tourist information office in the Sentral Station.

Be certain to ask for *The Official Guide for Oslo,* since it will aid you in seeing the various attractions in and around Oslo.

Getting Around in Oslo

Both tourist offices plus most Oslo hotels sell the **"Oslo Card,"** which provides unlimited use of city transportation by bus, train, tram, suburban railway, and ferry within Oslo's boundaries as well as up to four fare-stages within **Akershus.** The card includes free admission to more than 50 attractions and museums, various sight-seeing discounts, a free tour by boat (May through mid-August), discounts at local eateries such as Restaurant Dan Turell and Tryvannstua, and a surprise on the menu at Holmenkollen Restaurant and Brasserie 45. Reductions are also available at several shops (don't leave town without an authentic Norwegian sweater), ski lift tickets, theme parks and even Oslo by Horse.

The Oslo Card can be valid for 24, 48, or 72 hours and may be purchased at the following NOK rates: 24 hours, 180; 48 hours, 290; 72 hours, 410. Children's cards are 60, 80, and 110 NOK and family rates are 400 NOK.

Sights/Attractions/Tours

Visitors desiring personal-guide services can contact Guideservice or *Tel:* 22–427020 for reservations and tariffs. Students, taxi drivers, and couriers are not permitted to arrange paid guided tours in Oslo and for the museums.

A variety of tours in and around the city are available. For details call at the tourist information office or consult your hotel. You may book the standard sightseeing bus tours, which normally take 3 hours to complete, or you may want to opt for one of the more specialized tours combining bus and boat transportation. You will find them listed in *What's On in Oslo* and *The Official Guide for Oslo and Surrounding Area.*

With so much good weather on hand, it is only natural that the majority of Oslo's sight-seeing services concentrate their schedules into the summer months. In the period beginning with April and ending with October, a myriad of sight-seeing opportunities are available to visitors. Fjord cruises from 50 minutes' duration to several hours are available. Likewise, there are land-and-water combinations to select from that include (among other attractions) a visit to the **Kon-Tiki Raft Museum,** a cruise on the **Oslofjord,** and a view from the top of the famous **Holmenkollen ski jump.**

The usual types of city bus tours are also available, along with a wide selection of things to be seen. There's an old adage that when the weather is nice, you will never find anyone home in Oslo. That is true. Chances are, you will find that many of the passengers on your tour bus or boat are townspeople enjoying the view along with you.

Information describing **Bygdoy** and many other attractions in Oslo is available at the tourist information office, at the Oslo Sentral Station, or from the Tourist Information Centre.

Visit Oslo's famous **Vigeland Park** while you are in town. Among the 193 granite and bronze statues by sculptor Gustav Vigeland, you will be able to examine *The Monolith,* the world's largest granite sculpture.

All members of the family will enjoy a visit to **Akershus,** a medieval castle built in the twelfth century and reconstructed as a fortress during the seventeenth century. Standing at the front of Oslo's City Hall, you can see the fort off to your left. Akershus's military atmosphere is aided by the presence of two military museums. The **Norwegian Resistance Museum** chronicles Norway's struggle against the Nazis, and the **Norwegian Armed**

Forces Museum traces the country's military history from the Vikings to World War II. The fort maintains a garrison of armed sentries who patrol the grounds in dress uniform and plumed headdress.

During your stay in Scandinavia's oldest capital—Oslo was established in 1050 by Harald Hardrade—you should plan to visit the world-famous **Kon-Tiki** raft, the polar vessel **Fram,** and the collection of viking ships on exhibition at Bygdoy, across the harbor from the city hall. Each vessel bears a proud history in nautical accomplishments.

Day Excursions

When you consider that Norway is larger than the British Isles, you can readily appreciate why we deviate from our usual Base City–Day Excursion format for Oslo. An "out-and-back" excursion between Oslo and **Bergen** offers an almost limitless variety of travel modes and a visit to the fjord at **Flam.**

Within our usual Base City–Day Excursion concept, we selected a variety of daytime trips that will permit you to see the beautiful fjords, lakes, and mountains without daily packing and unpacking.

A day excursion to the towns of **Larvik** and **Skien** takes you into Norway's seacoast towns for a look at some breathtaking scenery as well as a close look at the country's ports.

Hamar lies to the north of Oslo. Its day excursion affords inspection of the countryside surrounding the town and its extensive railroad museum.

The northernmost day excursion takes you to **Lillehammer,** site of the 1994 Winter Olympics and one of Norway's best known summer-and-winter resorts.

OSLO

Day Excursion to

Bergen
And the Fjord at Flam

Depart from Oslo Sentral Station
Distance by Train: 293 miles (471 km)
Average Train Time: 6 hours, 40 minutes
Tourist Information Office: Vågsallmenningen 1
Tel: 55 32 14 80; **Fax:** 55 32 14 64
Internet: www.visitBergen.com
E-mail: info@visitBergen.com
Hours: June–August, 0830–2200 daily; May and September, 0900–2000. Rest of year, 0900–1600 Monday–Saturday.
Notes: Located by the fish market harbor. There is a map in the station that will point the way. When you exit the main door of the rail station, continue straight ahead for about 600–700 meters. There is also an information desk at the ticket office in the rail station where you can obtain a city map and purchase the Bergen Card.

B ergen is Norway's second largest city. It is beautifully framed by seven mountains. One cable car and one funicular terminate at mountaintop restaurants overlooking the city. Bergen has a fish market that also has live fish, a sixteenth-century town hall, and a twelfth-century cathedral. **Troldhaugen** is the home of Edvard Grieg (1843–1907), the most distinguished Norwegian composer of the nineteenth century. The city has a 300-year-old wooden village (**"Old Bergen"**), a symphony orchestra founded in 1765, and the oldest performing theater in Norway. Inseparable from the sea, Bergen also has the largest aquarium in northern Europe.

Founded in 1070 by King Olaf Kyrre, Bergen grew quickly as a commercial center, and during the twelfth and thirteenth centuries, it was the capital of Norway. Built mainly of wood, the buildings were highly susceptible to fire, and the city suffered severe fires in 1702, 1855, and 1916. Bergen was badly damaged during World War II, when it was occupied by the Germans.

This excursion has more route options than a cat has lives. The variations are such that we can list only a few. The daily train service between Oslo and Bergen has three daytime trains and one overnight train in each direction. During summer, a fourth train operates daily except Saturday. The overnight trains haul sleeping cars between Oslo and Bergen.

Express boats cruise between Bergen and Flam from mid-May to mid-September. As a result, many options are available in both time and mode. Before examining some of the options, let's look at the destinations and some of the reasons for going.

Flam is the terminus of a famously spectacular railway—the **Flam Railway** (Flamsbanen). As the train journeys through the steep and narrow Flam Valley, you're surrounded by astonishing waterfalls and mighty mountain peaks. The train slowly climbs 2,838 feet in only 12½ miles. From mid-April to mid-October, it makes a photo stop near the breathtaking Kjosfossen Waterfalls. The Flam Railways is not included on railpasses; however, holders of Eurailpass, Eurail Selectpass, Scanrailpass, and Norway Railpass receive a 30 percent discount.

Option 1, Oslo–Bergen:	June 17– September 16	September 17– January 5
Train from Oslo	0631	0811
To Myrdal	1153	1246
Change trains and depart from Myrdal	1203	1255
To Flam	1300	1345
Boat from Flam	1500	1500
To Gudvangen	1700	1700
Bus from Gudvangen	1715	1715
To Voss	1835	1815
Train from Voss	1915	1915
To Bergen	2035	2035

Option 2, Bergen–Oslo:	September 17–January 5
Train from Bergen	0840
To Voss	0953
Bus from Voss	1000
To Gudvangen	1125
Boat from Gudvangen	1130
To Flam	1330
Train from Flam	1655
To Myrdal	1735
Train from Myrdal	1750*
To Oslo	2228

* $10 (U.S.) per person seat reservation required.

Notes on Oslo-Bergen railway "New Express": About 30 minutes after stopping at Drammen, the railway travels above the timberline. When you reach Finse, you'll see the looming Hardanger Glacier. Further west, you enter the Finse Tunnel, the highest point on your way to Myrdal. As you descend toward Bergen, you pass through the longest tunnel on this route—the 5-mile Ulriken Tunnel.

To see **"Norway in a Nutshell"** with the Norwegian State Railways's Combination Tours, call Scantours, Inc. in the U.S. at (800) 223–7226, or fax (310) 390–0493, or visit www.scantours.com.

OSLO *Bergen*

Day Excursion to

Hamar
Heart of Norway's Lake Country

Depart from Oslo Sentral Station
Distance by Train: 78 miles (126 km)
Average Train Time: 1 hour, 45 minutes
Tourist Information Office: Hamar Rådhus, 2326 Hamar
Tel: 62510200; *Fax:* 62544211
E-mail: touristinfo@hamarregionen.net
Hours: 0800–1700 Monday–Friday, 1000–1500 Saturday
Notes: Located to the left just outside the railway station.

On September 17, 1976, en route to Hamar for the first time, we wrote, "This train passes through some of God's most beautiful countryside along one of His most beautiful lakes." That has not changed.

The countryside is the rich farmland of **Hedemarken,** and the lake is Norway's largest, **Lake Mjosa.** The lake is 75 miles long, and every foot of it is beautiful.

For a special treat cruise Lake Mjosa on the oldest operating paddle steamer in the world, the *Skibladner,* built in 1856. Ask the tourist office for excursion timetables and fares. For information in advance *E-mail:* skibladner@online.no; *Internet:* www.skibladner.no.

Hamar is situated on the eastern side of Lake Mjosa at its widest point. The train from Oslo traverses the river Vorma from Eidsvoll to Mirucsund and then continues along the eastern shore of Lake Mjosa to Hamar. Watch for the bridge that the train crosses about 1 hour and 10 minutes out of Oslo. Station yourself on the right side of the coach for a spectacular view down the lake from the vantage point of the bridge as the train crosses.

It seems that you have hardly settled in your seat when the train glides to a stop in Hamar. Time will pass even more quickly here, for there is much to see and do in this most pleasant city. Two of its feature attractions are the **Hedmark Museum** and the **Norwegian State Railways Museum.** These are not stuffy old buildings crowded with relics. Both are spacious, outdoor areas with fascinating displays of what rural and railroad life was like in Norway's earlier times.

Check with the tourist office regarding transportation to the museums. Both can be reached by public bus. If you prefer a taxi, you will find a taxi stand on your right when leaving the station. Fares by taxi to either museum are about NOK 50–60 one-way for a maximum of four persons.

Within the Hedmark Museum boundaries is the **Hamardomen,** enclosing the remains of a medieval cathedral built in 1152. Designed by architect Kjell Lund of Lund & Slaatto Arkitekter, Ltd., and completed in 1998, the glass-and-steel protective enclosure is a unique architectural and technical masterpiece. It is climate controlled to prevent any further deterioration of the cathedral's remains. The ruins reveal that it was one of the most magnificent churches in Scandinavia. History proves that the town of Hamar suffered along with the demise of the stately church. Years of civil strife and the Reformation practically wiped out what was once a thriving city.

It was not until 1849 that Hamar once again enjoyed the status and charter of a town. Marking this return to status, the present Hamar Cathedral, replacing its medieval predecessor, was built in 1886.

The museum area also includes forty buildings from the county of Hedmark. Most of them date back from the fifteenth to the eighteenth centuries. One unusual building, the house of a Norwegian emigrant, was built in North Dakota in 1871 and moved to the museum in 1973.

The **Odden Restaurant,** on the museum grounds, is open for business from mid-May to mid-September each year. From mid-June through mid-August, the museum is open from 1000 to 1800 daily. During the balance of the year, it is open for groups by appointment only.

The railway museum rivals anything the Disney folks have come up with to date. If you are a railroad buff, don't miss this stop. Included in its collection of rolling stock are the old royal train, several "stagecoach" types, and even an old fourth-class (or, shall we say, no-class) wagon—without seats.

Oslo—Hamar

DEPART OSLO SENTRAL	TRAIN NUMBER	ARRIVE HAMAR	NOTES
0757	IC 307	0927	Mon–Sat
0837	Et 43	0956	R
0857	IC 309	1023	Mon–Fri
0957	IC 311	1130	
1157	IC 315	1326	

DEPART HAMAR	TRAIN NUMBER	ARRIVE OSLO SENTRAL	NOTES
1504	IC 322	1634	exc. Sat
1610	IC 324	1734	
1810	IC 328	1934	
2009	IC 332	2134	
2130	Et 46	2253	R

Daily, unless otherwise noted
R Reservations required
Distance: 78 miles (126 km)

Norway's first railway station is among the many buildings found on the 7½-acre tract covered by the museum. It is open daily from mid-May through mid-September, 1000–1600, and during July 1000–1800.

When the Norwegian government closed the Aurskog-Hoeland railway in 1960, two steam locomotives and a selection of rolling stock from the narrow-gauge line were given to the railway museum together with many structures from this private railway that began operation in 1896. The museum also has eleven standard-gauge and four narrow-gauge engines—all in operating condition.

Hamar's railway museum is the oldest in Scandinavia, and it is also the oldest technical museum in Norway. No doubt it will still be in full operation during the Norwegian Railway Bicentennial in 2054.

Hamar is also a sporting town, and its Olympic halls can attest to that. Visit Hamar's **Olympia Hall**, the "Viking Ship," and the **Hamar Olympic Amphi Hall** (or the "Northern Lights Hall"). The Viking Ship is one of the largest sports halls in the world and was the architectural symbol of the 1994 Winter Olympics. The Northern Lights Hall is the world's largest wooden building. Check with the tourist office for opening times.

Day Excursion to
Larvik and Skien
Fjord Country

Depart from Oslo Sentral Station
Distance by Train: 120 miles (193 km) to Skien
Average Train Time: 2 hours, 30 minutes
Tourist Information Offices:
Larvik: Larvik Tourist Office, Box 200, Storgate 48, 3251 Larvik (located across from
    the rail station.)
    Tel: 47 33 13 91 00; **Fax:** 47 33 13 91 11
    Internet: www.visitlarvik.no
Skien: Skien Turist Kontor, Nedre Hjellegat 18, 3724 Skien
    Tel: 47 3590–5520; **Fax:** 47 3590–5530
    Hours: Monday–Friday, 0830–1600; summer (May–August), Monday–Friday
        0830–1900 and Saturday–Sunday 0900–1600
    Internet: www.grenland.no
    E-mail: info@grenland.no

If there's a fjord in your future, you'll probably find it on this day excursion. The greater part of that huge seaway known as the Oslofjord unfolds its grandeur as the train wends its way to Larvik and Skien. The sight of huge tankers and ocean liners miles from the ocean, plying between tree-covered mountains, is a breathtaking sight. You are certain to enjoy this outing.

As the train leaves Larvik en route to Skien, you'll also leave the fjords but begin to travel in an area of beautiful lakes connected by streams running through a wooded countryside. This, too, is fascinating and well worth the trip.

Because a train departs the Oslo Sentral Station on the Oslo–Drammen–Larvik–Skien line every 2 hours throughout the day, you might consider leaving the train at any point that catches your interest and returning to board the train that follows to continue your journey. It's a nice option to take.

You'll need to seek out the local tourist information office in some of the places you elect to stop, and the train gives you an excellent preview of what each town has to offer as you approach. Basically, the route through Larvik takes you to typical Norwegian seafaring towns, and each seems to offer a different type of land- and seascape. In a sense, you'll be window shopping, so be prepared to leave the train on impulse.

A summary of the cities the train passes follows. Be sure to take along a copy of the Norwegian State Railways schedule for this line in order to plan the follow-on portion of your trip as you go.

OSLO

Larvik and Skien

Drammen (40 kilometers from Oslo): Important center of Norway's timber and paper industries. There are many attractive buildings in town dating back to the seventeenth century. Have your camera handy—the city covers the headwaters of the Drammensfjorden, where it joins the river, and the docks teem with seafaring activities.

Tonsberg (103 kilometers from Oslo): The oldest town in Norway and the seat for centuries of its Viking kings. The Oseberg Viking ship now resting in the Oslo Viking Museum was found in a nearby burial mound. The ruins of a Viking castle overlook the town.

Sandefjord (127 kilometers from Oslo): Home of the Norwegian whaling fleet. Regardless of your opinions about this industry, there's a whaling museum in town, and there's a spectacular whaling monument in the center of the town square. The coastline around Sandefjord is spotted with many islands and inlets, making it very photogenic.

Larvik (146 kilometers from Oslo): The city has its own fjord, which connects to the Lagen River. The beautiful lake country we mentioned begins immediately beyond its city limits. An interesting museum is housed in **Herregarden,** a seventeenth-century manor house built for the counts of Larvik. The building is one of Norway's best-preserved wooden structures. A world-famous mineral water, Farris, originates here. Many of the small fishing harbors along the coast are accessible by bus. For ferry service from Larvik to **Frederikshavn,** Denmark, *Tel:* (625) 810–00811.

Prior to your visit, write to the Larvik Tourist Office for interesting booklets describing the Larvik district tourist attractions. Otherwise, when in Larvik visit the tourist office at Storgate 48, across from the rail station.

Skien (193 kilometers from Oslo): Situated where the Skien River and Lake Hjelle meet, this city has been an active trading center since A.D. 900. Sawmills were an important part of its industry. The first began here in the sixteenth century. Skien is the birthplace of Henrik Ibsen (1828–1906), famous Norwegian playwright. Ibsen's well-constructed plays dealing realistically with psychological and social problems won him recognition as the Father of Modern Drama.

Brekke Park, which looks out over the river and the town of Skien, warrants a visit. There you will find the **Museum of Telemark and Grenland.** (Skien is the administrative center for the district of Telemark.) In the park there are a number of old houses from different parts of the district, including a reconstruction of Ibsen's childhood home, **Venstøp.** The **Telemark Canal** starts in Skien and stretches 105 kilometers into the country. Canal boats sail daily in the summer. For more information contact the Skien tourist office.

Rather than return to Oslo by retracing your route back through Larvik and the other coastal towns, you might want to return to Oslo via the main rail line running from Stavanger on the North Sea. Board train 2582, which departs from Skien at 1454 to Nordagutu, where you'll arrive at 1526. Look around Nordagutu, then board train 80 at 1702, bound for Oslo. You will arrive in the Oslo Sentral Station promptly at 1858.

A. Oslo—Larvik—Skien—Oslo

Depart Oslo Sentral	Train Number	Depart Larvik	Arrive Skien
0739	IC 805	0947	1030
0939	IC 809	1147	1230
1139	IC 813	1347	1430
1339	IC 817	1547	1631

Depart Skien	Train Number	Depart Larvik	Arrive Oslo Sentral
1305	IC 822	1349	1552
1505	IC 826	1549	1752
1700	IC 830	1749	1952
1900	IC 834	1949	2152
2100	IC 838	2149	2352

other departures during week and seasonally.

B. Oslo—Skien—Larvik—Oslo (circuitous route via Nordagutu)

Depart Oslo Sentral	Train Number	Arrive Nordagutu	Depart Nordagutu	Train Number	Arrive Skien	Notes
0711	E 73	0856	1013	R 2575	1045	R
1111	E 77	1300	1422	R 2579	1454	R

Depart Skien	Train Number	Aarrive Nordagutu	Depart Nordagutu	Train Number	Arrive Oslo Sentral	Notes
1454	R 2582	1526	1702	E 80	1858	R
1819	R 2588	1851	1914	E 82	2058	R

See tables in section A above for return from Skien via Larvik to Oslo Sentral.

Daily, unless otherwise noted
R Reservations required
Distance: 120 miles (193 km) to Skien

Day Excursion to

Lillehammer
Norway's Vacation Center

Depart from Oslo Sentral Station
Distance by Train: 114 miles (184 km)
Average Train Time: 2 hours, 35 minutes
Tourist Information Office: 19 Elvegata
Tel: 61 25 92 99; **Fax:** 61 26 96 55
Internet: www.lillehammerturist.no
E-mail: info@lillehammerturist.no
Hours: Summer, Monday–Saturday, 0900–2100; Sunday 1100–1800. The office remains open a few extra hours during late June, July, and early August. The remainder of the year, the office is open Monday–Friday 0900–1600 and Saturday 1000-1400.
Notes: The office is only about a 5-minute walk from the rail station. Just follow the signs.

This day excursion is one of the most northerly of any appearing in *Europe by Eurail.* Thanks to its latitude, Lillehammer is a famous summer resort and an important winter-sports center as well, with more than 300 miles of prepared ski runs. Snow conditions for skiing are good from December until April, and the long summer evenings are perfect for enjoying the town's beautiful parks and recreation areas. No matter what the season, outdoors is how to enjoy Lillehammer.

If you have succumbed to the charm of Hamar, then you have already been introduced to the beauty of its Lake Mjosa. The train ride to Lillehammer will permit you to see the balance of the lake, because Lillehammer lies 35 miles to the north of Hamar. Here, Lake Mjosa narrows to the Lagen River and, in doing so, provides a scenic blend of green forest-lands and the special green color of the river. If you have ever wondered what most of the world was like before pollution, here is your answer.

Lillehammer served as the site for the 1994 Olympic Winter Games. The ski-jumps tower, with a view of the entire town, is open 0900–2000 in the summer and 1100–1600 in the winter. For those of us not in attendance at the 1994 games, the **Norwegian Olympic Museum** in Håkons Hall offers a chance to revisit them. History of both summer and winter games plus the relevance of sport in society are highlighted from the beginning of the Olympics to present day. The exhibit is translated into four languages, including English; the entrance fee includes a ticket for Maihaugen Museum.

Among the city's attractions, the **Museum of Historical Vehicles** opens at 1000 from mid-June through mid-August and at 1100 the remainder of

Oslo–Lillehammer

DEPART OSLO SENTRAL	TRAIN NUMBER	ARRIVE LILLEHAMMER	NOTES
0837	Et 43	1036	R
0957	IC 311	1215	
1157	IC 315	1416	
1357	IC 319	1616	

DEPART LILLEHAMMER	TRAIN NUMBER	ARRIVE OSLO SENTRAL	NOTES
1519	IC 324	1734	
1719	IC 328	1934	
1851	E 44	2053	R, exc. Sat
1917	IC 332	2134	
2046	Et 46	2253	R

Daily, unless otherwise noted
R Reservations required
Distance: 114 miles (184 km)

the year. Just north of Lillehammer you may visit **Lilleputhammer,** a scale model town of 62 miniature houses, where kids can romp at **Hunderfossen Family Park.** Ask the tourist office for details.

The city's stellar attraction is a 100-acre open-air museum known as **Maihaugen.** It is within easy walking distance of the tourist information office. The office can provide you with a city map as well as several brochures describing the Maihaugen Museum. The museum area is divided into three sections, and each depicts a different mode of Norwegian life. Its origins spring from the private collection of a dentist, Dr. Anders Sandvig.

As a young dentist just out of school, Dr. Sandvig came to Lillehammer in 1885. He soon learned that many of his patients preferred to pay him with products rather than cash. Sometimes it was a farm implement or a piece of furniture. Dr. Sandvig's practice grew, and so did his collection. Eventually, he laid out the museum area and began filling it with old buildings, which he acquired and transported to Lillehammer. Apparently, the museum business was more rewarding than dentistry, for Dr. Sandvig retired from the profession to run the museum personally, which he did until 1946, when he died at the age of eighty-four.

The museum was founded in 1887. There are 185 old buildings in the museum with handicrafts sections of 60 workshops demonstrating skills of the local artisans. Museum hours: June–August 15, 0900–1800 daily; August 16–September 30, 1000–1700 daily; October 1–May 16, 1100–1600 Tuesday–Sunday (closed Monday); May 18–May 31, 1000–1700 daily. For more information *E-mail:* post@maihaugen.museum.no or visit *Internet:*

OSLO
Lillehammer

www.maihaugen.museum.no. One of the most interesting objects of Norway's past on exhibit in the museum is the **Garmo Stave Church,** which was built in the Ottadal Valley area in the eleventh century and reassembled at the museum in 1920. Another interesting exhibit is "Slowly We Conquered Our Country," Norwegian history from the Ice Age until tomorrow.

In the dock area of the city from mid-June to mid-August, you can see the *Skibladner,* a paddle-wheel steamer launched in 1856 and still in service today. Its nickname is *White Swan.* True to tradition, salmon and strawberries are served onboard. It is really difficult to accept the fact that the vessel is now more than 130 years old and is in as good a condition now as the day it was launched. Some things do get better with age!

Art lovers will not want to miss the **Lillehammer Art Museum,** one of the leading visual-art centers of Norway. Exhibits alternate between international and Norwegian art from the 1800s through today, with the core of the permanent collection composed of works by artists such as Dahl, Gude, and Munch. Guided tours run Saturday and Sunday 1400–1500 or by prearrangement with the museum. Open Tuesday through Sunday 1100–1600, closed Monday. Tickets are adults NOK 50; children under 16, free; and group rate NOK 40. *Internet:* www.lillehammerartmuseum.com. *E-mail:* post@lilleham-merartmuseum.com for further information.

After visiting Lillehammer, if you would like to return to Oslo via a different route, board the bus to **Gjovik** in front of the railway station at 1550. You arrive in Gjovik at 1650. Board the train for Oslo that departs at 1934. This train returns to Oslo by a different route and arrives in the Oslo Sentral Station at 2139. The train service is one-class only, but it's always clean and neat.

The bus fare from Lillehammer to Gjovik is NOK 85. You will have time to do some fast sight-seeing in this charming little town on the west shore of Lake Mjosa before departing on the 1934 train to Oslo.

Portugal

Visitors to Portugal will find old world traditions, charm, and culture well preserved. Each province retains its own heritage and individual characteristics, and its history can be traced through its medieval cities and ancient palaces, castles, and cathedrals.

An independent kingdom since 1143, Portugal is one of the oldest nations in Europe. In fact, 10,000-year-old cave paintings have been uncovered in the northern reaches of Portugal and are said to be Europe's greatest outdoor gallery of Stone Age art. Portugal's museums contain some of the finest collections in the world, reflecting its exposure to rich cultures explored by Portuguese navigators of the fifteenth and sixteenth centuries.

But Portugal is more than antiquity. Its geography is diverse, making it a popular holiday destination for travelers from all over the world. You will find wonderful white-sand beaches, crystal-clear mountain streams, and some of the finest golf courses in all of Europe. You'll even find fun and games at glamorous casinos and discos.

Portuguese is the national language, with English and French being the second languages. Though some words are similar to the Spanish language, Portuguese is its own language and not a Spanish dialect. According to the Portuguese National Tourist Office, Portugal is "a vision for the future." For more information about Portugal, contact the Portuguese National Tourist Office of North America: *Internet:* **www. portugal.org.**

New York: 590 Fifth Avenue, Fourth Floor, New York, NY 10036. *Tel:* (212) 719–3985 or (800) PORTUGAL; *Fax:* (212) 719–4091

Montreal: 500 Sherbrooke Street West, Suite 940, Montreal QC H3A 3C6. *Tel:* (514) 282–1264; *Fax:* (514) 499–1450

Toronto: 60 Bloor Street, Suite 1005, Toronto, Ontario M4W 3B8. *Tel:* (416) 921–7376; *Fax:* (416) 921–1353

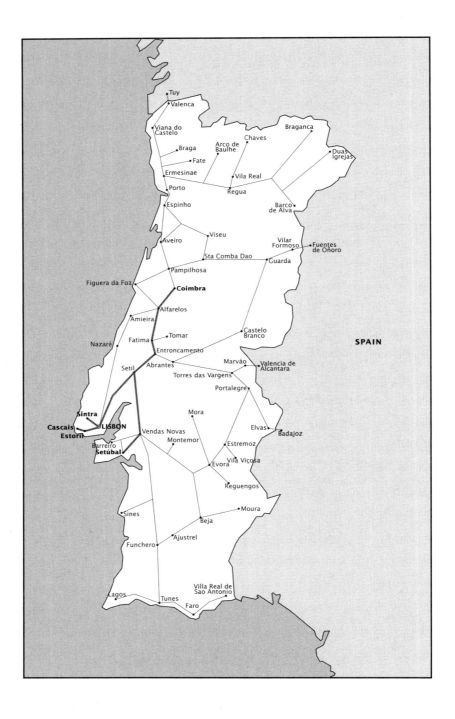

Tuy
Valenca

Viana do
Castelo
Braganca
Chaves
Arco de
Braga   Baulhe
Fate   Duas
Ermesinae   Vila Real   Igrejas
Porto   Regua
Espinho   Barco
de Alva

Aveiro   Viseu
Vilar   Fuentes
Formoso   de Oñoro
Sta Comba Dao   Guarda
Pampilhosa
Figuera da Foz   Coimbra

Alfarelos
Amieira
Fatima   Tomar   Castelo
Nazaré   Branco
Entroncamento
Setil   Abrantes   Marváo   Valencia de
Torres das Vargens   Alcantara
Portalegre
Sintra   Mora
Cascais LISBON   Elvas
Estoril   Badajoz
Barreiro Vendas Novas
Setúbal   Montemor Estremoz
Vila Viçosa
Evora
Reguengos

Sines   Moura
Beja
Funchero Ajustrel

Villa Real de
Sao Antonio
Lagos Tunes
Faro

SPAIN

Banking

- **Currency:** Euro (€)
- **Exchange rate at press time:** €1.10 = U.S. $1.00

Communications

- **Country Code:** 351
  Portugal Telecom operates the public telephones, including pay, Credifone, and TLP Card telephones.
  Use 00 before the country code to dial internationally from Portugal.

Rail Travel in Portugal

Portugal's rail system, **Caminhos de Ferro Portugueses** (CP), offers rail information by telephone. CP Information: *Tel:* (01) 888–4025, available 0800–2300 for Alfa and Intercity Lines; *Tel:* (01) 888–5092, available 0800–2300; or *Tel:* (01) 790–1004, 24 hours. *Internet:* www.cp.pt

The CP accepts **Eurail passes, Europass,** the **Iberic Flexipass,** and the **Portuguese RailPass.** The Portuguese RailPass is valid for first-class travel for any 4 days within a 15-day period, $103. Children age 4–11 are half fare. The Iberic Flexipass is valid for unlimited rail travel for 3 days within 2 months in Portugal and Spain. First class, $205; additional days are $45 each (a maximum of 7 extra days may be purchased). Supplements are required on the AVE and Talgo high-speed trains. Children 4–11 travel at half the adult fare, and children under age 4 travel free.

Interregional trains commute through the various regions of Portugal, while CP's Intercity service links about 60 Portuguese cities to Lisbon or Porto. The express **Alfa** service connects Lisbon, Porto, and Braga with four trains in each direction conveying both first- and second-class service. Alfa and Intercity should be reserved at least 24 hours in advance.

Two other international train connections are available between Porto and Vigo (Spain) and between Lisbon and Badajoz (Spain).

PORTUGAL

Base City:
Lisbon
(Lisboa)

City Dialing Code: 21

Lisbon (Lisboa), Portugal's largest city, is the capital and primary gateway for visitors from North America. It's also the center of the country's rail network and the major industrial and commercial area.

Built on the terraced sides of the hills overlooking the harbor, languid Lisbon is an excellent gateway to the Iberian peninsula and a good base for rail travel thoughout Portugal.

Arriving by Air

Lisbon International Airport (Portela), 5 miles north of Lisbon. *Tel:* 841–6990.

Airport–City Links: Passengers connect to Lisbon's Santa Apolonia railway station via the Green line (*Linha Verde*) every 15 minutes, 0700–2100. Fare, €1.30, but luggage space is limited.

Taxi fare from the airport to the city center (journey time: 15–20 minutes) averages about €6–10, depending on your destination and how much luggage you have. Taxis are metered; a tip is appreciated. The new "Taxi Voucher," a system of pre-paid travel vouchers for €10.97 or €13.97 (depending on the number of zones covered by the journey) may be purchased at the Lisbon Tourist Association desk.

Tourist information at the airport, *Tel:* 844–6473. Open 0600–2400 daily. Look for the sign ASSOCIACÃO DE TURISMO DE LISBOA.

Arriving by Train

Lisbon has four stations and a ferryboat terminal and is the main gateway to other cities in Portugal. **Santa Apolonia** station is Lisbon's international link and the western terminus of most European rail traffic. However, you can also arrive in Lisbon at the "Terreiro do Paço" south railway station, with the train departing from Vila Real St. Antónia to

Barreiro (and then the ferry connection) if you come from Seville (Spain).

- **Money exchange** is on the left side as you exit from the trains, beyond Porta (Gate) 47.
- **Rail information** (CP) **and tourist information:** Turn to the right as you exit from the trains and walk past ticket window No. 1. Hours: 0900–2200.
- **Railpass validation:** Porta (Gate) 47. Hours 1000–1800 daily. Buses No. 9, 39, and 46 run from Santa Apolónia Station to the Rossio Station in downtown Lisbon. The fare may be minimal, but buses frequently are crowded, making it rather difficult for you and your suitcase to board the same bus at the same time. Because taxi fares are reasonable and metered, leave your forays on Lisbon's public transportation system for when your luggage is safely stowed in your hotel room.

Rossio Station, at Praça do Rossio (Rossio Square), is located in the heart of Lisbon in a lovely nineteenth-century Neo-Gothic building. It is on the immediate left of the Teatro Nacional D. Maria II (National Theater). Rossio Station serves as the commuter station to locations west of Lisbon (from Cacem Station to Figueira da Foz). Trains depart for Sintra on tracks 4 and 5 every 16 minutes.

Campolide Station, the first station past Rossio, is the stop for the Alcantara commuter to Cascais or for travel to Azambuja.

Cais do Sodre Station is where trains from Estoril and Cascais terminate.

Terreiro do Paco Station is the ferryboat terminal for crossings to Barreiro Station on the east bank of the Tagus River. From Barreiro trains depart for cities in the Algarve.

Tourist Information/Hotel Reservations

Internet: www.cm-lisboa.pt/turismo/

Available in rail stations, at Praça dos Restauradores in the Palácio Foz building (*Tel:* 346–6307; Hours: 0900–2000 daily); or at the Lisbon Card office in the same building (*Tel:* 343–3314; Hours: 0900–1800).

To reach it, take a taxi or bus No. 9, 46, or 39 to Praça dos Restauradores. It is opposite the post office, near Rossio Station. The building, Palácio Foz (Foz Palace), has three main doors. Enter the one on the left marked Turismo. Hours: 0930–1800.

Hotel reservations can be made at the rail stations' combined train and tourist information offices.

Getting Around in Lisbon

Electric, cable-car–like trams provide inexpensive and enjoyable transport to many parts of the city. Historic Belem, for instance, can be reached via tram 15—an alternative to taking the train from Cais do Sodre station.

Train Connections to Other Base Cities from Lisbon (Lisboa)

Depart	Train Number	Arrive	Notes
		Madrid Chamartin	
2205	TLG 335	0825+1	R, Sleeper
		Paris Gare Montparnasse	
1805	311/TGV 8530	1620+1	R, 1, Sleeper

Daily, unless otherwise noted
R Reservations required
+1 Arrive next day
1. Change in Hendaye.

Of super value is the **Lisboa Card,** which provides unlimited travel on the public transportation system (CARRIS), including buses, trams, and the metro (underground) system; free entry to 26 museums, monuments, and other attractions that normally charge admission; and discounts at certain shops. It is truly your "password" to the city.

The Lisboa Card is available at the Central Office, at Palácio Foz; at Jerónimos Monastery, Praça do Imperio; at the National Museum of Ancient Art, Rua das Janelas Verdes; and at various CARRIS offices.

One-day Lisboa Card, €10.97; 2-day, €17.96; 3-day, €22.94; children age 5–11 pay €4.39, €6.18, and €8.73, respectively.

Other value cards also may be purchased at the tourist information offices, including:

* The "Lisboa Restaurant Card," which offers no less than 10 percent discount on your bill at more than 40 restaurants, within a 72–hour validity period.
* The "Lisboa Shopping Card," which provides 5–20 percent discount at more than 200 shops.

Attractions/Tours

Tourist offices or your hotel can arrange for a sight-seeing tour of Lisbon. Or, ask the tourist office for the guide booklet *Lisboa Step by Step,* purchase a Lisboa Card, and conduct your own tour. Highlights of any tour will include the sixteenth-century **Jerónimos Monastery** and the **Tower of Belém** in the Belém district. Lisbon's more modern side can be seen by visiting the **Discoveries Monument** (Centro Cultural das Descobertas), inaugurated in 1960. Another symbol of Lisbon is the **25 de April Bridge** spanning the Tagus River, which is equal to the Golden Gate Bridge of San Fransisco in its structural beauty.

Completed for Expo '98, Lisbon's **Vasco da Gama bridge** is a massive engineering feat. The bridge is 17 kilometers long—making it the longest bridge in Europe—1 kilometer longer than the one between Sweden and

Denmark. Besides providing another modern symbol of Lisbon, it provides much-needed relief of traffic congestion crossing the Tagus River, especially during the summer. The **Vasco da Gama Steel Tower** (the tallest building in Portugal) and the impressive **Lisboa Oceanarium** contribute to the east side's modern attractions.

Lisbon has three distinct districts—the shopping areas clustered around **Rossio, Baixa,** and **Chiado;** the more ancient areas, such as the Moorish quarter **Alfama** and **Castelo;** and the "new Lisbon," with postmodern high-rise structures, **Amoreiras,** stretching out to the airport and to the north. Just 5 minutes from the airport is the new Gare Intermodal de Lisboa multistation complex, also known as Oriental Station, which serves long-distance and suburban trains, the underground railway system, a bus and motorcoach terminal, and a taxi stop. A day can easily be spent in any one of its districts.

Of particular interest to Western visitors is the Alfama district, which suffered the least damage during the Great Lisbon Earthquake of 1755 and has thereby been able to preserve much of its old facade and narrow, winding cobblestone streets. **St. George's Castle** offers a splendid view of the city. The tourist office has several excellent illustrated brochures describing Lisbon, one of which lists walking tours *From the Castle to Alfama via Mouraria,* where examples of Moorish and medieval architecture prevail. A city map is also available.

Spend at least one evening in Lisbon's famous nightlife district— **Bairro Alto.** It can be reached via the Elevador da Gloria, which operates from the west side of the Praça dos Restauradores at Calcada da Gloria. Dine in a typical Portuguese restaurant/music bar, called "Fado houses," and listen to *Fado* (meaning "fate")—the plaintive, nostalgic, dramatic music of the *fadista* (Fado singer) that is unique to the Portuguese. Lisbon has its own type of Fado, which is considered to be more emotional and dramatic than that performed elsewhere.

Such Fado establishments are abundant in Lisbon, particularly in the Alfama and Bairro Alto districts. One of our favorites is **Adega Mesquita** at Rua Diário de Notícias, No. 107. Phone ahead for reservations: *Tel:* (21) 321 92 80; *Fax:* (21) 346 71 31.

In Alfama on Largo do Chafariz de Dentro, visit **Casa do Fado e da Guitarra Portuguesa,** the Fado museum. According to the tourist office, "It gives an insight and enables one to better understand the development, identity, and soul of this incomparable form of urban musical expression that was born in Lisbon in the 19th century." It's open daily except Tuesday 1000–1700. *Tel:* (21) 882 34 70.

Day Excursions

Cascais and **Estoril,** resort towns along the beautiful beaches of Costa do Estoril, are frequented by celebrities, royalty, and just plain folk. **Coimbra** reveals Portugal's academic nature. This fine old university town

LISBON

was at one time the capital of Portugal. **Setúbal** is a city of beautiful beaches, hillside castles, and excellent seafood. Castle buffs and romantics will enjoy **Sintra,** with its ancient castles and nearby Cape Roca, the westernmost point of Europe.

Day Excursion to

Cascais and Estoril
Lisbon's Riviera

Depart from Lisbon Cais do Sodré Station
Distance by Train: 16 miles (26 km)
Average Train Time: 30 minutes
City Dialing Code: 21
Tourist Information Office: Arcadas do Parque, 2769-503 Estoril
Tel: 466 38 13; *Fax:* 467 22 80
Internet: www.estorilcoast-tourism.com
E-mail: estorilcoast@mail.telepac.pt
Hours: 0900–2000
Notes: Tourist office is near the rail station. Use the underpass from the ocean side (the trains run on the left) to the city side.

Portugal boasts miles and miles of sun-drenched, white-sand beaches. Probably the most famous stretch lies just to the west of Lisbon along the Costa do Estoril. Here the two resort towns of Cascais and Estoril offer a wide variety of scenes to suit everyone's tastes.

We recommend you make **Costa do Estoril** your first stop on your visit to this coastal area, because Estoril is two stops before Cascais, which is the end of the rail line. Estoril has long been famous as a chic resort for royalty and a playground for the rich and famous. Besides the white-sand beach with its excellent facilities and the new seawater pool, the beautifully landscaped **Casino complex** of gaming rooms, restaurants, bars, and art gallery is a major attraction. But new, moderately priced hotels now make Estoril a major attraction for everyone.

Those who are sports minded can enjoy championship 18-hole golf courses that offer temporary memberships. **The Estoril Golf Course,** with its splendid seascape, has been home to the Portuguese Open. Tennis, horseback riding, and sailing are also available.

Cascais, which is only 4 minutes beyond Estoril, maintains a slightly lower-key atmosphere than its chic neighbor. Its beaches are smaller but more intimate. Reflecting the traditions of its fishing-village past, Cascais's Wednesday-morning and first and third Sunday market is well worth the trip from Lisbon. Locals in traditional garb hawk everything imaginable. Farmers' wives, suspicious of supermarket packaging, can be seen scrutinizing live chickens.

To reach the marketplace, bear to the right around the plaza in front of the rail station and continue to the right onto Avenue 25 de April. Two short blocks farther, and you will see the market—probably hear it, too. Bring your own market basket.

Worth visiting are the **Castro Guimarães Museum**, the **Sea Museum, Church of Cascais**, and **Marechal Carmona Park.**

Some rail travelers base themselves in a local resort hotel in or near Cascais or Estoril and then make day excursions into Lisbon for sightseeing or for continuing on with other day excursions. The fast and frequent rail service and the abundance of hotels to fit any budget make this concept a feasible one. The cosmopolitan night life is worth the stay. Cabarets, theaters, restaurants, and discotheques are all over the area. The **Estoril Casino** is the largest in Europe and is open every day 1500–0300. *Tel:* (21) 466 77 00.

Lisbon (Lisboa)—Estoril—Cascais

Trains depart Lisbon's Cais do Sodré Station at 0530, 0600, then 3–5 trains per hour depart until 2300, and then every 30 minutes 2330–0200. Two to three trains per hour depart on weekends until 2300.
Journey time:
Lisbon–Estoril, 28 minutes
Lisbon–Cascais, 32 minutes
Distance: 16 miles (26 km)

Day Excursion to

Coimbra
University Town

Depart from Lisbon Santa Apolonia Station
Distance by Train: 135 miles (218 km)
Average Train Time: 2 hours
City Dialing Code: 39
Tourist Information Office: Largo da Portagem, 3000 Coimbra
Tel: (39) 83 30 19/82 38 86/83 30 28; *Fax:* (39) 82 55 76
Hours: Monday–Friday 0900–1900; Saturday–Sunday 1400–1730
Notes: Trains from Lisbon stop at the Coimbra B. Station, a short distance north of the city center. Either take a taxi to Largo da Portagem or take a shuttle train into the main station. The tourist office is at the approach to the great bridge

Lisbon (Lisboa)—Coimbra

DEPART LISBON SANTA APOLONIA	TRAIN NUMBER	ARRIVE COIMBRA B (JUNCTION)	NOTES
0705	IC 511	0913	
0755	IC 531	1007	
0809	IR 811	1044	
0905	IR 831	1140	
0955	AP 123	1159	exc. Sun
1055	AP 521	1307	
1205	IR 833	1440	

DEPART COIMBRA B (JUNCTION)	TRAIN NUMBER	ARRIVE LISBON SANTA APOLONIA	NOTES
1354	IR 832	1635	
1518	AP 126	1720	
1715	IC 512	1920	
1754	IR 834	2035	
1818	AP 128	2020	
1855	IR 810	2135	
1954	IR 836	2235	
2018	AP 132	2220	Sun
2100	IR 812	2335	
2122	IC 532	2340	

Reservations required on all trains

spanning the Mondego River. If you take the shuttle to the main station, walk four blocks away from the station, upstream along the river, until you come to the bridge approach.

Coimbra is one of Portugal's most charming cities, uniquely blending the old and the new. Site of the oldest university in Portugal, its ancient buildings seem to blend perfectly with the modern spirit of its students. Founded in 1290 in Lisbon, the university was transferred to its present site in 1537 to compensate for moving Portugal's capital from Coimbra to Lisbon.

Coimbra University sits on a hilltop overlooking the river. In keeping with tradition, many students wear black suits and capes, marked with ribbons in tones that denote their scholarship.

There is an air of antiquity surrounding Coimbra. It is the scene of the largest Roman archaeological site in Portugal. Coimbra's cathedral is said to be the finest Romanesque building in Portugal. Gothic tombs and an art collection are housed in this twelfth-century monument.

An unusual attraction for "children" of all ages is the **Portugal dos Pequeninos** (Portugal of the Little Ones), in which you will find a miniaturized version of architectural styles of continental Portugal, Coimbra, Portuguese monuments, insular Portugal, and its overseas territories.

In the city center, you can visit the **monastery of the Holy Cross, Santa Cruz,** constructed in the twelfth century. Later additions include a charming Renaissance sacristy and a magnificently carved facade. A pictorial record of the explorer Vasco da Gama's voyages adorns the choir loft.

Day Excursion to

Setúbal
Seaside and Castles

Depart from Lisbon Terreiro do Paço Ferry Terminal and Barreiro Station
Distance by Train: 18 miles (29 km) from Barreiro
Average Train Time: 35 minutes
City Dialing Code: 265
Tourist Information Office: Região de Turismo de Setúbal, Travessa Frei Gaspar, 10, Apartado 73, 2901 Setúbal
Tel: (265) 53 91 20; *Fax:* (265) 53 91 27/8
Internet: www.costa-azul.rts.pt
E-mail: costa.azul@mail.telepac.pt
Hours: 0900–1230/1400–1900 Monday and Saturday; 0900–1900 Tuesday–Friday; 0900–1230 Sunday
Town Hall Tourist Information: Praca do Quebedo; Tel: 534 222
Hours: 0900–1230/1400–1730 Monday–Friday
Notes: Take a taxi from the station to the regional tourist office (Região de Turismo de Setúbal) or to the tourist office in the Town Hall, located across from the park, Praca do Quebedo.

Aday excursion to **Setúbal** begins at Lisbon's Terreiro do Paço ferry terminal with a 25-minute ferryboat ride across the Tagus River to Barreiro Station, where you board a southbound train to Setúbal. You may cross the 25 de April Bridge by train until Fogueteiro and board a bus to Setúbal or just ride the bus over both bridges.

Although Setúbal is Portugal's third largest city, its location on the estuary of the Sado River provides a more restful, rural-type atmosphere. It can best be enjoyed from **Saint Philip's Castle,** which overlooks Setúbal from its highest point. The sixteenth-century castle was converted into a pousada (inn, or resting place), and it commands an impressive view of both land and sea. A local taxi can take you there. It's a perfect spot for a lunch in its fine restaurant or for an overnight stay.

Setúbal has a remarkable assemblage of monuments and grand old buildings. The **Church of Jesus** is said to be one of the most beautiful small churches ever built. Next door, the Town Museum displays a priceless collection of old masters. There are also a Maritime Museum and the

Lisbon (Lisboa)—Setúbal

FERRY FROM LISBON TERREIRO DO PAÇO DOCK	ARRIVE BARREIRO PIER	DEPART BARREIRO STATION	TRAIN NUMBER	ARRIVE SETÚBAL STATION	NOTES
0810	0840	0853	IR 871	0922	1

plus hourly local service (2nd class) Barreiro Station–Setúbal from 0700 until 2300, and at 0730 and 0830 Mon–Sat

DEPART SETÚBAL STATION	TRAIN NUMBER	ARRIVE BARREIRO STATION	DEPART BARREIRO PIER	ARRIVE LISBON TERREIRO DO PAÇO DOCK	NOTES
2133	IR 872	2205	2245	2345	1
2203	IC 572	2226	2300	2330	Sun

plus hourly local service (2nd class) Setúbal–Barreiro Station at 11 minutes past each hour until 2311 and at 1741, 1841, 1941, and 2041 Mon–Fri

Daily, unless otherwise noted
1. Reservations recommended on all IR trains.
Distance: 18 miles (29 km) from Barreiro

Bocage Monument, which honors the city's great poet.

About 5 or 6 miles from Setúbal at the nearby seaport Sesimbra, the **Pousada do Castelo de Palmela** (Palmela Castle) offers a fantastic view of the surrounding countryside from high atop a hillside. Again, the best way to get there is via taxi.

Day Excursion to

Sintra
Mountain Peaks and Palaces

Depart from Lisbon Rossio Station
Distance by Train: 17 miles (28 km)
Average Train Time: 45 minutes
City Dialing Code: 21
Tourist Information Office: Praca da Republica 23, 2710–616 Sintra
Tel: (21) 9231157 or (21) 9241700; *Fax:* (21) 9235176
Internet: www.cm-sintra.pt
E-mail: cm.sintra@mail.telepac.pt
Hours: Open daily (except January 1, Easter, May 1, and Christmas) 0900–2000 June–September; 0900-1900 October–May
Notes: The main tourist office is about 1 kilometer from the rail station. Reach it by taxi or by boarding the bus Sintra Line No. 433, which leaves from near the station (at Correnteza). The bus stops a short distance from the National Palace of Sintra and the main tourist office. On foot, it is an interesting 15-minute walk.

Lisbon (Lisboa)—Sintra

Suburban trains run every 15 minutes between Lisbon's Rossio Station and Sintra, from 0552 to 2237, then every 30 minutes until 0137. The journey takes 45 minutes. All trains are one class only. Ride the train to the end of the line. Distance: 17 miles (28 km)

According to the Sintra tourist information office, "Sintra is a location which is not to be talked about, its history discussed or its countryside described—it is a location to be felt." **Sintra**, with its ancient castles and palaces towering above the countryside, is the former home of Portuguese kings. Surrounded by mountains and close by **Cape Roca**, the westernmost point of continental Europe "where the land ends and the sea begins," its beauty is unparalleled. This is the place Lord Byron termed "a glorious Eden," and it's all only 45 minutes from Lisbon by train.

There is public transportation to most of the places of tourist interest, except to the Gardens of Monserrate. Taxis and horse-drawn carriages are also available. Since the taxis do not have meters, the fare usually includes up to four passengers plus a fixed amount of time for you to complete your sight-seeing.

Of all the sights in the area, you'll probably want to visit the exquisite **Sintra National Palace** (Paço Real or Palácio da Vila) first. It is closed on Wednesday, and there are no guides. There is a nominal admission charge to the palace grounds. Inside, it possesses the most extensive collection of *Mudejar azulejos*—colored glazed tiles—in the world.

Pena Palace's commanding position from the highest peak in the area makes it well worth the visit. *Tel:* (21) 910 5340; *Fax:* (21) 910 5341. *Hours:* June–September: Tuesday–Sunday 1000–1830; October–May: Tuesday–Sunday 1000–1700. Hungry? Try Pena Palace's 100-seat restaurant offering fine traditional and contemporary Portuguese cuisine.

The **Queluz Palace** captures the style of Versailles, but on a smaller scale. It houses a gourmet restaurant in its former kitchen area. This palace is closed on Tuesday.

For a different experience, visit **Sintra Toy Museum** (open Tuesday–Sunday 1000–1800). Joao Arbués Moreira believed one could better understand the history of humankind through toys. He began his toy collection at the age of 14 with toys from his grandparents, parents, and others. As he acquired money, he began purchasing more toys. He spent a lifetime researching their manufacture and history and collected more than 20,000 different toys. You, too, can view this extraordinary collection at the Museu do Brinquedo, the Toy Museum, located in the old Sintra Fireman's Headquarters. *Tel:* (21) 9242171. There's a toy restoration workshop, and the gift shop is a great place to purchase that special memento. Or visit the Sintra street market on the second and fourth Sunday of each month at S. Pedro for a unique bauble to bring back home.

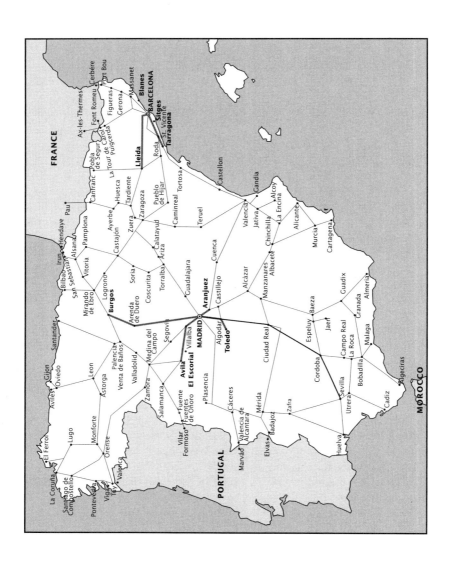

Spain

S pain is a delightful dichotomy—futuristic in many ways, yet respectful of its rich history and tradition. In 2001, Spain was the third most popular tourist destination in the world.

From the *delicato* music of Flamenco to swashbuckling matadors, Spain's culture and tradition are as widely varied as its geography. Flamenco is a genuine southern Spanish art form influenced by diverse cultures throughout Spain's history, including the Gypsies, the legendary Tartessos, and the Muslims.

Spain shares the Iberian Peninsula with its neighbor to the west, Portugal. France and the tiny country of Andorra lie to the north. Castilian Spanish is spoken throughout Spain, but Catalan, Valencian, Basque, and Galician are still spoken in their respective autonomous regions.

One social custom that visitors will notice immediately is that Spaniards get up later in the morning and usually stay out later at night than other Europeans. If you want to dance until dawn, you're visiting the right country. The nightlife in Spain is intensely zealous, with bars and discotheques remaining open until the wee hours of the morning, especially in the larger, more cosmopolitan cities of Barcelona and Madrid.

Arriving from North America, our base city Madrid is the primary gateway, with Barcelona being second. During summer, however, there are some direct flights to Malaga on the Mediterranean Sea.

For more information about Spain, contact the Tourist Offices of Spain in North America: (*Internet:* **www.okspain.org**; *E-mail:* oetny@tourspain.es):

Chicago: 845 North Michigan Avenue, Suite 915 East, Water Tower Place, Chicago, IL 60611. *Tel:* (312) 642–1992; *Fax:* (312) 642–9817

Los Angeles: San Vicente Plaza Building, 8383 Wilshire Boulevard, Suite 960, Beverly Hills, CA 90211. *Tel:* (323) 658–7188; *Fax:* (323) 658–1061

New York: 666 Fifth Avenue, Thirty-fifth Floor, New York, NY 10103. *Tel:* (212) 265–8822; *Fax:* (212) 265–8864

Toronto: 2 Bloor Street West, Thirty-fourth Floor, Toronto, Ontario M4W
3E2. *Tel:* (416) 961–3131; *Fax:* (416) 961–1992
Miami: 1221 Brickell Avenue, Suite 1850, Miami, FL 33131. *Tel:* (305)
358–1992; *Fax:* (305) 358–8223

Banking

- **Currency:** Euro (€)
- **Exchange rate at press time:** €1.10=U.S. $1.00
- **Hours:** Open Monday–Friday 0900–1400, with some open Saturday
0900–1430

Credit and ATM transfers at machines are the best exchange rate, since
no commission is charged.

Communications

- **Country Code:** 34
- **Direct Dial:** AT&T: 900 99 00 11; MCI: 900 99 00 14; Sprint: 900
99 00 13

Public telephones are available most everywhere in Spain; they offer
instructions in English and may be used to call most parts of the world. Some
phones are equipped to take credit cards. Since calling from Spain to America
is about ten times more expensive than calling from America to Spain, it is
advisable to access your American calling card connection.

When in Spain, dial 00 to telephone outside of Spain. When calling
Spain from abroad, include Spain's country code. It is then necessary to dial
the provincial codes for each province. When calling *within* Spain, the
provincial codes begin with 9.

Some provincial codes include Alicante, 96; Avila, 920; Barcelona, 93;
Burgos, 947; Cordoba, 957; Madrid, 91; Malaga, 95; Seville, 95; Toledo,
925; and Valencia, 96.

Rail Travel in Spain

With **RENFE** (Red Nacional de Ferrocarriles Españoles, or Spanish
National Railways), the trains in Spain run mainly on time—98 percent on
time. *Internet:* www.renfe.es. RENFE accepts **Eurailpass, Europass,** the
Iberic Flexipass, and **Spain Flexipass,** but it deviates from the basic railpass concept in that certain trains, such as AVE ("Alta Velocidad Espanola,"
or Spanish High Speed) trains and Talgos operating on high-speed lines, are
not included, but railpass holders do receive substantial discounts. (Please
see the Appendix for Iberic Flexipass, Eurailpass, and Europass types and
costs.) Special sight-seeing/tour trains such as *Al Andalus* and the narrow-
gauge FEVE are not included on the railpasses either, but tickets may be
purchased separately.

The Eurailpass bonus for Spain includes

- 20 percent discount on the Transmediterranea Line ships between
Barcelona–Menorca
Barcelona–Palma de Mallorca

Barcelona–Ibiza
Valencia–Palma de Mallorca and Menorca
Algeciras–Tanger (Morocco)
- 30 percent discount on full published standard double room rate, Hilton Hotel, Barcelona.

The Spain Flexipass may be purchased for a minimum of 3 days of unlimited rail travel in Spain within a 2-month period.

Spain Flexipass

	1st Class	2nd Class
3 days in 2 months	$200	$155
Additional days	$35	$30

Seven-day maximum additional rail days. The AVE and Talgo 200 trains require additional supplements. Children ages 4–11 travel half price.

Not to be outdone by French high-speed TGVs and Germany's ICEs, RENFE's sleek **AVEs** are derivations of the French TGV (*Train a Grand Vitesse,* or Train of Great Speed) *Atlantique.* Dynamic RENFE has been "on the move" since the first AVEs cruised into service as the main rail link between Madrid and Seville due to the opening of the International Exposition of Seville—Expo 1992. Via AVE, the Madrid-Seville trip can be done in only 2 hours, 15 minutes.

Reservations for AVE trains are required. Choose Turista, Preferente, or Club class. All three classes include television sets with individual earphones and four music channels, family areas with games for kids, facilities for the disabled, telephones, cafeteria, and a beverage machine. Club and Preferente Classes also include access to AVE club lounges, newspapers, and magazines. In-seat food/beverage service is provided only in Club Class.

For AVE information *Tel:* 902 240202.

Ultramodern Talgo 200 trains link Madrid and Malaga in a little more than 4 hours. These gauge-changing, high-speed trains also have significantly reduced the travel time between Madrid and Cadiz/Huelva.

The attractive blue and white **Euromed** (*Velocidad Alta Mediterranea* or Mediterranean High Speed) trains provide services on the Barcelona–Valencia–Alicante route with a cruising speed of 200 km/hour. These trains offer two classes of service—Preferente and Turista.

Remember—reservations are **required** on Spanish trains.

Base City:

Barcelona

Internet: www.barcelonaturisme.com or www.bcn.es
City Dialing Code: 93

Barcelona as it is today, the **New Barcelona**, was created only in 1874 by joining 27 separate municipalities. It has become Spain's most prosperous port and has developed a thriving industrial complex as well. The center of this new metropolitan area is the **Plaça de Catalunya**, a square rimmed with trees and highlighted by sculptures and fountains—and an abundance of pigeons. This square is where Old and New Barcelona meet.

Founded in ancient times by the Phoenicians and occupied by the Romans, **Old Barcelona** is composed of three districts: Barri Gòtic, or the Gothic Quarter, and the Ribera, and Raval districts. A visit to the History Museum in Plaça del Rei square provides insight to Barcelona's rich and ancient past.

At the other end of the spectrum, the World Trade Center (WTC) complex provides insight to Barcelona's promising future. According to the Tourist Office of Spain, the WTC association (including 300 centers in 97 countries) was created "to stimulate world trade and to increase cultural exchange and the development of nations." This stunning waterfront complex solidifies Barcelona's position as a major portal to European and Mediterranean markets.

Arriving by Air

Barcelona has one of the most modern international airports in Europe. About 8 miles from the city, transportation to and from is easily available and inexpensive. Foreign currency exchange and ATMs are available in both Terminals A and B. Look for signs ARGENTARIA or LA CAIXA. Tourist information is also available in both terminals from 0900–2100 daily.

Airport–City Links: Cercanias/Rodalie local line No. 1 **trains** connect travelers to Barcelona Sants Station in 18 minutes and depart every half hour from the airport 0600–2230 daily. The station is connected to the airport terminals by moving walkways. Follow the pictograms. Trains depart from track No. 1 in Barcelona Sants Station every half hour to the airport; Fare, €1.83 Monday–Friday; €2.10 weekends/holidays.

The **Aerobus** service departs the airport every 15 minutes 0530–2215 Monday–Friday and 0630–2220 on weekends and holidays. Time en route is 40–45 minutes. It stops at all three terminals on the way to and from Plaça de Catalunya. Aerobuses are equipped to handle wheelchairs. Fare: €3.00.

Approximate **taxi** fare from the airport to city center is €15–21.

Arriving by Train

Barcelona Sants Station (Estacio de Sants), Plaça Països Catalans

The Sants Station is the center of Barcelona's transportation system. Most bus lines, all metro lines (through transfers), and both regional and long distance trains are available here. The high-speed **Euromed** trains to Alicante, Castellón, Tarragona, and Valencia depart from the Sants Station, as well as direct trains to Montpellier for connections to Paris and Geneva on TGVs (French high-speed trains).

Twelve tracks are located beneath the main floor of the station, accessible by escalators or elevators. TV screens and a large display above the ticket windows show which trains leave from which platforms. There is a red desk, marked with a **M** where you can purchase tickets for both the metro and bus systems. They can also provide metro and bus system maps.

- **Train Information:** *Tel:* 902 24 02 02—24 hours, RENFE (Spain's national rail company) help line; *Tel:* 934 95 64 62—Passengers with disabilities; *Internet:* www.renfe.es. This easy-to-use Web site provides timetables for all travel originating in Spain (in English and Spanish).
- **Seat/Sleeper Reservations:** For same-day travel, go to the windows marked "venta immediate," which are on the right side of the station from the front entrance. For later travel, go to the "venta anticipada" windows on the left-hand side of the station. Usually, you need to take a number from the machine and watch for your number to appear on the digital display board. It will also indicate which window number you should go to. There are usually lines. We suggest you make your reservation as far in advance of your expected departure date as possible. **Railpass validation** can be made at any of these windows.
- **Money Exchange** may be made at the "kiosk" on the ground floor level in the center of the station. Hours: 0800–2200 daily. There are also numerous ATMs scattered throughout the station–four of which are opposite the "venta anticipada" windows.
- **Tourist Information** is available in the center of the station. For more extensive information and services, go to the one located at 17-S Plaça de Catalunya.

Other RENFE stations include Barcelona França, Passeig de Gràcia, Plaça de Catalunya, Clot-Arago, and Saint Andreu Comtal. All of the day excursions detailed in this edition, however, may be visited by departing from the Sants Station.

Tourist Information/Hotel Reservations

- *Turisme de Barcelona Tourist Information Offices:*

Plaça de Catalunya, 17-S.
National calls: *Tel:* 906 30 12 82
International calls: *Tel:* 93 304 34 21
Hours: 0900–2100 daily; closed January 1 and December 25
Located below street level. The mostly bilingual staff can provide a lot of information and change money as well.

Plaça Sant Jaume, 1.
Hours: 1000–2000 Monday–Saturday; 1000–1400 Sunday/holidays.

Sants Railway Station, Plaça Països Catalans (center of station).
Hours: Summer, 0800–2000 daily; winter, 0800–2000 Monday–Friday and 0800–1400 Saturday–Sunday/holidays.

Also, the "Red Jackets" (Cassaques Vermelles), tourism officials in red coats, patrol the Las Ramblas and Barri Gòtic areas, providing maps and information in summer.

Getting Around in Barcelona

Transportation in and around Barcelona is plentiful and easy to use. (*Internet:* www.tmb.net) The Barcelona Metro has 5 lines covering more than 80 kilometers and includes 112 stations. Trains run 0500–2300 Monday–Thursday; 0500–0200 Friday–Saturday; and 0600–2400 Sunday. Bus services generally run 0630–2200, although there is a special *Nitbus* (night bus) that runs 1000–0400. The price for a single bus or metro ticket is €0.90. A good deal is the ten-trip package for €5.32, which can be used on the bus and the metro, and it's transferable. Unlimited transfers can be made within one hour, 15 minutes.

The **Barcelona Card** is a real bargain. It provides free public transport, discounts of up to 50 percent at the city's major attractions, at several shops and restaurants, and a discount on the Aerobus to/from the airport. Purchase at airport Terminals A and B, tourist information offices, and at the Sants rail station:

	Adults	Children
1 Day	€15.62	€12.62
2 Days	€18.63	€15.62
3 Days	€21.63	€18.63

Train Connections to Other Base Cities from Barcelona

Depart Barcelona Sants Station

DEPART	TRAIN NUMBER	ARRIVE	NOTES
		Brussels (Bruxelles) Midi/Zuid	
2105	Hotel 475	1120+1	R, 1, Sleeper
		Lisbon (Lisboa) Santa Apolonia	
1530	TAL 379	0820+1	R, 2, 3
		Madrid Chamartin	
0830	TAL 41	1450	R
1030	TAL 179	1733	R
1200	TAL 377	1905	R
1530	TAL 379	2200	R
2200	Hotel 947	0528*+1	R, Sleeper
2203	Estr 373	0700	R, Sleeper
2300	Hotel 875	0800+1	R, 3, Sleeper exc. Sat
		Nice Ville	
0845	TAL 73	1909	R, 5
1920	471	0745+1	R, 4
		Paris Gare de Lyon	
0845	TAL 73	1725	R, 5
1804	TAL 374	0727+1	R, 4, 6
2105	Hotel 475	0900+1 (0848 Sa, Su)	R, 6, Sleeper

Daily, unless otherwise noted
R Reservations required
+1 Arrive next day.
* Arrives Madrid Puerta de Atocha Station.
1. Via Paris. Arrive Paris Austerlitz station 0900+1 (0848 +1 Sat, Sun); transfer to Paris Nord station for Thalys 9321, departing at 0955. Thalys high-speed trains require supplement.
2. Via Madrid. Arrive Madrid Chamartin station. Transfer to Spanish TrenHotel 332; the *Lusitania*. Depart 2245.
3. Spanish TrenHotel train. Deluxe sleeping accommodations (including toilet and shower in the compartment) are available. Special fares applicable.
4. Change trains in Cerbère.
5. Change trains in Montpellier.
6. Arrive Paris Austerlitz.

Sights/Attractions/Tours

Barcelona is a beautiful and immensely varied city. **La Rambla**, the world-renowned main avenue of the "Old City," is one interesting part of an outstanding whole. An entire day can easily be spent wandering up and down this lively, fascinating street that stretches 2 kilometers between the Plaça de Catalunya and the port. Begin at the "Diagonal" metro sign on Plaça de Catalunya (near the tourist information office) and head down towards the harbor area. Along the way, watch the numerous entertaining street performers and peruse the variety of wares displayed on every available inch of pavement.

On your right is **La Bouqueria,** declared to be Barcelona's "best market." Farther on, to the right, you will see the **Gran Teatre del Liceu** (the rebuilt old opera house), where you can take a 40-minute tour that includes the Hall of Mirrors. The **Plaça Reial** is off to the left. Built on the site of a former Capuchin convent, this delightful square contains the *Fountain of the Three Graces,* designed by Antoni Gaudí, Barcelona's most famous "native son." If you're tired of walking, this is also a good spot (as is Plaça de Catalunya) to board the **Bus Turistic** (tourist bus) for a great overview of the city, complete with recorded commentary in multiple languages. You can hop on and off the bus along two sightseeing routes with the same ticket. Fare: 1 day €13.22; 2 days €16.82; 3 days €21.63 (reduced rates for children).

Continuing on foot, the **Palau Güell,** designed by Gaudí as the palatial residence of Count Güell, will be on your right (closed on weekends/holidays). Near the harbor is the impressive **Mirador de Colón,** the Monument of Christopher Columbus. Take the elevator up 60 meters for an impressive panoramic view.

Like Las Ramblas, the **Barri Gótic (Gothic Quarter)** should not be missed. The most central metro stop is "Jaime I," but "Liceu" would also work. Within the Barri Gótic, you will find the **Picasso Museum** at Carrer Montcada, 15. *Tel:* 933 196 310; Hours: 1000–2000 Tuesday–Saturday, 1000–1500 Sunday, closed on Mondays. You will also find **La Catedral,** the largest cathedral in Barcelona, located at Plaça de la Seu.

Via metro, another good stop is "Sagrada Familia," only a five-minute walk to **La Sagrada Familia**—the huge church designed by Gaudí. Although it is not finished (and has been under construction since Gaudí died in 1926), the church is breathtaking. Love it or hate it, it is well worth seeing. Another Gaudí related sight, **Parc Güell,** is filled with mosaics he designed ("Vallarca" metro stop).

For a spectacular view, take the bus "Tibibús 2" from Plaça de Catalunya to **Plaça de Tibidabo** (or taxi—the metro does not run here), the highest point in Barcelona. Or, take Tramvia Blau (blue tram). Board the rides in the amusement park for even more spectacular views. The park is open mid-March to the end of October.

Attention, shoppers! In terms of quality and quantity of a variety of fashions and products, Barcelona is truly a city of international standing. To make it easy to spend your euros, Turisme de Barcelona plotted out a remarkable 5-kilometer-long **shopping route,** which includes Port Vell, Las Ramblas, Eixample, and the shopping district of the Diagonal. Take the special "Tombbus" bus service (look for the BARCELONA SHOPPING LINE sign on the bus). Ask for more details at the tourist information offices.

Barcelona also offers an impressive zoo, the Olympic Village from 1992, museums and art galleries, more than 4 kilometers of beach (Barceloneta), and a selection of wonderful restaurants featuring local and international cuisine. Barcelonian restaurants usually serve meals at much later times than other Europeans. Be prepared to eat your evening meals between 2100 and midnight.

Day Excursions from Barcelona

For a truly unique spiritual and cultural experience, take the metro from Plaça España to the Montserrat cable-car stop and board the cable car or funicular train up to the stunning Benedictine **Montserrat Monastery** (*Internet:* www.abadiamontserrat.net). Founded in the eleventh century, some 80 monks still live, work, and pray there. Montserrat, about 60 kilometers north of Barcelona, is also the home of the world's oldest boys' choir.

Other day excursions in this edition will take you to **Blanes**, also north of Barcelona, along the **Costa Brava** (Wild Coast), providing the breathtaking beauty of the Mediterranean coast and an opportunity to sample culinary delights from the sea. The citadel city of **Lleida**, stormed by Caesar's legions and conquered by the Moors, carries visitors far back into Spanish history. South of Barcelona along the beaches of Spain's Coasta Dorada (Gold Coast), picturesque **Sitges** attracts sun worshipers, gourmets, and wine connoisseurs alike. Farther south, the ancient city of **Tarragona's** first-century Roman ruins stir the imagination.

Day Excursion to

Blanes
Beaches, Bikinis, and Boats

Depart from Barcelona Sants (suburban section) station
Distance by Train: 42 miles (67 km)
Average Train Time: 1 hour, 10 minutes
City Dialing Code: 972
Tourist Information Office: Plaça Catalunya, 21
Tel: 972 330 348; **Fax:** 972 33 46 86
Internet: www.blanes.net
E-mail: turisme@blanes.net
Hours: Open June–September, Monday–Saturday 0900–2000, including July and August, Sundays 0930–1400; May–October, Monday–Friday 0900–1400/ 1600–1900, Saturday 0930–1330. Winter hours: Monday–Friday 0900–1400; Saturday 0930–1330
Notes: To get there from the rail station, board buses marked ESTACION-BLANES. They will take you into town to the bus terminal at Plaça de Catalunya. The tourist office is just a few steps from the bus terminal.

The **Costa Brava** is a breathtaking, 90-mile stretch of rugged coastline blessed with fantastic beaches and hidden coves. And it all begins at Blanes. Blanes is best described as a typical Spanish coastal village, where fishing is still the primary industry. Blanes curves around the Mediterranean

Trains depart Barcelona Sants daily, including holidays, from 0610, 0642, and every 30 minutes until 2042, then 2118, 2148, and 2218.

Trains depart Blanes to Barcelona Sants daily every 30 minutes until 2139 (Second class only).

Distance: 42 miles/67 km

much like Cannes on the French Riviera, but it is not a "resort" in the usual, more commercialized sense. As with most Spanish fishing villages, the pace is slow and the people friendly.

The rail station serving Blanes is perched on a hill about a half mile from the center of the village and the sea. Buses marked ESTACION-BLANES will take you into town to the bus terminal at Plaça de Catalunya, near the sea.

A stroll along the beach is delightful. It is fronted by fishermen's houses and dotted with boats lying at anchor in the curve of the bay. There is an auction of the day's catch each weekday evening at about 1700 at the breakwater. Blanes has plenty of fun-in-the-sun beaches, too.

Other diversions include a delightful botanical garden located near the breakwater where the fish auctions are held. Founded in 1924 by Karl Faust, the garden exhibits more than 4,000 species of regional and international flora. Hours: 0900–1800 daily April to mid-October (reduced hours in winter).

From Blanes, other ports along this rugged and beautiful coast can be accessed by local buses, cars, or cruise boats. The Crucerus Line, which identifies its vessels with a blue whale at each bow, operates from June to September. Boats sail north from Blanes to call at places like **Lloret de Mar,** famous for its new hotels and exciting nightlife; **Tossa;** and **San Feliu de Guixols.** Obtain details and schedules from the tourist office.

Day Excursion to

Lleida (Lerida)
From the Coast to the Mountains

Depart from Barcelona Sants Station
Distance by Train: 114 miles (184 km)
Average Train Time: 2 hours, 46 minutes
City Dialing Code: 73
Tourist Information Office: Oficina de Turismo de la Generalitat de Cataluna, 36 Madrid Avenue, 25002 Lleida
Tel: (97) 327–0997; **Fax:** (97) 327–0949
E-mail: oit.lleida@mailcat.net

Barcelona—Lleida (Lerida)

DEPART BARCELONA SANTS	TRAIN NUMBER	ARRIVE LLEIDA	NOTES
0703	TAL 177	0856	
0730	623	0924	2nd class only
0830	TAL 41	1016	
1003	D 11533	1218	Sat only
1200	TAL 377	1406	
1203	—	1437	2nd class only

DEPART LLEIDA	TRAIN NUMBER	ARRIVE BARCELONA SANTS	NOTES
1305	—	1600	2nd class only
1545	TAL 374	1800	
1620	IC 530	1850	
1755	—	2003	
1837	TAL 42	2030	
2010	TAL 378	2205	
2048	D620	2250	

Daily, unless otherwise noted

A reservation is required for all trains that have numbers. A reservation purchased onboard the train costs more than one purchased in advance. Higher fares incorporating a supplement are payable for travel by Talgo and InterCity trains.

Distance: 114 miles (184 km)

Hours: June–September, Monday–Friday 0900–2000 and Saturday 0900–1400; October–May, Monday–Friday 0900–1900 and Saturday 0900–1400

Notes: It's about a 15-minute walk from the rail station to the tourist information office. Exit the station and walk along Rambla de Ferran and Blondel Avenue to Madrid Avenue. The tourist office is in front of the University Bridge. A taxi can get you there in about 5 minutes.

A fast-moving Talgo or ELT (electrotren) diesel train takes passengers in comfort through the spectacular scenery of the rugged, steep slopes of Sierra de Montserrat in the Pyrenees to the Roman fortress city Lleida (Lerida). The train ride alone is worth the experience.

Be certain to make seat reservations well in advance of your day excursion date, since the train's early-morning departure does not allow sufficient time to make same-day reservations.

Your train stops briefly in Manresa, after which the scenery becomes more mountainous. Watch from the left side of the train as it approaches Lleida. The sight is unforgettable. Lleida's brooding **Seu Vella cathedral** stands as a sentinel atop a hill on the banks of the Segre River. The original cathedral makes Lleida's skyline very impressive.

Lleida served as an important Roman military outpost where Caesar's legions gathered to pursue their conquests. The Moors left a more lasting impression, which is reflected in the discernibly Mediterranean flavor of the city's marketplaces. Lleida's stormy history continued with Napoleon's attempts to annex it to France, and with artillery fire during the Spanish Civil War.

Constructed in the thirteenth century on the former site of a mosque, Seu Vella was converted from a church to a military fortress in 1707 by Philip V and then burned and pillaged in the wars that followed. It was restored and reconsecrated in 1950. The **Seu Nova** (new cathedral) stands on Carrer Major, the main street of the old town. The ancient fifteenth- to sixteenth-century **Hospital de Santa Maria** is just opposite and houses many fine Iberian and Roman archaeological excavation exhibits. If you are up to it, scale the tower for a panoramic view of the plain surrounding Lleida.

Lleida's picturesque "Old Quarter" teems with interesting pedestrian streets of shops with colorful awnings and generally lower prices than you'll find in Barcelona. Take time out to enjoy the simple yet high-quality cuisine of the region. Many dishes are flavored with olive oil of the Garrigues area—considered to be the best in the world. The annual **Agricultural Fair of Sant Miguel,** usually held at the end of September, shows off the best produce of the area. Top off your visit with a toast of one of the Costers del Segre wines.

Festival buffs will enjoy many of the other traditional celebrations of Lleida, including "Els Tres Tombs" (Feast of Saint Anthony) in mid-January, when the horses and cattle are led in procession through the streets of the city to be blessed; the "Aplec del Cargol" (Snail Feast), held on the first Sunday of May; and the Festival of the White Virgin, held in the beginning of October, when the city celebrates their patroness, the Madonna.

Day Excursion to

Sitges
Jewel on the Mediterranean

Depart from Barcelona Sants Station
Distance by Train: 25 miles (34 km)
Average Train Time: 30 minutes
City Dialing Code: 93
Tourist Information Office: Carrer Sínia Morera, 08870 Sitges (Barcelona)
Tel: 93 894 4251 or 93 894 5004; **Fax:** 93 894 4305
Internet: www.sitgestur.com (English version under construction)
E-mail: info@sitgestur.com
Hours: Daily in summer 1000–1330 and 1700–2100; remainder of the year: Monday–Friday 0900–1400/1600–1830
Notes: The tourist office is only about 3 minutes' walking time from the rail station.

Barcelona—Sitges

Trains depart daily from Barcelona Sants station at 6 and 36 minutes after the hour
from 0606 until 2236; journey time to Sitges is 30 minutes.

Trains depart daily from Sitges at 29 and 59 minutes after the hour throughout the
day until 2059, then at 2159; journey time to Barcelona Sants station is 30 minutes.
All second-class local service.

Distance: 25 miles (34 km)

Only 25 miles (40 km) south of Barcelona, Sitges can be accessed by train from several stations in Barcelona, but Sants and Passeig de Gracia stations are the most centralized. Sitges is one of the most cosmopolitan seaside resorts in Europe and a pleasant escape from Barcelona's summer heat.

Sitges, a member of the prestigious Jewels of European Tourism Club, boasts 17 golden beaches that stretch over 4 kilometers. It is also located in an important wine and "cava" champagne production area known as the Penedés region. Ask the tourist office about visiting the wine cellars in Vilafranca del Penedés and the Cava Cellars in Sant Sadurni de Noia.

Annually, Sitges hosts the national carnation show in June, when the town is awash with the brilliantly colored flowers. It coincides with the procession of Corpus Christi (June 2, 2002), one of the most renowned festivals in Spain, when streets are adorned with splendid carnation carpets, bands perform, and parades glide along narrow streets.

Fresh seafood is Sitges's specialty, but there are excellent meat and chicken dishes available as well at a multitude of fine restaurants. Typical Sitges dishes include *xato,* a salad of endive, tuna fish, salt-cod, anchovies, and olives, dressed with *nyora* peppers, roasted almonds, chilis, garlic, olive oil, more anchovies, and salt and vinegar. Or, try *arros a la sitgetana*—rice with a delicious mixture of shellfish, sausage, pork, peas, and peppers, seasoned with saffron and almonds. Follow it all with a glass of delicious Sitges's dessert wine, *Malvasia de Sitges.*

The **Carnival** (February 7–13, 2002), **June International Theater,** and the **October Film Festival** attract a varied mixture of participants and spectators, including international celebrities.

Other Sitges attractions include **Museu Romantic o Casa Llopis,** an outstanding exhibit of antique dolls housed in a refurbished eighteenth-century mansion; **Cau Ferrat,** the magnificent home of twentieth-century artist Santiago Rusinol, which displays Rusinol's best work as well as art by El Greco, Casas, and Picasso; and the **Maricel del Mar Museum.**

Day Excursion to

Tarragona
City of Roman Spain

Depart from Barcelona Sants Station
Distance by Train: 53 miles (85 km)
Average Train Time: 50 minutes
City Dialing Code: 977
Tourist Information Office: Patronat Municipal de Turisme, 39 Carrer Major, 43003 Tarragona
Tel: 977 245 203; **Fax:** 977 245 507
Internet: www.costadaurada.org
E-mail: turisme@tinet.fut.es
Hours: Monday–Friday 1000–2000
Notes: To reach the Patronat Municipal de Turisme, board a No. 2 bus across from the rail station. Get off at the Roman Wall, where you will see signs directing you to the tourist information office.

Tarragona can be reached via Barcelona's single-class suburban train system or by the faster, more stylish and comfortable Talgo trains, which require seat reservations.

Tarragona is rich in antiquity. It was once considered a jewel in the crown of the Roman Empire, with more than one-quarter of a million inhabitants (more than twice the present population) enjoying all the privileges of Rome. Tarragona's enormous stone walls were constructed in the first century B.C. As with the great pyramids of Egypt, modern engineers still wonder how the ancient Iberians could position such massive blocks of stone. Its attractive seascape of azure water, gold-colored beaches, and flower-laden cliffs has attracted visitors for centuries.

St. Paul supposedly preached at the site of Tarragona's twelfth-century cathedral, where a Roman temple to Jupiter once stood. Illustrations of his life are exhibited in the altar area.

A visit to the **Archeological Museum** is a journey into Tarragona's rich past, from Roman remains to reflecting the peoples who followed, including Visigoths, Moors, and Catalans. The penetrating stare of Medusa's eyes, cornices from the **Temple of Jupiter** (where the cathedral now stands), and age-old ceramics are on view. The museum operates on seasonal hours. Check with the tourist information office.

Hungry? While you're in the tourist office, ask for directions to the **Bufet el Tiberi Restaurant** at 5, Marti d'Ardenya or the **Restaurant el Celler** and **Restaurant el Trull.** Both feature local specialties.

Barcelona—Tarragona

DEPART BARCELONA SANTS	TRAIN NUMBER	ARRIVE TARRAGONA	NOTES
0630	—	0734	2nd class
0700	EM 1071	0748	1, 2, 3
0800	D 697	0851	1, 2
0803	—	0904	2nd class
0900	EM 1091	0949	1,2
0903	—	1004	2nd class
0930	D 693	1027	1
1003	D 11533	1104	4
1030	TAL 179	1123	2
1200	TAL 377	1252	2

DEPART TARRAGONA	TRAIN NUMBER	ARRIVE BARCELONA SANTS	NOTES
1532	TAL 460	1630	1, 2
1656	TAL 374	1800	1,2
1703	—	1805	
1738	A 1152	1833	1, 2
1807	EM 1162	1903	1, 2; except Sat
1934	D 694	2050	1, 2
1940	TAL 264	2033	1, 2
2005	EM 1182	2103	1, 2
2058	—	2201	2nd class
2140	A 1192	2235	1, 2
2205	EM 1202	2303	1, 2
2304	A 1212	2355	1, 2, 5

Daily, unless otherwise noted
1. A reservation is required for all journeys for which a train number is given in the tables. A reservation fee paid to the conductor onboard the train costs more than one purchased in advance.
2. Higher fares incorporating a supplement are payable for travel by Talgo (TAL) and InterCity (IC) trains. A special fare structure may apply for travel by EM trains (Euromed–200 km/hr high-speed trains, similar to AVE trains). Passengers wishing to travel on EM trains are advised to inquire at the Barcelona Sants station before boarding.
3. Mon–Sat
4. Sat only
5. Sun only

Distance: 53 miles (85 km)

Base City:

Madrid

Internet: www.munimadrid.es
City Dialing Code: 1

Madrid's central location in the very heart of Spain makes it a convenient base city and a major point of entry for Spain. Madrid, the capital of Spain, at first glance appears typical of any other modern capital that serves as a center for government and finance. But it is atypical of a busy metropolis in that the Spanish seem to move at a slower pace. They make time for friends and conversation, and as one Spanish writer noted, "Madrid is a city where no one is a stranger."

The Madrilenos are apparently connoisseurs of a variety of nightlife activities and have a flair for flamenco—the sensual, Gypsy-influenced form of singing and dancing. There are numerous specialized flamenco clubs in Madrid, including the Corral de la Moreria, Los Canasteros, and Torres Bermejas. It would appear that the Madrilenos never sleep!

According to the Spanish National Tourist Office, "Madrid has turned into the fable of Europe. It is called the capital of joy and of contentment. Describing our city in such terms means that it is welcoming, cordial, free, peaceful and universal."

Arriving by Air

Madrid's **Barajas International Airport,** about 9 miles (12 kilometers) northeast of the city.

- **Airport Information:** *Tel:* (91) 305–8343; 305–8344; 305–8345, and 305–8346. *Internet:* www.aena.es/madrid-barajas
- **INFORIBERIA:** *Tel:* (91) 902 400 500

Airport–City Links: Airport Bus (*Tel:* 431–6192), a yellow bus service, runs to and from Barajas Airport and the Plaça de Colón (Columbus Square) every 10–15 minutes 0600–0100. Journey time: about 30–60 minutes; fare, €2.31. Take a taxi from Plaça de Colón to your hotel.

The Atocha **metro** line is a link to metro-Madrid; numerous buses carry travelers to and from many locations in the city. RENFE (Spanish National Railways) office is on the ground floor of Terminal T2 (*Tel:* 91 305 85 44).

Taxi fare from the airport to city center is about €15–18, and the trip takes 30–60 minutes depending on traffic.

Arriving by Train

RENFE (Spanish National Railways)—For information on fares, schedules, and destinations: *Tel:* 328–9020; *Internet:* www.renfe.es.

Madrid's two main railway stations, **Chamartin** and **Atocha,** are connected by underground trackage via Madrid's metro system and by "Apeadero Cercanias" (local) trains or any through-trains scheduled to stop at both stations. The metro stop for Atocha Station is marked ATOCHA RENFE. Apeadero Cercanias stations also include **Nuevos Ministerios** in the government buildings area and **Recoletos** at the main post office. Railpasses are accepted on Apeadero Cercanias trains, but not on Madrid's metro.

Chamartin Station, San Agustin de Foxa Street, is Madrid's international station connecting with most European capitals, as well as the north, northeast, and south of Spain. The station is near the Chamartin metro stop, and buses Nos. 5 and 80 connect from the city and this railway station. High-speed AVE trains shuttle passengers quickly to and from **Seville** (about 2½ hours), with stops at **Cordoba** and **Ciudad Real.** Other fast trains depart to and arrive from various southern and southeastern Spanish destinations and from Portugal. There are 21 tracks.

- **Money exchange:** Opposite track Nos. 17 and 18. The sign reads CAJA ESPANA. Hours: 0830–1400 Monday–Friday. Banco Bilbao Vizcaya Argentaria, across from track 12. Hours: 0800–2200 daily (closed for lunch 1415–1500). ATM located next door.
- **Hotel reservations:** Opposite track Nos. 7 and 8. Hours: 0730–2300 daily. Nominal reservation fee. Be certain to ask for accommodations near one of the rail stations or close to public transportation. The check-in counter for Hotel Chamartin is near the luggage locker area.
- **Luggage lockers:** Available 0730–2330 daily. Follow the sign CONSIGNA AUTOMATICA.
- **Sala Club Intercity:** First-class lounge between entrances to track Nos. 13 and 14.
- **Tourist information:** Opposite track No. 19 (*Tel:* 91–315–9976). Hours: 0800–2000 Monday–Friday; 0900–1300 Saturday.
- **Train information, seat reservations,** and **railpass validation:** In the center of the station between track Nos. 11 and 12. Hours: 0830–2000. Take a number from the machine labeled RECOJA SU TURNO to reserve a place in line. Make certain the date (*fecha*) and departure time (*hora salida*) are correct on your reservation.

Remember: seat reservations are mandatory on all
express and international trains

Puerta de Atocha Station—High-speed AVE and Talgo 200 trains connect Madrid with Andalusia from this station. A pleasant tropical garden and cafe provide a respite from the heat and noise. The local/suburban Cercanias trains depart from the lower level and connect with Chamartin Station.

Sala Club Intercity: First-class lounge on the mezzanine level.

Principe Pio or Norte, near the Royal Palace on the west side of the city, links Madrid to cities in the north and northeast of Spain via the Cercanias, or suburban, trains. Other stations where you can board the suburban-type Cercanias trains include **Nuevos Ministerios** and **Recoletos.** Eurailpass, Europass, and the national Spain railpasses are accepted on these trains. Although considered "local" trains, they do extend to the surrounding countryside to our day excursions **Aranjuez** (Line C-3) and **El Escorial** (Line C-8a).

Tourist Information/Hotel Reservations

- *Offinas de Informacion de Turismo (Tourist Information Centers),* operated by the Madrid province: Opposite track No. 19 this tourist office can provide information about Madrid or nearby cities. Brochures describing all of the day-excursion points are usually available in English.
  Hours: Monday–Friday 0800–2000 and Saturday 0900–1300. *Tel:* (91) 315–9976. When closed, the hotel office opposite track Nos. 6 and 7 will assist you.
- **Hotel reservations** can be made for a nominal charge under the INFORMATCIO Y RESERVA HOTELERA sign opposite track Nos. 6 and 7. The office is open 0730–2300 daily. Madrid is a large city, so be certain that you ask for lodging near one of the rail terminals or close to public transportation.

Getting Around in Madrid

Madrid has an excellent Metro and bus system, Consorcio de Transportes de Madrid (CTM). Purchase reduced-fare 10-trip "metro-bus" tickets for €4.57 (single ticket, €0.87) at newspaper stands, tobacco stores, and all main bus stops. The tickets are magnetically encoded.

Although Madrid has no Spanish National Tourist offices, the following provincial and municipal offices provide general information about Spain. And while most of the tourist and rail personnel speak English, it's always polite to ask: *"¿Habla Ingles, por favor?"* (Do you speak English, please?).

- **Chamartin Railway Station** (*Tel:* 91–315–9976). Hours: Monday–Friday 0900–1900; Saturday 0930–1330.
- **Barajas Airport** (*Tel:* 91–305–8656) (international arrivals). Hours: Monday–Friday 0800–2000; Saturday 0800–1300.
- **Torre de Madrid in Plaça de España** (*Tel:* 91–541–2325).
- **Metro station: Plaça de España,** Duque de Medinaceli.

Train Connections to Other Base Cities from Madrid

Depart from Madrid Chamartin Station

DEPART	TRAIN NUMBER	ARRIVE	NOTES
		Barcelona Sants	
0700	TAL 178	1400	R
0900	TAL 176	1603	R
1100	TAL 374	1800	R
1400	TAL 42	2030	R
1530	TAL 378	2205	R
2200	370	0700+1	R, Sleeper
2300	Hotel 874	0758+1	R, 1
		Lisbon (Lisboa) Santa Apolonia	
2245	Hotel 332	0820+1	R, 1
		Paris Montparnasse	
1000	IC 203	2315	R, 2
1545	TAL 201	0710+1	R, 2, 3, Sleeper
1900	Hotel 407	0827+1	R, 1, 3
2245	205	1335+1	R, 2, Sleeper

Daily, unless otherwise noted
R Reservations required
+1 Arrive next day
1. Spanish TrenHotel train. Deluxe sleeping accommodations (including toilet and shower in the compartment) are available. Special fares applicable.
2. Change trains in Hendaye.
3. Arrive Paris Austerlitz station.

- **Outside the Palace Hotel** across the square from the Prado Museum (*Tel:* 91–429–4951). Hours: Monday–Friday 0900–1900; Saturday 0930–1330.
- **Metro station: Banco de España.** Hours: Monday–Friday 1000–1400/ 1600–1900; Saturday 1000–1330.
- **Metro station: Sol,** below Puerta del Sol.
- **Travelers' hot line** (*Tel:* 91–90220–2202) provides tourists with the latest information about accommodations. A wide variety of accommodations are available in Madrid, including the Palace Hotel, across the square from the Prado Museum. As the name implies, the hotel is on the site of a former palace (*Tel:* 360–8000). The Hotel Chamartin at Chamartin Station is convenient for those businesspersons and tourists traveling by train (*Tel:* 91–323–3087; *Fax:* 91–733–0214.)

Sights/Attractions/Tours

A convenient way to see the sights is on **Madrid Visions Touristic Bus.** For €10.82, you can jump on and off the bus at more than 14 various sights, museums, and churches.

Some "don't-miss" sights include **Puerta del Sol** (Gate of the Sun), the center of the old town and the terminus for the city's metro lines and many of the buses. Six of Spain's national freeways radiate from Kilometer Zero, a stone slab buried in the pavement from which all distances are measured in Spain. *El Oso y el Madrono,* the bush and the bear statue, is Madrid's emblem.

Proceed southwest along **Calle Mayor** to **Plaça de la Villa,** with two stunning buildings dating from the fifteenth century—the **Casa** (house) and the **Torre** (tower) **de los Lujanes.** Continuing to the right of Calle Mayor and beyond the Plaça de la Villa, turn into the alleyway leading to **San Nicolas de los Servitas,** to visit Madrid's oldest church.

Going north along the **Calle del Arenal,** one can view a famous El Greco at the Church of San Gines or visit Joy Eslava, the city's trendy disco. Farther on are the Royal Palace and the Opera House.

Other significant landmarks include the **Palacio Real** (Royal Palace). *Tel:* 541–0876; Hours: 0900–1800 Monday–Saturday and 1000–1430 Sunday). It is one of the best-conserved palaces in Europe. It's filled with paintings, frescoes, clocks, furniture, and porcelain. **Plaça Mayor,** behind Calle Mayor, is an exquisite seventeenth-century arcaded square.

A **Museum Pass,** which costs €6.31, is a bargain for visiting Madrid's fine museums. The incomparable **Prado Museum** at Paseo del Prado (*Tel:* 71–330–2800; hours 0900–1900 Tuesday–Saturday and 0900–1400 Sunday) houses more than 3,000 of the world's most precious works of art, including fine collections of the Spanish masters—Goya, Velazquez, El Greco, Murillo, and Zurbaran.

The **Thyssen–Bornemisza Museum** (*Tel:* 91–369–0151; hours 1000–1900 Tuesday–Sunday), in the Villahermosa Palace, features one of the world's most extensive private art collections now open to the public. The **Reina Sofia National Art Museum** has a fantastic collection of twentieth-century Spanish art, and the **National Chalcography Institute** includes 221 original copper and brass engraved plates by Goya.

If you plan to attend a bullfight in Madrid, remember what Ernest Hemingway wrote: "It is a tragedy; the death of the bull, which is played, more or less well by the bull and the man involved and in which there is danger for the man but certain death for the bull."

For people-watching visit several of Madrid's *chiringuitos,* a combination German-style beer garden and discotheque, and cafes that line the **Paseo de la Castellana** (which becomes Paseo del Prado as it nears the Prado Museum).

In the cuisine category, Madrid has some very old and very famous restaurants. The **Casa Botin** (*Tel:* 91–366–4217) is in the *Guinness Book of Records* as the oldest continuously operated restaurant and Hemingway's favorite for suckling pig and lamb. The **Zalacain** at Alvarez de Baena 4 (*Tel:* 561–5935) features Basque seafood and game.

Day Excursions

Aranjuez, Avila, El Escorial, and **Toledo** are four very different Spanish destinations easily accessed by train from Madrid.

Aranjuez and El Escorial are particularly picturesque. Aranjuez, on the fertile banks of the Tagus River, is set in a forested valley less than 1 hour's train journey south of Madrid. El Escorial is a village at the base of the Sierra de Guadarrama, 1 hour north of Madrid. Favorites of the royalty for centuries, they are now popular retreats for Madrilenos.

Avila and Toledo are cities with such different styles that they exemplify the diversity of this ancient land. Both are worth more than a day's visit to thoroughly explore and enjoy.

Burgos, home of El Cid, is about 3 hours' journey time from Madrid.

Day Excursion to
Aranjuez
Strawberries and Spanish Royal Retreat

Depart from Madrid Atocha Station
Distance by Train: 30 miles (49 km)
Average Train Time: 50 minutes
City Dialing Code: 91
Tourist Information Office: No. 9, Plaza de San Antonio (*Tel:* 91–891–0427)
Notes: We recommend taking a taxi from the station to the tourist office, located near Palacio Real.

In the eighteenth and nineteenth centuries, **Aranjuez** was a favorite hangout for Spanish royalty. Now, it's a popular place for "regular" Madrilenos to gather on weekends. You may want to make this day excursion during the week to avoid the weekend crowds.

Aranjuez has often been described as the "Oasis of Castille," in part because it nestles on the banks of the Tagus River that nurses dense groves of poplars, rich vegetation, and glorious crops of luscious strawberries and asparagus. Apparently, the jade green waters of the river favorably foster the growth of trees, as evidenced by the city's Circus of the Twelve Streets, a square from which twelve beautifully shaded avenues radiate.

The **Palacio Real** (Royal Palace) is a lavish palace that would vie with Versailles in extravagance. Its 18 magnificent rooms include the Porcelain Salon, the Throne Room, and The Museum of Royal Robes, which displays the court dress of sovereigns up to the nineteenth century. Another highlight is the grand staircase built during the reign of Philip V. During spring and summer, the palace is open 1000–1830 Tuesday–Sunday. It closes 1 hour earlier in autumn and winter.

The Farmer's Cottage, with its resplendent furnishings, can be reached through the Prince's Garden. The Casa de Marinos, the sailor's house that

MADRID–ARANJUEZ
Frequent service beginning at 0630 with last train out at 2330.

ARANJUEZ–MADRID
Frequent service beginning at 0640 with last train out at 2127.

Average journey time: 30–45 minutes. All trains 2nd class only.
Reservations available (not required). A reservation purchased onboard the train costs more than one purchased in advance.

Distance: 30 miles (49 km)

holds the royal vessels, displays Spain's dominant maritime history. And among the gardens, the Parterre Garden and the Jardinde la Isla (Island Garden) are most memorable.

You can purchase a combination ticket that includes a guided tour of the Royal Palace. The tours operate 1000–1815 April through August; 1000–1715 September through March. Note that all of the museums are closed on Monday.

Trains to Aranjuez depart every 20–30 minutes from Madrid's Atocha Cercanias station. For a real treat, take the nineteenth-century *El Tren del Fresa* (the Strawberry Train). Yes, strawberries are served on board by attendants in period costumes.

Day Excursion to

Avila

Walled City

Depart from Madrid Chamartin Station or Principe Pio
Distance by Train: 70 miles (112 km)
Average Train Time: 1 hour, 15 minutes
City Dialing Code: 920
Tourist Information Office: Plaça de la Catedral, 4, 05001 Avila
Tel: (920) 21 13 87; *Fax:* (920) 25 37 17
Internet: www.avila.net (in Spanish)
Hours: Monday–Friday 1000–1400/1700–2000; Saturday 0930–1430/1600–1900; Sunday 0930–1400/1600–1830
RENFE at Avila Railway Station: *Tel:* (920) 25 02 02
Notes: You can take a taxi to the information office. Taxis are to the far right of the rail station as you exit. Rail station is about 1 mile from city center.

Avila is the capital of the province of Avila, and at 1,127 meters it is the highest provincial capital in Spain and the best-preserved walled city in the world. The city is completely enclosed by 1.2 miles (2.5 kilometers) of twelfth-century walls averaging 33 feet high and 10 feet thick, with 90 towers and 9 gateways. The enormousness of this project becomes apparent when you realize it was constructed in 1085.

Viewed from **Los Cuatro Postes,** an observation post on the Salamanca Road outside the city, Avila is a breathtaking sight nestled on the Adaja River against the mountains. From here, the walled city appears to be a fascinating giant stage all set for a medieval drama.

Avila is most remembered for Saint Teresa. Her presence is most evident in the convent **Nuestra Senora de Gracia,** built at the site of her parents' home; the Monastery de la Encarnacion, which depicts her lifestyle; and "Las Madres" (Monastery de San Jose), her first foundation.

Across the street from the tourist office is the **Gran Hotel Palacio Valderrabonos.** This former noble's residence is an excellent place to have lunch. Its door dates from the fifteenth century.

Other sights in Avila include the cathedral, which forms a part of the great wall, thus giving it the distinctive look of a fortress rather than a church. Its somewhat austere exterior is in contrast to its interior, which has many beautiful details. In the cathedral's museum, you may view a portrait painted by El Greco and a colossal silver monstrance, weighing nearly 200 pounds, made by Juan de Arfe in 1571.

The cathedral was begun in the twelfth century in Romanesque style and finished in the fifteenth century with a facade of Gothic Towers, the Palacio de Polention, the Mansion de los Deanes, Mansion de Davila—all magnificent with art and architecture.

The cuisine of this area is fit for a king's palate. Trout from the Tormes River is renowned for its distinctive flavor; the roast suckling pig, lamb, or veal dishes are equally excellent and served with a hearty accompaniment of vegetables, followed by *yemas de Santa Teresa,* small sweets made of egg yolks.

Nearby *paradors* offer unique accommodations for those who prefer to "base" themselves here. *Paradors* are historic buildings and palaces that the Spanish government has converted into hotels.

Madrid—Avila

DEPART MADRID CHAMARTIN	TRAIN NUMBER	ARRIVE AVILA	NOTES
0800	TAL 131	0921	R
0830	8061	0952	1, 2nd class only
0900	TAL 61	1019	R
1000	IC 203	1120	R
1130	8001	1252	1, 2nd class only
1320	TAL 129	1520	R
1400	TAL 151	1520	R
1415	TAL 79	1620	R

plus other frequent service

DEPART AVILA	TRAIN NUMBER	ARRIVE MADRID CHAMARTIN	NOTES
1605	TAL 74	1735	R, Sat
1610	8004	1740	1, 2nd class only
1730	8012	1910	1, 2nd class only
1935	8006	2110	1, 2nd class only
1950	TAL 60	2120	R
2003	TAL 152	2130	R
2040	TAL 130	2212	R
2100	R 7202	2241	2nd class only
2115	IC 11202	2245	R, Sat only
2150	8014	2320	1, 2nd class only
2213	R 8790	2340	2nd class only

R Reservations required

Reservations required for all trains with categories (IC, TAL). A reservation fee paid to the conductor onboard the train costs more than one paid in advance. Higher fares incorporating a supplement are payable for travel by Talgo (TAL) and InterCity (IC) trains.

1. This train is a Castilla y León Exprés train; reservations are available.

Distance: 70 miles (112 km)

Burgos
Home of El Cid

Depart from Madrid Chamartin Station
Distance by Train: 211 miles (340 km)
Average Train Time: 3 hours
City Dialing Code: 947
Tourist Information Office: Plaça Alonso Martinez, 7 Bajo, 09003 Burgos
Tel: (947) 20 3125 or 20 1846; *Fax:* (947) 27 6529
Hours: 0900–1400/1700–1900 Monday–Friday; 1000–1400/1700–2000 Saturday–
Sunday and holidays
Notes: To reach the office on foot (about a 15-minute walk), exit the station and go
straight ahead until you cross the Arlanzon River. Turn right and proceed along
Paseo de la Isla Avenue to the arch where the walkway Paseo del Espolon begins.
Or, take a taxi.

Burgos is north of Madrid, approaching France, and on the crossroads to Portugal. Birthplace of the warrior El Cid, Burgos is the capital of Burgos province, one of the nine provinces of Castile and Leon.

El Cid and his wife, Ximena, are entombed in the **thirteenth-century cathedral,** one of the world's outstanding examples of Gothic architecture. Its twin spires rise to greet you long before your Talgo train comes to a halt in the Burgos Station.

The nave of the cathedral and the ambulatory and portals of El Sarmental and Coroneria date from its beginnings in 1221. The latest additions, dating from the sixteenth century, include Diego de Siloe's *Golden Stairs;* the chapels of La Consolation, Santiago, and Navidad; and Juan de Vallejo's exquisite lantern.

Burgos was the site where the Castilians initiated their campaigns against the Muslims to reclaim Madrid in 1083 and Toledo in 1085. In the twentieth century, Generalissimo Franco used Burgos as his headquarters during the Spanish Civil War and here declared the cease-fire in 1939.

The **Casa del Cordon,** a fifteenth-century house so named from the huge cord of rope carved in stone fronting its entrance, forms the backdrop for **El Cid's statue.** It was here that Christopher Columbus was received in formal audience by the Spanish monarchs on his return from his second voyage to the Americas.

For lunch, we suggest the **Ojeda Restaurant** at Calle Vitoria No. 5. It is quite pleasant to have a light snack or even a full meal at its outdoor tables in the summer.

DEPART MADRID CHAMARTIN	TRAIN NUMBER	ARRIVE BURGOS	NOTES
0830	8061	1226	2nd class
1000	IC 203	1326	R
1330	8063	1726	2nd class

DEPART BURGOS	TRAIN NUMBER	ARRIVE MADRID CHAMARTIN	NOTES
1500	8012	1910	2nd class
1903	TAL 200	2200	R, 1
1903	IC 11202	2240	R, Sat only
1921	8014	2320	2nd class

Daily, unless otherwise noted
R Reservations required
Reservation required for all trains with categories (e.g., IC, TAL). A reservation fee paid to the conductor onboard the train costs more than one paid in advance. Higher fares incorporating a supplement are payable for travel by Talgo (TAL) and InterCity (IC) trains.
1. Runs daily except Sat.
Distance: 211 miles (340 km)

Day Excursion to

El Escorial
World's Eighth Wonder

Depart from Madrid Atocha or Chamartin Stations
Distance by Train: 32 miles (52 km)
Average Train Time: 60 minutes
City Dialing Code: 91
Tourist Information Office: No.10 Calle Floridablanca
Tel: (91) 890–1554
Hours: 1000–1400/1500–1700 Monday–Friday; 1000–1400 Saturday
Notes: The rail station is about 1 mile from town. Taxis are to the left of the station exit. A taxi ride to the town square or the tourist office costs about €2.10. Buses are also available that will take you to the town square.

El Escorial is the name of the village and the immense palace-monastery, both havens of Phillip II, who personally supervised construction of the monumental structure to commemorate his victory over France at St. Quentin in 1557. Part monastery, part palace, part cathedral, El

Madrid—El Escorial

DEPART MADRID CHAMARTIN	TRAIN NUMBER	ARRIVE EL ESCORIAL
0616	RE 07109	0722
0847	R 07103	0943
1046	R 07105	1137
1348	R 07107	1444
1646	R 07109	1737
1932	R 07111	2023
2046	R 07113	2137

DEPART EL ESCORIAL	TRAIN NUMBER	ARRIVE MADRID CHAMARTIN
1515	R 07108	1607
1815	R 07110	1906
1937	R 07212	2026
2115	R 07112	2206
2126	R 08216	2209
2200	R 07202	2241

Daily, including holidays
All trains 2nd class.
Distance: 32 miles (52 km)

Escorial reflects its builder's vanity. The monastery and palace are open 1000–1800 in summer, until 1700 in winter; closed on Monday.

El Escorial encompasses 8 acres and has 9 towers, 16 courtyards, 86 staircases, 1,200 doors, and 2,673 leaded-glass windows. A force of 1,500 laborers worked 21 years to complete it. Wear your best pair of walking shoes—you'll need them.

The **Hall of Battles** epitomizes Spain's aggressive history in paintings by Italian artists Castello, Grenello, and Tavorone. Priceless artworks by Borsch, Rembrandt, Tintoretto, and Titian are also displayed throughout the palace. Tapestries of Spanish country life woven over sketches drawn by Goya also hang on the walls.

Prior to mounting the Armada against England, King Phillip tried to bring England into the Spanish empire by marrying Mary Tudor, known as "Bloody Mary" for her overzealous persecution of English Protestants. Forty years later, just before his death, Phillip had become a religious fanatic. He returned to the palace to live as though in poverty in a sparse second-floor apartment, which provides stark contrast to its surroundings—one of the grandest palaces in Europe.

Two other attractions of interest are the **Casita del Principe** (the Prince's

Cottage), which you pass en route to the station, and **Casita de Arriba,** a hunting lodge 2 miles farther on. Both are open 1000–1800 (1700 in winter); closed Monday. Both were constructed by Charles III (1759–1788). His friendship with France and hostility toward Great Britain led to the alliance in support of the American Revolution.

Day Excursion to

Toledo
City of History

Depart from Madrid Atocha Station
Distance by Train: 57 miles (91 km)
Average Train Time: 1 hour, 15 minutes
City Dialing Code: 925
Tourist Information Office: Puerta de Bisagra, 1, 45003 Toledo
Tel: (925) 220843; *Fax:* (925) 252648
Hours: 0900–1800 Monday–Friday; 0900–1900 Saturday; 0900–1500 Sunday
Notes: Public bus service from rail station into town. Buses depart every 15 minutes. Bus stops first at the tourist information office at Puerta de la Bisagra before terminating in the main square, Plaça de Zocodover (Marketplace). There is also an information office at the city hall, in front of the cathedral.

Toledo is (as is Avila) capital of a province with the same name. Toledo province is defined by mountain ranges, rivers, and rich rolling valleys; it abounds with game, aromatic plants, and delicate white-leafed rock roses—all of which distinguishes Toledo from the other provinces of La Mancha with their monotonous, flat expanses.

Divided by the River Tagus, Toledo has the rich and varied history of most river towns, and in Europe's south that means conquests by Romans, Visigoths, Moors, and ultimately Christians, who declared it Spain's Imperial City. It was ruled by the legendary El Cid. The impact of such a diverse history earned Toledo the UNESCO "Heritage of Mankind" status, defining it as one of the richest historically, culturally, and monumentally endowed cities in Spain.

A Cretan named Domenico Teotocopulo arrived in Toledo in 1577. His arrival might have gone unnoticed, except that Señor Teotocopulo, better known as El Greco, happened to be a painter of some renown. El Greco painted and bequeathed his best to Toledo. The **Museum of Santa Cruz** and the **El Greco museum** as well as the cathedral honor the achievements of one of Spain's most creative artists.

Although Toledo's history may be complicated, its charm is definitely

Madrid—Toledo

DEPART MADRID CHAMARTIN	DEPART MADRID ATOCHA	TRAIN NUMBER	ARRIVE TOLEDO	NOTES
0630	0644	7054	0753	Mon–Fri
0830	0844	7056	0947	
1014	1028	7058	0102	
1212	1226	7060	1325	

DEPART TOLEDO	ARRIVE MADRID ATOCHA	TRAIN NUMBER	ARRIVE MADRID CHAMARTIN
1425	7065	7054	1548
1630	7067	7056	1742
1857	7069	7058	2011
2058	7071	7060	2212

Daily, unless otherwise noted.
All train service to Toledo is second class only.
Reservations available on all trains (not required)

Distance: 57 miles (91 km)

not. Wander the city's narrow cobblestone streets; visit its friendly cafes, which remain open late into the night; and taste its fresh fruits from the open market in the morning.

In 1226, King Ferdinand III laid the first stone in the **Cathedral of Toledo,** and today it is renowned for its art and architecture. The thirteenth-century fortress **Alcazar** was a Roman Pretorian Palace in the third century.

Toledo also is well known for its crafters who work steel into some of the finest blades for knives and swords. The distinctive black-on-gold designs embellishing the handles of blades have been carried over to jewelry and other accessories available in shops throughout the city.

Although there are numerous eateries, most visitors seem to gather in the main square, **Plaça de Zocodover** (Marketplace). Here, you will find cafes and bars to sample local sandwiches and *tapas* (appetizers).

The **Parador Conde Orgaz** and the **Hotel Alfonso VI** are exceptional accommodations in Toledo, if you choose to stay.

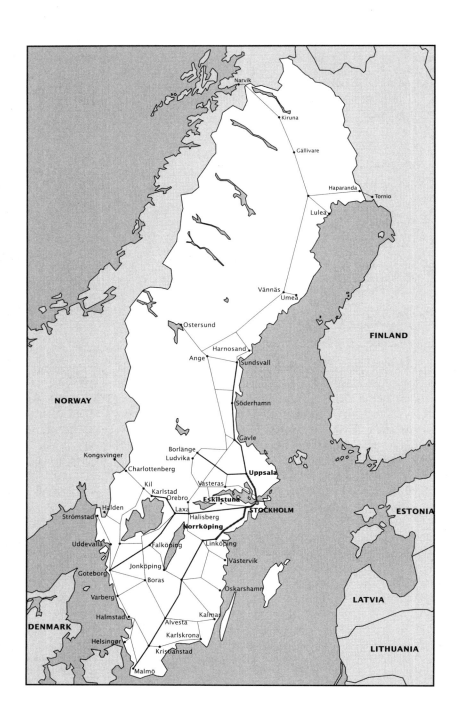

Sweden

I n size, Sweden is about the same size as the state of California or the country of Spain. It is half-covered by forests, dotted with nearly 100,000 lakes, and thousands of islands line its coastline. It is one of the largest and most prosperous countries in Europe and supports a large and efficient industrial complex. With a population of only 8.7 million inhabitants, however, it is not crowded, and its citizens enjoy a superb quality of life and one of the highest standards of living in the world.

Although Swedish, a Germanic language, is the language of the majority, Finland was a part of Sweden until 1809, and Finnish-speaking natives still occupy the northeastern area along with another minority group, the Sami (Lapp). Fortunately for English-speaking tourists, English is spoken by most Swedes who are involved in tourism, transportation, and international business.

From 1846 to 1930, approximately 1.3 million Swedes emigrated to North America. Thousands of visitors, including North Americans, trace their Swedish ancestry at the Swedish Emigrant Institute in Växjö, which houses and records memorabilia from that time period.

It is difficult to realize that only about a century ago, Sweden was one of the most backward countries in Europe. Today, Sweden is forward thinking—spending a large percentage of national output on industrial research and development. Since 1995, Sweden has played an important role as a member of the European Union. Sweden's strategic geographic location between the North Atlantic and Russia has affected its foreign policies and security strategies for all of Europe.

For more information about Sweden, visit *Internet:* **www.gosweden.org** *E-mail:* info@gosweden.org, or contact the Swedish Travel and Tourism Council:

New York: P.O. Box 4649, Grand Central Station, New York, NY
10163–4649; *Tel:* (212) 885–9700; *Fax:* (212) 885–9764

Banking

- **Currency:** Swedish Krona (SEK)
- **Exchange rate at press time:** SEK 10.64 = U.S. $1.00
- **Hours:** 0900–1700 Monday–Friday. Closes at 1500 on the day
  before a holiday, which the Swedes refer to as a *halvdag* (half day).

Communications

- **Country Dialing Code:** 46
  For telephone calls within Sweden dial zero (0) preceding area code.
- **Direct dial:** AT&T: 020–795–611; MCI: 020–795–922; Sprint:
  020–799–011

Rail Travel in Sweden

Swedish State Railways: Central Station, S-105 50 Stockholm
For calls within Sweden, call toll-free *Tel:* 020–757575. From outside of
Sweden call 46–8 696 7540; *Internet:* www.resor.sj.se.

The Swedish State Railways (SJ) operates about 7,000 miles of rail lines.
Its **X 2000** trains are Sweden's modern high-speed "tilting" trains, which
travel at 125 mph and serve most of the major cities in Sweden. In business
first class, meals are served at travelers' seats. There is also a bistro car,
which serves hot and cold meals, plus beverages at travelers' seats.

The combined rail and motorway connection via the 16-km Øresund
Bridge began July 1, 2000. This major infrastructure brought the cities of
Malmö, Sweden, and Copenhagen, Denmark, together to create the largest
northern European market. Express X2000 trains cut travel time between
Malmö and Copenhagen to 35 minutes.

InterCity trains operate between all of Sweden's major cities and
between Stockholm and Oslo and Stockholm and Copenhagen. These trains
often have a bistro car where you can purchase food, refreshments, or games
for the kids, and a "family car" with play areas available for children.
InterRegio trains operate between regions. These trains have radio sockets
at all seats and refreshments available. **Night trains** in Sweden offer several
different types of accommodations, ranging from exclusive compartments
with two beds, shower, and toilet to six-bedded couchettes with toilet and
washing facilities in the corridor.

Train platforms are referred to in Sweden as *spoors*. On most trains oper-
ated by the Scandinavian countries, drinking water is supplied at no charge.
Train reservations are mandatory for trips of more than 90 miles on all
X2000 and overnight trains.

SJ accepts the variety of **Eurail passes, ScanRail Pass,** and the **Sweden
RailPass** (see list of European RailPasses in the Appendix for prices and
ordering information for the multicountry passes and ScanRail Pass). Pass

prices do not include reservation fees, but a point-to-point ticket does. Bonuses for passholders include:

- Free ferry crossing on Silja Line: Stockholm–Helsinki, Finland (railpass must be valid in Finland), Stockholm–Turku and Umeå to Vaasa, Finland (pass must be valid in Finland);
- Free ferry crossing on Scandlines routes Helsingborg–Helsingør, Denmark (with valid railpass in Sweden and Denmark);
- 50 percent discount on Stena Line crossing Göteborg–Frederikshavn (no discount on cabin/couchette supplements);
- 50 percent discount on TT Line, Trelleborg–Travemünde, Germany;
- Free ferry crossing on TT Line Trelleborg–Sassnitz, Germany (valid railpass in Sweden and Germany);
- 50 percent discount on full fare ferry crossing with TR Line Trelleborg-Rostock, Germany.

Sweden RailPass

Unlimited travel on all routes operated by the Swedish Railways. Up to 2 children under 16 years of age travel free when accompanied by an adult. For additional children there are reduced prices available. Prices do not include reservation fees or supplement fees for sleepers or couchettes. The Sweden RailPass is valid on the night trains between Gothenburg/Stockholm-Umea/Boden/Kiruna/Vassijaure, which are operated by Tagkompaniet, a private company. (Night-train supplements are excluded.)

	Adult		Additional Child	
	1st class	2nd class	1st class	2nd class
3 days within 1 month	$211	$156	$148	$111
4 days within 1 month	$239	$177	$168	$124
5 days within 1 month	$268	$198	$188	$129

Special: Two children under age 16 travel free together per adult.

Base City:
Stockholm

Internet: www.stoinfo.se
City Dialing Code: 08

Stockholm declares intentions of retaining the old, then in the same breath states great love of progress and things modern; it provides visitors with the opportunity to experience Sweden's modern culture and to celebrate its ancient traditions.

Stockholm's **Gamla Stan** (Old Town) is located on a small island in the city center. Its narrow cobblestone streets wind their crooked ways over paths unchanged since the Middle Ages past houses bearing the same facades they had when they were built. But behind these old facades you find the most modern of business establishments and apartments whose decors rival those of similar dwellings anywhere in the world. With a delicate touch, Stockholm has made this dualism work in every way.

Another example is **Sergels Torg**, Stockholm's space-age city center. It is comfortably surrounded by other structures centuries older. Call it what you will, but most people call Stockholm absolutely beautiful.

Arriving by Air

Arlanda Airport lies 26 miles (42 kilometers) northwest of the city. *Tel:* (08) 797 60 00. Tourist information counter in the arrivals area.

Airport–City Links: Arlanda Express train service every 15 minutes to downtown Stockholm. *Internet:* www.arlandaexpress.com. Journey time: 20 minutes; fare, SEK 140 one-way for adults.

Flybussarna Airport Coach departures are every 10 minutes. Journey time: 35–40 minutes; fare, SEK 70 for adults. *Tel:* 600–1000; *Fax:* 686–1362. Coach terminates in Stockholm at the World Trade Centre, next to the Central Station. *Internet:* www.flygbussarna.com

SAS Limousine service (*Tel:* 797–3700; *Fax:* 797–4198) is available 24 hours per day (about U.S.$110/car) to Stockholm Central Station.

Taxis are available 24 hours daily. The taxi stand is located just outside the arrivals hall of the airport. Taxi fare is SEK 400–500. Journey time to city center: 30–40 minutes.

Arriving by Train

Stockholm has several suburban stations, but international trains stop only at the main rail station in the center of the city, Stockholm Central. All excursions out of Stockholm depart from Stockholm Central Station.

Stockholm's Central Station is modern, well organized, and easy to move about in. International trains usually arrive on track No. 17 or 18.

- **Luggage carts:** Insert a SEK 5 coin in the lock; coin will be refunded upon returning the cart to a rack.

The Central Station is close to several major hotels and directly connected to the Stockholm subway (the *Tunnelbanan*). The main taxi stand is across the street from the railway station.

The station does an excellent job of moving its passengers to and from the trains. It also provides a full complement of services for the traveler. An arcade of shops, on the lower station level in the proximity of the exits from track Nos. 17 and 18, provides all types of foodstuffs, beverages, tobacco, newspapers, and so forth.

The *Konsum*—Sweden's answer to the American supermarket—is a good place to restock your larder. It is located in the same area within the station. There are also shops in the main station–concourse area where you may purchase food and soft drinks.

The station's food-service facilities range from a cafeteria to a restaurant with its own gambling casino. The cafeteria is located on the main level of the station to the far right as you stand looking into the station from the train exit. It can be identified by its sign, CAFE OASEN. Cafeteria service is continuous Monday through Saturday 0630–2330 and Sunday 0700–2330; it is a good place to have breakfast, lunch, or dinner.

The **Centralens Restaurang** (restaurant) **Orientexpressen** has the previously mentioned casino. You'll see its sign on the right side of the station as you exit from the track area. In addition to the casino, the complex includes a pub and a restaurant with good food at reasonable prices. The all-you-can-eat breakfast in the restaurant section is a real bargain. The restaurant has an expansive but relatively inexpensive luncheon-and-dinner menu featuring many Swedish specialties (closed during July).

Across the street from Central Station, along the street Vasagatan, you can find a number of excellent food facilities ranging from fast to fancy.

- **Train information** is displayed on bulletins following the usual format. Departures are printed on yellow paper; arrivals appear on white. Train information is readily available throughout the station, including key positions just inside the main entrance and again in the corridors leading to the track areas. The office is in the main concourse to the left of the main exit. Hours: 0600–2300 Monday–Saturday; 0700–2300 Sunday.

Local train information, usually for commuter trains, is displayed by a bank of large-screen, closed-circuit television sets.

- **Train reservations** can be made in a large ticket office located in the main hall to the right as you proceed from the track area. A sign, FARD-BILJETTER PLATSBILJETTER, identifies it. Take a queue number for seat reservations and sleeping-car accommodations. Hours: Monday–Friday 0545–2100; Saturday 0545–1900; Sunday 0800–2100.

- **Railpass validation** should be completed before making your first train trip. Operating personnel aboard the trains can validate the pass, but they are required to charge for the service. Validation is free in any regular railway station. In Stockholm's Central Station, use the window marked INTERNATIONAL TICKETS to the right of the main exit.

- **Money exchange** is located in the main station concourse and to the right of the main exit as you proceed from the track area. The office displays the regular pictograph sign plus one reading FOREX (exchange office). Hours: 0700–2100 daily.

- **Hotel reservations** can be made at Stockholm Information Service, located in the main station concourse next to the post office. Look for the sign HOTELLCENTRAL TURISTINFORMATION. Hours: June–August, 0700–2100 daily; September–May, 0800–1900 daily. Small charges are made for obtaining hotel rooms and space in youth hostels. Advance payment is accepted to assure that the hotel or pension will hold your room until your arrival. If your accommodations are located some distance from the train station, this can be a welcomed service.

- **Tourist information** is available in the rail station at the same office, HOTELLCENTRAL TURISTINFORMATION, or in the main tourist center at Sweden House.

Tourist Information/Hotel Reservations

- *Stockholm Tourist Information Center:* Sweden House, Hamngatan 27 (Kungsträdgården); *Tel:* (08) 789–24–90, *Fax:* (08) 789–24–91; *Internet:* www.stoinfo.se; *E-mail:* info@stoinfo.se

Hours: May, 0900–1800 Monday–Friday and 0900–1500 Saturday–Sunday; June–August, 0800–1800 Monday–Friday and 0900–1700 Saturday–Sunday; September, 0900–1800 Monday–Friday and 0900–1500 Saturday–Sunday

Inquiries about the "Sweden at Home" plan of meeting Swedes with similar interests should be made at this information office. An excellent publication is the *Stockholm Guide.*

Getting Around in Stockholm

The city has excellent transportation facilities for sight-seeing in Stockholm. The extensive network of bus and subway systems makes it easy to reach practically any point in the city from any other point.

Train Connections to Other Base Cities from Stockholm

Depart from Stockholm Central Station

DEPART	TRAIN NUMBER	ARRIVE	NOTES
		Berlin Zoobahnhof	
0815	X2/521	1923	R, 1
1615	X2/541	0632+1	R, 2, Sleeper
		Copenhagen (København) H.	
0615	X2/521	1123	R
0815	X2/525	1323	R
1215	X2/533	1723	R
1615	X2/541	2123	R
1815	X2/545	2323	R
2300	INN 205	0711+1	R, 5, Sleeper
		Helsinki	
1700	Silja Line Ferry	0930+1	R, 3
1700	Viking Line Ferry	0955+1	R, 4
		Oslo Sentral	
0635	IC 51	1232	R
0905	X2 17427	1645	R, 6
1434	IC 53	2100	R

Daily, unless otherwise noted

R Reservations required. Seat reservations required on Swedish trains for journeys longer than 150 kilometers.

+1 Arrive next day

1. Change trains in Copenhagen then Hamburg.
2. Change trains in Malmö and Berlin-Ostbahnhof.
3. Silja Line ferries depart daily except Jan 21, 23, 25, September 12, 14, 16, and December 24 and 31. Silja Line docks are Stockholm Värtahamnen and Helsinki Eteläsatama. Refer to Appendix, Baltic Ferry Crossings, for details.
4. Viking Line ferries depart daily May 1–September 30. Viking Line docks are Stockholm Stadsgarden and Helsinki Katajanokka. Refer to Appendix, Baltic Ferry Crossings, for details.
5. Change trains in Malmö.
6. Change trains in Göteborg.

Your key to using these city transportation facilities is **The Stockholm Card,** which provides free admission to 70 of the city's museums and sights, as well as free sightseeing and transportation throughout the Stockholm area. Adult prices are SEK 220 for 24 hours, SEK 380 for 48 hours, and SEK 540 for 72 hours. Child rates are SEK 60 for 24 hours, SEK 120 for 48 hours, and SEK 180 for 72 hours. For additional children there are reduced rates available. The card is on sale at the tourist center in Sweden House and at the Central Station. It is sold undated and is stamped with the date and hour the first time you use it. With the card, you will be given a folder explaining its use and validation procedure.

Sights/Attractions/Tours

Gamla Stan—The Old Town dates back to 1290 and is Stockholm's oldest and most enchanting area. Besides containing many historical sights, such as the world's oldest existing bank (since 1656), the Royal Palace, and Parliament, you'll also find unusual shops, art galleries, antiques stores, and more than 30 restaurants.

With The Stockholm Card in your pocket, you can expand your day-excursion itinerary to include places of interest in and near Stockholm. For example, you can make a day excursion to **Norrtalje**, with its quaint port, and have lunch aboard a vintage steamer permanently moored there. You can also ride one of the Stockholm Transit Authority (SL) buses to **Furusund**, a narrow passage for ships entering and leaving the city's harbor. You can have lunch in a quaint Inn at Furusund. During high season, May–August, sightseeing boats can take you to the outer archipelago.

Yet another alternative use for the card would be to take a bus ride to historic **Vaxholm**, for a great Swedish lunch at the waterfront hotel overlooking the old fortress and shopping there at leisure. Stockholm has many museums to explore, so it is difficult to single out but a few recommendations. There is one, however, that we are sure you won't want to miss: the **Vasa Museum.**

In 1628, Sweden proudly launched what was then the world's largest warship and pride of the nation, the *Vasa*. Carrying the name of the royal family, along with sixty-four cannon, this ship was presumed to be unconquerable. But the nation's joy was short-lived. The *Vasa* capsized in the harbor during its maiden voyage. Raised in 1961, painstakingly restored, and now resting in a museum especially constructed for its preservation, the warship is enthroned in the middle of a great hall, displayed in all its grandeur. The cobblestone ground floor suggests a quay, and the restored warship can be viewed from various perspectives from four levels.

Vasa is unique since it is the oldest fully preserved warship in the world. Films of the raising and restoration of the *Vasa* are shown hourly in the museum, and guided tours following the film are conducted in the summer.

Winter travelers plan ahead to experience Stockholm's annual winter festival, events, and activities.

Day Excursions

We have selected a group of day excursions that will give you an excellent cross section of life in Sweden. **Eskilstuna** is often referred to as "Sweden's Sheffield," although it bears little resemblance to its English counterpart. Next is a trip southward through Ostergotland, where the city of **Norrköping** will unfold its industrial lifestyles.

Uppsala brings another contrast, that of a university town. Admittedly, planning day excursions in Sweden is made somewhat difficult by the distances involved between the centers of population, but all of these are within reasonable travel times and well worth the visit.

Eskilstuna
Sweden's Steel Center

Depart from Stockholm Central Station
Distance by Train: 73 miles (117 km)
Average Train Time: 1 hour
City Dialing Code: 16
Tourist Information Office: Nygatan 15
Tel: (016) 107000; *Fax:* (016) 514575
Internet: www.eskilstuna.se
E-mail: info@turism.eskilstuna.se
Hours: June–August: Monday–Friday 0900–1800 and Saturday 1000–1500, Sunday
   1100–1500; September–May: Monday–Friday 0900–1700
Notes: Exit by the front of the station and follow Drottninggatan Street two blocks
   down to Nygatan. Turn right onto Nygatan and continue two blocks. The tourist
   information office is on the corner of Nygatan/Alva Myrdals gata.

Eskilstuna is unique in that it has preserved its industrial birthplace in the midst of a great industrial expansion. In a quiet section in the center of Sweden's "steel town," the well-preserved **Rademacher Forges** stand today just as they have for the last 340 years. Be certain to include a visit to this area during your day excursion.

The forges were erected in 1658 under the supervision of Reinhold Rademacher. Originally twenty in number, six have been preserved as a tribute to the heritage of modern Eskilstuna. The entire area surrounding the forges was restored in 1959 to commemorate the city's tricentennial. Desecendants of the "smiths" are still at work forming gold, copper, and iron into colorful trinkets for sale. In the spring and early autumn, there is also a handicraft market in the area. The **Faktori museet** is situated in the old Musket Factory nearby. The museum includes, among other things, the city's historical exhibition, "Mellan sjöarna" ("Between the lakes.")

Eskilstuna is located in the most populous part of Sweden. Named after the eleventh-century English missionary Sam Eskil, Eskilstuna is the center of the Swedish steel industry. Its parks and open-area squares, however, make it unlike any other steel town. A statue of Saint Eskil stands in the churchyard of **Fors Kyrka.** Both the statue and the church are worth a visit. If you continue your walk along the riverside, you will find another monument of Saint Eskil on your way to **Kloster Kyrka,** which is easily recognized by its two towers.

Eskilstuna's town charter dates from 1659. In 1971, five surrounding rural communities and the town of Torshälla merged with Eskilstuna. Torshälla is more than 650 years old. Its name was derived from the Nordic

DEPART STOCKHOLM CENTRAL	TRAIN NUMBER	ARRIVE ESKILSTUNA STATION
0650	IC 909	0755
0755	IC 963	0856
0855	IC 915	1000

then hourly service at 55 minutes past the hour until 2255, plus 1000, 1625 and 1725.

DEPART ESKILSTUNA	TRAIN NUMBER	ARRIVE STOCKHOLM CENTRAL
1503	970	1605
1603	932	1705
1703	996	1811

then hourly until 2203, plus 1808 and 2008.

Daily
Distance: 73 miles (117 km)

god, Thor, who was worshipped at offertory gatherings of the barbarians occupying Torshälla.

Parken Zoo (zoo park) in Eskilstuna ranks as one of Sweden's most visited tourist attractions. Hours: May–September from 1000 daily. In addition to its zoological gardens, there are an amusement park known as the "Tivoli," a heated swimming pool with water slides, "Phantom Land," "Flamingo Valley," and a petting zoo. The zoo is well known for its collection of animals that are rare in Sweden, including the world's largest lizard, "the Komodo," and a family of white tigers. The white tiger is thought to be extinct in the wild, but at Parken Zoo, three little tigers were born in 2001.

The city is well endowed with works of art. The **Art Museum** (open daily except Monday 1200–1600) is especially proud of its collection of Swedish art from the seventeenth century to the present. Every three or four weeks, contemporary art exhibitions are changed.

Be certain to visit Tingsgarden, the glass-making center located in the old town, where you can view glass blowing and glass painting. There are also a gift shop, cafe, and restaurant. The eighteenth-century surroundings are well preserved and have been declared a historical monument.

Sunbyholm Castle is located 8 miles outside Eskilstuna. Built by an illegitimate son of a Swedish king, it has been restored to its original splendor and a restaurant has been added. The area also has a harbor, good swimming beach, and the 1000-year-old "strip cartoon"—the **Sigurd Carving** on stone—one of about 50 prehistoric monuments surrounding Eskilstuna. It illustrates some famous episodes from the ancient Icelandic saga of Sigurd the Dragon Slayer.

Day Excursion to

Norrköping
The Northern Cactus Center

Depart from Stockholm Central Station
Distance by Train: 101 miles (163 km)
Average Train Time: 1 hour, 17 minutes
City Dialing Code: 11
Tourist Information Office: Dalsgatan 16, 60181 Norrköping
Tel: 11 15 50 00; *Fax:* 11 15 50 74
Internet: www.destination.norrkoping.se
E-mail: info@destination.norrkoping.se
Hours: June 25–July 29; 0930–1900 Monday–Friday, 0930–1700 Saturday, and 0930–1400 Sunday; rest of the year: 1000–1800 Monday–Friday and 1000–1400 Saturday.
Notes: The tourist office is about a 10-minute walk from the rail station. Proceed down Drottninggatan. After crossing the bridge over the Motala River (Motala Ström), turn right on Hamngatan and take another right onto Gamla Rådstugugatan. Pass Repslagaregatan and take the next right to Dalsgatan. The tourist office is located in the Industrial Landscape, opposite Louis De Geer Concert and Congress Hall.

If you want to experience, in the same day, two different forms of land transportation that span one hundred years, now's your chance. Take the modern, high-speed X2000 train (seat reservations required and supplement payable) from Stockholm Central in the morning and arrive in Norrköping in only 1 hour, 17 minutes. Then, for an excellent introduction to Norrköping that includes the charm of yesteryear, ride the 1902 tram **Gamla Ettan,** "the Old Number One." There are only two cities in Sweden that still use the quaint, clean, and efficient tram system—Gothenburg and Norrköping.

Cactuses in Sweden? That's right. Just opposite the rail station, you may be surprised to see some 25,000 cactus plants in the Karl Johans Park. The plants are rearranged annually according to special motifs.

Norrköping is one of Sweden's most important industrial cities and is the eighth largest. If you proceed directly to the tourist office from the rail station, you'll be in the well preserved **Industrial Landscape area** (Industrilandskapet). Take a ride on one of the yellow trams to experience yesterday's history in today's environment and to discover the unique Industrial Landscape where the old spinning mills have been transformed. Or, take one of the many guided walks, such as "Johanna's Walk" to go back in time to 1910 and hear Johanna talk about life at that time.

The **Louis De Geer Concert and Congress Hall** is a prime example—it once was a paper mill. It no longer makes paper—it makes music—with performances by Norrköping's own symphony orchestra, as well as by many others. The hall is open to the public during the summertime, and guided tours are available.

One of Sweden's most beautiful industrial buildings sits in the middle of the Motala Ström (River). Shaped like an iron and called *strykjämet,* it houses the **Arbetets Museum** (the Museum of Work), with exhibitions, workshops, and a museum shop. (*Tel:* 11 18 92 00; *Fax:* 11 18 22 90; *Internet:* www.arbetetsmuseum.se. *Hours:* 1100–1700 daily, except for certain holiday weekends.) There's a spectacular view from the restaurant on the top floor.

Continuing in the old industrial area along the banks of the Motala Ström, visit the **Stadsmuseet** (City Museum) for a realistic view of life and the crafts and industries of nineteenth-century Norrköping. *Internet:* www.norrkoping.se/stadsmuseet. *Hours:* 1000–1700 Tuesday, Wednesday, and Friday; 1000–2000 Thursday; 1100–1700 Saturday and Sunday. Closed on Monday. No admission fee.

Farther along the banks of the Motala, you will come to an open-air museum, the **Färgargården** (Dyer's Workshop), which portrays the wool-dyeing processes of the mid-eighteenth century. For a great midday snack, stop in the cafe for waffles—Swedish style.

Norrköping successfully blends its industrial history with some of nature's most beautiful assets. Its many parks and beautiful flower displays provide an atmosphere of contentment and tranquillity.

Norrköping's history extends all the way back to the Bronze Age with the 3,000-year-old rock carvings in **Himmelstalundparken.** Guided tours of the rock carvings are available daily July 1–August 1 at 1400. There are also special exhibitions, rock-carving trips, and boat trips on the Motala. The rock-carving museum, **Hällristningsmuseet,** is open 1100–1600 May 11–June 14; 1100–1800 June 15–July 31; and 1100–1600 in August. Admission fee: SEK 30.

Only 25 kilometers north of Norrköping is the famous **Kolmårdens Zoo and Safari Park**—one of Europe's finest. Also, close to Norrköping, pleasure steamers ply the **Göta Canal** and the archipelago. Check with the tourist information office for more details on either of these great adventures.

Stockholm—Norrköping

DEPART STOCKHOLM CENTRAL	TRAIN NUMBER	ARRIVE NORRKÖPING	NOTES
0615	X 2000/521	0734	R
0715	X 2000/523	0833	R, Mon–Fri
0815	X 2000/525	0934	R
1015	X 2000/529	1134	R
1115	X 2000/531	1238	R
1215	X 2000/533	1336	R

DEPART NORRKÖPING	TRAIN NUMBER	ARRIVE STOCKHOLM CENTRAL	NOTES
1422	X 2000/534	1540	R
1520	X 2000/536	1640	R
1528	238	1715	
1622	X 2000/538	1740	R
1709	242	1905	Mon–Fri
1815	8340	2010	R
1822	X 2000/542	1940	
1922	X 2000.542	2040	except Sat
2022	X 2000/546	2140	R
2052	248	2245	except Sat
2220	X 2000/550	2340	

Daily, unless otherwise noted
R Reservations required on all X 2000 trains and for all journeys of more than 150 km on other trains. Special supplements payable on X 2000 trains.
Distance: 101 miles (163 km)

Day Excursion to

Uppsala
University City

Depart from Stockholm Central Station
Distance by Train: 40 miles (66 km)
Average Train Time: 43 minutes
City Dialing Code: 18
Tourist Information Office: Fyristorg 8, SE 753 10 Uppsala
Tel: (018) 27 48 00; Fax: (018) 13 28 95
Internet: http://res.till.uppland.nu
E-mail: tb@uppsalatourism.se
Hours: 1000–1800 Monday–Friday, 1000–1500 Saturday; Sunday 1200–1600 July–mid-August.
Notes: Five-minute walk from the railway station. Exit the station and walk diagonally

through the small park in front to the main street, Kungsgatan. Turn right, then turn left on Vaksalagatan (the next crossing). Walk until you reach the square (Stora Torget) where all the city buses meet. Follow the street Drottninggatan from the square and cross the small river Fyrisan. Turn right immediately after the bridge, and the tourist office is identified by the traditional i sign.

No other town in Sweden has such a long recorded history as Uppsala. This is where Sweden began. As far back as the sixth century, it was the political and religious center of the expanding Swedish kingdom. According to the ancient legends, pagans from all reaches of the kingdom came to Uppsala every ninth year to feast and offer sacrifices until the eleventh century, when Christianity began to take over. Legend has it that one of the kings of the period, King Aun, got all wrapped up in the nine-year cycle by sacrificing one of his sons each cycle. His tenth and last son put an end to old dad—and to the cycle, too!

Modern Uppsala won't remind you of Oxford or Heidelberg—or Bryn Mawr, for that matter. Uppsala is a university town with an academic environment distinctly its own. The city and the area surrounding it enshrine a great deal of Swedish history encompassing religion (pagan and Christian alike), academe, and politics. This composite results in a city of multifaceted interests, architecture, and customs.

Gamla Uppsala (Old Uppsala) lies 3 miles north of the present city center and is full of myth, legend, and history including the graves of the sixth-century Ynglinga Dynasty kings of Aun, Egil, and Adil (who worshiped the god Frej). (Take bus No. 2, 20, 24 or 54.) The pagan religion of the Vikings persisted here well into the eleventh century. A twelfth-century church, heralding the advent of Christianity, then replaced the pagan temple. Some say the ancient mounds were part of the lost civilization of Atlantis. The area is now an open-air museum, accessible to visitors daily year-round. Visit the **Gamla Historical Centre** celebrating the archaeological finds. Hours vary—check with the tourist information office. Admission is SEK 50 for adults; children are admitted free. *Tel:* 4618 23 9300; *Internet:* www.raa.se/gamlauppsala; *E-mail:* gamlauppsala@raa.se.

Uppsala Castle stands on a hill overlooking the city. Begun in the 1540s by King Gustav Vasa as a symbol of his power over the church, it was completed during the reign of Queen Christina. The king had cannon mounted on the castle pointing at the church. They still point that way today. Partially destroyed by fire in 1702, the castle has been restored. After the extensive renovation in 1994, you can now visit new parts of the castle on a 45-minute guided tour conducted in English at 1300 and 1500 from June 1 through August 27. You'll see the Hall of State and the castle church's uncovered altar wall.

The great **Hall of State** is frequently the scene of historic events. Both

Stockholm—Uppsala

Note: In addition to trains shown here, there is local train service between Stockholm and Uppsala; get information at Stockholm Central Station.

DEPART STOCKHOLM CENTRAL	TRAIN NUMBER	ARRIVE UPPSALA	NOTES
0855	824	0935	
1055	882	1135	Mon–Fri
1255	2228	1335	

DEPART UPPSALA	TRAIN NUMBER	ARRIVE STOCKHOLM CENTRAL	NOTES
1625	841	1705	except Sun
1825	857	1905	
2125	859	2205	except Sun
2155	849	2235	Mon–Fri

Daily, unless otherwise noted

Seat reservations presumably not needed since this trip is only 66 km, but passengers should check at the Stockholm Central Station before boarding these trains.

Distance: 40 miles (66 km)

the coronation banquet for Gustavus Adolphus and Queen Christina's abdication took place within the castle's walls. The castle is open 1100–1600 daily from May 2–August 27. A more restricted schedule is followed during the remainder of the year.

Three-quarters of Uppsala was destroyed by fire in 1702. It was in the subsequent period of reconstruction that the character of the city changed. The university and its scholars began to dominate, and the reputation of the university spread throughout the civilized world. The present university building was opened in 1887.

Among the collections in Exhibition Hall of The Uppsala University Library (located on Dag Hammarskjolds vag 1) are the Silver Bible from the sixth century, medieval manuscripts, and musical notations by Mozart. Take Bus No. 6, 7, 22, 26, or 52. *Tel:* 018 471 39 00. *Internet:* www.ub.uu.se. *Hours:* Summer (June 13–August 13): 0900–1700 Monday–Friday, 1000–1700 Saturday. Also open Sunday 1100–1600 from May 15–September 17. Winter: 0900–2000 Monday–Friday and 1000–1600 Saturday.

In Uppsala, Saint Erik, Saint Olof, and Saint Lars' church is usually referred to as **The Cathedral.** Two of its patron saints, Erik and Olof, were Christian kings in Scandinavia during the eleventh and twelfth centuries, when the Christians finally had the pagans on the run. Lars died a martyr's death in Rome in A.D. 258. Building of The Cathedral started in the late thirteenth century, and it took a century and a half to complete. It has been ravaged by fires, and its towers collapsed, but with Swedish determination it was restored. English-language tours of the Uppsala Cathedral are conducted several times a day in summer. *Internet:* www.uppsaladomkyrka.nu.

Switzerland

Switzerland is a year-round wonderland of astonishing beauty and one of the most multilingual countries in Europe. You can experience several different cultures encompassing four national languages—all within one neat little country. The German-speaking Swiss make up 65 percent of the population; French, 18 percent; Italian, 10 percent; and Romansch, 1 percent; and 70-plus dialects lend a special charisma to tiny villages and hamlets. And many Swiss can speak all four languages and English, too.

The diversity doesn't end there. From majestic snow-capped mountains to languid palm-fringed lakes, from cowbells and yodeling to craftsmanship and incredible feats of railroad engineering, Switzerland is surprising.

For more information about Switzerland, contact the Switzerland Tourism Offices of North America: (*Internet:* **www.switzerlandtourism.com**; *E-mail:* stnewyork@switzerland tourism.com):

Chicago: 150 North Michigan Avenue, Suite 2930, Chicago, IL 60601; *Tel:* (312) 630–5840

Los Angeles: 222 North Sepulveda Boulevard, Suite 1570, El Segundo, CA 90245; *Tel:* (310) 335–5980; *Fax:* (310) 335–5982

New York: 608 Fifth Avenue, New York, NY 10020; *Tel:* (212) 262–2090; *Fax:* (212) 262–6116

Toronto: 926 The East Mall, Etobicoke, Ontario M9B 6K1; *Tel:* (416) 695–2090; *Fax:* (416) 695–2774

Banking

- **Currency:** Swiss Franc (CHF)
- **Exchange rate at press time:** CHF 1.62 = U.S. $1.00
- **Hours:** 0830–1630 Monday–Friday

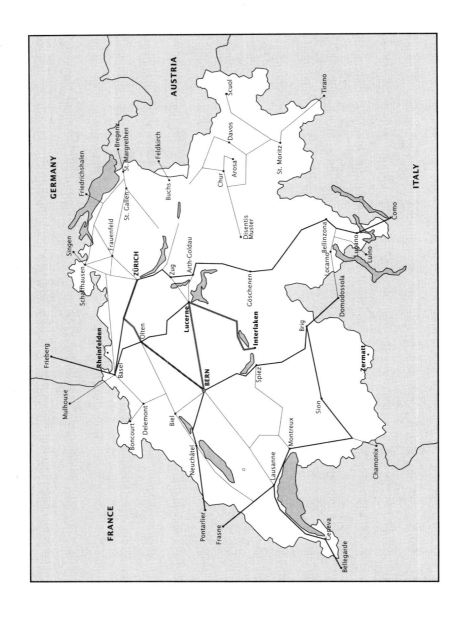

Communications

- **Country Dialing Code:** 41
  For telephone calls within Switzerland, dial zero (0) preceding area code. You can buy a calling card for calls within Switzerland at any Swiss post office. International calls can be placed from public phones at the post office and some major railway stations.
- **Direct dial:** AT&T: 0–800–890011; MCI: 0–800–890222; Sprint: 0–800–899777

Rail Travel in Switzerland

The Swiss are well known for their excellence in clock production, and they know how to run a railroad with the same finesse—on time. Rail travelers from North America may take advantage of the **"Fly Rail Baggage Service"** program by checking their luggage through from all airports and all airline companies to one of the 116 railway stations offering the service. When returning to North America, visitors can also check their luggage through to their destination airport (CHF 20 per bag). American carriers do not allow outbound service *from* Switzerland.

According to the Swiss, only the "Man in the Moon" knows how dense the network of railroads in Switzerland *really* is. Although Switzerland is only 216 miles from north to south and 137 miles from east to west, more than 13,000 miles of train, bus, and boat routes make up the Swiss Travel System network. Even mountains don't stop the Swiss. They either tunnel through them or scale their heights with funiculars or cog railways. Switzerland has one of the longest railroad tunnels, the highest railroad, plus more bridges, tunnels, and other engineering works per square mile than any other country in the world. New and beautiful **ICN (InterCity Neigezug) tilting trains** have shrunk travel times on many routes and frequency has increased to half-hourly service on most InterCity lines. New tilting trains and double-decker train equipment have also increased business, dining, family, and quiet-zone facilities. The innovative Swiss also have a **"grocery store on wheels"**! A rail car is stocked with food (in cooperation with the Coop grocery stores) and passengers can shop while the train is moving. Presently, there are five of these "grocery-store trains" on the Zürich-Bern route.

The Swiss Federal Railways (SBB/CFF/FFS) accepts the following rail-passes that can be purchased in advance of your departure for Europe: the 17-country **Eurailpass**, the 5-country **Europass**, the **Swiss Pass**, and **Swiss Card**. *Internet:* www.sbb.ch.

Swiss Federal Railways provides the following **Eurail** bonuses:

- 50 percent discount on Rhine River boats operated by URh, Constance-Schaffhausen
- Steamer services on lakes of Biel, Brienz, Geneva, Lucerne, Murten, Neuchâtel, Thun, and Zürich—free
- Alpnachstad–Mount Pilatus (see Lucerne section)—cable railway 35 percent discount
- Bürgenstock funicular—50 percent discount

Swiss Pass

Provides unlimited travel on the entire Swiss Travel System, including most of the private railroads, postal motor coaches, lake steamers, and urban transport systems in 35 cities. It also provides up to 25 percent discount on funiculars and cable cars.

Consecutive Days	1 adult		Saverpass*	
	1st Class	2nd Class	1st class	2nd class
4 days	$245	$160	$208	$136
8 days	$340	$225	$289	$192
15 days	$410	$270	$349	$230
22 days	$475	$315	$404	$268
1 month	$535	$350	$455	$298

*Price per person based on 2 people or more traveling together
Children under 16: free with parent (including step or foster parent). Children age 6–15 not accompanied by parent: half adult fare. Children under age 6: free.

Swiss Flexipass

Valid for non-consecutive days to be used within a 1-month period:

	1 Adult		Saverpass*	
	1st class	2nd class	1st class	2nd class
Any 3 days	$234	$156	$198	$132
Any 4 days	$276	$184	$234	$156
Any 5 days	$318	$212	$270	$180
Any 6 days	$360	$240	$306	$204
Any 8 days	$424	$282	$360	$240

*Price per person based on 2 adults or more traveling together. Children under 16: free with parent (including step or foster parent). Children age 6–15 not accompanied by parent: half adult fare. Children under age 6: free.

- Jungfrau Region Railways—25 percent discount
- Kriens–Mont Pilatus (near Lucerne) cable railway—30 percent discount
- 50 percent discount on boats operated by BSB, SBS and ÖBB on Lake Constance (May–October)
- Transportation Museum in Lucerne—35 percent off entrance fee
- Vitznau Rigi Railways—25 percent discount
- Stanserhorn funicular/cable railway—50 percent discount

The **Swiss Card** is valid for one free round trip plus 50 percent discount for additional trips (except for some mountain railroads that offer 25 percent discount) within a 1-month validity period. First class is $138; second class, $104. Children under age 16: free with parent. Children age 6–15 not accompanied by parent: half adult fare. Children under age 6: free.

The **Swiss Transfer Ticket** is great for skiers or for those who will only stay in one place. It provides for one round-trip ticket. First class: $107; second class: $71. Children under age 16 can travel round-trip free when accompanied by at least one parent. Children age 6–15 not accompanied by a parent: half adult fare. Children under age 6 travel free.

Some of Switzerland's most scenic railroads (descriptions follow) also accept Eurail or Europass; most private railroads, however, do not, although some offer discounts (aforementioned). Reservations are mandatory and cost extra. Remember to take along your passport for border crossings.

Some of Switzerland's most scenic routes by train include:

- *Bernina Express*—Chur–St. Moritz–Bernina Pass–Poschiavo–Tirano. Runs daily in the summer and only to and from Tirano in the winter. Trip is 2½ hours from St. Moritz or 4 hours from Chur. *Internet:* www.rhb.ch
- *Centovalli Railway*—Locarno–S. Maria Maggiore–Domodossola (Italy). Runs all year long.
- *Glacier Express*—Zermatt–Brig–Andermatt–Chur–Davos/St. Moritz. Journey runs daily in summer and winter. Trip is 7½ hours and passes through 91 tunnels and over 291 bridges. Eurail, Eurail Selectpass, and Europass valid only between Davos/St. Moritz and Disentis. You must purchase an additional point-to-point ticket for the portion from Disentis to Zermatt. *Internet:* www.glacierexpress.ch
- *Golden Pass*—Lucerne–Brünig Panoramic Express–Interlaken–Jungfraujoch–Salon bleu–Golden Pass Express–Montreux–Genève. Runs daily all year. Internet: www.goldenpass.ch
- *Swiss Chocolate Train*—Montreux-Gruyères-Broc-Montreux—a delight for chocolate lovers and rail buffs. Ride in a vintage 1915 "Belle Epoque" or an ultramodern panoramic rail car and visit Cailler-Nestlé chocolate factory in Broc for chocolate sampling. Operates once a week June–October. For exact dates and prices (holders of Swiss Pass/Swiss Flexi Pass pay reduced supplement), contact:

  GoldenPass Services   *Tel:* 011-41-21-989-8181 (from U.S.)
  GoldenPass Center   *Fax:* 011-41-21-863-8996
  CH-1820 Montreux   *Internet:* www.mob.ch
  Switzerland   *E-mail:* mob@mob.ch

- *William Tell Express*—Lucerne–Flüelen–St. Gotthard–Locarno/Lugano. Combination steamer and rail journey; includes gourmet Swiss lunch. Reservations compulsory; includes seats on the boat, train, journey documentation, and souvenir. Runs daily May–October. *Internet:* www.lakelucerne.ch

Rail Travel Note: A timetable bookshop is operated by the Swiss Federal Railways in St. Gallen, Switzerland, where you may purchase the current offical timetables of many European countries, as well as a wide range of rail travel literature and rail maps. St. Gallen is 1 hour by train from Zürich in the direction of Austria and Germany. Call at Room 224 in the St. Gallen rail station or telephone 071–222–1021, extension 208, ahead of time for details.

For an in-depth look at Switzerland's incredible rail system, *Switzerland by Train* (40 minutes) presents the adventure of some of the area's classic rail journeys. This video excites the novice and the expert alike. To order call Taylored Videos at (704) 366–0404.

Base City:

Bern

(Berne)

Internet: www.bernetourism.ch
City Dialing Code: 31

Bern (Berne) has the unique distinction of being the only city in Europe joined by all three of Europe's high-speed trains—the TGV from Paris, the ICE from Berlin, and the Cisalpino from Milan.

Bern, the federal capital of Switzerland, was founded in 1191 and is one of the few medieval cities which remains intact. Appropriately, Bern is a UNESCO World Heritage site. According to legend, it was named after the first animal caught in the area, a bear, and bears have played a part in its history ever since. The city's bear pits, where the animals are raised and displayed, are a must-see on any tour.

The most striking thing about Bern is its medieval appearance. Some of the buildings in the city's old town date from the thirteenth and fourteenth centuries. The low silhouette of its roof lines appears to be different from those of most of Europe's other cities with origins in the same era—and indeed it is, for there is a medieval ordinance still in effect today that mandates each roof line be at a different level from adjoining structures. This ancient architectural asset is most visible when you view the city from the Nydeggbrücke Bridge crossing the Aare en route to the bear pits. If you miss it, you'll have another opportunity when you view the city from the location of its rose gardens on the high bluff of the Aare's right bank.

Bern is a medieval city, yet it is a new city as well. Over the centuries, Bern's citizens have developed a remarkable means of combining modern living with the centuries-old facades of their surroundings. It is cosmopolitan, with more than 150 restaurants, and a wide selection of hotels, museums, and concert halls. Modern Bern has grown well beyond the curve of the Aare and into the surrounding foothills. The main commercial, cultural, and political activities of the city, however, still take place in its old sector.

The Aare River embraces Bern in a great natural bend. Like the river, you too will embrace this ancient Swiss city, once you have trod its cobblestone streets.

In summer, Bern leads you to believe it is the geranium capital of the world as well as being the federal capital of Switzerland. These flowers bloom everywhere in an eye-dazzling display of color. Bern was once voted Europe's most beautiful city of flowers. You will be bewitched by Bern, beguiled by its bears, and satisfied with its sights.

Arriving by Air

Switzerland's international airports, Basel, Geneva, and Zürich, connect incoming flights with trains to Bern. Bern is only 1 hour and 29 minutes away from Zürich's airport and 1 hour, 52 minutes from Geneva's by comfortable passenger trains that depart daily from the airports every 30 minutes. In Zürich, the rail station lies immediately beneath the airport's terminal. In Geneva, the rail station and the airport terminal are connected by a plaza. At the Bern-Belp Airport (9 kilometers south of the City Centre), direct connections can be made to and from many European cities, as well as shuttle bus service directly to Bern's railway station.

Arriving by Train

Bern's modern rail station is a small city within a city, with an impressive array of facilities, including a spacious underground arcade that connects at its surface entrances with the city's fabled, arcaded shopping walkways. Direct rail transport from Bern to Amsterdam, Berlin, Brussels, Luxembourg, Milan, Paris, Rome, Venice, and Zürich is available.

More than 70 trains a day depart Bern for Zürich Hauptbahnhof; 34 of these continue on to the Zürich airport following the city stop. More than 40 trains a day depart Bern for Geneva. Upon arrival in Geneva, stay aboard, and 8 minutes later you will be at the Geneva airport.

Bern's Railway Station. Parts of Bern's rail station have been rebuilt, making it a model of efficiency and functionalism. Trains are reached from its ground level via ramps, thus making the use of baggage carts practical.

With your baggage stacked in one of the station's baggage carts, leave the train platform by descending the ramp, then turn in the direction of track No. 1 and walk to the end of the passageway, where you will emerge into the station's underground arcade, with its myriad shops and services. You'll see the escalators directly ahead.

Escalators take you to the other levels of the station. Elevator service is also available. If you have your luggage on a cart, use the elevators. At street level you will find the **train information** and **Bern Tourismus** offices, plus additional facilities such as shops and restaurants. Snack bars and fruit stands prevail on the ground level; more extensive food-service facilities are on the upper levels, ending at the top of the escalators with a full-service restaurant.

- **Baggage storage.** Visitors burdened with baggage may want to use the coin lockers on the ground (train) level or find the area marked FLY BAGGAGE (baggage room) on the street level. Taxi service is available from the street level—follow the pictographs—but check with Bern Tourismus before attempting to use the public-bus and streetcar services. Their access ramps, fares, ticket machines, and so forth can be confusing.

A suburban train station is located on the underground arcade level. To reach it, continue past the escalators that run to the street level and watch for its entrance on the left side of the passageway. This system is operated by a private Swiss railroad. Swiss Passes are accepted, and Eurailpasses and Europasses are accepted by *some* private Swiss railroads such as RBS. Check prior to boarding the train.

The Bern station, like most of the major rail terminals in Switzerland, will accept your baggage and check it through the Zürich or Geneva airports directly to your U.S. port of entry (except if you're flying on American carriers). Trains for both airports depart the Bern station every 30 minutes throughout the day. Place your baggage on a train an hour or so in advance of your departure for the airport.

- **Money-exchange** facilities, two of them, are located on the ground level of the station. Both may be reached by turning right, just before the elevators, as you come out of the passageway leading from the trains. Both will be on your right as you proceed into the station's arcade. The first office, marked CHANGE SBB, is operated by the Swiss railroads. Hours: 0630–2100 daily. There is also an ATM.

  There are several banks in the plaza surrounding the station. The rates of exchange are standard throughout the city each day, however, and the rail-station money-exchange and ATM facilities are the most convenient. There is also a money-exchange machine available 24 hours a day near the station at Schwanengasse 4.

- **Train information, reservations,** and **railpass validations** can be obtained from the rail-reservations center immediately across the passageway from the tourist information office. Look for the blue i sign. Hours: 0800–1900 Monday–Friday; 0800–1700 Saturday. The center dispenses rail information, reservations, and other services, including validation of railpasses. Keep in mind that your Eurailpass or Europass is accepted on all of the Swiss federal railways and certain lake steamers; on the other hand, it is accepted only on a few of the private railroads. To be certain, check your day-excursions plans with the train information office. For example, if you plan to ascend the **Jungfrau**, a Eurailpass or Europass will take you to **Interlaken,** where you must purchase a ticket for the private railroads leading out of Interlaken to **Grindelwald** or **Lauterbrunnen** and **Wengen** en route to the Jungfrau.

- **Tourist information** and **hotel reservations** are available at **Bern Tourismus,** one of the most complete information centers in Europe.

Hotel line: (031) 328 1210; *Tel:* (031) 328 1212; *Fax:* (031) 312 2388; *Internet:* www.bernetourism.ch; *E-mail:* info-res@bernetourism.ch.

Turn left coming off the escalator from the ground level, then right at the passageway leading to the street. The office will be a few steps farther on your right. It is identified by a green **i** sign. Hours during summer (June–September), 0900–2030 daily; remainder of the year, 0900–1830 Monday–Saturday and 1000–1700 Sunday. There is no fee for hotel reservations.

Ask here for the booklets *Bern Information* and *Bern Excursions*, the latter being an informative publication listing more day excursions from Bern by rail, lake steamer, and postal buses.

- **Hotel reservations** can also be made by using an automatic telephone system located beside Bern Tourismus. The automatic telephone system makes finding and booking a hotel an easy task. There is a lighted board showing the locations of the hotels along with pictures of the hotels and their room rates. Press the button for your choice, and you'll be immediately connected with the hotel by telephone to discuss vacancies. For online bookings, visit www.bernetourism.ch.

Sights/Attractions/Tours

There are two excellent means of sight-seeing in Bern: on foot or by comfortable motor coach escorted by a multilingual guide. From April through October the bus departs from in front of the railway station at 1400 daily; November 1–March 31 on Saturday only at 1400. The bus tour takes 2 hours, and tickets may be purchased at the tourist office for CHF 24 (half fare for children).

If interested in the walking tour, ask at the tourist office for the *Short City Sightseeing Map*. It leads you right through the heart of Bern's ancient walled city to its famed **bear pits**. The tourist center is open daily 0900–1800 June 1–September 30; daily 1000–1600 October 1–31; Friday–Sunday 1100–1500 November 1–February 28; daily 1000–1600 March 1–May 31. Be certain to take in the multimedia *Bern Show*. Performances are every 20 minutes, and it's free! From there you return to your point of departure by a different route. According to the map, the entire route can be covered in approximately 1 hour, but without any stops en route. Plan for a minimum of 2 hours and consider yourself lucky if you make it in 3. (According to the tourist office, no one has ever returned within the hour.)

Be certain to see the *Zeitglockenturm*, the city's famous clock tower. It first began ticking in 1530, and it is still the city's official timepiece today. The clock's glockenspiel starts promptly at 4 minutes before the hour as accompaniment to a parade of armed bear figures following a rooster. It's quite a show. What makes it tick? Take the fascinating 45-minute guided tour, held at 1630 daily from May through October, (July through September, also at 1130) *inside* the clock tower. Purchase your ticket (CHF 8.00) at Bern Tourismus from the tour guide, or at your hotel. Another

Train Connections to Other Base Cities from Bern (Berne)

DEPART BERN	TRAIN NUMBER	ARRIVE	NOTES
		Amsterdam Centraal	
1149	EC 104	2054	
1249	IC 870	2154	1
2049	888	0856+1	2
		Berlin Zoobahnhof	
0949	ICE 72	1816	10
1049	EC 108	1919	3
1149	EC 104	2021	3
1949	IC 886	0723+1	R, 2, Sleeper
		Brussels (Bruxelles) Midi/Zuid	
1203	EC 90	1945	
2249	498	0645+1	R, Sleeper
		Budapest Keleti	
2117	IC 741	1133+1	R, Couchettes
		Hamburg Hauptbahnhof	
0749	IC 854	1532	1
0949	ICE 72	1733	
1049	EC 108	2110	exc. Sat
1149	EC 104	0014+1	1
1349	IC 972	0014	1
2049	IC 888	0833+1	R, 1, Sleeper
		Copenhagen (København) H.	
1749	IC 982	0959+1	R, 5, Sleeper
2049	IC 888	1359+1	R, 2, Sleeper then change in Hamburg
		Luxembourg	
1203	EC 90	1650	
1449	IC 874	1959	1
		Lyon Part-Dieu	
0747	IC 708	1223	R, 4
0832	TGV 9284	1402	R, 10
0947	IC 714	1419	R, 4
1047	IC 716	1435	R, 4

then hourly until 1347 followed by 1547, 1722, 1747 and 1947.

DEPART BERN	TRAIN NUMBER	ARRIVE	NOTES
		Milan (Milano) Centrale	
0734	CIS 45*	1050	R
1005	IC 331	1350	
1522	EC 91	1925	
		Munich (München)	
0612	IC 705	1157	6
0817	IC 711	1400	6
1217	IC 721	1701	6
1617	IC 729	2157	6
		Paris Gare de Lyon	
0630	TGV 9290	1117	R
0832	TGV 9284	1321	R
1047	IC 716	1710	7
1700	TGV 9288	2147	R

DEPART BERN	TRAIN NUMBER	ARRIVE	NOTES
		Rome (Roma) Termini	
0734	CIS 45*	1530	R, 8
1005	IC 331	1830	R, 8
2252	EN 313	0935+1	R, Sleeper
		Vienna (Wien)	
0817	IC 711	1850	R, 7
0949	ICE 72	2150	R, 11
1217	IC 721	2250	R, 6
2117	IC 743	0810+1	R, Sleeper

Zürich Hauptbahnhof

InterCity (IC) trains depart at 17 and 47 minutes past the hour. Journey time 1 hour 10 minutes; local trains depart at 52 minutes past the hour. Journey time 1 hour 41 minutes.

Daily, unless otherwise noted
R Reservations required
* Cisalpino (CIS) trains require supplement
+1 Arrive next day
1. Change trains in Basel.
2. Change to sleeper (R) train in Basel.
3. Change trains in Mannheim.
4. Change trains in Geneva (Genève).
5. Change trains in Basel, then in Frankfurt to sleeper.
6. Change trains in Zürich.
7. Change in Lausanne to a TGV (R) train.
8. Change to Eurostar *Italia* train (R) in Milan.
9. Change trains in Hannover.
10. Change trains in Dijon–Ville
11. Change trains in Frankfurt.

BERN

option is the stroll through the **Old Town,** which includes visits to the cathedral and the clock tower. Tours depart daily at 1100 from the station and cost CHF 14 (half price for children).

Another unusual feature of Bern is its **shopping arcades**—nearly 4 miles of them. They line the route of the walking tour suggested by Bern Tourismus and offer one of the finest selections of wares and food to be found anywhere in the world. The shopping arcades are completely covered, so they are weatherproof as well as traffic-free and totally delightful. On Tuesday and Saturday mornings, there are markets where Swiss farmers sell their meat and produce. Shop the city's arcades Monday–Friday 0900–1830 (until 2100 on Thursday), and 0900–1600 Saturday. Pick up a shopping guide at the tourist offices.

Or, if museums appeal to you, Bern has plenty to choose from, including the **Swiss Alpine Museum,** the **Museum of Communication,** the **Einstein House,** and even a **Museum of Psychiatry.**

For a view of Bern from an unusual perspective, take the **city tour by raft** on the river Aare (tickets cost CHF 30 for adults and CHF 20 for children).

The 1½-hour rafting tour departs at 1700 Tuesday, Thursday, Saturday and Sunday, June–September, from Schwellenmätteli (indicated on the city map) and includes a ten-passenger raft, life jackets, paddles, and, of course, a guide.

Day Excursions

Bern is an ideal base for day excursions to almost any point in Switzerland. Geneva is 1 hour and 40 minutes to the west by train; you can reach Zürich to the east by rail in only 1 hour and 10 minutes. Travel north and, in the same amount of time, your train will set you down in Basel on the banks of the Rhine.

The five day excursions that we have selected reveal the natural grandeur of the country. **The Golden Pass** adventure takes you through Alpine surroundings, in the comfort of a vista-dome rail car, to Lake Geneva and a cruise on the lake before returning to Bern. The outing to **Interlaken** unfolds a panorama of towering peaks along the shore of the Lake of Thun, where again you have the opportunity of a lake cruise to conclude a memorable day.

Picture-postcard perfect, **Lucerne** will charm you with its scenery, cuisine, and ambience. Promenade along its ancient walkways, scale nearby Mount Pilatus, or cruise the Lake of Lucerne during your visit.

For a peek at a Disney-type setting that has been going strong since the eleventh century, journey to **Rheinfelden,** where the mighty Rhine River swirls past a medieval setting that stirs the imagination. Or travel to Brig to catch the *Glacier Express* to **Zermatt** to view the magnificent Matterhorn.

Day Excursion to

The Golden Pass
The Alps a la Train

Depart from Bern
Distance by Train: 65 miles (104 km) to Montreux
Average Train Time: 1 hour, 25 minutes
Tourist Information Office (Montreux): Place du Debarcadere, 1820
Tel: 962-8484; *Fax:* 963-7895
Internet: www.montreux.ch
E-mail: tourism@montreuxtourism.ch
Hours: 1 January–15 April: 0900–1200 and 1330–1800 Monday–Friday; 1000–1400 Saturday–Sunday. 16 April–30 September: 0900–1900 daily

Dollar for dollar, or franc for franc, this day excursion is one of the best train-travel values in Europe. The Lucerne–Interlaken–

Montreux rail route provides an exciting variety of landscapes and cultures. The Montreux–Bernese–Oberland Railroad (MOB) operates the *Golden Pass Panoramic Express.* This train offers an unobstructed view of the breathtaking scenery between Zweisimmen and Montreux.

Before departure, check with Bern Tourismus. Inform them you are going on The Golden Pass trip and pick up the booklet *Bern Excursions.* (The booklet is usually available in the train information office as well.) Trains run through The Golden Pass rather frequently, and you may want to follow a different schedule. We selected the *Golden Pass Panoramic,* a luxury first-class train with panoramic-view windows and bar car on the portion of the route from Zweisimmen to Montreux and vice versa.

There is ample time for a leisurely lunch at the Majestic Hotel (located between the rail station and the city pier) in Montreux before boarding a lake steamer to Chillon. Disembark and go ashore to visit its famous castle. **Château de Chillon** is a beautifully restored eleventh-century castle that was made famous by Lord Byron in his poetic story of the imprisonment of François de Bonivard. After touring the castle, board another lake steamer back to Montreux. Then, ride the funicular adjacent to the steamer dock to the **Lausanne** train station, and board your train back to Bern. Whew! It's a day loaded with extras.

Check the weather report the night before embarking on this day excursion. The clearer the day, the better. You will be viewing some of the Alps's most spectacular scenery, and if it's shrouded in clouds, it just might spoil your day. To get the weather report in English, dial 162 on any Swiss telephone.

InterCity trains usually depart from the Bern railway station on track 6, but double-check just to be sure. The destination of this train is **Brig**, and it makes a stop at **Thun** (pronounced "tune") before it arrives at **Spiez**. At Thun, the beautiful Lake of Thun comes into view. As you approach Spiez, you'll see Mount Niesen (7,750 feet) towering over this quiet town on the southwestern shore of the lake.

In Spiez you have 11 minutes to cross a platform to board the next train—time enough to enjoy the breathtaking view. **Zweisimmen,** the next stop and transfer point, lies almost halfway between Spiez and Montreux. When you depart Spiez, you will enter The Golden Pass.

The transfer at Zweisimmen places you aboard MOB's *Golden Pass Panoramic Express* on a narrow-gauge railroad, with Montreux as its destination. The best instruction here is to "follow the crowd" as you move between the standard- and narrow-gauge trains.

A regular stop is **Gstaad**, which, you may recall, is the alpine-resort retreat of many famous movie stars, including Elizabeth Taylor and Roger Moore. During his lifetime, Richard Burton frequented the area, and the late David Niven maintained a chalet there on a mountainside for many years. **Château d'Oex** (pronounced "day") is an alpine resort, too, but more at the family level, frequented by the Genevese when they grow tired of viewing beautiful Lake Geneva—possibly because it's flat.

Bern (Berne)—The Golden Pass

Depart Bern 0926   Train IC 965   Arrive Spiez 0957
Depart Spiez 1002   Train 2364   Arrive Zweisimmen 1039
Depart Zweisimmen 1050   Train D 120   Arrive Montreux 1246
other departures also available.

Lake steamers depart Montreux pier at 1350 also other departures; stop at Château de Chillon is 10 to 13 minutes after leaving Montreux. (Summer schedules.)

Lake steamers depart Château de Chillon for Lausanne-Ouchy dock at 1538, 1628, and 1739; journey time to Lausanne-Ouchy is 1 hour and 27 to 46 minutes; steamers also stop at Montreux 12 to 17 minutes after departing Château de Chillon pier.

Mainline trains depart Montreux station for Lausanne on the hour and 39 minutes after the hour throughout the day; journey time to Lausanne is 21 minutes. There are other local trains that make several stops and take longer.

DEPART LAUSANNE STATION	TRAIN NUMBER	ARRIVE BERN HBF
1526	IR 1833	1638
1606	IC 733	1713
1626	IR 1835	1738
1706	IC 735	1813
1726	IR 1837	1838
1806	IC 737	1913
1826	IR 1839	1938
1906	IC 739	2013
1926	D 2741	2038

BERN *The Golden Pass*

Our "wood pile theory" can be tested—at least two-thirds of it—because you will be passing from a German-speaking area into one of French habitation. Based on research we have made during several decades of European rail travel, the theory is this: The Germans pile wood with precision, the Italians pile it artistically, and the French stack theirs with an air of independence. The two regular stops are Gstaad and Château d'Oex. Watch what happens to the wood piles between these two points. Gstaad, as the name may imply, is German; Château d'Oex lies in the French-speaking district.

Approaching Montreux, the train descends 2,000 feet to Lake Geneva in much the same manner as a jet airliner does when entering a landing pattern. It whirls through a series of hairpin curves for almost a half hour before coming to rest beside the main Montreux railway station. Have your camera handy, for you are going to see some sensational scenery during the descent.

You have several options while visiting Montreux. You can extend your shopping and sight-seeing in the city for 1 hour and 50 minutes if you forgo Chillon and yet board the same steamer for Lausanne and not miss any of your friends who may have elected to see the castle made famous by Lord

Byron. If it's stormy on Lake Geneva, you can still keep to the schedule by proceeding to Lausanne by rail.

Chillon-bound passengers should scurry to the castle as quickly as possible after the lake steamer docks to ensure maximum use of the time ashore. The steamer proceeds on to the French port of St. Gingolph and then returns to Chillon. Check at the Chillon dock for its return time. Should you miss the boat, you still have another option. Hail a cab back to Montreux, then board the train for Lausanne to join your friends in the dining car en route back to Bern.

Day Excursion to

Interlaken
Lake of Thun Cruise

Depart from Bern
Distance by Train: 37 miles (59 km)
Average Train Time: 50 minutes
City Dialing Code: 33
Tourist Information Office: Interlaken Tourismus, P.O. Box 369, Höheweg 37, CH–3800 Interlaken
Tel: (033) 826–5300; **Fax:** (033) 826–5375
Internet: www.interlakentourism.ch
E-mail: mail@interlakentourism.ch
Hours: July–September, 0800–1830 Monday–Friday; 0800–1700 Saturday; 1000–1200 and 1600–1800 Sunday. Hours are shorter the rest of the year, and the office is closed Sunday.
Notes: Interlaken Tourism Office is about a 5-minute walk down the Höheweg (the grand promenade), which starts at the West station and ends at Ost (East) station. It's on the left-hand side next to the Hotel Metropole.

Interlaken can best be described as the cultural and social focal point of Switzerland's Alpine areas. The English poet Lord Byron is said to have exclaimed, "It's a dream!" at his first sighting of Interlaken and its surroundings. Nestled between the **Lake of Thun** and the **Lake of Brienz**, Interlaken (Latin for "between the lakes") began in the twelfth century as a small cluster of buildings surrounding a monastery, traces of which can still be seen today.

The town's main thoroughfare, **Höheweg,** is lined with great hotels, shops, and even a grand casino that is set back from the main promenade and banked with such beautiful flowers that one might think it is a retirement home.

For Interlaken, the Höheweg plays the same part as does the Champs-Elysées for Paris or the Via Veneto for Rome—it is *the boulevard,* with the

Bern (Berne)—Interlaken

There is hourly InterCity (IC) train service from Bern Hauptbahnhof to Interlaken West and Interlaken Ost (East) stations; departures are at 26 minutes after the hour from 0726; journey time to Interlaken West is 50 minutes, and time to Interlaken Ost is 54 minutes.

Return hourly IC service departs Interlaken Ost at 40 minutes after the hour and departs Interlaken West at 45 minutes after the hour; journey time to Bern from Interlaken West is 48 minutes.

Distance: 37 miles (59 km)

Lake of Thun Cruise

DEPART INTERLAKEN PIER	ARRIVE THUN DOCK	DEPART THUN STATION	TRAIN NUMBER	ARRIVE BERN HBF
0940	1154	1214	IC 923	1234
1050	1240	1314	IC 972	1334
1210	1408	1414	IC 927	1434
1340	1608	1614	IC 935	1634

Note: Interlaken Pier is approximately 100 meters from Interlaken West station. Thun Dock is approximately 50 meters from Thun Station.

ambience for which the Swiss are famous. Just as in its larger counterparts, you'll find people on foot or aboard horse-drawn carriages taking in the sights along with those relaxing over coffee and pastries at the sidewalk cafes. Towering over this entire scene is the **Jungfrau** (*Internet:* www. jungfraubahn.ch), a massive mountain that tops out at 13,642 feet above sea level, a mere 11 miles south of Interlaken. On a clear day, the view is dazzling.

Believe it or not, the Jungfrau can be scaled by train. Beginning in Interlaken at the Ost (East) rail station, a private cog railroad terminates at the Jungfraujoch station, at 11,333 feet, the highest rail terminal in Europe. The round trip takes the better half of a day, and it should be made only in ideal weather. Furthermore, the round-trip fare is just as steep as the ascent, CHF 169.40 per person first class and CHF 159 for second class. Eurail passes, including Eurail Selectpass and Europass, do, however, provide a 25 percent discount. Plan your "assault" on the Jungfrau for a separate day after you have checked the weather—and your wallet.

If you *must* scale a mountain while in Interlaken, take the funicular running up to **Harderkulm,** which overlooks Interlaken to the south from 4,337 feet above sea level. On a clear day you can see both lakes surrounding Interlaken, as well as the Jungfrau. This can be done in about an hour for only CHF 21 per person. The Harderkulm station is only a short walk from Interlaken's Ost (East) station. Ask for directions at the tourist office.

Interlaken has two railway stations, west and east. Coming from Bern, you arrive first in the west station. Disembark here rather than riding another 5 minutes to the east station. Remember, however, if you are closer to the east station as your visit draws to a close, you can catch the same train from that point, too—but 5 minutes ahead of the west-station schedule.

An extra bonus offered with the Swiss Card is a 50 percent discount (25 percent with a Swiss Pass) on the **Brienz Rothorn Bahn**—Switzerland's oldest steam cog railway. Since 1892, it has climbed the 7,710 feet above sea level for a spectacular view from Rothorn Kulm. For further information *Tel:* (33) 952–2222 or *Fax:* (33) 952–2210.

The Höheweg starts at the west station, and the grand promenade extends to the east station. With a city map in hand, courtesy of the tourist office, you are all set to tour the town. If walking isn't your forte, you may prefer to see the sights from a surrey. These horse-drawn vehicles are available just outside the west station. Rates vary and must be arranged with the driver.

There are more than one hundred restaurants in Interlaken. We do have a favorite, although it's a bit off the beaten path—the **Hotel Rössli**, Hauptstrasse 10 (*Tel:* 33 822 78 16; *Fax:* 33 822 96 16; *E-mail:* roessli. hotels@bluewin.ch). It is run by a friendly gentleman who worked in New York City restaurants for many years before he moved to the German district of Switzerland. The result is German-Swiss food served with a French flair and an American accent—rather unusual.

Interlaken is a good base for explorations of the entire **Jungfrau Region.** We suggest that you devote one day to Interlaken and its immediate area and check with the tourist office regarding other day-excursion possibilities. In addition to the rail ascent to the Jungfrau, you can reach the **Schilthorn** and lunch in the restaurant **Piz Gloria** (at 10,000 feet), where James Bond escaped the murderous intents of the opposition by skiing down the world's longest ski slope in the film *On Her Majesty's Secret Service.*

Wearers of pacemakers should be wary of the higher altitudes, but there's no reason to miss out on the fun around Interlaken. The **Swiss Open-Air Museum** at nearby **Ballenberg** (open daily 1000–1700 mid-April through October) is an ideal alternative and easy to reach by either train or lake steamer departing from the city's east station. Ask for details at the tourist information office.

If the weather is agreeable, a cruise on the **Lake of Thun** before returning from Interlaken is a must. The ships depart from a pier that can be reached from either the west station by tunnel or the Bahnhofstrasse, where it intersects with the Höheweg alongside the station.

Day Excursion to

Lucerne (Luzern)
And Mount Pilatus

Depart from Bern
Distance by Train: 59 miles (95 km)
Average Train Time: 1 hour, 20 minutes
City Dialing Code: 041
Tourist Information Office: Zentralstrasse 5, CH–6002 Luzern
Tel: (041) 227 1717; *Fax:* (041) 227 1718
Internet: www.luzern.org
E-mail: luzern@luzern.org
Hours: June 16–September 15: Monday–Friday 0830–1930 and Saturday–Sunday
    0900–1930; September 16–June 15: Monday–Friday 0830–1800, Saturday–
    Sunday 0900–1800
Note: The tourist information office is located in the railway station at track No. 3.

This day excursion is weatherproof. Rain or shine, Lucerne (Luzern) has much to offer. So much, in fact, that you may want to return again and again until you have seen it all—a challenging task.

Lucerne is in its glory on a bright, sunny day, when the city and its surroundings sparkle with a brilliance that defies description. At the northwestern end of Lake Lucerne, where the Reuss River resumes its swift quest for the Rhine, Lucerne's lakefront, rimmed by the mighty Alps, is an unforgettable sight. But a rainy day in Lucerne (and that sort of thing does happen occasionally) won't dampen your spirits one bit, for there are many things to see that are under cover.

The *Kapellbrücke* covered bridge is one example. A symbol of Lucerne, the bridge was built at the beginning of the fourteenth century, together with the Wasserturm (water tower) at its side. During the seventeenth century, artists painted a total of 112 pictures under its eaves, depicting Swiss history, particularly that of Lucerne and its patron saints. The bridge was destroyed by fire in 1993, but the bridge and the artwork were re-created and reopened to the public in 1994.

The **Swiss Museum of Transport and Communications** in Lucerne is open daily April–October, 0900–1800; November–March, 1000–1700 daily. It is the largest and most modern museum in Europe—also one of the most visited. The museum is reached easily from the center of Lucerne by bus No. 6 or 8, which departs from the rail station every 6 minutes for the 10-minute trip, or by lake steamer to the Lido dock (Eurailpass, Europass, and Swiss Pass accepted).

Its special attraction is the **Longines Planetarium** at Sternenplatz 3, and the museum also vividly traces the development of Swiss transportation, including rail, road, aeronautical, and water navigation. Tourism since the

Bern (Berne)—Lucerne (Luzern)

DEPART BERN	TRAIN NUMBER	ARRIVE LUCERNE
0743	IR 1811	0903
0943	IR 1815	1103
1143	IR 1821	1303

and continuing daily at 2 hour intervals.

Other service at 2 hour intervals from 0649 requires a change of trains at Olten, with
arrival at Lucerne Hauptbahnhof in 1 hour, 28 minutes.

DEPART LUZERN	TRAIN NUMBER	ARRIVE BERN
1457	IR 1828	1617
1657	IR 1832	1817

and continuing daily at 1757, 1857, 2057, and 2157. Other service requiring a
change of trains at Olten departs at 1346 and every 2 hours until 1946, then
2254 and 2354; journey time to Bern Hauptbahnhof is 1 hour, 25 minutes.

Distance: 59 miles (95 km)

Lucerne (Luzern)—Pilatus

Via Pilatus cogwheel railway May–October. Discount for railpass holders on Pilatus
railway. Pilatus is 7,000 feet (2,132 meters) above sea level.

Train service from Lucerne to Alpnachstad throughout the day; departures at 0630,
0700, 0810, 0910, 1010, 1110, 1210, 1310, 1410, and 1510 through 2110,
then 2232 and 2332; journey time is 15–20 minutes.

Trains depart Alpnachstad for Lucerne at 29 minutes after the hour until 1929, then
2025, 2203, and 2310; journey time is 18 to 22 minutes.

Alpnachstad—Pilatus Kulm rack railway—operates daily, weather permitting.

Depart Alpnachstad at 0850, 0930, 1010, 1050, 1130, 1210, 1300 and continuing
until 1800–1900. Journey time to Pilatus Kulm is 30 minutes.

Depart Pilatus Kulm at 1205, 1255, 1335, 1420, 1500, 1545, 1625, 1705, 1745,
and Fri and Sat only June 2–Sept 23 at 1915, and 2120; journey time to
Alpnachstad is 40 minutes.

Distance: 3 miles (5 km) Pilatus cogwheel railway

nineteenth century is also highlighted. Kids from 7 to 77 will be fascinated
by the operating scale model of the Gotthard tunnel railroad, and everyone
will end up breathless following a visit to the museum's spectacular
Swissorama and IMAX Filmtheater. With three restaurants to choose from,
you can really plan to spend an entire day.

If you don't mind mixing fondue with frivolity, by all means eat at the
Stadtkeller Restaurant at Sternenplatz 3, just two blocks north of the
Kapellbrücke's right-bank entrance. It may be a bit "touristy," but if you like
yodeling, alphorn blowing, cowbell ringing, beer drinking, and flag throwing,
this is the place. At lunchtime, you should be there no later than 1130. It's a
tour-bus lunch stop and fills up rapidly. *Tel:* 041 4104733 for reservations

or ask the tourist office. You can watch those poor, tired bus passengers try to determine what country they are seeing today.

For a sobering experience, follow up lunch with a visit to **The Dying Lion** of Lucerne. One of the world's most famous monuments, it was hewn from natural rock in commemoration of the heroic, fatal defense by Swiss guards of Louis XVI at the Tuileries in Paris at the beginning of the French Revolution in 1792. Mark Twain described the Lion of Lucerne as "the saddest and most poignant piece of rock in the world."

Next door, you will find Lucerne's **Glacier Garden Museum,** which contains remnants of Lucerne's prehistoric past that were discovered in 1872. Twenty million years ago, Lucerne was a subtropical palm beach on the ocean; 20,000 years ago, Lucerne was covered by more than a mile of glacial ice. Don't miss it.

On your way to the Lion Monument and the Glacier Garden Museum, you will pass one of Switzerland's most outstanding and attractive restaurants, the **Old Swiss House.** Built in 1859, the restaurant contains an antique collection of rare beauty. The oil paintings are all originals. Call ahead for reservations (*Tel:* 041 410 61 71; *Internet:* www.oldswisshouse.ch; *E-mail:* osh@tic.ch), because the Old Swiss House is frequented by the locals for its exquisite Swiss and French cuisine. Meals are served 1100–2300 Tuesday–Sunday.

Visit **Mount Pilatus** as a side adventure during your Lucerne day excursion. Be certain to go on a clear day, for there is nothing more disappointing than a fog-shrouded peak. The world-famous Pilatus electric railway, with its maximum gradient of 48 percent, is the steepest cog railway in the world. Discounts are available for Eurailpass and Europass holders. It's best to purchase tickets at the tourist information office at Zentralstrasse 5. If you have a lot of time, you can take a lake steamer to **Alpnachstad.** For a breathtaking view and a beautiful way to end your day in Lucerne, descend Mount Pilatus in a cable car to **Kriens** and catch the bus to Lucerne. Check with the tourist information office for details and discounts available to railpass holders.

Day Excursion to

Rheinfelden
Walled City on the Rhine

Depart from Bern
Distance by Train: 76 miles (122 km)
Average Train Time: 1 hour, 30 minutes
City Dialing Code: 61
Tourist Information Office: Am Zähringerplatz, CH–4310 Rheinfelden

Tel: (061) 833–0525 *Fax:* (061) 833–0529
Internet: www.rheinfelden.ch (in German)
E-mail: tourismus@rheinfelden.ch
Hours: 0800–1200 and 1300–1730 Monday–Friday
Notes: To reach the tourist information office, proceed downhill on Bahnhofstrasse
(Station Street) to the bottom of the hill, where it meets Marktgasse, the pedestrian
shopping area.

A medieval jewel set on the banks of the swift-moving Rhine River just above Basel, Rheinfelden stirs the imagination. Much of its wall and many of its watch towers are still standing, and they were erected back in the eleventh century. An island on the Swiss side of the river's channel forms an important part of a bridge linking Switzerland to Germany. In the thirteenth century, it was the site of the famed "Emperor's Palace" described by Schiller in the tale of William Tell. The castle is gone now, and the island serves mainly as a city park; but the swirls and eddies of the mighty Rhine continue to stimulate one's sense of the centuries of history that have unfolded there.

During World War II, the bridge over the Rhine was the center of intrigue and mystery. Many downed, but uncaptured American and British aviators seeking the sanctuary of Switzerland attempted to flee Nazi Germany from there. Some made it; some were apprehended. We have talked with residents who still remember those days and the risks that were taken. One person recalled for us her perilous escape across the Rhine's waters in a rowboat.

Be certain to pick up a city map during your stop at the tourist office. Armed with the map, you can easily wind your way through the labyrinth-like streets to any point of interest and still find your way back to the train station in time for your return to Bern.

Check out the shops lining the Rhine. Here you can find bargains in jewelry, clothing, and sporting equipment. Most shops and restaurants are closed on Monday.

When your stomach (or your watch) tells you it's lunchtime, you have several excellent eating places to choose from in Rheinfelden. Our favorites are the **Hotel Schiff** and the **Café Confiserie Graf**, close to the river.

Rheinfelden is home of Switzerland's largest brewery, **Feldschlösschen**. Tours are available on an irregular basis. Excellent restaurants and beer stubes are located at the brewery.

Clustered about the bridge entrance are several eating places offering menus ranging from light snacks to full-course meals. Want to picnic by the Rhine? Pick up some cheese, bread, and wine at one of the market stalls and have your repast on the island as the Rhine provides the background.

Saline deposits were discovered under the town in 1844, and Rheinfelden quickly developed into an international spa. Its natural brine, which is one of the strongest in Europe, is piped from a depth of more than 600 feet to

Bern (Berne)–Basel–Rheinfelden

DEPART BERN	TRAIN NUMBER	ARRIVE BASEL	DEPART BASEL	ARRIVE RHEINFELDEN
0649	IC 952	0756	0815	0830
0749	IC 854	0856	0915	0930
0849	IC 864.	0956	1015	1030

plus other departures.

DEPART RHEINFELDEN	TRAIN NUMBER	ARRIVE BASEL	DEPART BASEL	ARRIVE BERN
1525	SS 1	1542	1604 IC 887	1711
1625	SS 1	1642	1704 EC 109	1811
1725	SS 1	1742	1904 IC 893	2011

and continuing at hourly intervals until 2325 plus other departures.

Alternative route via Brugg:

DEPART BERN	TRAIN NUMBER	ARRIVE BRUGG	DEPART BRUGG	ARRIVE RHEINFELDEN
0652	D 2709	0803	0825	0853
0752	D 2711	0903	0925	0953
0852	D 2713	1003	1025	1053
0952	D 2715	1103	1125	1153

Alternative return route:

DEPART RHEINFELDEN	TRAIN NUMBER	ARRIVE BRUGG	DEPART BRUGG	ARRIVE BERN
1504	IR 1777	1533	1555	1708
1604	IR 1779	1633	1655	1808
1704	IR 1783	1733	1755	1908
1804	IR 1785	1833	1855	2008
1904	EC 97	1933	1955	2108
2004	IR 1789	2033	2055	2208
2104	IR 1791	2133	2155	2308

Distance: 76 miles (122 km)

BERN *Rheinfelden*

454

several bathing facilities in town. The tourist office can provide full details. The structures housing the pumps that bring the brine to the surface from the deep wells bear a striking resemblance to the original oil fields of western Pennsylvania, where oil refining first began in North America.

There is an unusual inside-outside saltwater swimming pool that you should see. You can reach it on foot by walking along the Rhine in an upstream direction. The brine-well structures may be seen nearby.

River steamers ply between Rheinfelden and **Basel**. Returning to Bern via Basel and a boat trip on the Rhine becomes an attractive option between May and September, when the service is in operation. Schedules are posted at the Schifflande (boat landing) opposite the island. Information on the steamer service to Basel, as well as cruises on the Rhine, is also available in the Rheinfelden tourist information office. Rhine steamers, unlike the lake steamers, do not accept Eurailpass or Europass, but the rates to Basel are nominal.

Zermatt
Via the Glacier Express

Depart from Bern
Distance by Train: 99 miles (160 km)
Average Train Time: 2 hours, 28 minutes
City Dialing Code: 27
Tourist Information Office: Zermatt Tourist Office, Bahnhofplatz, 3920 Zurich
(Located at the railway station)
Tel: (27) 967 01 81
Internet: www.zermatt.ch
E-mail: Zermatt@wallis.ch
Hours: Mid-June–mid-October: 0830–1800 Monday-Friday, 0830–1830 Saturday, 0930–1200 and 1600–1830 Sunday; mid-December–mid-April: 0830–1200 and 1400–1900 Monday–Friday, 0830–1900 Saturday, 0930–1200 and 1600–1900 Sunday; remainder of the year: 0830–1200 and 1330–1800 Monday–Friday, 0830–1200 Saturday.

How about a cheese fondue luncheon in Zermatt while viewing the **Matterhorn?** A great place to have lunch is at the Winter Garden in the Alex Hotel. It is all glass and provides an endless view. *Tel:* (027) 966–7070; *Fax:* (027) 966–7090; *E-mail:* hotel.alex.zermatt@spectraweb. ch. Located in the middle of the Alps at 1,620 meters (about 5,300 feet) above sea level, Zermatt can be visited very easily during your stay in Bern. Board the 0734 *Cisalpino* or the 0822 *InterCity Express* from Bern to Brig. In Brig, you can connect with the *Glacier Express* private railroad (reservations required) to Zermatt. Eurail and Europass holders can travel to Brig on the railpasses, but must purchase a ticket for the portion from Brig to Zermatt. The entire route is included for Swiss Pass holders.

Taking the 0734 departure from Bern will have you in Zermatt at the newly reconstructed rail station at 1043; the later one at 0822 will still get you there in time for that luncheon at 1143. In fact, you could stay in Zermatt for an early dinner, too. There are more than 38 restaurants to choose from, offering specialty Swiss, Italian, French, and Asian cuisine. By leaving Zermatt at 1952 and changing trains in Brig and Spiez, you could still be back in Bern at 2339—all in the same day!

Famous for its perfect snow conditions, Zermatt has the longest skiing season in the Alps. Summers offer exquisite scenery for hiking, walking, and golfing. If visiting between the end of June to the middle of August, you'll see the most famous goats in the world as they travel in and out of town along the main street. And, Zermatt is car-free—only electric cars and horse-drawn conveyances are allowed.

Check with Bern Tourismus for information. The rail information office is across the hallway. Advance Glacier Express reservations can be made through RailPass.com (*Tel:* 877–RAILPASS; *Fax:* 614–764–0711). Don't miss "God's perfect little place" at the foot of the Matterhorn.

Base City:

Zürich

Internet: www.zurich-tourism.ch
City Dialing Code: 1

Some describe it as a garden city by a lake. Others picture it as one of the most elegant cities in Europe. Statisticians term it the largest in Switzerland, and anyone engaged in international business knows it is a world center for industry and commerce. Bankers seem content in knowing that it all begins and ends right there. Zürich, known as "Downtown Switzerland" can be all things to all people.

Zürich is packed with surprising contrasts. A charming tree-shaded avenue named Bahnhofstrasse runs from the railway station to Lake Zürich, yet it houses the headquarters of the great world banks and some of the most elegant shops to be found in Europe. A few short blocks away, the scene yields to the Middle Ages around St. Peter's Church near the Limmat River, and the bridge that crosses the river leads into Niederdorfstrasse, the city's roistering nightclub area.

Zürich is a major hub for European rail transportation. Trains between Milan in the south, Munich in the east, and the great trunk line crossing Switzerland glide in and out of its Hauptbahnhof (central train station) in a never-ending procession.

Arriving by Air

Zürich's **Kloten International Airport** lies 10 miles northeast of the city.

(*Internet:* www.uniqueairport.com; *Tel:* 157 10 60 [flight information].)

Zurich Airport is undergoing extensive expansion to be completed in 2004, making it one of the largest shopping areas in Switzerland. The new terminal, Dock Midfield, is scheduled to open at the end of 2002.

Airport–City Links

Train: SBB trains depart every 10–15 minutes for Zürich Hauptbahnhof from 0611–0020; journey time 10 minutes; fare CHF 10.40 first class, CHF 6.20 second class. Trains return from Zürich Hauptbahnhof to the airport every 15 minutes from 0526–2345. Also, direct rail connections are available from Zürich Airport to Bern, Chur, Geneva, Interlaken, Lucerne, and others.

Hotel Bus: Many hotels offer shuttle bus service. The hotel guest pick-up point is at the Arrivals level between Terminals A and B.

Regional Bus: Bus connections available to towns and villages in the Zürich region. Bus terminal is opposite Parking Level B.

Taxi: Taxi queues are in front of the Arrivals halls of Terminals A and B; journey time 20–30 minutes; average fare to downtown Zurich, CHF 55.

Arriving by Train

Zürich Hauptbahnhof (main railway station) is one of the most up-to-date and complete railway stations in Europe. All EuroCity, InterCity, ICN, and express trains stop here. There are three other suburban terminals within the city. Train departures are displayed on digital boards.

The **Rail Travel Centre** is located on the same level as the trains, opposite track 13. It contains all the elements required by the average rail traveler, including railpass validation. The rail information desks are staffed by 25–30 multilingual rail travel specialists to assist you in obtaining train information, tickets, reservations, plus many other travel services. An efficient numbering system is used—just take a number from the machine upon entering. Hours: 0630-2130 daily.

- **Money exchange** office (open 0630–2245) is located on the left side of the main arrival hall. If you don't have Swiss francs upon arrival, stock up on them. Not only is Zürich expensive, but the Swiss prefer their francs.
- **Baggage lockers** are one level down using the escalators. Two levels down are the shops and food services.

Tourist Information/Hotel Reservations

- *Zürich Tourist Information:* Hauptbahnhof; Zürich 8023; *Tel:* 215–4000; *Fax:* 215–4044; *Internet:* www.zuerich.com; *E-mail:* information@zuerich.com

  Hours: April–October: 0800–2030 Monday–Saturday, 0830–1900 Sunday; November–March, 0830–1900 Monday–Friday and 0900–1830 Saturday–Sunday

  Hotel reservations: *Tel:* 215–4040; *Fax:* 215–4044; *E-mail:* hotel@zuerich.com

Notes: To reach the Zürich tourist office, exit from the trains, turning right at the end of the tracks, and proceed directly through the main hall. The office will be on your left. The tourist office can also make hotel reservations. A city map and a brochure describing the Zürich public transportation system are available.

Getting Around in Zürich

The *Ride with Us* brochure is particularly helpful because it explains how to use the self-service facilities of the city's transportation system, including rail (S-Bahn), trams, buses, and funiculars. The Swiss Passes include travel on the city network, but the variety of Eurail passes and Europasses are accepted only on the S-Bahn network. If you have any type of Eurail pass/Europass, we recommend that you purchase a 1-day or multiple-day pass to cover the remaining public transport network in Zürich:

- Welcome 24 Ticket—24 hours in the city and between Zürich–Airport, CHF 10.80
- Welcome 48 Ticket—48 hours in the city, Zürich area (such as Uetilberg), CHF 25.00

Sights/Attractions/Tours

Obtain a copy of the brochure *Zürich City Tours and Excursions* from the tourist office. This brochure describes city sight-seeing, excursions by motor coach or by trolley, cruises on the Limmat River as well as those on Lake Zürich, ascension of Mount Uetliberg for a panoramic view of the city and Alps, and how to see Zürich by night.

Escorted and unescorted tours are available at various times throughout the week during certain seasons of the year, so be sure to check with the train-information office or the tourist office. Some of these excursions require Eurailpass or Europass holders to pay supplemental charges. Payment of these charges, along with reservations for the excursions, can be made at these offices.

For a relaxed "Classic Trolley Tour," board a vintage Swiss trolley. For this 2-hour tour, you can sit and see the sights. April–October, tours depart from the Hauptbahnhof at 0945, 1200, and 1400; November–March, departures are at 1200 and 1400. Fare: CHF 32.

Lake steamers at the far end of the Bahnhofstrasse at the Schiffstation (boat station) offer several interesting cruises, including one to the eastern end of the lake to an interesting old Swiss town, **Rapperswil.**

Zürich has its share of cathedrals. The **Grossmünster Cathedral** stands brooding on the east bank of the Limmat River. The cathedral has a statue of Charlemagne, who is said to have built the original church. Almost opposite on the other side of the river stands the **Fraümunster Cathedral,** reached by crossing the Münsterbrücke (Cathedral Bridge). Here, you can view the cathedral's famously beautiful Chagall windows. Alongside the central station is the **Swiss National Museum.** On exhibition are authentic rooms of the sixteenth and seventeenth centuries, removed from their original sites and rebuilt within the museum. Zürich is not totally old in face. Its **Kunsthaus** (Fine Arts Museum) is an attractive, modern building with a magnificent collection of modern art.

There is no shortage of fine dining in Zürich. One of our favorite places that combines an elegant medieval atmosphere with fine Swiss food specialties and wines at reasonable prices is **Zunfthaus zur Zimmerleuten** "Carpenters' Guildhouse," located at Limmatquai 40, along the Limmat River in the Old Town. You can get there on tram No. 4; get off at the *Rathaus* (Town Hall) stop. *Tel:* 252 08 34; *Fax:* 252 08 48.

Day Excursions

Zürich provides an alternative base city to Bern for those arriving via Zürich International Airport. The city's proximity to Lucerne and Rheinfelden decreases travel time for these day excursions when compared to Bern, but this time saving comes at a price. Zürich maintains a reputation for being one of Europe's most expensive cities. Budget-minded travelers may do well to use Bern as their base city and save Zürich for a day excursion and as a gateway city.

Train Connections to Other Base Cities from Zürich

DEPART ZURICH	TRAIN NUMBER	ARRIVE	NOTES
		Amsterdam Centraal	
1002	EC 102	1856	1
1202	ICE 70	2054	R, 2
1302	EC 2	2154	
2200	IR 1794	0856+1	R, 3, Sleeper
		Berlin Zoobahnhof	
0557	ICE 78	1416	4
0802	ICE 76	1626	4
1002	EC 102	1821	5
1202	ICE 70	2016	4
1302	EC 2	2215	5
1733	EC 93	0705+1	R, 6, Sleeper
		Bern (Berne)	

Approx. 36 direct trains daily; most depart at 04 and 34 min. past the hour; average journey time, 1 hr 09 min.

		Brussels (Bruxelles) Midi/Zuid	
0713	TGV 9284	1620	R, 7
1202	ICE 70	1945	3
1500	EC 96	2246	
2200	IR 1794	0645+1	R, Sleeper
		Budapest Keleti	
0933	EC 163	2233	8
2233	EN 467	1133+1	R, Sleeper

DEPART ZURICH	TRAIN NUMBER	ARRIVE	NOTES
Copenhagen (København) H.			
0802	ICE 76	2159	R, 9
2044	CNL 470	1359+1	R, 9, Sleeper
Hamburg			
0557	ICE 78	1332	
0802	ICE 76	1532	
1202	ICE 70	1932	
2044	CNL 470	0833+1	R, Sleeper
Luxembourg			
1202	ICE 70	1650	3
1500	EC 96	1959	
Lyon Part-Dieu			
0707	IR 508	1223	10
0834	IC 714	1419	10

then hourly until 1534 followed by 1607, 1634, 1834, and 2107.

DEPART ZURICH	TRAIN NUMBER	ARRIVE	NOTES
Milan (Milano) Centrale			
0630	CIS 151*	1015	R
0704	CIS 153*	1045	R
0830	IC 357	1245	R
0907	IC 355	1335	R
1107	IC 383	1535	R
1307	CIS 155*	1645	R
1507	IC 387	1935	R
1707	IC 381	2135	R
1907	CIS 157*	2245	R
Munich (München)			
0733	EC 99	1157	
0933	EC 197	1400	
1333	ICE 95	1748	
1733	EC 93	2157	
Nice Ville			
1007	D 1563	1958	11
1034	IC 718	2006	R, 10
2000	IR 1788	0911	R, 3, 12, Sleeper
Paris Gare de l'Est			
0713	TGV 9284	1321	R
1545	TGV 9288	2147	R
2300	IR 468	0646+1	R, Sleeper
Rome (Roma) Termini			
0704	CIS 153*	1630	R, 13
0907	IC 355	1830	R, 14
1107	IC 383	2030	R, 14
1307	CIS 155*	2230	R, 14
2207	EN 303	0915+1	R, 15, Sleeper
Vienna (Wien)			
0933	EC 163	1850	
1333	EC 161	2250	
2233	EN 467	0810+1	R, Sleeper

Daily, unless otherwise noted
R Reservations required
+1 Arrive next day
* Cisalpino (CIS) trains require supplement
1. Change trains in Duisburg.
2. Change trains in Freiburg.
3. Change trains in Basel.
4. Change trains in Hannover.
5. Change trains in Mannheim.
6. Change trains in Munich.
7. Change trains in Paris.
8. Change trains in Vienna.
9. Change trains in Hamburg
10. Change trains in Geneva.
11. Change trains in Arth-Goldau.
12. Change trains in Mulhouse-Ville.
13. Change trains in Bologna.
14. Change trains in Milan.
15. Change trains in Florence.

ZÜRICH

Appendix

RAIL–TOUR ITINERARIES

Three sample rail-tour itineraries are presented in response to readers' requests for sample itineraries combining several base cities and day excursions into a rail-tour package. These itineraries are similar to those used in previous tour programs and are considered "route-tested."

The base cities and day excursions in these itineraries are described elsewhere in this edition. Each itinerary may be completed with a 15-day Eurailpass, or a 15-day-in-2-months Eurail Flexipass or Saverpass.

Gateway cities are an important pretrip consideration. Discuss them with your travel agent before buying air tickets or before purchasing them yourselves on-line. We have included airport information in base city descriptions for your assistance. When suggested gateways are cities other than the rail-tour base cities, we have included rail schedules to assist in your planning, but as stated previously in this edition, our rail schedules are for planning purposes only. *Europe by Eurail* and its publisher cannot be held responsible for the consequences of either schedule or train changes occuring after press time or for inadvertent inaccuracies.

The following rail-tour schedules have been compiled on the basis of what we consider to be the best trains running at the best times; however, in almost every case, there are several other trains departing at other times that may be more convenient for your purposes. For this reason you may want to contact RailPass.com toll-free at (877) RAILPASS (877–724–5727) or visit the Point-to-Point section for scheduling at www.railpass.com.

Hotels suggested for the itineraries have been selected for their convenient locations near the railway stations and/or close to public transportation. Hotel price ranges are quoted in euros or local currencies for planning purposes only and are subject to change without prior notice. To convert the rates to U.S. dollars, consult the Foreign Exchange listing in the financial section of your hometown newspaper, contact your bank, or visit **www.oanda.com** and go to the cheat sheet for travelers page (you can print the rates for the countries on your itinerary and carry them with your other travel papers); another great site is **www.xe.net** for universal currency exchanges.

Confirm hotel rates either through your travel agent or directly with the hotel. Most of the hotels listed have U.S. representatives through whom your travel agent can make reservations at no additional cost to you.

Europe à la Carte

A rail tour using the *Europe by Eurail* base cities Munich, Bern, and Paris is an adventure through the very heart of Europe.

Base Cities

Munich: Germany's fun capital. Plan ample time for shopping and sightseeing before beginning your exciting rail adventure. Allow for jet lag, too.

Bern: Medieval elegance in the heart of Switzerland. An all-weather shopping center. Save the sunny days for Bern's eye-filling day excursions.

Paris: The City of Light and everyone's "second" city is the only one of its kind. Mix Paris's pleasures with its unusual array of day excursions.

Gateways

Open Jaw: Munich inbound, Paris outbound. Discuss with your travel agent for professional advice. Other gateways include:

Frankfurt Hbf: ICE 797 to Munich departs 1549 and arrives 1924 or ICE 799 departs 1649 and arrives 2025. Return to Frankfurt on ICE 990, departing 0630 and arriving 0951 or ICE 796, 1036–1410.

Amsterdam: EC 3 to Munich departs at 0755; arrives Mannheim at 1329. Change to ICE 593, departing 1332 and arriving Munich 1622. Return to Amsterdam on ICE 794, departing Munich at 1237; arrive Mannheim 1526. Change to EC 104 Mannheim to Amsterdam, 1529–2054.

Paris: Depart Paris Est on EC 65 *Mozart* to Munich at 0749; arrive Munich 1615. Return to Paris on EC 66 *Maurice Ravel,* at 0742; arrive Paris Est 1622.

Base-City Hotels

Munich: The InterCity Hotel, located in the station, is first choice. Quiet, good restaurant, but usually booked months in advance. Drei Lowen, one block from the station, is convenient. Balance of hotels listed are clustered nearby. Hilton and Sheraton properties in suburbs have easy tram connections to city center.

Bern: Schweizerhof, on the station plaza, is tops in location, restaurant, and price. Hotel Baeren and Hotel Bristol are more economical and 3 minutes' walk to station. Other hotels listed are also within a short walk of station and maintain highest Swiss standards.

Paris: For economy and excellent location for rail travelers, choose Hotel Albert Ier, situated between Gare du Nord and Gare de l'Est. Hotel Lyon-Palace-Paris, one short block away from Gare de Lyon's rail, Métro, and RER

EUROPE À LA CARTE BASE-CITY TRANSFER SCHEDULE

FROM	TO	DEPART	TRAIN NUMBER	ARRIVE	NOTES
Munich	*Zürich*	0814	EC 92	1227	R
Zürich	*Bern*	1234	IC 724	1343	R, 1
Bern	*Paris Lyon*	0832	TGV 9284	1321	R

EUROPE À LA CARTE DAY-EXCURSION SUGGESTIONS

BASE CITY	EXCURSION	DEPART	ARRIVE	RETURN	ARRIVE	NOTES
Munich	Berchtesgaden	0741	1021	1747	2020	2
	Garmisch-Partenkirchen	0800	0921	1831	1955	
	Innsbruck	0730	0922	1837	2030	
	Nuremberg	0747	0930	1830	2012	
	Salzburg	0725	0855	1905	2036	
Bern	Interlaken	0826	0920	1940	2033	
	Lucerne	0743	0903	1857	2017	
	Milan	0734	1050	1710	2024	R
Paris	Annecy	0644	1029	1902	2231	R
	Rennes	0805	1020	1835	2040	R
	Fontainebleau	0827	0904	1719	1802	
	Lyon	0730	0931	1900	2101	
	Rouen	0915	1021	1801	1907	

Note: All trains are daily.

R Reservations required or recommended

1. Half-hourly service Zürich–Bern

2. Change trains in Freilassing.

connections, has excellent neighborhood-restaurant section.

Europe à la Carte 15-Day Rail Itinerary

Day 1   Munich–Salzburg: Visit Mozart's birthplace and listen to Salzburg's sound of music.

Day 2   Munich–Garmisch–Partenkirchen: Home of the Winter Olympic Park and gateway to ascent of the mighty Zugspitze.

Day 3   Munich–Berchtesgaden: Explore salt mines, then soar to Hitler's ill-famed Eagle's Nest.

Day 4   Munich–Innsbruck: World famous for winter Olympics, with year-round exhilarating scenery.

Day 5   Munich–Nuremberg: Germany's leading toy producers spice activities with fresh gingerbread.

Day 6   Munich–Bern: Base-city transfer via Zürich.

Day 7   Bern–Interlaken: A day in alpine splendor; return to Bern by Lake of Thun steamer.

Day 8   Bern–Lucerne: A rain-or-shine outing with Mount Pilatus and Swiss cheese fondue.

Day 9   Bern–Milan: A change of pace, a change of place to Italy's bustling northern capital.

Day 10   Bern–Paris: Base-city transfer via Geneva.

Day 11   Paris–Rouen: Visit historic site of France's Joan of Arc.

Day 12   Paris–Rennes: Half-timbered houses and a ride on the TGV Atlantique.

Day 13   Paris–Fontainebleau: Visit the scene where Napoleon ruled and later was vanquished.

Day 14   Lyon–Annecy: Breathtaking scenery, sparkling water, and a charming medieval marketplace.

Day 15   Paris–Lyon: City of contrast visited after exciting journey aboard TGV, one of the world's fastest trains.

Tour Tips: Make seat reservations immediately on arrival in Munich. At minimum, reserve all base-city legs. Reservations are obligatory on TGV and many EuroCity trains. Don't overlook The Romantic Road and The Golden Pass day-excursion possibilities.

European Escapade

A more than passing acquaintance with some of Europe's most fascinating sights and cities. From gateway Luxembourg, you travel to Bern, Amsterdam, and Paris, with shopping in Brussels.

Base Cities

Luxembourg: Fortress city, steeped in European and American history. Virtually a tax-free city; save some of your dollars for Luxembourg shops.

EUROPEAN ESCAPADE BASE-CITY TRANSFER SCHEDULE

FROM	TO	DEPART	TRAIN NUMBER	ARRIVE	NOTES
Luxembourg	Bern	1002	EC 91	1511	R
Bern	Amsterdam	1149	EC 104	2054	R
Amsterdam	Paris Nord	0856	Thalys 9324*	1305	R
Paris Est	Luxembourg	1054	357	1435	R

EUROPEAN ESCAPADE DAY-EXCURSION SUGGESTIONS

BASE CITY	EXCURSION	DEPART	ARRIVE	DEPART	ARRIVE	NOTES
Luxembourg	Clervaux	0815	0906	1854	1945	
Bern	Koblenz	0822	1039	1716	1933	1
	Interlaken	0826	0920	1940	2033	
	Lucerne	0743	0903	1857	2017	
	Milan	0734	1050	1710	2024	R
Amsterdam	Alkmaar	0822	0853	1737	1811	
	Enkhuizen	0819	0923	1738	1844	
	Hoorn	0819	0858	1734	1814	
Paris	Annecy	0644	1029	1902	2231	R
	Rennes	0805	1020	1835	2040	R
	Chartres	0856	0953	1644	1757	
	Fontainebleau	0827	0904	1712	1800	
	Lyon	0730	0904	1801	1907	

Note: All trains are daily.

R Reservations required or recommended

* Thalys trains require supplement

1. Change trains in Trier.

Bern: Medieval settings in the heart of the Swiss Alps. Bern's arcaded walkways make shopping and sight-seeing easy even in bad weather.

Amsterdam: Canals, cheese shops, diamond cutters, and Rembrandt's finest masterpieces await you.

Paris: City of Light. Mix Paris's pleasures with an array of action-packed day excursions.

Gateways

Discuss all gateway possibilities with your travel agent, because the tour's circular itinerary provides a wide selection, including all of the base cities in this itinerary plus Brussels. Depart Brussels Midi for Luxembourg at 0716 on EC 91 for arrival in Luxembourg at 0952; EuroCity service returns you to Brussels at end of tour.

Base City Hotels

Luxembourg: Pick a price. Most of the hotels listed are near the station. Book well in advance, particularly in summer tour season.

Bern: Schweizerhof for luxury, but the other listed hotels offer only a shade less at varying prices. All are within walking distance of the station.

Amsterdam: Victoria Park Plaza Hotel, a scant block from the station, is most convenient and highly recommended. Grand Hotel Krasnapolsky is just another stone's throw away but posh, with prices to match.

Paris: Best bargain and good location is Hotel Albert Ier between Gare du Nord and Gare de l'Est. Same for independent Lyon-Palace-Paris Hotel, close to Gare de Lyon.

European Escapade 15–Day Rail Itinerary

Day 1	Luxembourg–Clervaux: An opportunity to visit site of World War II Battle of the Bulge.
Day 2	Luxembourg–Koblenz: A rail excursion along the Mosel to the Rhine in German wine country.
Day 3	Luxembourg–Bern: Base-city transfer via France.
Day 4	Bern–Interlaken: View of mighty Jungfrau and cruise on Lake of Thun highlight exciting rail tour.
Day 5	Bern–Lucerne: Sparkling highlights of Switzerland's lake city plus Mount Pilatus ascent.
Day 6	Bern–Milan: Cross into Italy for a delightful day of sight-seeing in fascinating Milan.
Day 7	Bern–Amsterdam: Base-city transfer via Rhine.
Day 8	Amsterdam–Enkhuizen: Visit the Zuider Zee museum, depicting the Dutch battle with the sea.
Day 9	Amsterdam–Hoorn: Steam-engine ride from Hoorn to Medemblik; the old Dutch Market on Wednesday.
Day 10	Amsterdam–Alkmaar: World-famous cheese market and site of Dutch revolt against Spanish rule.
Day 11	Amsterdam–Paris: Base-city transfer via Brussels.

SCANDINAVIAN SPLENDOR BASE-CITY TRANSFER SCHEDULE

FROM	TO	DEPART	TRAIN NUMBER	ARRIVE	NOTES
Copenhagen	*Oslo*	2216	392	0700+1	R, Sleeper
Oslo	*Stockholm*	0730	IC 55	1325	
Stockholm	*Helsinki*	1700	Silja ferry	0930+1	R
Helsinki	*Stockholm*	1800	Silja ferry	0900+1	R
Stockholm	*Copenhagen*	0815	X 2000/525	1323	R
		1215	X 2000/533	1723	R

SCANDINAVIAN SPLENDOR DAY-EXCURSION SUGGESTIONS*

BASE CITY	EXCURSION	DEPART	ARRIVE	DEPART	ARRIVE	NOTES
Copenhagen	Aarhus	0756	1044	1830	2122	R
	Helsingør	0821	0913	1645	1738	
	Odense	0800	0929	1806	1922	
	Roskilde	0830	0851	1826	1848	
Oslo	Hamar	0837	0954	1810	1934	R
	Larvik	0933	1143	1949	2152	2nd class
	Lillehammer	0837	1036	1851	2053	R
Stockholm	Eskilstuna	0855	0957	1703	1810	
	Norrköping	0815	0934	1622	1740	R
	Uppsala	0840	0920	1910	1950	R

* See appropriate base-city chapters for additional day-excursion suggestions.
Note: All trains are daily unless otherwise noted.
R Reservations required
+1 Arrive next day

Day 12   Paris–Chartres: Palaces and castles abound along with Gothic Cathedral of Notre Dame.
Day 13   Paris–Rennes: Experience TGV *Atlantique* at 186 miles per hour.
Day 14   Paris–Fontainebleau: Visit palace where Napoleon relaxed with Josephine—and a few others.
Day 15   Paris–Lyon: "Newest" city of France, with Roman history, visited aboard one of the world's fastest trains, a TGV.

Tour Tips: Book all seat reservations when you arrive in Luxembourg. Depart Luxembourg (Day 2) at 0822, arriving Koblenz at 1039 (transfer in Trier). In Koblenz, board EC 29 at 1053 for Mainz, arriving there at 1144. You'll get a great view of the Rhine from the train. Lunch in the Mainz station restaurant and depart at 1253 in the direction of Koblenz, but get off in Bingen at 1308. Board the steamer ship from the Bingen pier at 1415. Then relax on the Rhine until reaching Koblenz at 1800. Service operates April–October. Have dinner at the Weindorf. Catch RE 22014 at 2013 back to Luxembourg (transfer in Trier).

En route to Amsterdam from Bern (Day 7), after departing Mainz, watch on the right-hand side of the train for spectacular Rhine scenery to Koblenz.

Scandinavian Splendor

Tour the Scandinavian capitals of Copenhagen, Helsinki, Oslo, and Stockholm and board the Silja Line's finest cruise ship for adventure on the Baltic.

Base Cities

Copenhagen: Jovial, entertaining, the fun capital of Scandinavia. Save it for the grand finale.
Helsinki: Daughter of the Baltic. A glittering gem set in a picture-book harbor. Make the best of your "shore leave" by enjoying every moment.
Oslo: Friendly, pleasant, and compact. Take the Bergen–Flam excursion option if time permits.
Stockholm: Striking harbor skyline, a city of islands and waterways. Sightseeing must include a visit to Old Town, where it all began centuries ago.

Gateways

All the base cities have direct U.S. air service, even Helsinki. The circular nature of the tour's itinerary makes it possible to select any one of the aforementioned base cities as both the inbound and outbound gateway. Our choice would be Copenhagen; which is yours?

Base-City Hotels

Copenhagen: Palace Hotel gets the tourists' nod for convenient location, midrange rates, and so on. The Plaza, facing the station, is great but difficult to book in high season.

Helsinki: No listing, because we recommend using the Silja Line's accommodations for this tour's out-and-back day excursion, but we can recommend the *Presidenti* if you elect to extend your stay in Helsinki.

Oslo: The Grand Hotel features old-world elegance with modern conveniences—with the exception of price. The Hotel Nobel, with a wider rate range, is near the Grand Hotel.

Stockholm: Take your pick. All three hotels listed face Central Station. Price is probably the deciding factor. All have acceptable restaurants and are clean and well managed.

Scandinavian Splendor 15–Day Rail Itinerary

If Copenhagen is selected as the in-out gateway, spend jet-lag adjustment time there before validating your Eurailpass, Eurail Selectpass, or Scanrailpass and leaving for Oslo.

Day 1   Copenhagen–Oslo: Scenic base-city transfer.

Day 2   Oslo–Larvik: Put a fjord in your future with an excursion to Larvik and on to Skien.

Day 3   Oslo–Hamar: Drink in the beauty of Lake Mjosa before exploring the rail museum in Hamar.

Day 4   Oslo–Lillehammer: Lillehammer can provide an insight into Norway's culture.

Day 5   Oslo–Stockholm: Colorful base-city transfer.

Day 6   Stockholm–Uppsala: Spend an interesting day in a city that dates from pagan times.

Day 7   Stockholm–Eskilstuna: See Sweden's "steel city" and visit 300-year-old Rademacher Forges.

Day 8   Stockholm–Norrköping: Surprises such as cacti growing in Sweden await your arrival.

Day 9   Stockholm–Silja Line cruise to Helsinki: Cruise the Baltic in luxury to Finland.

Day 10   Helsinki–Stockholm: Set sail again for Sweden after an exciting day ashore in Helsinki.

Day 11   Stockholm–Copenhagen: Arrive in Denmark's capital after overland rail through Sweden.

Day 12   Copenhagen–Aarhus: Ferry and rail transportation join to make an exciting day excursion.

Day 13   Copenhagen–Helsingør: A rail visit to north Zealand to inspect Hamlet's castle.

Day 14   Copenhagen–Odense: A rail visit to the birthplace of Hans Christian Andersen.

Day 15   Copenhagen–Roskilde: Five Viking ships await your inspection in Roskilde's museum.

Tour Tips: Make the Silja Line cruise to Helsinki and back a highlight of your tour. Book a round-trip cabin and spend a carefree day ashore in Helsinki sans luggage. In Helsinki, ride tram 3T for a quick view of this remarkable city. The Silja Line can also arrange extended shore leave in Helsinki if desired.

BASE-CITY HOTELS AND INFORMATION

All hotel rates, given in local currencies applicable at press time, are subject to change. Rates range from the price of a single to double occupancy. The hotels listed are close to the railway stations and/or public transport facilities. The hotel's street location is below the hotel name.

When writing, the postal code, city, and country name should follow the hotel name and street address; for example, 1012 JS Amsterdam, The Netherlands.

Amsterdam Hotels

To telephone or fax the Amsterdam hotels from the United States, dial 011–31, then the number listed below.

Grand Hotel Krasnapolsky ★★★★★ *Tel:* (20) 5549111
Dam 9 €250–290 *Fax:* (20) 5547010
1012 JS
Internet: www.krasnapolsky.nl or www.goldentulip.com; *E-mail:* book@
krasnapolsky.nl
Breakfast €19.50

Victoria Hotel ★★★★ *Tel:* (20) 6234255
Damrak 1–5 €238–295 *Fax:* (20) 6252997
1012 LG
Breakfast €16.50
Internet: www.parkplazaamsterdam.com; *E-mail:* vicres@parkplazahotels.nl

Damrak Hotel ★★★ *Tel:* (20) 6262498
Damrak 49 €66–134* *Fax:* (20) 6250997
1012 LL
*Breakfast included in rates

Tulip Inn Amsterdam ★★★ *Tel:* (20) 4204545
Spuistraat 288–292 €150–177 *Fax:* (20) 4204300
1012 VX
Internet: www.goldentulip.com

Bern Hotels

To telephone or fax the Bern hotels from the United States, dial 011–41, then the number listed.

Gauer Schweizerhof ★★★★★ *Tel:* (31) 3268080
Bahnhofplatz 11 CHF 240–460 *Fax:* (31) 3268090
CH–3001
Internet: www.schweizerhof-bern.ch

Bern-Hotel ★★★★ *Tel:* (31) 3121021
Zeughausgasse 9 CHF 150–240 *Fax:* (31) 3121147
CH–3011
Internet: www.hotelbern.ch

Best Western Bristol ★★★★ *Tel:* (31) 3110101
Schauplatzgasse 10 CHF 180–250 *Fax:* (31) 3119479
CH–3011
Internet: www.bristolbern.ch
Buffet breakfast included.

City Am Bahnhof ★★★ *Tel:* (31) 3115377
Bahnhofplatz CHF 118–218 *Fax:* (31) 3110636
CH–3011
Internet: www.fassbind-hotels.ch; *E-mail:* city-ab@fassbind-hotels.ch
Buffet breakfast CHF 18.00; continental breakfast CHF 9.00

Hotel Metropole ★★★ *Tel:* (31) 3115021
Zeughausgasse 26 CHF 115–195 *Fax:* (31) 3121153
CH 3000
Internet: www.hotelmetropole.ch; *E-mail:* hotel@hotelmetropole.ch

Copenhagen Hotels

To telephone or fax hotels in Copenhagen from the United States, dial
011–45, then the number as listed.

The Palace Hotel ★★★★ *Tel:* (33) 144050
Rådhuspladsen 57 DKK 1,525–2,495[*] *Fax:* (33) 145279
DK–1550
Internet: www.palace-hotel.dk; *E-mail:* booking@principle.dk
[*]Some 5★ rooms available; rates include VAT, service charge, and breakfast

Sofitel Plaza Copenhagen ★★★★ *Tel:* (33) 149262
Bernstorffsgade 4 DKK 1,695–2,095 *Fax:* (33) 939362
DK–1577
Internet: www.accorhotel.dk; *E-mail:* sofitel@accorhotel.dk

Best Western,
The Mayfair Hotel ★★★ *Tel:* (45) 33314801
Helgolandsgade 3 DKK 975–1475 *Fax:* (45) 33239686
DK–1653
Internet: www.themayfairhotel.dk; *E-mail:* info@themayfairhotel.dk

Comfort Hotel Europa ★★★ Tel: (33) 213333
Colbjørnsgade 5-11 DKK 1095–1495 Fax: (33) 313399
DK–1652
Internet: www.choicehotels.dk; E-mail: info.europa@comfort.choicehotels.dk

Luxembourg Hotels

To telephone or fax Luxembourg hotels from the United States, dial 011–352, then the numbers as listed.

Note: Government of Luxembourg does not usually rate hotels.
*Rates include buffet breakfast and taxes

Golden Tulip Central ★★★★
Molitor Hotel Tel: 489911
28 Avenue de la Liberté €94–154* Fax: 483382
L–1930
Internet: www.hotelmolitor.lu or www.goldentulip.com; E-mail: molitor@pt.lu

President Hotel ★★★★ Tel: 486161
32 Place de la Gare €136–174* Fax: 486180
L–1024 (lower weekend rates)
Internet: www.president.lu; E-mail: info@president.lu

Hotel Italia
15–17 rue d'Anvers Tel: 4866261
L–1130 €65–81 Fax: 480807
E-mail: italia@euro.lu

Nobilis Hotel Tel: 494971
47 Avenue de la Gare €88–97 Fax: 403101
L–1611

Munich Hotels

To telephone or fax Munich hotels from the United States, dial 011–49, then the numbers as listed.

Atrium ★★★★ Tel: (89) 514190
Landwehrstrasse 59 €158–189 Fax: (89) 535066
D–80336

Best Western Hotel Cristal   ★★★★   *Tel:* (89) 551110
Schwanthalerstrasse 36   €120–140   *Fax:* (89) 55111992
80336
Internet: www.cristal.bestwestern.de or www.bestwestern.com;
Email: info@cristal.bestwestern.de

Drei Löwen   ★★★★   *Tel:* (89) 551040
Schillerstrasse 8   €100–187*   *Fax:* (89) 55104905
D–80336
*Breakfast included in rate

Top InterCity Hotel Munich   ★★★★   *Tel:* (89) 545560
Bayerstrasse10   €107–250*   *Fax:* (89) 5456610
D–80335
* Breakfast included
Internet: www.intercity-hotel.de; *E-mail:* reservierung@intercity-hotel.de
Located in Munich Hauptbahnhof (rail station)

Germania   ★★★   *Tel:* (49) 59046140
Schwanthalerstrasse 28   €57–95   *Fax:* (49) 591171
80336

Oslo Hotels

To telephone or fax Oslo hotels from the United States, dial 011–47, then
the numbers as listed.

Grand Hotel   ★★★★   *Tel:* (22) 429390
Karl Johansgate 31   NOK 1,520–3,150 *Fax:* (22) 421225
N–0101
E-mail: reservations@grand-hotel.no

Best Western
Hotell Bondeheimen   ★★★   *Tel:* (23) 214100
Rosenkrantz gate 8   NOK 575–1,245* *Fax:* (23) 214101
N-0159
*Breakfast included in rates
Internet: www.bestwestern.com; *E-mail:* booking@bondeheimen.com

Norlandia Karl Johan Hotel   ★★★   *Tel:* (23) 161700
Karl Johansgate 33   NOK 690–1,450   *Fax:* (23) 420519
N–0162
Internet: www.norlandia.no; *E-mail:* service@karljohan.norlandia.no

Paris Hotels

To telephone or fax the Paris hotels from the United States, dial 011-33, then the numbers as listed.

Hotel Ambassador   ★★★★   *Tel:* (1) 44834040
16, Blvd. Haussmann   €259–434   *Fax:* (1) 42461984
F–75009
Internet: www.concorde-hotels.com; *E-mail:* ambass@concord-hotels.com

Best Western
Anjou–Lafayette   ★★★   *Tel:* (1) 42468344
4, rue Riboutté   €77–90   *Fax:* (1) 48000897
F–75009
Internet: www.bestwestern.com; *E-mail:* hotel.anjou.lafayette@wanadoo.fr

Hotel Albert Ier ★★★   *Tel:* (1) 40368240
162, rue LaFayette   €82–96   *Fax:* (1) 40357252
F–75010
Internet: www.escapade-paris.com; *E-mail:* albert.premier@escapade-paris.com

Lyon-Palace-Paris   ★★★   *Tel:* (1) 43072949
11, rue de Lyon   €70–88   *Fax:* (1) 46289155
F–75012

Maine Atlantique   ★★★   *Tel:* (1) 45428143
55, rue des Plaisance   €60–77   *Fax:* (1) 45429787
F–75014

Plaza Elysées   ★★★   *Tel:* (1) 45639383
177, Blvd. Haussmann   €128–142   *Fax:* (1) 45611430
F–75008

Stockholm Hotels

To telephone or fax the Stockholm hotels from the United States, dial 011–46, then the numbers as listed.

Best Western Hotel
Terminus   ★★★★   *Tel:* (8) 440 1670
Vasagatan 20   SEK 1435–1650   *Fax:* (8) 440 1671
S–10125
E-mail: hotel.terminus@swipnet.se

Sheraton Stockholm
Hotel & Towers ★★★★ *Tel:* (8) 4123400
Tegelbacken 6, Box 195 SEK 1,380–2,300[*] *Fax:* (8) 4123409
S–10123
*Breakfast included

Internet: www.sheratonstockholm.com; *E-mail:* sheraton_stockholm@
sheraton.com

Scandic Hotel Continental ★★★ *Tel:* (8) 51734200
Vasagatan Box 120 SEK 1,667–2,074 *Fax:* (8) 51734211
S–10122
Located by Central rail station
Internet: www.scandic-hotels.com; *E-mail:* continental@scandic-hotels.com

FERRY CROSSINGS

In addition to unlimited rail travel and other conveniences, Eurail provides railpass holders with deck passage on ferries conveying train passengers within the Eurail countries. In some instances, passengers must detrain and board the ferries, but on most major rail lines, the passenger coaches are loaded directly onto the ferry. In either case, the ferries are equipped with amenities such as restaurants, bars, boutiques, and, when traveling between countries, money exchanges and tax-free shops.

Three major international ferry crossings exist; they are between Italy and Greece, Finland and Sweden, and Ireland and France. The distances are considerable and usually involve overnight travel. (Sleeping accommodations are extra.) Other ferry crossings of international importance to railpass travelers include the lines between Ireland and Britain.

Italy–Greece and v.v.

If your railpass is valid in Greece, you are granted free deck passage between Ancona or Bari, Italy, and Patras or Igoumenitsa, Greece, by **Superfast Ferries.** Railpass holders are also granted free deck passage between Brindisi, Italy, and Corfu, Igoumenitsa and Patras on ferries operated by **Hellenic Mediterranean Lines** and **Blue Star Ferries.**

You must present your railpass to the shipping-company office in the port and have a ticket and a boarding pass issued before boarding. Reservation fees, port taxes, meals, reclining chairs, or sleeping accommodations are not included. Reclining chairs are a great bargain for the budget-minded traveler. During July and August there is a high-season surcharge of about $20 (U.S.).

Superfast Ferries (www.superfast.com)
Superfast Ferries operate daily, departing in the evening for arrival the following morning.

Italy–Greece

Routes	Depart	Arrive	Hours
Ancona–Patras	1700	1300+1	19
Via Igoumenitsa	1900	1730+1	21.5
Ancona–Igoumenitsa	1900	1100+1	15
Bari–Patras			
Via Igoumenitsa	2000	1230+1	15.5
Bari–Igoumenitsa	2000	0630+1	9.5

Greece–Italy

Routes	Depart	Arrive	Hours
Patras–Ancona	2100	1500+1	19
Via Igoumenitsa	1700	1330+1	21.5
Igoumenitsa–Ancona	2330	1330+1	15
Patras–Bari	1800	0830+1	15.5
Igoumenitsa–Bari	2359	0830+1	9.5

- +1 = following day
- Departures and arrivals in local time.
- Schedules subject to change. Contact Superfast Ferries for bookings, prices for sleeping accommodations, exact sailing dates/times, and non-departure dates due to ships' maintenance.

Contacts:

Greece
Athens Superfast Ferries
30 Amalias Ave
105 58 Syntagma
Tel: (30) 1 3313252; *Fax:* (30) 1 3310369
E-mail: info.Athens@superfast.com

Italy
F.LLI Morandi & Co.
Via XXIX Settembre 2/0
I-60122 Ancona
Tel: (39) 071 202033/4; *Fax:* (39) 071 20 22 19
E-mail: info.anconaport@superfast.com

United States
Kompas
2929 E. Commercial Blvd.,Suite 201
Fort Lauderdale FL 33308
Tel: (954) 771-9200; *Fax:* (954) 771-9841
E-mail: kompas@superfast.com

Hellenic Mediterranean Lines (HML) (www.ferries.gr/hml)

Brindisi Depart	ITALY–GREECE Igoumenitsa Arrive	Corfu Arrive	Patras Arrive
Mon 1930	—	—	1130+1
Wed 1930	—	0600+1	1400
Fri 1930	0700+1	0900	
Sat 1930	—	—	1130+1

Patras Depart	GREECE–ITALY Igoumenitsa Depart	Corfu Depart	Brindisi Arrive
Tue 1930	—	—	1000+1
Thu 1930	—	0630+1	1400
	Sat 0700	Sat 0900	1545
Sun 1930	—	—	1000+1

- +1 = following day
- Departures and arrivals in local time.
- Schedules subject to change. Contact HML for bookings, prices for sleeping accommodations, exact sailing dates/times, and non-departure dates due to ships' maintenance.

Contact:
Hellenic Mediterranean Lines
HSAP Building
Pl. Looudovikou 4, P.O. Box 80057
GR-185 10 Pireaus, Greece
Tel: (30) 1 4225341; *Fax:* (30) 1 4225317
Tel: in Brindisi, Italy (39) 831528531; *Fax:* (39) 831526872
E-mail: prenato@hml.it

Blue Star Ferries

Italy–Greece		Greece–Italy	
Brindisi Depart	Igoumenitsa* Arrive	Igoumenitsa Depart	Brindisi** Arrive
1030	2000	2330	0700+1

Brindisi Depart	Corfu Arrive	Corfu Depart	Brindisi Arrive
1030	1830	0100	0700

*via Corfu on Mon, Wed, Thu
**via Corfu on Mon, Fri, Sat
- Daily departures

- +1 = following day
- Departures and arrivals in local time.
- Schedules subject to change. Contact Blue Star Ferries for bookings, prices for sleeping accommodations, exact sailing dates/times, and non-departure dates due to ships' maintenance.

Contact:
Blue Star Ferries
26, Akti Posidonos
185 31 Piraeus
Tel: (30) 1 422 5000; *Fax:* (30) 1 422 5265

Brindisi, Italy, Ferry Terminal: A 15-minute walk downhill to the Seno di Levante pier at the foot of Corso (Umberto), Corso Garibaldi, and Via del Mera, the streets leading to the waterfront. The terminal is on the right, just before the pier. It opens daily two hours prior to departure times.

Attenzione (That's "attention" in Italian): From the time you arrive in Brindisi until you are safely aboard the ferry, beware of "entrepreneurs" approaching you with offers to help. Many are garbed in official-looking uniforms or are wearing "Official Guide" headgear. They bear alarming messages such as, "I have bad news. All of the deck space for tonight's sailing has been sold out." Then they relate the good news: "You are fortunate in meeting me, for I can take you to an agency where a few cabins are still available." With that, he'll reach for your baggage unless, by now, you have interrupted his presentation with a firm, "No, thank you." If he insists, *polizia* (police) is another good word to inject into the conversation.

Patras, Greece, Ferry Terminal: To reach the terminal from the railway station, turn left as you exit the station. Walk along the street side of the quay approximately 300 yards, to the office marked CENTRAL AGENCY Summer hours are 0900–2200 daily. Winter hours are 0900–1300 and 1700–2200. Report on day of embarkation only. No baggage checking is available.

Author's suggestion: The port cities of Brindisi and Patras are interesting, charming, and steeped in history. Why not take a day to see them at a leisurely pace? Plan to arrive a day before your scheduled ferry departure. Ask your hotel to call ahead for a reservation. Also ask the concierge to check on your ferry reservation. The address and telephone numbers of the city tourist information offices are posted in the arrival halls of the rail stations.

Finland–Sweden and v.v.

There are two competing ferry services between Helsinki and Stockholm: Silja Line and Viking Line. Holders of Eurail passes, Eurail Selectpass (provided that Finland and Sweden were chosen as two of the three bordering countries), and Scanrail Pass are valid for deck passage. Pass holders must pay extra for cabin space.

Crossing between Sweden and Finland, you may select between two routes: Stockholm–Helsinki direct; or Stockholm–Turku, with train connections or the Silja Line express bus service between Turku and Helsinki. Our preference is the direct route between the two capitals because it gives you a few more hours aboard ship to enjoy the scenery, which is spectacular. Both routes traverse the breathtaking archipelago between the two countries. Although your railpass entitles you to travel on the ferry, you also need to obtain a boarding pass before embarking. If you need a boarding pass, you should be at the ferry terminal 1½–2 hours before ship departure.

Silja Line ferries depart daily from Helsinki Olympiaterminaali (Olympia Terminal) at Eteläsatama port at 1700 and arrive Stockholm Värtahamnen port at 0930 the next day. Tram 3B and 3T service, adjacent to the Olympia Terminal, connects with Helsinki city center. Shuttle bus service (extra charge) is available from Stockholm Värtan Terminal at Värtahamnen port to Ropsten Metro (underground/subway) station, where there are trains to Stockholm Central Station.

For more details, schedules, and/or to reserve cabin space, contact:

Silja Line, Main Office
Mannerheimintie 2
FIN-00100 Helsinki, Finland
Tel: (358) 9 180 4422; *Fax:* (358) 9 180 4279
Internet: www.silja.fi or www.silja.com/english

Silja Line's U.S. Sales Agent:
Norwegian Coastal Voyage
405 Park Avenue
New York, NY 10022
Tel: (212) 319–1300 or (800) 323–7436; *Fax:* (212) 319–1390
Internet: www.silja.com; *E-mail:* info@coastalvoyage.com

Viking Line ferries depart Helsinki Katajanokka dock at 1730 daily*. Arrive Stockholm Stadsgården dock 0930 the next day. Tram 4 service operates daily between the vicinity of Viking Line Terminal and Helsinki city center; or bus no. 13 operates between Katajanokka Terminal–Helsinki rail station in connection with departure/arrival of ships. Bus service between Stockholm Stadsgården port and Cityterminalen (bus terminal) near Stockholm Central Station runs in connection with arrival/departure of ships. For more detailed information on Viking Line services or to reserve cabin space, contact:

Viking Line, Main Office
PO Box 35
FIN-2201 Mariehamn, Finland
Tel: (358) 18 26011; *Fax:* (358) 18 15811
Internet: www.vikingline.fi

Train/Ferry Connections Helsinki—Stockholm via Turku

DEPART HELSINKI	TRAIN NUMBER	ARRIVE TURKU HARBOR
0550	121	0823
1804	143	2032

Note: Arrives Turku Satama (harbor train station)

Silja Line ferries depart Turku Harbor daily at 0910, arrive Stockholm Värtahamnen Port 1915; depart at 2115 for arrival at 0700 next day.*

Viking Line ferries depart Turku Linnansatama dock daily at 0845, arrive Stockholm Stadsgården dock at 1855; depart at 2100 for arrival at 0630 next day. Bus sevice between Stadsgården port and Cityterminalen (bus terminal) near Stockholm Central Station in connection with arrival/departure of ships.

*2002 sailing date exceptions unavailable at press time.

Ireland—Britain and v.v.

Stena Line, the world's largest international ferry company, operates on 16 routes in northwestern Europe, including the Irish Sea and the English Channel. Stena's HSS (High-speed Sea Service) ships cruise between Belfast in Northern Ireland and Stranraer in Scotland in only 105 minutes. Stena Line's Superferry service offers leisurely crossings with duty-free shopping, meals, and even a movie (on some routes). The Superferry *Koningin Beatrix* on the Rosslare–Fishguard route, capable of carrying 2,100 passengers and 500 automobiles, is the largest and most luxurious ferry to operate on the southern Irish Sea. *Internet:* www.stenaline.com.

Irish Ferries can take you from Dublin to Holyhead, and P&O Irish Sea ferries serve on the Larne–Cairnryan route. *Internet:* www.irishferries.com.

Coming from London by train requires a transfer to either a Stena Line or Irish Ferries ferry at Holyhead. The Stena Line ferries serve the port of Dun Laoghaire, a suburb of Dublin, where passengers can transfer to the center of the city by the local train service, DART.

Stena Line to Britain

ROUTE	JOURNEY
Rosslare–Fishguard	3 hours, 30 minutes Superferry or 100 minutes Stena Lynx Catamaran
Dublin–Holyhead	3 hours, 45 minutes Superferry
Dun Läoghaire–Holyhead	100 minutes HSS fast ferry
Belfast–Stranraer	3 hours and 15 minutes Superferry or 105 minutes HSS fast ferry

Irish Ferries

	DEPART	ARRIVE
Dublin to Holyhead	0945	1300
	2145	0100
Holyhead to Dublin	1545	1900
	0330	0645
	(Crossing time: 3 hours and 15 minutes)	
Rosslare to Pembroke	0915	1300
	2130	0115
Pembroke to Rosslare	1500	1845
	0315	0700
	(Crossing time: 3 hours and 45 minutes)	

Ireland—France and v.v.

Trains connecting Dublin with the Irish Ferries services that sail from the port of Rosslare, south of Dublin, to the French ports of Cherbourg and Roscoff use Dublin's Connolly Station. A sign directing visitors to the nearby tourist information office on O'Connell Street is located on the right side of the concourse. Connolly Station is also the terminal in Dublin for trains arriving from Northern Ireland.

Eurail travelers are entitled to a 50 percent discount for deck passage on the Irish Ferries route between Rosslare and Cherbourg or Roscoff. Meals and sleeping accommodations are extra. Sailings operate April–September: Advance booking is highly recommended. Journey time between Rosslare–Cherbourg is 16.5 hours; between Rosslare–Roscoff, 18 hours. All passages are overnight. Check-in points are usually open 2 hours prior to sailing times. Passengers are requested to check in no later than 1 hour prior to sailing times.

For sailing schedules, cabin rates, availability and reservations, visit www.irishferries.com or contact the Irish Ferries General Sales Agent, USA and Canada:

Scots-American Travel Advisors
1140 Seventh Court, Suite A
Vero Beach, FL 32960
Tel: (561) 563–2856; *Fax:* (561) 563–2087
E-mail: info@scotsamerican.com
24-hour Information line in Ireland: from the U.S., dial 011 44 01 6610715
Online bookings (in Euro dollars): www.irishferries.com

Rosslare Port, Irish Ferries Port Office *Tel:* 053 33158. Trains from Dublin and Limerick connect with the Irish Ferries on the Rosslare Harbor pier. There are no transfer costs.

Cherbourg Port, Irish Ferries Port Office *Tel:* 02 33 23 44 44. Taxi service available for transfer to/from Cherbourg's railway station to the Irish Ferries Terminal.

Roscoff Port, Irish Ferries Port Office *Tel:* 02 98 61 17 17. Rail connections available for Brittany, west coast, and southwestern France.

INTERNATIONAL CALLING

The following chart provides the country codes and city codes you will need when calling from one country to another. The country codes should be used when dialing to that country from another country. In most cases you will also need to dial a city or area code prior to the local number.

Calling Europe from North America:

To use these codes from within North America, dial 011 + country code, city code, and the local number you wish to reach. If the European city code is prefaced with a "0," omit it when dialing from North America.

Calling North America from Europe with a calling card:

Your local long-distance phone company will have a number for you to dial while in Europe (either a toll-free or a local call) to connect to an operator in your home country. For more information call one of the following:
AT&T Direct Service: (800) 331–1140; from abroad, (412) 553–7458; www.att.com/traveler
MCI WorldPhone: (800) 996–7535; www.mci.com
SprintExpress: (800) 877–4646; www.sprint.com
Canada Primus: (800) 565–4708

CELL PHONE HIRE

Most U.S. and Canadian cellular phones do not work outside North America. Those travelers who need or want to use a cell phone in Europe can rent one from Cellhire. GMS (Global System for Mobiles) covers Europe, including Eastern Europe. (Satellite phones provide coverage worldwide, but they are considerably more expensive.)

GMS rental from Cellhire includes free delivery of a fully tested and sanitized handset by high-end manufacturers such as Motorola, Ericsson, or Nokia and come with VoiceMail as standard. You also get two batteries, a rapid charger, travel adapter, instruction booklet, and a return pack with a prepaid waybill. Call RailPass.com toll free at (877) 724–5727 for a free brochure; or call Cellhire toll free at (888) 476–7368 and refer to Code #3429 to order; or download an order form at www.railpass.com.

	Country/City Code	AT&T	MCI	Sprint
AUSTRIA	43	022–903–011	022–903–012	022–903–014
Vienna	1			
Baden	2252			
Innsbruck	512			
Melk	27			
Salzburg	662			

Country/City Code		AT&T	MCI	Sprint
BELGIUM	32	0–800–100–10	0800–10012	0800–100–14
Brussels	2			
Antwerp	3			
Bruges	50			
Ghent	9			
Namur	81			
DENMARK	45	8001–0010	8001–0022	800–10–877
City codes not required. All points are 8 digits or 45 plus 121				
FINLAND	358	9800–100–10	08001–102–80	0800–110–284
Helsinki	9			
Hanko	19			
Lahti	3			
Tampere	3			
Turku	2			
FRANCE	33	0800 99 00 11	0800 99 00 19	0800 99 00 87
City codes not required; regional codes are included.				
GERMANY	49	0800–2255–288	0800–888–8000	0800–888–0013
Berlin	30			
Dresden	351			
Leipzig	341			
Potsdam	331			
Hamburg	40			
Bremen	421			
Hameln	5151			
Hannover	511			
Lübeck	451			
Munich	89			
Berchtesgaden	8652			
Garmisch-Partenkirchen	8821			
Nuremberg	911			
Rothenburg	9851			
(Romantic Road)				
Ulm	731			
Koblenz	261			
Trier	651			
GREECE	30	00–800–1311	00–800–1211	00–800–1411
Athens	1			
Argos	751			
Corinth	741			
Patras	61			
Piraeus	1			
HUNGARY	36	00** 800–01111	00**800–01411	00**800–01877
Budapest	1			
Key: ** = wait for second dial tone				
IRELAND	353	1–800–550–000	1–800–551–001	1–800–552–001
Dublin	1			
Cork	21			
Galway	91			
Kilkenny	56			
Killarney	64			

Country/City Code		AT&T	MCI	Sprint
ITALY	39	172–1011	172–1022	172–1877
Milan	2			
Bologna	51			
Genoa	10			
Venice	41			
Rome	6			
Anzio	06			
Florence	55			
Naples	81			
Pisa	50			
LUXEMBOURG	352	0–800–0111	0800–0112	0800–0115
City codes not required.				
MONACO	377	800–90–288	800–90–019	800–90–087
Monte Carlo	no code required			
THE NETHERLANDS	31	0800–022–9111	0800–022–9122	0800–022–9119
Amsterdam	20			
Alkmaar	72			
Enkhuizen	228			
Haarlem	23			
Hoorn	299			
NORWAY	47	800–190–11	800–19912	800–19–877
City codes not required				
PORTUGAL	351	0800–800–128	050–17–1234	0800–800–187
Lisbon	1			
Cascais and Estoril	1			
Coimbra	39			
Setúbal	65			
Sintra	1			
SPAIN	34	900–99–0011	900–99–0014	900–99–0013
When calling in Spain, use 9 before dialing city codes.				
Barcelona	3			
Blanes	72			
Lleida	73			
Sitges	3			
Tarragona	77			
Madrid	1			
Aranjuez	1			
Avila	20			
Burgos	47			
El Escorial	1			
Toledo	25			
SWEDEN	46	020–795–611	020–795–922	020–799–011
Stockholm	8			
Eskilstuna	16			
Norrköping	11			
Uppsala	18			
SWITZERLAND	41	0–800–89–0011	0–800–89–0222	0800–89–9777
Bern	31			
Interlaken	33			
Lucerne	41			
Lake Lugano	91			
Rheinfelden	61			
Zürich	1			

TRAIN TRAVEL TERMINOLOGY

English	French	Italian	German	Spanish
On the train:				
aisle	couloir	corridoio	gang	pasillo
car	compartement	vettura	wagen	vagón
couchette	couchette	cuccetta	liegeplatz	couchette
restaurant car	voiture-restaurant	carrozza-restaurante	speisewagen	coche-restaurante
seat	place	posto	sitzplätz	asiento
sleeper	wagon-lit	cabina	bettplätz	cama
sleeping car	voiture-lit	vagone letto	schlafwagen	coche-cama
smoking	fumeur	per fumatori	raucher	fumadores
nonsmoking	non fumeur	non fumatori	nichtraucher	no fumadores
table	table	tavolo	tisch	mesa
toilets	toilettes	tolette	toiletten	servicios
window	fenêtre	finestrino	fenster	ventana
In the station:				
entrance	entrée	entrata	eingang	entrada
exit	sortie	uscita	ausgang	salida
Gentlemen	Hommes	Signori	Herren	Caballeros
Information	Renseignements	Informazioni	Information	Información
Ladies	Femmes	Signore	Damen	Señoras
left luggage	consigne	bagaglio depositato	gepäckauf-bewahrung	consigna
lost and found	objets trouvés	oggetti smarriti	fundbüro	oficina de objeto perdidos
luggage	bagages	bagagli	gepäck	equipaje
luggage lockers	consigne automatique	armadietti per bagagli	schließfächer	consigna automática
station	gare	stazione	bahnhof	estación
subway/underground	Métro	Metropolitana	die U-bahn	Metro
track/platform	quai	binario	bahnsteig	andén
telephone	téléphone	telefono	telefon	teléfono
ticket office	guichet	biglietteria	fahrkarten-sshalter	despacho de billetes
train	train	treno	zug	tren

English	French	Italian	German	Spanish
At the ticket window:				
arrival	arrivée	arrivo	ankunft	llegada
arrives	arrive	arriva	kommt an	llega
change at	correspondance	cambiare a	umsteigen in	cambiar en
first class	première classe	prima classe	erste klasse	primera clase
second class	seconde classe	seconda classe	zweite klasse	segunda clase
connection	correspondance	coincidenza	anschluß	conexión
departure	départ	partenza	abfhart	salida
departs	part	parte	fährt ab	sale
domestic tickets	billets	biglietti nazionali	fahrkarten inland	billetes nacionales
earlier	plus tôt	più presto	früher	más temprano
express	express	espresso	schnellzug	expreso
fast	rapid	rapido	schnell	rápido
from Rennes	(en provenance) de Rennes	(proviene) da Rennes	von Rennes	(procede) de Rennes
international tickets	billets internationaux	biglietti internazionali	fahrkarten ausland	billetes internacionales
not available	non disponible	non disponibile	nicht erhältlich	no disponible
later	plus tard	più tardi	später	más tarde
local service	service local	servizio locale	personenzug	servicio local
next train	prochain train	prossimo treno	nächst zug	próximo tren
reservation	reservation	prenotazione	reservierung	reservación
schedule/ timetable	horaires	orario	fahrplan	horari
supplement payable	avec supplément	con pagamento di supplemento	zuschlag- pflichtig	con pago de suplemento
to Oslo	vers Oslo, à destination de Oslo	a Oslo	nach Oslo	a Oslo
via	via	via	über	via

RAIL FARES BETWEEN MAJOR CITIES

First-class one-way fares (*without a railpass*) between major cities are listed in U.S. dollars but do not include seat reservation fees or sleeping car accommodation charges. Rates applicable as of press time and subject to change without notice. Second-class fares are approximately one-third less than first class. To purchase point-to-point tickets and for other points not listed, contact **RailPass.com** toll-free at (877) 724–5727; *Fax:* (614) 764–0711; *Internet:* www.railpass.com.

	AMS	ATH	BAR	BAS	BER	BRN	BRU	BUD	COL	CPH	FLO	FRA	GEN	HAM	LIS	LUX	LYN	MAD	MIL	MUC	NCE	OSL	PAR	ROM	STK	VCE	VEN
Amsterdam																											
Athens	437																										
Barcelona	282	262																									
Basel	185	232	192																								
Berlin	157	231	416	224																							
Bern	224	234	231	39	263																						
Brussels	45	357	286	94	190	133																					
Budapest	308	302	381	189	229	220	283																				
Cologne	57	393	322	130	146	169	47	237																			
Copenhagen	181	568	497	305	130	118	210	255	193																		
Florence	324	134	160	138	293	134	241	159	252	434																	
Frankfurt	122	347	287	95	150	150	107	187	59	225	124																
Geneva	202	238	112	80	350	56	210	255	210	367	355	175															
Hamburg	103	423	400	208	76	247	147	297	102	79	322	146	288														
Lisbon	319	402	140	332	556	308	302	521	304	549	207	340	252	423													
Luxembourg	62	323	252	60	200	99	35	263	54	264	150	69	140	162	271												
Lyon	214	266	116	61	337	91	133	256	194	419	247	170	42	316	253	80											
Madrid	336	323	67	259	483	298	319	448	321	546	40	357	179	467	73	288	183										
Milan	284	156	140	107	288	78	201	146	237	412	99	202	91	315	280	167	110	207									
Munich	210	217	308	116	194	155	188	120	153	287	60	117	180	206	448	155	222	375	94								
Nice	242	174	100	180	337	156	173	195	310	447	585	258	100	364	240	136	80	167	49	143							
Oslo	333	653	630	438	242	477	377	527	332	149	213	376	518	230	630	392	546	697	545	436	594						
Paris	114	300	168	75	277	120	97	285	99	324	46	135	109	218	205	66	95	222	184	165	123	448					
Rome	349	88	174	164	356	146	258	176	305	461	597	259	150	335	314	235	178	235	68	129	86	565	212				
Stockholm	345	665	642	450	233	489	389	539	344	161	35	388	242	242	782	404	558	709	557	362	606	110	432	577			
Venice	304	152	184	133	394	113	294	124	272	384	124	223	197	312	324	261	145	251	35	106	72	542	208	64	468		
Vienna	264	236	236	151	194	182	271	44	202	353	124	152	217	262	404	219	259	331	124	85	168	492	226	148	504	96	
Zürich	224	231	135	39	263	52	133	168	166	326	117	134	87	280	275	99	129	202	83	93	132	510	114	143	522	111	130

PASSPORT INFORMATION

Internet: www.travel.state.gov

The phone numbers of the passport office call centers that follow provide a recorded message that describes the documents you need and the application process for obtaining a passport. The message will direct you to the proper agencies for information regarding naturalization, travel advisories, customs regulations, and shots required by various countries. Applying several months in advance is advised. Passport forms are available at over 4,500 facilities nationwide, including many post offices, Federal, state, and probate courts, some libraries, and a number of country and municipal offices. Most of the 13 agencies listed here are for urgent departures and appointments are required.

The National Passport Information Center at (900) CALLNPIC provides telephone operators for prompt and accurate response to any questions you may have.

The regional offices are as follows:

Boston: Thomas P. O'Neill Federal Building, 10 Causeway Street, Suite 247, Boston, Massachusetts 02222–1094; (617) 565–6990.

Chicago: Kluczynski Office Building, 230 South Dearborn Street, Room 380, Chicago, Illinois 60604–1564; (312) 353–7155. *

Honolulu: First Hawaii Tower, 1132 Bishop Street, Suite 500, Honolulu, Hawaii 96813–2309; (808) 522–8283 or (808) 522–8286.

Houston: Mickey Leland Federal Building, 1919 Smith Street, Suite 1100, Houston, Texas 77002–8049; (713) 209–3153. *

Los Angeles: Federal Building, 11000 Wilshire Boulevard, Room 11000, Los Angeles, California 90024–3615; (310) 575–5700. *

Miami: Claude Pepper Federal Office Building, 51 Southwest First Avenue, Third Floor, Miami, Florida 33130–1680; (305) 539–3600. *

New Orleans: Postal Services Building, 701 Loyal Avenue, T-12005, New Orleans, Louisiana 70113–1931; (504) 589–6728 or (504) 589–6161.

New York: Greater Manhattan Federal Building, 367 Hudson Street, New York, New York 10014; (212) 206–3500. *

Philadelphia: U.S. Customs House, 200 Chestnut Street, Room 103, Philadelphia, Pennsylvania 19106–2970; (215) 597–7480.

San Francisco: 95 Hawthorne Street, Fifth Floor, San Francisco, California 94105–3901; (415) 744–4010 or (415) 744–4444.

Seattle: Federal Building, 915 Second Avenue, Room 992, Seattle, Washington 98174–1091; (206) 220–7788.

Stamford: One Landmark Square, Broad and Atlantic Streets, Stamford, Connecticut 06901–2667; (203) 325–3530. *

Washington, D.C.: 1111 19th Street NW, Washington, D.C. 20524–1705; (202) 647–0518.

* These offices use an appointment system.

EUROPEAN TOURIST OFFICES
IN NORTH AMERICA

Austrian National Tourist Office—www.anto.com;
E-mail: antonyc@ibm.net

New York: P.O. Box 1142, 500 Fifth Avenue, Suite #800, New York, NY
10110. *Tel:* (212) 944–6880; *Fax:* (212) 730–4568.

Toronto: 2 Bloor Street East, Suite 3330, Toronto, Ontario M4W 1A8, Canada.
Tel: (416) 967–3381; *Fax:* (416) 967–4101.

Belgium Tourist Office—www.visitbelgium.com;
E-mail: belinfo@nyxfer.blythe.org

New York: 780 Third Avenue, Suite 1501, New York, NY 10017–7076.
Tel: (212) 758–8130; *Fax:* (212) 355–7675.

British Tourist Authority—www.visitbritain.com

New York: 551 Fifth Avenue, Suite 701, New York, NY 10176–0799. *Tel:*
(800) 462–2748 or (212) 986–2200; *Fax:* (212) 986–1188.

Chicago: 625 North Michigan Avenue, Suite 1510, Chicago, IL 60611.
Tel: (312) 787–0464; *Fax:* (312) 787–7746.

Montreal: P.O. Box 760, Succursale NDG Montreal, Quebec H4A 3S2 Canada.
Tel: (514) 484–3594; *Fax:* (514) 489–8965.

Czech Service Center—www.czech.cz

New York: 1109 Madison Avenue, New York, NY 10028. *Tel:* (212)
288–0830; *Fax:* (212) 288–0971.

French Government Tourist Office—www.francetourism.com;
E-mail: info@francetourism.com

For information on France by telephone, dial (900) 990–0040 in the
United States (charge is 95 cents per minute). Or call (410) 286–8310 for
information requests.

New York: 444 Madison Avenue, Sixteenth Floor, New York, NY
10022–6903. *Tel:* (212) 838–7800; *Fax:* (212) 838–7855.

Chicago: 676 North Michigan Avenue, Suite 336, Chicago, IL 60611. *Tel:*
(312) 751–7800; *Fax:* (312) 337–6339.

Los Angeles: 9454 Wilshire Boulevard, Suite 715, Beverly Hills, CA
90212–2967. *Tel:* (310) 271–6665; *Fax:* (310) 276–2835.

Montreal: 1981 McGill College Avenue, Suite 490, Montreal, Quebec PQH3A
2W9, Canada. *Fax:* (514) 845–4868.

Toronto: 30 St. Patrick Street, Suite 700, Toronto, Ontario M5T 3A3, Canada.
Fax: (416) 979–7587.

German National Tourist Office—www.germany-tourism.de;
E-mail: gnotony@aol.com

New York: 122 East Forty-second Street, Fifty-second Floor, Chanin Building, New York, NY 10168–0072. *Tel:* (212) 661–7200; *Fax:* (212) 661–7174.

Greek National Tourist Organization—www.gogreece.com;
E-mail: gnto@orama.com

New York: 645 Fifth Avenue, Olympic Tower, Fifth Floor, New York, NY 10022. *Tel:* (212) 421–5777; *Fax:* (212) 826–6940; *E-mail:* gnto@aurora.eexi.gr.

Hungarian National Tourist Office—www.gotohungary.com;
E-mail: huntour@ldt.com

New York: c/o Embassy of the Republic of Hungary, 150 East Fifty-eighth Street, Thirty-third Floor, New York, NY 10155–3398. *Tel:* (212) 355–0240; *Fax:* (212) 207–4103.

Irish Tourist Board—www.ireland.travel.ie;
E-mail: info@irishtouristboard.com

New York: 345 Park Avenue, New York, NY 10154. *Tel:* (212) 418–0800 or (800) 223–6470; *Fax:* (212) 371–9052.
Toronto: 160 Bloor Street East, Suite 1150, Toronto, Ontario M4W 1B9, Canada. *Tel:* (416) 929–2777; *Fax:* (416) 929–6783.

Italian Government Tourist Board—www.italiantourism.com

New York: 630 Fifth Avenue, Suite 1565, New York, NY, 10111. *Tel:* (212) 245–4822; *Fax:* (212) 586–9249.
Chicago: 401 North Michigan Avenue, Suite 3030, Chicago, IL 60611. *Tel:* (312) 644–9448; *Fax:* (312) 644–3019.
Los Angeles: 12400 Wilshire Boulevard, Suite 550, Los Angeles, CA 90025. *Tel:* (310) 820–0098; *Fax:* (310) 820–6357.
Montreal: 1 Place Ville Marie, Suite 1914, Montreal, Quebec, H3B 3M9, Canada. *Tel:* (514) 866–7667; *Fax:* (514) 392–1429.

Luxembourg National Tourist Office—www.visitluxembourg.com; E-mail:
luxnto@aol.com

New York: 17 Beekman Place, New York, NY 10022. *Tel:* (212) 935–8888; *Fax:* (212) 935–5896.

Malta National Tourist Office—www.visitmalta.com; E-mail:
104452.2005@compuserve.com

New York: Empire State Building, 350 Fifth Avenue, Suite 4412, New York, NY 10118. *Tel:* (212) 695–9520; *Fax:* (212) 695–8229.

Monaco Government Tourist/Convention Bureau— www.monaco-tourism.com

New York: 565 Fifth Avenue, New York, NY 10017. *Tel:* (800) 753–9696 or (212) 286–3330; *Fax:* (212) 286–9890.

Netherlands Board of Tourism—www.goholland.com; E-mail: info@goholland.com

New York: 365 Lexington Avenue, New York, NY 10017–6603. *Tel:* (212) 370–7360 or (888) GO HOLLAND (888–464–6552); *Fax:* (212) 370–9507.

Northern Ireland Tourist Board—www.northernireland.tourism.com

New York: 551 Fifth Avenue, Suite 701, New York, NY 10176. *Tel:* (800) 326–0036 or (212) 922–0101; *Fax:* (212) 922–0099.
Toronto: 3 Bloor Street West, Suite 1501, Toronto, Ontario M4W 3E2. *Tel:* (800) 576–8174 or (416) 925–6368; *Fax:* (416) 925–6033.

Portuguese National Tourist Office—www.portugal.org

New York: 590 Fifth Avenue, Fourth Floor, New York, NY 10036–4704. *Tel:* (212) 719–3985 or (800) PORTUGAL; *Fax:* (212) 719–4019.
Montreal: 500 Sherbrooke Street West, Suite 940, Montreal, Canada, QC H3A 3C6. *Tel:* (514) 282–1264; *Fax:* (514) 499–1450.
Toronto: 60 Bloor Street, Suite 1005, Toronto, Ontario M4W 3B8, Canada. *Tel:* (416) 921–7376; *Fax:* (416) 921–1353.

Scandinavian Tourist Boards of Denmark, Finland, Iceland, Norway, and Sweden—www.goscandinavia.com; E-mail: info@goscandinavia.com

New York: P.O. Box 4649, Grand Central Station, New York, NY 10163–4649. *Tel:* (212) 885–9700; *Fax:* (212) 885–9710.

Tourist Office of Spain—www.okspain.org; E-mail: oetny@okspain.org

New York: 666 Fifth Avenue, Thirty-fifth Floor, New York, NY 10103. *Tel:* (888) OK SPAIN or (212) 265–8822; *Fax:* (212) 265–8864.
Chicago: 845 North Michigan Avenue, Water Tower Place, Suite 915 E, Chicago, IL 60611. *Tel:* (312) 642–1992; *Fax:* (312) 642–9817.
Los Angeles: San Vicente Plaza Building, 8383 Wilshire Boulevard, Suite 956, Beverly Hills, CA 90211. *Tel:* (213) 658–7188; *Fax:* (213) 658–1061.
Toronto: 2 Bloor Street West, Thirty-fourth Floor, Toronto, Ontario M4W 3E2, Canada. *Tel:* (416) 961–3131; *Fax:* (416) 961–1992.
Miami: 1221 Brickell Avenue, Miami, FL 33131. *Tel:* (305) 358–1992; *Fax:* (305) 358–8223.

Switzerland Tourism—www.switzerlandtourism.com;
E-mail: stnewyork@switzerlandtourism.com

New York: 608 Fifth Avenue, New York, NY 10020. *Tel:* (212) 757–5944; *Fax:* (212) 262–6116.

Chicago: 150 North Michigan Avenue, Suite 2930, Chicago, IL 60601. *Tel:* (312) 630–5840.

Los Angeles: 222 North Sepulveda Boulevard, Suite 1570, El Segundo, CA 90245. *Tel:* (310) 335–5980; *Fax:* (310) 335–5982.

Toronto: 926 The East Mall, Etobicoke, Ontario M9B 6K1, Canada. *Tel:* (416) 695–2090; *Fax:* (416) 695–2774.

AIRLINE NUMBERS AND WEB SITES
(Dialing from the United States)

Aer Lingus (EI) 800–Irish–air/223–6537
www.aerlingus.ie

Air Canada (AC)...................... 888–247–2262
www.aircanada.ca

Air France (AF) 800–237–2747
www.airfrance.com

American Airlines, Inc. (AA) .. 800–433–7300
www.aa.com

Austrian Airlines (OS) 800–843–0002
www.austrianair.com

British Airways (BA)...................800–AIRWAYS
www.britishairways.com

Continental Airlines (CO) 800–231–0856
www.continental.com

CSA Czech Airlines
Airlines (OK) 800–628–6107
www.csa.cz

Delta Air Lines, Inc. (DL) 800–241–4141
www.delta.com

Finnair (AY) 800–950–5000
www.us.finnair.com

Icelandair (FI)......................... 800–223–5500
www.icelandair.com

KLM Royal Dutch Airlines (KL) 800–374–7747
www.klm.com

Lufthansa German
Airlines (LH) 800–645–3880
www.lufthansa-usa.com

Northwest Airlines,
Inc. (NW) 800–447–4747
www.nwa.com

Olympic Airways (OA) 800–223–1226
www.olympic-airways.gr

Sabena Belgian World
Airlines (SN) 800–955–2000
www.sabena.com

Scandinavian Airlines
System (SK)..................... 800–221–2350
www.scandinavian.net

Swissair (SR)............................ 800–221–4750
www.swissair.com

TAP Air Portugal (TO) 800–221–7370
www.tap-airportugal.pt

Trans World Airlines, Inc.
(TWA) 800–221–2000
www.twa.com

United Air Lines, Inc. (UA) 800–241–6522
www.ual.com

USAirways (US) 800–428–4322
www.usairways.com

Virgin Atlantic Airways
Ltd. (VS) 800–862–8621
www.virgin-atlantic.com

AIRPORT–CITY CONNECTIONS

Those arriving in many popular European cities will find direct rail service between central stations and airports at a growing number of European airports. Service includes:

CITY	AIRPORT	DISTANCE	TRANSPORT TYPE	BUS #	CITY TERMINAL
Alacant	Alicante	12 km	Bus services daily	C6	Plaça del Mar
Amsterdam	Schiphol	14 km	Train every 15 min.	—	Centraal Station
Athens (Athinai)	Ellinikon	14 km	Bus every 30 min.	A&B	Syndagma Square/ Amalias Avenue
Barcelona	Barcelona	10 km	Train every 30 min.	—	Barcelona Sants
Basel	Basel/Mulhouse/ Freiburg	9 km	Bus every 20–30 min.	50	SBB Station/ Kannenfeldplatz
Belfast	Belfast International	26 km	Bus every 30 min.	300 (airbus) Sundays #60	Europa Buscentre, Glengall Street
Berlin	Schönefeld	18 km	S-Bahn train every 30 min.	—	Bahnhof Zoo/Ost rail stations
Berlin	Tegel	7 km	Bus every 10 min.	X9 & 109	Bahnhof Zoo rail station
Bordeaux	Merignac	12 km	Bus 15 services daily	—	Gare St. Jean
Bristol	Bristol	13 km	Bus 10 services daily	331	Bus station, also Temple Meads Station
Brussels	Nationaal	12 km	Train every 20 min.	—	Midi/Zuid Station also calls at Central and Nord
Budapest	Ferihegy	16 km	Bus every 30 min.	—	Bus Station, Erzébet tér
Dublin	Dublin	11 km	Bus "Airlink" every 15–25 min.	—	Heuston Rail Station/ Busaras Bus Station
Düsseldorf	Düsseldorf	7 km	Train S7 (S-Bahn) every 20 min	—	Hauptbahnhof

STATION	AIRPORT	DISTANCE	TRANSPORT	BUS #	CITY TERMINAL
Florence (Firenze)	Firenze Peretola	7 km	Bus every 25 min.	ATAF 62	Stazione FS
Frankfurt am Main	Frankfurt International	10 km	Train S8 (S-Bahn) 4–5 hourly	—	Hauptbahnhof
Gèneve	Gèneve	4 km	Train, 4 times hourly	—	Cornavin Station
Genova (Genoa)	Cristoforo Colombo	7 km	"Volabus" 12–14 services daily	—	Brignole and Principe stations; Piazza de Ferrari
Göteburg	Landvetter	25 km	Bus every 15 min. Mon–Fri; every 20–30 min. Saturday, Sunday, and holidays	—	City Air Terminal/ Central Station
Grenoble	Lyon Satolas	85 km	Bus (Cars Faure) 9–13/day 0500–1915	—	Gare routière (bus station)
Hamburg	Fuhlsbüttel	11 km	Bus (Jasper) every 20 min.	—	Hauptbahnhof/ Kirchenallee
Hannover	Langenhagen	13 km	S-Bahn trains every 15–30 min.	58	Bus station at Hauptbahnhof
Helsinki	Vantaa	19 km	Bus every 15–20 min.	—	City Air Terminal/ Rail Station
Copenhagen (København)	Kastrup	9 km	Train every 20 min.	—	Central Station
Cologne (Köln)	Koln/Bonn	20 km	Bus every 20 min.	670	Hauptbahnhof
Lisbon (Lisboa)	Portela	7 km	Bus every 20 min. 0700–2100	AeroBus 91	Cais do Sodré
London	City	10 km	Bus every 10 min. 0650–2050 Mon–Fri, exc. holidays; 0710–1150 Sat; 1100–2050 Sun	—	Liverpool Street Station
London	Gatwick	44 km	Train every 15 min.	—	Victoria Station
London	Heathrow	24 km	Train, every 15 min.	—	London Underground/ Paddington Station

STATION	AIRPORT	DISTANCE	TRANSPORT	BUS #	CITY TERMINAL
Luxembourg	Findel	7 km	Bus every 15–30 min.	9	Gare Centrale
Lyon	Saint Exupéry	25 km	Bus (Navette Aéroport) every 20 min.	—	Perrache Station, via Part Dieu Station
Madrid	Barajas	12 km	Metro train, Bus every 10 min.	—	Plaza Colón
Málaga	Málaga	7 km	Train every 30 min.	—	Málaga Station Centre-Alameda & RENFE Stations
Marseille	Marseille/Provence	28 km	Bus every 20 min.	—	Gare St. Charles
Milan (Milano)	Linate	9 km	Bus every 30 min.	—	Piazza S. Babila/Milano Centrale Station
Milan (Milano)	Milano-Malpensa	45 km	Train "Malpensa Express" (FNM) every 30 min.	—	Cadorna rail Stations
Munich (Munchen)	Strauss	28 km	Train, S-Bahn, every 20 min.	S8	Hauptbahnhof
Naples (Napoli)	Capodichino	7 km	Bus every 20 min.	14	Piazza Garibaldi (Central Station)
Nice	Nice-Côte d'Azur	7 km	Bus every 20 min. / Bus every 20 min.	23 / 20	Gare Routière /SNCF rail station
Oslo	Gardermoen	49 km	Airport Express Trains 2–4/hour	—	Central Station
Palma de Mallorca	Palma	11 km	Bus every 30 min.	—	Plaça España
Paris	Charles de Gaulle	25 km	RER train (Line B) every 7–15 min.	—	Gare du Nord/ Châtelet les Halles & St. Michel stations
Paris	Orly	15 km	RER train every 15 min. (Line C)	—	Austerlitz, St. Michel, Musée d'Orsay and Invalides stations

STATION	AIRPORT	DISTANCE	TRANSPORT	BUS #	CITY TERMINAL
Pisa	Pisa (Galilei)	2 km	Train, 11 daily Bus	— 7	Pisa Centrale (trains continue to/from Firenze)
Porto	Pedras Rubras	17 km	Bus every 15–30 min.	—	Praça do Carmo
Prague (Praha)	Ruzyne	17 km	Bus (CSA) every 30 min.	—	CSA office, Vcelnici (100 m from Masarykovo rail station)
Rome (Roma)	Fiumicino	26 km	Train every 20–30 min.	—	Roma Tiburtina/ Ostiense/Termini stations
Salzburg	Salzburg	5 km	Bus every 15 min.	77	Salzburg Bahnhof
Stockholm	Arlanda	44 km	Arlanda Express Train every 15 minutes	—	Central rail station
Strasbourg	Entzheim	12 km	Bus every 15–30 min.	—	Etoile Homme de Fer/ Central Rail Station
Stuttgart	Echterdingen	14 km	Train S2, S3 S-Bahn every 20–30 min.	—	Hauptbahnhof
Turin (Torino)	Caselle	16 km	Bus every 45 min.	—	Corso Inghilterra 3
Toulouse	Blagnac	8 km	Bus every 20 min.	—	Gare Routiére/ Place Jeanne d'Arc
Valencia	Manises	9 km	Train every 30–60 min.	—	Nord Rail Station
Venice (Venezia)	Marco Polo	13 km	Bus every 30–60 min. (summer/winter)	5	Pizzale Roma
Vienna (Wien)	Schwechat	17 km	Train every 30 min. Bus every 20–30 mins.	—	Wien Mitte and Wien Nord Stations
Zürich	Zürich (Kloten)	12 km	Train 7 times per hour	—	Zürich Hauptbahnhof

In addition, rail service to other cities via the Airport Station may be available.

HOTEL RESERVATIONS NUMBERS

(Dialing from the United States)

Best Western International 800–780–7234
www.bestwestern.com

Choice Hotels
International, Inc. 800–4–CHOICE
www.hotelchoice.com

Consort Hotels Ltd 800–55–CONSORT
www.consorthotels.com

European Tours Limited 800–722–3679
www.europeantourslimited.com

Forte & Meridian Hotels.......... 800–225–5843
www.forte-hotels.com

Golden Tulip International 800–344–1212
www.goldentulips.com

Hilton Reservations
Worldwide 800–HILTONS
www.hilton.com

Holiday Inns Worldwide 800–HOLIDAY
www.basshotels.com

Hyatt Worldwide
Reservation Centres 800–233–1234
www.hyatt.com

Inter-Continental
Hotels Corp 800–327–0200
www.interconti.com

ITT Sheraton Corporation 800–325–3535
www.sheraton.com

Kempinski International 800–426–3135
www.kempinski.com

Leading Hotels of the World 800–223–6800
www.lhw.com

Loews Representation Int'l........800–223–0888
www.loewshotel.com

Marriott Corporation 800–228–9290
www.marriott.com

MinOtels Int'l 800–336–4668
www.minotel.com

Movenpick Hotels Int'l 800–34–HOTEL
www.ctmtravelgroup.com

Nikko Hotels International 800–645–5687
www.nikkohotels.com

Preferred Hotels & Resorts
Worldwide 800–323–7500
www.preferredhotels.com

Radisson Hotels, Int'l 800–333–3333
www.radisson.com

Ramada International Hotels
& Resorts........................ 800–854–7854
www.ramada.com

SRS World Hotels Service 800–223–5652
www.srs-worldhotels.com

Swisshotel 800–63–SWISS
www.swisshotel.com

**To order, call toll-free (877) RAILPASS (877–724–5727) or (614) 793–7651
or visit the RailPass.com Web site at www.railpass.com.**

EURAIL PASSES

Eurail Passes entitle you to unlimited travel on Europe's extensive 100,000-mile
rail network in 17 countries of Europe (England, Scotland, and Wales not
included) as follows:

Austria • Belgium • Denmark • Finland • France • Germany • Greece • Hungary
Ireland (Republic of) • Italy • Luxembourg • Netherlands • Norway
Portugal • Spain • Sweden • Switzerland

Eurail Pass		Eurail Saverpass	
Consecutive-day travel on any or all days for the duration of the pass.		Rail travel for 2-5 people traveling together at all times.	
1ST CLASS		Price is per person.	
15 days	$572	$486	
21 days	$740	$610	
1 month	$918	$780	
2 months	$1,298	$1,106	
3 months	$1,606	$1,366	

Children 4-11, half adult fare. Under age 4 travel free.

Eurail Flexipass

Choose your travel days and use them within 60 days.

1ST CLASS

10 days in 2 months	$674
15 days in 2 months	$888

Children 4-11, half adult fare. Under age 4 travel free.

Eurail Saver Flexipass

Rail travel for 2-5 people traveling together at all times. Price is per person.

$574
$756

Eurail Youth Pass*

2ND CLASS

15 days	$401
21 days	$518
1 month	$644
2 months	$910
3 months	$1,126

Eurail Youth Flexipass*

2ND CLASS

10 days in 2 months	$473
15 days in 2 months	$622

*Available for passengers age 12–25 on their first date of travel.

Eurail SelectPass

Eurail Selectpass gives travelers the option to customize a railpass by choosing any 3 bordering Eurail countries that are connected by train or by ship. The Benelux countries of Belgium, Luxembourg, and The Netherlands count as a single country.

EURAIL SELECTPASS

Travel on any or all days for the duration of the pass in any 3 adjoining Eurailpass countries.

	ADULT 1ST CLASS	YOUTH* 2ND CLASS
5 days in 2 months	$346	$243
6 days in 2 months	$380	$266
8 days in 2 months	$444	$310
10 days in 2 months	$502	$352

*Youth price available for passengers 12–26. Children 4–11 half adult fare. Under age 4 travel free.

EURAIL SELECTPASS SAVER

For 2 or more persons traveling together at all times. Travel on any or all days for the duration of the pass in any 3 adjoining Eurailpass countries.

	ADULT 1ST CLASS
5 days in 2 months	$294
6 days in 2 months	$322
8 days in 2 months	$378
10 days in 2 months	$428

Children 4–11 half adult fare. Under age 4 travel free.

EUROPASS

The Europass features unlimited travel in the 5 most frequently visited countries of Europe: France, Germany, Italy, Spain, and Switzerland.

You determine the number of travel days from 5, 6, 8, 10, or 15 travel days needed in a 2-month period, making the Europass the most flexible railpass available. In addition you may add up to 2 of the following Associate Country areas to extend the geographic area of the pass (does not extend the pass length in days):

Benelux (Belgium, Luxembourg, and the Netherlands)

Austria/Hungary
Greece and Ferry Crossing to Italy
Portugal

Europass

Valid for rail travel in: France, Germany, Italy, Spain, and Switzerland.

	ADULT 1ST CLASS	YOUTH* 2ND CLASS
5 days in 2 months	$360	$253
6 days in 2 months	$400	$282
8 days in 2 months	$474	$332
10 days in 2 months	$544	$382
15 days in 2 months	$710	$497

*Youth price available for passengers 12–25. Children 4-11, half adult fare; under age 4 travel free.

Europass SaverPass

Valid for First Class rail travel for 2–5 people traveling together at all times in the countries of: France, Germany, Italy, Spain, and Switzerland. Prices are per person.

	ADULT 1ST CLASS
5 days in 2 months	$306
6 days in 2 months	$340
8 days in 2 months	$404
10 days in 2 months	$464
15 days in 2 months	$604

Children 4-11, half adult fare; under age 4 travel free.

Associate Countries

May add up to 2 of the following zones to extend the geographic area of the Europass: Benelux, Austria/Hungary, Greece, and Portugal.

	ADULT 1ST CLASS	YOUTH* 2ND CLASS	SAVERPASS 1ST CLASS
1 Add-on Zone	$62	$43	$54
2 Add-on Zones	$102	$72	$88

Children 5–11, half adult fare; under age 4 travel free.

COUNTRY AND REGIONAL PASSES

Austrian Railpass

	ADULT 1ST CLASS	2ND CLASS
3 days in 15	$158	$107
Additional Days	$20	$15

Children 6–12, half adult fare; 5 and under travel free. 5 day maximum additional rail days. Bonuses include discounts on steamers, local trains, and bicycle rentals.

Balkan Flexipass

Valid for rail travel in Bulgaria, Greece, Former Yugoslav Republic of Macedonia, Montenegro, Romania, Serbia, and Turkey.

	1ST CLASS	
	ADULT	YOUTH
5 days in 1 month	$152	$90

10 days in 1 month	$264	$156
15 days in 1 month	$317	$190

Children 4–12, half adult fare. Youth 13–25.
Senior: Available only for passengers 60 and over.

Benelux Tourrail Pass

Valid for rail travel in Belgium, Luxembourg, and the Netherlands.

5 days in 1 month	1ST CLASS	2ND CLASS
Adult	$217	$155
Youth	—	$104

Youth 4–25; under age 4 travel free.

Benelux Tourrail for Two

Valid for rail travel in Belgium, Luxembourg, and the Netherlands. Prices are per person based on two people traveling together at all times.

	1ST CLASS	2ND CLASS
5 days in 1 month	$163	$116.50

Czech FlexiPass

	1ST CLASS	2ND CLASS
5 days in 15 days	$69	$48
Additional days	$9	$6

Children 4–11, half adult fare; under age 4 travel free.
Up to 5 additional days can be added.

European East Pass

Valid for rail travel in Austria, Czech Republic, Hungary, Poland, and Slovak Republic.

	1ST CLASS
5 days in 1 month	$210
Additional Days	$24

Up to 5 additional days can be added. Children 4–11, half adult fare; under 4 free.

FinnRail Pass

Valid for any 3, 5, or 10 days of rail travel within one month.

	ADULT		CHILD	
	1ST CLASS	2ND CLASS	1ST CLASS	2ND CLASS
3 days in 1 month	$162	$108	$81	$54
5 days in 1 month	$216	$144	$108	$72
10 days in 1 month	$291	$194	$145.50	$97

France Pass

	ADULT		SAVERPASS*	
	1ST CLASS	2ND CLASS	1ST CLASS	2ND CLASS
4 days in 1 month	$240	$210	$171	$146
Additional days	$30	$30	$30	$30

	SENIORPASS	
	1ST CLASS	2ND CLASS
3 days in 1 month	$199	$159
Additional days	$30	$27

	YOUTH (2ND CLASS ONLY)
4 days in 2 months	$170
Additional days	$20

Maximum of 6 additional days. Youth 12–25; children 4–11, half adult fare; under age 4 travel free; Seniors 60+.
*Price per person based on 2 people traveling together at all times, includes 40% companion discount.

German Railpass

| | ADULT | | YOUTH |
	1ST CLASS	2ND CLASS	2ND CLASS
4 days in 1 month	$260	$180	$142
Additional rail days	$34	$22	$14

Maximum of 6 extra days may be added. Bonuses for passholders include free travel on KD River Steamers on certain Rhine, Main, and Moselle River sections and free travel on selected bus lines operated by Deutsche Touring/Europabus. Youth 12–25. Children 6–11, half adult fare; under age 6 travel free.

German Twinpass
Valid for two adults traveling together at all times.

| | ADULT | |
	1ST CLASS	2ND CLASS
4 days in 1 month	$390	$270
Additional rail days	$45	$33

Same extra day maximum and bonuses as German Railpass.

Greek Flexipass
Valid for 1st class rail travel in Greece.

	ADULT	YOUTH	CHILD
3 days in 1 month	$86	$62	$58
4 days in 1 month	$110	—	$74
5 days in 1 month	$120	$89	$85
6 days in 1 month	$144	—	$101

Bonuses include discounts on sea crossings to Italy, one day cruises from Athens to Aegina, Poros, and Hydra, and certain hotel specials. Youth 12–25. Children 2–11; under age 2 travel free.

Holland Railpass

| | ADULT | | YOUTH |
	1ST CLASS	2ND CLASS	2ND CLASS
3 days in 1 month	$98	$65	$52
5 days in 1 month	$147	$98	$79

| | SENIOR | | CHILD | |
	1ST CLASS	2ND CLASS	1ST CLASS	2ND CLASS
3 days in 1 month	$78	$52	$50	$33
5 days in 1 month	$119	$79	$74	$49

Youth 12–25. Seniors 60+. Children 4–11; under age 4 travel free.

Holland Rail TwinPass

| | ADULT | | YOUTH |
	1ST CLASS	2ND CLASS	2ND CLASS
3 days in 1 month	$148	$98	$78
5 days in 1 month	$221	$148	$120

| | SENIOR | | CHILD | |
	1ST CLASS	2ND CLASS	1ST CLASS	2ND CLASS
3 days in 1 month	$117	$78	$75	$50
5 days in 1 month	$180	$120	$111	$74

Youth 4–25. Children age 4–11; under age 4 travel free.

Hungarian Flexipass

	1ST CLASS
5 days in 15 days	$67
10 days in 1 month	$84

Children 5–14, half adult fare; under age 5 travel free.

Iberic Flexipass

Valid for unlimited rail travel in Spain and Portugal.

	1ST CLASS
3 days in 2 months	$205
Additional days	$45

Supplements required for travel on the AVE and Talgo high-speed trains. Maximum of 7 extra days may be added. Children 4–11, half adult fare. Under age 4 travel free.

Irish Rail & Bus Passes

Contact CIE Tours International to order Irish products: (800) 243–8687.

Irish Explorer—Rail

Unlimited rail travel on standard class Irish Rail in Republic of Ireland and local rail services in Dublin area.

	ADULT	CHILDREN
5 days in 15 days	$106	$53

Irish Explorer—Rail and Bus

Unlimited rail and bus travel on standard class Irish Rail in Republic of Ireland and local rail services in Dublin area; plus city bus services in Cork, Limerick, Galway, and Waterford.

	ADULT	CHILDREN
8 days in 15 days	$158	$79

Irish Rover—Rail

Unlimited rail travel on Irish Rail, Northern Ireland Rail and Suburban rail services in Northern Ireland plus local rail services in Dublin area.

	ADULT	CHILDREN
5 days in 15 days	$132	$66

Irish Rover—Rail and Bus

Unlimited rail travel on Irish Rail, Northern Ireland Rail, and suburban rail services in Northern Ireland plus local rail services in Dublin area plus bus services.

	ADULT	CHILDREN
5 days in 15 days	$316	$158

Emerald Card—Rail and Bus

Unlimited rail travel on standard class Irish Rail, Northern Ireland Rail, Irish Bus, Ulsterbus, local rail and bus services in Dublin; plus bus services in Belfast, Cork, Limerick, Galway, and Waterford.

	ADULT	CHILDREN
8 days in 15 days	$182	$91
15 days in 30 days	$316	$158

Italy Railcard

Valid for unlimited travel on the entire Italian Rail network including InterCity, EuroCity and Rapido trains with no surcharge. A supplement is required for Eurostar Italia trains.

	1ST CLASS	2ND CLASS
Consecutive days		
8 days	$299	$199

15 days	$373	$249
21 days	$433	$289
30 days	$522	$348
Flexi Rail Card		
4 days in 30 days	$239	$159
8 days in 30 days	$334	$223
12 days in 30 days	$429	$286

Children 4–11, half fare; under age 4 travel free.

Norway Railpass

	ADULT		SENIOR	
	1ST CLASS	**2ND CLASS**	**1ST CLASS**	**2ND CLASS**
3 days in 1 month	$181	$139	$144	$111
4 days in 1 month	$224	$172	$179	$139
5 days in 1 month	$252	$194	$202	$155

Children age 4–16 half the adult fare. Children under age 4 travel free; maximum of 2 children travel free per adult. Senior age 60+. Travel on the Flam Railway Line no longer included. A discount of 30% offered on the Flam Line. New "Signatur" Expresstrains run on the Southern Line and Dovreline; Bergen Line added. Supplement required, includes meals and refreshments.

Paris Plus Pass/Le Paris Visite

	ADULT	CHILD
2 Consecutive Days	$34	$17
3 Consecutive Days	$47	$24
5 Consecutive Days	$57	$29

Provides unlimited travel on all zones of the entire Paris Métro (subway), Paris bus routes, RER trains to the airports, Versailles, EuroDisney, and the funicular at the Sacré Coeur. Children under age 5 travel free.

Portuguese Railpass

	1ST CLASS
4 days in 15 days	$105

Children 4–11, half adult fare; under age 4 travel free. Not valid on the Luis de Cameos train.

Prague Excursion

Valid for rail transportation from any Czech border crossing to Prague and returning within seven days.

	1ST CLASS	2ND CLASS
Adult	$55	$35
Youth	$45	$30
Children	$28	$18

Youth 12–25. Children 4–11.

Romanian Railpass

	1ST CLASS
3 days in 15 days	$80

Children 4–11, half adult fare; under age 4 travel free.

ScanRail Pass

Valid for unlimited rail travel in Denmark, Finland, Norway and Sweden.

	ADULT		SENIOR	
	1ST CLASS	**2ND CLASS**	**1ST CLASS**	**2ND CLASS**
5 days in 2 months	$290	$214	$258	$190
10 days in 2 months	$388	$288	$345	$256
21 days	$448	$332	$399	$295

	YOUTH	
	1ST CLASS	2ND CLASS
5 days in 2 months	$218	$161
10 days in 2 months	$291	$216
21 days	$336	$249

Senior 60+. Youth 12–25. Children 4–11: half adult fare.

Spain Flexipass

	1ST CLASS	2ND CLASS
3 days in 2 months	$200	$155
Additional days	$35	$30

Maximum of 10 days. The AVE and Talgo 200 require an additional supplement. Children 4–11, half adult fare.

Sweden Railpass

	ADULT	
	1ST CLASS	2ND CLASS
3 days within 1 month	$211	$156
4 days within 1 month	$239	$177
5 days within 1 month	$268	$198

Special: Two children (under age 16) travel free together with one adult.

Swiss Card (Ideal for Skiers)

Valid for one round-trip rail journey plus 50 percent discount for additional trips (except for some mountain railroads that offer 25 percent discount) within a 1-month validity period.

	1ST CLASS	2ND CLASS
1 month - 1 round trip	$155	$110

Children under 16: free with parent. Children 6–15 not accompanied by parent: half adult fare. Children under age 6: free.

Swiss Museum Pass

Entrance to over 180 museums in Switzerland. Valid for one month of unlimited visits.

	ADULT	ADULT + CHILDREN*
Museum Pass	$25	$30

*Valid for one adult and up to five children.

Swiss Passes

Valid for consecutive-day unlimited travel. Choice of 1st class or 2nd class. Free Swiss Family Card: children under age 16 travel free when accompanied by at least one parent; half adult fare when not accompanied by parent. Includes travel lake steamers, transportation on 35 city systems, postal and private bus lines, and selected private railways, such as Glacier Express and Panoramic Express.

	SWISS PASS		SWISS SAVERPASS*	
	1ST CLASS	2ND CLASS	1ST CLASS	2ND CLASS
4 days	$245	$160	$208	$136
8 days	$340	$225	$289	$192
15 days	$410	$270	$349	$230
21 days	$475	$315	$404	$268
1 month	$535	$350	$455	$298

	SWISS FLEXIPASS		SWISS SAVER FLEXIPASS*	
	1ST CLASS	2ND CLASS	1ST CLASS	2ND CLASS
Any 3 days in 1 month	$234	$156	$198	$132
Any 4 days in 1 month	$276	$184	$234	$156
Any 5 days in 1 month	$318	$212	$270	$180
Any 6 days in 1 month	$360	$240	$306	$204
Any 8 days in 1 month	$424	$282	$360	$240

*Price per person based on 2 or more adults traveling together.

Swiss Transfer Ticket

Great for skiers or for those who will stay in one place. Provides for one-round trip ticket.

1ST CLASS	2ND CLASS
$118	$76

Children under age 16 free when accompanied by at least one parent; otherwise, children age 6–15 half adult fare. Children under age 6 travel free.

Railpass Protection

Entitles traveler to a 100% reimbursement on the unused portion of the railpass if lost or stolen while traveling in Britain or Europe.

$13 per pass

See "Railpass/Rail & Drive Protection" in the Appendix.

BRITRAIL PASSES

A BritRail consecutive-day or flexipass allows unlimited travel on the entire British rail network spanning England, Scotland, and Wales. Prices for 2001 are current as of press time, but are always subject to change without notice.

BritRail Classic Pass

Valid for consecutive days of rail travel throughout Britain (England, Scotland, and Wales.)

	ADULT		SENIOR	YOUTH STANDARD
	1ST CLASS	STANDARD CLASS	1ST CLASS	CLASS ONLY
8 days	$399	$265	$340	$215
15 days	$599	$399	$510	$280
22 days	$760	$505	$645	$355
1 month	$899	$599	$765	$420

Senior 60+. Youth 16-25. Children 5-15, half adult fare. Children under age 5 travel free.

BritRail Family Pass

Receive one free child pass (age 5–15) of the same type when purchasing one adult or senior BritRail Classic Pass, BritRail Flexipass, BritRail Pass + Ireland, BritRail Pass 'n Drive or a BritRail Party Pass (up to 2 children may travel free per BritRail Party Pass; not to exceed total of 5 persons, including child, on the Party Pass). Children under age 5 travel free.

BritRail Flexipass

Valid for unlimited rail travel in Britain for the days chosen within a 60-day period.

	ADULT		SENIOR	YOUTH STANDARD
	1ST CLASS	STANDARD CLASS	1ST CLASS	CLASS ONLY
4 days in 2 months	$349	$235	$299	$185
8 days in 2 months	$510	$340	$435	$240
15 days in 2 months	$770	$514	$656	$360

Senior 60+. Youth 16-25. Children 5-15, half adult fare. Children under age 5 travel free.

BritRail Party Pass

For parties of 3 or 4 passengers traveling together at all times, a 50-percent discount is offered on the third and fourth person's pass. Applies to the BritRail Classic and BritRail Flexipass (1st class only, Adult and Senior).

BritRail Pass + Ireland
Valid for travel in England, Scotland, Wales, Northern Ireland, and the Republic of Ireland.

	1ST CLASS	STANDARD CLASS
5 days within 1 month	$528	$396
10 days within 1 month	$753	$566

Children 5-15, half adult fare; under age 5 travel free.
Round-trip Stena Sealink service is included between Holyhead and Dun Laoghaire, Fishguard and Rosslare or Stranraer and Larne via ship, HSS or SeaLynx. Reservations are essential for Irish Sea services. Refunds not offered on dated or partially used passes; sea coupons are not refundable if unused.

BritRail SouthEast Pass
A Flexipass for a large section of southern England.

	ADULT		CHILD	
	1ST CLASS	STANDARD CLASS	1ST CLASS	STANDARD CLASS
3 days within 8 days	$106	$73	$31	$21
4 days within 8 days	$142	$106	$31	$21
7 days within 15 days	$189	$142	$31	$21

Children 5-15. Children under age 5 travel free.

Freedom of Scotland Travelpass

	STANDARD CLASS
4 days within 8 days	$135
8 days within 15 days	$189
12 days within 15 days	$206

Includes transportation on most Caledonian MacBrayne and Strathclyde ferries to the islands of Scotland. Discounts on several ferry operators and on certain CityLink bus services, plus covers Glasgow Underground. Discounts on some P&O ferry routes. Children 5–15, half adult fare. Children under age 5 travel free.

Wales Flexipass

	STANDARD CLASS	
	ADULT	CHILD
4 days within 8 days	$85	$60
8 days within 15 days	$159	$105

Includes unlimited travel on main rail lines in Wales and most major bus services. Discounts on several of Wales' preserved railways, selected attractions, and some bus tours. Monday–Friday valid after 0900 only. Unrestricted travel on Saturday and Sunday.

Gatwick Express

	1ST CLASS	STANDARD CLASS
	$28	$17

Travel by train from Gatwick Airport to London Victoria Station. Children 5-15, half adult fare.

Heathrow Express

	1ST CLASS	STANDARD CLASS
One way	$35	$21
Round trip	$69	$38

Travel by train from Heathrow Airport to London Paddington Station. Children age 5–15 half adult fare.

Great British Heritage Pass

Offers entrance to over 500 well-known public and privately owned castles, homes, gardens and other historic properties throughout Britain. Includes colorful guidebook and map.

	ADULT
7 days	$54
15 days	$75
1 month	$102

No discounts for children. The pass is nonrefundable/nonreturnable.

Guide Friday Sightseeing

Booklet of four sightseeing bus vouchers $45

Choice of 24 popular locations: Bath, Birmingham, Brighton, Cambridge, Cardiff, Chester, Cork, Dover, Dublin, Edinburgh, Galway, Glasgow, Hastings, Inverness, Lincoln, Llandudno and Conway, Norwich, Oxford, Plymouth, Stonehenge, Stratford-upon-Avon, Windsor, and York. Flexibility to use for 1 person for 4 different tour days, or 4 people for 1 tour day; each valid for a full day.

London Day Tour

ADULT	CHILD
$89	$81

Includes: an experienced guide, a luxury air-conditioned touring coach, pub lunch, cruise of the river Thames with afternoon tea, and all entrance fees. Operates daily. Children 5–15.

London Visitor Travel Card

Valid for unlimited consecutive day travel in all of the six zones of the London Underground and on the red double-decker buses. Also includes Heathrow Airport transfer, plus discounts to sites and attractions.

	ADULT	CHILD
3 days	$32	$14
4 days	$41	$15
7 days	$63	$24

Children 5-15. Children under age 4 travel free.

British Tours

Choose from a wide variety of interesting tours throughout the British countryside; day trips to Paris or Brussels; or Paris overnighters via the Eurostar. Call EuropeanVacation for a free brochure at 888–868–7404 or visit www.europeanvacation.com for more detailed information and to book a tour.

RAIL/DRIVE PASSES

BritRail Pass 'N Drive

Valid for any 5 days (3 rail, 2 car) within 2 months. No additional raildays can be added.

CAR CATEGORY	2 ADULTS		ADDITIONAL CAR DAY
	1ST CLASS	2ND CLASS	
Mini	$299	$219	$56
Compact	$319	$235	$75
Intermed.	$329	$249	$89
Compact automatic	$345	$260	$105
Intermed. automatic	$355	$275	$119
Luxury automatic	$475	$395	$239

CAR CATEGORY	1 ADULT 1ST CLASS	2ND CLASS	ADDITIONAL CAR DAY
Mini	$359	$279	$56
Compact	$389	$309	$75
Intermed.	$419	$339	$89
Compact automatic	$449	$359	$105
Intermed. automatic	$465	$385	$119
Luxury automatic	$709	$625	$239

CAR CATEGORY	2 SENIORS 1ST CLASS	1 SENIOR 1ST CLASS MINI
Compact	$280	$349
Intermed.	$290	$379
Compact automatic	$305	$409
Intermed. automatic	$320	$429
Luxury automatic	$438	$669

Rates for third and fourth person sharing car: 1st class for $244, 2nd class for $164.
Children 5–15: 1st class for $125, 2nd class for $85. Children under age 5 travel free.
Extra car days for seniors are the same as for adults.

Eurail/Drive Pass
Any 6 days (4 rail, 2 car) within 2 months for travel in any of the seventeen Eurail countries. Add up to 5 additional rail days and unlimited number of car days.

CAR CATEGORY	2 ADULTS* 1ST CLASS	1 ADULT 1ST CLASS	ADD'L CAR DAY
Economy	$377	$435	$58
Compact	$397	$475	$78
Intermediate	$407	$495	$88
Compact auto.**	$422	$525	$103
Add'l. rail day	$42	$42	

Third and fourth person sharing car $319 per person. *Prices per person based on 2 people traveling together. **Cars with automatic shift are available at selected rental locations. Children 4–11 are $135 for the basic package. Extra rail days are $29 each.

Eurail Selectpass Drive
Any 5 days (3 rail, 2 Avis or Hertz car rental) within 2 months in any of the three bordering countries selected. Add up to 4 additional rail days and an unlimited number of car days.

CAR CATEGORY	2 ADULTS* 1ST CLASS	1 ADULT 1ST CLASS	ADD'L CAR DAY
Economy	$279	$329	$49
Compact	$289	$359	$65
Intermediate	$299	$379	$75
Small automatic**	$319	$409	$95

Extra rail days are $35 each.

*Prices per person based on 2 people traveling together. Third and fourth person sharing car $229 per person. Children 4–11, $119; under age 4, free. Hertz Eurail Selectpass Drive car not available in Norway, Finland, or Sweden.

**Small automatic with Hertz only in major locations.

Europass Drive

Any 5 days (3 rail, 2 car) within 2 months for travel in France, Germany, Italy, Spain, and Switzerland. No zones may be added. Add up to 7 additional rail days and an unlimited number of car days.

CAR CATEGORY	2 ADULTS* 1ST CLASS	1 ADULT 1ST CLASS	ADD'L CAR DAY
Economy	$291	$346	$55
Compact	$311	$386	$75
Intermediate	$321	$406	$85
Compact auto.**	$331	$426	$95
Add'l. rail day	$36	$36	

*Prices per person based on 2 people traveling together. Third and fourth person $236 each.
**Cars with automatic shift available at selected rental locations. Children 4–11 are $111 for the basic package. Extra rail days are $22 each.

France Rail 'N' Drive

Any 5 days (3 rail, 2 car) within 1 month for travel in France. Add up to 6 additional rail days and car days. 3rd and 4th persons may purchase railpasses only.

CAR CATEGORY	1ST CLASS 2 ADULTS*	1 ADULT	2ND CLASS 2 ADULTS*	1 ADULT	ADD'L. CAR DAY
Economy	$199	$275	$175	$245	$49
Compact	$209	$289	$185	$265	$55
Intermediate	$220	$319	$199	$289	$70
Compact auto.	$229	$339	$205	$305	$79
Add'l. rail day	$30	$30	$30	$30	

*Price per person.

German Rail/Drive

Any 4 days (2 rail, 2 car) within 2 months for travel in Germany. Add up to 3 additional rail days.

CAR CATEGORY	1ST CLASS 2 ADULTS*	1 ADULT	2ND CLASS 2 ADULTS*	1 ADULT	ADD'L. CAR DAY
Economy	$168	$223	$143	$198	$55
Compact	$188	$263	$163	$238	$75
Intermediate	$198	$283	$173	$258	$85
Compact auto.**	$208	$303	$183	$278	$95
Add'l. rail day	$50	$50	$42	$42	

*Price per person. Extra person $113 1st Class; $88 2nd Class.
**Cars with automatic transmission are available at selected locations.

Iberic Rail/Drive

Valid for 3 days of unlimited rail travel within 2 months and 3 days of car rental for travel in Spain and Portugal. Up to 2 additional rail days and an unlimited number of car days may be added.

CAR CATEGORY	2 ADULTS* 1ST CLASS	1 ADULT 1ST CLASS	ADD'L CAR DAY
Economy	$260	$315	$55
Compact	$280	$355	$75
Intermediate	$290	$375	$85
Compact auto.**	$300	$395	$95
Add'l. rail day	$45	$45	

*Price per person. Third and fourth persons or children sharing car need only to purchase railpasses. **Automatics not available in Portugal.

Italian Rail/Drive

Valid for 2 days of unlimited rail travel within 1 month and 2 days of car rental for travel in Italy. Up to 1 extra rail day and an unlimited number of car days may be added.

CAR CATEGORY	2 ADULTS* 1ST CLASS	1 ADULT 1ST CLASS	ADD'L CAR DAY
Economy	$215	$270	$55
Compact	$235	$310	$75
Intermediate	$245	$330	$85
Compact automatic**	$255	$350	$95
Add'l. rail day	$75	$75	

Third and fourth persons sharing car $160 per person. Need only to purchase railpasses for children.*Price per person. **Automatic transmission available at selected locations.

Spanish Rail/Drive

Valid for 5 days (3 rail, 2 car) within 2 months of travel in Spain. Up to 2 additional rail days and unlimited car days available.

CAR CATEGORY	2 ADULTS* 1ST CLASS	1 ADULT 1ST CLASS	ADD'L CAR DAY
Economy	$244	$299	$55
Compact	$264	$339	$75
Intermediate	$274	$359	$85
Compact automatic*	$284	$379	$95
Additional rail day	$34	$34	

Third and fourth person sharing car $189 each. Need only purchase railpasses for children. *Price per person. *Automatic transmission available at selected locations.

Scanrail/Drive

Valid for 5 days of unlimited rail travel and 2 days of car rental to be used within 15 days in the Scandinavian countries of Denmark, Finland, Norway, and Sweden. Unlimited number of car days may be added.

CAR CATEGORY	1ST CLASS 2 ADULTS*	1ST CLASS 1 ADULT	2ND CLASS 2 ADULTS*	2ND CLASS 1 ADULT	ADD'L. CAR DAY
Economy	$340	$410	$270	$340	$70
Compact	$360	$450	$290	$380	$90
Intermediate	$370	$470	$300	$400	$100
Comp. auto**	$380	$490	$310	$420	$110

Third and fourth person need only purchase railpasses. Car rental not available in Finland. Automatics not available in Norway. *Price per person. **Automatic transmission available at selected locations.

Railpass/Rail & Drive Protection

This program entitles you to a 100 percent reimbursement on the unused portion of a rail- or a combination Railpass/Rail & Drive program if lost or stolen while traveling in Spain or Europe.

$13 per railpass or for the driver
$13 for each additional person

There's no better way to see Europe than by rail. Our experts have years of experience in helping plan the perfect trip. Rail travel offers much more freedom than packaged tours and many advantages over renting a car.

www.EUROTRIPS.com

Let Us Help Plan the Perfect European Rail Excursion for you!

Visit www.EUROTRIPS.com see **a sample of some of our** ost **popular self-guided rail tours,** f you are interested in having us buil special itinerary just for you, e-mail at **info@eurotrips.com**.